MW00788302

ANDREW MURRAY

COLLECTED WORKS
ON PRAYER

ANDREW MURRAY

COLLECTED WORKS ON PRAYER

WHITAKER
HOUSE

Unless otherwise indicated, all Scripture quotations are taken from the King James Version of the Holy Bible. Scripture quotations marked (ASV) are taken from the American Standard Edition of the Revised Version of the Holy Bible. Scripture quotations marked (RV) are taken from the Revised Version of the Holy Bible.

ANDREW MURRAY COLLECTED WORKS ON PRAYER

Titles included in this anthology:
Abide in Christ
ISBN: 978-0-88368-860-1 © 1979 by Whitaker House
The Prayer Life
ISBN: 978-0-88368-102-2 © 1981 by Whitaker House
Waiting on God
ISBN: 978-0-88368-101-5 © 1981 by Whitaker House
With Christ in the School of Prayer
ISBN: 978-0-88368-106-0 © 1981 by Whitaker House
The Ministry of Intercession
ISBN: 978-0-88368-667-6 © 1982 by Whitaker House
The Secret of Intercession
ISBN: 978-0-88368-849-6 © 1995 by Whitaker House
Prayer Guide
ISBN: 978-0-88368-475-7 © 1992 by Whitaker House

ISBN: 978-1-60374-833-9
Printed in the United States of America
© 2013 by Whitaker House

Whitaker House
1030 Hunt Valley Circle
New Kensington, PA 15068
www.whitakerhouse.com

No part of this book may be reproduced or transmitted in any form or by any means, electronic or mechanical—including photocopying, recording, or by any information storage and retrieval system—without permission in writing from the publisher. Please direct your inquiries to permissionseditor@whitakerhouse.com.

3 4 5 6 7 8 9 10 11 12 13 **LU** 28 27 26 25 24 23 22 21 20

CONTENTS

ABIDE IN CHRIST

CONTENTS

PREFACE

During the life of Jesus on earth, the word He chiefly used when speaking of the relations of the disciples to Himself was: *"Follow me"* (Matthew 4:19). When about to leave for heaven, He gave them a new word, in which their more intimate and spiritual union with Himself in glory should be expressed. That chosen word was: *"Abide in me"* (John 15:4).

It is to be feared that there are many earnest followers of Jesus from whom the meaning of this word, with the blessed experience it promises, is very much hidden. While trusting in their Savior for pardon and for help, and seeking to some extent to obey Him, they have hardly realized to what closeness of union, to what intimacy of fellowship, to what wondrous one-ness of life and interest, He invited them when He said, *"Abide in me."* This is not only an unspeakable loss to themselves, but the church and the world suffer in what they lose.

If we ask the reason why those who have indeed accepted the Savior, and been made partakers of the renewing of the Holy Spirit, thus come short of the full salvation prepared for them, I am sure the answer will in very many cases be that ignorance is the cause of the unbelief that fails of the inheritance. If, in our orthodox churches, the abiding in Christ, the living union with Him, the experience of His daily and hourly presence and keeping, were preached with the same distinctness and urgency as His atonement and pardon through His blood, I am confident that many would be found to accept with gladness the invitation to such a life, and that its influence would be manifest in their experience of the purity and the power, the love and the joy, the fruit bearing, and all the blessedness that the Savior connected with the abiding in Him.

It is with the desire to help those who have not yet fully understood what the Savior meant with His command, or who have feared that it was a life beyond their reach, that these meditations are now published. It is only by frequent repetition that a child learns his lessons. It is only by continuously fixing the mind for a time on one of the lessons of faith that the believer is gradually helped to take and thoroughly assimilate them. I have the hope that to some, especially young believers, it will be a help to come for a month, day after day, and read over the precious words, *"Abide in me,"* with the lessons connected with them in the parable of the Vine. Step by step we will get to see how truly this promise-precept is meant for us, how surely grace is provided to enable us to obey it, how indispens-able the experience of its blessing is to a healthy Christian life, and how unspeakable the blessings are that flow from it. As we listen, meditate, and pray—as we surrender ourselves and accept in faith the whole Jesus as He offers Himself to us in it—the Holy Spirit will make the Word to be spirit and life. This word of Jesus, too, will become to us the power of God unto salvation, and through it will come the faith that grasps the long desired blessing.

I pray earnestly that our gracious Lord may be pleased to bless this little book, to help those who seek to know Him fully, as He has already blessed it in its original issue in the Dutch language. I pray still more earnestly that He would, by whatever means, make the multitudes of His dear children who are still living divided lives, to see how He claims them wholly for Himself, and how the wholehearted surrender to abide in Him alone brings the joy unspeakable that is full of glory. Oh, let each of us who has begun to taste the sweetness of this life, yield himself wholly to be a witness to the grace and power of our Lord to keep us united with Himself, and seek by word and walk to win others to follow Him fully. It is only in such fruit bearing that our own abiding can be maintained.

In conclusion, I ask to be permitted to give one word of advice to my reader. It is this. It takes time to grow into Jesus the Vine; do not expect to abide in Him unless you will give Him that time. It is not enough to read God's Word, or meditations as here offered, and when we think we have hold of the thoughts and have asked God for His blessing, to go out in the hope that the blessing will abide. No, it requires day-by-day time with Jesus and with God. We all know the need of time for our meals each day. Every workman claims his hour for dinner; the hurried eating of so much food is not enough. If we are to live through Jesus, we must feed on Him (John 6:57); we must thoroughly take in and assimilate that heavenly food the Father has given us in His life. Therefore, my brother who wants to learn to abide in Jesus, take time each day, before you read, while you read, and after you read, to put yourself into living contact with the living Jesus, to yield yourself distinctly and consciously to His blessed influence, so will you give Him the opportunity of taking hold of you, of drawing you up and keeping you safe in His almighty life.

And now, to all God's children whom He allows me the privilege of pointing to the Heavenly Vine, I offer my fraternal love and salutations, with the prayer that to each one of them may be given the rich and full experience of the blessedness of abiding in Christ. And may the grace of Jesus, and the love of God, and the fellowship of the Holy Spirit, be their daily portion. Amen.

—*Andrew Murray*

JOHN 15:1–12

I am the true vine, and my Father is the husbandman. Every branch in me that beareth not fruit he taketh away: and every branch that beareth fruit, he purgeth it, that it may bring forth more fruit. Now ye are clean through the word which I have spoken unto you. Abide in me, and I in you. As the branch cannot bear fruit of itself, except it abide in the vine; no more can ye, except ye abide in me. I am the vine, ye are the branches: He that abideth in me, and I in him, the same bringeth forth much fruit: for without me ye can do nothing. If a man abide not in me, he is cast forth as a branch, and is withered; and men gather them, and cast them into the fire, and they are burned. If ye abide in me, and my words abide in you, ye shall ask what ye will, and it shall be done unto you. Herein is my Father glorified, that ye bear much fruit; so shall ye be my disciples. As the Father hath loved me, so have I loved you: continue ye in my love. If ye keep my commandments, ye shall abide in my love; even as I have kept my Father's commandments, and abide in his love. These things have I spoken unto you, that my joy might remain in you, and that your joy might be full. This is my commandment, That ye love one another, as I have loved you.

1

ALL YOU WHO HAVE COME TO HIM

Come unto me.
—Matthew 11:28

Abide in me.
—John 15:4

I t is to you who have heard and hearkened to the call, "*Come unto me,*" that this new invitation comes, "*Abide in me.*" The message comes from the same loving Savior. You doubtless have never repented having come at His call. You experienced that His word was truth; all His promises He fulfilled; He made you partakers of the blessings and the joy of His love. Was not His welcome most hearty, His pardon full and free, His love most sweet and precious? More than once, at your first coming to Him, you had reason to say, "*The half was not told me*" (1 Kings 10:7).

And yet you have had to complain of disappointment; as time went on, your expectations were not realized. The blessings you once enjoyed were lost; the love and joy of your first meeting with your Savior, instead of deepening, have become faint and feeble. And often you have wondered what the reason could be, that with such a Savior, so mighty and so loving, your experience of salvation should not have been a fuller one.

The answer is very simple. You wandered from Him. The blessings He bestows are all connected with His "*Come unto me*," and are only to be enjoyed in close fellowship with Him. You either did not fully understand, or did not rightly remember, that the call meant, "Come to Me to stay with Me." And yet this was indeed His object and purpose when first He called you to Himself. It was not to refresh you for a few short hours after your conversion with the joy of His love and deliverance, and then to send you forth to wander in sadness and sin. He had destined you to something better than a short-lived blessedness, to be enjoyed only in times of special earnestness and prayer, and then to pass away, as you had to return to those duties in which the far greater part of life has to be spent. He had prepared for you an abiding dwelling with Himself, where your whole life and every moment of it might be spent, where the work of your daily life might be done, and where all the while you might be enjoying unbroken communion with Him. It was even this He meant when to that first word, "*Come unto me*," He added this, "*Abide in me*." As earnest and faithful, as loving and tender, as the compassion that breathed in that blessed "*come*," was the grace that added this no less blessed "*abide*." As mighty as the attraction with which that first word drew you were the bonds with which this second, had you but listened to it, would have kept you. And as great as were the blessings with which that coming was rewarded, so large, yes, and much greater, were the treasures to which that abiding would have given you access.

And observe especially, it was not that He said, "Come to Me and abide with Me," but, "*Abide in me.*" The communion was not only to be unbroken, but most intimate and complete. He opened His arms to press you to His bosom; He opened His heart to welcome you there; He opened up all His divine fullness of life and love and offered to take you up into its fellowship to make you wholly one with Himself. There was a depth of meaning you cannot yet realize in His words: "*Abide in me.*"

And with no less earnestness than He had cried, "*Come unto me,*" did He plead, had you but noticed it, "*Abide in me.*" By every motive that had induced you to come, did He beseech you to abide. Was it the fear of sin and its curse that first drew you? The pardon you received on first coming could, with all the blessings flowing from it, only be confirmed and fully enjoyed on abiding in Him. Was it the longing to know and enjoy the infinite love that was calling you? The first coming gave but single drops to taste; it is only the abiding that can really satisfy the thirsty soul and give to drink of the rivers of pleasure that are at His right hand. Was it the weary longing to be made free from the bondage of sin, to become pure and holy, and so to find rest, the rest of God for the soul? This too can only be realized as you abide in Him—only abiding in Jesus gives rest in Him. Or if it was the hope of an inheritance in glory, and an everlasting home in the presence of the Infinite One, the true preparation for this, as well as its blessed foretaste in this life, are granted only to those who abide in Him. In very truth, there is nothing that moved you to come, that does not plead with thousandfold greater force: "Abide in Him." You did well to come; you do better to abide. Who would, after seeking the King's palace, be content to stand in the door, when he is invited in to dwell in the King's presence and share with Him in all the glory of His royal life? Oh, let us enter in and abide and enjoy to the full all the rich supply His wondrous love has prepared for us!

And yet I fear that there are many who have indeed come to Jesus, and who yet have to confess mournfully that they know but little of this blessed abiding in Him. With some, the reason is that they never fully understood that this was the meaning of the Savior's call. With others, though they heard the word, they did not know that such a life of abiding fellowship was possible, and indeed within their reach. Others will say that though they did believe that such a life was possible and did seek after it, they have never yet succeeded in discovering the secret of its attainment. And others, again, alas, will confess that it is their own unfaithfulness that has kept them from the enjoyment of the blessing. When the Savior would have kept them, they were not found ready to stay; they were not prepared to give up everything, and always, only, wholly to abide in Jesus.

To all such I come now in the name of Jesus, their Redeemer and mine, with the blessed message: *"Abide in me."* In His name I invite them to come, and for a season meditate with me daily on its meaning, its lessons, its claims, and its promises. I know how many, and, to the young believer, how difficult, the questions are that suggest themselves in connection with it. There is especially the question, with its various aspects, as to the possibility, in the midst of wearying work and continual distraction, of keeping up, or rather being kept in, the abiding communion. I do not undertake to remove all difficulties; this, Jesus Christ Himself alone must do by His Holy Spirit. But what I would gladly by the grace of God be permitted to do is, to repeat day by day the Master's blessed command, *"Abide in me,"* until it enters the heart and finds a place there, no more to be forgotten or neglected. I desire gladly that in the light of Holy Scripture we should meditate on its meaning, until the understanding, that gate to the heart, opens to apprehend something of what it offers and expects. So we will discover the means of its attainment and learn to know what keeps us from it, and what can help us to it; so we will feel its claims and be compelled to acknowledge that there can be no true allegiance to our King without simply and heartily accepting this one, too, of His commands. So we will gaze on its blessedness, until desire is inflamed and the will with all its energies is roused to claim and possess the unspeakable blessing.

Come, my fellow believers, and let us day by day set ourselves at His feet and meditate on this word of His, with an eye fixed on Him alone. Let us set ourselves in quiet trust before Him, waiting to hear His holy voice—the still small voice that is mightier than the storm that rends the rocks—breathing its quickening spirit within us, as He speaks, *"Abide in me.*" The soul that truly hears Jesus Himself speak the word, receives with the word the power to accept and to hold the blessing He offers.

And it may please You, blessed Savior, indeed, to speak to us; let each of us hear Your blessed voice. May the feeling of our deep need, and the faith of Your wondrous love, combined with the sight of the wonderfully blessed life You are waiting to bestow upon us, constrain us to listen and to obey, as often as You speak, *"Abide in me."* Let day by day the answer from our heart be "Savior, I do abide in You."

2

AND YOU SHALL FIND REST TO YOUR SOULS

Come unto me...and I will give you rest. Take my yoke upon you,
and learn of me; for I am meek and lowly in heart:
and ye shall find rest unto your souls.
—Matthew 11:28–29

Rest for the soul: such was the first promise with which the Savior sought to win the heavy-laden sinner. Simple though it appears, the promise is indeed as large and comprehensive as can be found. Rest for the soul—does it not imply deliverance from every fear, the supply of every need, the fulfillment of every desire? And now nothing less than this is the prize with which the Savior woos back the wandering one—who is mourning that the rest has not been so abiding or so full as he had hoped—to come back and abide in Him. Nothing but this was the reason that the rest has either not been found, or, if found, has been disturbed or lost again: you did not abide with, you did not abide in, Him.

Have you ever noticed how, in the original invitation of the Savior to come to Him, the promise of rest was repeated twice, with such a variation in the conditions as might have suggested that abiding rest could only be found in abiding nearness. First the Savior said, *"Come unto me...and I will give you rest"*; the very moment you come, and believe, I will give you rest—the rest of pardon and acceptance—the rest in My love. But we know that all that God bestows needs time to become fully our own; it must be held fast and appropriated and assimilated into our inmost being; without this not even Christ's giving can make it our very own, in full experience and enjoyment. And so the Savior repeats His promise, in words that clearly speak not so much of the initial rest with which He welcomes the weary one who comes, but of the deeper and personally appropriated rest of the soul that abides with Him. He now not only said, *"Come unto me,"* but *"Take my yoke upon you, and learn of me"*: become My scholars, yield yourselves to My training, submit in all things to My will, let your whole life be one with Mine—in other words, abide in Me. And then He adds, not only, *"I will give,"* but *"ye shall find rest unto your souls."* The rest He gave at coming will become something you have really found and made your very own—the deeper, the abiding, rest that comes from longer acquaintance and closer fellowship, from entire surrender and deeper sympathy. *"Take my yoke... and learn of me," "Abide in me"* (John 15:4)—this is the path to abiding rest.

Do not these words of the Savior reveal what you have perhaps often sought in vain to know, how it is that the rest you at times enjoy is so often lost? It must have been this: you had not understood how entire surrender to Jesus is the secret of perfect rest. Giving up one's whole life to Him, for Him alone to rule and order it; taking up His yoke and submitting to be led and taught, to learn of Him; abiding in Him, to be and do only what He wills—these are the conditions of discipleship without which there can be no thought of maintaining the rest that was bestowed on first coming to Christ. The rest is in Christ, and not something He gives apart from Himself, and so it is only in having Him that the rest can really be kept and enjoyed.

It is because so many a young believer fails to lay hold of this truth that the rest so speedily passes away. Some really did not know; they were never taught how Jesus claims the undivided allegiance of the whole heart and life; how there is not a spot in the whole of life over which He does not wish to reign; how in the very least things His disciples must only seek to please Him. They did not know how entire the consecration was that Jesus claimed. With others, who had some idea of what a very holy life a Christian ought to lead, the mistake was a different one: they could not believe such a life to be a possible attainment. Taking, and bearing, and never for a moment laying aside the yoke of Jesus, appeared to them to require such a strain of effort, and such an amount of goodness, as to be altogether beyond their reach. The very idea of always, all the day, abiding in Jesus, was too high—something they might attain to after a life of holiness and growth, but certainly not what a feeble beginner was to start with.

They did not know how, when Jesus said, *"My yoke is easy"* (Matt. 11:30), He spoke the truth; how just the yoke gives the rest, because the moment the soul yields itself to obey, the Lord Himself gives the strength and joy to do it. They did not notice how, when He said, *"Learn of me,"* He added, *"I am meek and lowly in heart,"* to assure them that His gentleness would meet their every need and bear them as a mother bears her feeble child. Oh, they did not know that when He said, *"Abide in me"* (John 15:4), He only asked the surrender to Himself; His almighty love would hold them fast and keep and bless them. And so, as some had erred from the lack of full consecration, so these failed because they didn't fully trust. These two, consecration and faith, are the essential elements of the Christian life—the giving up all to Jesus, the receiving all from Jesus. They are implied in each other; they are united in the one word: surrender. A full surrender is to obey as well as to trust, to trust as well as to obey.

With such misunderstanding at the outset, it is no wonder that the disciple life was not one of such joy or strength as had been hoped. In some things you were led into sin without knowing it, because you had not learned how wholly Jesus wanted to rule you, and how you could not keep right for a moment unless you had Him very near you. In other things you knew what sin was, but had not the power to conquer, because you did not know or believe how entirely Jesus would take charge of you to keep and to help you. Either way, it was not long before the bright joy of your first love was lost, and your path, instead of being like the path of the just, shining more and more unto the perfect day, became like Israel's wandering in the desert—ever on the way, never very far, and yet always coming short of the promised rest. Weary soul, since so many years driven to and fro like the panting hart, come and learn this day the lesson that there is a spot where safety and victory, where peace and rest, are always sure, and that that spot is always open to you: the heart of Jesus.

But, alas, I hear someone say, it is just this abiding in Jesus, always bearing His yoke, to learn of Him, that is so difficult, and the very effort to attain to this often disturbs the rest even more than sin or the world. What a mistake to speak thus, and yet how often the words are heard! Does it weary the traveler to rest in the house or on the bed where he seeks repose from his fatigue? Or is it a labor to a little child to rest in his mother's arms? Is it not the house that keeps the traveler within its shelter? Do not the arms of the mother sustain and keep the little one? And so it is with Jesus. The soul has but to yield itself to Him, to be still and rest in the confidence that His love has undertaken, and that His faithfulness will perform, the work of keeping it safe in the shelter of His arms. Oh, it is because the blessing is so great that our little hearts cannot rise to apprehend it. It is as if we cannot believe that Christ, the Almighty One, will indeed teach and keep us all the day. And yet this is just what He has promised, for without this He cannot really give us rest. It is as our heart takes in this truth that, when He said, "*Abide in me*" (John 15:4), "*Learn of me,*" He really meant it, and that it is His own work to keep us abiding when we yield ourselves to Him, that we will venture to cast ourselves into the arms of His love and abandon ourselves to His blessed keeping. It is not the yoke, but resistance to the yoke, that causes the difficulty; the wholehearted surrender to Jesus, as at once our Master and our Keeper, finds and secures the rest.

Come, my brother, and let us this very day commence to accept the word of Jesus in all simplicity. This is a distinct command: *"Take my yoke... and learn of me"*; *"Abide in me."* A command has to be obeyed. The obedient scholar asks no questions about possibilities or results; he accepts every order in the confidence that his teacher has provided for all that is needed. The power and the perseverance to abide in the rest, and the blessing in abiding—it belongs to the Savior to see to this. It is mine to obey; it is His to provide. Let us this day in immediate obedience accept the command and answer boldly, "Savior, I abide in You. At Your bidding I take Your yoke. I undertake the duty without delay; I abide in You." Let each consciousness of failure only give new urgency to the command and teach us to listen more earnestly than ever until the Spirit again allows us to hear the voice of Jesus saying, with a love and authority that inspire both hope and obedience, "Child, abide in Me." That word, listened to as coming from Himself, will be an end of all doubting—a divine promise of what will surely be granted. And with ever increasing simplicity, its meaning will be interpreted. Abiding in Jesus is nothing but the giving up of oneself to be ruled and taught and led, and so resting in the arms of Everlasting Love.

Blessed rest, the fruit and the foretaste and the fellowship of God's own rest, found of them who thus come to Jesus to abide in Him! It is the peace of God, the great calm of the eternal world, that passes all understanding, and that keeps the heart and mind (Phil. 4:7). With this grace secured, we have strength for every duty, courage for every struggle, a blessing in every cross, and the joy of life eternal in death itself.

O my Savior, if ever my heart should doubt or fear again, as if the blessing were too great to expect, or too high to attain, let me hear Your voice to quicken my faith and obedience: *"Abide in me"*; *"Take my yoke upon you, and learn of me...ye shall find rest unto your souls."*

3

TRUSTING HIM TO KEEP YOU

Not as though I had already attained,
either were already perfect: but I follow after, if that I may apprehend
that for which also I am apprehended of Christ Jesus.
—Philippians 3:12

More than one admits that it is a sacred duty and a blessed privilege to abide in Christ, but they shrink back continually before the question: Is a life of unbroken fellowship with the Savior possible? Eminent Christians, to whom special opportunities of cultivating this grace have been granted, may attain to it; for the large majority of disciples, whose life, by a divine appointment, is so fully occupied with the affairs of this life, it can scarcely be expected. The more they hear of this life, the deeper their sense of its glory and blessedness, and there is nothing they would not sacrifice to be made partakers of it. But they are too weak, too unfaithful; they never can attain to it.

Dear souls, how little they know that the abiding in Christ is just meant for the weak, and so beautifully suited to their feebleness. It is not the doing of some great thing and does not demand that we first lead a holy and devoted life. No, it is simply weakness entrusting itself to a Mighty One to be kept—the unfaithful one casting self on One who is altogether trustworthy and true. Abiding in Him is not a work that we have to do as the condition for enjoying His salvation, but a consenting to let Him do all for us, and in us, and through us. It is a work He does for us: the fruit and the power of His redeeming love. Our part is simply to yield, to trust, and to wait for what He has engaged to perform.

It is this quiet expectation and confidence, resting on the word of Christ that in Him there is an abiding place prepared, which is so sadly lacking among Christians. They scarcely take the time or the trouble to realize that when He said *"Abide in me"* (John 15:4), He offers Himself, the Keeper of Israel that slumbers not nor sleeps, with all His power and love, as the living home of the soul, where the mighty influences of His grace will be stronger to keep than all their feebleness to lead astray. The idea they have of grace is this: that their conversion and pardon are God's work, but that now, in gratitude to God, it is their work to live as Christians and follow Jesus. There is always the thought of a work that has to be done, and even though they pray for help, still the work is theirs. They fail continually and become hopeless, and the despondency only increases the helplessness. No, wandering one; as it was Jesus who drew you when He spoke *"Come"* (Matt. 11:28), so it is Jesus who keeps you when He said *"Abide"* (John 15:4). The grace to come and the grace to abide are alike from Him alone. That word *come*, heard, meditated on, accepted, was the cord of love that drew you near; that word *abide* is even so the band with which He holds you fast and binds you to Himself. Let the soul but take time to listen to the voice of Jesus. *"In me,"* He said, "is your place—in My almighty arms. It is I who love you so, who speak 'Abide in me'; surely you can trust Me." The voice of Jesus entering and dwelling in the soul cannot but call for the response: "Yes, Savior, In You I can, I will abide."

"*Abide in me.*" These words are no law of Moses, demanding from the sinful what they cannot perform. They are the command of love, which is ever only a promise in a different shape. Think of this until all feeling of burden and fear and despair pass away, and the first thought that comes as you hear of abiding in Jesus is one of bright and joyous hope: it is for me; I know I will enjoy it. You are not under the law, with its inexorable *do*, but under grace, with its blessed *believe* what Christ will do for you. And if the question is asked, "But surely there is something for us to do?" the answer is, "Our doing and working are but the fruit of Christ's work in us." It is when the soul becomes utterly passive, looking and resting on what Christ is to do, that its energies are stirred to their highest activity, that we work most effectively because we know that He works in us. It is as we see in those words *in me* the mighty energies of love reaching out after us to have us and to hold us, that all the strength of our will is roused to abide in Him.

This connection between Christ's work and our work is beautifully expressed in the words of Paul: "*I follow after, if that I may apprehend that for which also I am apprehended of Christ Jesus.*" It was because he knew that the mighty and the faithful One had grasped him with the glorious purpose of making him one with Himself, that he did his utmost to grasp the glorious prize. The faith, the experience, the full assurance, "Christ has apprehended me," gave him the courage and the strength to press on and apprehend that for which he was apprehended. Each new insight of the great end for which Christ had apprehended and was holding him, roused him afresh to aim at nothing less.

Paul's expression, and its application to the Christian life, can be best understood if we think of a father helping his child to mount the side of some steep precipice. The father stands above and has taken the son by the hand to help him on. He points him to the spot on which he will help him to plant his feet, as he leaps upward. The leap would be too high and dangerous for the child alone; but the father's hand is his trust, and he leaps to get hold of the point for which his father has taken hold of him. It is the father's strength that secures him and lifts him up and so urges him to use his utmost strength.

Such is the relation between Christ and you, O weak and trembling believer! Fix first your eyes on that for which He has apprehended you. It is nothing less than a life of abiding, unbroken fellowship with Himself to which He is seeking to lift you up. All that you have already received— pardon and peace, the Spirit and His grace—are but preliminary to this. And all that you see promised to you in the future—holiness and fruit- fulness and glory everlasting—are but its natural outcome. Union with Himself, and so with the Father, is His highest object. Fix your eyes on this, and gaze until it stands out before you clear and unmistakable: Christ's aim is to have me abiding in Him.

And then let the second thought enter your heart: unto this "*I am apprehended of Christ.*" His almighty power has laid hold on me and offers now to lift me up to where He would have me. Fix your eyes on Christ. Gaze on the love that beams in those eyes and that asks whether you cannot trust Him, who sought and found and brought you near, now to keep you. Gaze on that arm of power, and say whether you have reason to be assured that He is indeed able to keep you abiding in Him.

And as you think of the spot where He points—the blessed place for which He apprehended you—and keep your gaze fixed on Himself, hold- ing you and waiting to lift you up, say, could you not this very day take the upward step and rise to enter upon this blessed life of abiding in Christ? Yes, begin at once, and say, "O my Jesus, if You bid me, and if You engage to lift and keep me there, I will venture. Trembling, but trusting, I will say, 'Jesus, I do abide in You.'"

My beloved fellow believer, go, and take time alone with Jesus, and say this to Him. I dare not speak to you about abiding in Him for the mere sake of calling forth a pleasing religious sentiment. God's truth must at once be acted on. Oh, yield yourself this very day to the blessed Savior in the surrender of the one thing He asks of you: give up yourself to abide in

Him. He Himself will work it in you. You can trust Him to keep you trusting and abiding.

And if ever doubts again arise, or the bitter experience of failure tempt you to despair, just remember where Paul found His strength: "*I am apprehended of Christ Jesus.*" In that assurance you have a fountain of strength. From that you can look up to that for which He has set His heart, and set yours there too. From that you gather confidence that the good work He has begun He will also perform. And in that confidence you will gather courage, day by day, afresh to say, "'*I follow after, if that I may apprehend that for which also I am apprehended of Christ Jesus.*' It is because Jesus has taken hold of me, and because Jesus keeps me, that I dare to say: Savior, I abide in You."

4

AS THE BRANCH
IN THE VINE

I am the vine, ye are the branches.
—John 15:5

I t was in connection with the parable of the Vine that our Lord first used the expression, *"Abide in me"* (John 15:4). That parable, so simple, and yet so rich in its teaching, gives us the best and most complete illustration of the meaning of our Lord's command and the union to which He invites us.

The parable teaches us the nature of that union. The connection between the vine and the branch is a living one. No external, temporary union will suffice; no work of man can effect it. The branch, whether an original or an engrafted one, is such only by the Creator's own work, in virtue of which the life, the sap, the fatness, and the fruitfulness of the vine communicate themselves to the branch. And it is the same way with the believer too. His union with his Lord is no work of human wisdom or human will, but an act of God, by which the closest and most complete life union is effected between the Son of God and the sinner. *"God hath sent forth the Spirit of his Son into your hearts"* (Gal. 4:6). The same Spirit that dwelled and still dwells in the Son, becomes the life of the believer; in the unity of that one Spirit, and the fellowship of the same life that is in Christ, he is one with Him. As between the vine and branch, it is a life union that makes them one.

The parable teaches us the completeness of the union. So close is the union between the vine and the branch, that each is nothing without the other, that each is wholly and only for the other.

Without the vine the branch can do nothing. To the vine it owes its right of place in the vineyard, its life and its fruitfulness. And so the Lord said, *"Without me ye can do nothing"* (John 15:5). The believer can each day be pleasing to God only in that which he does through the power of Christ dwelling in him. The daily inflowing of the life sap of the Holy Spirit is his only power to bring forth fruit. He lives alone in Him and is for each moment dependent on Him alone.

Without the branch the vine can also do nothing. A vine without branches can bear no fruit. No less indispensable than the vine to the branch, is the branch to the vine. Such is the wonderful condescension of the grace of Jesus, that just as His people are dependent on Him, He has made Himself dependent on them. Without His disciples He cannot dispense His blessing to the world; He cannot offer sinners the grapes of the heavenly Canaan. Marvel not! It is His own appointment; and this is the high honor to which He has called His redeemed ones, that as indispensable as He is to them in heaven, that from Him their fruit may be found, so indispensable are they to Him on earth, that through them His fruit may be found. Believers, meditate on this, until your soul bows to worship in the presence of the mystery of the perfect union between Christ and the believer.

There is more: as neither vine nor branch is anything without the other, so is neither anything except for the other.

All the vine possesses belongs to the branches. The vine does not gather from the soil its fatness and its sweetness for itself—all it has is at the disposal of the branches. As it is the parent, so it is the servant of the branches. And Jesus, to whom we owe our lives, how completely does He give Himself for us and to us: *"The glory which thou gavest me I have given them"* (John 17:22); *"He that believeth on me, the works that I do shall he do also; and greater works...shall he do"* (John 14:12). All His fullness and all His riches are for you, believer, for the vine does not live for itself, keeps nothing for itself, but exists only for the branches. All that Jesus is in heaven, He is for us. He has no interest there separate from ours; as our representative He stands before the Father.

And all the branch possesses belongs to the vine. The branch does not exist for itself, but to bear fruit that can proclaim the excellence of the vine. It has no reason for existence except to be of service to the vine. This is a glorious image of the calling of the believer, and the entireness of his consecration to the service of his Lord. As Jesus gives Himself so wholly over to him, he feels himself urged to be wholly his Lord's. Every power of his being, every moment of his life, every thought and feeling, belong to Jesus, that from Him and for Him he may bring forth fruit. As he realizes what the vine is to the branch, and what the branch is meant to be to the vine, he feels that he has but one thing to think of and to live for, and that is, the will, the glory, the work, the kingdom of his blessed Lord—the bringing forth of fruit to the glory of His name.

The parable teaches us the object of the union. The branches are for fruit and fruit alone. *"Every branch...that beareth not fruit he taketh away"* (John 15:2). The branch needs leaves for the maintenance of its own life and the perfection of its fruit; the fruit itself it bears to give away to those around. As the believer enters into his calling as a branch, he sees that he has to forget himself and to live entirely for his fellowmen. To love them, to seek for them, and to save them, Jesus came. For this every branch on the Vine has to live as much as the Vine itself. It is for fruit, much fruit, that the Father has made us one with Jesus.

Wondrous parable of the Vine—unveiling the mysteries of the divine love, of the heavenly life, of the world of the Spirit—how little have I understood you! Jesus the living Vine in heaven, and I the living branch on earth! How little have I understood how great my need of, but also how perfect my claim to, all His fullness! How little understood, how great His need of, but also how perfect His claim to, my emptiness! Let me, in its beautiful light, study the wondrous union between Jesus and His people, until it becomes to me the guide into full communion with my beloved Lord. Let me listen and believe, until my whole being cries out, "Jesus is indeed to me the True Vine, bearing me, nourishing me, supplying me, using me, and filling me to the full to make me bring forth fruit abundantly." Then I will not fear to say, "I am indeed a branch to Jesus, the True Vine, abiding in Him, resting on Him, waiting for Him, serving Him, and living only that through me, too, He may show forth the riches of His grace and give His fruit to a perishing world."

It is when we try thus to understand the meaning of the parable, that the blessed command spoken in connection with it will come home to us in its true power. The thought of what the vine is to the branch, and Jesus to the believer, will give new force to the words, *"Abide in me"* (v. 4). It will be as if He says, "Think, soul, how completely I belong to you. I have joined Myself inseparably to you; all the fullness and fatness of the Vine are yours indeed. Now once you are in Me, be assured that all I have is wholly yours. It is My interest and My honor to have you be a fruitful branch; only abide in Me. You are weak, but I am strong; you are poor, but I am rich. Only abide in Me; yield yourself wholly to My teaching and rule; simply trust My love, My grace, My promises. Only believe; I am wholly yours; I am the Vine, you are the branch. Abide in Me."

What do you say, O my soul? Will I hesitate longer or withhold consent? Or will I not, instead of only thinking how hard and how difficult it is to live like a branch of the True Vine, because I thought of it as something I had to accomplish—will I not now begin to look upon it as the most blessed and joyful thing under heaven? Will I not believe that, now that I am in Him, He Himself will keep me and enable me to abide? On my part, abiding is nothing but the acceptance of my position, the consent to be kept there, the surrender of faith to the strong Vine still to hold the feeble branch. Yes, I will, I do abide in You, blessed Lord Jesus.

O Savior, how unspeakable is Your love! *"Such knowledge is too wonderful for me; it is high, I cannot attain unto it"* (Ps. 139:6). I can only yield myself to Your love with the prayer that, day by day, You would unfold to me something of its precious mysteries and so encourage and strengthen Your loving disciple to do what his heart longs to do indeed—ever, only, wholly to abide in You.

5

AS YOU CAME TO HIM, BY FAITH

As ye have therefore received Christ Jesus the Lord,
so walk ye in him: rooted and built up in him,
and stablished in the faith...abounding therein.
—Colossians 2:6–7

I n these words the apostle teaches us the weighty lesson that it is not only by faith that we first come to Christ and are united to Him, but that it is by faith that we are to be rooted and established in our union with Christ. Not less essential than for the commencement, is faith for the progress of the spiritual life. Abiding in Jesus can only be by faith.

There are earnest Christians who do not understand this, or, if they admit it in theory, they fail to realize its application in practice. They are very zealous for a free Gospel, with our first acceptance of Christ, and justification by faith alone. But after this they think everything depends on our diligence and faithfulness. While they firmly grasp the truth, the sinner "*is justified by faith*" (Rom. 3:28), they have hardly found a place in their scheme for the larger truth: "*The just shall live by faith*" (Rom. 1:17). They have never understood what a perfect Savior Jesus is and how He will each day do for the sinner just as much as He did the first day when he came to Him. They do not know that the life of grace is always and only a life of faith, and that in the relationship to Jesus the one daily and unceasing duty of the disciple is to believe, because believing is the one channel through which divine grace and strength flow out into the heart of man. The old nature of the believer remains evil and sinful to the last. It is only as he daily comes, all empty and helpless, to his Savior to receive His life and strength, that he can bring forth the fruits of right-eousness to the glory of God. Therefore it is: "*As ye have therefore received Christ Jesus the Lord, so walk ye in him: rooted…in him, and stablished in the faith…abounding therein.*" As you came to Jesus, so abide in Him, by faith.

And if you would know how faith is to be exercised in thus abiding in Jesus, to be rooted more deeply and firmly in Him, you have only to look back to the time when you first received Him. You remember well what obstacles at that time there appeared to be in the way of your believing. There was first your vileness and guilt: it appeared impossible that the promise of pardon and love could be for such a sinner. Then there was the sense of weakness and death: you did not feel the power for the sur-render and the trust to which you were called. And then there was the future: you dared not undertake to be a disciple of Jesus while you felt so sure that you could not remain standing, but would speedily again be unfaithful and fall. These difficulties were like mountains in your way. And how were they removed? Simply by the Word of God. That Word, as it were, compelled you to believe that, notwithstanding guilt in the past, and weakness in the present, and unfaithfulness in the future, the promise was sure that Jesus would accept and save you. On that Word you ventured to come and were not deceived: you found that Jesus did indeed accept and save.

Apply this, your experience in coming to Jesus, to the abiding in Him. Now, as then, the temptations to keep you from believing are many. When you think of your sins since you became a disciple, your heart is cast down with shame, and it looks as if it were too much to expect that Jesus should indeed receive you into perfect intimacy and the full enjoyment of His holy love. When you think how utterly, in times past, you have failed in keeping the most sacred vows, the consciousness of present weakness makes you tremble at the very idea of answering the Savior's command with the promise, "Lord, from henceforth I will abide in You." And when you set before yourself the life of love and joy, of holiness and fruitfulness, which in the future are to flow from abiding in Him, it is as if it only serves to make you still more hopeless: you, at least, can never attain to it. You know yourself too well. It is no use expecting it, only to be disappointed; a life fully and wholly abiding in Jesus is not for you.

Oh, that you would learn a lesson from the time of your first coming to the Savior! Remember, dear soul, how you then were led, contrary to all that your experience, and your feelings, and even your sober judgment said, to take Jesus at His word, and how you were not disappointed. He did receive you, and pardon you; He did love you and save you—you know it. And if He did this for you when you were an enemy and a stranger, do you not think, now that you are His own, He will not much more fulfill His promise? Oh, that you would come and begin simply to listen to His Word, and to ask only the one question: Does He really mean that I should abide in Him? The answer His Word gives is so simple and so sure: By His almighty grace you now are *in Him*; that same almighty grace will indeed enable you to abide in Him. By faith you became partakers of the initial grace; by that same faith you can enjoy the continuous grace of abiding in Him.

And if you ask what exactly it is that you now have to believe that you may abide in Him, the answer is not difficult. Believe first of all what He said, *"I am the vine"* (John 15:5). The safety and the fruitfulness of the branch depend upon the strength of the vine. Do not think so much of yourself as a branch, nor of the abiding as your duty, until you have first had your soul filled with the faith of what Christ as the Vine is. He really will be to you all that a vine can be—holding you fast, nourishing you, and making Himself every moment responsible for your growth and your fruit. Take time to know, set yourself heartily to believe, "my Vine, on whom I can depend for all I need, is Christ." A large, strong vine bears the feeble branch, and holds it more than the branch holds the vine. Ask the Father by the Holy Spirit to reveal to you what a glorious, loving, mighty Christ this is, in whom you have your place and your life; it is the faith in what Christ is, more than anything else, that will keep you abiding in Him. A soul filled with large thoughts of the Vine will be a strong branch and will abide confidently in Him. Be much occupied with Jesus, and believe much in Him as the True Vine.

And then, when faith can well say, "He is my Vine," let it further say, "I am His branch; I am in Him." I speak to those who say they are Christ's disciples, and on them I cannot too earnestly press the importance of exercising their faith in saying, "I am in Him." It makes the abiding so simple. If I realize clearly as I meditate that now I am in Him, I see at once that there is nothing lacking except just my consent to be what He has made me, to remain where He has placed me. I am in Christ: This simple thought, carefully, prayerfully, believingly uttered, removes all difficulty as if there were some great attainment to be reached. No, I am in Christ, my blessed Savior. His love has prepared a home for me with Himself when He says, "Abide in My love," and His power has undertaken to keep the door, and to keep me in, if I will but consent. I am in Christ. I have now but to say, "Savior, I bless You for this wondrous grace. I consent; I yield myself to Your gracious keeping. I do abide in You."

It is astonishing how such a faith will work out all that is further implied in abiding in Christ. There is in the Christian life great need of watchfulness and of prayer, of self-denial and of striving, of obedience and of diligence. But *"all things are possible to him that believeth"*

(Mark 9:23). *"This is the victory that overcometh...even our faith"* (1 John 5:4). It is the faith that continually closes its eyes to the weakness of the creature and finds its joy in the sufficiency of an Almighty Savior that makes the soul strong and glad. It gives itself up to be led by the Holy Spirit into an ever deeper appreciation of that wonderful Savior whom God has given us—the Infinite Immanuel. It follows the leading of the Spirit from page to page of the blessed Word, with the one desire to take each revelation of what Jesus is and what He promises as its nourishment and its life. In accordance with the promise, *"If that which ye have heard from the beginning shall [abide] in you, ye also shall [abide] in the Son, and in the Father"* (1 John 2:24), it lives by every word that proceeds out of the mouth of God (Matt. 4:4). And so it makes the soul strong with the strength of God to be and to do all that is needed for abiding in Christ.

Believer, you want to abide in Christ; only believe. Believe always; believe now. Bow even now before your Lord, and say to Him in childlike faith, that because He is your Vine, and you are His branch, you will this day abide in Him.

Author's Note

"I am the true vine" (John 15:1). He who offers us the privilege of an actual union with Himself is the great I Am, the almighty God, who upholds all things by the word of His power. And this almighty God reveals Himself as our perfect Savior, even to the unimaginable extent of seeking to renew our fallen natures by grafting them into His own divine nature.

To realize the glorious deity of Him whose call sounds forth to longing hearts with such exceeding sweetness, is no small step toward gaining the full privilege to which we are invited. But longing is by itself of no use; still less can there be any profit in reading of the blessed results to be gained from a close and personal union with our Lord, if we believe that union to be practically beyond our reach. His words are meant to be a living, an eternal, precious reality. And this they can never become unless we are sure that we may reasonably expect their accomplishment. But what could make the accomplishment of such an idea possible—what could make it reasonable to suppose that we poor, weak, selfish creatures, full of sin and full of failures, might be saved out of the corruption of our nature and made partakers of the holiness of our Lord—except the fact, the marvelous, unalterable fact, that He who proposes to us so great a transformation is Himself the everlasting God, as able as He is willing to fulfill His own Word. In meditating, therefore, upon these utterances of Christ, containing as they do the very essence of His teaching, the very concentration of His love, let us, at the outset, put away all tendency to doubt. Let us not allow ourselves so much as to question whether such erring disciples as we are can be enabled to attain the holiness to which we are called through a close and intimate union with our Lord. If there is any impossibility, any falling short of the proposed blessedness, it will arise from the lack of earnest desire on our part. There is no lack in any respect on His part who puts forth the invitation; with God there can be no shortcoming in the fulfillment of His promise.—*The Life of Fellowship; Meditations on John 15:1–2* by A. M. James.

It is perhaps necessary to say, for the sake of young or doubting Christians, that there is something more necessary than the effort to exercise faith in each separate promise that is brought under our notice. What is of even greater importance is the cultivation of a trustful disposition toward God, the habit of always thinking of Him, of His ways and His works, with bright confiding hopefulness. In such soil alone can the individual promises strike root and grow up. In a little work published by the Tract Society, *Encouragements to Faith*, by James Kimball, there will be found many most suggestive and helpful thoughts, all pleading for the right God has to claim that He will be trusted. *The Christian's Secret of a Happy Life* is another little work that has been a great help to many. Its bright and buoyant tone, its loving and unceasing repetition of the keynote—we may indeed depend on Jesus to do all He has said, and more than we can think—has breathed hope and joy into many a heart that was almost ready to despair of ever going on. In Frances Havergal's *Kept for the Master's Use,* there is the same healthful hope-inspiring tone.

6

GOD HIMSELF HAS UNITED YOU TO HIM

Of [God] *are ye in Christ Jesus, who was made unto us wisdom from God, both righteousness and sanctification, and redemption.*
—1 Corinthians 1:30 RV

My Father is the husbandman.
—John 15:1

Y e [are] *in Christ Jesus.*" The believers at Corinth were still feeble and carnal, only babes in Christ. And yet Paul wants them, at the outset of his teaching, to know distinctly that they are in Christ Jesus.

The whole Christian life depends on the clear consciousness of our position in Christ. Most essential to the abiding in Christ is the daily renewal of our faith's assurance, "I am in Christ Jesus." All fruitful preaching to believers must take this as its starting point: "*Ye* [are] *in Christ Jesus.*"

But the apostle has an additional thought, of almost greater importance: "*Of* [God] *are ye in Christ Jesus.*" He wants us not only to remember our union to Christ, but especially that it is not our own doing, but the work of God Himself. As the Holy Spirit teaches us to realize this, we will see what a source of assurance and strength it must become to us. If it is of God alone that I am in Christ, then God Himself, the Infinite One, becomes my security for all I can need or wish in seeking to abide in Christ.

Let me try to understand what it means, this wonderful "*Of* [God]… *in Christ.*" In becoming partakers of the union with Christ, there is a work God does and a work we have to do. God does His work by moving us to do our work. The work of God is hidden and silent; what we do is something distinct and tangible. Conversion and faith, prayer and obedience, are conscious acts of which we can give a clear account; while the spiritual quickening and strengthening that come from above are secret and beyond the reach of human sight. And so it comes that when the believer tries to say, "I am in Christ Jesus," he looks more to the work he did, than to that wondrous secret work of God by which he was united to Christ. Nor can it well be otherwise at the commencement of the Christian course. "I know that I have believed" is a valid testimony. But it is of great consequence that the mind should be led to see that at the back of our turning and believing and accepting of Christ, there was God's almighty power doing its work—inspiring our will, taking possession of us, and carrying out its own purpose of love in planting us into Christ Jesus. As the believer enters into this, the divine side of the work of salvation, he will learn to praise and to worship with new exultation, and to rejoice more than ever in the divineness of that salvation he has been made partaker of. At each step he reviews, the song will come, "This is the Lord's doing"—divine Omnipotence working out what eternal Love had devised. Of God I am in Christ Jesus.

The words will lead him even further and higher, even to the depths of eternity. *"Whom he did predestinate, them he also called"* (Rom. 8:30). The calling in time is the manifestation of the purpose in eternity. Before the world was, God had fixed the eye of His sovereign love on you in the election of grace and chosen you in Christ. That you know yourself to be in Christ is the stepping-stone by which you rise to understand in its full meaning the word, "Of God I am in Christ Jesus." With the prophet, your language will be, *"The LORD hath appeared of old unto me, saying, Yea, I have loved thee with an everlasting love: therefore with lovingkindness have I drawn thee"* (Jer. 31:3). And you will recognize your own salvation as a part of that *"mystery of his will, according to his good pleasure which he hath purposed in himself"* (Eph. 1:9) and join with the whole body of believers in Christ as these say, *"In whom also we have obtained an inheritance, being predestinated according to the purpose of him who worketh all things after the counsel of his own will"* (v. 11). Nothing will more exalt free grace, and make man bow very low before it, than this knowledge of the mystery *"Of [God]...in Christ."*

It is easy to see what a mighty influence it must exert on the believer who seeks to abide in Christ. What a sure standing ground it gives him, as he rests his right to Christ and all His fullness on nothing less than the Father's own purpose and work! We have thought of Christ as the Vine, and the believer as the branch; let us not forget that other precious word, *"My Father is the husbandman."* The Savior said, *"Every plant, which my heavenly Father hath not planted, shall be rooted up"* (Matt. 15:13), but every branch grafted by Him in the True Vine will never be plucked out of His hand. As it was the Father to whom Christ owed all He was, and in whom He had all His strength and His life as the Vine, so to the Father the believer owes his place and his security in Christ. The same love and delight with which the Father watched over the beloved Son Himself, watch over ever member of His body, everyone who is in Christ Jesus.

What confident trust this faith inspires, not only as to the being kept in safety to the end, but also especially as to the being able to fulfill in every point the object for which I have been united to Christ. The branch is as much in the charge and keeping of the husbandman as the vine; his honor as much concerned in the well-being and growth of the branch as of the vine. The God who chose Christ to be the Vine fitted Him thoroughly for the work He had as the Vine to perform. The God who has chosen me and planted me in Christ has thereby engaged to secure, if I will but let Him, by yielding myself to Him, that I in every way be worthy of Jesus Christ. Oh, that I would only fully realize this! What confidence and urgency it would give to my prayer to the God and Father of Jesus Christ! How it would quicken the sense of dependence and make me see that praying without ceasing is indeed the one need of my life—an unceasing waiting, moment by moment, on the God who has united me to Christ, to perfect His own divine work, to work in me both to will and to do of His good pleasure.

And what a motive this would be for the highest activity in the maintenance of a fruitful branch life! Motives are mighty powers; it is of infinite importance to have them high and clear. Here surely is the highest: you are God's workmanship, created in Christ Jesus unto good works (see Eph. 2:10), grafted by Him into Christ, unto the bringing forth of much fruit. Whatever God creates is exquisitely suited to its end. He created the sun to give light: how perfectly it does its work! He created the eye to see: how beautifully it fulfills its object! He created the new man unto good works: how admirably it is fitted for its purpose.

Of God I am in Christ, created anew, made a branch of the Vine, fitted for fruit bearing. Would to God that believers would cease looking most at their old natures, and complaining of their weaknesses, as if God called them to what they were unfitted for! If only they would believingly and joyfully accept the wondrous revelation of how God, in uniting them to Christ, has made Himself chargeable for their spiritual growth and fruitfulness! How all sickly hesitancy and sloth would disappear, and under the influence of this mighty motive—the faith in the faithfulness of Him of whom they are in Christ—their whole nature would rise to accept and fulfill their glorious destiny!

O my soul; yield yourself to the mighty influence of this word: *"Of [God] are ye in Christ Jesus"*! It is the same God of whom Christ is made all that He is for us, of whom we also are in Christ, and will most surely be made what we must be to Him. Take time to meditate and to worship, until the light that comes from the throne of God has shone into you, and you have seen your union to Christ as indeed the work of His almighty Father. Take time, day after day, and let, in your whole religious life, with all it has of claims and duties, of needs and wishes, God be everything. See Jesus, as He speaks to you, *"Abide in me"* (John 15:4), pointing upward and saying, *"'My Father is the husbandman.'* Of Him you are in Me, through Him you abide in Me, and to Him and to His glory will be the fruit you bear." And let your answer be, "Amen, Lord! So be it." From eternity Christ and I were ordained for each other; inseparably we belong to each other. It is God's will; I will abide in Christ. It is of God I am in Christ Jesus.

7

AS YOUR WISDOM

*Of [God] are ye in Christ Jesus, who was made unto us wisdom from
God, both righteousness and sanctification, and redemption.*
—1 Corinthians 1:30 RV

Jesus Christ is not only Priest to purchase and King to secure, but also Prophet to reveal to us the salvation that God has prepared for those who love Him. Just as at Creation the light was first called into existence, that in it all God's other works might have their life and beauty, so in our text wisdom is mentioned first as the treasury in which are to be found the three precious gifts that follow. The life is the light of man; it is in revealing to us, and making us behold the glory of God in His own face, that Christ makes us partakers of eternal life. It was by the tree of knowledge that sin came; it is through the knowledge that Christ gives that salvation comes. He is made of God unto us wisdom. In Him are hid all the treasures of wisdom and knowledge.

And of God you are in Him and have but to abide in Him to be made a partaker of these treasures of wisdom. In Him you are, and in Him the wisdom is. Dwelling in Him, you dwell in the very fountain of all light. Abiding in Him, you have Christ, the wisdom of God, leading your whole spiritual life and being ready to communicate, in the form of knowledge, just as much as is necessary for you to know. Christ is made unto us wisdom; you are in Christ.

It is this connection between what Christ has been made of God to us, and how we have it only as also being in Him, that we must learn to understand better. We will thus see that the blessings prepared for us in Christ cannot be obtained as special gifts in answer to prayer apart from the abiding in Him. The answer to each prayer must come in the closer union and the deeper abiding in Him; in Him, the unspeakable gift, all other gifts are treasured up, the gift of wisdom and knowledge, too.

How often have you longed for wisdom and spiritual understanding that you might know God better, whom to know is life eternal! Abide in Jesus: your life in Him will lead you to that fellowship with God in which the only true knowledge of God is to be had. His love, His power, His infinite glory will, as you abide in Jesus, be so revealed as it has not entered into the heart of man to conceive. You may not be able to grasp it with the understanding, or to express it in words, but the knowledge that is deeper than thoughts or words will be given—the knowing of God that comes from being known of Him. *"We preach Christ crucified...unto them which are called...Christ the power of God, and the wisdom of God"* (1 Cor. 1:23–24).

Or you would gladly *"count all things but loss for the excellency of the knowledge of Christ Jesus [your] Lord"* (Phil. 3:8). Abide in Jesus, and be found in Him. You will know Him in *"the power of his resurrection, and the fellowship of his sufferings"* (v. 10). Following Him, you will not walk in darkness, but have the light of life. It is only when God shines into the heart, and Christ Jesus dwells there, that the light of the knowledge of God in the face of Christ can be seen (2 Cor. 4:6).

Or would you understand His blessed work as He worked it on earth, or works it from heaven by His Spirit? Would you know how Christ can become our righteousness, and our sanctification, and redemption? It is just as bringing, and revealing, and communicating these that He is made unto us wisdom from God. There are a thousand questions that at times come up, and the attempt to answer them becomes a weariness and a burden. It is because you have forgotten you are in Christ, whom God has made to be your wisdom. Let it be your first care to abide in Him in undivided fervent devotion of heart. When the heart and the life are right, rooted in Christ, knowledge will come in such measure as Christ's own wisdom sees fit. And without such abiding in Christ the knowledge does not really profit but is often most hurtful. The soul satisfies itself with thoughts that are but the forms and images of truth, without receiving the truth itself in its power. God's way is ever first to give us, even though it is but as a seed, the thing itself, the life and the power, and then the knowledge. Man seeks the knowledge first, and often, alas, never gets beyond it. God gives us Christ, and in Him hid the treasures of wisdom and knowledge. Oh, let us be content to possess Christ, to dwell in Him, to make Him our life, and only in a deeper searching into Him, to search and find the knowledge we desire. Such knowledge is life indeed.

Therefore, believer, abide in Jesus as your wisdom, and expect from Him most confidently whatever teaching you may need for a life to the glory of the Father. In all that concerns your spiritual life, abide in Jesus as your wisdom. The life you have in Christ is a thing of infinite sacredness, far too high and holy for you to know how to act it out. It is He alone who can guide you, as by a secret spiritual instinct, to know what is becoming your dignity as a child of God, what will help and what will hinder your inner life, and especially your abiding in Him. Do not think of it as a mystery or a difficulty you must solve. Whatever questions come up as to the possibility of abiding perfectly and uninterruptedly in Him, and of really obtaining all the blessing that comes from it, always remember: He knows, all is perfectly clear to Him, and He is my wisdom. Just as much as you need to know and are capable of apprehending will be communicated, if you only trust Him. Never think of the riches of wisdom and knowledge hid in Jesus as treasures without a key, or of your way as a path without a light. Jesus your wisdom is guiding you in the right way, even when you do not see it.

In all your dealings with the blessed Word, remember the same truth: abide in Jesus, your wisdom. Study much to know the written Word, but study more to know the living Word, in whom you are of God. Jesus, the wisdom of God, is only known by a life of implicit confidence and obedience. The words He speaks are spirit and life to those who live in Him. Therefore, each time you read or hear or meditate upon the Word, be careful to take up your true position. Realize first your oneness with Him who is the wisdom of God. Know yourself to be under His direct and special training; go to the Word abiding in Him, the very fountain of divine light. In His light you will see light.

In all your daily life, its ways and its work, abide in Jesus as your wisdom. Your body and your daily life share in the great salvation: in Christ, the wisdom of God, provision has been made for their guidance, too. Your body is His temple, your daily life the sphere for glorifying Him. It is to Him a matter of deep interest that all your earthly concerns would be guided aright. Only trust His sympathy, believe His love, and wait for His guidance—it will be given. Abiding in Him, the mind will be calmed and freed from passion, the judgment cleared and strengthened; the light of heaven will shine on earthly things, and your prayers for wisdom, like Solomon's, will be fulfilled above what you ask or think.

And so, especially in any work you do for God, abide in Jesus as your wisdom. "*We are…created in Christ Jesus unto good works, which God hath before ordained that we should walk in them*" (Eph. 2:10); let all fear or doubt lest we should not know exactly what these works are be put far away. In Christ we are created for them. He will show us what they are and how to do them. Cultivate the habit of rejoicing in the assurance that the divine wisdom is guiding you, even where you do not yet see the way.

All that you can wish to know is perfectly clear to Him. As Man, as Mediator, He has access to the counsels of Deity, to the secrets of Providence, in your interest, and on your behalf. If you will but trust Him fully, and abide in Him entirely, you can be confident of having unerring guidance.

Yes, abide in Jesus as your wisdom. Seek to maintain the spirit of waiting and dependence that always seeks to learn and will not move but as the heavenly light leads on. Withdraw yourself from all needless distraction, close your ears to the voices of the world, and be as a docile learner, ever listening for the heavenly wisdom the Master has to teach. Surrender all your own wisdom; seek a deep conviction of the utter blindness of the natural understanding in the things of God; and both as to what you have to believe and have to do, wait for Jesus to teach and to guide. Remember that the teaching and guidance come not from without: it is by His life in us that the divine wisdom does His work. Retire frequently with Him into the inner chamber of the heart, where the gentle voice of the Spirit is only heard if all is still. Hold fast with unshaken confidence, even in the midst of darkness and apparent desertion, His own assurance that He is the light and the leader of His own. And live, above all, day by day in the blessed truth that, as He Himself, the living Christ Jesus, is your wisdom, your first and last care must ever be this alone: to abide in Him. Abiding in Him, His wisdom will come to you as the spontaneous outflowing of a life rooted in Him. I abide in Christ, who was made unto us wisdom from God; wisdom will be given me.

8

AS YOUR RIGHTEOUSNESS

Of [God] are ye in Christ Jesus, who was made unto us wisdom from
God, both righteousness and sanctification, and redemption.
—1 Corinthians 1:30 RV

The first of the great blessings that Christ our wisdom reveals to us as prepared in Himself, is righteousness. It is not difficult to see why this must be first. There can be no real prosperity or progress in a nation, a home, or a soul, unless there is peace. In the same way as a machine cannot do its work unless it is in rest, secured on a good foundation, quietness and assurance are indispensable to our moral and spiritual well-being. Sin had disturbed all our relations; we were out of harmony with ourselves, with men, and with God. The first requirement of a salvation that should really bring blessedness to us was peace. And peace can only come with right. Where everything is as God would have it, in God's order and in harmony with His will, there alone can peace reign. Jesus Christ came to restore peace on earth, and peace in the soul, by restoring righteousness. Because He is Melchizedek, King of Righteousness, He reigns as King of Salem, King of Peace. (See Heb. 7:2.) He so fulfills the promise the prophets held out: *"A king shall reign in righteousness....And the work of righteousness shall be peace; and the effect of righteousness quietness and assurance for ever"* (Isa. 32:1, 17). Christ is made of God unto us righteousness; of God we are in Him as our righteousness. We are made the righteousness of God in Him (2 Cor. 5:21). Let us try to understand what this means.

When first the sinner is led to trust in Christ for salvation, he, as a rule, looks more to His work than His person. As he looks at the Cross, and Christ suffering there, the Righteous One for the unrighteous, he sees in that atoning death the only but sufficient foundation for his faith in God's pardoning mercy. The substitution and the curse-bearing and the atonement of Christ dying in the stead of sinners are what give him peace. And as he understands how the righteousness that Christ brings becomes his very own, and how, in the strength of that, he is counted righteous before God, he feels that he has what he needs to restore him to God's favor: *"Being justified by faith, we have peace with God"* (Rom. 5:1). He seeks to wear this robe of righteousness in the ever renewed faith in the glorious gift of righteousness that has been bestowed upon him.

But as time goes on, and he seeks to grow in the Christian life, new needs arise. He wants to understand more fully how it is that God can thus justify the ungodly on the strength of the righteousness of another. He finds the answer in the wonderful teaching of Scripture as to the true union of the believer with Christ as the Second Adam. He sees that it is because Christ had made Himself one with His people, and they were one with Him; that it was in perfect accordance with all law in the kingdom of nature and of heaven, that each member of the body should have the full benefit of the doing and the suffering as of the life of the head. And so he is led to feel that it can only be in fully realizing his personal union with Christ as the Head that he can fully experience the power of

His righteousness to bring the soul into the full favor and fellowship of the Holy One. The work of Christ does not become less precious, but the person of Christ more so; the work leads up into the very heart, the love, and the life of the God-man.

And this experience sheds its light again upon Scripture. It leads him to notice, what he had scarcely remarked before, how distinctly the righteousness of God, as it becomes ours, is connected with the person of the Redeemer. "*This is his name whereby he shall be called, THE LORD OUR RIGHTEOUSNESS*" (Jer. 23:6). "*In the LORD have I righteousness and strength*" (Isa. 45:24). "*Christ Jesus, who of God is made unto us…righteousness*" (1 Cor. 1:30). "*That we might be made the righteousness of God in him*" (2 Cor. 5:21). That I may be found in Him, having the righteousness of God (Phil. 3:9).

He sees how inseparable righteousness and life in Christ are from each other: "*The righteousness of one…came upon all men unto justification of life*" (Rom. 5:18). "*They which receive…the gift of righteousness shall reign in life by one, Jesus Christ*" (v. 17). And he understands what deep meaning there is in the key word of the epistle to the Romans: "*The* [righteousness] *shall live by faith*" (Rom. 1:17).

He is not now content with only thinking of the imputed righteousness as his robe; but putting on Jesus Christ, and seeking to be wrapped up in, to be clothed upon with Himself and His life, he feels how completely the righteousness of God is his, because the Lord our righteousness is his. Before he understood this, he, too, often felt it difficult to wear his white robe all day long; it was as if he especially had to put it on when he came into God's presence to confess his sins and seek new grace. But now the living Christ Himself is his righteousness, that Christ who watches over and keeps and loves us as His own; it is no longer an impossibility to walk all day long enrobed in the loving presence with which He covers His people.

Such an experience leads still further. The life and the righteousness are inseparably linked, and the believer becomes more conscious than before of a righteous nature planted within him. The new man created in

Christ Jesus is *"created in righteousness and true holiness"* (Eph. 4:24). *"He that doeth righteousness is righteous, even as he is righteous"* (1 John 3:7). The union to Jesus has effected a change not only in the relation to God, but in the personal state before God. And as the intimate fellowship to which the union has opened up the way is maintained, the growing renewal of the whole being makes righteousness to be his very nature.

To a Christian who begins to see the deep meaning of the truth, "[He is] *made unto us...righteousness,"* it is hardly necessary to say, "Abide in Him." As long as he only thought of the righteousness of the Substitute, and our being counted judicially righteous for His sake, the absolute necessity of abiding in Him was not apparent. But as the glory of *"THE LORD OUR RIGHTEOUSNESS"* (Jer. 23:6) unfolds to the view, he sees that abiding in Him personally is the only way to stand, at all times, complete and accepted before God, as it is the only way to realize how the new and righteous nature can be strengthened from Jesus our Head. To the penitent sinner the chief thought was the righteousness that comes through Jesus dying for sin; to the intelligent and advancing believer, Jesus, the Living One, through whom the righteousness comes, is everything, because having Him he has the righteousness too.

Believer, abide in Christ as your righteousness. You bear about with you a nature altogether corrupt and vile, ever seeking to rise up and darken your sense of acceptance and of access to unbroken fellowship with the Father. Nothing can enable you to dwell and walk in the light of God, without even the shadow of a cloud between, but the habitual abiding in Christ as your righteousness. To this you are called. Seek to walk worthy of that calling. Yield yourself to the Holy Spirit to reveal to you the wonderful grace that permits you to draw near to God, clothed in a divine righteousness. Take time to realize that the King's own robe has indeed been put on, and that in it you need not fear entering His presence. It is the token that you are the man whom the King delights to honor. Take time to remember that as much as you need it in the palace, no less do you need it when He sends you forth into the world, where you are the King's messenger and representative. Live your daily life in the full consciousness of being righteous in God's sight, an object of delight and pleasure in Christ.

Connect every view you have of Christ in His other graces with this first one: of God, He is made to you righteousness. This will keep you in perfect peace. Thus will you enter into, and dwell in, the rest of God. So will your inmost being be transformed into being righteous and doing righteousness. In your heart and life it will become manifest where you dwell; abiding in Jesus Christ, the Righteous One, you will share His position, His character, and His blessedness: *"Thou lovest righteousness, and hatest wickedness: therefore God, thy God, hath anointed thee with the oil of gladness above thy fellows"* (Ps. 45:7). Joy and gladness above measure will be your portion.

9

AS YOUR SANCTIFICATION

Of [God] are ye in Christ Jesus, who was made unto us wisdom from God, both righteousness and sanctification, and redemption.
—1 Corinthians 1:30 RV

P aul...*unto the church of God which is at Corinth, to them that are sanctified in Christ Jesus, called to be saints*" (1 Cor. 1:1–2)—thus the chapter opens in which we are taught that Christ is our sanctification. In the Old Testament, believers were called the righteous; in the New Testament, they are called saints, the holy ones, sanctified in Christ Jesus. Holiness is higher than righteous. ("Holiness may be called spiritual perfection, as righteousness is legal completeness."—Horatius Bonar in *God's Way of Holiness*.) Holy, in God, has reference to His inmost being; righteous, to His dealings with His creatures. In man, righteousness is but a stepping-stone to holiness. It is in this he can approach most near to the perfection of God. (See Matt. 5:48; 1 Pet. 1:16.) In the Old Testament, righteousness was found, while holiness was only typified; in Jesus Christ, the Holy One, and in His people, His saints or holy ones, it is first realized.

As in Scripture, and in our text, so in personal experience, righteousness precedes holiness. When first the believer finds Christ as his righteousness, he has such joy in the newly made discovery that the study of holiness hardly has a place. But as he grows, the desire for holiness makes itself felt, and he seeks to know what provision his God has made for supplying that need. A superficial acquaintance with God's plan leads to the view that while justification is God's work, by faith in Christ, sanctification is our work, to be performed under the influence of the gratitude we feel for the deliverance we have experienced, and by the aid of the Holy Spirit. But the earnest Christian soon finds how little gratitude can supply the power. When he thinks that more prayer will bring it, he finds that, indispensable as prayer is, it is not enough. Often the believer struggles hopelessly for years, until he listens to the teaching of the Spirit, as He glorifies Christ again, and reveals Christ, our sanctification, to be appropriated by faith alone.

Christ is made of God unto us sanctification. Holiness is the very nature of God, and that alone is holy which God takes possession of and fills with Himself. God's answer to the question, "How could sinful man become holy?" is, "Christ, the Holy One of God." In Him, whom the Father sanctified and sent into the world, God's holiness was revealed incarnate and brought within reach of man. *"For their sakes I sanctify myself, that they also might be sanctified through the truth"* (John 17:19). There is no other way of our becoming holy but by becoming partakers of the holiness of Christ. And there is no other way of this taking place than by our personal spiritual union with Him, so that through His Holy Spirit, His holy life flows into us. *"Of [God] are ye in Christ Jesus, who was made unto us...sanctification."* Abiding by faith in Christ our sanctification is the simple secret of a holy life. The measure of sanctification will depend on the measure of abiding in Him; as the soul learns wholly to abide in Christ, the promise is increasingly fulfilled: *"the very God of peace sanctify you wholly"* (1 Thess. 5:23).

To illustrate this relation between the measure of the abiding and the measure of sanctification experienced, let us think of the grafting of a tree, that instructive symbol of our union to Jesus. The illustration is suggested by the Savior's words, *"Make the tree good, and his fruit good"* (Matt. 12:33). I can graft a tree so that only a single branch bears good fruit, while many of the natural branches remain and bear their old fruit—a type of believer in whom a small part of the life is sanctified, but in whom, from ignorance or other reasons, the carnal life still in many respects has full dominion. I can graft a tree so that every branch is cut off, and the whole tree becomes renewed to bear good fruit; and yet, unless I watch over the tendency of the stems to give sprouts, they may again rise and grow strong, and, robbing the new graft of the strength it needs, make it weak. Such are Christians who, when apparently powerfully converted, forsake all to follow Christ, and yet after a time, through unwatchfulness, allow old habits to regain their power and whose Christian life and fruit are but feeble. But if I want a tree wholly made good, I take it when young, and, cutting the stem clean off on the ground, I graft it just where it emerges from the soil. I watch over every bud that the old nature could possibly put forth, until the flow of sap from the old roots into the new stem is so complete, that the old life has, as it were, been entirely conquered and covered by the new. Here I have a tree entirely renewed—emblem of the Christian who has learned in entire consecration to surrender everything for Christ and, in a wholehearted faith, to abide wholly in Him.

If, in the last case, the old tree were a reasonable being that could cooperate with the gardener, what would his language be to it? Would it not be this: "Yield yourself now entirely to this new nature with which I have invested you; repress every tendency of the old nature to give buds or sprouts; let all your sap and all your life powers rise up into this graft from yonder beautiful tree, which I have put on you; so will you bring forth sweet and much fruit." And the language of the tree to the gardener would be: "When you graft me, spare not a single branch; let everything of the old self, even the smallest bud, be destroyed, that I may no longer live in my own, but in that other life that was cut off and brought and put upon me, that I might be wholly new and good." And, once again, could you afterwards ask the renewed tree, as it was bearing abundant fruit, what it could say of itself, its answer would be this: "In me, that is, in my roots, there dwells no good thing. (See Rom. 7:18.) I am ever inclined to evil; the sap I collect from the soil is in its nature corrupt and ready to show itself in bearing evil fruit. But just when the sap rises into the sunshine to ripen the fruit, the wise gardener has clothed me with a new life, through which my sap is purified, and all my powers are renewed to the bringing forth of good fruit. I have only to abide in that which I have received. He cares for the immediate repression and removal of every bud that the old nature still would put forth."

Christian, fear not to claim God's promises to make you holy. Listen not to the suggestion that the corruption of your old nature would render holiness an impossibility. In your flesh dwells no good thing (v. 18), and that flesh, though crucified with Christ, is not yet dead, but will continually seek to rise and lead you to evil. But the *"Father is the husbandman"* (John 15:1). He has grafted the life of Christ on your life. That holy life is mightier than your evil life; under the watchful care of the Husbandman, that new life can keep down the workings of the evil life within you. The evil nature is there, with its unchanged tendency to rise up and show itself. But the new nature is there too—the living Christ, your sanctification, is there—and through Him all your powers can be sanctified as they rise into life and be made to bear fruit to the glory of the Father.

And now, if you would live a holy life, abide in Christ your sanctification. Look upon Him as the Holy One of God who was made man that He might communicate to us the holiness of God. Listen when Scripture teaches that there is within you a new nature, a new man, created in Christ Jesus in righteousness and true holiness. Remember that this holy nature that is in you is singularly fitted for living a holy life and performing all holy duties, as much so as the old nature is for doing evil. Understand that this holy nature within you has its root and life in Christ in heaven and can only grow and become strong as the dealings between it and its source are uninterrupted. And above all, believe most confidently that Jesus Christ Himself delights in maintaining that new nature within you, and imparting to it His own strength and wisdom for its work.

Let that faith lead you daily to the surrender of all self-confidence, and the confession of the utter corruption of all there is in you by nature. Let it fill you with a quiet and assured confidence that you are indeed able to do what the Father expects of you as His child, under the covenant of His grace, because you have Christ strengthening you. Let it teach you to lay yourself and your services on the altar as spiritual sacrifices, holy and acceptable in His sight, a sweet-smelling savor. Look not upon a life of holiness as a strain and an effort, but as the natural outgrowth of the life of Christ within you. And let ever again a quiet, hopeful, cheerful faith hold itself assured that all you need for a holy life will most assuredly be given you out of the holiness of Jesus. Thus will you understand and prove what it is to abide in Christ our sanctification.

Author's Note

The thought that in the personal holiness of our Lord a new holy nature was formed to be communicated to us, and that we make use of it by faith, is the central idea of Marshall's invaluable work, *The Gospel Mystery of Sanctification*:

> One great mystery is, that the holy frame and disposition whereby our souls are furnished and enabled for immediate practice of the law, must be obtained by receiving it out of Christ's fullness, as a thing already prepared and brought to an existence for us in Christ, and treasured up in Him; and that, as we are justified by a righteousness wrought out in Christ, and imputed to us, so we are sanctified by such a holy frame and qualification as are first wrought out and completed in Christ for us, and then imparted to us. As our natural corruption was produced originally in the first Adam, and propagated from him to us, so our new nature and holiness is first produced in Christ, and derived from Him to us, or, as it were,

propagated. So that we are not at all to work together with Christ in making or producing that holy frame in us, but only to take it to ourselves, and use it in our holy practice, as made ready to our hands. Thus we have fellowship with Christ, in receiving that holy frame of spirit that was originally in Him; for fellowship is where several persons have the same things in common. This mystery is so great, that notwithstanding all the light of the Gospel, we commonly think that we must get a holy frame by producing it anew in ourselves, and by pursuing it and working it out of our own heart. (See Chapter 3.)

10

AS YOUR REDEMPTION

Of [God] are ye in Christ Jesus, who was made unto us wisdom from God, both righteousness and sanctification, and redemption.
—1 Corinthians 1:30 RV

Here we have the top of the ladder, reaching into heaven—the blessed end to which Christ and life in Him is to lead. The word *redemption*, though sometimes applied to our deliverance from the guilt of sin, here refers to our complete and final deliverance from all its consequences, when the Redeemer's work will become fully manifest, even to the redemption of the body itself. (See Romans 8:21–23; Ephesians 1:14, 4:30.) The expression points us to the highest glory to be hoped for in the future, and therefore also to the highest blessing to be enjoyed in the present in Christ. We have seen how, as a Prophet, Christ is our wisdom, revealing to us God and His love, with the nature and conditions of the salvation that love has prepared. As a Priest, He is our righteousness, restoring us to right relations to God, and securing us His favor and friendship. As a King, He is our sanctification, forming and guiding us into the obedience to the Father's holy will. As these three offices work out God's one purpose, the grand consummation will be reached, the complete deliverance from sin and all its effects will be accomplished, and ransomed humanity will regain all that it had ever lost.

Christ is made of God unto us redemption. The word invites us to look upon Jesus, not only as He lived on earth, teaching us by word and example; as He died, to reconcile us with God; as He lives again, a victorious King, rising to receive His crown; but also as, sitting at the right hand of God, He takes again the glory that he had with the Father, before the world began, and holds it there for us. It consists in this, that there His human nature, yes, His human body, freed from all the consequences of sin to which He once had been exposed, is now admitted to share the divine glory. As Son of Man, He dwells on the throne and in the bosom of the Father; the deliverance from what He had to suffer from sin is complete and eternal. The complete redemption is found embodied in His own person; what He as man is and has in heaven is the complete redemption. He is made of God to us redemption.

We are in Him as such. And the more intelligently and believingly we abide in Him as our redemption, the more we will experience, even here, of *"the powers of the world to come"* (Heb. 6:5). As our communion with Him becomes more intimate and intense, and we let the Holy Spirit reveal Him to us in His heavenly glory, the more we realize how the life in us is the life of One who sits upon the throne of heaven. We feel the power of an endless life working in us. We taste the eternal life. We have the foretaste of the eternal glory.

The blessings flowing from abiding in Christ as our redemption are great. The soul is delivered from all fear of death. There was a time when even the Savior feared death. But now no longer. He has triumphed over death; even His body has entered into the glory. The believer who abides in Christ as his full redemption realizes even now his spiritual victory over death. It becomes to him the servant that removes the last rags of the old carnal apparel, before he is clothed upon with the new body of glory. It carries the body to the grave, to lie there as the seed from which the new body will arise the worthy companion of the glorified spirit. The resurrection of the body is no longer a barren doctrine, but a living expectation, and even an incipient experience, because the Spirit of Him who raised Jesus from the dead, dwells in the body as the pledge that even our mortal bodies will be quickened. (See Rom. 8:11–23.) This faith exercises its sanctifying influence in the willing surrender of the sinful members of the body to be mortified and completely subjected to the dominion of the Spirit, as preparation for the time when the frail body will be changed and fashioned like to His glorious body.

This full redemption of Christ as extending to the body, has a depth of meaning not easily expressed. It was of man as a whole, soul and body, that it is said that he was made in the image and likeness of God. In the angels, God had created spirits without material bodies; in the creation of the world, there was matter without spirit. Man was to be the highest specimen of divine art: the combination in one being, of matter and spirit in perfect harmony, as type of the most perfect union between God and His own creation. Sin entered in and appeared to thwart the divine plan: the material obtained a fearful supremacy over the spiritual. *"The Word was made flesh"* (John 1:14); the divine fullness received an embodiment in the humanity of Christ, that the redemption might be a complete and perfect one, that the whole creation, which now groans and travails in pain together (Rom. 8:22), might be delivered from the bondage of corruption into the liberty of the glory of the children of God. God's purpose will not be accomplished, and Christ's glory will not be manifested fully, until the body, with that whole of nature of which it is part and head, has been transfigured by the power of the spiritual life and made the transparent apparel for showing forth the glory of the Infinite Spirit. Then only will we understand: Christ Jesus is made unto us complete redemption.

In the meantime we are taught to believe: of God are you in Christ as your redemption. This is not meant as a revelation to be left to the future; for the full development of the Christian life, our present abiding in Christ must seek to enter into and appropriate it. We do this as we learn to triumph over death. We do it as we learn to look upon Christ as the Lord of our body, claiming its entire consecration, securing even here, if faith will claim it, victory over the terrible dominion sin has had in the body. We do this as we learn to look on all nature as part of the kingdom of Christ, destined, even though it be through a baptism of fire, to partake in His redemption. We do it as we allow the powers of the coming world to possess us and to lift us up into a life in the heavenly places, to enlarge our hearts and our views, to anticipate, even here, the things which have never entered into the heart of man to conceive.

Believer, abide in Christ as your redemption. Let this be the crown of your Christian life. Seek it not first or only, apart from the knowledge of Christ in His other relations. But seek it truly as that to which they are meant to lead you up. Abide in Christ as your redemption. Nothing will fit you for this but faithfulness in the previous steps of the Christian life. Abide in Him as your wisdom, the perfect revelation of all that God is and has for you. Follow, in the daily ordering of the inner and the outer life, with meek docility His teaching, and you will be counted worthy to have secrets revealed to you that to most disciples are a sealed book. The wisdom will lead you into the mysteries of complete redemption. Abide in Him as your righteousness, and dwell clothed upon with Him as your righteousness, in that inner sanctuary of the Father's favor and presence to which His righteousness gives you access.

As you rejoice in your reconciliation, you will understand how it includes all things, and how they too wait the full redemption. *"For it pleased the Father...by him to reconcile all things unto himself; by him, I say, whether they be things in earth, or things in heaven"* (Col. 1:19–20). And abide in Him as your sanctification; the experience of His power to make you holy, spirit and soul and body, will quicken your faith in a holiness that will not cease its work until the bells of the horses and every pot in

Jerusalem will be holiness to the Lord. (See Zech. 14:20.) Abide in Him as your redemption, and live, even here, as the heir of the future glory. And as you seek to experience in yourself to the full, the power of His saving grace, your heart will be enlarged to realize the position man has been destined to occupy in the universe, as having all things made subject to him, and you will, for your part, be fitted to live worthy of that high and heavenly calling.

11

THE CRUCIFIED ONE

I am crucified with Christ: nevertheless I live;
yet not I, but Christ liveth in me.
—Galatians 2:20

We have been planted together in the likeness of his death.
—Romans 6:5

I am crucified with Christ." Thus the apostle expresses his assurance of
his fellowship with Christ in His sufferings and death, and his full
participation in all the power and the blessing of that death. And so really
did he mean what he said, and know that he was now indeed dead, that

he adds: *"Nevertheless I live; yet not I, but Christ liveth in me."* How blessed must be the experience of such a union with the Lord Jesus! To be able to look upon His death as mine, just as really as it was His—upon His perfect obedience to God, His victory over sin, and complete deliverance from its power, as mine; and to realize that the power of that death does by faith work daily with a divine energy in mortifying the flesh, and renewing the whole life into the perfect conformity to the resurrection life of Jesus! Abiding in Jesus, the Crucified One, is the secret of the growth of that new life that is ever begotten of the death of nature.

Let us try to understand this. The suggestive expression, *"Planted... in the likeness of his death"* will teach us what the abiding in the Crucified One means. When a graft is united with the stock on which it is to grow, we know that it must be kept fixed; it must abide in the place where the stock has been cut, been wounded, to make an opening to receive the graft. There is no graft without wounding—the laying bare and opening up of the inner life of the tree to receive the stranger branch. It is only through such wounding that access can be obtained to the fellowship of the sap and the growth and the life of the stronger stem. Even so with Jesus and the sinner. Only when we are planted into the likeness of His death will we also be in the likeness of His resurrection, partakers of the life and the power there are in Him. In the death of the cross, Christ was wounded, and in His opened wounds a place was prepared where we might be grafted in. And just as one might say to a graft, and does practically say as it is fixed in its place, "Abide here in the wound of the stem that is now to bear you"; so to the believing soul the message comes, "Abide in the wounds of Jesus; there is the place of union, and life, and growth. There you will see how His heart was opened to receive you; how His flesh was rent that the way might be opened for your being made one with Him and having access to all the blessings flowing from His divine nature."

You have also noticed how the graft has to be torn away from the tree where it by nature grew, and to be cut into conformity to the place prepared for it in the wounded stem. Even so the believer has to be made conformable to Christ's death—to be crucified and to die with Him. The wounded stem and the wounded graft are cut to fit into each other, into each other's likeness. There is a fellowship between Christ's sufferings and your sufferings. His experiences must become yours. The disposition He manifested in choosing and bearing the cross must be yours. Like Him, you will have to give full assent to the righteous judgment and curse of a holy God against sin. Like Him, you have to consent to yield your life, as laden with sin and curse, to death, and through it to pass to the new life. Like Him, you will experience that it is only through the self-sacrifice of Gethsemane and Calvary that the path is to be found to the joy and the fruit bearing of the resurrection life. The more clear the resemblance between the wounded stem and the wounded graft, the more exactly their wounds fit into each other, the surer and the easier and the more complete will be the union and the growth.

It is in Jesus, the Crucified One, I must abide. I must learn to look upon the Cross as not only an atonement to God, but also a victory over the Devil—not only a deliverance from the guilt, but also from the power of sin. I must gaze on Him on the cross as wholly mine, offering Himself to receive me into the closest union and fellowship, and to make me partaker of the full power of His death to sin and the new life of victory to which it is but the gateway. I must yield myself to Him in an undivided surrender, with much prayer and strong desire, imploring to be admitted into the ever closer fellowship and conformity of His death, of the Spirit in which He died that death.

Let me try to understand why the Cross is thus the place of union. On the cross the Son of God enters into the fullest union with man—enters into the fullest experience of what it says to have become a son of man, a member of a race under the curse. It is in death that the Prince of life conquers the power of death; it is in death alone that He can make me partaker of that victory. The life He imparts is a life from the dead; each new experience of the power of that life depends upon the fellowship of the death. The death and the life are inseparable. All the grace that Jesus the Saving One gives is given only in the path of fellowship with Jesus the Crucified One. Christ came and took my place; I must put myself in His place and abide there. And there is but one place that is both His and mine—that place is the Cross. His in virtue of His free choice; mine by reason of the curse of sin. He came there to seek me; there alone I can find Him.

When He found me there, it was the place of cursing; this He experienced, for *"cursed is every one that hangeth on a tree"* (Gal. 3:13). He made it a place of blessing; this I experienced, for Christ has delivered us from the curse, being made a curse for us (v. 13). When Christ comes in my place, He remains what He was, the beloved of the Father; but in the fellowship with me, He shares my curse and dies my death. When I stand in His place, which is still always mine, I am still what I was by nature, the accursed one, who deserves to die; but as united to Him, I share His blessing and receive His life. When He came to be one with me, He could not avoid the Cross, for the curse always points to the Cross as its end and fruit. And when I seek to be one with Him, I cannot avoid the Cross either, for nowhere but on the Cross are life and deliverance to be found. As inevitably as my curse pointed Him to the Cross as the only place where He could be fully united to me, His blessing points me to the Cross too as the only place where I can be united to Him. He took my cross for His own; I must take His Cross as my own; I must be crucified with Him. It is as I abide daily, deeply in Jesus the Crucified One, that I will taste the sweetness of His love, the power of His life, the completeness of His salvation.

Beloved believer, it is a deep mystery, this of the Cross of Christ. I fear there are many Christians who are content to look upon the cross, with Christ on it dying for their sins, who have little heart for fellowship with the Crucified One. They hardly know that He invites them to it. Or they are content to consider the ordinary afflictions of life, which the children of the world often have as much as they, as their share of Christ's Cross. They have no conception of what it is to be crucified with Christ, that bearing the cross means likeness to Christ in the principles which animated Him in His path of obedience. The entire surrender of all self-will, the complete denial to the flesh of its every desire and pleasure, the perfect separation from the world in all its ways of thinking and acting, the losing and hating of one's life, the giving up of self and its interests for the sake of others—this is the disposition which marks him who has taken up Christ's

Cross, who seeks to say, "I am crucified with Christ; I abide in Christ, the Crucified One."

Would you truly please your Lord, and live in as close fellowship with Him as His grace could maintain you in? Pray that His Spirit lead you into this blessed truth: this secret of the Lord for them that fear Him. We know how Peter knew and confessed Christ as the Son of the living God while the Cross was still an offense. (See Matt. 16:16–17, 21–23.) The faith that believes in the blood that pardons, and the life that renews, can only reach its perfect growth as it abides beneath the Cross, and in living fellowship with Him seeks for perfect conformity with Jesus the Crucified. O Jesus, our crucified Redeemer, teach us not only to believe on You, but to abide in You, to take Your cross not only as the ground of our pardon, but also as the law of our life. Teach us to love it not only because on it You did bear our curse, but because on it we enter into the closest fellowship with Yourself, and are crucified with You. And teach us, that as we yield ourselves wholly to be possessed of the Spirit in which You did bear the Cross, we will be made partakers of the power and the blessing to which the Cross alone gives access.

12

GOD HIMSELF WILL ESTABLISH YOU IN HIM

He which stablisheth us with you in Christ…is God.
—2 Corinthians 1:21

These words of Paul teach us a much needed and most blessed truth—that just as our first being united with Christ was the work of divine omnipotence, so we may look to the Father, too, for being kept and being fixed more firmly in Him. *"The LORD will perfect that which concerneth me"* (Ps. 138:8)—this expression of confidence should ever accompany the prayer, *"Forsake not the works of thine own hands"* (v. 8). In all his longings and prayers to attain to a deeper and more perfect abiding in Christ, the believer must hold fast his confidence: *"He which hath begun a good work in you will perform it until the day of Jesus Christ"* (Phil. 1:6). There is nothing that will so help to root and ground him in Christ as this faith: *"He which stablisheth us…in Christ…is God."*

How many there are who can witness that this faith is just what they need! They continually mourn over the variableness of their spiritual life. Sometimes there are hours and days of deep earnestness, and even of blessed experience of the grace of God. But how little is needed to mar their peace, to bring a cloud over the soul! And then, how their faith is shaken! All efforts to regain their standing appear utterly fruitless, and neither solemn vows nor watching and prayer avail to restore to them the peace they for a while had tasted. Could they but understand how just their own efforts are the cause of their failure, because it is God alone who can establish us in Christ Jesus. They would see that just as in justification they had to cease from their own working, and to accept in faith the promise that God would give them life in Christ, so now, in the matter of their sanctification, their first need is to cease from striving themselves to establish the connection with Christ more firmly and to allow God to do it. *"God is faithful, by whom ye were called unto the fellowship of his Son Jesus Christ"* (1 Cor. 1:9). What they need is the simple faith that the establishing in Christ, day by day, is God's work—a work that He delights to do, in spite of all our weakness and unfaithfulness, if we will but trust Him for it.

To the blessedness of such a faith, and the experience it brings, many can testify. What peace and rest to know that there is a Husbandman who cares for the branch, to see that it grows stronger, and that its union with the Vine becomes more perfect, who watches over every hindrance and danger, who supplies every needed aid! What peace and rest, fully and finally to give up our abiding into the care of God, and never have a wish or thought, never to offer a prayer or engage in an exercise connected with it, without first having the glad remembrance that what we do is only the manifestation of what God is doing in us! The establishing in Christ is His work: He accomplishes it by stirring us to watch and wait and work. But this He can do with power only as we cease interrupting Him by our self-working—as we accept in faith the dependent posture which honors Him and opens the heart to let Him work. How such a faith frees the soul from care and responsibility! In the midst of the rush and bustle of the world's stirring life, amid the subtle and ceaseless temptations of sin, amid all the daily cares and trials that so easily distract and lead to failure, how blessed it would be to be an established Christian—always abiding in Christ! How blessed even to have the faith that one can surely become it—that the attainment is within our reach!

Dear believer, the blessing is indeed within your reach. He who establishes you with us in Christ is God. What I want you to take in is this: that believing this promise will not only give you comfort, but will be the means of your obtaining your desire. You know how Scripture teaches us that in all God's leadings of His people, faith has everywhere been the one condition of the manifestation of His power. Faith is the ceasing from all nature's efforts, and all other dependence; faith is confessed helplessness casting itself upon God's promise and claiming its fulfillment; faith is the putting ourselves quietly into God's hands for Him to do His work. What you and I need now is to take time, until this truth stands out before us in all its spiritual brightness: it is God Almighty, God the faithful and gracious One, who has undertaken to establish me in Christ Jesus.

Listen to what the Word teaches you: *"The Lord shall establish thee an holy people unto himself"* (Deut. 28:9); *"O Lord God…[establish] their heart unto thee"* (1 Chron. 29:18); *"Thy God loved Israel, to establish them for ever"* (2 Chron. 9:8); *"Now to him that is of power to stablish you…be glory…for ever"* (Rom. 16:25, 27); *"To the end he may stablish your hearts unblameable in holiness"* (1 Thess. 3:13); *"The Lord is faithful, who shall stablish you, and keep you from evil"* (2 Thess. 3:3); *"The God of all grace, who hath called us… by Christ Jesus…make you perfect, stablish, strengthen, settle you"* (1 Pet. 5:10). Can you take these words to mean anything less than that you too—however fitful your spiritual life has hitherto been, however unfavorable your natural character or your circumstances may appear—can be established in Christ Jesus, can become an established Christian? Let us but take time to listen, in simple childlike teachableness, to these words as the truth of God, and the confidence will come: as surely as I am in Christ, I will also, day by day, be established in Him.

The lesson appears so simple, and yet most of us take so long to learn it. The chief reason is that the grace the promise offers is so large, so godlike, so beyond all our thoughts, that we do not take it really to mean what it says. The believer who has once come to see and accept what it brings, can bear witness to the wonderful change that comes over the spiritual life. Up to this time he had taken charge of his own welfare; now he has a God to take charge of it. He now knows himself to be in the school of God, a Teacher who plans the whole course of study for each of His pupils with infinite wisdom and delights to have them come daily for the lessons He has to give. All he asks is to feel himself constantly in God's hands and to follow His guidance, neither lagging behind nor going before. Remembering that it is God who works both to will and to do (see Phil. 2:13), he sees his only safety to be in yielding himself to God's working. He lays aside all anxiety about his inner life and its growth, because the *"Father is the husbandman"* (John 15:1) under whose wise and watchful care each plant is well secured. He knows that there is the prospect of a most blessed life of strength and fruitfulness to everyone who will take God alone and wholly as his hope.

Believer, you must admit that such a life of trust must be a most blessed one. You say, perhaps, that there are times when you do, with your whole heart, consent to this way of living, and do wholly abandon the care of your inner life to your Father. But somehow it does not last. You forget again, and instead of beginning each morning with the joyous transference of all the needs and cares of your spiritual life to the Father's charge, you again feel anxious, burdened, and helpless. Is it not, perhaps, my brother, because you have not committed to the Father's care this matter of daily remembering to renew your entire surrender? Memory is one of the highest powers in our nature. By it day is linked to day, the unity of life through all our years is kept up, and we know that we are still ourselves. In the spiritual life, recollection is of infinite value. For the sanctifying of our memory, in the service of our spiritual life, God has provided most beautifully. The Holy Spirit is the One who reminds us, the Spirit of recollection. Jesus said, *"He shall…bring all things to your remembrance"* (John 14:26). *"He which stablisheth us with you in Christ…is God; who hath also sealed us, and given the earnest of the Spirit in our hearts"* (2 Cor. 1:21–22). It is just for the establishing of us in Him that the Holy Remembrancer has been given. Each day God will enable you to remember His blessed promises and your unceasing acts of faith and surrender in accepting them. The Holy Spirit is—blessed be God—the memory of the new man.

Apply this to the promise of the text: "*He which stablisheth us...in Christ...is God.*" As you now, at this moment, abandon all anxiety about your growth and progress to the God who has undertaken to establish you in the Vine and feel what a joy it is to know that God alone has charge, ask and trust Him by the Holy Spirit ever to remind you of this your blessed relation to Him. He will do it, and with each new morning your faith may grow stronger and brighter: I have a God to see that each day I become more firmly united to Christ.

And now, beloved fellow believer, "*the God of all grace, who hath called us... by Christ Jesus...make you perfect, stablish, strengthen, settle you*" (1 Pet. 5:10). What more can you desire? Expect it confidently; ask it fervently. Count on God to do His work. And learn in faith to sing the song, the notes of which each new experience will make deeper and sweeter: "*Now to him that is of power to stablish you...be glory...for ever. Amen*" (Rom. 16:25, 27). Yes, glory to God, who has undertaken to establish us in Christ!

13

EVERY MOMENT

In that day sing ye unto her, A vineyard of red wine.
I the Lord do keep it; I will water it every moment: lest any hurt it,
I will keep it night and day.
—Isaiah 27:2–3

The vineyard was the symbol of the people of Israel, in whose midst the True Vine was to stand. The branch is the symbol of the individual believer, who stands in the Vine. The song of the vineyard is also the song of the Vine and its every branch. The command still goes forth to the watchers of the vineyard—if only they obeyed it and sang until every feeble-hearted believer had learned and joined the joyful strain—"*Sing ye unto her...I the Lord do keep it; I will water it every moment: lest any hurt it, I will keep it night and day.*"

What an answer from the mouth of God Himself to the question so often asked: Is it possible for the believer always to abide in Jesus? Is a life of unbroken fellowship with the Son of God indeed attainable here in this earthly life? Truly not, if the abiding is our work, to be done in our strength. But the things that are impossible with men are possible with God. (See Luke 18:27.) If the Lord Himself will keep the soul night and day, yes, will watch and water it every moment, then surely the uninterrupted communion with Jesus becomes a blessed possibility to those who can trust God to mean and to do what He says. Then surely the abiding of the branch of the Vine day and night, summer and winter, in a never ceasing life fellowship, is nothing less than the simple but certain promise of your abiding in your Lord.

In one sense, it is true, there is no believer who does not always abide in Jesus; without this there could not be true life. *"If a man abide not in me, he is cast forth"* (John 15:6). But when the Savior gives the command, *"Abide in me"* (v. 4), with the promise, *"He that abideth in me…bringeth forth much fruit"* (v. 5), He speaks of that willing, intelligent, and wholehearted surrender by which we accept His offer and consent to the abiding in Him as the only life we choose or seek. The objections raised against our right to expect that we will always be able thus voluntarily and consciously to abide in Jesus are chiefly two.

The one is derived from the nature of man. It is said that our limited powers prevent our being occupied with two things at the same moment. God's providence places many Christians in business, where for hours at a time the closest attention is required to the work they have to do. How can such a man, it is asked, with his whole mind on the work he has to do, be at the same time occupied with Christ and keeping up fellowship with Him? The consciousness of abiding in Jesus is regarded as requiring such a strain, and such a direct occupation of the mind with heavenly thoughts, that to enjoy the blessing would imply a withdrawing of oneself from all the ordinary activities of life. This is the same error as drove the first monks into the wilderness.

Blessed be God, there is no necessity for such a going out of the world. Abiding in Jesus is not a work that needs the mind to be engaged each moment, or the affections to be directly and actively occupied with it. It is an entrusting of oneself to the keeping of the eternal love, in the faith that it will abide near us, and with its holy presence watch over us and ward off the evil, even when we have to be most intently occupied with other things. And so the heart has rest and peace and joy in the consciousness of being kept when it cannot keep itself.

In ordinary life we have abundant illustration of the influence of a supreme affection reigning in and guarding the soul, while the mind concentrates itself on work that requires its whole attention. Think of the father of a family, separated for a time from his home, that he may secure for his loved ones what they need. He loves his wife and children, and longs much to return to them. There may be hours of intense occupation when he has not a moment to think of them, and yet his love is as deep and real as when he can call up their images; all the while his love and the hope of making them happy urge him on and fill him with a secret joy in his work. Think of a king: in the midst of work and pleasure and trial, he all the while acts under the secret influence of the consciousness of royalty, even while he does not think of it. A loving wife and mother never for one moment loses the sense of her relation to the husband and children: the consciousness and the love are there, amid all her engagements. And can it be thought impossible for Everlasting Love so to take and keep possession of our spirits, that we too will never for a moment lose the secret consciousness: we are in Christ, kept in Him by His almighty power?

Oh, it is possible; we can be sure it is. Our abiding in Jesus is even more than a fellowship of love—it is a fellowship of life. In work or in rest, the consciousness of life never leaves us. And even so can the mighty power of the eternal life maintain within us the consciousness of its presence. Or rather, Christ, who is our life, Himself dwells within us, and by His presence maintains our consciousness that we are in Him.

The second objection has reference to our sinfulness. Christians are so accustomed to looking upon sinning daily as something absolutely inevitable, that they regard it as a matter of course that no one can keep up abiding fellowship with the Savior: we must sometimes be unfaithful and fail. As if it were not just because we have a nature that is nothing but a very fountain of sin that the abiding in Christ has been ordained for us as our only, and our sufficient, deliverance! As if it were not the Heavenly Vine, the living, loving Christ, in whom we have to abide, and whose almighty power to hold us fast is to be the measure of our expectations! As if He would give us the command, *"Abide in me"* (John 15:4) without securing the grace and the power to enable us to perform it! As if, above all, we had not the Father as the Husbandman (v. 1) to keep us from falling, and that not in a large and general sense, but according to His own precious promise: night and day, every moment! Oh, if we will only look to our God as the Keeper of Israel, of whom it is said, *"The LORD shall preserve thee from all evil; he shall preserve thy soul"* (Ps. 121:7), we will learn to believe that conscious abiding in Christ every moment, night and day, is indeed what God has prepared for those who love Him.

My beloved fellow Christians, let nothing less than this be your aim. I know well that you may not find it easy to attain, that there may come more than one hour of weary struggle and bitter failure. Were the church of Christ what it should be; were older believers to younger converts what they should be, witnesses to God's faithfulness, like Caleb and Joshua, encouraging their brothers to go up and possess the land with their, *"we are well able to overcome…if the LORD delight in us, then he will bring us into this land"* (Num. 13:30, 14:8); were the atmosphere that the young believer breathes as he enters the fellowship of the saints that of a healthy, trustful, joyful consecration; abiding in Christ would come as the natural outgrowth of being in Him. But in the sickly state in which such a great part of the body is, souls that are pressing after this blessing are sorely hindered by the depressing influence of the thought and the life around them. It is not to discourage that I say this, but to warn and to urge to a more entire casting of ourselves upon the Word of God Himself. There may come more than one hour in which you are ready to yield to despair, but be of good courage. Only believe. He who has put the blessing within your reach will assuredly lead to its possession.

The way in which souls enter into the possession may differ. To some it may come as the gift of a moment. In times of revival, in the fellowship with other believers in whom the Spirit is working effectually, under the leading of some servant of God who can guide, and sometimes in solitude too, it is as if all at once a new revelation comes upon the soul. It sees, as in the light of heaven, the strong Vine holding and bearing the feeble branches so securely, that doubt becomes impossible. It can only wonder how it ever could have understood the words to mean anything else than this: to abide unceasingly in Christ is the portion of every believer. It sees it, and to believe and rejoice and love come as of itself.

To others it comes by a slower and more difficult path. Day by day, amid discouragement and difficulty, the soul has to press forward. Be of good cheer; this way, too, leads to the rest. Only seek to keep your heart set upon the promise: *"I the* LORD *do keep it...night and day."* Take from His own lips the watchword: *"Every moment."* In that you have the law of His love, and the law of your hope. Be content with nothing less. Think no longer that the duties and the cares, that the sorrows and the sins, of this life must succeed in hindering the abiding life of fellowship. Take rather for the rule of your daily experience the language of faith: I am persuaded that neither death with its fears, nor life with its cares, nor things present with their pressing claims, nor things to come with their dark shadows, nor height of joy, nor depth of sorrow, nor any other creature, will be able, for one single moment, to separate us from the love of God which is in Christ Jesus our Lord, and in which He is teaching me to abide. (See Rom. 8:38–39.) If things look dark and faith would fail, sing again the song of the vineyard: *"I the* LORD *do keep it; I will water it every moment: lest any hurt it, I will keep it night and day."* And be assured that, if Jehovah keeps the branch night and day, and waters it every moment, a life of continuous and unbroken fellowship with Christ is indeed our privilege.

14

DAY BY DAY

And the people shall go out and gather the portion of a day in its day.
—Exodus 16:4

The day's portion in its day: such was the rule for God's giving and man's working in the ingathering of the manna. It is still the law in all the dealings of God's grace with His children. A clear insight into the beauty and application of this arrangement is a wonderful help in understanding how one, who feels himself utterly weak, can have the confidence and the perseverance to hold on brightly through all the years of his earthly course. A doctor was once asked by a patient who had met with a serious accident, "Doctor, how long will I have to lie here?" The answer, "Only a day at a time," taught the patient a precious lesson. It was the same lesson

God had recorded for His people of all ages long before: the day's portion in its day.

It was, without doubt, with a view to this and to meet man's weakness, that God graciously appointed the change of day and night. If time had been given to man in the form of one long unbroken day, it would have exhausted and overwhelmed him; the change of day and night continually recruits and recreates his powers. As a child, who easily makes himself master of a book, when each day only the lesson for the day is given him, would be utterly hopeless if the whole book were given him at once; so it would be with man, if there were no divisions in time. Broken small and divided into fragments, he can bear them; only the care and the work of each day have to be undertaken—the day's portion in its day. The rest of the night fits him for making a fresh start with each new morning; the mistakes of the past can be avoided, its lessons improved. And he has only each day to be faithful for the one short day, and long years and a long life take care of themselves without the sense of their length or their weight ever being a burden.

Most sweet is the encouragement to be derived from this truth in the life of grace. Many a soul is disquieted with the thought as to how it will be able to gather and to keep the manna needed for all its years of travel through such a barren wilderness. It has never learned what unspeakable comfort there is in the thought: the day's portion for its day. It takes away all care for tomorrow most completely. Only today is yours; tomorrow is the Father's. The question—What security have you that during all the years in which you have to contend with the coldness, or temptations, or trials of the world, you will always abide in Jesus?—is one you need not, yes, may not ask. Manna, as your food and strength, is given only by the day; faithfully to fill the present is your only security for the future. Accept, and enjoy, and fulfill with your whole heart the part you have this day to perform. His presence and grace enjoyed today will remove all doubt whether you can entrust tomorrow to Him too.

How great the value which this truth teaches us to attach to each single day! We are so easily led to look at life as a great whole, and to neglect the little today, to forget that the single days do indeed make up the whole, and that the value of each single day depends on its influence on the whole. One day lost is a link broken in the chain, which it often takes more than another day to mend. One day lost influences the next and makes its keeping more difficult. Yes, one day lost may be the loss of what months or years of careful labor had secured. The experience of many a believer could confirm this.

Believer, would you abide in Jesus, let it be day by day. You have already heard the message: moment by moment; the lesson of day by day has something more to teach. Of the moments, there are many where there is no direct exercise of the mind on your part; the abiding is in the deeper recesses of the heart, kept by the Father, to whom you entrusted yourself. But just this is the work that with each new day has to be renewed for the day—the distinct renewal of surrender and trust for the life of moment by moment. God has gathered up the moments and bound them up into a bundle, for the very purpose that we might take measure of them. As we look forward in the morning, or look back in the evening, and weigh the moments, we learn how to value and how to use them rightly. And even as the Father, with each new morning, meets you with the promise of just sufficient manna for the day for yourself and those who have to partake with you, meet Him with the bright and loving renewal of your acceptance of the position He has given you in His beloved Son. Accustom yourself to look upon this as one of the reasons for the appointment of day and night. God thought of our weakness and sought to provide for it. Let each day have its value from your calling to abide in Christ. As its light opens on your waking eyes, accept it on these terms: A day, just one day only, but still a day, given to abide and grow up in Jesus Christ. Whether it be a day of health or sickness, joy or sorrow, rest or work, of struggle or victory, let the chief thought with which you receive it in the morning thanksgiving be this: "This is a day that the Father has given; in it I may, I must, become more closely united to Jesus." As the Father asks, "Can you trust Me just for this one day to keep you abiding in Jesus, and Jesus to keep you fruitful?" you cannot help but give the joyful response: "I will trust and not be afraid."

The day's portion for its day was given to Israel in the morning very early. The portion was for use and nourishment during the whole day, but the giving and the getting of it was the morning's work. This suggests how greatly the power to spend a day aright, to abide all the day in Jesus, depends on the morning hour. If the firstfruits are holy, the lump is holy. During the day there come hours of intense occupation in the rush of business or the throng of men, when only the Father's keeping can maintain the connection with Jesus unbroken. The morning manna fed all the day; it is only when the believer in the morning secures his quiet time in secret to renew distinctly and effectually loving fellowship with his Savior, that the abiding can be kept up all the day. But what cause for thanksgiving that it may be done! In the morning, with its freshness and quiet, the believer can look out upon the day. He can consider its duties and its temptations, and pass them through beforehand, as it were, with his Savior, throwing all upon Him who has undertaken to be everything to him. Christ is his manna, his nourishment, his strength, his life: he can take the day's portion for the day, Christ as his for all the needs the day may bring, and go on in the assurance that the day will be one of blessing and of growth.

And then, as the lesson of the value and the work of the single day is being taken to heart, the learner is all unconsciously being led on to get the secret of "*day by day continually*" (Exod. 29:38). The blessed abiding grasped by faith for each day apart is an unceasing and ever increasing growth. Each day of faithfulness brings a blessing for the next, makes both the trust and the surrender easier and more blessed. And so the Christian life grows: as we give our whole heart to the work of each day, it becomes all the day and from that every day. And so each day separately, all the day continually, day by day successively, we abide in Jesus. And the days make up the life: what once appeared too high and too great to attain is given to the soul that was content to take and use every day its portion, "*as the duty of every day required*" (Ezra 3:4). Even here on earth the voice is heard: "*Well done, good and faithful servant; thou hast been faithful over a few things, I will make thee ruler over many things: enter thou into the joy of thy lord*" (Matt. 25:23). Our daily life becomes a wonderful interchange of God's daily grace and our daily praise: "*Daily [He] loadeth us with benefits*" (Ps. 68:19); "*That I may daily perform my vows"* (Ps. 61:8). We learn to understand God's reason for daily giving, as He most certainly gives, only enough, but also fully enough, for each day. And we get into His way, the way of daily asking and expecting only enough, but most certainly fully enough, for the day. We begin to number our days not from the sun's rising over the world, or by the work we do or the food we eat, but the daily renewal of the miracle of the manna—the blessedness of daily fellowship with Him who is the Life and the Light of the world. The heavenly life is as unbroken and continuous as the earthly; the abiding in Christ each day has for that day brought its blessing; we abide in Him every day, and all the day. Lord, make this the portion of each one of us.

15

AT THIS MOMENT

Behold, now is the accepted time; behold, now is the day of salvation.
—2 Corinthians 6:2

The thought of living moment by moment is of such central importance—looking at the abiding in Christ from our side—that I want once more to speak of it. And to all who desire to learn the blessed art of living only a moment at a time, I want to say: the way to learn it is to exercise yourself in living in the present moment. Each time your attention is free to occupy itself with the thought of Jesus—whether it is with time to think and pray, or only for a few passing seconds—let your first thought be to say: Now, at this moment, I do abide in Jesus. Use such time, not in vain regrets that you have not been abiding fully, or still more hurtful fears that you will not be able to abide, but just at once take the position the Father has given you: "I am in Christ; this is the place God has given me. I accept it; here I rest; I do now abide in Jesus." This is the way to learn to abide continually.

You may be yet so feeble as to fear to say of each day, "I am abiding in Jesus," but the feeblest can, each single moment, say, as he consents to occupy his place as a branch in the vine, "Yes, I do abide in Christ." It is not a matter of feeling—it is not a question of growth or strength in the Christian life—it is the simple question whether the will at the present moment desires and consents to recognize the place you have in your Lord, and to accept it. If you are a believer, you are in Christ. If you are in Christ, and wish to stay there, it is your duty to say, though it is but for a moment, "Blessed Savior, I abide in You now; You keep me now."

It has been well said that in that little word *now* lies one of the deepest secrets of the life of faith. At the close of a conference on the spiritual life, a minister of experience rose and spoke. He did not know that he had learned any truth he did not know before, but he had learned how to use correctly what he had known. He had learned that it was his privilege at each moment, whatever surrounding circumstances might be, to say, "Jesus saves me *now*." This is indeed the secret of rest and victory. If I can say, "Jesus is to me at this moment all that God gave Him to be: life, and strength, and peace," I have but as I say it to hold still, and rest, and realize it, and for that moment I have what I need. As my faith sees how of God I am in Christ, and takes the place in Him my Father has provided, my soul can peacefully settle down: now I abide in Christ.

Believer, when striving to find the way to abide in Christ from moment to moment, remember that the gateway is to abide in Him at this present moment. Instead of wasting effort in trying to get into a state that will last, just remember that it is Christ Himself, the living, loving Lord, who alone can keep you and is waiting to do so. Begin at once, and act by faith in Him for the present moment: this is the only way to be kept the next. To attain the life of permanent and perfect abiding is not ordinarily given at once as a possession for the future; it comes mostly step by step. Avail yourself, therefore, of every opportunity of exercising the trust of the present moment. Each time you bow in prayer, let there first be an act of simple devotion: "Father, I am in Christ; I now abide in Him." Each time you have, amid the bustle of duty, the opportunity of self-recollection, let its first involuntary act be: "I am still in Christ, abiding in Him now." Even when overtaken by sin, and the heart within is all disturbed and excited, let your first look upwards be with the words: "Father, I have sinned; and yet I come—though I blush to say it—as one who is in Christ. Father, here I am; I can take no other place; of God I am in Christ; I *now* abide in Christ." Yes, Christian, in every possible circumstance, every moment of the day, the voice is calling: Abide in me, do it now. And even now, as you are reading this, come at once, and enter upon the blessed life of always abiding, by doing it at once: do it now.

In the life of David there is a beautiful passage which may help to make this thought clearer. David had been anointed king in Judah. The other tribes still followed Ishbosheth, Saul's son. Abner, Saul's chief captain, resolved to lead the tribes of Israel to submit to David, the God-appointed king of the whole nation. He spoke to the elders of Israel: "*Ye sought for David in times past to be king over you: now then do it: for the* LORD *hath spoken of David, saying, By the hand of my servant David I will save my people Israel out of the hand of the Philistines, and out of the hand of all their enemies*" (2 Sam. 3:17–18). And they did it and anointed David a second time to be king, now over all Israel, as at first only over Judah (2 Sam. 5:3)—a most instructive type of the way in which a soul is led to the life of entire surrender and undivided allegiance, to the full abiding.

First you have the divided kingdom: Judah faithful to the king of God's appointment; Israel still clinging to the king of its own choosing. As a consequence, the nation was divided against itself and had no power to conquer the enemies—a picture of the divided heart. Jesus accepted as King in Judah, the place of the holy mount, in the inner chamber of the soul, but the surrounding territory, the everyday life, not yet brought to subjection;

more than half the life still ruled by self-will and its hosts. And so no real peace within and no power over the enemies.

Then there is the longing desire for a better state: "*Ye sought for David in times past to be king over you.*" There was a time, when David had conquered the Philistines, that Israel believed in him, but they had been led astray. Abner appealed to their own knowledge of God's will, that David must rule over all. So the believer, when first brought to Jesus, did indeed want Him to be Lord over all, had hoped that He alone would be King. But, alas, unbelief and self-will had come in, and Jesus could not assert His power over the whole life. And yet the Christian is not content. How he longs—sometimes without daring to hope that it can be—for a better time!

Then follows God's promise. Abner said: "*The LORD hath spoken... By the hand of...David I will save my people...out of the hand of...all their enemies.*" He appealed to God's promise: as David had conquered the Philistines, the nearest enemy in time past, so he alone could conquer those farther off. He would save Israel from the hand of all their enemies. Beautiful type of the promise by which the soul is now invited to trust Jesus for the victory over every enemy, and a life of undisturbed fellowship! "*The LORD hath spoken*"—this is our only hope. On that word rests the sure expectation:

> As he spake...that we should be saved from...the hand of all that hate us; to perform...the oath which he sware...that he would grant unto us, that we being delivered out of the hand of our enemies might serve him without fear, in holiness and righteousness before him, all the days of our life. (Luke 1:70–75)

David reigning over every corner of the land and leading a united and obedient people on from victory to victory: this is the promise of what Jesus can do for us, as soon as in faith in God's promise all is surrendered to Him, and the whole life given up to be kept abiding in Him.

"*Ye sought for David in times past to be king over you*" (2 Sam. 3:17) spoke Abner, and added, "*Now then do it*" (v. 18). Do it *now* is the message that this story brings to each one of us who longs to give Jesus unreserved supremacy. Whatever the present moment is, however unprepared the message finds you, however sad the divided and hopeless state of the life may be, still I come and urge Christ's claim to an immediate surrender—this very moment. I know well that it will take time for the blessed Lord to assert His power, and order all within you according to His will, to conquer the enemies and train all your powers for His service. This is not the work of a moment. But there are things which are the work of a moment—of this moment. The one is your surrender of all to Jesus; your surrender of yourself entirely to live only in Him. As time goes on, and exercise has made faith stronger and brighter, this surrender may become clearer and more intelligent. But for this no one may wait. The only way ever to attain to it is to begin at once. Do it now. Surrender yourself this very moment to abide wholly, only, always in Jesus. It is the work of a moment. And just so, Christ's renewed acceptance of you is the work of a moment. Be assured that He has you and holds you as His own, and that each new "Jesus, I do abide in You," meets with an immediate and most hearty response from the Unseen One. No act of faith can be in vain. He does indeed anew take hold on us and draw us close to Himself. Therefore, as often as the message comes, or the thought of it comes, Jesus says: Abide in me, do it at once. Each moment there is the whisper: Do it now.

Let any Christian begin, then, and he will speedily experience how the blessing of the present moment is passed on to the next. It is the unchanging Jesus to whom he links himself; it is the power of a divine life, in its unbroken continuity, that takes possession of him. The "do it now" of the present moment—a little thing though it seems—is nothing less than the beginning of the ever present now, which is the mystery and the glory of eternity. Therefore, Christian, abide in Christ: do it now.

16

FORSAKING ALL FOR HIM

I have suffered the loss of all things, and do count them but dung,
that I may win Christ, and be found in him.
—Philippians 3:8–9

Wherever there is life, there is a continual interchange of taking in and giving out, receiving and restoring. The nourishment I take is given out again in the work I do; the impressions I receive, in the thoughts and feelings I express. The one depends on the other—the giving out ever increases the power of taking in. In the healthy exercise of giving and taking is all the enjoyment of life.

It is so in the spiritual life too. There are Christians who look on its blessedness as consisting all in the privilege of ever receiving; they do not know how the capacity for receiving is only kept up and enlarged by continual giving up and giving out—how it is only in the emptiness that comes from the parting with what we have, that the divine fullness can flow in. It was a truth our Savior continually insisted on. When He spoke of selling all to secure the treasure, of losing our life to find it, of the hundredfold to those who forsake all, He was expounding the need of self-sacrifice as the law of the kingdom for Himself as well as for His disciples. If we are really to abide in Christ, and to be found in Him—to have our life always and wholly in Him—we must each in our measure say with Paul, *"I count all things but loss for the excellency of the knowledge of Christ Jesus my Lord…that I may win Christ, and be found in him"* (vv. 8–9).

Let us try and see what there is to be forsaken and given up. First of all, there is sin. There can be no true conversion without the giving up of sin. And yet, owing to the ignorance of the young convert of what really is sin, of what the claims of God's holiness are, and of the extent to which the power of Jesus can enable us to conquer sin, the giving up of sin is but partial and superficial. With the growth of the Christian life there comes the want of a deeper and more entire purging out of everything that is unholy. And it is especially when the desire to abide in Christ uninterruptedly, to be always found in Him, becomes strong, that the soul is led to see the need of a new act of surrender, in which it afresh accepts and ratifies its death to sin in Christ and parts indeed with everything that is sin. Availing himself, in the strength of God's Spirit, of that wonderful power of our nature by which the whole of one's future life can be gathered up and disposed of in one act of the will, the believer yields himself to sin no more—to be only and wholly a servant of righteousness. He does it in the joyful assurance that every sin surrendered is gain indeed—room for the inflowing of the presence and the love of Christ.

Next to the parting with unrighteousness, is the giving up of self-righteousness. Though we contend most earnestly against our own works or merits, it is often long before we come really to understand what it is to refuse self the least place or right in the service of God. Unconsciously we allow the actings of our own mind and heart and will free scope in

God's presence. In prayer and worship, in Bible reading and working for God, instead of absolute dependence on the Holy Spirit's leading, self is expected to do a work it never can do. We are slow to learn the lesson, *"In me (that is, in my flesh,) dwelleth no good thing"* (Rom. 7:18). As it is learned, and we see how corruption extends to everything that is of nature, we see that there can be no entire abiding in Christ without the giving up of all that is of self in religion—without giving it up to the death, and waiting for the breathings of the Holy Spirit as alone able to work in us what is acceptable in God's sight.

Then, again, there is our whole natural life, with all the powers and endowments bestowed upon us by the Creator, with all the occupations and interests with which Providence has surrounded us. It is not enough that, when once you are truly converted, you have the earnest desire to have all these devoted to the service of the Lord. The desire is good, but can neither teach the way nor give the strength to do it acceptably. Incalculable harm has been done to the deeper spirituality of the church, by the idea that when once we are God's children the using of our gifts in His service follows as a matter of course. No; for this there is indeed needed very special grace. And the way in which the grace comes is again that of sacrifice and surrender.

I must see how all my gifts and powers are, even though I am a child of God, still defiled by sin and under the power of the flesh. I must feel that I cannot at once proceed to use them for God's glory. I must first lay them at Christ's feet, to be accepted and cleansed by Him. I must feel myself utterly powerless to use them correctly. I must see that they are most dangerous to me, because through them the flesh, the old nature, self, will so easily exert its power. In this conviction I must part with them, giving them entirely up to the Lord. When He has accepted them, and set His stamp upon them, I receive them back, to hold them as His property, to wait on Him for the grace to use them correctly day by day, and to have them act only under His influence. And so experience proves it true here too, that the path of entire consecration is the path of full salvation. Not only is what is thus given up received back again to become doubly our own, but the forsaking all is followed by the receiving all. We abide in Christ more fully as we forsake all and follow Him. As I count all things loss for His sake, I am found in Him.

The same principle holds good of all the lawful occupations and possessions with which we are entrusted of God. Such were the fishnets on the Sea of Galilee, and the household duties of Martha of Bethany—the home and the friends of many a one among Jesus' disciples. Jesus taught them indeed to forsake all for Him. It was no arbitrary command, but the simple application of a law in nature to the kingdom of His grace: that the more perfectly the old occupant is cast out, the more complete the possession of the new can be, and the more entire the renewal of all within.

This principle has a still deeper application. The truly spiritual gifts that are the working of God's own Holy Spirit within us—these surely need not be thus given up and surrendered? They do indeed; the interchange of giving up and taking in is a life process and may not cease for a moment. No sooner does the believer begin to rejoice in the possession of what he has, than the inflow of new grace is retarded, and stagnation threatens. It is only into the thirst of an empty soul that the streams of living waters flow. Ever thirsting is the secret of never thirsting. Each blessed experience we receive as a gift of God must at once be returned back to Him from whom it came, in praise and love, in self-sacrifice and service; so only can it be restored to us again, fresh and beautiful with the bloom of heaven. Is this not the wonderful lesson Isaac on Moriah teaches us? Was he not the son of promise, the God-given life, the wonder gift of the omnipotence of Him who quickens the dead? (See Rom. 4:17.) And yet even he had to be given up, and sacrificed, that he might be received back again a thousandfold more precious than before—a type of the Only Begotten of the Father, whose pure and holy life had to be given up before He could receive it again in resurrection power, and could make His people partakers of it. A type, too, of what takes place in the life of each believer, as, instead of resting content with past experiences or present grace, he presses on, forgetting and giving up all that is behind, and reaches out to the fullest possible apprehension of Christ, His life.

And such surrender of all for Christ, is it a single step, the act and experience of a moment, or is it a course of daily renewed and progressive attainment? It is both. There may be a moment in the life of a believer when he gets a first sight, or a deeper insight, of this most blessed truth, and when made willing in the day of God's power, he does indeed, in an act of the will, gather up the whole of life yet before him into the decision of a moment, and lay himself on the altar a living and an acceptable sacrifice. Such moments have often been the blessed transition from a life of wandering and failure to a life of abiding and power divine. But even then his daily life becomes what the life must be of each one who has no such experience, the unceasing prayer for more light on the meaning of entire surrender, the ever renewed offering up of all he has to God.

Believer, I desire that you would abide in Christ, and see here the blessed path. Nature shrinks back from such self-denial and crucifixion in its rigid application to our life in its whole extent. But what nature does not love and cannot perform, grace will accomplish and make to you a life of joy and glory. If you will but yield up yourself to Christ your Lord, the conquering power of His incoming presence will make it joy to cast out all that before was most precious. *"An hundredfold"* in this life (see Mark 10:30): this word of the Master comes true to all who, with wholehearted faithfulness, accept His commands to forsake all. The blessed receiving soon makes the giving up most blessed too. And the secret of a life of close abiding will be seen to be simply this: as I give myself wholly to Christ, I find the power to take Him wholly for myself; and as I lose myself and all I have for Him, He takes me wholly for Himself and gives Himself wholly to me.

17

THROUGH THE HOLY SPIRIT

The anointing which ye have received of him abideth in you...
and even as it hath taught you, ye shall abide in him.
—1 John 2:27

How beautiful the thought of a life always abiding in Christ! The longer we think of it, the more attractive it becomes. And yet how often it is that the precious words, *"Abide in me"* (John 15:4) are heard by the young disciple with a sigh! It is as if he understands so little what they really mean and can realize so little how this full enjoyment can be attained. He longs for someone who could make it perfectly clear and continually again remind him that the abiding is indeed within his reach. If such a one would but listen to the word we have from John this day, what hope and joy it would bring! It gives us the divine assurance that we have the anointing of the Holy Spirit to teach us all things, also to teach us how to abide in Christ.

Alas, someone answers, this word does not give me comfort, it only depresses me more. For it tells of another privilege I so little know to enjoy: I do not understand how the teaching of the Spirit is given—where or how I can discern His voice. If the Teacher is so unknown, no wonder that the promise of His teaching about the abiding does not help me much.

Thoughts like these come from an error which is very common among believers. They imagine that the Spirit, in teaching them, must reveal the mysteries of the spiritual life first to their intellect, and afterwards in their experience. And God's way is just the contrary of this. What holds true of all spiritual truth is especially true of the abiding in Christ: we must live and experience truth in order to know it. Life fellowship with Jesus is the only school for the science of heavenly things. *"What I do thou knowest not now; but thou shalt know hereafter"* (John 13:7) is a law of the kingdom, especially true of the daily cleansing of which it first was spoken, and the daily keeping. Receive what you do not comprehend, submit to what you cannot understand, accept and expect what to reason appears a mystery, believe what looks impossible, walk in a way that you know not—such are the first lessons in the school of God. "If you abide in My word, you will understand the truth"—in these and other words of God we are taught that there is a habit of mind and life which precedes the understanding of the truth. True discipleship consists in first following and then knowing the Lord. The believing surrender to Christ, and the submission to His Word to expect what appears most improbable, is the only way to the full blessedness of knowing Him.

These principles hold especially good in regard to the teaching of the Spirit. That teaching consists in His guiding the spiritual life within us to what God has prepared for us, without our always knowing how. On the strength of God's promise, and trusting in His faithfulness, the believer yields himself to the leading of the Holy Spirit, without claiming to have it first made clear to the intellect what He is to do, but consenting to let Him do His work in the soul and afterwards to know what He has wrought there. Faith trusts the working of the Spirit unseen in the deep recesses of the inner life. And so the Word of Christ and the gift of the Spirit are to the believer sufficient guarantee that he will be taught by the Spirit to abide in Christ. By faith he rejoices in what he does not see or feel; he knows and is confident that the blessed Spirit within is doing His work silently but surely, guiding him into the life of full abiding and unbroken communion. The Holy Spirit is the Spirit of life in Christ Jesus; it is His work, not only to breathe, but ever to foster and strengthen, and so to perfect the new life within. And just in proportion as the believer yields himself in simple trust to the unseen but most certain law of the Spirit of life working within him, his faith will pass into knowledge. It will be rewarded by the Spirit's light revealing in the Word what has already been wrought by the Spirit's power in the life.

Apply this now to the promise of the Spirit's teaching us to abide in Christ. The Holy Spirit is indeed the mighty power of God. And He comes to us from the heart of Christ, the Bearer of Christ's life, the Revealer and Communicator of Christ Himself within us. In the expression, the *"fellowship of the Spirit"* (Phil. 2:1), we are taught what His highest work is. He is the bond of fellowship between the Father and the Son; by Him they are one. He is the bond of fellowship between all believers; by Him they are one. Above all, He is the bond of fellowship between Christ and believers; He is the life sap through which Vine and branch grow into real and living oneness. By Him we are one. And we can be assured of it that if we do but believe in His presence and working, if we do but watch not to grieve Him, because we know that He is in us, if we wait and pray to be filled with Him, He will teach us how to abide. First guiding our will to a wholehearted cleaving to Christ, then quickening our faith into ever larger confidence and expectation, then breathing into our hearts a peace and joy that pass understanding (see Phil. 4:7), He teaches us to abide, we scarcely know how. Then coming through the heart and life into the understanding, He makes us know the truth—not as mere thought truth, but as the truth that is in Christ Jesus, the reflection into the mind of the light of what He has already made a reality in the life. *"The life was the light of men"* (John 1:4).

In view of such teaching, it is clear how, if we would have the Spirit to guide us into the abiding life, our first need is quiet, restful faith. Amid all the questions and difficulties that may come up in connection with our striving to abide in Christ, amid all the longing we may sometimes feel to have a Christian of experience to aid us, amid the frequent painful consciousness of failure, of ignorance, of helplessness—do let us hold fast the blessed confidence: we have the unction of the Holy One to teach us to abide in Him. (See 1 John 2:20.) *"The anointing which ye have received of him abideth in you...and even as it hath taught you, ye shall abide in him."* Make this teaching of His in connection with the abiding a matter of special exercise of faith.

Believe that as surely as you have part in Christ, you have His Spirit too. Believe that He will do His work with power, if only you do not hinder Him. Believe that He is working, even when you cannot discern it. Believe that He will I work mightily if you ask this from the Father. It is impossible to live the life of full abiding without being full of the Holy Spirit; believe that the fullness of the Spirit is indeed your daily portion. Be sure and take time in prayer to dwell at the footstool of the throne of God and the Lamb, whence flows the river of the water of life. It is there, and only there, that you can be filled with the Spirit. Cultivate carefully the habit of daily, yes, continually honoring Him by the quiet, restful confidence that He is doing His work within. Let faith in His indwelling make you jealous of whatever could grieve Him: the spirit of the world or the acting of self and the flesh. Let that faith seek its nourishment in the Word and all it says of the Spirit, His power, His comfort, and His work. Above all, let that faith in the Spirit's indwelling lead you especially to look away to Jesus; as we have received the anointing of Him, it comes in ever stronger flow from Him as we are occupied with Him alone. Christ is the Anointed One. As we look up to Him, the holy anointing comes, *"the precious ointment upon the head [of Aaron]...that went down to the skirts of his garments"* (Ps. 133:2). It is faith in Jesus that brings the anointing; the anointing leads to Jesus and to the abiding in Him alone.

Believer, abide in Christ, in the power of the Spirit. What do you think: should the abiding be a fear or a burden? Surely not. Oh, if we did but know the graciousness of our Holy Comforter and the blessedness of wholly yielding ourselves to His leading, we should indeed experience the divine comfort of having such a teacher to secure our abiding in Christ. The Holy Spirit was given for this one purpose—that the glorious redemption and life in Christ might with divine power be conveyed and communicated to us. We have the Holy Spirit to make the living Christ, in all His saving power, and in the completeness of His victory over sin, ever present within us. It is this that constitutes Him the Comforter; with Him we need never mourn an absent Christ. Let us therefore, as often as we read, or meditate, or pray in connection with this abiding in Christ, reckon upon it as a settled thing that we have the Spirit of God Himself within us, teaching, and guiding, and working. Let us rejoice in the confidence that we must succeed in our desires, because the Holy Spirit is working all the while with secret but divine power in the soul that does not hinder Him by its unbelief.

18

IN STILLNESS OF SOUL

*In returning and rest shall ye be saved; in quietness and in
confidence shall be your strength.*
—Isaiah 30:15

[Be silent to] *the* Lord, *and wait patiently for him.*
—Psalm 37:7

Truly my soul waits silently upon God.
—Psalm 62:1

There is a view of the Christian life that regards it as a sort of partnership, in which God and man have each to do their part. It admits that there is but little that man can do, and that little is defiled with sin; still he must do his utmost—then only can he expect God to do His part. To those who think thus, it is extremely difficult to understand what Scripture means when it speaks of our being still and doing nothing, of our resting and waiting to see the salvation of God. It appears to them a perfect contradiction, when we speak of this quietness and ceasing from all effort as the secret of the highest activity of man and all his powers. And yet this is just what Scripture does teach.

The explanation of the apparent mystery is to be found in this, that when God and man are spoken of as working together, there is nothing of the idea of a partnership between two partners who each contribute their share to a work. The cooperation is a very different one. The true idea is that of cooperation founded on subordination. As Jesus was entirely dependent on the Father for all His words and all His works, so the believer can do nothing of himself. What he can do of himself is altogether sinful. He must therefore cease entirely from his own doing, and wait for the working of God in him. As he ceases from self-effort, faith assures him that God does what He has undertaken, and works in him. And what God does is to renew, to sanctify, and to waken all his energies to their highest power. So that just in proportion as he yields himself a truly passive instrument in the hand of God, will he be wielded of God as the active instrument of His almighty power. The soul in which the wondrous combination of perfect passivity with the highest activity is most completely realized, has the deepest experience of what the Christian life is.

Among the lessons to be learned of those who are studying the blessed art of abiding in Christ, there is none more necessary and more profitable than this one of stillness of soul. In it alone can we cultivate that teachableness of spirit, to which the Lord will reveal His secrets, that meekness to which He shows His ways. It is the spirit exhibited so beautifully in all the three Marys. In her whose only answer to the most wonderful revelation ever made to human beings was, *"Behold the handmaid of the Lord; be it unto me according to thy word"* (Luke 1:38); and of whom, as mysteries multiplied around her, it is written: *"Mary kept all these things, and pondered them in her heart"* (Luke 2:19). And in her who *"sat at Jesus' feet, and heard his* word" (Luke 10:39) and who showed, in anointing Him for His burial, how she had entered more deeply into the mystery of His death than even the beloved disciple. And in her, too, who sought her Lord in the house of the Pharisee, with tears that spoke more than words. (See Luke 7:37–38.) It is a soul silent unto God that is the best preparation for knowing Jesus, and for holding fast the blessings He bestows. It is when the soul is hushed in silent awe and worship before the Holy Presence that reveals itself within, that the still small voice of the blessed Spirit will be heard.

Therefore, beloved Christian, as often as you seek to understand better the blessed mystery of abiding in Christ, let this be your first thought: "My soul, only be silent unto God; '*for my expectation is from him*' (Ps. 62:5)." Do you indeed hope to realize the wondrous union with the Heavenly Vine? Do you know that flesh and blood cannot reveal it unto you, but only the Father in heaven? "*Cease from thine own wisdom*" (Prov. 23:4). You have but to bow in the confession of your own ignorance and impotence; the Father will delight to give you the teaching of the Holy Spirit. If only your ears are open, and your thoughts brought into subjection, and your heart prepared in silence to wait upon God, and to hear what He speaks, He will reveal to you His secrets. And one of the first secrets will be the deeper insight into the truth, that as you sink low before Him in nothingness and helplessness, in a silence and a stillness of soul that seeks to catch the faintest whisper of His love, teachings will come to you that you had never heard before because of the rush and noise of your own thoughts and efforts. You will learn how your great work is to listen and hear and believe what He promises; to watch and wait and see what He does; and then, in faith and worship and obedience, to yield yourself to His working who works in you mightily.

One would think that no message could be more beautiful or welcome than this, that we may rest and be quiet, and that our God will work for us and in us. And yet how far this is from being the case! And how slow many are to learn that quietness is blessedness, that quietness is strength, that quietness is the source of the highest activity—the secret of all true abiding in Christ! Let us try to learn it and to watch against whatever interferes with it. The dangers that threaten the soul's rest are not a few.

There is the dissipation of soul that comes from entering needlessly and too deeply into the interests of this world. Everyone of us has his divine calling; and within the circle pointed out by God Himself, interest in our work and its surroundings is a duty. But even here the Christian needs to exercise watchfulness and sobriety. And still more do we need a holy temperance in regard to things not absolutely imposed upon us by God. If abiding in Christ really is our first aim, let us beware of all needless excitement. Let us watch even in lawful and necessary things against the wondrous power these have to keep the soul so occupied, that there remains but little power or zest for fellowship with God. Then there is the restlessness and worry that come of care and anxiety about earthly things; these eat away the life of trust and keep the soul like a troubled sea. There the gentle whispers of the Holy Comforter cannot be heard.

No less hurtful is the spirit of fear and distrust in spiritual things; with its apprehensions and its efforts, it never comes really to hear what God has to say. Above all, there is the unrest that comes through seeking in our own way and in our own strength the spiritual blessing that comes alone from above. The heart occupied with its own plans and efforts for doing God's will, and securing the blessing of abiding in Jesus, must fail continually. God's work is hindered by our interference. He can do His work perfectly only when the soul ceases from its work. He will do His work mightily in the soul that honors Him by expecting Him to work both to will and to do.

And, last of all, even when the soul seeks truly to enter the way of faith, there is the impatience of the flesh, which forms its judgment of the life and progress of the soul not after the divine but the human standard.

In dealing with all this, and so much more, blessed is the man who learns the lesson of stillness and fully accepts God's Word: *"In quietness and in confidence shall be your strength."* Each time he listens to the Word of the Father, or asks the Father to listen to his words, he dares not begin his Bible reading or prayer without first pausing and waiting, until the soul is hushed in the presence of the Eternal Majesty. Under a sense of the divine nearness, the soul, feeling how self is always ready to assert itself and intrude even into the holiest of all with its thoughts and efforts, yields itself in a quiet act of self-surrender to the teaching and working of the divine Spirit. It is still and waits in holy silence, until all is calm and ready to receive the revelation of the divine will and presence. Its reading and prayer then indeed become a waiting on God with ear and heart opened and purged to receive fully only what He says.

Abide in Christ! Let no one think that he can do this if he does not daily have his quiet time, his seasons of meditation and waiting on God. In these, a habit of soul must be cultivated in which the believer goes out into the world and its distractions with the peace of God that passes all understanding keeping the heart and mind. (See Phil. 4:7.) It is in such a calm and restful soul that the life of faith can strike deep root, that the Holy Spirit can give His blessed teaching, that the Holy Father can accomplish His glorious work. May each one of us learn every day to say, "Truly my soul is silent unto God." And may every feeling of the difficulty of attaining this only lead us simply to look and trust Him whose presence makes even the storm a calm. Cultivate the quietness as a means to the abiding of Christ; expect the ever deepening quietness and calm of heaven in the soul as the fruit of abiding in Him.

19

IN AFFLICTION AND TRIAL

Every branch that beareth fruit, he purgeth it,
that it may bring forth more fruit.
—John 15:2

In the whole plant world there is not a tree to be found so specially suited to the image of man in his relation to God as the vine. There is none of which the fruit and its juice are so full of spirit, so quickening and stimulating. But there is also none of which the natural tendency is so entirely evil—none where the growth is so ready to run into wood that is utterly worthless except for the fire. Of all plants, not one needs the pruning knife so unsparingly and so unceasingly. None is so dependent on cultivation and training, but with this none yields a richer reward to the husbandman. In His wonderful parable, the Savior, with a single word, refers to this need of pruning in the vine and the blessing it brings. But from that single word what streams of light pour in upon this dark world, so full of suffering and of sorrow to believers! What treasures of teaching and comfort to the bleeding branch in its hour of trial: *"Every branch that beareth fruit, he purgeth it, that it may bring forth more fruit."* And so He has prepared His people, who are so ready when trial comes to be shaken in their confidence, and to be moved from their abiding in Christ, to hear in each affliction the voice of a messenger that comes to call them to abide still more closely. Yes, believer, most especially in times of trial, abide in Christ.

Abide in Christ! This is indeed the Father's object in sending the trial. In the storm the tree strikes deeper roots in the soil; in the hurricane the inhabitants of the house abide within and rejoice in its shelter. So by suffering the Father would lead us to enter more deeply into the love of Christ. Our hearts are continually prone to wander from Him; prosperity and enjoyment all too easily satisfy us, dull our spiritual perception, and make us unfit for full communion with Himself. It is an unspeakable mercy that the Father comes with His chastisement, makes the world around us all dark and unattractive, and leads us to feel more deeply our sinfulness and for a time lose our joy in what was becoming so dangerous. He does it in the hope that, when we have found our rest in Christ in time of trouble, we will learn to choose abiding in Him as our only portion, and so that when the affliction is removed, we will have so grown more firmly into Him, that in prosperity He still will be our only joy. So much has He set His heart on this, that though He has indeed no pleasure in afflicting us, He will not keep back even the most painful chastisement; He can thereby guide His beloved child to come home and abide in the beloved Son. Christian, pray for grace to see in every trouble, small or great, the Father's finger pointing to Jesus, and saying, "Abide in Him."

Abide in Christ; so will you become partaker of all the rich blessings God designed for you in the affliction. The purposes of God's wisdom will become clear to you, your assurance of the unchangeable love become stronger, and the power of His Spirit will fulfill in you the promise:

"He [chastens us] *for our profit, that we might be partakers of his holiness*" (Heb. 12:10). Abide in Christ, and your cross becomes the means of fellowship with His cross, and access into its mysteries—the mystery of the curse that He bore for you, of the death to sin in which you partake with Him, of the love in which, as sympathizing High Priest, He descended into all your sorrows. Abide in Christ; as you are growing in conformity to your blessed Lord in His sufferings, deeper experience of the reality and the tenderness of His love will be yours. Abide in Christ; in the fiery oven, one like the Son of Man will be seen as never before; the purging away of the cross and the refining of the gold will be accomplished, and Christ's own likeness will be reflected in you. Oh, abide in Christ; the power of the flesh will be mortified; the impatience and self-will of the old nature will be humbled to make place for the meekness and gentleness of Christ. A believer may pass through much affliction, and yet secure but little blessing from it all. Abiding in Christ is the secret of securing all that the Father meant the chastisement to bring us.

Abide in Christ: in Him you will find sure and abundant consolation. With the afflicted, comfort is often first, and the profit of the affliction second. The Father loves us so, that with Him our real and abiding profit is His first object, but He does not forget to comfort too. When He comforts, it is so that He may turn the bleeding heart to Himself to receive the blessing in fellowship with Him; when He refuses comfort, His object is still the same. It is in making us partakers of His holiness that true comfort comes. The Holy Spirit is the Comforter, not only because He can suggest comforting thoughts of God's love, but far more, because He makes us holy and brings us into close union with Christ and with God. He teaches us to abide in Christ; and because God is found there, the truest comfort will come there too. In Christ the heart of the Father is revealed, and higher comfort there cannot be than to rest in the Father's bosom. In Him the fullness of the divine love is revealed, combined with the tenderness of a mother's compassion—and what can comfort like this? In Him you see a thousand times more given you than you have lost; see how God only took from you that you might have room to take from Him what is so much better. In Him suffering is consecrated and becomes the foretaste of eternal glory; in suffering it is that the Spirit of God and of glory rests on us. Believer, would you have comfort in affliction? Abide in Christ.

Abide in Christ; so will you bear much fruit. Not a vine is planted but the owner thinks of the fruit, and the fruit only. Other trees may be planted for ornament, for the shade, for the wood—the vine only for the fruit. And of each vine the husbandman is continually asking how it can bring forth more fruit, much fruit. Believer, abide in Christ in times of affliction, and you will bring forth more fruit. The deeper experience of Christ's tenderness and the Father's love will urge you to live to His glory. The surrender of self and self-will in suffering will prepare you to sympathize with the misery of others, while the softening that comes of chastisement will fit you for becoming, as Jesus was, the servant of all. The thought of the Father's desire for fruit in the pruning will lead you to yield yourself afresh, and more than ever, to Him, and to say that now you have but one object in life—making known and conveying His wonderful love to fellowmen. You will learn the blessed art of forgetting self, and, even in affliction, availing yourself of your separation from ordinary life to plead for the welfare of others. Dear Christian, in affliction abide in Christ. When you see it coming, meet it in Christ; when it has come, feel that you are more in Christ than in it, for He is nearer you than affliction ever can be; when it is passing, still abide in Him. And let the one thought of the Savior, as He speaks of the pruning, and the one desire of the Father, as He does the pruning, be yours too: *"Every branch that beareth fruit, he purgeth it, that it may bring forth more fruit."*

So will your times of affliction become your times of choicest blessing—preparation for richest fruitfulness. Led into closer fellowship with the Son of God, and deeper experience of His love and grace; established in the blessed confidence that He and you entirely belong to each other; more completely satisfied with Him and more wholly given up to Him than ever before, with your own will crucified afresh, and the heart brought into deeper harmony with God's will—you will be a vessel cleansed, fit for the Master's use, prepared for every good work (2 Tim. 2:21). True believer! Try to learn the blessed truth, that in affliction your first, your only, your blessed calling is to abide in Christ. Be much with Him alone. Beware of the comfort and the distractions that friends so often bring. Let Jesus Christ Himself be your chief companion and comforter. Delight yourself in the assurance that closer union with Him, and more abundant fruit through Him, are sure to be the results of trial, because it is the Husbandman Himself who is pruning and will ensure the fulfillment of the desire of the soul that yields lovingly to His work.

20

THAT YOU MAY
BEAR MUCH FRUIT

*He that abideth in me, and I in him, the same bringeth forth much
fruit....Herein is my Father glorified, that ye bear much fruit.*
—John 15:5, 8

We all know what fruit is: the produce of the branch, by
which men are refreshed and nourished. The fruit is not
for the branch, but for those who come to carry it away. As soon as the
fruit is ripe, the branch lets it go, to commence afresh its work of charity,
and anew prepare its fruit for another season. A fruit-bearing tree lives
not for itself, but wholly for those to whom its fruit brings refreshment

131

and life. And so the branch exists only and entirely for the sake of the fruit. To make glad the heart of the husbandman is its object, its safety, and its glory.

Beautiful image of the believer: abiding in Christ! He not only grows in strength, the union with the Vine becoming ever surer and firmer, he also bears fruit, yes, much fruit. He has the power to offer that to others of which they can eat and live. Amid all who surround him he becomes like a tree of life, of which they can taste and be refreshed. He is in his circle a center of life and of blessing, and that simply because he abides in Christ, and receives from Him the Spirit and the life of which he can impart to others. Learn thus, if you would bless others, to abide in Christ, and that if you do abide, you will surely bless. As surely as the branch abiding in a fruitful vine bears fruit, so surely, yes, much more surely, will a soul abiding in Christ with His fullness of blessing be made a blessing.

The reason for this is easily understood. If Christ, the Heavenly Vine, has taken the believer as a branch, then He has pledged Himself, in the very nature of things, to supply the sap and spirit and nourishment to make it bring forth fruit. *"From me is thy fruit found"* (Hos. 14:8); these words derive new meaning from our parable. The soul need but have one care: to abide closely, fully, wholly. He will give the fruit. He works all that is needed to make the believer a blessing.

Abiding in Him, you receive of Him His Spirit of love and compassion toward sinners, making you desirous to seek their good. By nature the heart is full of selfishness. Even in the believer, his own salvation and happiness are often too much his only object. But abiding in Jesus, you come into contact with His infinite love; its fire begins to burn within your heart; you see the beauty of love; you learn to look upon loving and serving and saving your fellowmen as the highest privilege a disciple of Jesus can have. Abiding in Christ, your heart learns to feel the wretchedness of the sinner still in darkness, and the fearfulness of the dishonor done to your God. With Christ you begin to bear the burden of souls, the burden of sins not your own. As you are more closely united to Him, something of that passion for souls that urged Him to Calvary begins to breathe within you, and you are ready to follow His footsteps, forsake the heaven of your own happiness, and devote your life to win the souls Christ has taught you to love. The very spirit of the Vine is love; the spirit of love streams into the branch that abides in Him.

The desire to be a blessing is but the beginning. As you undertake to work, you speedily become conscious of your own weakness and the difficulties in your way. Souls are not saved at your bidding. You are ready to be discouraged and to relax your effort. But abiding in Christ, you receive new courage and strength for the work. Believing what Christ teaches, that it is He who through you will give His blessing to the world, you understand that you are but the feeble instrument through which the hidden power of Christ does its work, that His strength may be perfected and made glorious in your weakness. It is a great step when the believer fully consents to his own weakness, and the abiding consciousness of it, and so works faithfully on, fully assured that his Lord is working through him. He rejoices that the excellence of the power is of God, and not of us. (See 2 Cor. 4:7.) Realizing his oneness with his Lord, he considers no longer his own weakness, but counts on the power of Him of whose hidden working within he is assured. It is this secret assurance that gives a brightness to his look and a gentle firmness to his tone and a perseverance to all his efforts, which of themselves are great means of influencing those he is seeking to win.

He goes forth in the spirit of one to whom victory is assured; for this is the victory that overcomes, even our faith (1 John 5:4). He no longer counts it humility to say that God cannot bless his unworthy efforts. He claims and expects a blessing, because it is not he, but Christ in him, that works. The great secret of abiding in Christ is the deep conviction that we are nothing, and He is everything. As this is learned, it no longer seems strange to believe that our weakness need be no hindrance to His saving power. The believer who yields himself wholly up to Christ for service in the spirit of a simple childlike trust will assuredly bring forth much fruit. He will not fear even to claim his share in the wonderful promise: *"He that believeth on me, the works that I do shall he do also; and greater works than these shall he do; because I go unto my Father"* (John 14:12). He no longer thinks that He cannot have a blessing, and must be kept unfruitful so that he may be kept humble. He sees that the most heavily laden branches bow the lowest. Abiding in Christ, he has yielded assent to the blessed agreement between the Vine and the branches, that of the fruit all the glory will go to the Husbandman, the blessed Father.

Let us learn two lessons. If we are abiding in Jesus, let us begin to work. Let us first seek to influence those around us in daily life. Let us accept distinctly and joyfully our holy calling, that we are even now to live as the servants of the love of Jesus to our fellowmen. Our daily life must have for its object the making of an impression favorable to Jesus. When you look at the branch, you see at once the likeness to the Vine. We must live so that something of the holiness and the gentleness of Jesus may shine out in us. We must live to represent Him. As was the case with Him when on earth, the life must prepare the way for the teaching. What the church and the world both need is this: men and women full of the Holy Spirit and of love, who, as the living embodiments of the grace and power of Christ, witness for Him, and for His power on behalf of those who believe in Him. Living so, with our hearts longing to have Jesus glorified in the souls He is seeking after, let us offer ourselves to Him for direct work. There is work in our own home. There is work among the sick, the poor, and the outcast. There is work in a hundred different paths that the Spirit of Christ opens up through those who allow themselves to be led by Him. There is work perhaps for us in ways that have not yet been opened up by others. Abiding in Christ, let us work. Let us work, not like those who are content if they now follow the fashion and take some share in religious work. No; let us work as those who are growing more like Christ, because they are abiding in Him, and who, like Him, count the work of winning souls to the Father the very joy and glory of heaven begun on earth.

And the second lesson is: if you work, abide in Christ. This is one of the blessings of work if done in the right spirit—it will deepen your union with your blessed Lord. It will discover your weakness and throw you back on His strength. It will stir you to much prayer, and in prayer for others is the time when the soul, forgetful of itself, unconsciously grows deeper into Christ. It will make clearer to you the true nature of branch life: its absolute dependence, and at the same time its glorious sufficiency, independent of all else, because dependent on Jesus. If you work, abide in Christ. There are temptations and dangers. Work for Christ has sometimes drawn away from Christ and taken the place of fellowship with Him. Work can sometimes give a form of godliness without the power. As you work, abide in Christ. Let a living faith in Christ working in you be the secret spring of all your work; this will inspire at once humility and courage. Let the Holy Spirit of Jesus dwell in you as the Spirit of His tender compassion and His divine power. Abide in Christ, and offer every faculty of your nature freely and unreservedly to Him, to sanctify it for Himself. If Jesus Christ is really to work through us, it requires an entire consecration of ourselves to Him, daily renewed. But we understand now, just this is abiding in Christ; just this it is that constitutes our highest privilege and happiness. To be a branch bearing much fruit—nothing less, nothing more—should be our only joy.

21

SO YOU WILL
HAVE POWER IN PRAYER

If ye abide in me, and my words abide in you,
ye shall ask what ye will, and it shall be done unto you.
—John 15:7

Prayer is both one of the means and one of the fruits of union to Christ. As a means it is of unspeakable importance. All the things of faith, all the pleadings of desire, all the yearnings after a fuller surrender, all the confessions of shortcoming and of sin, all the exercises in which the soul gives up self and clings to Christ, find their utterance in prayer. In each meditation on abiding in Christ, as some new feature of what Scripture teaches concerning this blessed life is apprehended, the first impulse of the believer is at once to look up to the Father and pour out the heart into His, and ask from Him the full understanding and the full possession of what he has been shown in the Word. And it is the believer who is not content with this spontaneous expression of his hope, but who takes time in secret prayer to wait until he has received and laid hold of what he has seen, who will really grow strong in Christ. However feeble the soul's first abiding, its prayer will be heard, and it will find prayer to be one of the great means of abiding more abundantly.

But it is not so much as a means, but as a fruit of the abiding, that the Savior mentions it in the parable of the Vine. He does not think so much of prayer—as we, alas, too exclusively do—as a means of getting blessing for ourselves, but as one of the chief channels of influence by which, through us as fellow workers with God, the blessings of Christ's redemption are to be dispensed to the world. He sets before Himself and us the glory of the Father, in the extension of His kingdom, as the object for which we have been made branches; and He assures us that if we but abide in Him, we will be Israels, having power with God and man. Ours will be the effectual, fervent prayer of the righteous man, availing much, like Elijah's for ungodly Israel. (See James 5:16–17.) Such prayer will be the fruit of our abiding in Him and the means of bringing forth much fruit.

To the Christian who is not abiding wholly in Jesus, the difficulties connected with prayer are often so great as to rob him of the comfort and the strength it could bring. Under the guise of humility, he asks how one so unworthy could expect to have influence with the Holy One. He thinks of God's sovereignty, His perfect wisdom and love, and cannot see how his prayer can really have any distinct effect. He prays, but it is more because he cannot rest without prayer, than from a loving faith that the prayer will be heard. But what a blessed release from such questions and perplexities is given to the soul who is truly abiding in Christ! He realizes increasingly how it is in the real spiritual unity with Christ that we are accepted and heard. The union with the Son of God is a life union; we are indeed one with Him—our prayers ascend as His prayer. It is because we abide in Him that we can ask what we will, and it is given to us.

There are many reasons why this must be so. One is, that abiding in Christ, and having His words abiding in us, teach us to pray in accordance with the will of God. With the abiding in Christ our self-will is kept down, and the thoughts and wishes of nature are brought into captivity to the thoughts and wishes of Christ. Like-mindedness to Christ grows upon us; all our working and willing become transformed into harmony with His. There is deep and oft-renewed heart searching to see whether the surrender has indeed been entire; there is fervent prayer to the heart-searching Spirit that nothing may be kept back. Everything is yielded to the power of His life in us, that it may exercise its sanctifying influence even on ordinary wishes and desires. His Holy Spirit breathes through our whole being, and without our being conscious how, our desires, as the breathings of the divine life, are in conformity with the divine will and are fulfilled. Abiding in Christ renews and sanctifies the will; we ask what we will, and it is given to us.

In close connection with this is the thought that the abiding in Christ teaches the believer in prayer only to seek the glory of God. In promising to answer prayer, Christ's one thought is this, *"that the Father may be glorified in the Son"* (John 14:13). In His intercession on earth (see John 17), this was His one desire and plea; in His intercession in heaven, it is still His great object. As the believer abides in Christ, the Savior breathes this desire into him. The thought, "only the glory of God," becomes more and more the keynote of the life hid in Christ. At first this subdues, quiets, and makes the soul almost afraid to dare entertain a wish, lest it should not be to the Father's glory. But when once its supremacy has been accepted, and everything yielded to it, it comes with mighty power to elevate and enlarge the heart, and open it to the vast field open to the glory of God. Abiding in Christ, the soul learns not only to desire, but spiritually to discern what will be for God's glory; and one of the first conditions of acceptable prayer is fulfilled in it when, as the fruit of its union with Christ, the whole mind is brought into harmony with that of the Son as He said, *"Father, glorify thy name"* (John 12:28).

Once more: abiding in Christ, we can fully avail ourselves of the name of Christ. Asking in the name of another means that the other authorized me and sent me to ask, and wants to be considered as asking himself; he wants the favor done to him. Believers often try to think of the name of Jesus and His merits, and to argue themselves into the faith that they will be heard, while they painfully feel how little they have of the faith of His name. They are not living wholly in Jesus' name; it is only when they begin to pray that they want to take up that name and use it. This cannot be. The promise *"Whatsoever ye shall ask in my name"* (John 14:13) may not be severed from the command, *"Whatsoever ye do...do all in the name of the Lord Jesus"* (Col. 3:17). If the name of Christ is to be wholly at my disposal, so that I may have the full command of it for all I will, it must be because I first put myself wholly at His disposal, so that He has free and full command of me. It is the abiding in Christ that gives the right and power to use His name with confidence. To Christ, the Father refuses nothing. Abiding in Christ, I come to the Father as one with Him. His righteousness is in me, His Spirit is in me; the Father sees the Son in me and gives me my petition. It is not—as so many think—by a sort of imputation that the Father looks upon us as if we were in Christ, though we are not in Him. No; the Father wants to see us living in Him; thus will our prayers really have power to prevail. Abiding in Christ not only renews the will to pray aright, but secures the full power of His merits to us.

Again: abiding in Christ also works in us the faith that alone can obtain an answer. *"According to your faith be it unto you"* (Matt. 9:29); this is one of the laws of the kingdom. *"Believe that ye receive...and ye shall have"* (Mark 11:24). This faith rests upon, and is rooted in the Word, but is something infinitely higher than the mere logical conclusion: God has promised, I will obtain. No; faith, as a spiritual act, depends upon the words abiding in us as living powers, and so upon the state of the whole inner life. Without fasting and prayer (see Mark 9:29), without humility and a spiritual mind (see John 5:44), without a wholehearted obedience (see 1 John 3:22), there cannot be this living faith. But as the soul abides in Christ, and grows into the consciousness of its union with Him and sees how entirely it is He who makes it and its petition acceptable, it dares to claim an answer because it knows itself one with Him. It was by faith it learned to abide in Him; as the fruit of that faith, it rises to a larger faith in all that God has promised to be and to do. It learns to breathe its prayers in the deep, quiet, confident assurance: we know we have the petition we ask of Him.

Abiding in Christ, further, keeps us in the place where the answer can be bestowed. Some believers pray earnestly for blessing, but when God comes and looks for them to bless them they are not to be found. They never thought that the blessing must not only be asked, but waited for and received in prayer. Abiding in Christ is the place for receiving answers. Outside of Him the answer would be dangerous—we should consume it on our lusts. (See James 4:3.) Many of the richest answers—say for spiritual grace or for power to work and to bless—can only come in the shape of a larger experience of what God makes Christ to us. The fullness is in Him; abiding in Him is the condition of power in prayer, because the answer is treasured up and bestowed in Him.

Believer, abide in Christ, for there is the school of prayer—mighty, effectual, answer-bringing prayer. Abide in Him, and you will learn what to so many is a mystery: that the secret of the prayer of faith is the life of faith—the life that abides in Christ alone.

22

AND IN HIS LOVE

As the Father hath loved me, I also have loved you:
abide ye in my love.
—John 15:9 RV

Blessed Lord, enlighten our eyes to see properly the glory of this wondrous word. Open to our meditation the secret chamber of Your love, that our souls may enter in and find there their everlasting dwelling place. How else will we know anything of a love that passes knowledge? (See Eph. 3:19.)

Before the Savior speaks the word that invites us to abide in His love, He first tells us what that love is. What He says of it must give force to His invitation and make the thought of not accepting it an impossibility: "As *the Father hath loved me, I also have loved you!" "As the Father hath loved me."* How will we be able to form right conceptions of this love? Lord, teach us. *"God is love"* (1 John 4:8). Love is His very being. Love is not an attribute but the very essence of His nature, the center around which all His glorious attributes gather. It was because He was love that He was the Father, and that there was a Son. Love needs an object to whom it can give itself away, in whom it can lose itself, with whom it can make itself one. Because God is love, there must be a Father and a Son. The love of the Father to the Son is that divine passion with which He delights in the Son and speaks, *"My beloved Son, in whom I am well pleased"* (Matt. 3:17). The divine love is as a burning fire; in all its intensity and infinity it has but one object and but one joy, and that is the only begotten Son. When we gather together all the attributes of God—His infinity, His perfection, His immensity, His majesty, His omnipotence—and consider them but as the rays of the glory of His love, we still fail in forming any conception of what that love must be. It is a love that passes knowledge. (See Eph. 3:19.)

And yet this love of God to His Son must serve, O my soul, as the glass in which you are to learn how Jesus loves you. As one of His redeemed ones, you are His delight, and all His desire is to you, with the longing of a love that is stronger than death and that many waters cannot quench. His heart yearns after you, seeking your fellowship and your love. Were it needed, He could die again to possess you. As the Father loved the Son and could not live without Him—could not be God the blessed without Him—so Jesus loves you. His life is bound up in yours; you are to Him inexpressibly more indispensable and precious than you ever can know. You are one with Himself. *"As the Father hath loved me, I also have loved you."* What a love!

It is an eternal love. From before the foundation of the world—God's Word teaches us this—the purpose had been formed that Christ should be the Head of His church, that He should have a body in which His glory could be set forth. In that eternity He loved and longed for those who had been given to Him by the Father, and when He came and told His disciples that He loved them, it was indeed not with a love of earth and of time but with the love of eternity. And it is with that same infinite love that His eye still rests upon each of us here seeking to abide in Him, and in each breathing of that love there is indeed the power of eternity. *"I have loved thee with an everlasting love"* (Jer. 31:3).

It is a perfect love. It gives all, and holds nothing back. *"The Father loveth the Son, and hath given all things into his hand"* (John 3:35). And just so Jesus loves His own: all He has is theirs. When it was needed, He sacrificed His throne and crown for you: He did not count His own life and blood too dear to give for you. His righteousness, His Spirit, His glory, even His throne, all are yours. This love holds nothing, nothing back, but, in a manner which no human mind can fathom, makes you one with itself. What wondrous love, to love us even as the Father loved Him, and to offer us this love as our everyday dwelling!

It is a gentle and most tender love. As we think of the love of the Father to the Son, we see in the Son everything so infinitely worthy of that love. When we think of Christ's love to us, there is nothing but sin and unworthiness to meet the eye. And the question comes: How can that love within the bosom of the divine life and its perfections be compared to the love that rests on sinners? Can it indeed be the same love? Blessed be God, we know it is so. The nature of love is always one, however different the objects. Christ knows of no other law of love but that with which His Father loved Him. Our wretchedness only serves to call out more distinctly the beauty of love, such as could not be seen even in heaven. With the tenderest compassion He bows to our weakness; with patience inconceivable He bears with our slowness; with the gentlest loving-kindness He meets our fears and our follies. It is the love of the Father to the Son: beautified and glorified in its condescension, in its exquisite adaptation to our needs.

And it is an unchangeable love. *"Having loved his own which were in the world, he loved them unto the end"* (John 13:1). *"The mountains shall depart, and the hills be removed; but my kindness shall not depart from thee"* (Isa. 54:10). The promise with which it begins its work in the soul is this: *"I will not leave thee, until I have done that which I have spoken to thee of"* (Gen. 28:15). And just as our wretchedness was what first drew it to us, so the sin, with which it is so often grieved, and which may well cause us to fear and doubt, is but a new motive for it—to hold to us all the more. And why? We can give no reason but this: *"As the Father hath loved me, I also have loved you."*

And now, does not this love suggest the motive, the measure, and the means of that surrender by which we yield ourselves wholly to abide in Him?

This love surely supplies a motive. Only look and see how this love stands and pleads and prays. Gaze, oh, gaze on the divine form, the eternal glory, the heavenly beauty, the tenderly pleading gentleness of the crucified love, as it stretches out its pierced hands and says, "Oh, will you not abide with me? Will you not come and abide in me?" It points you up to the eternity of love from where it came to seek you. It points you to the Cross, and all it has borne to prove the reality of its affection and to win you for itself. It reminds you of all it has promised to do for you, if you will but throw yourself unreservedly into its arms. It asks you whether, so far as you have come to dwell with it and taste its blessedness, it has not done well by you. And with a divine authority, mingled with such an inexpressible tenderness that one might almost think he heard the tone of reproach in it, it says, "Soul, 'as the Father hath loved me, I also have loved you'; abide in my love." Surely there can be but one answer to such pleading: "Lord Jesus Christ! Here I am. From now on, Your love will be the only home of my soul; in Your love alone will I abide."

That love is not only the motive, but also the measure of our surrender to abide in it. Love gives all, but asks all. It does so, not because it grudges us anything, but because without this it cannot get possession of us to fill us with itself. In the love of the Father and the Son, it was so. In the love of Jesus to us, it was so. In our entering into His love to abide there, it must be so too; our surrender to it must have no other measure than its surrender to us. Oh, that we understood how the love that calls us has infinite riches and fullness of joy for us, and that what we give up for its sake will be rewarded a hundredfold in this life! Or rather, would that we understood that it is a love with a height and a depth and a length and a breadth that passes knowledge! (See Eph. 3:19.) How all thought of sacrifice or surrender would pass away, and our souls be filled with wonder at the unspeakable privilege of being loved with such a love, of being allowed to come and abide in it forever.

Doubt may again suggest the question: But is it possible, can I always abide in His love? Then, listen how that love itself supplies the only means for the abiding in Him: it is faith in that love that will enable us to abide in it. If this love is indeed so divine, such an intense and burning passion, then surely I can depend on it to keep me and to hold me fast. Then surely all my unworthiness and feebleness can be no hindrance. If this love is indeed so divine, with infinite power at its command, I surely have a right to trust that it is stronger than my weakness, and that with its almighty arm it will clasp me to its bosom, and allow me to go out no more. I see how this is the one thing my God requires of me. Treating me as a reasonable being endowed with the wondrous power of willing and choosing, He cannot force all this blessedness on me but waits until I give the willing consent of the heart. In His great kindness, He has ordered the token of this consent to be faith—that faith by which utter sinfulness casts itself into the arms of love to be saved and utter weakness to be kept and made strong. Oh, Infinite Love! Love with which the Father loved the Son! Love with which the Son loves us! I can trust You; I do trust You. Oh, keep me abiding in You.

23

AS CHRIST IN THE FATHER

As the Father hath loved me, I also have loved you:
abide ye in my love…even as I…abide in his love.
—John 15:9–10 RV

Christ had taught His disciples that to abide in Him was to abide in His love. The hour of His suffering is near, and He cannot speak much more to them. They doubtless have many questions to ask as to what the abiding in Him and His love is. He anticipates and meets their wishes, and gives them His own life as the best exposition of His command. As example and rule for their abiding in His love, they have to look to His abiding in the Father's love. In the light of His union with the

Father, their union with Him will become clear. His life in the Father is the law of their life in Him.

The thought is so high that we can hardly take it in, and is yet so clearly revealed that we dare not neglect it. Do we not read in John 6:57, "As...I live by the Father: so he that eateth me, even he shall live by me"? And the Savior prays so distinctly, "that they may be one, even as we are one: I in them, and thou in me" (John 17:22–23). The blessed union of Christ with the Father and His life in Him is the only rule of our thoughts and expectations in regard to our living and abiding in Him.

Think first of the origin of that life of Christ in the Father. They were one—one in life and one in love. In this His abiding in the Father had its root. Though dwelling here on earth, He knew that He was one with the Father, that the Father's life was in Him and His love on Him. Without this knowledge, abiding in the Father and His love would have been utterly impossible. And it is thus only that you can abide in Christ and His love. Know that you are one with Him—one in the unity of nature. By His birth He became man and took your nature that He might be one with you. By your new birth, you become one with Him and are made a partaker of His divine nature (2 Pet. 1:4). The link that binds you to Him is as real and close as bound Him to the Father—the link of a divine life. Your claim on Him is as sure and always availing as was His on the Father. Your union with Him is as close.

And as it is the union of a divine life, it is one of an infinite love. In His life of humiliation on earth He tasted the blessedness and strength of knowing Himself the object of an infinite love, and of dwelling in it all the day; from His own example He invites you to learn that herein lies the secret of rest and joy. You are one with Him; yield yourself now to be loved by Him. Let your eyes and heart open to the love that shines and presses in on you on every side. Abide in His love.

Think then too of the mode of that abiding in the Father and His love that is to be the law of your life. "I have kept my Father's commandments, and abide in his love" (John 15:10). His was a life of subjection and dependence, and yet most blessed. To our proud self-seeking nature, the thought of dependence and subjection suggests the idea of humiliation and servitude; in the life of love that the Son of God lived, and to which He invites us, they are the secret of blessedness. The Son is not afraid of losing anything by giving up all to the Father, for He knows that the Father loves Him and can have no interest apart from that of the beloved Son. He knows that as complete as is the dependence on His part is the communication on the part of the Father of all He possesses. Hence, when He had said, "*The Son can do nothing of himself, but what he seeth the Father do*" (John 5:19), He added at once, "*What things soever* [the Father] *doeth, these also doeth the Son likewise. For the Father loveth the Son, and showeth him all things that himself doeth*" (vv. 19–20).

The believer who studies this life of Christ as the pattern and the promise of what his may be, learns to understand how the "*Without me ye can do nothing*" (John 15:5) is but the forerunner of "*I can do all things through Christ which strengtheneth me*" (Phil. 4:13). We learn to glory in infirmities, to take pleasure in necessities and distresses for Christ's sake; for "*when I am weak, then am I strong*" (2 Cor. 12:10). We rise above the ordinary tone, in which so many Christians speak of their weakness while they are content to abide there, because we have learned from Christ that in the life of divine love the emptying of self and the sacrifice of our will is the surest way to have all we can wish or will. Dependence, subjection, self-sacrifice, are for the Christian, as for Christ, the blessed path of life. As Christ lived through and in the Father, even so the believer lives through and in Christ.

Think of the glory of this life of Christ in the Father's love. Because He gave Himself wholly to the Father's will and glory, the Father crowned Him with glory and honor. He acknowledged Him as His only representative; He made Him partaker of His power and authority; He exalted Him to share His throne as God. And even so will it be with him who abides in Christ's love. If Christ finds us willing to trust ourselves and our interests to His love, if in that trust we give up all care for our own will and honor, if we make it our glory to exercise and confess absolute dependence on Him in all things, if we are content to have no life but in Him, He will do for us what the Father did for Him. He will lay of His glory on us: as the name of our Lord Jesus is glorified in us, we are glorified in Him. (See 2 Thess. 1:12.) He acknowledges us as His true and worthy representatives; He entrusts us with His power. He admits us to His counsels, as He allows our intercession to influence His rule of His church and the world. He makes us the vehicles of His authority and His influence over men. His Spirit knows no other dwelling than such and seeks no other instruments for His divine work. Blessed life of love for the soul that abides in Christ's love, even as He in the Father's!

Believer, abide in the love of Christ. Take and study His relation to the Father as pledge of what your own can become. As blessed, as mighty, as glorious as was His life in the Father, can yours be in Him. Let this truth, accepted under the teaching of the Spirit in faith, remove every vestige of fear, as if abiding in Christ were a burden and a work. In the light of His life in the Father, let it henceforth be to you a blessed rest in the union with Him, an overflowing fountain of joy and strength. To abide in His love, His mighty, saving, keeping, satisfying love, even as He abode in the Father's love—surely the very greatness of our calling teaches us that it never can be a work we have to perform; it must be with us as with Him, the result of the spontaneous outflowing of a life from within, and the mighty inworking of the love from above. The only thing we need is this: to take time and study the divine image of this life of love set before us in Christ. We need to have our souls still unto God, gazing upon that life of Christ in the Father until the light from heaven falls on it and we hear the living voice of our Beloved whispering gently to us personally the teaching He gave to the disciples. Soul, be still and listen; let every thought be hushed until the word has entered your heart too: "Child! I love you, even as the Father loved Me. Abide in My love, even as I abide in the Father's love. Your life on earth in Me is to be the perfect counterpart of Mine in the Father."

And if the thought will sometimes come: "Surely this is too high for us; can it be really true?" only remember that the greatness of the privilege is justified by the greatness of the object He has in view. Christ was the revelation of the Father on earth. He could not be this if there were not the most perfect unity, the most complete communication of all the Father had to the Son. He could be it because the Father loved Him, and He abode in that love. Believers are the revelation of Christ on earth. They cannot be this unless there is perfect unity, so that the world can know that He loves them and has sent them. But they can be it if Christ loves them with the infinite love that gives itself and all it has, and if they abide in that love.

Lord, show us Your love. Make us with all the saints to know the love that passes knowledge. (See Eph. 3:19.) Lord, show us in Your own blessed life what it is to abide in Your love. And the sight will so win us, that it will be impossible for us one single hour to seek any other life than the life of abiding in Your love.

24

OBEYING HIS COMMANDMENTS

*If ye keep my commandments, ye shall abide in my love; even as I have
kept my Father's commandments, and abide in his love.*
—John 15:10

How clearly we are taught here the place that good works are to occupy in the life of the believer! Christ as the beloved Son was in the Father's love. He kept His commandments, and so He abode in the love. So the believer, without works, receives Christ and is in Him; he keeps the commandments, and so abides in the love. When the sinner, in coming to Christ, seeks to prepare himself by works, the voice of the Gospel sounds, *"Not of works"* (Eph. 2:9). When once in Christ, lest the flesh should abuse the word, *"Not of works,"* the Gospel lifts its voice as loud: *"Created in Christ Jesus unto good works"* (Eph. 2:10). To the sinner out of Christ, works may be his greatest hindrance, keeping him from the union with the Savior. To the believer in Christ, works are strength and blessing, for by them faith is made perfect (James 2:22), the union with Christ is cemented, and the soul established and more deeply rooted in the love of God. *"If a man love me, he will keep my words: and my Father will love him"* (John 14:23). *"If ye keep my commandments, ye shall abide in my love."*

The connection between this keeping the commandments and the abiding in Christ's love is easily understood. Our union with Jesus Christ is not a thing of the intellect or sentiment, but a real vital union in heart and life. The holy life of Jesus, with His feelings and disposition, is breathed into us by the Holy Spirit. The believer's calling is to think and feel and will just what Jesus thought and felt and willed. He desires to be partaker, not only of the grace, but also of the holiness of his Lord; or rather, he sees that holiness is the chief beauty of grace. To live the life of Christ means to him to be delivered from the life of self; the will of Christ is to him the only path of liberty from the slavery of his own evil self-will.

To the ignorant or slothful believer there is a great difference between the promises and commands of Scripture. The former he counts his comfort and his food, but to him who is really seeking to abide in Christ's love, the commands become no less precious. As much as the promises, they are the revelation of the divine love; they are guides into the deeper experience of the divine life, blessed helpers in the path to a closer union with the Lord. He sees how the harmony of our will with His will is one of the chief elements of our fellowship with Him. The will is the central faculty in the divine as in the human being. The will of God is the power that rules the whole moral as well as the natural world. How could there be fellowship with Him without delight in His will? It is only as long as salvation is to the sinner nothing but a personal safety, that he can be careless or afraid of the doing of God's will. No sooner is it to him what Scripture and the Holy Spirit reveal it to be—the restoration to communion with God and conformity to Him—than he feels that there is no law more natural or more beautiful than this: keeping Christ's commandments the way to abide in Christ's love. His inmost soul approves when he hears the beloved Lord make the larger measure of the Spirit, with the manifestation of the Father and the Son in the believer, entirely dependent upon the keeping of His commandments. (See John 14:15–16, 21, 23.)

There is another thing that opens to him a deeper insight and secures a still more cordial acceptance of this truth. It is this, that in no other way did Christ Himself abide in the Father's love. In the life which Christ led upon earth, obedience was a solemn reality. The dark and awful power that led man to revolt from his God, came upon Him too, to tempt Him. To Him as man its offers of self-gratification were not matters of indifference; to refuse them, He had to fast and pray. He suffered, being tempted. He spoke very distinctly of not seeking to do His own will, as a surrender He had continually to make. He made the keeping of the Father's commandments the distinct object of His life, and so abode in His love. Does He not tell us, *"I do nothing of myself; but as the Father hath taught me, I speak these things. And he that sent me is with me: the Father hath not left me alone; for I do always those things that please him"* (John 8:29–29)? He thus opened to us the only path to the blessedness of a life on earth in the love of heaven, and when, as from our Vine, His Spirit flows in the branches, this keeping the commands is one of the surest and highest elements of the life He inspires.

Believer, if you would abide in Jesus, be very careful to keep His commandments. Keep them in the love of your heart. Be not content to have them in the Bible for reference, but have them transferred by careful study, by meditation and by prayer, by a loving acceptance, by the Spirit's teaching, to the *"fleshly tables of the heart"* (2 Cor. 3:3). Be not content with the knowledge of some of the commands, those most commonly received among Christians, while others lie unknown and neglected. Surely, with your new covenant privileges, you would not be behind the Old Testament saints who spoke so fervently: *"I esteem all thy precepts concerning all things to be right"* (Ps. 119:128). Be assured that there is still much of your Lord's will that you do not yet understand. Make Paul's prayer for the Colossians yours for yourself and all believers, *"that ye might be filled with the knowledge of his will in all wisdom and spiritual understanding"* (Col. 1:9); and that of wrestling Epaphras, *"that ye may stand perfect and complete in all the will of God"* (Col. 4:12). Remember that this is one of the great elements of spiritual growth—a deeper insight into the will of God concerning you.

Imagine not that entire consecration is the end—it is only the beginning—of the truly holy life. See how Paul, after having taught believers to lay themselves upon the altar, whole and holy burnt offerings to their God (see Rom. 12:1), at once proceeds to tell them what the true altar life is: being ever more and more renewed in their minds to prove what is the good and perfect and acceptable will of God (see v. 2). The progressive renewal of the Holy Spirit leads to growing like-mindedness to Christ; then comes a delicate power of spiritual perception—a holy instinct—by which the soul *"of quick understanding in the fear of the* LORD*"* (Isa. 11:3) knows to recognize the meaning and the application of the Lord's commands to daily life in a way that remains hidden to the ordinary Christian. Keep them dwelling richly within you, hide them within your heart, and you will taste the blessedness of the man whose *"delight is in the law of the* LORD*; and in his law doth he meditate day and night"* (Ps. 1:2). Love will assimilate into your inmost being the commands as food from heaven. They will no longer come to you as a law standing outside and against you but as the living power that has transformed your will into perfect harmony with all your Lord requires.

And keep them in the obedience of your life. It has been your solemn vow—has it not?—no longer to tolerate even a single sin: *"I have sworn, and I will perform it, that I will keep thy righteous judgments"* (Ps. 119:106). Labor earnestly in prayer to *"stand perfect and complete in all the will of God"* (Col. 4:12). Ask earnestly for the discovery of every secret sin—of anything that is not in perfect harmony with the will of God. Walk up to the light you have, faithfully and tenderly, yielding yourself in an unreserved surrender to obey all that the Lord has spoken. When Israel took that vow (see Exodus 19:8, 24:7), it was only to break it all too soon. The new covenant gives the grace to make the vow and to keep it too. (See Jeremiah 31:31–34.) Be careful of disobedience even in little things. Disobedience dulls the conscience, darkens the soul, deadens our spiritual energies; therefore, keep the commandments of Christ with implicit obedience. Be a soldier who asks for nothing but the orders of the commander.

And if even for a moment the commandments appear grievous, just remember whose they are. They are the commandments of Him who loves you. They are all love; they come from His love; they lead to His love. Each new surrender to keep the commandments, each new sacrifice in keeping them, leads to deeper union with the will, the spirit, and the love of the Savior. The double recompense of reward will be yours—a fuller entrance into the mystery of His love, a fuller conformity to His own blessed life. And you will learn to prize these words as among your choicest treasures: *"If ye keep my commandments, ye shall abide in my love; even as I have kept my Father's commandments, and abide in his love."*

25

THAT YOUR JOY
MAY BE FULL

*These things have I spoken unto you, that my joy might [abide] in you,
and that your joy might be full.*
—John 15:11

Abiding fully in Christ is a life of exquisite and overflowing happiness. As Christ gets more complete possession of the soul, it enters into the joy of its Lord. His own joy, the joy of heaven, becomes its own, and that in full measure and as an ever abiding portion. Just as joy on earth is everywhere connected with the vine and its fruit, so joy is an essential characteristic of the life of the believer who fully abides in Christ, the Heavenly Vine.

We all know the value of joy. It alone is the proof that what we have really satisfies the heart. As long as duty or self-interest or other motives influence me, men cannot know what the object of my pursuit or possession is really worth to me. But when it gives me joy, and they see me delight in it, they know that to me at least it is a treasure. Hence there is nothing so attractive as joy, no preaching so persuasive as the sight of hearts made glad. Just this makes gladness such a mighty element in the Christian character: there is no proof of the reality of God's love and the blessing He bestows, which men so soon feel the force of, as when the joy of God overcomes all the trials of life. And for the Christian's own welfare, joy is no less indispensable: the joy of the Lord is his strength; confidence, and courage, and patience find their inspiration in joy. With a heart full of joy no work can weary and no burden can depress; God Himself is strength and song.

Let us hear what the Savior said of the joy of abiding in Him. He promised us His own joy: *"My joy."* As the whole parable refers to the life His disciples should have in Him when ascended to heaven, the joy is that of His resurrection life. This is clear from those other words of His: *"I will see you again, and your heart shall rejoice, and your joy no man taketh from you"* (John 16:22). It was only with the resurrection and its glory that the power of the never changing life began, and only in it that the never ceasing joy could have its rise. With it was fulfilled the word: *"Therefore God, thy God, hath anointed thee with the oil of gladness above they fellows"* (Ps. 45:7). The day of His crowning was the day of the gladness of His heart. That joy of His was the joy of a work fully and forever completed, the joy of the Father's bosom regained, and the joy of souls redeemed. These are the elements of His joy; of them the abiding in Him makes us partakers.

The believer shares so fully His victory and His perfect redemption, that his faith can without ceasing sing the conqueror's song: *"Thanks be unto God, which always causeth* [me] *to triumph"* (2 Cor. 2:14). As the fruit of this, there is the joy of the undisturbed dwelling in the light of the Father's love—not a cloud to intervene if the abiding is unbroken. And then, with this joy in the love of the Father, as a love received, there is the joy of the love of souls, as love going out and rejoicing over the lost. Abiding in Christ, penetrating into the very depths of His life and heart, seeking for the most perfect oneness, these the three streams of His joy flow into our hearts. Whether we look backward and see the work He has done, or upward and see the reward He has in the Father's love that passes knowledge (Eph. 3:19), or forward in the continual accessions of joy as sinners are brought home, His joy is ours. With our feet on Calvary, our eyes on the Father's countenance, and our hands helping sinners home, we have His joy as our own.

And then He spoke of this joy as abiding—a joy that is never to cease or to be interrupted for a moment: *"That my joy might* [abide] *in you." "Your joy no man taketh from you"* (John 16:22). This is what many Christians cannot understand. Their view of the Christian life is that it is a succession of changes, now joy and now sorrow. And they appeal to the experiences of a man like the apostle Paul, as a proof of how much there may be of weeping and sorrow and suffering. They have not noticed how Paul gave the strongest evidence as to this unceasing joy. He understood the paradox of the Christian life as the combination at one and the same moment of all the bitterness of earth and all the joy of heaven. *"As sorrowful, yet alway rejoicing"* (2 Cor. 6:10)—these precious golden words teach us how the joy of Christ can overrule the sorrow of the world, can make us sing while we weep, and can maintain in the heart, even when cast down by disappointment or difficulties, a deep consciousness of a joy that is unspeakable and full of glory. There is but one condition: *"I will see you again, and your heart shall rejoice, and your joy no man taketh from you"* (John 16:22). The presence of Jesus, distinctly manifested, cannot but give joy. Abiding in Him consciously, how can the soul but rejoice and be glad? Even when weeping for the sins and the souls of others, there is the fountain of gladness springing up in the faith of His power and love to save.

And this His own joy abiding with us, He wants to be full. Of the full joy our Savior spoke three times on the last night. Once here in the parable of the Vine: *"These things have I spoken unto you…that your joy might be full,"* and every deeper insight into the wonderful blessedness of being the branch of such a Vine confirms His Word. Then He connects it with our prayers being answered: *"Ask, and ye shall receive, that your joy may be full"* (John 16:24). To the spiritual mind, answered prayer is not only a means of obtaining certain blessings, but something infinitely higher. It is a token of our fellowship with the Father and the Son in heaven, of their delight in us, and our having been admitted and having had a voice in that wondrous interchange of love in which the Father and the Son hold counsel and decide the daily guidance of the children on earth. To a soul abiding in Christ that longs for manifestations of His love and that understands to take an answer to prayer in its true spiritual value as a response from the throne to all its utterances of love and trust, the joy which it brings is truly unutterable. The word is found true: *"Ask, and ye shall receive, that your joy may be full."*

And then the Savior said, in His high-priestly prayer to the Father, *"These things I speak...that they might have my joy fulfilled in themselves"* (John 17:13). It is the sight of the Great High Priest entering the Father's presence for us, ever living to pray and carry on His blessed work in the power of an endless life, that removes every possible cause of fear or doubt and gives us the assurance and experience of a perfect salvation. Let the believer who seeks, according to the teaching of John 15, to possess the full joy of abiding in Christ and, according to John 16, the full joy of prevailing prayer, press forward to John 17. Let him there listen to those wondrous words of intercession spoken, that his joy might be full. Let him, as he listens to those words, learn the love that even now pleads for him in heaven without ceasing, the glorious objects for which it is pleading, and which, through its all-prevailing pleading, are hourly being realized, and Christ's joy will be fulfilled in him.

Christ's own joy, abiding joy, fullness of joy—such is the portion of the believer who abides in Christ. Why, oh, why is it that this joy has so little power to attract? The reason simply is: men, yes, even God's children, do not believe in it. Instead of the abiding in Christ being looked upon as the happiest life that ever can be led, it is regarded as a life of self-denial and of sadness. They forget that the self-denial and the sadness are owing to the not abiding, and that to those who once yield themselves unreservedly to abide in Christ as a bright and blessed life, their faith comes true; the joy of the Lord is theirs. The difficulties all arise from the lack of the full surrender to a full abiding.

Child of God who seeks to abide in Christ, remember what the Lord said. At the close of the parable of the Vine, He added these precious words: "*These things have I spoken unto you, that my joy might* [abide] *in you, and that your joy might be full.*" Claim the joy as part of the branch life—not the first or chief part, but as the blessed proof of the sufficiency of Christ to satisfy every need of the soul. Be happy. Cultivate gladness. If there are times when it comes of itself, and the heart feels the unutterable joy of the Savior's presence, praise God for it, and seek to maintain it. If at other times feelings are dull, and the experience of the joy not such as you could wish it, still praise God for the life of unutterable blessedness to which you have been redeemed. In this, too, the word holds good: "*According to your faith be it unto you*" (Matt. 9:29). As you claim all the other gifts in Jesus, ever claim this one too—not for your own sake, but for His and the Father's glory. "*My joy…in you*"; "*that my joy might* [abide] *in you*"; "*my joy fulfilled in themselves*" (John 17:13)—these are Jesus' own words. It is impossible to take Him wholly and heartily, and not to get His joy too. Therefore, "*Rejoice in the Lord alway: and again I say, Rejoice*" (Phil. 4:4).

26

AND IN LOVE
TO FELLOW BELIEVERS

This is my commandment, That ye love one another,
as I have loved you.
—John 15:12

As the Father hath loved me, so have I loved you" (John 15:9); "as I have loved you...ye also love one another" (John 13:34). God became man; divine love began to run in the channel of a human heart; it becomes the love of man to man. The love that fills heaven and eternity is ever to be daily seen here in the life of earth and of time.

"*This is my commandment,*" the Savior said, "*that ye love one another, as I have loved you.*" He sometimes spoke of commandments, but the love, which is the fulfilling of the law, is the all-including one, and therefore is called His commandment—the new commandment. It is to be the great evidence of the reality of the new covenant, of the power of the new life revealed in Jesus Christ. It is to be the one convincing and indisputable token of discipleship: *"By this shall all men know that ye are my disciples"* (John 13:35); *"That they also may be one in us: that the world may believe"* (John 17:21); *"That they may be made perfect in one; and that the world may know that thou hast…loved them, as thou hast loved me"* (v. 23). To the believer seeking perfect fellowship with Christ, the keeping of this commandment is at once the blessed proof that he is abiding in Him and the path to a fuller and more perfect union.

Let us try to understand how this is so. We know that God is love, and that Christ came to reveal this, not as a doctrine but as a life. His life, in its wonderful self-abasement and self-sacrifice, was, above everything, the embodiment of divine love, the showing forth to men, in such human manifestations as they could understand, how God loves. In His love to the unworthy and the ungrateful, in His humbling Himself to walk among men as a servant, in His giving Himself up to death, He simply lived and acted out the life of the divine love that was in the heart of God. He lived and died to show us the love of the Father.

And now, just as Christ was to show forth God's love, believers are to show forth to the world the love of Christ. They are to prove to men that Christ loves them, and in loving fills them with a love that is not of earth. They, by living and by loving just as He did, are to be perpetual witnesses to the love that gave itself to die. He loved so that even the Jews cried out, as at Bethany, *"Behold how he loved!"* (John 11:36). Christians are to live so that men are compelled to say, "See how these Christians love one another." In their daily dealings with each other, Christians are made a display to God and to angels and to men; and in the Christlikeness of their love to each other, they are to prove what manner of spirit they are of. Amid all diversity of character or of creed, of language or of station, they are to prove that love has made them members of one body, and of each other, and has taught them each to forget and sacrifice self for the sake of the other. Their life of love is the chief evidence of Christianity, the proof to the world that God sent Christ, and that He has shed abroad in them the same love with which He loved Him. Of all the evidences of Christianity, this is the mightiest and most convincing.

This love of Christ's disciples to each other occupies a central position between their love to God and to all men. Of their love to God, whom they cannot see, it is the test. The love to one unseen may so easily be a mere sentiment, or even an imagination; in the interactions with God's children, love to God is really called into exercise and shows itself in deeds that the Father accepts as done to Himself. So alone can it be proved to be true. The love to the believers is the flower and fruit of the root, unseen in the heart, of love to God. And this fruit again becomes the seed of love to all men; dealings with each other is the school in which believers are trained and strengthened to love their fellowmen, who are yet out of Christ, not simply with the liking that rests on points of agreement, but with the holy love that takes hold of the unworthiest and bears with the most disagreeable for Jesus' sake. It is love to each other as disciples that is ever put in the foreground as the link between love to God alone and to men in general.

In Christ's dealings with His disciples, this brotherly love finds the law of its conduct. As it studies His forgiveness and forbearance toward His friends, with the seventy times seven as its only measure (see Matt. 18:21–22)—as it looks to His unwearied patience and His infinite humility, as it sees the meekness and lowliness with which He seeks to win for Himself a place as their servant, wholly devoted to their interests—it accepts with gladness His command, "*Ye should do as I have done*" (John 13:15). Following His example, each lives not for himself but for the other. The law of kindness is on the tongue, for love has vowed that never will one unkind word cross its lips. It refuses not only to speak, but even to hear or to think evil; of the name and character of the fellow Christian it is more jealous than of its own. My own good name I may leave to the Father; my brother's my Father has entrusted to me. In gentleness and loving-kindness, in courtesy and generosity, in self-sacrifice and beneficence, in its life of blessing and of beauty, the divine love, which has been shed abroad in the believer's heart, shines out as it shone in the life of Jesus.

Christian, what say you of this your glorious calling to love like Christ? Does not your heart bound at the thought of the unspeakable privilege of thus showing forth the likeness of the Eternal Love? Or are you rather ready to sigh at the thought of the inaccessible height of perfection to which you are thus called to climb? Brother, sigh not at what is indeed the highest token of the Father's love, that He has called us to be like Christ in our love, just as He was like the Father in His love. Understand that He who gave the command in such close connection with His teaching about the Vine and the abiding in Him, gave us in that the assurance that we only have to abide in Him to be able to love like Him. Accept the command as a new motive to a fuller abiding in Christ. Regard the abiding in Him more than ever as an abiding in His love; rooted and grounded daily in a love that passes knowledge (see Eph. 3:19), you receive of its fullness and learn to love. With Christ abiding in you, the Holy Spirit sheds abroad the love of God in your heart, and you love the believers, the most trying and unlovable, with a love that is not your own, but the love of Christ in you. And the command about your love to the believers is changed from a burden into a joy, if you but keep it linked, as Jesus linked it, to the command about His love to you: "*Abide in my love....Love one another, as I have loved you*" (John 15:10, 12).

"*This is my commandment, That ye love one another, as I have loved you.*" Is not this now some of the much fruit that Jesus has promised we will bear—indeed, a cluster of grapes of Eshcol, with which we can prove to others that the land of promise is indeed a good land? (See Numbers 13:23–24.) Let us try in all simplicity and honesty to go out to our homes to translate the language of high faith and heavenly enthusiasm into the plain prose of daily conduct, so that all men can understand it. Let our temper be under the rule of the love of Jesus: He cannot alone curb it—He can make us gentle and patient. Let the vow, that not an unkind word about others will ever be heard from our lips, be laid trustingly at His feet. Let the gentleness that refuses to take offense, that is always ready to excuse, to think and hope the best, mark our dealings with all. Let the love that seeks not its own, but ever is ready to wash others' feet, or even to give its life for them, be our aim as we abide in Jesus. Let our life be one of self-sacrifice, always studying the welfare of others, finding our highest joy in blessing others. And let us, in studying the divine art of doing good, yield ourselves as obedient learners to the guidance of the Holy Spirit. By His grace, the most commonplace life can be transfigured with the brightness of a heavenly beauty, as the infinite love of the divine nature shines out through our frail humanity. Fellow Christian, let us praise God! We are called to love as Jesus loves, as God loves.

"Abide in my love....Love...as I have loved" (John 15:10, 12). Bless God, it is possible. The new holy nature we have, and which grows ever stronger as it abides in Christ the Vine, can love as He did. Every discovery of the evil of the old nature, every longing desire to obey the command of our Lord, every experience of the power and the blessedness of loving with Jesus' love, will urge us to accept with fresh faith the blessed injunctions: *"Abide in me, and I in you"* (v. 4); *"abide in my love"* (v. 10).

27

THAT YOU MAY NOT SIN

In him is no sin. Whosoever abideth in him sinneth not.
—1 John 3:5–6

The apostle had said, "*Ye know that he was manifested to take away our sins,*" (1 John 3:5) and had thus indicated salvation from sin as the great object for which the Son was made man. The connection shows clearly that the taking away has reference not only to the atonement and freedom from guilt, but to deliverance from the power of sin, so that the believer no longer does it. It is Christ's personal holiness that constitutes His power to effect this purpose. He admits sinners into life union with Himself; the result is that their life becomes like His. "*In him is no sin. Whosoever abideth in him sinneth not.*" As long as he abides, and as far as he abides, the believer does not sin. Our holiness of life has its roots in the personal holiness of Jesus. *"If the root be holy, so are the branches"* (Rom. 11:16).

The question at once arises: How is this consistent with what the Bible teaches of the abiding corruption of our human nature, or with what John himself tells of the utter falsehood of our profession, *"if we say that we have no sin…that we have not sinned"* (1 John 1:8, 10)? It is just this passage that, if we look carefully at it, will teach us to understand our text correctly. Note the difference in the two statements, *"If we say that we have no sin"* (v. 8), and, *"If we say that we have not sinned"* (v. 10). The two expressions cannot be equivalent; the second would then be an unmeaning repetition of the first. Having sin in verse eight is not the same as doing sin in verse ten. Having sin is having a sinful nature. The holiest believer must each moment confess that he has sin within him: the flesh, namely, in which *"dwelleth no good thing"* (Rom. 7:18). Sinning or doing sin is something very different; it is yielding to indwelling sinful nature and falling into actual transgression.

And so we have two admissions that every true believer must make. The one is that he has still sin within him (see 1 John 1:8); the second, that that sin has in former times broken out into sinful actions (see v. 10). No believer can say either, "I have no sin in me," or "I have in time past never sinned." If we say we have no sin at present, or that we have not sinned in the past, we deceive ourselves. But no confession, though we have sin in the present, is demanded that we are doing sin in the present too; the confession of actual sinning refers to the past. It may, as appears from 1 John 2:2, be in the present also, but is expected not to be. And so we see how the deepest confession of sin in the past (as Paul's of his having been a persecutor), and the deepest consciousness of having still a vile and corrupt nature in the present, may consist with humble but joyful praise to Him who keeps from stumbling.

But how is it possible that a believer, having sin in him—sin of such intense vitality, and such terrible power as we know the flesh to have—that a believer having sin should yet not be doing sin? The answer is: *"In him is no sin. Whosoever abideth in him sinneth not.*" When the abiding in Christ becomes close and unbroken, so that the soul lives from moment to moment in the perfect union with the Lord its keeper, He does, indeed, keep down the power of the old nature, so that it does not regain dominion over the soul. We have seen that there are degrees in the abiding. With most Christians the abiding is so feeble and intermittent that sin continually obtains the ascendency and brings the soul into subjection. The divine promise given to faith is: "*Sin shall not have dominion over you*" (Rom. 6:14). But with the promise is the command: "*Let not sin therefore reign in your mortal body*" (v. 12). The believer who claims the promise in full faith has the power to obey the command, and sin is kept from asserting its supremacy. Ignorance of the promise or unbelief or unwatchfulness opens the door for sin to reign. And so the life of many believers is a course of continual stumbling and sinning. But when the believer seeks full admission into, and a permanent abode in Jesus, the Sinless One, then the life of Christ keeps from actual transgression. "*In him is no sin. Whosoever abideth in him sinneth not.*" Jesus does indeed save him from his sin—not by the removal of his sinful nature, but by keeping him from yielding to it.

I have read of a young lion whom nothing could awe or keep down but the eye of his keeper. With the keeper you could come near him, and he would crouch, his savage nature all unchanged, and thirsting for blood, trembling at the keeper's feet. You might put your foot on his neck, as long as the keeper was with you. To approach him without the keeper would be instant death. And so it is that the believer can have sin and yet not do sin. The evil nature, the flesh, is unchanged in its enmity against God, but the abiding presence of Jesus keeps it down. In faith the believer entrusts himself to the keeping, to the indwelling, of the Son of God; he abides in Him and counts on Jesus to abide in him too. The union and fellowship is the secret of a holy life: "*In him is no sin. Whosoever abideth in him sinneth not.*"

And now another question will arise: Admitted that the complete abiding in the Sinless One will keep us from sinning, is such abiding possible? May we hope to be able so to abide in Christ, say, even for one day, that we may be kept from actual transgressions? The question has only to be fairly stated and considered; it will suggest its own answer. When Christ commanded us to abide in Him, and promised us such rich fruit bearing to the glory of the Father, and such mighty power in our intercessions, can He have meant anything but the healthy, vigorous, complete union of the branch with the Vine? When He promised that as we abide in Him He would abide in us, could He mean anything but that His dwelling in us would be a reality of divine power and love? Is not this way of saving from sin just that which will glorify Him? It is keeping us daily humble and helpless in the consciousness of the evil nature, watchful and active in the knowledge of its terrible power, dependent and trustful in the remembrance that only His presence can keep the lion down. Oh, let us believe that when Jesus said, *"Abide in me, and I in you"* (John 15:4), He did indeed mean that, while we were not to be freed from the world and its tribulation, from the sinful nature and its temptations, we were at least to have this blessing fully secured to us—grace to abide wholly, only, even in our Lord. The abiding in Jesus makes it possible to keep from actual sinning; and Jesus Himself makes it possible to abide in Him.

Beloved Christian! I do not wonder if the promise of the text appears almost too high. Do not, I pray, let your attention be diverted by the question as to whether it would be possible to be kept for your whole life, or for so many years, without sinning. Faith has ever only to deal with the present moment. Ask this: Can Jesus at the present moment, as I abide in Him, keep me from those actual transgressions that have been the stain and the weariness of my daily life? You cannot but say, "Surely He can." Take Him then at this present moment, and say, "Jesus keeps me now; Jesus saves me now." Yield yourself to Him in the earnest and believing prayer to be kept abiding, by His own abiding in you—and go into the next moment and the succeeding hours, with this trust continually renewed.

As often as the opportunity occurs in the moments between your occupations, renew your faith in an act of devotion: Jesus keeps me now; Jesus saves me now. Let failure and sin, instead of discouraging you, only urge you still more to seek your safety in abiding in the Sinless One.

Abiding is a grace in which you can grow wonderfully, if you will but make at once the complete surrender and then persevere with ever larger expectations. Regard it as His work to keep you abiding in Him and His work to keep you from sinning. It is indeed your work to abide in Him, but it is that, only because it is His work as Vine to bear and hold the branch. Gaze upon His holy human nature as what He prepared for you to be partaker of with Himself, and you will see that there is something even higher and better than being kept from sin—that is but the restraining from evil. There is the positive and larger blessing of being now a vessel purified and cleansed, of being filled with His fullness, and made the channel of showing forth His power, His blessing, and His glory.

Author's Note:
Is Daily Sinning an Inevitable Necessity?

Why is it that, when we possess a Savior whose love and power are infinite, we are so often filled with fear and despondency? We are wearied and faint in our minds, because we do not look steadfastly unto Jesus, the author and finisher of faith, who is set down at the right hand of God—unto Him whose omnipotence embraces both heaven and earth, who is strong and mighty in His feeble saints.

While we remember our weakness, we forget His all-sufficient power. While we acknowledge that apart from Christ we can do nothing, we do not rise to the height or depth of Christian humility: *"I can do all things through Christ which strengtheneth me"* (Phil. 4:13). While we trust in the power of the death of Jesus to cancel the guilt of sin, we do not exercise a reliant and appropriating faith in the omnipotence of the living Savior to deliver us from the bondage and power of sin in our daily life. We forget that Christ worketh in us mightily, and that, one with Him, we possess strength sufficient to overcome every temptation. We are apt either to forget our nothingness, and imagine that in our daily path we can live without sin, that the duties and trials of our everyday life can be performed and borne in our own strength; or we do not avail ourselves of the omnipotence of Jesus, who is able to subdue all things to Himself, and to keep us from the daily infirmities and falls which we are apt to imagine an inevitable necessity. If we really depended in all things and at all times on Christ, we would in all things and at all times gain the victory through Him whose power is infinite, and who is appointed by the Father to be the Captain of our salvation. Then all our deeds would be wrought, not merely before, but in God. We would then do all things to the glory of the Father, in the all-powerful name of Jesus, who is our sanctification. Remember that unto Him all power is given in heaven and on earth, and live by the constant exercise of faith in His power. Let us most fully believe that we have and are nothing, that with man it is impossible, that in ourselves we have no life which can bring forth fruit; but that Christ is all—that abiding in Him, and His word dwelling in us, we can bring forth fruit to the glory of the Father.—From *Christ and the Church*, sermons by Adolph Saphir

28

AS YOUR STRENGTH

All power is given unto me in heaven and in earth.
—Matthew 28:18

Be strong in the Lord, and in the power of his might.
—Ephesians 6:10

My power is made perfect in weakness.
—2 Corinthians 12:9 RV

There is no truth more generally admitted among earnest Christians than that of their utter weakness. There is no truth more generally misunderstood and abused. Here, as elsewhere, God's thoughts are heaven-high above man's thoughts.

The Christian often tries to forget his weakness; God wants us to remember it, to feel it deeply. The Christian wants to conquer his weakness and to be freed from it; God wants us to rest and even rejoice in it. The Christian mourns over his weakness; Christ teaches His servant to say, "I take pleasure in infirmities. *'Most gladly…will I…glory in my infirmities'* (2 Cor. 12:9)." The Christian thinks his weakness his greatest hindrance in the life and service of God; God tells us that it is the secret of strength and success. It is our weakness, heartily accepted and continually realized, that gives us our claim and access to the strength of Him who has said, "*My strength is made perfect in weakness*" (v. 9).

When our Lord was about to take His seat upon the throne, one of His last words was: "*All power is given unto me in heaven and in earth.*" Just as His taking His place at the right hand of the power of God was something new and true—a real advance in the history of the God-man—so was this clothing with all power. Omnipotence was now entrusted to the man Christ Jesus, that from henceforth through the channels of human nature it might put forth its mighty energies. Hence He connected with this revelation of what He was to receive, the promise of the share that His disciples would have in it: "When I am ascended, '*ye shall receive power*' (Acts 1:8) '*from on high*' (Luke 24:49)". It is in the power of the omnipotent Savior that the believer must find his strength for life and for work.

It was thus with the disciples. During ten days they worshipped and waited at the footstool of His throne. They gave expression to their faith in Him as their Savior, to their adoration of Him as their Lord, to their love to Him as their Friend, to their devotion and readiness to work for Him as their Master. Jesus Christ was the one object of thought, of love, of delight. In such worship of faith and devotion their souls grew up into intensest communion with Him upon the throne, and when they were prepared, the baptism of power came. It was power within and power around.

The power came to qualify for the work to which they had yielded themselves—of testifying by life and word to their unseen Lord. With some the chief testimony was to be that of a holy life, revealing the heaven and the Christ from whom it came. The power came to set up the kingdom within them, to give them the victory over sin and self, to fit them by living experience to testify to the power of Jesus on the throne to make men live in the world as saints. Others were to give themselves up entirely to the speaking in the name of Jesus. But all needed and all received the gift of power, to prove that now Jesus had received the kingdom of the Father, that all power in heaven and earth was indeed given to Him, and by Him imparted to His people just as they needed it, whether for a holy life or effective service. They received the gift of power to prove to the world that the kingdom of God, to which they professed to belong, was not in word but in power. (See 1 Cor. 4:20.) By having power within, they had power without and around. The power of God was felt even by those who would not yield themselves to it. (See Acts 2:43, 4:13, 5:13.)

And what Jesus was to these first disciples, He is to us too. Our whole life and calling as disciples find their origin and their guarantee in the words: *"All power is given unto me in heaven and in earth."* What He does in and through us, He does with almighty power. What He claims or demands, He works Himself by that same power. All He gives, He gives with power. Every blessing He bestows, every promise He fulfills, every grace He works—all, all is to be with power. Everything that comes from this Jesus on the throne of power is to bear the stamp of power. The weakest believer may be confident that in asking to be kept from sin, to grow in holiness, to bring forth much fruit, he may count upon these his petitions being fulfilled with divine power. The power is in Jesus; Jesus is ours with all His fullness; it is in us, His members, that the power is to work and be made manifest.

And if we want to know how the power is bestowed, the answer is simple: Christ gives His power in us by giving His life in us. He does not, as so many believers imagine, take the feeble life He finds in them and impart a little strength to aid them in their feeble efforts. No; it is in giving His own life in us that He gives us His power. The Holy Spirit came down to the disciples direct from the heart of their exalted Lord, bringing down into them the glorious life of heaven into which He had entered. And so

His people are still taught to be strong in the Lord and in the power of His might. When He strengthens them, it is not by taking away the sense of feebleness, and giving in its place the feeling of strength. By no means. But in a very wonderful way leaving and even increasing the sense of utter impotence, He gives them along with it the consciousness of strength in Him. *"We have this treasure in earthen vessels, that the excellency of the power may be of God, and not of us"* (2 Cor. 4:7). The feebleness and the strength are side by side; as the one grows, the other too, until they understand the saying, *"When I am weak, then am I strong....I...glory in my infirmities, that the power of Christ may rest upon me"* (2 Cor. 12:10, 9).

The believing disciple learns to look upon Christ on the throne, Christ the Omnipotent, as his life. He studies that life in its infinite perfection and purity, in its strength and glory; it is the eternal life dwelling in a glorified man. And when he thinks of his own inner life, and longs for holiness, to live well pleasing unto God, or for power to do the Father's work, he looks up and, rejoicing that Christ is his life, he confidently reckons that that life will work mightily in him all he needs. In things little and things great, in the being kept from sin from moment to moment for which he has learned to look, or in the struggle with some special difficulty or temptation, the power of Christ is the measure of his expectation. He lives a most joyous and blessed life, not because he is no longer feeble, but because, being utterly helpless, he consents and expects to have the mighty Savior work in him.

The lessons these thoughts teach us for practical life are simple, but very precious. The first is, that all our strength is in Christ, laid up and waiting for use. It is there as an almighty life, which is in Him for us, ready to flow in according to the measure in which it finds the channels open. But whether its flow is strong or feeble, whatever our experience of it is, there it is in Christ: all power in heaven and earth. Let us take time to study this. Let us get our minds filled with the thought that Jesus might be to us a perfect Savior; the Father gave Him all power. That is the qualification that fits Him for our needs: all the power of heaven over all the powers of earth, over every power of earth in our heart and life too.

The second lesson is: this power flows into us as we abide in close union with Him. When the union is feeble, little valued or cultivated, the inflow of strength will be feeble. When the union with Christ is rejoiced in as our highest good, and everything sacrificed for the sake of maintaining it, the power will work: His strength will be made perfect in our weakness. (See 2 Cor. 12:9.) Our one care must therefore be to abide in Christ as our strength. Our one duty is to be strong in the Lord, and in the power of His might. Let our faith cultivate large and clear understanding of the exceeding greatness of God's power in them that believe, even that power of the risen and exalted Christ by which He triumphed over every enemy. (See Eph. 1:19–21.) Let our faith consent to God's wonderful and most blessed arrangement: nothing but feebleness in us as our own; all the power in Christ, and yet within our reach as surely as if it were in us. Let our faith daily go out of self and its life into the life of Christ, placing our whole being at His disposal for Him to work in us. Let our faith, above all, confidently rejoice in the assurance that He will indeed, with His almighty power, perfect His work in us. As we thus abide in Christ, the Holy Spirit, the Spirit of His power, will work mightily in us, and we too will sing, "The LORD is my strength and song" (Exod. 15:2). "In the LORD have I righteousness and strength" (Isa. 45:24). "I can do all things through Christ which strengtheneth me" (Phil. 4:13).

29

AND NOT IN SELF

In me (that is, in my flesh,) dwelleth no good thing.
—Romans 7:18

To have life in Himself is the prerogative of God alone, and of the Son, to whom the Father has also given it. To seek life, not in itself, but in God, is the highest honor of the creature. To live in and to himself is the folly and guilt of sinful man; to live to God in Christ is the blessedness of the believer. To deny, to hate, to forsake, to lose his own life, such is the secret of the life of faith. *"I live; yet not I, but Christ liveth in me"* (Gal. 2:20); *"Not I, but the grace of God which was with me"* (1 Cor. 15:10)— this is the testimony of each one who has found out what it is to give up his own life and to receive instead the blessed life of Christ within us. There is no path to true life, to abiding in Christ, than that which our Lord traveled before us—through death.

At the first commencement of the Christian life, this begins, but few see this. In the joy of pardon, new believers feel constrained to live for Christ and trust with the help of God to be enabled to do so. They are as yet ignorant of the terrible enmity of the flesh against God and its absolute refusal in the believer to be subject to the law of God. They know not yet that nothing but death, the absolute surrender to death of all that is of nature, will suffice, if the life of God is to be manifested in them with power. But bitter experience of failure soon teaches them the insufficiency of what they have yet known of Christ's power to save, and deep heart longings are awakened to know Him better. He lovingly points them to His cross. He tells them that as there, in the faith of His death as their substitute, they found their title to life, so there they will enter into its fuller experience too. He asks them if they are indeed willing to drink of the cup of which He drank—to be crucified and to die with Him. He teaches them that in Him they are indeed already crucified and dead—all unknowing, at conversion they become partakers of His death. But what they need now is to give a full and intelligent consent to what they received before they understood it, by an act of their own choice to will to die with Christ.

This demand of Christ's is one of unspeakable solemnity. Many a believer shrinks back from it. He can hardly understand it. He has become so accustomed to a low life of continual stumbling, that he hardly desires, and still less expects, deliverance. Holiness, perfect conformity to Jesus, unbroken fellowship with His love, can scarcely be counted distinct articles of his creed. Where there is not intense longing to be kept to the utmost from sinning, and to be brought into the closest possible union with the Savior, the thought of being crucified with Him can find no entrance. The only impression it makes is that of suffering and shame; such a one is content that Jesus bore the cross, and so won for him the crown he hopes to wear. How different the light in which the believer who is really seeking to abide fully in Christ looks upon it. Bitter experience has taught him how, both in the matter of entire surrender and simple trust, his greatest enemy in the abiding life is self. Now it refuses to give up its will; then again, by its working, it hinders God's work.

Unless this life of self, with its willing and working, is displaced by the life of Christ, with His willing and working, to abide in Him will be impossible. And then comes the solemn question from Him who died on the cross: "Are you ready to give up self to the death? You yourself, the living person born of God, are already in Me dead to sin and alive to God; but are you ready now, in the power of this death, to mortify your members, to give up self entirely to its death of the cross, to be kept there until it is wholly destroyed?" The question is a heart-searching one. Am I prepared to say that the old self will no longer have a word to say, that it will not be allowed to have a single thought, however natural; not a single feeling, however gratifying; not a single wish or work, however right?

Is this indeed what He requires? Is not our nature God's handiwork, and may not our natural powers be sanctified to His service? They may and must indeed. But perhaps you have not yet seen how the only way they can be sanctified is that they be taken from under the power of self and brought under the power of the life of Christ. Think not that this is a work that you can do, because you earnestly desire it and are indeed one of His redeemed ones. No, there is no way to the altar of consecration but through death. As you yielded yourself a sacrifice on God's altar as one alive from the dead (see Rom. 6:13, 12:1), so each power of your nature— each talent, gift, possession that is really to be holiness to the Lord—must be separated from the power of sin and self and laid on the altar to be consumed by the fire that is ever burning there. It is in the mortifying, the slaying of self, that the wonderful powers with which God has fitted you to serve Him, can be set free for a complete surrender to God, and offered to Him to be accepted and sanctified and used. And though, as long as you are in the flesh, there is no thought of being able to say that self is dead, yet when the life of Christ is allowed to take full possession, self can be so kept in its crucifixion place, and under its sentence of death, that it will have no dominion over you, not for a single moment. Jesus Christ becomes your second self.

Believer, if you want to truly and fully abide in Christ, prepare yourself to part forever from self and not to allow it, even for a single moment, to have anything to say in your inner life. If you are willing to come entirely away out of self, and to allow Jesus Christ to become your life within you, inspiring all your thinking, feeling, acting, in things temporal and spiritual, He is ready to undertake the charge. In the fullest and widest sense the word *life* ever can have, He will be your life, extending His interest and influence to each one, even the minutest, of the thousand things that make up your daily life. To do this He asks but one thing: come away out of self and its life, abide in Christ and the Christ life, and Christ will be your life. The power of His holy presence will cast out the old life.

To this end give up self at once and forever. If you have never yet dared to do it, for fear you might fail of your engagement, do it now, in view of the promise Christ gives you that His life will take the place of the old life. Try to realize that though self is not dead, you are indeed dead to self. Self is still strong and living, but it has no power over you. You, your renewed nature—you, your new self, begotten again in Jesus Christ from the dead—are indeed dead to sin and alive to God. Your death in Christ has freed you completely from the control of self; it has no power over you, except as you, in ignorance or unwatchfulness or unbelief, consent to yield to its usurped authority. Come and accept by faith simply and heartily the glorious position you have in Christ. As one who, in Christ, has a life dead to self, as one who is freed from the dominion of self, and has received His divine life to take the place of self, to be the animating and inspiring principle of your life, venture boldly to plant the foot upon the neck of this enemy of yours and your Lord's. Be of good courage; only believe. Fear not to take the irrevocable step and to say that you have once for all given up self to the death for which it has been crucified in Christ (Rom. 6:6). And trust Jesus the Crucified One to hold self to the cross and to fill its place in you with His own blessed resurrection life.

In this faith, abide in Christ! Cling to Him; rest on Him; hope on Him. Daily renew your consecration; daily accept afresh your position as ransomed from your tyrant and now in turn made a conqueror. Daily look with holy fear on the enemy, self, struggling to get free from the cross, seeking to allure you into giving it some little liberty, or else ready to deceive you by its profession of willingness now to do service to Christ. Remember, self seeking to serve God is more dangerous than self refusing obedience. Look upon it with holy fear, and hide yourself in Christ; in Him alone is your safety; abide thus in Him; He has promised to abide in you. He will teach you to be humble and watchful. He will teach you to be happy and trustful. Bring every interest of your life, every power of your nature, all the unceasing flow of thought and will and feeling that make up life, and trust Him to take the place that self once filled so easily and so naturally. Jesus Christ will indeed take possession of you and dwell in you, and in the restfulness and peace and grace of the new life you will have unceasing joy at the wondrous exchange that has been made—the coming out of self to abide in Christ alone.

Author's Note

In his work on sanctification, Marshall, in the twelfth chapter, on "Holiness through Faith Alone," puts with great force the danger in which the Christian is of seeking sanctification in the power of the flesh, with the help of Christ, instead of looking for it to Christ alone, and receiving it from Him by faith. He reminds us how there are two natures in the believer, and so two ways of seeking holiness, according as we allow the principles of the one or other nature to guide us. The one is the carnal way, in which we put forth our utmost efforts and resolutions, trusting Christ to help us in doing so. The other the spiritual way, in which, as those who have died, and can do nothing, our one care is to receive Christ day by day, and at every step to let Him live and work in us.

Despair of purging the flesh or natural man of its sinful lusts and inclinations, and of practicing holiness by your willing and resolving to do the best that lies in your own power, and trusting on the grace of God and Christ to help you in such resolutions and endeavors. Rather resolve to trust on Christ to work in you to will and to do by His own power according to His own good pleasure.

They that are convinced of their own sin and misery do commonly first think to tame the flesh, and to subdue and root out its lusts, and to make their corrupt nature to be better natured and inclined to holiness by their struggling and wrestling with it; and if they can but bring their hearts to a full purpose and resolution to do the best that lies in them, they hope that by such a resolution they shall be able to achieve great enterprises in the conquests of their lusts and performance of the most difficult duties. It is the great work of some zealous [theologians] in their preachings and writings to stir up people to this resolution, wherein they place the chiefest turning point from sin to godliness. And they think that this is not contrary to the life of faith, because they trust in the grace of God through Christ to help them in all such resolutions and endeavors. Thus they endeavor to reform their old state, and to be made perfect in the flesh, instead of putting it off and walking according to the new state in Christ. They trust on low carnal things for holiness, and upon the acts of their own will, their purposes, resolutions, and endeavors, instead of Christ; and they trust to Christ to help them in this carnal way; whereas true faith would teach them that they are nothing, and that they do but labor in vain.

30

AS THE SURETY
OF THE COVENANT

Jesus [was] *made a surety of a better testament.*
—Hebrews 7:22

O f the old covenant, Scripture speaks as not being faultless, and God complains that Israel had not continued in it; and so He regarded them not (Heb. 8:7–9). It had not secured its apparent object, in the uniting of Israel and God; Israel had forsaken Him, and He had not regarded Israel. Therefore, God promised to make a new covenant, free from the faults of the first, and effectual to realize its purpose. If it were to accomplish its end, it would need to secure God's faithfulness to His people, and His people's faithfulness to God. And the terms of the new covenant expressly declare that these two objects will be attained. *"I will put my laws into their mind"* (Hebrews 8:10); thus God proposes to secure their unchanging faithfulness to Him. *"Their sins…will I remember no more"* (v. 12); thus He assures His unchanging faithfulness to them. A pardoning God and an obedient people: these are the two parties who are to meet and to be eternally united in the new covenant.

The most beautiful provision of this new covenant is that of the surety in whom its fulfillment on both parts is guaranteed. Jesus was made the surety of the better covenant. To man He became surety that God would faithfully fulfill His part, so that man could confidently depend upon God to pardon and accept and never more forsake. And to God He likewise became surety that man would faithfully fulfill his part, so that God could bestow on him the blessing of the an everlasting covenant. And the way in which He fulfills His suretyship is this: as one with God, and having the fullness of God dwelling in His human nature, He is personally security to men that God will do what He has engaged. All that God has is secured to us in Him as man. And then, as one with us, and having taken us up as members into His own body, He is security to God that His interests will be cared for. All that man must be and do is secured in Him. It is the glory of the new covenant that it has in the person of the God-man its living surety, its everlasting security. And it can easily be understood how, in proportion as we abide in Him as the surety of the covenant, its objects and its blessings will be realized in us.

We will understand this best if we consider it in the light of one of the promises of the new covenant. Take the following in Jeremiah 32:40: *"I will make an everlasting covenant with them, that I will not turn away from them, to do them good; but I will put my fear in their hearts, that they shall not depart from me."*

With what wonderful condescension the infinite God here bows Himself to our weakness! He is the faithful and unchanging One, whose word is truth; and yet more abundantly to show to the heirs of the promise the immutability of His counsel, He binds Himself in the covenant that He will never change: *"I will make an everlasting covenant…that I will not turn away from them.*" Blessed is the man who has thoroughly appropriated this and finds his rest in the everlasting covenant of the Faithful One!

But in a covenant there are two parties. And what if man becomes unfaithful and breaks the covenant? Provision must be made, if the covenant is to be well ordered in all things and sure (2 Sam. 23:5), that this cannot be, and that man too remain faithful. Man never can undertake to give such an assurance. And see, here God comes to provide for this too. He not only undertakes in the covenant that He will never turn from His people, but also to put His fear in their hearts, that they do not depart from Him. In addition to His own obligations as one of the covenanting parties, He undertakes for the other party too: *"I will...cause you to walk in my statutes, and ye shall keep my judgments, and do them"* (Ezek. 36:27). Blessed is the man who understands this half of the covenant too! He sees that his security is not in the covenant that he makes with His God, and that he would but continually break again. He finds that a covenant has been made, in which God stands good, not only for Himself, but for man too. He grasps the blessed truth that his part in the covenant is to accept what God has promised to do, and to expect the sure fulfillment of the divine engagement to secure the faithfulness of His people to their God: *"I will put my fear in their hearts, that they shall not depart from me"* (Jer. 32:40).

It is just here that the blessed work comes in of the surety of the covenant, appointed of the Father to see to its maintenance and perfect fulfillment. To Him the Father has said, *"I...give thee for a covenant of the people"* (Isa. 42:6). And the Holy Spirit testifies, *"All the promises of God in him are yea, and in him Amen, unto the glory of God by us"* (2 Cor. 1:20). The believer who abides in Him has a divine assurance for the fulfillment of every promise the covenant ever gave.

Christ was made surety of a better testament. It is as our Melchisedec that Christ is surety. (See Hebrews 7.) Aaron and his sons passed away; of Christ it is witnessed that He lives. He is priest in the power of an endless life. Because He continues ever, He has an unchangeable priesthood. And because He ever lives to make intercession, He can save to the uttermost;

He can save completely. It is because Christ is the Ever Living One that His suretyship of the covenant is so effectual. He lives ever to make intercession, and can therefore save completely. Every moment the unceasing pleadings that secure to His people the powers and the blessings of the heavenly life rise up from His holy presence to the Father. And every moment the mighty influences of His unceasing intercession, conveying to them uninterruptedly the power of the heavenly life, go out from Him downward to His people. As surety with us for the Father's favor, He never ceases to pray and present us before Him; as surety with the Father for us, He never ceases to work and reveal the Father within us.

The mystery of the Melchisedec priesthood, which the Hebrews were not able to receive (see Heb. 5:10–14), is the mystery of the resurrection life. It is in this that the glory of Christ as surety of the covenant consists: He ever lives. He performs His work in heaven in the power of a divine, an omnipotent life. He ever lives to pray; there is not a moment that as surety His prayers do not rise Godward to secure the Father's fulfillment to us of the covenant. He performs His work on earth in the power of that same life; there is not a moment that His answered prayers—the powers of the heavenly world—do not flow downward to secure for His Father our fulfillment of the covenant. In the eternal life there are no breaks, never a moment's interruption; each moment has the power of eternity in it. He ever, every moment, lives to pray. He ever, every moment, lives to bless. He can save to the uttermost, completely and perfectly, because He ever lives to pray. (See Heb. 7:25.)

Believer, come and see here how the possibility of abiding in Jesus every moment is secured by the very nature of this ever living priesthood of your surety. Moment by moment, as His intercession rises up, its efficacy descends. And because Jesus stands good for the fulfillment of the covenant—*"I will put my fear in their hearts, that they shall not depart from me"* (Jer. 32:40)—He cannot afford to leave you one single moment to yourself. He dares not do so, or He would fail of His undertaking. Your unbelief may fail of realizing the blessing; He cannot be unfaithful. If you will but consider Him, and the power of that endless life after which He was made and is a High Priest, your faith will rise to believe that an endless, ever continuing, unchangeable life of abiding in Jesus is nothing less than what is waiting you.

It is as we see what Jesus is, and is to us, that the abiding in Him will become the natural and spontaneous result of our knowledge of Him. If His life unceasingly, moment by moment, rises to the Father for us, and descends to us from the Father, then to abide moment by moment is easy and simple. Each moment of conscious communion with Him we simply say, "Jesus, Surety, Keeper, Ever Living Savior, in whose life I dwell, I abide in You." Each moment of need or darkness or fear, we still say, "O You Great High Priest, in the power of an endless, unchangeable life, I abide in You." And for the moments when direct and distinct communion with Him must give place to necessary occupations, we can trust His suretyship, His unceasing priesthood, in its divine efficacy, and the power with which He saves to the uttermost (see Heb. 7:25), still to keep us abiding in Him.

31

THE GLORIFIED ONE

Your life is hid with Christ in God. When Christ, who is our life,
shall appear, then shall ye also appear with him in glory.
—Colossians 3:3–4

He who abides in Christ the Crucified One, learns to know what it is to be crucified with Him, and in Him to be indeed dead unto sin. He who abides in Christ the Risen and Glorified One, becomes in the same way partaker of His resurrection life and of the glory with which He has now been crowned in heaven. Unspeakable are the blessings that flow to the soul from the union with Jesus in His glorified life.

This life is a life of perfect victory and rest. Before His death, the Son of God had to suffer and to struggle, could be tempted and troubled by sin and its assaults; as the Risen One, He has triumphed over sin; and, as the Glorified One, His humanity has entered into participation of the glory of Deity. The believer who abides in Him as such, is led to see how the power of sin and the flesh are indeed destroyed; the consciousness of complete and everlasting deliverance becomes increasingly clear, and the blessed rest and peace, the fruit of such a conviction that victory and deliverance are an accomplished fact, take possession of the life. Abiding in Jesus, in whom he has been raised and set in the heavenly places, he receives of that glorious life streaming from the Head through every member of the body.

This life is a life in the full fellowship of the Father's love and holiness. Jesus often gave prominence to this thought with His disciples. His death was a going to the Father. He prayed: *"O Father, glorify thou me with thine own self with the glory which I had with thee"* (John 17:5). As the believer, abiding in Christ the Glorified One, seeks to realize and experience what his union with Jesus on the throne implies, he apprehends how the unclouded light of the Father's presence is His highest glory and blessedness, and in Him the believer's portion too. He learns the sacred art of always, in fellowship with His exalted Head, dwelling in the secret of the Father's presence. Further, when Jesus was on earth, temptation could still reach Him; in glory, everything is holy, and in perfect harmony with the will of God. And so the believer who abides in Him experiences that, in this high fellowship, his spirit is sanctified into growing harmony with the Father's will. The heavenly life of Jesus is the power that casts out sin.

This life is a life of loving beneficence and activity. Seated on His throne, He dispenses His gifts, bestows His Spirit, and never ceases in love to watch and to work for those who are His. The believer cannot abide in Jesus the Glorified One without feeling himself stirred and strengthened to work; the Spirit and the love of Jesus breathe the will and the power to be a blessing to others. Jesus went to heaven with the very object of obtaining power there to bless abundantly. He does this as the Heavenly Vine only through the medium of His people as His branches. Whoever, therefore, abides in Him, the Glorified One, bears much fruit, for he receives of the Spirit and the power of the eternal life of his exalted Lord and becomes the channel through which the fullness of Jesus, who has been exalted to be a Prince and a Savior, flows out to bless those around him.

There is one more thought in regard to this life of the Glorified One, and ours in Him. It is a life of wondrous expectation and hope. It is so with Christ. He sits at the right hand of God, expecting until all His enemies be made His footstool, looking forward to the time when He will receive His full reward, when His glory will be made manifest and His beloved people be ever with Him in that glory. The hope of Christ is the hope of His redeemed: *"I will come again, and receive you unto myself; that where I am, there ye may be also"* (John 14:3). This promise is as precious to Christ as it ever can be to us. The joy of meeting is surely no less for the coming Bridegroom than for the waiting bride. The life of Christ in glory is one of longing expectation; the full glory only comes when His beloved are with Him.

The believer who abides closely in Christ will share with Him in this spirit of expectation. Not so much for the increase of personal happiness, but from the spirit of enthusiastic allegiance to his King, he longs to see Him come in His glory, reigning over every enemy, the full revelation of God's everlasting love. "Until He comes" is the watchword of every true-hearted believer. *"Christ...shall appear, then shall* [we] *also appear with him in glory."*

There may be very serious differences in the exposition of the promises of His coming. To one it is plain as day that He is coming very speedily in person to reign on earth, and that speedy coming is his hope and his stay. To another, loving his Bible and his Savior not less, the coming can mean nothing but the Judgment Day—the solemn transition from time to eternity, the close of history on earth, the beginning of heaven; and the thought of that manifestation of his Savior's glory is no less his joy and his strength. It is Jesus, Jesus coming again, Jesus taking us to Himself, Jesus adored as Lord of all, that is to the whole church the sum and the center of its hope.

It is by abiding in Christ the Glorified One that the believer will be quickened to that truly spiritual looking for His coming, which alone brings true blessing to the soul. There is an interest in the study of the things which are to be, in which the discipleship of a school is often more marked than the discipleship of Christ the meek, in which contendings for opinions and condemnation of believers are more striking than any signs of the coming glory. It is only the humility that is willing to learn from those who may have other gifts and deeper revelations of the truth than we, and the love that always speaks gently and tenderly of those who see not as we do, and the heavenliness that shows that the Coming One is indeed already our life, that will persuade either the church or the world that this our faith is not in the wisdom of men, but in the power of God. To testify of the Savior as the Coming One, we must be abiding in and bearing the image of Him as the Glorified One. Neither the correctness of the views we hold, nor the earnestness with which we advocate them, will prepare us for meeting Him, but only the abiding in Him. Then only can our being manifested in glory with Him be what it is meant to me—a transfiguration, a breaking out and shining forth of the indwelling glory that had been waiting for the day of revelation.

Blessed life! The *"life...hid with Christ in God,"* set in the heavenlies in Christ (Eph. 1:20), abiding in Christ the glorified! Once again the question comes: Can a feeble child of dust really dwell in fellowship with the King of Glory? And again the blessed answer has to be given: To maintain that union is the very work for which Christ has all power in heaven and earth at His disposal. The blessing will be given to him who will trust his Lord for it, who in faith and confident expectation ceases not to yield himself to be wholly one with Him. It was an act of wondrous though simple faith in which the soul yielded at first to the Savior. That faith grows up to clearer insight and faster hold of God's truth that we are one with Him in His glory. In that same wondrous faith, wondrously simple but wondrously mighty, the soul learns to abandon itself entirely to the keeping of Christ's almighty power and the actings of His eternal life. Because it knows that it has the Spirit of God dwelling within to communicate all that Christ is, it no longer looks upon it as a burden or a work, but allows the divine life to have its way, to do its work; its faith is the increasing abandonment of self, the expectation and acceptance of all that the love and the power of the Glorified One can perform. In that faith, unbroken fellowship is maintained, and growing conformity realized. As with Moses, the fellowship makes partakers of the glory, and the life begins to shine with a brightness not of this world.

Blessed life! It is ours, for Jesus is ours. Blessed life! We have the possession within us in its hidden power, and we have the prospect before us in its fullest glory. May our daily lives be the bright and blessed proof that the hidden power dwells within, preparing us for the glory to be revealed. May our abiding in Christ the Glorified One be our power to live to the glory of the Father, our fitness to share in the glory of the Son.

And now, little children, abide in him; that, when he shall appear,
we may have confidence, and not be ashamed before him at his coming.
—1 John 2:28

THE PRAYER LIFE

CONTENTS

PREFACE

A few words with regard to the origin of this book and the object with which it was written will help to put the reader into the right position for understanding its teaching. It was the outcome of a conference of ministers at Stellenbosch, South Africa, April 11–14, 1912. The occasion of the conference was as follows: Professor de Vos of our theological seminary had written a letter to the ministers of our church (Dutch Reformed Church) concerning the low state of spiritual life which marked the church universal generally, which, he said, ought to lead to the inquiry as to how far that statement included our church too. What had been said in the book *The State of the Church* called for deep searching of heart. He thought there could be no doubt about the truth of the statement in regard to the lack of spiritual power. He asked whether it was not time for us to come together and in God's presence to find out what might be the cause of the evil. He wrote: "If only we study the conditions in all sincerity, we shall have to acknowledge that our unbelief and sin are the cause of the lack of spiritual power; that this condition is one of sin and guilt before God, and nothing less than a direct grieving of God's Holy Spirit."

His invitation met with a hearty response. Our four theological professors, with more than two hundred ministers, missionaries, and theological students, came together with the above words as the keynote of our meeting. From the very first in the addresses there was the tone of confession as the only way to repentance and restoration. At a subsequent meeting the opportunity was given for testimony as to what might be the sins that made the life of the church so feeble. Some began to mention failings that they had seen in other ministers, either in conduct or in doctrine or in service. It was soon felt that this was not the right way; each must acknowledge that in which he himself was guilty.

The Lord graciously so ordered it that we were gradually led to the sin of prayerlessness as one of the deepest roots of the evil. No one could plead himself free from this. Nothing so reveals the defective spiritual life in minister and congregation as the lack of believing and unceasing prayer. Prayer is indeed the pulse of the spiritual life. It is the great means of bringing to the minister and people the blessing and power of heaven. Persevering and believing prayer means a strong and an abundant life.

When once the spirit of confession began to prevail, the question arose as to whether it would be indeed possible to expect to gain the victory over all that had in the past hindered our prayer lives. In smaller conferences held previously, it had been found that many were most anxious to make a new beginning, and yet they had not the courage to expect that they would be able to maintain that prayer life that they saw to be in accordance with the Word of God. They had often made the attempt but had failed. They did not dare to make any promise to the Lord to live and pray as He would have them; they felt it impossible. Such confessions gradually led to the great truth that the only power for a new prayer life is to be found in an entirely new relationship to our blessed Savior. It is as we see in Him the Lord who saves us from sin—the sin of prayerlessness, too—and our faith yields itself to a life of closer communion with Him, that a life in His love and fellowship will make prayer to Him the natural expression of our soul's life. Before we parted, many were able to testify that they were returning with new light and new hope to find in Jesus Christ strength for a new prayer life.

Many felt that this was only a beginning. Satan, who had so long prevailed in the inner chamber, would do his utmost with his temptations to make us yield once again to the power of the flesh and the world. Nothing but the teaching and the fellowship of Christ Himself could ever give the power to remain faithful.

The need was felt for some statement of the truths that had been dealt with at the conference, to remind those who had been present of what they had learned and of what would help them in the new endeavor after that prayer life that is so essential to a minister's success. It was also needed for those who had been prevented from coming and for the eldership in our church, who had in many cases felt the deepest interest in hearing what the purpose was for which their ministers had gone from home.

Early copies of the book were sent out with the thought that if the leaders of the church, ministers and elders, begin to see that in spiritual work everything depends upon prayer, and that God Himself is the helper of those who wait on Him, it would indeed be a day of hope for our church. It was at the same time meant for all believers who long for a life of more entire separation to the Lord. For all who desired to pray more and pray better, it sought to point them to the glory of God in the inner chamber, and the way in which that glory can rest upon the soul.

When first asked to have the book translated into English, I felt as if its composition had been too hurried and its tone, owing to the close connection with the meetings that had preceded, too colloquial to make this desirable. And my own limited strength made it impossible for me to think of rewriting it. When, however, my friend, Reverend W. M. Douglas, asked permission to translate it, I gave my consent. If God has a message through the book to any of His servants, I would count it a privilege to tell what He has done here in our church, as a suggestion of what He may do in other churches.

I close with my greetings to all the ministers of the Gospel and to the church members who may read these pages. I pray fervently that the grace of God would work among us conviction of sin, confession of deep need and helplessness, and then give the vision and the faith of what Jesus Christ can do for those who trust Him. May He give to more than one who reads, the courage to take counsel with his brothers and to seek for and obtain that full fellowship with God in prayer which is the very essence of the Christian life. It has been said: "It is only the prayerless who are too proud to own up to prayerlessness." Let us believe that there are many hearts waiting for the call inviting them to united and whole-hearted confession of shortcoming, as the only but the sure way of a return and restoration to God's favor, and the experience of what He will do in answer to prayer.

I wish to add one word more, in regard to "the Pentecostal prayer meetings" held throughout our church. These have had a very interesting and important place in our work. At the time of the great revival in America and Ireland in 1858 and following years, some of our elder ministers issued a circular urging the churches to pray that God might visit us too. In 1860, the revival broke out in various parishes. In April 1861, there was very deep interest shown in the Paarl, in one of our oldest congregations. During the week preceding Pentecost, the minister, who ordinarily preached only once on a Sunday, announced that in the afternoon there would be a public prayer meeting in the church. The occasion was one of extraordinary interest, and many hearts were deeply touched. As one result the minister suggested that in the future the ten days between Ascension and Pentecost should be observed by daily prayer meetings. This took place the following year. The blessing then received was such that all the neighboring congregations took up the suggestion, and now for fifty years the ten days of prayer have been observed throughout the whole church. Each year notes were issued as subjects of addresses and prayer, and the result has been that throughout our whole church Christians have been educated in the knowledge of what God's Word teaches regarding the Holy Spirit, and have been stirred to seek and to yield themselves to His blessed leading. These ten days have often proved the occasion for special effort with the unconverted, and of partial revival. And they have been the means of untold blessing in leading ministers and people to recognize the place that the Holy Spirit ought to have as the executive of the Godhead in the heart of the believer, in the dealing with souls, and in consecration to the service of the kingdom.

There is still very much indeed lacking of the full knowledge and power of the Holy Spirit, but we feel that we cannot be sufficiently grateful to God for what He has done through His leading us to dedicate these days to special prayer for the movings of His Holy Spirit.

I have written this with the thought that there may be some who will be glad to know of it, and in their sphere to unite in the observance.

—Andrew Murray

1

THE SIN
OF PRAYERLESSNESS

I n order for our conscience to do its work and for our hearts to be thoroughly repentant, it is necessary for each individual to mention his sin by name. The confession must be severely personal. In a meeting of ministers there is probably no single sin which each one of us ought to acknowledge with deeper shame—"Guilty, verily guilty"—than the sin of prayerlessness.

What is it, then, that makes prayerlessness such a great sin? At first it is looked upon merely as a weakness. There is so much talk about lack of time and all sorts of distractions that the deep guilt of the situation is not recognized. Let it be our honest desire that, for the future, the sin of prayerlessness may be to us truly sinful. Consider the following.

1. What a reproach it is to God. There is the holy and most glorious God who invites us to come to Him, to converse with Him, to ask from Him such things as we need, and to experience what a blessing there is in fellowship with Him. He has created us in His own image and has redeemed us by His own Son, so that in prayer with Him we might find our highest glory and salvation.

What use do we make of this heavenly privilege? How many there are who take only five minutes for prayer! They say that they have no time and that the heart desire for prayer is lacking; they do not know how to spend half an hour with God! It is not that they absolutely do not pray; they pray every day—but they have no joy in prayer, as a token of communion with God that shows that God is everything to them.

If a friend comes to visit them, they have time, they make time, even at the cost of sacrifice, for the sake of enjoying conversation with him. Yes, they have time for everything that really interests them, but no time to practice fellowship with God and delight themselves in Him! They find time for a creature who can be of service to them; but day after day, month after month passes, and there is no time to spend one hour with God.

Do not our hearts begin to acknowledge what a dishonor this is to God, that I dare to say I cannot find time for fellowship with Him? If this sin begins to appear plain to us, will we not with deep shame cry out: "'*Woe is me! for I am undone*' (Isa. 6:5), O God; be merciful to me and forgive this awful sin of prayerlessness"?

2. It is the cause of a deficient spiritual life. It is a proof that, for the most part, our lives are still under the power of the flesh. Prayer is the pulse of life; by it the doctor can tell what is the condition of the heart. The sin of prayerlessness is a proof for the ordinary Christian or minister that the life of God in the soul is in deadly sickness and weakness.

Much is said and many complaints are made about the feebleness of the church to fulfill her calling, to exercise an influence over her members, to deliver them from the power of the world, and to bring them to a life of holy consecration to God. Much is also spoken about her indifference to the millions of heathen whom Christ entrusted to her that she might make known to them His love and salvation. What is the reason that many thousands of Christian workers in the world do not have a greater influence? Nothing except this—the prayerlessness of their service. In the midst of all their zeal in the study and in the work of the church, of all their faithfulness in preaching and conversation with the people, they lack that ceaseless prayer that has attached to it the sure promise of the Spirit and the *"power from on high"* (Luke 24:49). It is nothing but the sin of prayerlessness that is the cause of the lack of powerful spiritual life!

3. The church suffers a dreadful loss as a result of prayerlessness of the minister. It is the business of a minister to train believers up to a life of prayer, but how can a leader do this if he himself has little understanding of the art of conversing with God and of receiving from the Holy Spirit, every day, out of heaven, abundant grace for himself and for his work? A minister cannot lead a congregation higher than he is himself. He cannot with enthusiasm point out a way, or explain a work, in which he is not himself walking or living.

How many thousands of Christians there are who know next to nothing of the blessedness of prayer fellowship with God! How many there are who know something of it and long for a further increase of this knowledge, but in the preaching of the Word they are not persistently urged to keep on until they obtain the blessing! The reason is simply and only that the minister understands so little about the secret of powerful prayer and does not give prayer the place in his service that, in the nature of the case and in the will of God, is indispensably necessary. Oh, what a difference we would notice in our congregations if ministers could be brought to see in its right light the sin of prayerlessness and were delivered from it!

4. It is impossible to preach the Gospel to all men—as we are commanded by Christ to do—so long as this sin is not overcome and cast out.

Many feel that the great need of missions is the obtaining of men and women who will give themselves to the Lord to strive in prayer for the salvation of souls. It has also been said that God is eager and able to deliver and bless the world He has redeemed, if His people were but willing, if they were but ready, to cry to Him day and night. But how can congregations be brought to that unless there comes first an entire change in ministers, that they begin to see that the indispensable thing is not preaching, not pastoral visitation, not church work, but fellowship with God in prayer until they are clothed with *"power from on high"* (Luke 24:49)?

Oh, that all thought and work and expectation concerning the kingdom might drive us to the acknowledgment of the sin of prayerlessness! God help us to root it out! God deliver us from it through the blood and power of Christ Jesus! God teach every minister of the Word to see what a glorious place he may occupy if he first of all is delivered from this root of evils; so that with courage and joy, in faith and perseverance, he can go on with his God!

The sin of prayerlessness! May the Lord lay the burden of it so heavy on our hearts that we cannot rest until it is taken far from us through the name and power of Jesus. He will make this possible for us.

A Witness from America

In 1898, there were two members of the Presbytery in New York who attended the Northfield Conference for the deepening of their spiritual lives. They returned to their work with the fire of a new enthusiasm. They endeavored to bring about a revival in the entire Presbytery. In a meeting that they held, the chairman was guided to ask the other believers a question concerning their prayer life: "Brothers," said he, "let us today make confession before God and each other. It will do us good. Will everyone who spends half an hour every day with God in connection with his work hold up a hand?" One hand was held up. He made a further request: "All who thus spend fifteen minutes hold up a hand." Not half of the hands were held up. Then he said, "Prayer, the working power of the church of Christ, and half of the workers make hardly any use of it! All who spend five minutes hold up a hand." All hands went up. But one man came later with the confession that he was not quite sure if he spent five minutes in prayer every day. "It is," said he, "a terrible revelation of how little time I spend with God."

The Cause of Prayerlessness

In an elder's prayer meeting, a brother asked the question: "What, then, is the cause of so much prayerlessness? Is it not unbelief?"

The answer was: "Certainly; but then comes the question—what is the cause of that unbelief?" When the disciples asked the Lord Jesus: *"Why could not we cast [the Devil] out?"* (Matt. 17:19), His answer was, *"Because of your unbelief"* (v. 20). He went further and said: *"Howbeit this kind goeth not out but by prayer and fasting"* (v. 21). If the life is not one of self-denial, of fasting—that is, letting the world go—of prayer—that is, laying hold of heaven—faith cannot be exercised. A life lived according to the flesh and not according to the Spirit—it is in this that we find the origin of the prayerlessness of which we complain. As we came out of the meeting, a brother said to me: "That is the whole difficulty; we wish to pray in the Spirit and at the same time walk after the flesh, and this is impossible."

If one is sick and desires healing, it is of prime importance that the true cause of the sickness be discovered. This is always the first step toward recovery. If the particular cause is not recognized, and attention is directed to subordinate causes, or to supposed but not real causes, healing is out of the question. In the same way, it is of the utmost importance for us to obtain a correct insight into the cause of the sad condition of deadness and failure in prayer in the inner chamber, which should be such a blessed place for us. Let us seek to realize fully what is the root of this evil.

Scripture teaches us that there are but two conditions possible for the Christian. One is a walk according to the Spirit, the other a walk according to the flesh. These two powers are in irreconcilable conflict with each other. So it comes to pass, in the case of the majority of Christians, that, while we thank God that they are born again through the Spirit and have received the life of God—yet their ordinary daily life is not lived according to the Spirit but according to the flesh. Paul wrote to the Galatians: *"Are ye so foolish? having begun in the Spirit, are ye now made perfect by the flesh?"* (Gal. 3:3). Their service lay in fleshly outward performances. They did not understand that where *"the flesh"* is permitted to influence their service for God, it soon results in open sin.

So he mentions not only grave sins as the work of the flesh, such as adultery, murder, drunkenness; but also the more ordinary sins of daily life—wrath, strife, variance—and he gives the exhortation: *"Walk in the Spirit, and ye shall not fulfil the lust of the flesh....If we live in the Spirit, let us also walk in the Spirit"* (Gal. 5:16, 25). The Spirit must be honored not only as the Author of a new life, but also as the Leader and Director of our entire walk. Otherwise we are what the apostle calls "carnal."

The majority of Christians have little understanding of this matter. They have no real knowledge of the deep sinfulness and godlessness of that carnal nature that belongs to them and to which unconsciously they yield. *"God...condemned sin in the flesh"* (Rom. 8:3)—in the Cross of Christ. *"They that are Christ's have crucified the flesh with the affections and lusts"* (Gal. 5:24). *"The flesh"* cannot be improved or sanctified. *"The carnal mind is enmity against God: for it is not subject to the law of God, neither indeed can be"* (Rom. 8:7). There is no means of dealing with the flesh except as Christ dealt with it, bearing it to the cross. *"Our old man is crucified with him"* (Rom. 6:6); so we by faith also crucify it, and regard and treat it daily as an accursed thing that finds its rightful place on the accursed cross.

It is saddening to consider how many Christians there are who seldom think or speak earnestly about the deep and immeasurable sinfulness of the flesh: *"In me (that is, in my flesh,) dwelleth no good thing"* (Rom. 7:18). The man who truly believes this may well cry out: *"I see another law in my members...bringing me into captivity to the law of sin....O wretched man that I am! who shall deliver me from the body of this death?"* (vv. 23–24). Happy is he who can go further and say: *"I thank God through Jesus Christ our Lord.... For the law of the Spirit of life in Christ Jesus hath made me free from the law of sin and death"* (Rom. 7:25, 8:2).

Would that we might understand God's counsels of grace for us! The flesh on the cross—the Spirit in the heart and controlling the life.

This spiritual life is too little understood or sought after; yet it is literally what God has promised and will accomplish in those who unconditionally surrender themselves to Him for this purpose.

Here then we have the deep root of evil as the cause of a prayerless life. The flesh can say prayers well enough, calling itself religious for so doing and thus satisfying conscience. But the flesh has no desire or strength for the prayer that strives after an intimate knowledge of God, that rejoices in fellowship with Him, and that continues to lay hold of His strength. So, finally, it comes to this: the flesh must be denied and crucified.

The Christian who is still carnal has neither desire nor strength to follow after God. He rests satisfied with the prayer of habit or custom. But the glory, the blessedness of secret prayer is a hidden thing to him, until one day his eyes are opened, and he begins to see that the flesh, in its disposition to turn away from God, is the archenemy that makes powerful prayer impossible for him.

I had once, at a conference, spoken on the subject of prayer and made use of strong expressions about the enmity of the flesh as a cause of prayerlessness. After the address, the minister's wife said that she thought I had spoken too strongly. She was also guilty of having too little desire for prayer, but she believed her heart was sincerely set on seeking God. I showed her what the Word of God said about the flesh, and that everything that prevents the reception of the Spirit is nothing else than a secret work of the flesh. Adam was created to have fellowship with God and enjoyed it before his Fall. After the Fall, however, there came immediately a deep-seated aversion to God, and he fled from Him. This incurable aversion is the characteristic of the unregenerate nature and the chief cause of our unwillingness to surrender ourselves to fellowship with God in prayer. The following day she told me that God had opened her eyes; she confessed that the enmity and unwillingness of the flesh was the hidden hindrance in her defective prayer life.

Oh, my fellow believers, do not seek to find in circumstances the explanation of this prayerlessness over which we mourn; seek it where God's Word declares it to be, in the hidden aversion of the heart to a holy God.

When a Christian does not yield entirely to the leading of the Spirit—and this is certainly the will of God and the work of His grace—he lives, without knowing it, under the power of the flesh. This life of the flesh manifests itself in many different ways. It appears in the hastiness of spirit, or the anger that so unexpectedly arises in you, or the lack of love for which you have so often blamed yourself. It also appears in the pleasure found in eating and drinking when your conscience chides you; in that seeking for your own will and honor, that confidence in your own wisdom and power, that pleasure in the world, of which you are sometimes ashamed before God. All this is life after the flesh. *"Ye are yet carnal"* (1 Cor. 3:3)—that text, perhaps, disturbs you at times; you have not full peace and joy in God.

I pray that you will take time and give an answer to the question: Have I not found here the cause of my prayerlessness, of my powerlessness to effect any change in the matter? I live in the Spirit, I have been born again, but I do not walk after the Spirit—the flesh lords it over me. The carnal life cannot possibly pray in the spirit and power. God forgive me. The carnal life is evidently the cause of my sad and shameful prayerlessness.

The Storm Center on the Battlefield

Mention was made in the conference of the expression "strategic position" used so often in reference to the great strife between the kingdom of heaven and the powers of darkness.

When a general chooses the place from which he intends to strike the enemy, he pays the most attention to those points that he thinks are the most important in the fight. Thus there was on the battlefield of Waterloo a farmhouse that Wellington immediately saw as the key to the situation. He did not spare his troops in his endeavor to hold that point; the victory depended on it. So he won the victory. It is the same in the conflict between the believer and the powers of darkness. The inner chamber is the place where the decisive victory is obtained.

The Enemy uses all his power to lead the Christian, and above all the minister, to neglect prayer. He knows that however admirable the sermon may be, however attractive the service, however faithful the pastoral visitation, none of these things can damage him or his kingdom if prayer is neglected. When the church shuts herself up to the power of the inner chamber, and the soldiers of the Lord have received on their knees *"power from on high"* (Luke 24:49), then the powers of darkness will be shaken and souls will be delivered. In the church, on the mission field, with the minister and his congregation, everything depends on the faithful exercise of the power of prayer.

In the week of the conference I found the following in *The Christian:*

Two persons quarrel over a certain point. We call them Christian and Apollyon. Apollyon notices that Christian has a certain weapon that would give him a sure victory. They meet in deadly strife, and Apollyon resolves to take away the weapon from his opponent and destroy it. For the moment the main cause of the strife has become subordinate; the great point now is who will get possession of the weapon on which everything depends? It is of vital importance to get hold of that.

So it is in the conflict between Satan and the believer. God's child can conquer everything by prayer. Is it any wonder that Satan does his utmost to snatch that weapon from the Christian, or to hinder him in the use of it?

Now how does Satan hinder prayer? By temptation to postpone or curtail it, by bringing in wandering thoughts and all sorts of distractions, or through unbelief and hopelessness. Happy is the prayer hero who, through it all, takes care to hold fast and use his weapon. Like our Lord in Gethsemane, the more violently the Enemy attacked, the more earnestly He prayed and did not cease until He had obtained the victory. After all the other parts of the armor had been named, Paul added, *"With all prayer and supplication in the Spirit"* (Eph. 6:18). Without prayer, the helmet of salvation, the shield of faith, and the sword of the Spirit, which is God's Word, have no power. All depends on prayer. May God teach us to believe this and to hold fast!

2

THE FIGHT AGAINST PRAYERLESSNESS

As soon as the Christian becomes convinced of his sin in this matter, his first thought is that he must begin to strive, with God's help, to gain the victory over it. But alas, he soon experiences that his striving is worth little, and the discouraging thought comes over him, like a wave, that such a life is not for him—he cannot continue faithfully! At conferences on the subject of prayer, held during the past years, many a minister has openly said that it seemed impossible for him to attain such a strict life.

Recently, I received a letter from a minister, well-known for his ability and devotion, in which he wrote: "As far as I am concerned, it does not seem to help me to hear too much about the life of prayer, about the strenuous exertion for which we must prepare ourselves, and about all the time and trouble and endless effort it will cost us. These things discourage me; I have heard them so often. I have time after time put them to the test, and the result has always been sadly disappointing. It does not help me to be told: 'You must pray more, and hold a closer watch over yourself, and become altogether a more earnest Christian.'"

My reply to him was as follows: "I think in all I spoke at the conference or elsewhere, I have never mentioned exertion or struggle, because I am so entirely convinced that our efforts are futile unless we first learn how to abide in Christ by a simple faith."

My correspondent said further: "The message I need is this: 'See that your relationship to your living Savior is what it ought to be. Live in His presence, rejoice in His love, rest in Him.'" A better message could not be given, if it is only rightly understood. "See that your relationship to the living Savior is what it ought to be." But this is just what will certainly make it possible for one to live the life of prayer.

We must not comfort ourselves with the thought of standing in a right relationship to the Lord Jesus while the sin of prayerlessness has power over us, and while we, along with the whole church, have to complain about our feeble lives that make us unfit to pray for ourselves, for the church, or for missions, as we ought. But if we recognize that a right relationship to the Lord Jesus includes prayer, with both the desire and power to pray according to God's will, then we have something that gives us the right to rejoice in Him and to rest in Him.

I have related this incident to point out how discouragement will naturally be the result of self-effort and will shut out all hope of improvement or victory. And this indeed is the condition of many Christians when called on to persevere in prayer as intercessors. They feel it is something entirely beyond their reach. They believe that they do not have the power for the self-sacrifice and consecration necessary for such prayer. They shrink from the effort and struggle that will, as they suppose, make them unhappy. They have tried in the power of the flesh to conquer the flesh—a wholly impossible thing. They have endeavored by Beelzebub to cast out Beelzebub—this can never happen. It is Jesus alone who can subdue the flesh and the Devil.

We have spoken of a struggle that will certainly result in disappointment and discouragement. This is the effort made in our own strength. But there is another struggle that will certainly lead to victory. The Scripture speaks of *"the good fight of faith"* (1 Tim. 6:12), that is to say, a fight that springs from and is carried on by faith. We must get right conceptions about faith and stand fast in our faith. Jesus Christ is always the Author and Finisher of our faith (Heb. 12:2). It is when we come into right relationship with Him that we can be sure of the help and power He bestows. Just as earnestly as we must, in the first place, say, "Do not strive in your own strength; cast yourself at the feet of the Lord Jesus, and wait upon Him in the sure confidence that He is with you and works in you"; so do we, in the second place, say, "Strive in prayer; let faith fill your heart; so will you be strong in the Lord and in the power of His might."

An illustration will help us to understand this. A devoted Christian woman who conducted a large Bible class with zeal and success came to see her minister quite troubled. In her earlier years she had enjoyed much blessing in the inner chamber, in fellowship with the Lord and His Word. But this had gradually been lost and, do what she would, she could not get right. The Lord had blessed her work, but the joy had gone out of her life. The minister asked what she had done to regain the lost blessedness. "I have done everything," said she, "that I can think of, but all in vain."

He then questioned her about her experience in connection with her conversion. She gave an immediate and clear answer: "At first I spared no pains in my attempt to become better and to free myself from sin, but it was all useless. At last I began to understand that I must lay aside all my efforts, and simply trust the Lord Jesus to bestow on me His life and peace, and He did it."

"Why then," said the minister, "do you not try this again? As you go to your inner chamber, however cold and dark your heart may be, do not try in your own might to force yourself into the right attitude. Bow before Him, and tell Him that He sees in what a sad state you are and that your only hope is in Him. Trust Him with a childlike trust to have mercy upon you, and wait upon Him. In such a trust you are in a right relationship to Him. You have nothing; He has everything." Some time later she told the minister that his advice had helped her. She had learned that faith in the love of the Lord Jesus is the only method of getting into fellowship with God in prayer.

Do you begin to see, my reader, that there are two kinds of warfare— the first when we seek to conquer prayerlessness in our own strength? In that case, my advice to you is: "Give over your restlessness and effort; fall helpless at the feet of the Lord Jesus. He will speak the word, and your soul will live." If you have done this, then, second, comes the message: "This is but the beginning of everything. It will require deep earnestness and the exercise of all your power and a watchfulness of the entire heart—eager to detect the least backsliding. Above all, it will require a surrender to a life of self-sacrifice that God really desires to see in us and which He will work out for us."

3

HOW TO BE DELIVERED
FROM PRAYERLESSNESS

The greatest stumbling block in the way of victory over prayerlessness is the secret feeling that we will never obtain the blessing of being delivered from it. We have often put forth effort in this direction, but in vain. Old habits and the power of the flesh, our surroundings with their attractions, have been too strong for us. What good is it to attempt that which our heart assures us is out of our reach? The change needed in the entire life is too great and too difficult. If the question is asked, "Is a change possible?" our sighing heart says, "Alas, for me it is entirely impossible!" Do you know why that reply comes? It is simply because you have received the call to prayer as the voice of Moses and as a command of the law. Moses and his law have never yet given anyone the power to obey.

Do you really long for the courage to believe that deliverance from a prayerless life is possible for you and may become a reality? Then you must learn the great lesson that such a deliverance is included in the redemption that is in Christ Jesus, that it is one of the blessings of the new covenant that God Himself will impart to you through Christ Jesus. As you begin to understand this, you will find that the exhortation, *"Pray without ceasing"* (1 Thess. 5:17) conveys a new meaning. Hope begins to spring up in your heart that the Spirit—who has been bestowed on you to cry constantly, *"Abba, Father"* (Gal. 4:6)—will make a true life of prayer possible for you. Then you will hearken, not in the spirit of discouragement, but in the gladness of hope, to the voice that calls you to repentance.

Many a one has turned to his inner chamber, under bitter self-accusation that he has prayed so little, and has resolved for the future to live in a different manner. Yet no blessing has come; there was not the strength to continue faithfully, and the call to repentance had no power, because his eyes had not been fixed on the Lord Jesus. If he had only understood, he would have said, "Lord, you see how cold and dark my heart is; I know that I must pray, but I feel I cannot do so. I lack the urgency and desire to pray."

He did not know that at that moment the Lord Jesus in His tender love was looking down upon him and saying: "You cannot pray; you feel that all is cold and dark: why not give yourself over into My hands? Only believe that I am ready to help you in prayer. I long greatly to shed My love abroad in your heart, so that you, in the consciousness of weakness, may confidently rely on Me to bestow the grace of prayer. Just as I will cleanse you from all other sins, so also will I deliver you from the sin of prayerlessness—only do not seek the victory in your own strength. Bow before Me as one who expects everything from his Savior. Let your soul keep silence before Me, however sad you feel your state to be. Be assured of this—I will teach you how to pray."

Many a one will acknowledge, "I see my mistake. I had not thought that the Lord Jesus must deliver and cleanse me from this sin also. I had not understood that He was with me every day in the inner chamber, in His great love ready to keep and bless me, however sinful and guilty I felt myself to be. I had not supposed that just as He will give all other graces in answer to prayer, so, above all and before all, He will bestow the grace of a praying heart. What folly to think that all other blessings must come from Him, but that prayer, on which everything else depends, must be obtained by personal effort! Thank God I begin to comprehend that the Lord Jesus is Himself in the inner chamber watching over me and holding Himself responsible to teach me how to approach the Father. He only demands this: that I, with childlike confidence, wait upon Him and glorify Him."

Brothers and sisters, have we not seriously forgotten this truth? From a defective spiritual life, nothing better can be expected than a defective prayer life. It is vain for us, with our defective spiritual life, to endeavor to pray more or better. It is an impossibility. Nothing less is necessary than that we should experience that he who is in Christ Jesus *"is a new creature: old things are passed away; behold, all things are become new"* (2 Cor. 5:17). This is literally true for the man who understands and experiences what it is to be in Jesus Christ.

Our whole relationship to the Lord Jesus must be a new thing. I must believe in His infinite love, which really longs to have communion with me every moment and to keep me in the enjoyment of His fellowship. I must believe in His divine power, which has conquered sin and will truly keep me from it. I must believe in Him who, as the great Intercessor, through the Spirit, will inspire each member of His body with joy and power for communion with God in prayer. My prayer life must be brought entirely under the control of Christ and His love. Then, for the first time, will prayer become what it really is, the natural and joyous breathing of the spiritual life, by which the heavenly atmosphere is inhaled and then exhaled in prayer.

Do you not see that, just as this faith possesses us, the call to a life of prayer that pleases God will be a welcome call? The cry, "Repent of the sin of prayerlessness," will not be responded to by a sigh of helplessness or by the unwillingness of the flesh. The voice of the Father will be heard as He sets before us a widely opened door and receives us into blessed fellowship with Himself. When we pray for the Spirit's help, it will no longer be in the fear that prayer is too great an effort for us. Instead, we will simply fall down at the Lord's feet in our weakness. There we will find the victory and power that comes from His love.

The question may arise in our minds: "Will this continue?" And with it the fear comes: "You know how often you have tried and been disappointed." But faith will find its strength, not in the thought of what you will or do, but in the unchanging faithfulness and love of Christ, who has assured you, once again, that those who wait on Him will not be ashamed.

If fear and hesitation still remain, I pray that by the mercies of God in Jesus Christ, and by the unspeakable faithfulness of His tender love, you dare to cast yourselves at His feet. Only believe with your whole heart that there is deliverance from the sin of prayerlessness. *"If we confess our sins, he is faithful and just to forgive us our sins, and to cleanse us from all unrighteousness"* (1 John 1:9). In His blood and grace there is complete deliverance from all unrighteousness and from all prayerlessness. Praise be His name forever!

How Deliverance from Prayerlessness May Continue

What we have said about deliverance from the sin of prayerlessness also applies to the question: "How may the experience of deliverance be maintained?" Redemption is not granted to us piecemeal, or as something that we may make use of from time to time. It is bestowed as a fullness of grace stored up in the Lord Jesus, which may be enjoyed in a new fellowship with Him every day. It is so necessary that this great truth should be driven home and fastened in our minds that I will once more mention it. Nothing can preserve you from carelessness, or make it possible for you to persevere in living, powerful prayer, except a daily close fellowship with Jesus our Lord.

He said to His disciples: *"Ye believe in God, believe also in me....Believe me that I am in the Father, and the Father in me....He that believeth on me, the works that I do shall he do also; and greater works than these shall he do"* (John 14:1, 11–12). The Lord wished to teach His disciples that all they had learned from the Old Testament concerning the power and holiness and love of God must now be transferred to Him. They must not believe merely in certain written documents but in Him personally. They had to believe that He was in the Father, and the Father in Him, in such a sense that they had one life, one glory. All that they knew about Christ they would find in God. He laid much emphasis on this because it was only through such a faith in Him and His divine glory that they could do the works that He did, or even greater works. This faith would lead them to know that just as Christ and the Father are one, so also they were in Christ and Christ was in them.

It is this intimate, spiritual, personal, uninterrupted relationship to the Lord Jesus that manifests itself powerfully in our lives, and especially in our prayer lives. Let us consider this and see what it means: that all the glorious attributes of God are in our Lord Jesus Christ. Think of the following.

1. The omnipresence of God. His presence fills the world and every moment is present in everything. Just as it is with the Father, so now our Lord Jesus is everywhere present, above all with each of His redeemed ones. This is one of the greatest and most important lessons that our faith must learn. We can clearly understand this from the example of our Lord's disciples. What was the special privilege of these disciples, who were always in fellowship with Him? It was uninterrupted enjoyment of the presence of the Lord Jesus. It was because of this they were so sorrowful at the thought of His death. They would be deprived of that presence. He would no longer be with them. How, under these circumstances, did the Lord Jesus comfort them? He promised that the Holy Spirit from heaven would so work in them a sense of the fullness of His life and of His personal presence that

He would be even more intimately near and have more unbroken fellowship with them than they had ever experienced while He was upon earth.

This great promise is now the inheritance of every believer, although so many of them know so little about it. Jesus Christ, in His divine personality, in that eternal love that led Him to the cross, longs to have fellowship with us every moment of the day and to keep us in the enjoyment of that fellowship. This ought to be explained to every new convert: "The Lord loves you so much that He would have you near Him without a break, that you may experience His love." This is what every believer must learn who has felt his powerlessness for a life of prayer, of obedience, and of holiness. This alone will give us power as intercessors to conquer the world and to win souls out of it for our Lord.

2. The omnipotence of God. How wonderful is God's power! We see it in creation; we see it in the wonders of redemption recorded in the Old Testament. We see it in the wonderful works of Christ that the Father wrought in Him, and above all in His resurrection from the dead. We are called on to believe in the Son, just as we believe in the Father. Yes, the Lord Jesus, who in His love is so unspeakably near us, is the Almighty One with whom nothing is impossible. Whatever may be in our hearts or flesh that will not submit to us, He can and will conquer. Everything that is promised in God's Word, all that is our inheritance as children of the new covenant, the Almighty Jesus can bestow upon us. If I bow before Him in my inner chamber, then I am in contact with the eternal, unchanging power of God. If I commit myself for the day to the Lord Jesus, then I may rest assured that it is His eternal almighty power that has taken me under its protection and that will accomplish everything for me.

Oh, if we would only take time for the inner chamber so that we might experience in full reality the presence of this Almighty Jesus! What a blessedness would be ours through faith! An unbroken fellowship with an omnipotent and almighty Lord.

3. The holy love of God. This means that He, with His whole heart, offers all His divine attributes for our service and is prepared to impart Himself to us. Christ is the revelation of His love. He is the Son of His love, the gift of His love, the power of His love. This Jesus has sought on the cross to give an overwhelming proof of His love in His death and bloodshed, so as to make it impossible for us not to believe in that love. It is this Jesus who comes to meet us in the inner chamber and gives the positive assurance that unbroken fellowship with Him is our inheritance and will, through Him, become our experience. The holy love of God that sacrificed everything to conquer sin and bring it to nothing, comes to us in Christ to save us from every sin.

Brothers and sisters, take time to think over that word of our Lord: *"Ye believe in God, believe also in me"* (John 14:1). *"Believe me that I am in the Father....And ye in me, and I in you"* (vv. 11, 20). That is the secret of the life of prayer. Take time in the inner chamber to bow down and worship, and wait on Him until He unveils Himself and takes possession of you and goes out with you to show how a man may live and walk in abiding fellowship with an unseen Lord.

Do you long to know how you may always experience deliverance from the sin of prayerlessness? Here you have the secret. Believe in the Son of God, and give Him time in the inner chamber to reveal Himself in His ever present nearness, as the Eternal and Almighty One, the Eternal Love who watches over you. You will experience what, up until now, you have perhaps not known—that it has not entered into the heart of man what God can do for those who love Him. (See 1 Cor. 2:9.)

4

THE BLESSING OF VICTORY

If now we are delivered from the sin of prayerlessness and understand how this deliverance may continue to be experienced, what will be the fruit of our liberty? He who sees this correctly will, with renewed earnestness and perseverance, seek after this liberty. His life and experience will indeed be an evidence that he has obtained something of unspeakable worth. He will be a living witness of the blessing which victory has brought. Consider the following.

1. The blessedness of unbroken fellowship with God. Think of the confidence in the Father that will take the place of the reproach and self-condemnation that was the earlier characteristic of our lives. Think of the

235

deep consciousness that God's almighty grace has effected something in us, to prove that we really bear His image and are fitted for a life of communion with Him and are prepared to glorify Him. Think how we, notwithstanding our conviction of our nothingness, may live as true children of a King, in communion with their Father, and may manifest something of the character of our Lord Jesus in the holy fellowship with His Father that He had when on earth. Think how in the inner chamber the hour of prayer may become the happiest time in the whole day for us, and how God may use us to take a share in the carrying out of His plans, and make us fountains of blessing for the world around us.

2. The power that we may have for the work to which we are called. The preacher will learn to receive his message directly from God, through the power of the Holy Spirit, and to deliver it in that power to the congregation. He will know where he can be filled with the love and zeal that will enable him, in his rounds of pastoral visiting, to meet and help each individual in a spirit of tender compassion. He will be able to say with Paul, "*I can do all things through Christ which strengtheneth me*" (Phil. 4:13). "*We are more than conquerors through him that loved us*" (Rom. 8:37). "*We are ambassadors for Christ…we pray you in Christ's stead, be ye reconciled to God*" (2 Cor. 5:20). These are no vain dreams or pictures of a foolish imagination. God has given us Paul as an illustration, so that, however we may differ from him in gifts or calling, yet in inner experience we may know the all-sufficiency of grace that can do all things for us as it did for him.

3. The prospect that opens before us for the future—to be consecrated to take part as intercessors in the great work of bearing on our hearts the need of the entire church and world. Paul sought to encourage men to pray for all saints, and he tells us what a conflict he had for those who had not yet seen his face. In his personal presence he was subject to conditions of time and place, but in the Spirit he had power in the name of Christ to pray for blessing on those who had not yet heard of the Savior. In addition to his life in connection with men here on earth, far or near, he lived another, a heavenly life—one of love and of a wonderful power in prayer which he continually exercised. We can hardly form a conception of the power God will bestow, if only we get freed from the sin of prayerlessness and pray with the daring that reaches heaven and brings down blessing in the almighty name of Christ.

What a prospect! Minister and missionaries brought by God's grace to pray, let us say twice as much as formerly, with twofold faith and joy! What a difference it would make in the preaching, in the prayer meeting, in the fellowship with others! What a gentle power would come down in an inner chamber, sanctified by communion with God and His love in Christ! What an influence would be exercised on believers, in urging them forward to the work of intercession! How greatly this influence would be felt in the church and among the heathen! What power might be exercised over ministers of other churches, and who knows how God might use us for His church throughout the whole world! Is it not worthwhile to sacrifice everything, and to beseech God without ceasing to give us real and full victory over the prayerlessness that has covered us with such shame?

Why do I now write these things and extol so highly the blessedness of victory over *"the sin which doth so easily beset us"* (Heb. 12:1) and that has so terribly robbed us of the power that God has intended for us? I can give an answer. I know all too well what low thoughts we have concerning the promises and the power of God and how prone we are always to backslide, to limit God's power, and to deem it impossible for Him to do greater things than we have seen. It is a glorious thing to get to know God in a new way in the inner chamber. That, however, is but the beginning. It is something still greater and more glorious to know God as the All-sufficient One and to wait on His Spirit to open our hearts and minds wide to receive the great things, the new things that He really longs to bestow on those who wait for Him.

God's object is to encourage faith and to make His children and servants see that they must take trouble to understand and rely upon the unspeakable greatness and omnipotence of God, so that they may take literally and in a childlike spirit this word: *"Unto him that is able to do exceeding abundantly above all that we ask or think...be glory...throughout all ages"* (Eph. 3:20–21). Oh, that we knew what a great and glorious God we have!

Someone may ask: "Couldn't this note of certain victory become a snare and lead to levity and pride?" Undoubtedly. What is the highest and best on earth is always liable to abuse. How, then, can we be saved from this? Through nothing so surely as through true prayer, which brings us into real contact with God. The holiness of God, sought for in persistent prayer, will cover our sinfulness. The omnipotence and greatness of God will make us feel our nothingness. Fellowship with God in Jesus Christ will lead us to the experience that there is no good thing in us, and that we can have fellowship with God only as our faith becomes a humbling of ourselves as Christ humbled Himself and we truly live in Him as He is in the Father.

Prayer is not merely coming to God to ask something from Him. It is, above all, fellowship with God and being brought under the power of His holiness and love, until He takes possession of us and stamps our entire nature with the lowliness of Christ, which is the secret of all true worship.

Yes, it is in Christ Jesus that we draw near to the Father as those who have died with Christ and are entirely done with their own lives, as those in whom He lives and whom He enables to say, *"Christ liveth in me"* (Gal. 2:20). What we have said about the work that the Lord Jesus does in us to deliver us from prayerlessness is true not only of the beginning of the life of prayer, and of the joy which a new experience of power to pray brings us; it is true for the whole life of prayer all the day long. *"Through him"* we have access to the Father (Eph. 2:18). In this always, as in the whole spiritual life, *"Christ is all"* (Col. 3:11). *"They saw no man, save Jesus only"* (Matt. 17:8).

May God strengthen us to a belief that there is certain victory prepared for us and that the blessing will be what the heart of man has not conceived! God will do this for those who love Him.

This does not come to us all at once. God has great patience with His children. He bears with us in our slow progress with Fatherly patience. Let each child of God rejoice in all that God's Word promises. The stronger our faith, the more earnestly will we persevere to the end.

The More Abundant Life

Our Lord spoke this word concerning the more abundant life when He said that He had come to give His life for His sheep: *"I am come that they might have life, and that they might have it more abundantly"* (John 10:10). A man may have life, and yet, through lack of nourishment, or through illness, there may be no abundance of life or power. This was the distinction between the Old Testament and the New. In the former there was indeed life, under the law, but not the abundance of grace of the New Testament. Christ had given life to His disciples, but they could receive the abundant life only through His resurrection and the gift of the Holy Spirit.

All true Christians have received life from Christ. The greater portion of them, however, know nothing about the more abundant life that He is willing to bestow. Paul speaks constantly of this. He said about himself that the grace of God was *"exceeding abundant"* (1 Tim. 1:14). *"I can do all things through Christ which strengtheneth me"* (Phil 4:13). *"Thanks be unto God, which always causeth us to triumph in Christ"* (2 Cor. 2:14). *"We are more than conquerors through him that loved us"* (Rom. 8:37).

We have spoken of the sin of prayerlessness and the means of deliverance and how to be kept free from this sin. What has been said in these points is all included in that expression of Christ: *"I am come that they might have life, and that they might have it more abundantly."* It is of the utmost importance in order for us to understand this more abundant life, that we clearly see that for a true life of prayer nothing less is necessary than walking in an ever increasing experience of that overflow life.

It is possible for us to begin this conflict against prayerlessness depending on Christ, and looking to Him to be assisted and kept in it, and yet to be disappointed. This is the case when prayerlessness is looked upon as the one sin against which we must strive. It must be recognized as part of the whole life of the flesh and as closely connected with other sins that spring from the same source. We forget that the entire flesh with all its affections, whether manifested in the body or soul, must be regarded as crucified and be handed over to death. We must not be satisfied with a feeble life, but must seek for an abundant life. We must surrender ourselves entirely, that the Spirit may take full possession of us. We must manifest that abundant life so completely that there may come an entire transformation in our spiritual being, by which the complete mastery of Christ and the Spirit is recognized.

What is it, then, that especially constitutes this abundant life? We cannot too often repeat it: the abundant life is nothing less than the full Jesus having the full mastery over our entire beings, through the power of the Holy Spirit. As the Spirit makes known in us the fullness of Christ, and the abundant life that He gives, it will be chiefly in three aspects.

1. As the Crucified One. Not merely as the One who died for us, to atone for our sins, but as He who has taken us up with Himself on the cross to die with Him, and who now works out in us the power of His cross and death. You have the true fellowship with Christ when you can say, "*I am crucified with Christ*' (Gal. 2:20); He, the Crucified One, lives in me." The feelings and the disposition that were in Him, His lowliness and obedience even to the death of the cross—these were what He referred to when He said of the Holy Spirit, "*He shall take of mine, and shall show it unto you*" (John 16:15)—not as an instruction, but as childlike participation of the same life that was in Him.

Do you desire that the Holy Spirit should take full possession of you, so as to cause the crucified Christ to dwell in you? Understand then that this is just the end for which He has been given, and this He will surely accomplish in all who yield themselves to Him.

2. As the Risen One. The Scripture frequently mentions the resurrection in connection with the wonder-working power of God, by which Christ was raised from the dead, and from which comes the assurance of "*the exceeding greatness of his power to us-ward who believe, according to the working of his mighty power, which he wrought in Christ, when he raised him from the dead*" (Eph. 1:19–20). Do not pass hastily over these words. Turn back and read them once more, and learn the great lesson that, however power-less and weak you feel, the omnipotence of God is working in you; and, if you only believe, He will give you in daily life a share in the resurrection of His Son.

Yes, the Holy Spirit can fill you with the joy and victory of the resurrection of Christ, as the power of your daily life, here in the midst of the trials and temptations of this world. Let the Cross humble you to death. God will work out the heavenly life in you through His Spirit. Ah, how little have we understood that it is entirely the work of the Holy Spirit to make us partakers of the crucified and risen Christ, and to conform us to His life and death!

3. As the Glorified One. The glorified Christ is He who baptizes with the Holy Spirit. When the Lord Jesus Himself was baptized with the Spirit, it was because He had humbled Himself and offered Himself to take part in John's baptism of repentance—a baptism for sinners—in Jordan. Even so, when He took upon Himself the work of redemption, He received the Holy Spirit to fit Him for His work from that hour until on the cross He *"offered himself without spot to God"* (Heb. 9:14). Do you desire that this glorified Christ should baptize you with the Holy Spirit? Offer yourself then to Him for His service, to further His great work of making known to sinners the love of the Father.

May God help us to understand what a great thing it is to receive the Holy Spirit with power from the glorified Jesus! It means a willingness—a longing of the soul—to work for Him and, if need be, to suffer for Him. You have known and loved your Lord and have worked for Him and have had blessing in that work, but the Lord has more than that to bestow. He can so work in us, and in our brothers and sisters around us, and in the ministers of the church, by the power of the Holy Spirit, as to fill our hearts with adoring wonder.

Have you laid hold of it, my reader? The abundant life is neither more nor less than the full life of Christ as the Crucified, the Risen, the Glorified One, who baptizes with the Holy Spirit and reveals Himself in our hearts and lives as Lord of all within us.

I read not long ago an expression, "Live in what must be." Do not live in your human imagination of what is possible. Live in the Word—in the love and infinite faithfulness of the Lord Jesus. The faith that always thanks Him—not for experiences, but for the promises on which it can rely—goes on from strength to strength, still increasing in the blessed assurance that God Himself will perfect His work in us.

5

THE EXAMPLE OF OUR LORD

The connection between the prayer life and the Spirit life is close and indissoluble. It is not merely that we can receive the Spirit through prayer, but the Spirit life requires, as an indispensable thing, a continuous prayer life. I can be led continually by the Spirit only as I continually give myself to prayer.

This was very evident in the life of our Lord. A study of His life will give us a wonderful view of the power and holiness of prayer.

Consider His baptism. It was when He was baptized and prayed that heaven was opened and the Holy Spirit came down upon Him. (See Luke 3:21–22.) God desired to crown Christ's surrender of Himself to the sinner's baptism in Jordan, which was also a surrender of Himself to the sinner's death, with the gift of the Spirit for the work that He must accomplish. But this could not have taken place had He not prayed. In the fellowship of worship the Spirit was bestowed on Him to lead Him out into the desert to spend forty days there in prayer and fasting. Turn to Mark 1:32–33, 35:

> *And at even, when the sun did set, they brought unto him all that were diseased, and them that were possessed with devils. And all the city was gathered together at the door....And in the morning, rising up a great while before day, he went out, and departed into a solitary place, and there prayed.*

The work of the day and evening had exhausted Him. In His healing of the sick and casting out devils, power had gone out of Him. While others still slept, He went away to pray and to renew His strength in communion with His Father. He had need of this; otherwise He would not have been ready for the new day. The holy work of delivering souls demands constant renewal through fellowship with God.

Think again of the calling of the apostles as given in Luke 6:12–13:

> *And it came to pass in those days, that he went out into a mountain to pray, and continued all night in prayer to God. And when it was day, he called unto him his disciples: and of them he chose twelve, whom also he named apostles.*

Is it not clear that if anyone wishes to do God's work, he must take time for fellowship with Him, to receive His wisdom and power? The dependence and helplessness of which this is an evidence open the way and give God the opportunity of revealing His power. How great was the importance of the choosing of the apostles for Christ's own work, for the early church, and for all time! It had God's blessing and seal; the stamp of prayer was on it.

Read Luke 9:18, 20: *"And it came to pass, as he was alone praying, his disciples were with him: and he asked them, saying, Whom say the people that I am?...Peter answering said, The Christ of God."* The Lord had intended that the Father might reveal to them who He was, and for this purpose He had chosen the twelve apostles. (See John 17:6–8.) After a night of prayer, *"he chose twelve, whom also he named apostles"* (Luke 6:13). It was one of these, Peter, who said, *"Thou art the Christ, the Son of the living God"* (Matt. 16:16); and the Lord then said, *"Flesh and blood hath not revealed it unto thee, but my Father which is in heaven"* (v. 17). This great confession was the fruit of prayer.

Read further:

> He took Peter and John and James, and went up into a mountain to pray. And as he prayed, the fashion of his countenance was altered.... And there came a voice out of the cloud, saying, This is my beloved Son: hear him. (Luke 9:28–29, 35)

Christ had desired that, for the strengthening of their faith, God might give them an assurance from heaven that He was the Son of God. Prayer obtained for our Lord Jesus Himself, as well as for His disciples, what happened on the Mount of Transfiguration.

Does it not become still more clear that what God wills to accomplish on earth needs prayer as its indispensable condition? And there is but one way for Christ and believers. A heart and mouth open toward heaven in believing prayer will certainly not be put to shame.

Read Luke 11:1: *"As he was praying in a certain place, when he ceased, one of his disciples said unto him, Lord, teach us to pray."* And then He gave them that inexhaustible prayer: *"Our Father which art in heaven"* (v. 2). In this He showed what was going on in His heart, when He prayed that God's name might be hallowed, and His kingdom come, and His will be done, and all of this *"as in heaven, so in earth"* (v. 2). How will this ever come to pass?

Through prayer. This prayer has been uttered through the ages by count-less millions, to their unspeakable comfort. But do not forget this—it was born out of the prayer of our Lord Jesus. He had been praying, and there-fore was able to give that glorious answer.

Read John 14:16: *"I will pray the Father, and he shall give you another Comforter."* The entire dispensation of the New Testament, with the won-derful outpouring of the Holy Spirit, is the outcome of the prayer of the Lord Jesus. In answer to the prayer of the Lord Jesus, and later of His dis-ciples, the Holy Spirit will surely come. But it will be in answer to prayer like that of our Lord, in which He took time to be alone with God and in that prayer offered Himself wholly to God.

Read John 17, the most holy High Priestly Prayer! Here the Son prays first for Himself, that the Father will glorify Him by giving Him power for the Cross, by raising Him from the dead, by setting Him at His right hand. These great things could not take place except through prayer. Prayer had the power to obtain them.

Afterward He prayed for His disciples, that the Father might preserve them from the Evil One, might keep them from the world, and might sanctify them. And then, further, He prayed for all those who through their word might believe on Him, that all might be one in love, even as the Father and the Son were One. This prayer gives us a glimpse into the won-derful relationship between the Father and the Son and teaches us that all the blessings of heaven come continually through the prayer of Him who is at God's right hand and ever prays for us. But it teaches us, also, that all these blessings must in the same manner be desired and asked for by us. The whole nature and glory of God's blessings consist in this: they must be obtained in answer to prayer, by hearts entirely surrendered to Him, and hearts that believe in the power of prayer.

Now we come to the most remarkable instance of all. In Gethsemane we see that our Lord, according to His constant habit, consulted and arranged with the Father the work He had to do on earth. First He besought Him in agony and bloody sweat to let the cup pass from Him. When He under-stood that this could not be, then He prayed for strength to drink it, and surrendered Himself with the words: *"Thy will be done"* (Matt. 26:42). He was able to meet the enemy full of courage, and in the power of God He gave Himself over to the death of the cross. He had prayed.

Oh, why is it that God's children have so little faith in the glory of prayer as the great power for subjecting our own wills to that of God, as well as for the confident carrying out of the work of God in spite of our great weakness? If only we might learn from our Lord Jesus how impossible it is to walk with God, to obtain God's blessing or leading, or to do His work joyously and fruitfully, apart from close, unbroken fellowship with Him who is ever a living fountain of spiritual life and power!

Let every Christian think over this simple study of the prayer life of our Lord Jesus and endeavor from God's Word to learn what the life is that the Lord Jesus Christ bestows upon him and supports in him. It is nothing else than a life of daily prayer. Let each minister especially recognize how entirely vain it is to attempt to do the work of our Lord in any other way than that in which He did it. Let us, as workers, begin to believe that we are set free from the ordinary business of the world that we may, above everything, have time, in our Savior's name and with His Spirit and in oneness with Him, to ask for and obtain blessing for the world.

6

THE HOLY SPIRIT
AND PRAYER

I s it not sad that our thoughts about the Holy Spirit are so often coupled with grief and self-reproach? Yet He bears the name of Comforter and is given to lead us to find in Christ our chief delight and joy. But there is something still more sad: He who dwells within us to comfort us is often grieved by us because we will not permit Him to accomplish His work of love. What a cause of inexpressible pain to the Holy Spirit is all this prayerlessness in the church. It is the cause also of the low vitality and utter impotence that are so often found in us, because we are not prepared to permit the Holy Spirit to lead us.

God grant that our meditation on the work of the Holy Spirit may be a matter for rejoicing and for the strengthening of our faith!

The Holy Spirit is the Spirit of prayer. He is definitely called by this name in Zechariah 12:10: "*The spirit of grace and of supplications.*" Twice in Paul's Epistles there is a remarkable reference to Him in the matter of prayer. "*Ye have received the Spirit of adoption, whereby we cry, Abba, Father*" (Rom. 8:15). "*God hath sent forth the Spirit of his Son into your hearts, crying, Abba, Father*" (Gal. 4:6). Have you ever meditated on these words, "*Abba, Father*"? In that name our Savior offered His greatest prayer to the Father, accompanied by the entire surrender and sacrifice of His life and love. The Holy Spirit is given for the express purpose of teaching us, from the very beginning of our Christian life onward, to utter that word in childlike trust and surrender. In one of these passages we read, "we cry"; in the other, "He cries." What a wonderful blending of the divine and human cooperation in prayer. What a proof that God—if I may say so—has done His utmost to make prayer as natural and effectual as though it were the cry of a child to an earthly father, as he says, "*Abba, Father.*"

Is it not proof that the Holy Spirit is to a great extent a stranger in the church, when prayer, for which God has made such provisions, is regarded as a task and a burden? And does this not teach us to seek for the deep root of prayerlessness in our ignorance of, and disobedience to, the divine Instructor whom the Father has commissioned to teach us to pray?

If we desire to understand this truth still more clearly we must notice what is written in Romans 8:26–27:

> *Likewise the Spirit also helpeth our infirmities: for we know not what we should pray for as we ought: but the Spirit itself maketh intercession for us with groanings which cannot be uttered. And he that searcheth the hearts knoweth what is the mind of the Spirit, because he maketh intercession for the saints according to the will of God.*

Is it not clear from this that the Christian, if left to himself, does not know how to pray? God has stooped to meet us in this helplessness of ours by giving us the Holy Spirit Himself to pray for us. His operation is deeper than our thoughts or feelings and is noticed and answered by God.

Our first work, therefore, ought to be to come into God's presence, not with our ignorant prayers, not with many words and thoughts, but in the confidence that the divine work of the Holy Spirit is being carried on within us. This confidence will encourage reverence and quietness and will also enable us, in dependence on the help that the Spirit gives, to lay our desires and heart needs before God. The great lesson for every prayer is to see to it, first of all, that you commit yourself to the leading of the Holy Spirit and, with entire dependence on Him, give Him the first place. For through Him your prayers will have a value you cannot imagine, and through Him also you will learn to speak out your desires in the name of Christ.

What a protection this faith would be against deadness and despondency in the inner chamber! Only think of it! In every prayer the Triune God takes a part: the Father who hears, the Son in whose name we pray, the Spirit who prays for us and in us. How important it is that we should be in right relationship to the Holy Spirit and understand His work!

The following points demand serious consideration.

1. Let us firmly believe, as a divine reality, that the Spirit of God's Son, the Holy Spirit, is in us. Do not imagine that you know this and have no need to consider it. It is a thought so great and divine that it can gain an entrance to our hearts and be retained there only by the Holy Spirit Himself. *"The Spirit itself beareth witness with our spirit"* (Rom. 8:16). Our position ought to be that of reckoning with full assurance of faith that our heart is His temple, yes, that He dwells within us and rules soul and body. Let us thank God heartily as often as we pray that we have His Spirit in us to teach us to pray. Thanksgiving will draw our hearts out to God and keep us engaged with Him; it will take our attention from ourselves and give the Spirit room in our hearts.

Oh, it is no wonder that we have been prayerless and have felt this work too heavy for us, if we have sought to hold fellowship with the Eternal God apart from His Spirit, who reveals the Father and the Son.

2. In the practice of this faith, in the certainty that the Spirit dwells and works in us, there must also be the understanding of all that He desires to accomplish in us. His work in prayer is closely connected with His other work. We have seen in an earlier chapter that His first and greatest work is to reveal Christ in His omnipresent love and power. So the Holy Spirit will in prayer constantly remind us of Christ, of His blood and name, as the sure ground of our being heard.

He will, further, as *"the spirit of holiness"* (Rom. 1:4), teach us to recognize, and hate, and be done with sin. He is the Spirit of light and wisdom (Eph. 1:17) who leads us into the heavenly secret of God's overflowing grace. He is the Spirit of love and power (see 2 Tim. 1:7) who teaches us to witness for Christ and to labor for souls with tender pity. The more closely I associate all these blessings with the Spirit, the more I will be convinced of His deity and will be ready to commit myself to His guidance, as I give myself to prayer. What a different life mine would be if I knew the Spirit as the Spirit of prayer!

There is still another thing that I need constantly to learn afresh:

3. The Spirit desires to have full possession of my life. We pray for more of the Spirit, and we pray well, if alongside this prayer we set the truth that the Spirit wants more of me. The Spirit would possess me entirely. Just as my soul has my whole body for its dwelling place and service, so the Holy Spirit wants to have my body and soul as His dwelling place, entirely under His control. No one can continue long and earnestly in prayer without beginning to perceive that the Spirit is gently leading to an entirely new consecration, of which previously he knew nothing: "I seek You with my whole heart." (See Psalm 119:2.) The Spirit will make such words more and more the motto of our lives. He will cause us to recognize that what remains in us of double-mindedness is truly sinful. He will reveal Christ as the Almighty Deliverer from all sin, who is always near to defend us. He will lead us in this way in prayer, to forget ourselves and make us willing to offer ourselves for training as intercessors, to whom God can entrust the carrying out of His plans, and who day and night cry to Him to avenge His church of her adversary.

God help us to know the Spirit and to reverence Him as the Spirit of prayer!

7

SIN VERSUS
THE HOLINESS OF GOD

To understand grace, to understand Christ properly, we must understand what sin is. And how otherwise can we come to this understanding than through the light of God and His Word? Come with me to the beginning of the Bible. See there man created by God, after His image, and pronounced by his Creator to be very good. Then sin entered as rebellion against God. Adam was driven out of Paradise and was brought, along with the untold millions of following generations, under curse and ruin. That was the work of sin. Here we learn its nature and power.

Come further on, and see the ark of Noah on Ararat. So terrible had godlessness become among men, God saw nothing but to destroy man from off the earth. That was the work of sin.

Come once more with me to Sinai. God wished to establish His covenant with a new nation—with the people of Israel. But because of man's sinfulness, He could do this only by appearing in darkness and lightning so terrible that Moses said, "*I exceedingly fear and quake*" (Heb. 12:21). And before the end of the giving of the law, that awful message came: "*Cursed is every one that continueth not in all things which are written in the book of the law to do them*" (Gal. 3:10). It was sin which made that necessary.

Come once more with me, and this time to Calvary. There see what sin is, and the hatred and enmity with which the world cast out and crucified the Son of God. There sin reached its climax. There Christ was, by God Himself, made sin and became a curse, as the only way to destroy sin. In the agony in which He prayed in Gethsemane, that He might not drink the terrible cup, and in the agony in which on the cross, in the deep darkness of desertion, He cried out, "*My God, my God, why hast thou forsaken me?*" (Matt. 27:46), we obtain at least some faint idea of the curse and indescribable suffering which sin brings. If anything can make us hate and detest sin, it is Christ on the cross.

Come once again with me to the judgment seat of the Great Day, and see the bottomless pit of darkness wherein countless souls will be plunged under the sentence, "*Depart from me, ye cursed, into everlasting fire*" (Matt. 25:41). Oh, will not these words soften our hearts and fill us with a never-to-be-forgotten horror of sin, so that we may hate it with a perfect hatred?

And now is there anything else that can help us to understand what sin is? Yes, there is. Turn your eyes inward, and behold your own heart, and see sin there. Remember that all you have already seen of the hatefulness and godlessness of sin should teach you what sin in your own heart means; all the enmity against God, all the ruin of men, all of its inner nature of hatefulness, lie hidden in the sin you have committed. And when you acknowledge that you are a child of God and yet commit sin, allowing it sometimes to fulfill its lusts, is it not fitting that you should cry out with shame: "Woe is me, because of my sin"? *"Depart from me; for I am a sinful man, O Lord"* (Luke 5:8).

One great power of sin is that it blinds men so that they do not recognize its true character. Even the Christian himself finds an excuse in the thought that he can never be perfect and that daily sin is a necessity. He is so accustomed to the thought of sinning that he has almost lost the power and ability of mourning over sin. And yet there can be no real progress in grace apart from an increased consciousness of the sin and guilt of every transgression against God. And there cannot be a more important question than this: "How can I regain the lost tenderness of conscience and become prepared really to offer to God the sacrifice of a broken heart?"

Scripture teaches us the way. Let the Christian remember what God thinks about sin—the hatred with which His holiness burns against it, the solemn sacrifice that He made to conquer sin and deliver us from it. Let him tarry in God's presence until His holiness shines upon him, and he cries out with Isaiah: *"Woe is me! for I am undone"* (Isa. 6:5).

Let him remember the cross, and what the love of Christ had to endure there, through the unspeakable pain that sin caused Him. And let him ask if this will not teach him to hearken to the voice which says, *"Oh, do not this abominable thing that I hate"* (Jer. 44:4). Let him take time, so that the blood and love of the cross may exercise their full influence on him, and let him think of sin as nothing less than giving his hand to Satan and to his power. Is this not a terrible result of our prayerlessness and of our short and hasty tarrying before God that the true knowledge of sin is almost lost?

Let the believer think not only of what redemption has cost Christ, but also of the fact that Christ is offered to him, by the Holy Spirit, as a gift of inconceivable grace, through whom divine forgiveness and purification and renewing have taken possession of him. Then let him ask himself with what return such love should be repaid. If only time were taken to tarry in God's presence and ask such questions, the Spirit of God would accomplish His work of conviction of sin in us and would teach us to take an entirely new standpoint and would give us a new view of sin. The thought would begin to arise in our hearts that we have truly been redeemed, so that in the power of Christ we may live every day as partners in the great victory that Christ obtained over sin on the cross and manifest it in our walk.

What do you think? Do you begin to see that the sin of prayerlessness has had a more terrible effect than you thought at first? It is because of the hasty and superficial conversation with God that the sense of sin is so weak and that no motives have power to help you to hate and flee from sin as you should. Nothing, nothing, except the hidden, humble, constant fellowship with God can teach you, as a child of God, to hate sin as God wants you to hate it. Nothing, nothing but the constant nearness and unceasing power of the living Christ can make it possible for you to rightly understand what sin is and to detest it. And without this deeper understanding of sin, there will be no thought of appropriating the victory that is made possible for you in Christ Jesus and will be wrought in you by the Spirit.

O my God, cause me to know my sin and teach me to tarry before You and to wait on You until Your Spirit causes something of Your holiness to rest upon me! O my God, cause me to know my sin, and let this drive me to listen to the promise, "*Whosoever abideth in him sinneth not*" (1 John 3:6), and to expect the fulfillment from You!

The Holiness of God

It has often been said that the conception of sin and of the holiness of God has been lost in the church. In the inner chamber we have the place where we may learn again how to give God's holiness the position it should have in our faith and life. If you do not know how to spend half an hour in prayer, take up the subject of God's holiness. Bow before Him. Give yourself time, and give God also time, that He and you may come into touch with one another. It is a great work but one overflowing with great blessing.

If you wish to strengthen yourself in the practice of this Holy Presence, take up the Holy Word. Take, for instance, the book of Leviticus, and notice how God gives the command seven times in various forms: "Ye shall be holy; for I am holy." (See Leviticus 11:44, 45; 19:2; 20:7, 26; 21:8; 22:32.) Still more frequent is the expression, "*I am the* LORD *that doth sanctify you*" (Exod. 31:13). This great thought is taken over into the New Testament. Peter said, "*Be ye holy in all manner of conversation; because it is written, Be ye holy; for I am holy*" (1 Pet. 1:15–16). Paul wrote in his epistle, "*To the end he may stablish your hearts unblameable in holiness….God hath… called us…unto holiness….Faithful is he that calleth you, who also will do it*" (1 Thess. 3:13, 4:7, 5:24).

Nothing but the knowledge of God, as the Holy One, will make us holy. And how are we to obtain that knowledge of God, except in the inner chamber, our private place of prayer? It is a thing utterly impossible unless we take time and allow the holiness of God to shine on us. How can any man on earth obtain intimate knowledge of another man of remarkable wisdom, if he does not associate with him and place himself under his influence? And how can God Himself sanctify us, if we do not take time to be brought under the power of the glory of His holiness? Nowhere can we get to know the holiness of God, and come under its influence and power, except in the inner chamber. It has been well said: "No man can expect to make progress in holiness who is not often and long alone with God."

And what now is this holiness of God? It is the highest and most glorious and most all-embracing of all the attributes of God. *Holiness* is the most profound word in the Bible. It is a word that is at home in heaven. Both the Old and New Testaments tell us this. Isaiah heard the seraphs with veiled faces cry out, "*Holy, holy, holy, is the* LORD *of hosts*" (Isa. 6:3). John heard the four living creatures say, "*Holy, holy, holy, Lord God Almighty*" (Rev. 4:8). This is the highest expression of God's glory in heaven by beings who live in His immediate presence and bow low before Him. And dare we imagine that we, by thinking and reading and hearing, can understand or become partakers of the holiness of God? What folly! Oh, that we might begin to thank God that we have a place in the inner chamber, a place where we can be alone with Him, and take time for the prayer: "Let Your holiness, O Lord, shine more and more into our hearts, that they may become holy."

And let our hearts be deeply ashamed of our prayerlessness, through which we have made it impossible for God to impart His holiness to us. Let us beseech God fervently to forgive us for this sin and to allure us by

His heavenly grace and to strengthen us to have fellowship with Him, the holy God.

I have said that the meaning of the words, *the holiness of God*, is not easily expressed. But we may begin by saying that they imply the unspeakable aversion and hatred with which God regards sin. And if you wish to understand what that means, remember that He preferred to see His Son die, rather than that sin should reign. Think of the Son of God, who gave up His life rather than act in the least matter against the will of the Father. Still further, He had such a hatred of sin that He preferred to die rather than that men should be held in sin's power. That is something of the holiness of God, which is a pledge that He will do everything for us— for you and me—to deliver us from sin. Holiness is the fire of God that will consume sin in us and make us holy sacrifices, pure and acceptable before Him. (See Rom. 12:1.) It was for this reason that the Spirit came down as fire. He is the Spirit of God's holiness, the Spirit of sanctification in us.

Oh, think over the holiness of God, and bow in lowliness before Him, until your heart is filled with the assurance of what the Holy One will do for you. Take a week, if necessary, to read and reread the words of God on this great truth, until your heart is brought under the conviction: this is the glory of the inner chamber, to converse with God the Holy One, to bow in deep humility and shame before Him, because we have so despised Him and His love through our prayerlessness. There we will receive the assurance that He will again take us into fellowship with Himself. No one can expect to understand and receive the holiness of God who is not often and long alone with God.

Someone has said that the holiness of God is the expression of the unspeakable distance by which He in His righteousness is separated from us, and yet also of the unspeakable nearness in which He in His love longs to hold fellowship with us and dwell in us. Bow in humble reverence, as you think of the immeasurable distance between you and God. Bow in childlike confidence in the unspeakable desire of His love to be united with you in the deepest intimacy, and reckon most confidently on Him to reveal something of His holiness to the soul that thirsts after Him and waits upon Him and is quiet before Him.

Notice how the two sides of the holiness of God are united in the Cross. So terrible was the aversion and anger of God against our sin that Christ was left in the thick darkness, because God, when sin was laid upon Jesus, had to hide His face from Him. And yet so deep was the love of God toward us and so deep His desire to be united to us, that He spared not His Son but gave Him over to unutterable sufferings. This was so that He might receive us, in union with Christ, into His holiness, and press us to His heart as His beloved children. It was of this suffering that our Lord Jesus said, "*I sanctify myself, that they also might be sanctified through the truth*" (John 17:19). Thus He has become of God our sanctification, and we are holy in Him.

I beseech you, do not think little of the grace that you have a holy God who longs to make you holy. Do not think little of the voice of God that calls you to give time to Him in the stillness of the inner chamber, so that He may cause His holiness to rest on you. Let it be your business every day, in the secrecy of the inner chamber, to meet the holy God. You will be repaid for the trouble it may cost you. The reward will be sure and rich. You will learn to hate sin and to regard it as accursed and conquered. The new nature will give you a horror of sin. The living Jesus, the holy God, will, as Conqueror, be your power and strength. And you will begin to believe the great promise contained in 1 Thessalonians 5:23–24: "*The very God of peace sanctify you wholly.....Faithful is he that calleth you, who also will do it.*"

8

OBEDIENCE AND
THE VICTORIOUS LIFE

In opposition to sin stands obedience. *"For as by one man's disobedi-ence many were made sinners, so by the obedience of one shall many be made righteous.....Ye became the servants of righteousness"* (Rom. 5:19, 6:18). In connection with all that has been said about sin and the new life and the reception of the Holy Spirit, we must always give to obedience the place assigned to it by God.

It was because Christ humbled Himself and became obedient unto death, yes, the death of the cross, that God so highly exalted Him. (See Phil. 2:8–9.) And Paul, in this connection, exhorts us: *"Let this mind be in you, which was also in Christ Jesus"* (v. 5). We see, above everything else, that the obedience of Christ, which was so pleasing to God, must become really the characteristic of our nature and of our entire walk. Just as a servant knows that he must first obey his master in all things, so the surrender to an implicit and unquestionable obedience must become the essential characteristic of our lives.

How little this is understood by Christians! How many there are who allow themselves to be misled, and rest satisfied with the thought that sin is a necessity, that one must sin every day! It would be difficult to say how great the harm is which has been done by this mistake. It is one of the chief causes why the sin of disobedience is so little recognized. I have myself heard Christians, speaking about the cause of darkness and weakness, say, half laughingly, "Yes, it is just disobedience again." We try to get rid of a servant as speedily as possible who is habitually disobedient, but it is not regarded as anything extraordinary that a child of God should be disobedient every day. Disobedience is daily acknowledged, and yet there no turning away from it.

Is this not the reason why so much prayer for the power of the Holy Spirit is offered, and yet so few answers come? Do we not read that God has given His Holy Spirit to those who obey Him (Acts 5:32)? Every child of God has received the Holy Spirit. If he uses the measure of the Holy Spirit that he has, with the definite purpose of being obedient to the utmost, then God can and will favor him with further manifestations of the Spirit's power. But if he permits disobedience to get the upper hand, day by day, he need not wonder if his prayer for more of the Spirit remains unanswered.

We have already said that we must not forget that the Spirit desires to possess more of us. How can we wholly surrender ourselves to Him other than by being obedient? The Scripture says that we must be led by the Spirit, that we must walk by the Spirit. My right relationship to the Holy Spirit is that I allow myself to be guided and ruled by Him. Obedience is the great factor in our whole relationship to God. *"Obey my voice, and I will be your God"* (Jer. 7:23).

Mark how the Lord Jesus, on the last night, when giving His great promise about the Holy Spirit, lays emphasis on this point. *"If ye love me, keep my commandments. And I will pray the Father, and he shall give you another Comforter"* (John 14:15–16). Obedience was essential as a preparation for the reception of the Spirit. And this thought is often repeated by Him. *"He that hath my commandments, and keepeth them, he it is that loveth me: and he that loveth me shall be loved of my Father, and I will love him, and will manifest myself to him"* (v. 21). So also in verse 23: *"If a man love me, he will keep my words: and my Father will love him, and we will come unto him, and make our abode with him."* *"If ye abide in me, and my words abide in you, ye shall ask what ye will, and it shall be done unto you"* (John 15:7). *"If ye keep my commandments, ye shall abide in my love"* (v. 10). *"Ye are my friends, if ye do whatsoever I command you"* (v. 14).

Can words more plainly or impressively declare that the whole life, following the resurrection of Christ, depends on obedience? That is the Spirit of Christ. He lived to do not His own will, but the will of the Father. And He cannot with His Spirit make an abiding home in the heart of one who does not surrender himself utterly to a life of obedience.

Alas, how few there are who are truly concerned because of this disobedience! How little it is believed that Christ really asks for and expects this from us, because He has undertaken to make it possible for us! How much is it manifested in prayer, or walk, or in the depths of the soul life, that we really endeavor to be well pleasing to the Lord in all things? We say too little in regard to our disobedience, "I will be sorry for my sin."

But is obedience really possible? It is certain for the man who believes that Christ Jesus is his sanctification and relies on Him. Just as it is possible for a man to see that Christ can at once forgive his sin, it is also possible to have faith that in Christ is a sure promise of power to accomplish all that God desires from His child. Just as through faith we found the fullness of forgiveness, so through a new act of faith we obtain a real deliverance from the dominion of the sin which has so easily beset. Then the abiding blessing of the keeping power of Christ becomes ours. This faith obtains a new insight into promises, the meaning of which was not previously understood: "*The God of peace…make you perfect in every good work to do his will, working in you that which is wellpleasing in his sight, through Jesus Christ*" (Heb. 13:20–21). "*Unto him that is able to keep you from falling…be glory and majesty*" (Jude 24–25). "*Give diligence to make your calling and election sure: for if ye do these things, ye shall never fall*" (2 Pet. 1:10). "*To the end he may stablish your hearts unblameable in holiness*" (1 Thess. 3:13). "*But the Lord is faithful, who shall stablish you, and keep you from evil*" (2 Thess. 3:3).

The soul must understand that the fulfillment of these and other promises is secured for us in Christ, and that, as certainly as the forgiveness of sin is assured to us in Him, so also is power against new or fresh attacks of sin assured to us. Then for the first time is the lesson learned accurately that faith can confidently rely upon a full Christ and His abiding protection.

This faith sheds a wholly new light on the life of obedience. Christ holds Himself responsible to work this out in me every moment, if I only trust Him for it. Then I begin to understand the important phrase with which Paul begins and closes his epistle to the Romans, "The obedience of faith." (See Romans 1:5, 16:26.) Faith brings me to the Lord Jesus, not only to obtain the forgiveness of sin, but also that I may enjoy the power that will make it possible for me, as a child of God, to abide in Him and to be numbered among His obedient children. As His obedient children, it is written that He who has called them is holy, so they also may be holy in all manner of conversation. (See 1 Pet. 1:15.) Everything depends on whether or not I believe on the whole Christ, that with the fullness of His grace He will, not now and then but every moment, be the strength of my life. Such faith will lead to an obedience which will enable me to "*walk worthy of the Lord unto all pleasing, being fruitful in every good work…strengthened with all might, according to his glorious power*" (Col. 1:10–11).

The soul that feeds on such promises will experience, instead of the disobedience of self-effort, what the obedience of faith means. All such promises have their measure, their certainty, and their strength in the living Christ.

The Victorious Life

In another chapter, we viewed the matter chiefly from the side of our Lord Jesus. We saw that there is to be found in Him—the Crucified, the Risen, and the Glorified One who baptizes with the Holy Spirit—all that is needed for a life of abundant grace. In speaking of the victorious life, we will now look at the matter from another standpoint. We want to see how a Christian can really live as a victor. We have already said that the prayer life is not something that can be improved by itself. It is so intimately bound up with the entire spiritual life that it is only when that whole life, previously marked by lack of prayer, becomes renewed and sanctified that prayer can have its rightful place of power. We must not be satisfied with less than the victorious life to which God calls His children.

You remember how our Lord, in the seven letters to the churches in the Revelation of John, concludes with a promise to those who overcome. Take the trouble of going over that seven times repeated "him that overcometh" (see Revelation 2:7, 11, 17, 26; 3:5, 12, 21) and notice what unspeakable glorious promises are given there. And they were given even to churches like Ephesus, which had lost its first love (see Rev. 2:4), and Sardis, which had *"a name that thou livest, [but] art dead"* (Rev. 3:1); and Laodicea, with her lukewarmness and self-satisfaction. (See vv. 13–16.) If only they would repent, they would win the crown of victory. The call comes to every Christian to strive for the crown. It is impossible to be a healthy Christian, still more impossible to be a preacher in the power of God, if everything is not sacrificed to gain the victory.

The answer to the question, as to how we attain to it, is simple. All is in Christ. *"Thanks be unto God, which always causeth us to triumph in Christ"* (2 Cor. 2:14). *"In all these things we are more than conquerors through him that loved us"* (Rom. 8:37). All depends on our right relationship to Christ, our entire surrender, perfect faith, and unbroken fellowship with Him. But you wish to know how to obtain all this. Listen once more to the simple directions as to the way by which the full enjoyment of what is prepared for you in Christ may be yours. These are a new discovery of sin, a new surrender to Christ, and a new faith in the power that will make it possible for you to persevere.

1. A new discovery of sin. In Romans 3, you find described the knowledge of sin that is necessary, in repentance, for forgiveness: *"That every mouth may be stopped, and all the world may become guilty before God"* (v. 3:19). There you took your stand, you recognized your sin more or less consciously and confessed it, and you obtained mercy. But if you would lead the victorious life, something more is needed. This comes with the experience that in you, that is, in your flesh, there *"dwelleth no good thing"* (Rom. 7:18). You have a delight in the law of God after the inner man, but you see another law in your members bringing you into captivity to the law of sin and compelling you to cry out, *"O wretched man that I am! who shall deliver me from the body of this death?"* (v. 24). It is not, as it was at conversion, when you thought over your few or many sins. This work goes much deeper. You find that, as a Christian, you have no power to do the good that you wish to do. You must be brought to a new and deeper insight into the sin of your nature and into your utter weakness, even though you are a Christian, to live as you ought. And you will learn to cry out: "Who shall deliver me; I, wretched man, a prisoner bound under the law of sin?"

The answer to this question, is, *"I thank God through Jesus Christ our Lord"* (v. 25). Then follows the revelation of what there is in Christ. It is not just as given in Romans 3. It is more: I am in Christ Jesus, and *"the law of the Spirit of life in Christ Jesus hath made me free from the law of sin and death"* (Rom. 8:2), under which I was bound. It is the experience that the law or power of the life of the Spirit in Christ has made me free and now calls on me, in a new sense and by a new surrender, to acknowledge Christ as the bestower of the victory.

2. A new surrender to Christ. You may have used these words *surrender* and *consecration* many times but without rightly understanding what they mean. You have been brought by the teaching of Romans 7 to a complete sense of the hopelessness of leading a true Christian life, or a true prayer life, by your own efforts. In the same way, you feel that the Lord Jesus must take you up, by His own power, in an entirely new way and must take possession of you, by His Spirit, in an entirely new measure. This alone can preserve you from constantly sinning afresh. Only this can make you really victorious. This leads you to look away from yourself, really to get free from yourself, and to expect everything from the Lord Jesus.

If we begin to understand this, we are prepared to admit that in our nature there is nothing good, that it is under a curse and is nailed with Christ to His cross. We come to see what Paul meant when he said that we are dead to sin by the death of Christ. Thus do we obtain a share of the glorious resurrection life there is in Him. By such an insight we are encouraged to believe that Christ, through His life in us, through His continual indwelling, can keep us. Just as, at our conversion, we had no rest until we knew He had received us, so now we feel the need of coming to Him to receive from Him the assurance that He has really undertaken to keep us by the power of His resurrection life. And we feel then that there must be an act as definite as His reception of us at conversion, by which He gives us the assurance of victory. And although it appears to us to be too great and too much, the man who casts himself, without plea, into the arms of Christ will experience that He does indeed receive us into such a fellowship as will make us, from the beginning onward, *"more than conquerors"* (Rom. 8:37).

3. A new faith in the power that will make it possible for you to persevere in your surrender. Christ is prepared to take upon Himself the care and preservation of our lives every day, and all the day long, if we trust Him to do it. In the testimony given by many, this thought is emphasized. They have told us that they felt themselves called to a new surrender, to an entire consecration of life to Christ, reaching to the smallest things, but they were hindered by the fear of failure. The thirst after holiness, after an unbroken fellowship with Jesus, after a life of persevering childlike obedience, drew them one way. But the question arose: "Will I continue to be faithful?" And to this question there came no answer, until they believed that the surrender must be made, not in their own strength, but in a power that was bestowed by a glorified Lord. He would not only keep them for the future, but He must first make possible for them the surrender of faith that expects that future grace. It was in the power of Christ Himself that they were able to present themselves to Him.

Oh, Christian, only believe that there is a victorious life! Christ, the Victor, is your Lord, who will undertake for you in everything and will enable you to do all that the Father expects from you. Be of good courage. Will you not trust Him to do this great work for you, He who has given His life for you and has forgiven your sins? Only dare, in His power, to surrender yourself to the life of those who are kept from sin by the power of God. Along with the deepest conviction that there is no good in you, confess that you see in the Lord Jesus all the goodness you need for the life of a child of God, and begin literally to live *"by the faith of the Son of God, who loved [you], and gave himself for [you]"* (Gal. 2:20).

Let me, for your encouragement, give the testimony of Bishop Moule, a man of deep humility and tender piety. When he first heard of Keswick,[1] he was afraid of perfectionism and would have nothing to do with it. Unexpectedly, during a vacation in Scotland, he came in contact with some friends at a small convention. There he heard an address by which he was convinced how entirely the teaching was according to Scripture. There was no word about sinlessness in the flesh or in man. It was a setting forth of how Jesus can keep a man with a sinful nature from sin. The light shone into his heart. He who had always been counted a tender Christian came into touch now with a new experience of what Christ is willing to do for one who gives himself entirely to Him.

Listen to what he said concerning the text from Philippians 4:13, *"I can do all things through Christ which strengtheneth me"*:

I dare to say that it is possible for those who really are willing to count on the power of the Lord to keep them, to lead a life in which His promises are taken as they stand and are found to be true. It is possible to cast all our care on Him daily and to enjoy deep peace in doing it. It is possible to have the thoughts and imaginations of our hearts purified in the deepest meaning of the word, through faith. It is possible to see the will of God in everything and to receive it, not with sighing, but with singing. It is possible, in

---

1. A town in England where a revival began with a major emphasis on God's power to keep man from sin.

the inner life of desire and feeling, to lay aside all bitterness, wrath, anger, and evil-speaking, every day and every hour. It is possible, by taking complete refuge in divine power, to become strong through and through. We find that the things that formerly upset all our resolves to be patient or pure or humble furnish today an opportunity, through Him who loved us and works in us an agreement with His will and a blessed sense of His presence and His power, to make sin powerless. These things are divine possibilities. And because they are His work, the true experience of them will always cause us to bow lower at His feet and to learn to thirst and long for more. We cannot possibly be satisfied with anything less than— each day, each hour, each moment in Christ, through the power of the Holy Spirit—to walk with God.

Thank God, a life of victory is sure for those who have a knowledge of their inward ruin and are hopeless in themselves, but who, in the confidence of despair, have looked to Jesus. Then in faith in His power to make the act of surrender possible for them, they have done it, in His might, and now rely on Him alone every day and every hour.

9

HINTS FOR
THE INNER CHAMBER

At the conference there was a brother who had earnestly confessed his neglect of prayer, but who was able, later, to declare that his eyes had been opened to see that the Lord really supplied grace for all that He required from us. In sincerity he asked if some hints could not be given as to the best way of spending time profitably in the inner chamber. There was no opportunity then for giving an answer. Perhaps the following thoughts may be of help.

1. As you enter the inner chamber, let your first work be to thank God for the unspeakable love that invites you to come to Him and to

converse freely with Him. If your heart is cold and dead, remember that religion is not a matter of feeling but has to do first with the will. Raise your heart to God and thank Him for the assurance you have that He looks down on you and will bless you. Through such an act of faith you honor God and draw your soul away from being occupied with itself. Think also of the glorious grace of the Lord Jesus, who is willing to teach you to pray and to give you the disposition to do so. Think, too, of the Holy Spirit who was purposely given to cry, *"Abba, Father"* (Gal. 4:6), in your heart and to help your weakness in prayer. Five minutes spent thus will strengthen your faith for your work in the inner chamber. Once more I say, begin with an act of thanksgiving and praise God for the inner chamber and the promise of blessing there.

2. You must prepare yourself for prayer by prayerful Bible study. The great reason why the inner chamber is not attractive is that people do not know how to pray. Their stock of words is soon exhausted, and they do not know what to say further. This happens because they forget that prayer is not a soliloquy, where everything comes from one side, but it is a dialogue, where God's child listens to what the Father says, replies to it, and then asks for the things he needs.

Read a few verses from the Bible. Do not concern yourself with the difficulties contained in them. You can consider these later; but take what you understand, apply it to yourself, and ask the Father to make His Word light and power in your heart. Thus you will have material enough for prayer from the Word that the Father speaks to you; you will also have the liberty to ask for things you need. Keep on in this way, and the inner chamber will become at length, not a place where you sigh and struggle only, but one of living fellowship with the Father in heaven. Prayerful study of the Bible is indispensable for powerful prayer.

3. When you have thus received the Word into your heart, turn to prayer. But do not attempt it hastily or thoughtlessly, as though you knew well enough how to pray. Prayer in our own strength brings no blessing. Take time to present yourself reverently and in quietness before God. Remember His greatness and holiness and love. Think over what you wish to ask from Him. Do not be satisfied with going over the same things every day. No child goes on saying the same thing day after day to his earthly father.

Conversation with the Father is colored by the needs of the day. Let your prayers be something definite, arising either out of the Word that you have read, or out of the real soul needs that you long to have satisfied. Let your prayers be so definite that you can say as you go out, "I know what I have asked from my Father, and I expect an answer." It is a good plan sometimes to take a piece of paper and write down what you wish to pray for. You might keep such a paper for a week or more and repeat the prayers until some new need arises.

4. We are allowed to pray that we may help also in the needs of others. What has been said is in reference your own needs. One great reason why prayer in the inner chamber does not bring more joy and blessing is that it is too selfish, and selfishness is the death of prayer.

Remember your family, your congregation, with its interests, your own neighborhood, and the church to which you belong. Let your heart be enlarged and take up the interests of missions and of the church throughout the whole world. Become an intercessor, and you will experience for the first time the blessedness of prayer, as you find out that God will make use of you to share His blessing with others through prayer. You will begin to feel that there is something worth living for, as you find that you have something to say to God, and that from heaven He will do things in answer to your prayers that otherwise would not have been done.

A child can ask his father for bread. A full-grown son converses with him about all the interests of his business and about his further purposes. A weak child of God prays only for himself, but a full-grown man in Christ understands how to consult with God over what must take place in the kingdom. Let your prayer list bear the names of those for whom you pray: your minister, and all other ministers, and the different missionary affairs with which you are connected. Thus the inner chamber will really become a wonder of God's goodness and a fountain of great joy. It will become the most blessed place on earth. It is a great thing to say, but it is the simple truth, that God will make it a Bethel, where His angels will ascend and descend, and where you will cry out, "*The* Lord [shall] *be my God*" (Gen. 28:21). He will make it also Peniel, where you will see the face of God, as a prince of God, as one who wrestled with the angel and overcame him. (See Gen. 32:30.)

5. Do not forget the close bond between the inner chamber and the outer world. The attitude of the inner chamber must remain with us all the day. The object of the inner chamber is to so unite us with God that we may have Him always abiding with us. Sin, thoughtlessness, and yielding to the flesh or to the world make us unfit for the inner chamber and bring a cloud over the soul. If you have stumbled or fallen, return to the inner chamber; let your first work be to invoke the blood of Jesus and to claim cleansing by it. Do not rest until by confession you have repented of and put away your sin. Let the precious blood really give you a fresh freedom of approach to God. Remember that the roots of your life in the inner chamber strike far out in body and soul so as to manifest themselves in business life. Let "*the obedience of faith*" (Rom. 16:26), in which you pray in secret, rule you constantly. The inner chamber is intended to bind man to God, to supply him with power from God, to enable him to live for God alone. Let God be thanked for the inner chamber and for the blessed life that He will enable us to experience and nourish there.

Time

Before the creation of the world, time did not exist. God lived in eternity in a way that we little understand. With creation, time began, and everything was placed under its power. God has placed all living creatures under a law of slow growth. Think of the length of time it takes for a child to become a man in body and mind. In learning, in wisdom, in business, in handicraft, and in politics, everything somehow depends on patience and perseverance. Everything needs time.

It is just the same in religion. There can be no communion with a holy God, no fellowship between heaven and earth, no power for the salvation

of the souls of others, unless much time is set apart for it. Just as it is necessary for a child, for long years, to eat and learn every day, so the life of grace
depends entirely on the time men are willing to give to it day by day.

The minister is appointed by God to teach and help those who are
engaged in the ordinary avocations of life to find time and to use it properly
for the preservation of the spiritual life. The minister cannot do this unless
he himself has a living experience of a life of prayer. His highest calling
is not preaching, or speaking, or parochial visitation, but it is to cultivate
the life of God daily and to be a witness of what the Lord teaches him and
accomplishes in him.

Was it not so with the Lord Jesus? Why did He, who had no sin to
confess, sometimes have to spend all night in prayer to God? Because the
divine life had to be strengthened in communication with His Father. His
experience of a life in which He took time for fellowship with God has
enabled Him to share that life with us.

Oh, that each minister might understand that he has received his time
from God so that he might serve Him with it! God must have the first
and the best of your time for fellowship with Himself. Without this, your
preaching and labor have little power. Here on earth I may spend my time
for the money or the learning which I receive in exchange. The minister
can exchange his time for the divine power and the spiritual blessings to be
obtained from heaven. That, and nothing else, makes him a man of God
and ensures that his preaching will be in the demonstration of the Spirit
and power.

10

THE EXAMPLE OF PAUL

Be ye followers of me, even as I also am of Christ.
—1 Corinthians 11:1

Paul was a minister who prayed much for his congregation. Let us read his words prayerfully and calmly so that we may hear the voice of the spirit. What food for meditation!

Night and day praying exceedingly that we…might perfect that which is lacking in your faith.…The Lord make you to increase…to the end he may stablish your hearts umblameable in holiness.

(1 Thess. 3:10, 12–13)

The very God of peace sanctify you wholly. (1 Thess. 5:23)

Now our Lord Jesus Christ himself...comfort your hearts, and stablish you in every good word and work. (2 Thess. 2:16–17)

Without ceasing I make mention of you always in my prayers; making request...impart unto You some spiritual gift, to the end ye may be established. (Rom. 1:9–11)

My heart's desire and prayer to God for Israel is, that they might be saved. (Rom. 10:1)

I...cease not...making mention of you in my prayers; that...God...may give unto you the spirit of wisdom and revelation in the knowledge of him...that ye may know...what is the exceeding greatness of his power to us-ward who believe. (Eph. 1:15–19)

For this cause I bow my knees unto the Father...that he would grant you...to be strengthened with might by his Spirit in the inner man; that Christ may dwell in your hearts by faith; that ye, being rooted...in love... might be filled with all the fulness of God. (Eph. 3:14, 16–17, 19)

Always in every prayer of mine for you all making request with joy....I pray, that your love may abound yet more and more...that ye may be sincere...filled with the fruits of righteousness. (Phil. 1:4, 9–11)

But my God shall supply all your need according to his riches in glory by Christ Jesus. (Phil. 4:19)

We...do not cease to pray for you, and to desire that ye might be filled with the knowledge of his will...that ye might walk worthy of the Lord...

strengthened with all might, according to his glorious power.
                                                    (Col. 1:9–11)

*I would that ye knew what great conflict I have for you…as many as
have not seen my face in the flesh; that their hearts might be comforted,
being knit together in love.*   (Col. 2:1–2)

What a study for the inner chamber! These passages teach us that
unceasing prayer formed a large part of Paul's service in the Gospel. We
see the high spiritual aim that he set before himself in his work on behalf
of believers, and the tender and self-sacrificing love with which he ever continued to think of the church and its needs. Let us ask God to bring each
one of us, and all the ministers of His Word, to a life of which such prayer
is the healthy and natural outflow. We will need to turn again and again to
these pages if we would really be brought by the Spirit to the apostolic life
that God has given us as an example.

Paul was a minister who asked his congregation to pray much. Read
again with prayerful attention:

*I beseech you, brethren, for the Lord Jesus Christ's sake, and for the love
of the Spirit, that ye strive together with me in your prayers to God for
me; that I may be delivered from them that do not believe in Judaea.*
                                                    (Rom. 15:30–31)

*We…trust…in God…that he will yet deliver us; ye also helping together
by prayer for us.*   (2 Cor. 1:9–11)

*Praying always with all prayer and supplication in the Spirit, and
watching thereunto with all perseverance and supplication for all saints;
and for me, that utterance may be given unto me, that I may open my
mouth boldly, to make known the mystery of the gospel…as I ought to
speak.*   (Eph. 6:18–20)

For I know that this shall turn to my salvation through your prayer, and the supply of the Spirit of Jesus Christ. (Phil. 1:19)

Continue in prayer, and watch in the same with thanksgiving; withal praying also for us, that God would open unto us a door of utterance, to speak...as I ought to speak. (Col. 4:2–4)

Finally, brethren, pray for us, that the word of the Lord may have free course, and be glorified, even as it is with you. (2 Thess. 3:1)

What a deep insight Paul had as to the unity of the body of Christ and the relation of the members one to another! It is as we permit the Holy Spirit to work powerfully in us that He will reveal this truth to us, and we too will have this insight. What a glimpse Paul gives us of the power of the spiritual life among these Christians, by the way in which he reckoned that at Rome and Corinth and Ephesus and Colosse and Philippi, there were men and women on whom he could rely for prayer who would reach heaven and have power with God! And what a lesson for all ministers, to lead them to inquire if they truly appreciate the unity of the body at its right value, if they are endeavoring to train up Christians as intercessors, and if they indeed understand that Paul had that confidence because he was himself so strong in prayer for the congregation!

Let us learn the lesson and beseech God that ministers and congregations together may grow in the grace of prayer, so that their entire service and Christian life may witness that the Spirit of prayer rules them. Then we may be confident that God will avenge His own elect who cry out day and night to Him. (See Luke 18:7.)

Ministers of the Spirit

What is the meaning of the expression, "The minister of the Gospel is a minister of the Spirit"? (See 2 Corinthians 3:6–8.) It means the following.

1. The preacher is entirely under the power and control of the Spirit, so that he may be led and used by the Spirit as He wills.

2. The Spirit must have you entirely, and always, and in all things under His power. Many pray for the Spirit, that they may make use of Him and His power for their work. This is certainly wrong. It is He who must use you. Your relationship toward Him must be one of deep dependence and utter submission.

3. It is the Spirit in and through the preacher who will bring the Word to the heart. There are many who think they must preach the Word only, and that the Spirit will make the Word fruitful. They do not understand that they need the Spirit. I must not be satisfied with praying to God to bless, through the operation of His Spirit, the Word that I preach. The Lord wants me to be filled with the Spirit; then I will speak properly, and my preaching will be in the manifestation of the Spirit and power.

We see this on the day of Pentecost. They were filled with the Spirit and began to speak, and spoke with power through the Spirit who was in them.

Thus we learn what the relationship of the minister toward the Spirit should be. He must have a strong belief that the Spirit is in him, that the Spirit will teach him in his daily life and will strengthen him to bear witness to the Lord Jesus in his preaching and visiting. He must live in ceaseless prayer that he may be kept and strengthened by the power of the Spirit.

When the Lord promised the apostles that they would receive power when the Holy Spirit had come upon them and commanded them to wait for Him, it was as though He had said: "Do not dare to preach without this power. It is the indispensable preparation for your work. Everything depends on it."

What then is the lesson we may learn from the phrase "ministers of the Spirit"? Alas, how little we have understood this! How little we have lived in it! How little we have experienced the power of the Holy Spirit! What must we do then? There must be deep confession of guilt that we have so constantly grieved the Spirit because we have not lived daily as

His ministers. And there must be simple childlike surrender to His lead-ing in sure confidence that the Lord will work a change in us. Finally, we must have daily fellowship with the Lord Jesus in ceaseless prayer. He will bestow on us the Holy Spirit as *"rivers of living water"* (John 7:38).

11

THE WORD
AND PRAYER

Little of the Word with little prayer is death to the spiritual life. Much of the Word with little prayer gives a sickly life. Much prayer with little of the Word gives more life, but without steadfastness. A full measure of the Word and prayer each day gives a healthy and powerful life. Think of the Lord Jesus: in His youth and manhood He treasured the Word in His heart. In the temptation in the wilderness, and on every opportunity that presented itself—until He cried out on the cross in death, *"My God, my God, why hast thou forsaken me?"* (Matt. 27:46)—He showed that the Word of God filled His heart. And in His prayer life He manifested two things: first, that the Word supplies us with material for prayer and encourages us in expecting everything from God. The second is that it is only by prayer that we can live such a life that every word of God can be fulfilled in us.

How can we come to the place where the Word and prayer may each have its undivided right over us? There is only one answer. Our lives must be wholly transformed. We must get a new, a healthy, a heavenly life in which the hunger after God's Word and the thirst after God express themselves in prayer as naturally as do the needs of our earthly life. Every manifestation of the power of the flesh in us and the weakness of our spiritual life must drive us to the conviction that God will, through the powerful operation of His Holy Spirit, work out a new and strong life in us.

Oh, that we but understood that the Holy Spirit is essentially the Spirit of the Word and the Spirit of prayer! He will cause the Word to become a joy and a light in our souls, and He will also most surely help us in prayer to know the mind and will of God, and find in it our delight. If ministers wish to explain these things and to train God's people for the inheritance that is prepared for them, then they must commit ourselves from this moment forward to the leading of the Holy Spirit. They must, by faith in what He will do in them, appropriate the heavenly life of Christ as He lived it here on earth. They must have the certain expectation that the Spirit, who filled Jesus with the Word and prayer, will also accomplish that work in them.

Yes, let us believe that the Spirit who is in us is the Spirit of the Lord Jesus and that He is in us to make us truly partakers of His life. If we firmly believe this and set our hearts upon it, then there will come a change in our use of the Word and prayer such as we could not have thought possible. Believe it firmly; expect it surely.

Perhaps you are familiar with the vision of the valley of dry bones. The Lord said to the prophet, "*Prophesy upon these bones....Behold, I will cause breath to enter into you, and ye shall live*" (Ezek. 37:4–5). When he had done this, there was a noise, and bone came together to its bone, and flesh came up, and skin covered them—but there was no breath in them. The prophesying to the bones—the preaching of the Word of God—had a powerful influence. It was the beginning of the great miracle which was about to happen, and there lay an entire army of men newly made. It was the beginning of the work of life in them, but there was no spirit there.

Then the Lord said to the prophet, *"Propehsy unto the wind...Thus saith the Lord GOD; Come from the four winds, O breath, and breathe upon these slain, that they may live"* (Ezek.37:9). And when the prophet had done this, the Spirit came upon them, and they lived and stood on their feet, a very great army. Prophesying to the bones, that is, preaching, had accomplished a great work. There lay the beautiful new bodies. But the prophesying to the Spirit, "Come, O Spirit," that is, prayer, accomplished a far more wonderful thing. The power of the Spirit was revealed through prayer.

Is not the work of our ministers mostly this prophesying to dry bones in making known the promises of God? This is followed sometimes by great results. Everything that belongs to the form of godliness has been brought to perfection; a careless congregation becomes regular and devout. But, "There is no life in them," remains true for the most part. Preaching must be followed by prayer. The preacher must come to see that his preaching is comparatively powerless to bring in a new life until he begins to take time for prayer and, according to the teaching of God's Word, strives and labors and continues in prayer, and takes no rest, and gives God no rest, until He bestows the Spirit in overflowing power.

Do you not feel that a change must come in our work? We must learn from Peter to continue in prayer, in our ministry of the Word. Just as we are zealous preachers, we must be zealous in prayer. We must, with all our power, pray unceasingly like Paul. For the prayer: *"Come...breathe on these slain,"* the answer is sure.

Wholeheartedness

Experience teaches us that if anyone is engaged in a work in which he is not wholehearted, he will seldom succeed. Just think of a student, or his teacher, a man of business, or a soldier. He who does not give himself wholeheartedly to his calling is not likely to succeed. And that is still more true of religion, and above all, of the high and holy task of communion in prayer with a holy God and of being always well pleasing to Him. It is because of this that God has said so impressively, *"Ye shall seek me, and find me, when ye shall search for me with all your heart"* (Jer. 29:13).

More than one of God's servants has said, "I seek You with my whole heart." Have you ever thought how many Christians there are of whom it is all too plain that they do not seek God with their whole hearts? When they were in trouble over their sins, they seemed to seek God with their whole hearts. But then they discovered that they had been pardoned; one could see by their lives that they were religious. But no one would think, "This man has surrendered himself with his whole heart to follow God and to serve Him as the supreme work of his life."

How is it with you? What does your heart say? While you, as a minister for instance, have given yourself up with wholehearted devotion to fulfill your office faithfully and zealously, will you not perhaps acknowledge, "I fear, or rather I am convinced, that my unsatisfactory prayer life is to be attributed to nothing else than that I have not lived with a wholehearted surrender of all on earth that could hinder me in fellowship with God." What a deeply important question to consider in the inner chamber and to give the answer to God! How important to arrive at a plain answer and to utter it all before God! Prayerlessness cannot be overcome as an isolated thing. It is in the closest relationship to the state of the heart. True prayer depends on an undivided heart.

You may say, "But I cannot give myself that undivided heart that enables me to say, 'I seek God with my whole heart.'" No, that is impossible for you, but God will do it. "I will give them hearts to fear me." (See Jeremiah 32:40.) "I will write my law (as a power of life) in their hearts." (See Jeremiah 31:33.) Such promises serve to awaken desire. However weak the desire may be, if there is but the sincere determination to strive after what God holds out to us, then He will Himself work in our hearts both to will and to do. It is the great work of the Holy Spirit in us to make us willing and to enable us to seek God with the whole heart.

12

"FOLLOW ME"

The Lord did not speak the words, *"Follow me"* (Matt. 4:19), to all who believed on Him, or who hoped to be blessed by Him, but only to those whom He would make fishers of men. He said this not only at the first calling of the apostles, but also later on to Peter, *"Henceforth thou shalt catch men"* (Luke 5:10). The holy art of winning souls, of loving and saving them, can be learned only in close and persistent communion with Christ. What a lesson for ministers and for Christian workers and others! This communion was the great and special privilege of His disciples. The Lord chose them that they might always be with and near Him. We read of the choice of the twelve apostles in Mark 3:14: *"And he ordained twelve, that they should be with him, and that he might send them forth to preach."* So also our Lord said on the last night, *"And ye also shall bear witness, because ye have been with me from the beginning"* (John 15:27).

This fact was noticed by outsiders—thus, for instance, the woman who spoke to Peter, *"This man was also with him"* (Luke 22:56). So in the Sanhedrin, *"They took knowledge of them, that they had been with Jesus"* (Acts 4:13). The chief characteristic and indispensable qualification for the man who will bear witness to Christ is that he has been with Him. Continuous fellowship with Christ is the only school for the training of believers in the Holy Spirit. What a lesson for all Christians! It is only he who, like Caleb (see Numbers 14:24), follows the Lord fully who will have power to teach other souls the art of following Jesus. But what an unspeakable grace that the Lord Jesus Himself would train us after His own likeness, so that others may learn from us! Then we might say with Paul to our converts, *"Ye became followers of us, and of the Lord"* (1 Thess. 1:6) *"Be ye followers of me, even as I also am of Christ"* (1 Cor. 11:1).

Never was there a teacher who took such trouble with his scholars as Jesus Christ will with us who preach His Word. He will spare no pains; no time will be too precious or too long for Him. In the love that brought Him to the cross, He would have intimate conversation with us, fashion us, sanctify us, and make us fit for His holy service. Dare we still complain that it is too much for us to spend so much time in prayer? Will we not commit ourselves entirely to the love which gave up all for us, and look upon it as our greatest happiness now to hold fellowship with Him daily? Oh, all you who long for blessing in your ministry, He calls you to be with Him! Let this be the greatest joy of your life; it will be the surest preparation for blessing in your service. Oh, my Lord, draw me, help me, hold me fast, and teach me how to daily live in Your fellowship by faith.

The Holy Trinity

1. God is an ever flowing fountain of pure love and blessedness.

2. Christ is the reservoir wherein the fullness of God was made visible as grace, and has been opened for us.

3. The Holy Spirit is the stream of living water that flows from under the throne of God and of the Lamb.

4. The redeemed, God's believing children, are the channels through which the love of the Father, the grace of Christ, and the powerful operation of the Spirit are brought to the earth, there to be imparted to others.

What an impression we gain here of the wonderful partnership into which God takes us up as dispensers of the grace of God! Prayer, when we chiefly pray for ourselves, is but the beginning of the life of prayer. The glory of prayer is that we have power as intercessors to bring the grace of Christ, and the energizing power of the Spirit, upon those souls which are still in darkness.

The more surely the channel is connected with the reservoir, the more certainly will the water flow unhindered through it. The more we are occupied in prayer with the fullness of Christ and with the Spirit who proceeds from Him, and the more firmly we abide in fellowship with Him, the more surely will our lives be happy and strong. This, however, is still only a preparation for the reality. The more we give ourselves up to fellowship and converse with the Triune God, the sooner will we receive the courage and ability to pray down blessing on souls, on ministers, and on the church around us.

Are you truly a channel that is always open, so that the water may flow through you to the thirsty ones in the dry land? Have you offered yourself unreservedly to God, to become a bearer of the energizing operations of the Holy Spirit?

Is it not, perhaps, because you have thought only of yourself in prayer that you have experienced so little of the power of prayer? Do you understand that the new prayer life into which you have entered in the Lord Jesus can be sustained and strengthened only by the intercession in which you labor for the souls around you, to bring them to know the Lord? Oh, meditate on this—God an ever flowing fountain of love and blessing, and I, His child, a living channel through which the Spirit and life can be brought to the earth every day!

Life and Prayer

Our lives have a great influence on our prayers, just as in the same way our prayers influence our lives. The entire life of man is a continuous prayer, to nature or to the world, to provide for his wants and make him happy. This natural prayer and desire of the heart can be so strong in a man who also prays to God that the words of prayer that his mouth utters cannot be heard. At times God cannot hear the prayer of your lips because the desires of your heart after the world cry out to Him much more strongly and loudly.

Life exercises a mighty influence over prayer. A worldly life, a self-seeking life, makes prayer powerless and an answer impossible. With many Christians there is a conflict between life and prayer, and life holds the upper hand. But prayer can also exercise a mighty influence over life. If I give myself entirely to God in prayer, then prayer can conquer the life of the flesh and sin. The entire life may be brought under the control of prayer. Prayer can change and renew the whole life, because prayer calls in and receives the Lord Jesus and the Holy Spirit to purify and sanctify the life.

Many think that they must, with their defective spiritual life, work themselves up to pray more. They do not understand that only in proportion as the spiritual life is strengthened can the prayer life increase. Prayer and life are inseparably connected. What do you think? Which has the stronger influence over you, prayer for five or ten minutes, or the whole day spent in the desires of the world? Let it not surprise you if your prayers are not answered. The reason may easily lie here; your life and your prayers are at strife with each other; your heart is more wholly devoted to living than to prayer. Learn this great lesson: my prayer must rule my whole life. What I request from God in prayer is not decided in five or ten minutes. I must learn to say, "I have prayed with my whole heart." What I desire from God must really fill my heart the whole day; then the way is open for a certain answer.

Oh, the sacredness and power of prayer if it takes possession of the heart and life! It keeps one constantly in fellowship with God. We can then literally say, "I wait on You all the day." Let us be careful to consider not only the length of the time we spend with God in prayer, but the power with which our prayers take possession of our whole lives.

Perseverance in Prayer

"It is not reason," said Peter, "that we should leave the word of God, and serve tables" (Acts 6:2). For that work deacons were chosen. And this word of Peter serves for all time and for all who are set apart as ministers. "We will give ourselves continually to prayer, and to the ministry of the word" (v. 4). Dr. Alexander Whyte, in an address, once said: "I sometimes wonder, when my salary is paid to me so punctually, and the deacons have performed their part faithfully; have I been so faithful in my part, in persevering in prayer and the ministry of the Word?" Another minister has said: "How surprised people would be if I proposed to divide my time between these two equally—one-half given to prayer, the other to the ministry of the Word!"

Notice, in the case of Peter recorded in Acts, chapter 10, what perseverance in prayer meant. He went up on the roof to pray. There, in prayer, he received heavenly instruction as to his work among the heathen. There, the message from Cornelius came to him. There, the Holy Spirit said to him, "Arise...and go with them" (v. 20). And from there he went to Caesarea, where the Spirit was so unexpectedly outpoured on the heathen. All this is to teach us that it is through prayer God will give the instruction of His Spirit to make us understand His will, to let us know with whom we are to speak, to give us the assurance that His Spirit will make His Word powerful through us.

Have you ever earnestly thought over why ministers have a salary and a parsonage and are set free from the need of following earthly business? It is for nothing else than that they should continue in prayer and the ministry of the Word. That will be their wisdom and power. That will be the secret of a blessed service of the Gospel.

No wonder there is complaint about the ineffective spiritual life in minister and congregation, when what is of prime importance, perseverance in prayer, does not hold its rightful place—the first place.

Peter was able to speak and act as he did because he was filled with the Spirit. Let us not be satisfied with anything less than hearty surrender to an undivided appropriation of the Spirit, as Leader and Lord of our lives. Nothing less will help us. Then, for the first time, we will be able to say, "[God] *hath made us able ministers of...the spirit*" (2 Cor. 3:6).

Carnal or Spiritual?

There is a great difference between these two states that is little understood or pondered. The Christian who walks in the Spirit and has crucified the flesh is spiritual. (See Gal. 5:24.) The Christian who walks after the flesh and wishes to please the flesh is carnal. (See Rom. 13:14.) The Galatians, who had begun in the Spirit, were ending in the flesh. Yet there were among them some spiritual members who were able to restore the wandering with meekness.

What a difference between the carnal and the spiritual Christian! (See 1 Corinthians 3:1–3.) With the carnal Christian there may be much religion and much zeal for God and for the service of God. But it is for the most part in human power. With the spiritual, on the other hand, there is a complete subjection to the leading of the Spirit, a deep sense of weakness and entire dependence on the work of Christ; it is a life of abiding fellowship with Christ, wrought out by the Spirit.

How important it is for me to find out and plainly acknowledge before God whether I am spiritual or carnal! A minister may be very faithful in his orthodoxy, and be most zealous in his service, and yet be so chiefly in the power of human wisdom and zeal. And one of the signs of this is that there is little pleasure or perseverance in fellowship with Christ through prayer. Love of prayer is one of the marks of the Spirit.

What a change is necessary for a Christian who is chiefly carnal to become truly spiritual! At first he cannot understand what must happen, or how it can come to pass. The more the truth dawns upon him, the more he is convinced that it is impossible, unless God does it. Yet to believe truly that God will do it requires earnest prayer. Quiet retirement and meditation are indispensable, along with the death of all confidence in ourselves. But along this road there ever comes the faith that God can, God is willing, God will do it. The soul that earnestly clings to the Lord Jesus will be led by the Spirit to this faith.

How will you be able to avoid having someone say to you, "I...could not speak unto you as unto spiritual, but as unto carnal, even as unto babes in Christ" (1 Cor. 3:1)? It is impossible unless you have the experience of having passed from the one state to the other. God will teach you. Persevere in prayer and faith.

13

GEORGE MÜLLER AND HUDSON TAYLOR

Just as God gave the apostle Paul as an example in his prayer life for Christians of all time, so He has also given George Müller in these latter days as a proof to His church how literally and wonderfully He still always hears prayer. It is not only that He gave him in his lifetime over a million pounds sterling to support his orphanages, but Mr. Müller also stated that he believed that the Lord had given him more than thirty thousand souls in answer to prayer. And that not only from among the orphans, but also many others for whom he—in some cases for fifty years—had prayed faithfully every day, in the firm faith that they would be saved. When he was asked on what ground he so firmly believed this, his answer was, "There are five conditions which I always endeavor to fulfill; by observing these I have the assurance of answer to my prayer:

1. I have not the least doubt because I am assured that it is the Lord's will to save them, for He wills that all men should be saved and come to the knowledge of the truth (see 1 Tim. 2:4); and we have the assurance *'that, if we ask any thing according to his will, he heareth us'* (1 John 5:14).

2. I have never pleaded for their salvation in my own name, but in the blessed name of my precious Lord Jesus, and on His merits alone. (See John 1:14.)

3. I always firmly believed in the willingness of God to hear my prayers. (See Mark 11:24.)

4. I am not conscious of having yielded to any sin, for *'if I regard iniquity in my heart, the Lord will not hear me'* (Ps. 66:18) when I call.

5. I have persevered in believing prayer for more than fifty-two years for some, and will continue until the answer comes: *'Shall not God avenge his own elect, which cry day and night unto him?'* (Luke 18:7)."

Take these thoughts into your hearts and practice prayer according to these rules. Let prayer be not only the utterance of your desires, but a fellowship with God, until we know by faith that our prayers are heard. The way George Müller walked is the new and living way to the throne of grace, which is open for us all.

Hudson Taylor

When Hudson Taylor, as a young man, had given himself unreservedly to the Lord, there came to him a strong conviction that God would send him to China. He had read of George Müller and how God had answered his prayers for his own support and that of his orphans, and he began to ask the Lord to teach him how to trust Him in the same way. He felt that if he would go to China with such faith, he must first begin to live by faith in England. He asked the Lord to enable him to do this. He had a position as a doctor's dispenser and asked God to help him not to ask for his salary, but to leave it to God to move the heart of the doctor to pay him at the right time. The doctor was a good-hearted man, but very irregular in payment. This cost Taylor much trouble and struggle in prayer because he believed, as did George Müller, that the word, *"Owe no man any thing"* (Rom. 13:8) was to be taken literally, and that debt should not be incurred.

So he learned the great lesson to move men through God—a thought of deep meaning, which later on became an unspeakably great blessing to him in his work in China. He relied on this truth: in the conversion of the Chinese, in the awakening of Christians to give money for the support of the work, and in finding suitable missionaries who would hold to faith's rule of conduct, that we should make our desires known to God in prayer, and then rely on God to move men to do what He would have done.

After he had been in China for some years, he prayed that God would give twenty-four missionaries, two for each of the eleven provinces and Mongolia, each with millions of souls and with no missionaries. God did it. But there was no society to send them out. He had indeed learned to trust God for his own support, but he dared not take upon himself the responsibility of the twenty-four, if possibly they had not sufficient faith. This cost him severe conflict, and he became very ill under it, until at last he saw that God could as easily care for the twenty-four as for himself. He undertook it in a glad faith. And so God led him, through many severe trials of faith, to trust Him fully. These twenty-four increased, in the course of time, to a thousand missionaries who relied wholly on God for support. Other missionary societies have acknowledged how much they have learned from Hudson Taylor, as a man who stated and obeyed this law: Faith may rely on God to move men to do what His children have asked of Him in prayer.

Light from the Inner Chamber

But thou, when thou prayest, enter into thy closet, and when thou hast shut thy door, pray to thy Father which is in secret; and thy Father which seeth in secret shall reward thee openly. (Matt. 6:6)

Our Lord had spoken of the prayer of the hypocrites who desire to be seen of men and also of the prayer of the heathen who trust in the multitude of their words. They do not understand that prayer has no value unless it is addressed to a personal God who sees and hears. In Matthew 6:6, our Lord teaches us a wonderful lesson concerning the inestimable blessing which the Christian may have in his inner chamber. In order to understand the lesson properly, we must notice the light that the inner chamber sheds on the following.

1. The wonderful love of God. Think of God, His greatness, His holiness, His unspeakable glory, and then on the inestimable privilege to which he invites His children, that each one of them, however sinful or feeble he may be, may have access to Him every hour of the day and converse with Him as long as he wishes. If he enters his inner chamber, then God is ready to meet him, to have fellowship with him, to give him the joy and strength that he needs with the living assurance in his heart that He is with him and will undertake for him in everything. In addition, He promises that He will enrich him in his outward life and work with those things that he has asked for in secret. Should we not cry out with joy? What an honor! What a salvation! What an overflowing supply for every need!

One may be in the greatest distress, or may have fallen into the deepest sin, or may in the ordinary course of life desire temporal or spiritual blessing; he may desire to pray for himself or for those belonging to him, or for his congregation or church; he may even become an intercessor for the whole world—the promise for the inner chamber covers all: *"Pray to thy Father which is in secret; and thy Father...shall reward thee openly."*

We might well suppose that there is no place on earth so attractive to the child of God as the inner chamber with the presence of God promised, where he may have unhindered communion with the Father. The happiness of a child on earth if he enjoys the love of his father, the happiness of a friend as he meets a beloved benefactor, the happiness of a subject who has free access to his king and may stay with him as long as he wishes, these are nothing compared with this heavenly promise. In the inner chamber you can converse with your God as long and as intimately as you desire; you can rely on His presence and fellowship.

Oh, the wonderful love of God in the gift of an inner chamber sanctified by such a promise! Let us thank God every day of our lives for it as the gift of His wonderful love. In this sinful world He could devise nothing more suitable for our needs than a fountain of unspeakable blessing.

2. The deep sinfulness of man. We might have thought that every child of God would have availed himself with joy of such an invitation. But, see! What is the response? There comes a cry from all lands that prayer in the inner chamber is, as a general rule, neglected by those who call themselves believers. Many make no use of it; they go to church, they confess Christ, but they know little of personal communication with God. Many make a little use of it, but in a spirit of haste, and more as a matter of custom, or for the easing of conscience. Therefore, they cannot speak of any joy or blessing in it. And, what is sadder, many who know something of its blessedness confess that they know little about faithful, regular, and happy fellowship with the Father, all the day, as something that is as necessary as their daily bread.

Oh, what is it, then, that makes the inner chamber so powerless? Is it not the deep sinfulness of man, and the aversion of his fallen nature for God, which make the world with its fellowship more attractive than being alone with the heavenly Father?

Is it not that Christians do not believe the Word of God where that Word declares that the flesh that is in them is enmity against God (see Rom. 8:7), and that they walk too much after the flesh, so that the Spirit cannot strengthen them for prayer? Is it not that Christians allow themselves to be deprived by Satan of the use of the weapon of prayer, so that they are powerless to overcome him? Oh, the deep sinfulness of man! We have no greater proof of it than this dishonor that is done to the unspeakable love that has given us the inner chamber.

And what is still sadder is that even ministers of Christ acknowledge that they know they pray too little. The Word tells them that their only power lies in prayer; through that only, and through that certainly, they can be clothed with power from on high for their work. But it seems as though the power of the world and the flesh have deceived them. While they devote time to, and manifest zeal in, their work, what is the most necessary of all is neglected. And there is not the desire or strength for prayer to obtain the indispensable gift of the Holy Spirit to make their work fruitful. God give us grace to understand in the light of the inner chamber the deep sinfulness of our nature.

3. The glorious grace of Christ Jesus. Is there, then, no hope of a change? Must it always be this way? Or is there a means of recovery? Thank God, there is!

The man through whom God has made known to us the message of the inner chamber is no other than our Lord Jesus Christ, who saves us from our sins. He is able and willing to deliver us from this sin, and He will deliver. He has not undertaken to redeem us from all our other sins and leave us to deal with the sin of prayerlessness in our own strength. No, in this also we may come to Him and cry out, *"Lord, if thou wilt, thou canst make me clean"* (Matt. 8:2). *"Lord, I believe; help thou mine unbelief"* (Mark 9:24).

Do you wish to know how you may experience this deliverance? By none other than the well-known way along which every sinner must come to Christ. Begin by acknowledging, by confessing before Him in a childlike and simple manner, the sin of neglecting and desecrating the inner chamber. Bow before Him in deep shame and sorrow. Tell Him that your heart has deceived you by the thought that you could pray as you ought. Tell Him that through the weakness of the flesh, and the power of the world, and self-confidence, you have been led astray and that you have no strength to do better. Let this be done heartily. You cannot by your resolution and effort put things right.

Come in your sin and weakness to the inner chamber, and begin to thank God, as you have never thanked Him, that the grace of the Lord Jesus will surely make it possible for you to converse with your Father as a child ought to do. Hand over afresh to the Lord Jesus all your sin and misery, as well as your whole life and will, that He may cleanse and take possession of you and rule over you as His very own.

Even though your heart is cold and dead, persevere in the exercise of faith that Christ is an almighty and faithful Savior. You may be sure that deliverance will come. Expect it, and you will begin to understand that the inner chamber is the revelation of the glorious grace of the Lord Jesus. This grace makes it possible for us to do what we could not do ourselves; that is, to have fellowship with God and to experience the desire and power of remaining in that intimate fellowship as we walk with God.

14

THE SPIRIT OF THE CROSS

We seek sometimes for the operation of the Spirit, with the object of obtaining more power for work, more love in life, more holiness in the heart, more light on Scripture or on our path. And yet all these gifts are only subordinate to what is the great purpose of God. The Father has bestowed the Spirit on the Son, and the Son has given Him to us, with the one great object of revealing and glorifying Christ Jesus Himself in us.

The heavenly Christ must become for us a real living personality, always with us and in us. Our life on earth must be lived every day in the unbroken and holy fellowship of our Lord Jesus in heaven. This must be the first and the greatest work of the Holy Spirit in believers, that they should know and experience Christ as the life of their lives. God desires that we should become strengthened with might by His Spirit in the inner man, that Christ may dwell in our hearts through faith, and that we may be filled with His love unto all the fullness of God (Eph. 3:16–19).

This was the secret of the joy of the first disciples. They had received the Lord Jesus, whom they feared they had lost, as the heavenly Christ into their hearts.

And this was their preparation for Pentecost: they were entirely taken up with Him. He was literally their all. Their hearts were empty of everything, so that the Spirit might fill them with Christ. In the fullness of the Spirit they had power for a life and service such as the Lord desired. Is this, now, the great object in our desires, in our prayers, in our experience? May the Lord teach us to know that the blessing for which we have so earnestly prayed can be preserved and increased in no other way than through intimate fellowship with Christ in the inner chamber, practiced and cultivated every day.

And yet it has seemed to me that there was a still deeper secret of Pentecost to be discovered. The thought came that perhaps our conception of the Lord Jesus in heaven was limited. We think of Him in the splendor, the glory of God's throne. We also think of the unsearchable love that moved Him to give Himself for us. But we forget too often that, above all, it is as the Crucified One He was known here on earth, and that, above all, it is as the Crucified One He has His place on the throne of God. *"And, lo, in the midst of the throne…stood a Lamb as it had been slain"* (Rev. 5:6).

Yes, it is as the Crucified One that He is the object of the Father's eternal good pleasure and of the worship of the entire creation. And it is, therefore, of the first importance that we here on earth should know and have experience of Him as the Crucified One, so that we may make men see what His nature and ours is, and what the power is that can make them partakers of salvation.

The Cross is Christ's highest glory. The Holy Spirit neither has done nor can do anything greater or more glorious than He did when He empowered

Jesus to go to that cross: "*Christ…through the eternal Spirit offered himself without spot to God*" (Heb. 9:14). In the same way, the Holy Spirit can do nothing greater or more glorious for us than to take us up into the fellowship of that Cross, and to work in us the same spirit of the Cross that was seen in our Lord Jesus. In a word, the question arose whether this was not the real reason why our prayers for the powerful operation of the Holy Spirit could not be answered, because we had sought too little to receive the Spirit, in order that we might know and become like the glorified Christ in the fellowship of His Cross.

Is this not the deepest secret of Pentecost? The Spirit comes to us from the cross, where He strengthened Christ to offer Himself to God. He comes from the Father, who looked down with unspeakable good pleasure at the humiliation and obedience and self-sacrifice of Christ, as the highest proof of His surrender to Him. He comes from Christ, who through the cross was prepared to receive from the Father the fullness of the Spirit, that He might share it with the world. He comes to reveal Christ to out hearts, as the Lamb slain in the midst of the throne, so that we on earth may worship Him as they do in heaven. He comes, chiefly, to impart to us the life of the crucified Christ, so that we may be able to say truly, "*I am crucified with Christ: nevertheless I live; yet not I, but Christ liveth in me*" (Gal. 2:20).

To understand this secret in any way, we must first meditate on what the meaning and what the worth of the Cross is.

The Mind That Was in the Crucified Christ

The Cross must necessarily be viewed from two standpoints. The first is the work it has accomplished—the pardon and conquest of sin. This is the first message with which the Cross comes to the sinner. It proclaims to him free and full deliverance from the power of sin. And then the second is the spirit or inner nature that was manifested there. We find this expressed in Philippians 2:8: "*He humbled himself, and became obedient unto death, even the death of the cross.*" Here we see self-abasement to the lowest place that could be found under the burden of our sin and curse, obedience to the uttermost to all the will of God, self-sacrifice to the death of the cross.

These three words reveal to us the holy perfection of His Person and work. Therefore, God has so greatly exalted Him. It was the spirit of the Cross that made Him the object of His Father's good pleasure, of the worship of the angels, of the love and confidence of all the redeemed. The self-abasement of Christ, His obedience to the will of God even to death, His self-sacrifice even to the death of the cross—these made Him the *"Lamb, as it had been slain,"* standing *"in the midst of the throne"* (Rev. 5:6).

The Spirit of the Cross in Us

All that Christ was, He was for us and desires to become in us. The spirit of the Cross was His blessedness and glory. It should be this even more for us. He desires to manifest His likeness in us and to give us a full share of all that is His. Thus Paul wrote the words we have so often quoted: *"Let this mind be in you, which was also in Christ Jesus"* (Phil. 2:5). Elsewhere he wrote, *"We have the mind of Christ"* (1 Cor. 2:16). The fellowship of the Cross in not only a holy duty for us, but an unspeakably blessed privilege, which the Holy Spirit Himself will make ours according to the promise: *"He shall take of mine, and shall show it unto you"* (John 16:15); *"He shall glorify me"* (v. 14). The Holy Spirit worked this disposition in Christ and will also work it in us.

15

TAKING UP THE CROSS

When the Lord told His disciples that they must take up the cross and follow Him, they could have little understanding of His meaning. He wished to encourage them to earnest thought and so prepare them for the time when they would see Him carrying His cross. From the Jordan, where He had presented Himself to be baptized and reckoned among sinners, onward, He carried the Cross always in His heart. That is to say, He was always conscious that the sentence of death, because of sin, rested on Him, and that He must bear it to the uttermost. As the disciples thought on this and wondered what He meant by it, only one thing was clear to them: it was the thought of a man who was sentenced to death, and carried his cross to the appointed place.

Christ had said at the same time, *"He that loseth his life… shall find it"* (Matt. 10:39). He taught them that they must hate their own lives. Their natures were so sinful that nothing less than death could meet their needs; they deserved nothing less than death.

So the conviction gradually dawned upon them that the taking up of the cross meant, "I am to feel that my life is under sentence of death, and that under the consciousness of this sentence I must constantly surrender my flesh, my sinful nature, to death." So they were slowly prepared to see later on that the cross that Christ had carried was the one power truly to deliver from sin, and that they must first receive from Him the true Cross spirit. They must learn from Him what self-humiliation in their weakness and unworthiness was to mean; what the obedience was that crucified their own will in all things, in the greatest as well as in the least; what the self-denial was that did not seek to please the flesh or the world. *"Take up [your] cross, and follow me"* (Matt. 16:24)—that was the word with which Jesus prepared His disciples for the great thought that His mind and inner nature might become theirs, that His cross might indeed become their own.

Crucified with Christ

The lesson that the Lord wished His disciples to learn from His statement concerning the taking up of the cross and the losing of their life finds its expression in the words of Paul. Naturally, he was speaking after Christ had died on the cross and been exalted on high, and the Spirit had been poured out. Paul said, *"I am crucified with Christ"* (Gal. 2:20); *"God forbid that I should glory, save in the cross of our Lord Jesus Christ, by whom the world is crucified unto me, and I unto the world"* (Gal. 6:14). He wished that every believer would live in a manner that proved he was crucified with Christ. He wished us to understand that the Christ who comes to dwell in our hearts is the crucified Christ who will Himself, through His life, impart to us the true mind of the Cross. He tells us that *"our old man is crucified with him"* (Rom. 6:6). Yes, more, *"They that are Christ's have crucified the flesh"* (Gal. 5:24). When they received by faith the crucified Christ, they gave over the flesh to the death sentence that was executed to the full on Calvary. Paul said, *"We have been planted together in the likeness of his death"* (Rom. 6:5), and that therefore we must reckon that we are dead to sin in Christ Jesus.

These words of the Holy Spirit, through Paul, teach us that we must abide constantly in the fellowship of the Cross, in fellowship with the crucified and living Lord Jesus. It is the soul that continuously lives under the cover, shelter, and deliverance of the cross that alone can expect to continuously glory in Christ Jesus and in His abiding nearness.

The Fellowship of the Cross

There are many who place their hope for salvation in the redemption of the Cross who understand little about the fellowship of the Cross. They rely on what the Cross has purchased for them, on forgiveness of sin and peace with God. But they can often live for a length of time without fellowship with the Lord Himself. They do not know what it means to strive every day after heart communion with the crucified Lord as He is seen in heaven: *"A Lamb…in the midst of the throne"* (Rev. 5:6). Oh, that this vision might exercise its spiritual power upon us. Then we will really experience every day that as truly as the Lamb is seen there on the throne, so we may have the power and experience of His presence here!

Is it possible? Without a doubt it is. Why did that great miracle happen, and why was the Holy Spirit given from heaven, if it were not to make the glorified Jesus, the Lamb standing, as slain, in the midst of the throne, present with us here in our earthly surroundings?

16

THE HOLY SPIRIT AND THE CROSS

The Holy Spirit always leads us to the cross. It was so with Christ. The Spirit taught Him and enabled Him to offer Himself without spot to God. (See Heb. 9:14.) It was so with the disciples. The Spirit, with whom they were filled, led them to preach Christ as the Crucified One. Later on He led them to glory in the fellowship of the Cross when they were deemed worthy to suffer for Christ's sake.

And the Cross directed them again to the Spirit. When Christ had borne the cross, He received the Spirit from the Father, that the Spirit might be poured out. When the three thousand bowed before the Crucified

One (see Acts 2:41), they received the promise of the Holy Spirit. When the disciples rejoiced in their experience of the fellowship of the Cross, they received the Holy Spirit afresh. The union between the Spirit and the Cross is indissoluble; they belong inseparably to one another. We see this especially in the epistles of Paul.

> *Jesus Christ hath been evidently set forth, crucified among you....*
> *Received ye the Spirit by the works of the law, or by the hearing of*
> *faith?* (Gal. 3:1–2)

> *Christ hath redeemed us from the curse of the law...that we might*
> *receive the promise of the Spirit through faith.* (Gal. 3:13–14)

> *God sent forth his Son...to redeem them that were under the law...*
> *and...hath sent forth the Spirit of his Son into your hearts.*
> (Gal. 4:4–6)

> *And they that are Christ's have crucified the flesh....If we live in the*
> *Spirit, let us also walk in the Spirit.* (Gal. 5:24–25)

> *Ye also are become dead to the law by the body of Christ....that we*
> *should serve in newness of spirit.* (Rom. 7:4, 6)

> *For the law of the Spirit of life in Christ Jesus hath made me free from*
> *the law of sin and death. For...God...condemned sin in the flesh: that*
> *the righteousness of the law might be fulfilled in us, who walk not after*
> *the flesh, but after the Spirit.* (Rom. 8:2–4)

In everything and always the Spirit and the cross are inseparable. Yes, even in heaven. The Lamb, as it had been slain, standing in the midst of the throne had "*seven eyes, which are the seven Spirits of God sent forth into all the earth*" (Rev. 5:6). Again, "*He showed me a pure river of water of life, clear as crystal* [Is this other than the Holy Spirit?], *proceeding out of the throne of God and of the Lamb*" (Rev. 22:1). When Moses smote the rock, the water streamed out and Israel drank. When the Rock, Christ, was actually smitten, and He had taken His place as the slain Lamb on the throne of God, there flowed out from under the throne the fullness of the Holy Spirit for the whole world.

How foolish it is to pray for the fullness of the Spirit if we have not first placed ourselves under the full power of the Cross! Just think of the one hundred and twenty disciples. The crucifixion of Christ had touched, broken, and taken possession of their entire hearts. They could speak or think of nothing else, and when the Crucified One had shown them His hands and His feet, He said to them, "*Receive ye the Holy Ghost*" (John 20:22). And so also, with their hearts full of the crucified Christ, now received up into heaven, they were prepared to be filled with the Spirit. They dared to proclaim to the people, "Repent and believe in the Crucified One," and they also received the Holy Spirit.

Christ gave Himself up entirely to the Cross. The disciples also did the same. The Cross demands this also from us; it would have our entire lives. To comply with this demand requires nothing less than a powerful act of the will, for which we are unfit. It also requires a powerful act of God that will assuredly come to those who cast themselves unreservedly on Him.

The Spirit

Why aren't there more men and women who can witness, in the joy of their hearts, that the Spirit of God has taken possession of them and given them new power to witness for Him? Yet more urgently arises the heart-searching question to which an answer must be given: What is it that hinders? The Father in heaven is more willing than any earthly father to give bread to His child, and yet the cry arises, "Is the Spirit restricted? Is this His work?"

Many will acknowledge that the hindrance undoubtedly lies in the fact that the church is too much under the sway of the flesh and the world. They understand too little of the heart-piercing power of the Cross of Christ. So it comes to pass that the Spirit does not have the vessels into which He can pour His fullness.

Many complain that the subject is too high or too deep for them. This is proof of how little we have appropriated and brought into practice the teaching of Paul and Christ about the Cross. I bring you a message of joy. The Spirit who is in you, in however limited a measure, is prepared to take you under His teaching, to lead you to the Cross, and, by His heavenly instruction, to make you know something of what the crucified Christ wills to do for you and in you.

But then He wants you to spend time with Him, so that He may reveal the heavenly mysteries to you. He wants to make you see how neglecting the inner chamber has hindered fellowship with Christ, the knowledge of the Cross, and the powerful operations of the Spirit. He will teach you what is meant by the denial of self, the taking up of your cross, the losing of your life, and following Him.

In spite of all that you have felt of your ignorance, and lack of spiritual insight, He is able and willing to take you under His teaching and to make known to you the secret of the spiritual life above all your expectations.

Begin at the beginning. Be faithful in the inner chamber. Thank Him that you can count on Him to meet you there. Although everything appears cold, dark, and strained, bow in silence before the loving Lord Jesus, who so longs after you. Thank the Father that He has given you the Spirit. And be assured that all you do not yet know—about the flesh, and the world, and the cross—the Spirit of Christ, who is in you, will surely make known to you. Oh, soul, only believe that this blessing is for you! Christ belongs entirely to you. He longs to obtain full possession of you. He can and will possess you through the Holy Spirit. But for this, time is necessary. Oh, give Him time in the inner chamber every day. You can rest assured that He will fulfill His promise in you. *"He that hath my commandments, and keepeth them, he it is that loveth me: and he that loveth me shall be loved of my Father, and I will love him, and will manifest myself to him"* (John 14:21).

Persevere, in addition to all that you ask for yourself, in prayer for your congregation, your church, your minister, for all believers, for the whole church of God, that God may strengthen them with power through His Spirit, so that Christ may dwell in their hearts by faith. (See Eph. 3:16–17.) Blessed time when the answer comes! Continue in prayer. The Spirit will reveal and glorify Christ and His love, Christ and His Cross, as the Lamb slain standing in the midst of the throne. (See Rev. 5:6.)

The Cross and the Flesh

These two are deadly enemies. The cross desires to condemn and put to death the flesh. The flesh desires to cast aside and conquer the cross. Many, as they hear of the Cross as the indispensable preparation for the fullness of the Holy Spirit, will find out what is in them which must still be crucified. We must understand that our entire nature is sentenced to death and becomes dead by the Cross, so that the new life in Christ may come to rule in us. We must obtain such an insight into the fallen condition of our nature and its enmity against God that we become willing, even desirous, to be wholly freed from it.

We must learn to say with Paul, *"In me (that is, in my flesh,) dwelleth no good thing"* (Rom. 7:18). *"The* [mind of the flesh] *is enmity against God: for it is not subject to the law of God, neither indeed can be"* (Rom. 8:7). It is its very essence to hate God and His holy law. This is the wonder of redemption, that Christ has borne on the cross the judgment and curse of the flesh and has forever nailed it to the cursed tree. If a man only believes God's Word about this cursed mind of the flesh, and then longs to be delivered from it, he learns to love the Cross as his deliverer from the power of the enemy.

"Our old man is crucified" with Christ (Rom. 6:6), and our one hope is to receive this by faith and to hold it fast. *"They that are Christ's have crucified the flesh"* (Gal. 5:24). They have willingly declared that they will daily regard the flesh that is in them as the enemy of God, the enemy of Christ, the enemy of their soul's salvation, and will treat it as having received its deserved reward in being nailed to the cross.

This is one part of the eternal redemption that Christ has brought to us. It is not something that we can grasp with our understanding or accomplish with our strength. It is something that the Lord Jesus Himself will give us if we are willing to abide in His fellowship day by day and to receive everything from Him. It is something that the Holy Spirit will teach us. He will impart it to us as an experience and will show how He can give victory in the power of the Cross over all that is of the flesh.

The Cross and the World

What the flesh is in the smallest circle of my own person, that the world is in the larger circle of mankind. The flesh and the world are two manifestations of the same god of this world who is served by both. When the cross deals with the flesh as accursed, we at once discover what the nature and power of the world are. "*They…hated both me and my Father*" (John 15:24). The proof of this was that they crucified Christ. But Christ obtained the victory on the cross and freed us from the power of the world. And now we can say, "*God forbid that I should glory, save in the cross of our Lord Jesus Christ, by whom the world is crucified unto me, and I unto the world*" (Gal. 6:14).

Every day the Cross was to Paul a holy reality, both in what he had to suffer from the world and in the victory that the Cross constantly gave. John also wrote, "*The whole world lieth in wickedness*" (1 John 5:19). "*Who is he that overcometh the world, but he that believeth that Jesus is the Son of God? This is he that came by water and blood, even Jesus Christ.…And it is the Spirit that beareth witness, because the Spirit is truth*" (vv. 5–6). Against the two great powers of the god of this world, God has given us two great powers from heaven, namely, the Cross and the Spirit.

EPILOGUE

I t is not enough that one should understand and appropriate the thought of the writer, and then rejoice because of the new insight he has obtained and the pleasure that knowledge has brought. There is something else that is of great importance. I must surrender myself to the truth so that I will be ready, with an undivided will, to immediately perform all that I will learn to be God's will.

In a book such as this, dealing with the life of prayer and hidden fellowship with God, it is indispensable that we should be prepared to receive and obey all that we see to be according to the Word and will of God. When this inner desire is lacking, knowledge only serves to make it more difficult for the heart to receive abundant life. Satan endeavors to become master of the Christian's inner chamber because he knows that if there has been unfaithfulness in prayer, then that Christian will bring little loss to Satan's kingdom. Spiritual power to lead the unsaved to the Lord or to build up the children of God will not be experienced under it. Persevering prayer, through which alone this power comes, has been lacking.

The great question has been: Will we really set ourselves to win back again the weapon of believing prayer that Satan has, in a measure, taken away from us? Let us set before ourselves the serious importance of this conflict. As far as each minister is concerned, everything depends on whether or not he is a man of prayer—one who in the inner chamber must be clothed each day with power from on high. We, in common with the church throughout the whole world, have to complain that prayer does not have the place in our service of God that it ought to have, according to the will and promise of God and according to the need of minister, congregation, and church.

The public consecration that many a believer has been led to make of himself at conferences in not an easy thing. And even when the step is taken, old custom and the power of the flesh will tend to bring it to nothing. The power of faith is not yet vigorous. It will cost strife and sacrifice to conquer the Devil in the name of Christ. Our churches are the battlefield where Satan will bring forth all his power to prevent us from becoming men of prayer, powerful in the Lord to obtain the victory in heaven and on earth. How much depends on this for ourselves, for our congregations, and for the kingdom!

Do not be surprised if I say that it is with fear and trembling, and with much prayer, that I have written what I trust will help to encourage believers in the conflict. It is with a feeling of deep unworthiness that I venture to offer myself as a guide to the inner chamber, which is the way to holiness and to fellowship with God.

Do not wonder that I have asked the Lord to give this book a place in some inner chambers, that He may assist the reader. The end result is so that as the reader sees what God's will is, he may immediately give himself up to do it. In war, everything depends on each soldier being obedient to the word of command, even though it costs him his life. In our strife with Satan, we will not conquer unless each one of us holds himself ready, even in the reading of this simple book, to say from the heart, "What God says I will do. And if I see that anything is according to His will, I will immediately receive it and act upon it." Do not wonder that I have written this message to remind believers that everything depends on the spirit of surrender to immediate obedience, according to the Word of God.

God grant that, in His great grace, this book may prove a bond of fellowship by which we may think of and help one another. I pray that we might strengthen each other for the conflict in prayer by which the Enemy may be overcome and the life of God may be gloriously revealed!

WAITING ON GOD

CONTENTS

FOREWORD

Before my trip to England, I had been very impressed by the thought of how, in all our Christianity, personal and public, we need more of God. I felt that we needed to train our people to wait on God more, to cultivate a deeper sense of His presence, to seek more direct contact with Him, and to rest in entire dependence on Him. These must be the definite aims of our ministry. At a welcome breakfast in Exeter Hall, I expressed this thought very simply in connection with all our spiritual work. I have already said elsewhere that I was surprised at the response the sentiment met with. I saw that God's Spirit had been working the same desire in many hearts.

The experiences of the past year, both personal and public, have greatly deepened the conviction. It is as if I myself am only beginning to see the deepest truth concerning God and our relationship to Him. It must be centered in this waiting on God, and how very little, in our life and work, we have been surrounded by its spirit. The following pages are the outcome of my conviction and of desire to direct the attention of all God's people to the one great remedy for all our needs. More than half the pieces were written on board ship. I fear they bear the marks of being somewhat crude and hasty. I have felt that I should write them over again. But, this I cannot do now. And so, I send them out with the prayer that He who loves to use the feeble may give His blessing with them.

I do not know if it will be possible for me to put into a few words the chief things we need to learn. But, what I want to say here is this: the great lack of our faith is that we do not know God. The answer to every complaint of feebleness and failure, the message to every congregation or convention seeking instruction on holiness, ought to simply be, "What is the matter? Do you not have God?" If you really believe in God, He will make everything all right. God is willing and able by His Holy Spirit. Cease from expecting the least good from yourself, or the least help from anything there is in man. Just yield yourself unreservedly to God to work in you. He will do all for you.

How simple this looks! And yet, this is the Gospel we so little know. I feel ashamed as I send forth these very defective teachings; I can only cast them on the love of my fellow believers, and of our God. May He use them to draw us all to Himself, to learn in practice and experience the blessed art of waiting only upon God. If only God would show us the right conception of what the influence would be on a life spent, not in thought or imagination or effort, but in the power of the Holy Spirit, wholly waiting upon God.

With my greeting in Christ to all God's saints it has been my privilege to meet, and, no less to those I have not met, I subscribe myself, your brother and servant,

—Andrew Murray

1

THE GOD OF
OUR SALVATION

My soul waiteth in silence for God only:
from him cometh my salvation.
—Psalm 62:1 ASV

If salvation truly comes from God and is entirely His work, just as our creation was, it follows that our first and highest duty is to wait on Him and to do that work that pleases Him. Waiting then becomes the only way to the experience of a full salvation—the only way to truly know God as the God of our salvation. All the difficulties that are brought forward, as keeping us back from full salvation, have their cause in this one thing: the defective knowledge and practice of waiting upon God. All that the church and its members need for the manifestation of the mighty power of God in the world is the return to our true place, the place that belongs to us, both in creation and redemption, the place of absolute and unceasing dependence upon God. Let us strive to see what elements make up this most blessed and necessary waiting upon God. It may help us if we discover the reasons why this grace is so little cultivated. We must feel how infinitely desirable it is that the church, that we ourselves, should learn its blessed secret at any price.

The deep need for this waiting on God lies equally in the nature of man and the nature of God. God, as Creator, formed man to be a vessel in which He could show forth His power and goodness. Man was not to have, in himself, a fountain of life or strength or happiness. The ever living and only living One was each moment to communicate to man all that he needed. Man's glory and blessedness was not to be independent, or dependent upon himself, but dependent on a God of such infinite riches and love. Man was to have the joy of constantly receiving from the fullness of God. This was his blessedness as an unfallen creature.

When he fell from God, he was still more absolutely dependent on Him. There was not the slightest hope of his recovery out of his state of death, but in God, His power, and His mercy. It is God alone who began the work of redemption. It is God alone who continues and carries it on each moment in each individual believer. Even in the regenerate man, there is no power of goodness in himself. He has and can have nothing that he does not each moment receive. Waiting on God is just as indispensable, and must be just as continuous and unbroken, as the breathing that maintains his natural life.

It is then because Christians do not know their relationship to God as absolute poverty and helplessness that they have no sense of the need of absolute and unceasing dependence or of the unspeakable blessedness of continually waiting on God. But, once a believer begins to see it and consent to it—that he must, by the Holy Spirit, each moment receive what God each moment works—waiting on God becomes his brightest hope and joy. As he begins to understand how God, as God, as infinite Love, delights to impart His own nature to His child as fully as He can—how God is not weary of keeping charge of his life and strength—he wonders why he ever thought that God could not be waited on all day. God unceasingly giving and working and His child unceasingly waiting and receiving—this is the blessed life.

"Truly my soul waiteth upon God: from him cometh my salvation" (Ps. 62:1). First, we wait on God for salvation. Then, we learn that salvation is only to bring us to God and teach us to wait on Him. Then, we find what is better still, that waiting on God is itself the highest salvation. It is ascribing to Him the glory of being All; it is experiencing that He is All to us. May God teach us the blessedness of waiting on Him!

My soul, wait thou only upon God!
—Psalm 62:5

2

THE KEYNOTE OF LIFE

I have waited for thy salvation, O LORD.
—Genesis 49:18

I t is not easy to say in what exact sense Jacob used these words in the midst of his prophecies in regard to the future of his sons. But, they certainly do indicate that, both for himself and for them, his expectation was from God alone. It was God's salvation he waited for, a salvation that God had promised and that God Himself alone could work out. He knew himself and his sons to be under God's charge. Jehovah, the everlasting God, would show them what His saving power is and does. The words point forward to that wonderful history of redemption that is not yet finished, and to the glorious future in eternity to which it is leading.

They suggest to us how there is no salvation but God's salvation, and how waiting on God for that, whether for our personal experience or in wider circles, is our first duty, our true blessedness.

Let us think of ourselves and the inconceivably glorious salvation God has worked out for us in Christ and is now going to perfect in us by His Spirit. Let us meditate until we realize that every participation of this great salvation, from moment to moment, must be the work of God Himself. God cannot part with His grace or goodness or strength as an external thing that He gives us, as He gives the raindrops from heaven. No, He can only give it, and we can only enjoy it, as He works it Himself directly and unceasingly. And, the only reason that He does not work it more effectually and continuously is that we do not let Him. We hinder Him either by our indifference or by our self-effort, so that He cannot do what He wants to do.

What He asks of us, in the way of surrender, obedience, desire, and trust, is all comprised in this one word: waiting on Him, waiting for His salvation. It combines the deep sense of our entire helplessness and our perfect confidence that our God will work all in His divine power.

Again, I say, let us meditate on the divine glory of the salvation God purposes to work out in us, until we know the truths it implies. Our heart is the scene of a divine operation more wonderful than creation. We can do as little toward the work as toward creating the world, except as God works in us to will and to do. God only asks us to yield, to consent, to wait upon Him, and He will do it all. Let us meditate and be still until we see how right and blessed it is that God alone do all. Our soul will, of itself, sink down in deep humility to say, *"I have waited for thy salvation, O LORD."* And the deep, blessed background of all our praying and working will be, *"Truly my soul waiteth upon God"* (Ps. 62:1).

The application of the truth to wider circles, to those we labor among or intercede for, to the church of Christ around us, or throughout the world, is not difficult. There can be no good but what God works. To wait upon God, and have the heart filled with faith in His working, and in that faith to pray for His mighty power to come down, is our only wisdom. Oh, for the eyes of our heart to be opened to see God working in ourselves and in others. If only we could see how blessed it is to worship and to wait for His salvation!

Our private and public prayers are our chief expressions of our relationship to God. It is in them chiefly that our waiting upon God must be exercised. If our waiting begins by quieting the activities of nature, and being still before God; if it bows and seeks to see God in His universal and almighty operation, alone able and always ready to work all good, then it will be the strength of the soul. If it yields itself to Him in the assurance that He is working and will work in us; if it maintains the place of humility and stillness, and surrenders until God's Spirit has quickened the faith that He will perfect His work, it will indeed become the joy of the soul. Life will become one deep, blessed cry, "I have waited for Your salvation, O Lord."

My soul, wait thou only upon God!

3

THE TRUE PLACE OF MAN

These wait all for thee, that thou mayest give them their food in
due season. Thou givest unto them, they gather;
thou openest thy hand, they are satisfied with good.
—Psalm 104:27–28 ASV

This psalm is in praise of the Creator of the birds and the beasts of the forest, of the young lions, and man going forth to his work, of the great sea, where things exist, both small and great beasts. And, it sums up the whole relationship of all creation to its Creator, and its continuous and universal dependence upon Him, in the one word, "*these wait all for thee*"! Just as much as it was God's work to create, it is His work to maintain. As little as man could create himself, is he left to provide for himself. The whole creation is ruled by the one unalterable law of waiting upon God!

The word is the simple expression of that for the sake of which alone man was brought into existence, the very groundwork of his constitution. The one object for which God gave life to mankind was that in them He might prove and show forth His wisdom, power, and goodness. He would be, each moment, their life and happiness, and pour forth unto them the riches of His goodness and power. And just as this is the very place and nature of God, to be unceasingly the supplier of every want, so the very place and nature of man is nothing but this: to wait upon God and receive from Him what He alone can give, what He delights to give.

If we are at all to understand what waiting on God is to be to the believer, to practice it and to experience its blessedness, it is of great importance that we begin at the very beginning and see the deep reasonableness of the call that comes to us. We will then understand how the duty is no arbitrary command. We will see how it is not only rendered necessary by our sin and helplessness; it is simply and truly our restoration to our original destiny and our highest nobility, to our true place and glory as people blessedly dependent on the all-glorious God.

Once our eyes are opened to this precious truth, all nature will become a preacher, reminding us of the relationship that, founded in creation, is now taken up in grace. As we read this psalm, and learn to look upon all life in nature as continually maintained by God Himself, waiting on God will be seen to be the very necessity of our being. As we think of the young lions and the ravens crying to Him, of the birds and the fishes and every insect waiting on Him, until He gives them their meat in due season, we will see that it is the very nature and glory of God that He is a God who is to be waited on. Every thought of what nature is, and of what God is, will give new force to the call, *"wait thou only upon God"* (Ps. 62:5).

"These wait all for thee, that thou mayest give." It is God who gives all: let this faith enter deeply into our hearts. Before we fully understand all that is implied in our waiting upon God, and before we have even been able to cultivate the habit, let the truth enter our souls. Waiting on God,

unceasing and entire dependence upon Him, is, in heaven and earth, the only true faith, the one unalterable and all-comprehensive expression for the true relationship to the ever blessed One in whom we live.

Let us resolve at once that it will be the one characteristic of our life and worship, a continual, humble, truthful waiting upon God. We may rest assured that He who made us for Himself, that He might give Himself to us and in us, will never disappoint us. In waiting on Him, we will find rest and joy and strength, and the supply of every need.

My soul, wait thou only upon God!

4

FOR SUPPLIES

The LORD upholdeth all that fall, and raiseth up all those
that be bowed down. The eyes of all wait upon thee;
and thou givest them their meat in due season.
—Psalm 145:14–15

Psalm 104 is a psalm of Creation, and the words, *"These wait all upon thee"* (v. 27), were used with reference to the animal creation. Here, we have a psalm of the kingdom, and *"the eyes of all wait upon thee"* appears especially to point to the needs of God's saints, of all who fall and are heavy laden. What the universe and the animal creation does unconsciously, God's people are to do intelligently and voluntarily. Man is to be the interpreter of nature. He is to prove that there is nothing nobler or more blessed in the exercise of our free will than to use it in waiting upon God.

If any army has been sent out to march into an enemy's country, and news is received that it is not advancing, the question is at once asked, What is the cause of the delay? The answer will very often be: "waiting for supplies." All the stores of provisions or clothing or ammunition have not arrived. Without these, it dare not proceed. It is likewise in the Christian life: day by day, at every step, we need our supplies from above. And, there is nothing so necessary as to cultivate that spirit of dependence on God and of confidence in Him, which refuses to go on without the needed supply of grace and strength.

If the question is asked whether this is anything different from what we do when we pray, the answer is that there may be much praying with very little waiting on God. In praying, we are often occupied with ourselves, with our own needs, and with our own efforts in the presentation of them. In waiting upon God, the first thought is of the God upon whom we wait. We enter His presence and feel we need just to be quiet, so that He, as God, can overshadow us with Himself. God longs to reveal Himself, to fill us with Himself. Waiting on God gives Him time to come to us in His own way and divine power.

It is especially at the time of prayer that we ought to set ourselves to cultivate this spirit.

Before you pray, bow quietly before God, just to remember and realize who He is, how near He is, how certainly He can and will help. Just be still before Him, and allow His Holy Spirit to waken and stir in your soul the childlike disposition of absolute dependence and confident expectation. Wait upon God as a living Being, as the living God, who notices you. He is just longing to fill you with His salvation. Wait on God until you know you have met Him; prayer will then become so different.

And when you are praying, let there be intervals of silence, reverent stillness of soul, in which you yield yourself to God, in case He may have other things He wishes to teach you or to work in you. Waiting on Him will become the most blessed part of prayer, and the blessing thus obtained will be doubly precious as the fruit of such fellowship with the Holy One. God has so ordained it, in harmony with His holy nature, and with ours, that waiting on Him should be the honor we give Him. Let us bring Him the service gladly and truthfully. He will reward it abundantly.

"*The eyes of all wait upon thee; and thou givest them their meat in due season.*" Dear soul, God provides in nature for the creatures He has made. How much more will He provide in grace for those He has redeemed! Learn to say of every want and every failure and every lack of needed grace: I have waited too little upon God, or He would have given me in due season all I needed. And say then, too,

My soul, wait thou only upon God!

5

FOR INSTRUCTION

Show me thy ways, O Lord; teach me thy paths.
Lead me in thy truth, and teach me: for thou art the God of my
salvation; on thee do I wait all the day.
—Psalm 25:4–5

I spoke of an army on the point of entering an enemy's territories. The answer to the question as to the cause of delay was: "waiting for supplies." The answer might also have been: "waiting for instructions," or "waiting for orders." If the last dispatch had not been received, with the final orders of the commander in chief, the army dared not move. It is even so in the Christian life—as deep as the need of waiting for supplies is that of waiting for instructions.

See how beautifully this comes out in Psalm 25. The writer knew and loved God's laws exceedingly, and he meditated in that law day and night. But, he knew that this was not enough. He knew that for the right spiritual understanding of the truth, and for the right personal application of it to his own particular circumstances, he needed a direct, divine teaching.

The psalm has at all times been a very special one because of its reiterated expression of the felt need of the divine teaching and of the childlike confidence that that teaching would be given. Study the psalm until your heart is filled with the two thoughts: the absolute need and the absolute certainty of divine guidance. And with these, how entirely it is in this connection that he speaks, *"On thee do I wait all the day."* Waiting for guidance, waiting for instruction, all the day, is a very blessed part of waiting upon God.

The Father in heaven is so interested in His child, and so longs to have his life at every step in His will and His love, that He is willing to keep his guidance entirely in His own hand. He knows so well that we are unable to do what is really holy and heavenly, except as He works it in us, that He means His very demands to become promises of what He will do, in watching over and leading us all the day. We may count on Him to teach us His way and show us His path in special difficulties and times of perplexity, as well as in the common course of everyday life.

And what is necessary for us to receive this guidance? One thing: waiting for instructions, waiting on God. *"On thee do I wait all the day."* We want, in our times of prayer, to give clear expression to our sense of need and our faith in His help. We want to definitely become conscious of our ignorance as to what God's way may be. We must be aware of our need of the divine light shining within us if our way is to be as the sun, shining more and more unto the perfect day. (See Prov. 4:18.) And we want to wait quietly before God in prayer until the deep, restful assurance fills us. It will be given: *"the meek will he guide in...his way"* (Ps. 25:9).

"On thee do I wait all the day." The special surrender to the divine guidance in our seasons of prayer must cultivate, and be followed up by, the habitual looking upward *"all the day."* As simple as it is to walk all day in

the light of the sun, so simple and delightful can it become to a soul, practiced in waiting on God, to walk all day in the enjoyment of God's light and leading. What is needed to help us to such a life is just one thing: the real knowledge and faith of God as the only source of wisdom and goodness, as ever ready, and longing much to be to us all that we can possibly require. Yes, this is the one thing we need! If we only saw our God in His love, if we only believed that He waits to be gracious, that He waits to be our life and to work all in us—how this waiting on God would become our highest joy, the natural and spontaneous response of our hearts to His great love and glory!

My soul, wait thou only upon God!

6

FOR ALL SAINTS

Let none that wait on thee be ashamed.
—Psalm 25:3

Let us now, each one forgetting himself, think of the great company of God, and the saints throughout the world who are all waiting on Him. And let us all join in the fervent prayer for each other: *"Let none that wait on thee be ashamed."*

Just think for a moment of the many waiting ones who need that prayer, how many are sick and weary and alone and feel as if their prayers are not answered. They sometimes begin to fear that their hope will be put to shame. And then, think of how many servants of God, ministers or missionaries, teachers or workers, of various names, whose hopes in their work

351

have been disappointed, and whose longing for power and blessing remains unsatisfied. And then, too, think of how many who have heard of a life of rest and perfect peace, of abiding light and fellowship, of strength and victory, and who cannot find the path. With all these, it is only that they have not yet learned the secret of full waiting upon God. They just need what we all need, the living assurance that waiting on God can never be in vain. Let us remember, all who are in danger of fainting or being weary, and unite in the cry, *"Let none that wait on thee be ashamed"*!

If this intercession for all who wait on God becomes part of our waiting on Him for ourselves, we will help to bear each other's burdens, and so fulfill the law of Christ. (See Gal. 6:2.)

There will be introduced into our waiting on God that element of unselfishness and love, which is the path to the highest blessing and the fullest communion with God. Love to believers and love to God are inseparably linked. In God, the love to His Son and to us are one: *"That the love wherewith thou hast loved me may be in them"* (John 17:26). In Christ, the love of the Father to Him, and His love to us, are one: *"As the Father hath loved me, so have I loved you"* (John 15:9). In us, He asks that His love to us be ours to our brothers and sisters: *"that ye love one another; as I have loved you"* (John 13:34). All the love of God, and of Christ, are inseparably linked with love to brothers and sisters. And how can we, day by day, prove and cultivate this love except by praying daily for each other? Christ did not seek to enjoy the Father's love for Himself; He passed it all on to us. All true seeking of God, and His love for ourselves, will be inseparably linked with the thought and the love of our brothers and sisters in prayer for them.

"Let none that wait on thee be ashamed." Twice in the psalm David speaks of his waiting on God for himself; here he thinks of all who wait on Him. Let this be the message to all God's tried and weary ones, that there are more people praying for them than they know about. Let it stir them and us in our waiting to make a point of at times forgetting ourselves, and to enlarge our hearts and say to the Father: *"These wait all upon thee; that thou mayest give them their meat in due season"* (Ps. 104:27). Let it inspire us all

with new courage, for who is there who is not at times ready to faint and be weary? *"Let none that wait on thee be ashamed"* is a promise in a prayer. "They who wait on You will not be ashamed!" From many a witness, the cry comes to everyone who needs help—brother, sister, tried one, *"Wait on the* Lord: *be of good courage, and he shall strengthen thine heart: wait, I say, on the* Lord*"* (Ps. 27:14). *"Be of good courage, and he shall strengthen thine heart,"* all who wait on the Lord.

Blessed Father, we humbly beseech You, let none who wait on You be ashamed; no, not one. Some are weary, and the time of waiting appears long. And some are feeble and scarcely know how to wait. And some are so entangled in the effort of their prayers and their work, they think that they can find no time to wait continually. Father, teach us all how to wait! Teach us to think of each other and pray for each other. Teach us to think of You, the God of all waiting ones. Father, let none who wait on You be ashamed! For Jesus' sake. Amen.

My soul, wait thou only upon God!

7

A PLEA IN PRAYER

Let integrity and uprightness preserve me; for I wait on thee.
—Psalm 25:21

For the third time in this psalm we have the word *wait*. As before in verse 5, "*on thee do I wait all the day*," so here, too, the believing supplicant appeals to God to remember that he is waiting on Him, looking for an answer. It is a great thing for a soul not only to wait upon God, but to be filled with such a consciousness that its whole spirit and position is that of a waiting one. It can, in childlike confidence, say, "Lord, You know, I wait on You!" It will prove a mighty plea in prayer, giving ever increasing boldness of expectation to claim the promise, "They who wait on Me will not be ashamed!"

The prayer in connection with which the plea is put forth here is one of great importance in the spiritual life. If we draw near to God, it must be with a true heart. There must be perfect integrity and wholeheartedness in our dealing with God. As we read in the next psalm, *"Judge me, O LORD; for I have walked in mine integrity....As for me, I will walk in mine integrity"* (Ps. 26:1, 11), there must be perfect uprightness of single-heartedness before God, as it is written, "His righteousness is for the upright in heart." (See Ps. 36:10.) The soul must allow nothing sinful, nothing doubtful, if it is indeed to meet the Holy One and receive His full blessing. This can only be done with a heart wholly and singly given up to His will. The whole spirit that animates us in the waiting must be, *"let integrity and uprightness"*—You see that I desire to come so to You; You know I am looking to You to work them perfectly in me—let them *"preserve me; for I wait on thee."*

And, if at our first attempt to truly live the life of fully and always waiting on God, we begin to discover how much that perfect integrity is lacking, this will just be one of the blessings that the waiting was meant to work. A soul cannot seek close fellowship with God, or attain the abiding consciousness of waiting on Him all the day, without a very honest and entire surrender to all His will.

"For I wait on thee." It is not only in connection with the prayer of our text, but with every prayer that this plea may be used. To use it often will be a great blessing to us. Let us, then, study the words well until we know all their meanings. It must be clear to us what we are waiting for. There may be very different things. It may be waiting for God in our times of prayer to take His place as God and to work in us the sense of His holy presence and nearness. It may be a special petition to which we are expecting an answer. It may be our whole inner life, in which we are on the lookout for God putting forth His power. It may be the whole state of His church and saints, or some part of His work, for which our eyes are ever toward Him. It is good that we remember and keep track of the things we are waiting for on God. As we say definitely to each of them, *"On thee do I wait"* (Ps. 25:5), we will be able to claim the answer, *"For I wait on thee."*

Whom we are waiting on must also be clear to us. Not an idol, a God of whom we have made an image by our conceptions of what He is. No, but the living God, such as He really is in His great glory, His infinite holiness, His power, wisdom, and goodness, in His love and nearness. It is the presence of a beloved or a dreaded master that awakens the whole attention of the servant who waits on him. It is the presence of God, as He can in Christ by His Holy Spirit make Himself known, and keep the soul under its covering and shadow, that will awaken and strengthen the true waiting spirit. Let us be still and wait and worship until we know how near He is, and then say, "*On thee do I wait.*"

And then, let it be very clear, too, that we are waiting. Let that become so much our consciousness that the utterance comes spontaneously, "*On thee do I wait all the day....I wait on thee*" (Ps. 25:5, 21). This will indeed imply sacrifice and separation, a soul entirely given up to God as its all, its only joy. This waiting on God has hardly been acknowledged as the only true Christianity. And yet, if it is true that God alone is goodness and joy and love, if it is true that our highest blessedness is in having as much of God as we can, if it is true that Christ has redeemed us wholly for God and made a life of continual abiding in His presence possible, nothing less ought to satisfy us than to be ever breathing this blessed atmosphere, "*I wait on thee.*"

My soul, wait thou only upon God!

8

STRONG AND
OF GOOD COURAGE

Wait on the LORD: be strong, and let thine heart take courage;
yea, wait thou on the LORD.
—Psalm 27:14 RV

The psalmist has just said, "*I had fainted, unless I had believed to see the goodness of the LORD in the land of the living*" (v. 13). If it had not been for his faith in God, his heart would have fainted. But, in the confident assurance in God that faith gives, he urges himself and us to remember one thing above all—to wait upon God. "*Wait on the LORD: be strong, and let thine heart take courage; yea, wait thou on the LORD.*" One of the chief needs in our waiting upon God, one of the deepest secrets of its blessedness and blessing, is a quiet, confident persuasion that it is not in vain. Have courage and believe that God will hear and help. We are waiting on a God who could never disappoint His people.

"*Be strong, and let thine heart take* [good] *courage.*" These words are frequently found in connection with some great and difficult enterprise, in prospect of the combat with the power of strong enemies, and the utter insufficiency of all human strength. Is waiting on God a work so difficult that such words are needed: "*Be strong, and let thine heart take courage*"? Yes, indeed. The deliverance for which we often have to wait is from enemies, in whose presence we are so weak. The blessings for which we plead are spiritual and all unseen—things impossible with men—heavenly, supernatural, divine realities. Our hearts may well faint and fail.

Our souls are so little accustomed to hold fellowship with God; the God on whom we wait so often appears to hide Himself. We who have to wait are often tempted to fear that we do not wait enough, that our faith is too feeble, that our desire is not as upright or as earnest as it should be, that our surrender is not complete. Amid all these causes of fear or doubt, how blessed to hear the voice of God: "*Wait on the* Lᴏʀᴅ: *be strong, and let thine heart take courage; yea, wait thou on the* Lᴏʀᴅ." Let nothing in heaven or earth or hell keep you from waiting on your God in full assurance that it cannot be in vain.

The one lesson our text teaches us is this, that when we set ourselves to wait on God we ought, beforehand, to resolve that it will be with the most confident expectation of God's meeting and blessing us. We ought to make up our minds to this, that nothing was ever so sure as that waiting on God will bring us untold and unexpected blessing. We are so accustomed to judge the work of God in us by what we feel, that the great probability is that when we begin to cultivate the waiting on Him, we will be discouraged because we do not find any special blessing from it. The message comes to us: "Above everything, when you wait on God, do so in the spirit of abounding hopefulness. It is God in His glory, in His power, in His love longing to bless you that you are waiting on."

If you say that you are afraid of deceiving yourself with vain hope, because you do not see or feel any evidence in your present state for such special expectations, my answer is, it is God who is the reason for your expecting great things. Oh, do learn the lesson! You are not going to wait on yourself to see what you feel and what changes come to you. You are going to wait on God, to know first what He is, and then after that, what He will do. The whole duty and blessedness of waiting on God has its roots in this, that He is such a blessed Being, full to overflowing of goodness and power and life and joy, that we, however wretched, cannot for any time come into contact with Him without that life and power secretly, silently beginning to enter into us and blessing us. *"God is love"* (1 John 4:8)! That is the only and all-sufficient warrant of your expectation. Love seeks not its own. (See 1 Cor. 13:4–5.) God's love is just His delight to impart Himself and His blessedness to His children.

Come, and however feeble you feel, just wait in His presence. As a feeble, sickly invalid is brought out into the sunshine to let its warmth go through him, come with all that is dark and cold in you into the sunshine of God's holy, omnipotent love. Sit and wait there, with the one thought: here I am, in the sunshine of His love. As the sun does its work in the weak one who seeks its rays, God will do His work in you. Oh, do trust Him fully! *"Wait on the* LORD: *be strong, and let thine heart take courage; yea, wait thou on the* LORD."

My soul, wait thou only upon on God!

9

WITH THE HEART

Be strong, and let your heart take courage,
all ye that wait for the Lord.
—Psalm 31:24 rv

The words are nearly the same as in our last meditation. But I gladly avail myself of them again to stress a much needed lesson for all who desire to truly and fully learn what waiting on God is. The lesson is this: it is with the heart that we must wait upon God. *"Let your heart take courage."* All our waiting depends on the state of the heart. As a man's heart is, so is he before God. We can advance no further or deeper into the holy place of God's presence to wait on Him there, than our heart is prepared for it by the Holy Spirit. The message is, *"Let your heart take courage, all ye that wait for the* LORD.*"*

The truth appears so simple that some may ask, "Do not all admit this? Where is the need of insisting on it so specially?" Because very many Christians have no sense of the great difference between the Christianity of the mind and the Christianity of the heart, and the former is far more diligently cultivated than the latter. They do not know how infinitely greater the heart is than the mind. It is this that causes much of the feebleness of our Christian life. And it is only as this is understood that waiting on God will bring its full blessing. Proverbs 3:5 may help to make my meaning clear. Speaking of a life in the fear and favor of God, it says, *"Trust in the* LORD *with all thine heart; and lean not unto thine own understanding."* In all faith, we have to use these two powers. The mind has to gather knowledge from God's Word and prepare the food by which the heart with the inner life is to be nourished. But, here is the terrible danger of our leaning to our own understanding and trusting in our own comprehension of divine things.

People imagine that if they are occupied with the truth, the spiritual life, will as a matter of course, be strengthened. This is by no means the case. The understanding deals with conceptions and images of divine things, but it cannot reach the real life of the soul. Hence the command, *"Trust in the* LORD *with all thine heart; and lean not unto thine own understanding."* It is with the heart that man believes and comes into touch with God. It is in the heart that God has given His Spirit to be the presence and the power of God working in us. In all our faith, it is the heart that must trust, love, worship, and obey. My mind is utterly unable to create or maintain the spiritual life within me. The heart must wait on God for Him to work it in me.

It is in this even as in the physical life. My reason may tell me what to eat and drink, and how the food nourishes me. But, in the eating and feeding, my reasons can do nothing; the body has its organs for that special purpose. Just so, reason may tell me what God's Word says, but it can do nothing to the feeding of the soul on the bread of life; this the heart alone can do by its faith and trust in God. A man may be studying the nature and effects of food or sleep. When he wants to eat or sleep he sets aside his thoughts and study, and uses the power of eating or sleeping. And so, the Christian always needs, when he has studied or heard God's Word, to cease from his thoughts, to put no trust in them, to awaken his heart to open itself before God, and seek the living fellowship with Him.

This is now the blessedness of waiting upon God: that I confess the utter weakness of all my thoughts and efforts and set myself still to bow my heart before Him in holy silence and to trust Him to renew and strengthen His own work in me. And this is just the lesson of our text, *"Let your heart take courage, all ye that wait for the* LORD.*"* Remember the difference between knowing with the mind and believing with the heart. Beware of the temptation of leaning upon your understanding, with its clear, strong thoughts. They only help you to know what the heart must get from God; in themselves they are only images and shadows.

"Let your heart take courage, all ye that wait for the LORD.*"* Present it before Him as that wonderful part of your spiritual nature in which God reveals Himself, and by which you can know Him. Cultivate the greatest confidence that though you cannot see into your heart, God is working there by His Holy Spirit. Let the heart wait at times in perfect silence and quiet; in its hidden depths God will work. Be sure of this, and just wait on Him. Give your whole heart, with its secret workings, into God's hands continually. He wants the heart. He takes it and, as God, dwells in it. *"Be strong, and let your heart take courage, all ye that wait for the* LORD.*"*

My soul, wait thou only upon God!

10

IN HUMBLE FEAR
AND HOPE

*Behold, the eye of the LORD is upon them that fear him, upon them
that hope in his mercy; to deliver their soul from death,
and to keep them alive in famine. Our soul waiteth for the LORD:
he is our help and our shield. For our heart shall rejoice in him,
because we have trusted in his holy name. Let thy mercy, O LORD, be
upon us, according as we [wait for] thee.*
—Psalm 33:18–22

God's eye is upon His people; their eyes are upon Him. In waiting upon God, our eyes, looking up to Him, meet His looking down upon us. This is the blessedness of waiting upon God, that it takes our eyes and thoughts away from ourselves, even our needs and desires, and occupies us with our God. We worship Him in His glory and love, with His all-seeing eye watching over us, that He may supply our every need. Let us consider this wonderful meeting between God and His people, and notice what we are taught here of them on whom God's eye rests, and of Him on whom our eye rests.

"*The eye of the* LORD *is upon them that fear him, upon them that hope in his mercy.*" Fear and hope are generally thought to be in conflict with each other. In the presence and worship of God, they are found side by side in perfect and beautiful harmony. And this is so, because in God Himself all apparent contradictions are reconciled. Righteousness and peace, judgment and mercy, holiness and love, infinite power and infinite gentleness, a majesty that is exalted above all heaven, and a condescension that bows very low, meet and kiss each other.

There is indeed a fear that has torment, that is cast out entirely by perfect love (1 John 4:18). But, there is a fear that is found in the very heavens. In the song of Moses and the Lamb they sing, "*Who shall not fear thee, O Lord, and glorify thy name?*" (Rev. 15:4). And out of the very throne the voice came, "*Praise our God, all ye his servants, and ye that fear him*" (Rev. 19:5). Let us in our waiting ever seek to "*fear this glorious and fearful name,* THE LORD THY GOD" (Deut. 28:58). The deeper we bow before His holiness in holy fear and adoring awe, in deep reverence and humble self-abasement, even as the angels veil their faces before the throne, the more His holiness will rest upon us. Then, we will be filled to have God reveal Himself. The deeper we enter into the truth "*that no flesh should glory in his presence*" (1 Cor. 1:29), will it be given us to see His glory. "*The eye of the* LORD *is upon them that fear him.*"

"*Upon them that hope in his mercy.*" So far will the true fear of God be from keeping us back from hope, it will stimulate and strengthen it. The lower we bow, the deeper we feel we have nothing to hope in but His mercy. The lower we bow, the nearer God will come and make our hearts bold to trust Him. Let every exercise of waiting, let our whole habit of waiting on God, be pervaded by abounding hope—a hope as bright and boundless as

God's mercy. The fatherly kindness of God is such that, in whatever state we come to Him, we may confidently hope in His mercy.

Such are God's waiting ones. And now, think of the God on whom we wait. "*The eye of the* LORD *is upon them that fear him, upon them that hope in his mercy; to deliver their soul from death, and to keep them alive in famine.*" Not to prevent the danger of death and famine—this is often needed to stir the waiting on Him—but to deliver and keep alive. For the dangers are often very real and dark; the situation, whether in the temporal or spiritual life, may appear to be utterly hopeless. There is always one hope: God's eye is on them.

That eye sees the danger, sees in tender love His trembling, waiting child, sees the moment when the heart is ripe for the blessing, and sees the way in which it is to come. This living, mighty God, oh, let us fear Him and hope in His mercy! And, let us humbly but boldly say, "*Our soul waiteth for the* LORD; *he is our help and our shield....Let thy mercy, O* LORD, *be upon us, according as we* [wait for] *thee.*"

Oh, the blessedness of waiting on such a God! A very present help in every time of trouble (Ps. 46:1), a shield and defense against every danger. Children of God, will you not learn to sink down in entire helplessness and inability, and in stillness to wait and see the salvation of God! In the utmost spiritual famine, and when death appears to prevail, oh, wait on God! He does deliver; He does keep alive. Say it not only in solitude, but say it to each other—the psalm speaks not of one but of God's people: "*our soul waiteth for the* LORD: *he is our help and our shield.*" Strengthen and encourage each other in the holy exercise of waiting, that each may not only say of himself, but of his brothers, "*We have waited for him, we will be glad and rejoice in his salvation*" (Isa. 25:9).

My soul, wait thou only upon God!

11

PATIENTLY

Rest in the LORD, and wait patiently for him....
Those that wait upon the LORD, they shall inherit the earth.
—Psalm 37:7, 9

In patience possess your souls. (See Luke 21:19.) *"Ye have need of patience"* (Heb. 10:36). *"Let patience have her perfect work, that ye may be perfect and entire"* (James 1:4). Such words of the Holy Spirit show us what an important element, in the Christian life and character, patience is. And nowhere is there a better place for cultivating or displaying it than in waiting on God. There we discover how impatient we are and what our impatience means. We confess, at times, that we are impatient with men and circumstances that hinder us, or with ourselves and our slow progress in the Christian life. If we truly set ourselves to wait upon God, we will find that it is with Him we are impatient, because He does not at once, or as soon as we would wish, do our bidding. It is in waiting upon God that our eyes are opened to believe in His wise and sovereign will. Then, we will see that the sooner and the more completely we absolutely yield to it, the more surely His blessing can come to us.

"It is not of him that willeth, nor of him that runneth, but of God that showeth mercy" (Rom. 9:16). We have as little power to increase or strengthen our spiritual life as we had to originate it. We *"were born, not...of the will of the flesh, nor of the will of man, but of God"* (John 1:13). Even so, our willing and running, our desire and effort, avail nothing; all is *"of God that showeth mercy."*

All the exercises of the spiritual life, our reading and praying, our willing and doing, have their value. But, they can go no farther than this, that they point the way and prepare us in humility to look to and depend upon God Himself, and in patience to wait His good time and mercy. The waiting is to teach us our absolute dependence upon God's mighty working, and to make us, in perfect patience, place ourselves at His disposal. They who wait on the Lord will inherit the land (see Ps. 37:34), the promised land and its blessing. The heirs must wait; they can afford to wait.

"Rest in the LORD, and wait patiently for him." The margin gives for *"Rest in the LORD,"* *"Be still before the Lord"* (ASV). It is resting in the Lord, in His will, His promise, His faithfulness, and His love, that makes patience easy. And the resting in Him is nothing but being silent unto Him, still before Him—having our thoughts and wishes, our fears and hopes, hushed into calm and quiet in that great peace of God that passes all understanding. (See Phil. 4:7.) That peace keeps the heart and mind when we are anxious for anything, because we have made our requests known to Him. (See v. 6.) The rest, the silence, the stillness, and the patient waiting, all find their strength and joy in God Himself.

The need for patience, and the reasonableness and the blessedness of patience, will be disclosed to the waiting soul. Our patience will be seen to be the counterpart of God's patience. He longs far more to bless us fully than we can desire it. But, as the husbandman has long patience until the fruit ripens, so God bows Himself to our slowness and bears long with us. Let us remember this, and wait patiently. Of each promise and every answer to prayer the word is true, "*I the LORD will hasten it in his time*" (Isa. 60:22).

"*Rest in the LORD, and wait patiently for him.*" Yes, for Him. Seek not only the help, the gift; seek Himself; wait for Him. Give God His glory by resting in Him, by trusting Him fully, by waiting patiently for Him. This patience honors Him greatly. It leaves Him, as God on the throne, to do His work. It yields self wholly into His hands. It lets God be God. If your waiting is for some special request, wait patiently. If your waiting is more an exercise of the spiritual life seeking to know and have more of God, wait patiently. Whether it is in the shorter specific periods of waiting, or as the continuous habit of the soul, rest in the Lord, be still before the Lord, and wait patiently. "*Those that wait upon the LORD, they shall inherit the earth.*"

My soul, wait thou only upon God!

12

KEEPING HIS WAYS

Wait on the Lord, and keep his way,
and he shall exalt thee to inherit the land.
—Psalm 37:34

If we desire to find a man whom we long to meet, we inquire as to the places in which he is to be found. When waiting on God, we need to be very careful that we keep His ways; outside of these we never can expect to find Him. *"Thou meetest him that rejoiceth and worketh righteousness, those that remember thee in thy ways"* (Isa. 64:5). We may be sure that God is never and nowhere to be found but in His way. There, by the soul who seeks and patiently waits, He is always most surely to be found. *"Wait on the Lord, and keep his way, and he shall exalt thee."*

How close is the connection between the two parts of the injunction, "*Wait on the* LORD"—which has to do with worship and disposition—"*and keep his way*"—which deals with walk and work. The outer life must be in harmony with the inner; the inner must be the inspiration and the strength for the outer. It is our God who has made His way known in His Word for our conduct and invites our confidence for His grace and help in our heart. If we do not keep His way, our waiting on Him can bring no blessing. The surrender to a full obedience to all His will is the secret of full access to all the blessings of His fellowship.

Notice how strongly this comes out in the psalm. It speaks of the evil-doer who prospers in his way and calls on the believer not to worry himself. When we see men around us prosperous and happy while they forsake God's ways, and ourselves left in difficulty or suffering, we are in danger of first fretting at what appears so strange, and then gradually yielding to seek our prosperity in their path. Psalm 37 says,

> *Fret not thyself....Trust in the* LORD, *and do good....Rest in the* LORD, *and wait patiently for him....Cease from anger, and forsake wrath....Depart from evil, and do good....The* LORD...*forsaketh not his saints....The righteous shall inherit the land....The law of his God is in his heart; none of his steps shall slide.*
>
> (vv. 1, 3, 7–8, 27–29, 31)

And then follows—the word *wait* occurs for the third time in the psalm—"*Wait on the* LORD, *and keep his way.*" Do what God asks you to do; God will do more than you can ask Him to do.

And, let no one give way to the fear: I cannot keep His way. It is this that robs believers of every confidence. It is true you have not the strength yet to keep His way. But, carefully keep those for which you have received strength already. Surrender yourself willingly and trustingly to keep all God's ways, in the strength that will come in waiting on Him. Give up your whole being to God without reserve and without doubt. He will prove Himself God to you, and work in you that which is pleasing in His sight through Jesus Christ.

Keep His ways as you know them in the Word. Keep His ways, as nature teaches them, in always doing what appears right. Keep His ways as providence points them out. Keep His ways as the Holy Spirit suggests. Do not think of waiting on God while you say you are not willing to work in His path. However weak you feel, only be willing, and He who has worked to will, will work to do by His power.

"Wait on the LORD, and keep his way." It may be that the consciousness of shortcoming and sin makes our text look more like a hindrance than a help in waiting on God. Let it not be so. Have we not said more than once that the very starting point and groundwork of this waiting is utter and absolute weakness? Why then do you not come with everything evil you feel in yourself, every memory of unwillingness, unwatchfulness, unfaithfulness, and all that causes such unceasing self-condemnation? Put your power in God's omnipotence, and find your deliverance in waiting on God.

Your failure has been due to only one thing. You sought to conquer and obey in your own strength. Come and bow before God until you learn that He is the God who alone is good, and alone can work any good thing. Believe that in you, and all that nature can do, there is no true power. Be content to receive from God each moment the inworking of His mighty grace and life. Then, waiting on God will become the renewal of your strength to run in His ways and not be weary, to walk in His paths and never faint. *"Wait on the LORD, and keep his way"* will be command and promise in one.

My soul, wait thou only upon God!

13

FOR MORE THAN
WE KNOW

And now, Lord, what wait I for? my hope is in thee.
Deliver me from all my transgressions.
—Psalm 39:7–8

There may be times when we feel as if we do not know what we are waiting for. There may be other times when we think we do know, and when it would be good for us to realize that we do not know how to ask as we ought. God is able to do for us exceeding abundantly above what we ask or think. (See Eph. 3:20.) And, we are in danger of limiting Him when we confine our desires and prayers to our own thoughts of them. It is a great thing at times to say, as our psalm says, *"And now, Lord, what wait I for?"* I scarcely know or can tell; this only I can say, *"My hope is in thee."*

How we see this limiting of God in the case of Israel! When Moses promised them meat in the wilderness, they doubted, saying, *"Can God furnish a table in the wilderness?...He smote the rock, that the waters gushed out... can he give bread also? can he provide flesh for his people?"* (Ps. 78:19–20). If they had been asked whether God could provide streams in the desert, they would have answered, Yes. God had done it; He could do it again. But, when they thought of God doing something new, they limited Him. Their expectation could not rise beyond their past experience, or their own thoughts of what was possible.

Even so, we may be limiting God by our conceptions of what He has promised or is able to do. Do let us beware of limiting the Holy One of Israel in our prayers. Let us believe that the very promises of God we plead have a divine meaning, infinitely beyond our thoughts of them. Let us believe that His fulfillment of them can be, in a power and an abundance of grace, beyond our largest grasping of thought. And, let us, therefore, cultivate the habit of waiting on God, not only for what we think we need, but for all that His grace and power are ready to do for us.

In every true prayer, there are two hearts in exercise. The one is your heart, with its little, dark, human thoughts of what you need and God can do. The other is God's great heart, with its infinite, its divine, purposes of blessing. What think you? To which of these two ought the larger place be given in your approach to Him? Undoubtedly, to the heart of God. Everything depends upon knowing and being occupied with that. But, how little this is done. This is what waiting on God is meant to teach you. Just think of God's wonderful love and redemption, in the meaning these words must have to Him. Confess how little you understand what God is willing to do for you, and say each time as you pray, *"And now, Lord, what wait I for?"* My heart cannot say. God's heart knows and waits to give. *"My hope is in thee."* Wait on God to do more for you than you can ask or think.

Apply this to the prayer that follows, *"Deliver me from all my transgressions."* You have prayed to be delivered from temper or pride or self-will.

It is as if it is in vain. May it not be that you have had your own thoughts about the way or the extent of God's doing it, and have never waited on the God of glory, according to the riches of His glory, to do for you what the hearts of man cannot conceive?

Learn to worship God as the God who does wonders, who wishes to prove in you that He can do something supernatural and divine. Bow before Him, wait upon Him, until your soul realizes that you are in the hands of a divine and almighty worker. Consent but to know what and how He will work. Expect it to be something altogether godlike, something to be waited for in deep humility, and received only by His divine power. Let the *"And now, Lord, what wait I for? my hope is in thee"* become the spirit of every longing and every prayer. He will, in His time, do His work.

Dear soul, in waiting on God you may often be weary, because you hardly know what to expect. I pray you, be of good courage—this ignorance is often one of the best signs. He is teaching you to leave all in His hands, and to wait on Him alone. *"Wait on the LORD: be of good courage… wait, I say, on the LORD"* (Ps. 27:14).

My soul, wait thou only upon God!

14

THE WAY TO THE
NEW SONG

I waited patiently for the Lord; and he inclined unto me,
and heard my cry....And he hath put a new song in my mouth,
even praise unto our God.
—Psalm 40:1, 3

Come and listen to the testimony of one who can speak from experience of the sure and blessed outcome of patient waiting upon God. True patience is so foreign to our self-confident nature, it is so indispensable in our waiting upon God, it is such an essential element of true faith, that we would do well to once again meditate on what the Word has to teach us.

The word *patience* is derived from the Latin word for suffering. It suggests the thought of being under the constraint of some power from which we would gladly be free. At first, we submit against our will. Experience teaches us that when it is vain to resist, patient endurance is our wisest course. In waiting on God, it is of infinite consequence that we not only submit, because we are compelled to, but because we lovingly and joyfully consent to be in the hands of our blessed Father. Patience then becomes our highest blessedness and our highest grace. It honors God, and gives Him time to have His way with us. It is the highest expression of our faith in His goodness and faithfulness. It brings the soul perfect rest in the assurance that God is carrying on His work. It is the token of our full consent that God should deal with us in such a way and time as He thinks best. True patience is the losing of our self-will in His perfect will.

Such patience is needed for the true and full waiting on God. Such patience is the growth and fruit of our first lesson in the school of waiting. To many, it will appear strange how difficult it is to truly wait upon God. The great stillness of soul before God that sinks into its own helplessness and waits for Him to reveal Himself must be waited for. The deep humility that is afraid to let its own will or own strength work except as God works to will and to do requires patience. The meekness that is content to be and to know nothing except as God gives His light takes time. The entire resignation of the will that only wants to be a vessel in which His holy will can move and mold is not found at once. But, each will come in measure as the soul maintains its position, and continually says, *"Truly my soul waiteth upon God: from him cometh my salvation. He only is my rock and my salvation"* (Ps. 62:1–2).

Have you ever noticed what proof we have that patience is a grace for which very special grace is given? Notice these words of Paul: *"Strengthened with all might, according to his glorious power, unto all"*—what?—*"patience and longsuffering with joyfulness"* (Col. 1:11). Yes, we need to be strengthened with all God's might, according to the measure of His glorious power, if we are to wait on God in all patience. It is God revealing Himself in us as our life and strength that will enable us, with perfect patience, to leave all in His hands. If any are inclined to despond because they do not have such patience, let them be of good courage. It is in the course of our feeble and very imperfect waiting that God Himself, by His hidden power, strengthens us and works out in us the patience of the saints, the patience of Christ Himself.

Listen to the voice of one who was deeply tried: *"I waited patiently for the Lord; and he inclined unto me, and heard my cry."* Hear what he passed through: *"He brought me up also out of an horrible pit, out of the miry clay, and set my feet upon a rock, and established my goings. And he hath put a new song in my mouth, even praise unto our God"* (Ps. 40:2–3). Patient waiting upon God brings a rich reward; the deliverance is sure. God Himself will put a new song into your mouth. Oh, soul, do not be impatient, whether it is in the exercise of prayer and worship that you find it difficult to wait, in the delay of definite requests, or in the fulfillment of your heart's desire for the revelation of God Himself in a deeper spiritual life! Fear not, but rest in the Lord, and wait patiently for Him.

And, if you sometimes feel as if patience is not your gift, then remember it is God's gift, and take that prayer: *"The Lord direct your hearts into the...patience of Christ"* (2 Thess. 3:5 ASV). Into the patience with which you are to wait on God, He Himself will guide you.

My soul, wait thou only upon God!

15

FOR HIS COUNSEL

They soon forgat his works; they waited not for his counsel.
—Psalm 106:13

This refers to the sin of God's people in the wilderness. He had wonderfully redeemed them and was prepared to supply their every need just as wonderfully. But, when the time of need came, *"they waited not for his counsel."* They did not think that the Almighty God was their Leader and Provider. They did not ask what His plans might be. They simply thought the thoughts of their own hearts, and tempted and provoked God by their unbelief. *"They waited not for his counsel."*

How this has been the sin of God's people in all ages! In the land of Canaan, in the days of Joshua, the only three failures of which we read were owing to this one sin. In going up against Ai, in making a covenant with the Gibeonites, in settling down without going up to possess the whole land, *"they waited not for his counsel."* And so, even the advanced believer is in danger from this most subtle of temptations: taking God's Word, thinking his own thoughts of it, and not waiting for His counsel. Let us heed the warning and see what Israel teaches us. And, let us especially regard it not only as a danger to which the individual is exposed, but as one against which God's people, in their collective capacity, need to be on their guard.

Our whole relationship to God is ruled in this, that His will is to be done in us and by us as it is in heaven. He has promised to make known His will to us by His Spirit, the Guide into all truth. And, our position is to be that of waiting for His counsel as the only guide of our thoughts and actions. In our church worship, in our prayers meetings, in our conventions, in all our gatherings as managers or directors or committees or helpers in any part of the work for God, our first object must always be to ascertain the mind of God. God always works according to the counsel of His will. The more that counsel of His will is sought and found and honored, the more surely and mightily will God do His work for us and through us.

The great danger in all such assemblies is that in our consciousness of having our Bible, in our past experience of God's leading, in our sound creed and our honest wish to do God's will, we trust in these and do not realize that with every step we need and may have a heavenly guidance. There may be elements of God's will, application of God's Word, experience of the close presence and leading of God, manifestations of the power of His Spirit, of which we know nothing as yet. God may be willing, no, God is willing to open up these to the souls who are intently set upon allowing Him to have His way entirely, and who are willing, in patience, to wait for Him to make it known.

When we come together praising God for all He has done and taught and given, we may, at the same time, be limiting Him by not expecting greater things. It was when God had given the water out of the rock that they did not trust Him for bread. It was when God had given Jericho into his hands that Joshua thought the victory over Ai was sure and did not wait for counsel from God. And so, while we think that we know and trust the power of God for what we may expect, we may be hindering Him by not giving Him time, and not definitely cultivating the habit of waiting for His counsel.

A minister has no more solemn duty than to teach people to wait upon God. Why was it that in the house of Cornelius, when *"Peter yet spake these words, the Holy Ghost fell on all them which heard"* (Acts 10:44)? They had said, *"Now therefore are we all here present before God, to hear all things that are commanded thee of God"* (v. 33). We may come together to give and to listen to the most earnest exposition of God's truth with little spiritual profit if there is no waiting for God's counsel.

And so, in all our gatherings we need to believe in the Holy Spirit as the Guide and Teacher of God's saints. They must wait to be led by Him into the things that God has prepared and that the heart cannot conceive.

More stillness of soul to realize God's presence; more consciousness of ignorance of what God's great plans may be; more faith in the certainty that God has greater things to show us; that He Himself will be revealed in new glory—these must be the marks of the assemblies of God's saints if they would avoid the reproach, *"They waited not for his counsel."*

My soul, wait thou only upon God!

16

AND HIS LIGHT IN
THE HEART

I wait for the LORD, *my soul doth wait, and in his word do I hope.*
My soul waiteth for the Lord more than they that watch for the
morning: I say, more than they that watch for the morning.
—Psalm 130:5–6

How intensely the morning light is often waited for: by the mariners in a shipwrecked vessel; by a benighted traveler in a dangerous country; by an army that finds itself surrounded by an enemy. The morning light will show what hope of escape there may be. The morning may bring life and liberty. And so, the saints of God in darkness have longed for the light of His countenance, more than watchmen for the morning.

They have said, *"My soul waiteth for the Lord more than they that watch for the morning."* Can we say that, too? Our waiting on God can have no higher object than simply having His light shine on us, in us, and through us, all day.

God is light. God is a sun. Paul said, *"God…hath shined in our hearts, to give the light"* (2 Cor. 4:6). What light? *"The light of the…glory of God in the face of Jesus Christ"* (v. 6). Just as the sun shines its beautiful, life-giving light on and into our earth, so God shines into our hearts the light of His glory, of His love, in Christ His Son. Our hearts are meant to have that light filling and gladdening them all day. They can have it because God is our sun, and it is written, *"Thy sun shall no more go down"* (Isa. 60:20). God's love shines on us without ceasing.

But, can we indeed enjoy it all day? We can. And how can we? Let nature give us the answer. Those beautiful trees and flowers, with all the green grass, what do they do to keep the sun shining on them? They do nothing; they simply bask in the sunshine when it comes. The sun is millions of miles away, but over all that distance it comes, its own light and joy. And the tiniest flower that lifts its little head upward is met by the same exuberance of light and blessing as flood the widest landscape. We do not have to provide for the light we need for our day's work. The sun cares and provides and shines the light around us all day. We simply count upon it, receive it, and enjoy it.

The only difference between nature and grace is this, that what the trees and the flowers do unconsciously, as they drink in the blessing of the light, is to be, for us, a voluntary and loving acceptance. Faith, simple faith in God's Word and love, is to be the opening of the eyes and the heart, to receive and enjoy the unspeakable glory of His grace. And just as the trees, day by day and month by month, stand and grow into beauty and fruitfulness, just welcoming whatever sunshine the sun may give, so it is the very highest exercise of our Christian life just to abide in the light of God. Let it, and let Him, fill us with the life and the brightness it brings.

And if you ask, But can it really be, that just as naturally and heartily as I recognize and rejoice in the beauty of a bright sunny morning, I can rejoice in God's light all day? It can, indeed. From my breakfast table I look out on a beautiful valley, with trees and vineyards and mountains. In our spring and autumn months, the light in the morning is exquisite, and almost involuntarily we say, How beautiful! And the question comes, Is it only the light of the sun that is to bring such continual beauty and joy? And is there no provision for the light of God being just as much an unceasing source of joy and gladness? There is, indeed, if the soul will only be still and wait on Him. Only let God shine.

Dear soul, learn to wait on the Lord, more than watchers for the morning! All within you may be very dark. But, is that not the very best reason for waiting for the light of God? The beginnings of light may be just enough to discover the darkness, and painfully to humble you on account of sin. Can you not trust the light to expel the darkness? Do believe it will. Just bow, even now, in stillness before God, and wait on Him to shine into you. Say, in humble faith, God is light, infinitely brighter and more beautiful than that of the sun. God is light—the Father. The eternal, inaccessible, and incomprehensible light—the Son. The light concentrated, embodied, and manifested—the Spirit, the light entering and dwelling and shining in our hearts. God is light, and is here shining on my heart. I have been so occupied with the candles of my thoughts and efforts that I have never opened the shutters to let His light in. Unbelief has kept it out.

I bow in faith—God, light, is shining into my heart. The God of whom Paul wrote, "God...hath shined in our hearts" (2 Cor. 4:6), is my God. What would I think of a sun that could not shine? What would I think of a God who does not shine? No, God shines! God is light! I will take time, just be still, and rest in the light of God. My eyes are feeble, and the windows are not clean, but I will wait on the Lord. The light does shine; the light will shine in me and make me full of light. And I will learn to walk all day in the light and joy of God. My soul waits on the light of the Lord, more than the watchers for the morning.

My soul, wait thou only upon God!

17

IN TIMES OF DARKNESS

I will wait upon the Lord,
that hideth his face from the house of Jacob, and I will look for him.
—Isaiah 8:17

ere we have a servant of God waiting upon Him, not on behalf of himself, but of his people, from whom God was hiding His face. It suggests to us how our waiting upon God, though it commences with our personal needs, with the desire for the revelation of Himself, or of the answer to personal petitions, need not, may not, stop there. We may be walking in the full light of God's countenance, and yet God may be hiding His face from His people around us. Far from our being content to think that this is nothing but the just punishment of their sin, or the consequence of their indifference, we are called with tender hearts to think of their sad estate, and to wait on God on their behalf. The privilege of waiting upon God is one that brings great responsibility. Even as Christ, when He entered God's presence, at once used His place of privilege and honor as intercessor, so we, no less, if we know what it is to really enter in and wait upon God, must use our access for our less favored brothers and sisters. "*I will wait upon the* Lord, *that hideth his face from the house of Jacob.*"

You worship with a certain congregation. Possibly, there is not the spiritual life or joy either in the preaching or in the fellowship that you desire. You belong to a church with its many services. There is so much error or worldliness, so much seeking after human wisdom and culture, or so much trust in ordinances and observances, that you are not surprised that God hides His face in many cases. It is no wonder that there is little power for conversion or true edification.

Then, there are branches of Christian work with which you are connected—a Sunday school, a gospel hall, a young men's association, a mission work abroad—in which the feebleness of the Spirit's working appears to indicate that God is hiding His face. You think, too, you know the reason. There is too much trust in men and money. There is too much formality and self-indulgence. There is too little faith and prayer; too little love and humility; too little of the spirit of the crucified Jesus. At times, you feel as if things are hopeless and that nothing will help.

Do believe that God can and will help. Let the spirit of the prophet come into you, as you value his words, and set yourself to wait on God, on behalf of His erring children. Instead of the tone of judgment or condemnation, of despondency or despair, realize your calling to wait upon God. If others fail in doing it, give yourself doubly to it. The deeper the darkness, the greater the need of appealing to the only Deliverer. The greater the self-confidence around you, that knows not that it is poor and wretched and blind, the more urgent the call to be at your post waiting upon God. Say on each new occasion, when you are tempted to speak or to sigh, "*I will wait upon the* Lord, *that hideth his face from the house of Jacob.*"

There is a still larger circle—the Christian church throughout the world. Think of Greek, Roman Catholic, and Protestant churches, and the state of the millions who belong to them. Or, think only of the Protestant churches with their open Bible and orthodox creeds. How much nominal profession and formality! How much of the rule of the flesh and of man in the very temple of God! And what abundant proof that God does hide His face!

What are those who see and mourn this to do? The first thing to be done is this: *"I will wait upon the LORD, that hideth his face from the house of Jacob."* Let us wait on God, in the humble confession of the sins of His people. Let us take time and wait on Him in this exercise. Let us wait on God in tender, loving intercession for all saints, our beloved brothers and sisters, however wrong their lives or their teaching may appear. Let us wait on God in faith and expectation, until He shows us that He will hear. Let us wait on God, with the simple offering of ourselves to Himself, and the earnest prayer that He would send us to our brothers and sisters. Let us wait on God, and give Him no rest until He makes Zion a joy in the earth.

Yes, let us rest in the Lord and wait patiently for Him who now hides His face from so many of His children. And let us say of the lifting up of the light of His countenance that we long for all His people, *"I wait for the LORD, my soul doth wait, and in his word do I hope"* (Ps. 130:5). *"My soul waiteth for the Lord more than they that watch for the morning: I say, more than they that watch for the morning"* (v. 6).

My soul, wait thou only upon God!

18

TO REVEAL HIMSELF

And it shall be said in that day, Lo, this is our God;
we have waited for him, and he will save us: this is the LORD;
we have waited for him, we will be glad and rejoice in his salvation.
—Isaiah 25:9

In this passage, we have two precious thoughts. The one, that it is the language of God's people who have been unitedly waiting on Him. The other, that the fruit of their waiting has been that God has so revealed Himself, that they could joyfully say, *"Lo, this is our God...this is the LORD."* The power and the blessing of united waiting is what we need to learn.

Note that this phrase is repeated twice, *"We have waited for him."* In some time of trouble, the hearts of the people had been drawn together, and they had, ceasing from all human hope or help, with one heart set themselves to wait for their God. Is this not just what we need in our churches and conventions and prayer meetings? Is not the need of the church and the world great enough to demand it? Are there not in the church of Christ evils to which no human wisdom is equal? Have we not ritualism and rationalism, formalism and worldliness, robbing the church of its power? Have we not culture and money and pleasure threatening its spiritual life? Are not the powers of the church utterly inadequate to cope with the powers of infidelity and iniquity and wretchedness in Christian countries and in heathendom? And, is there not, in the promise of God and in the power of the Holy Spirit, a provision made that can meet the need and give the church the restful assurance that she is doing all her God expects of her? And would not united waiting upon God for the supply of His Spirit most certainly seem the needed blessing? We cannot doubt it.

The object of a more definite waiting upon God in our gatherings would be very much the same as in personal worship. It would mean a deeper conviction that God must and will do all. It would require a more humble and abiding entrance into our deep helplessness, and the need of entire and unceasing dependence upon Him. We need a more living consciousness that the essential thing is to give God His place of honor and of power. We must have a confident expectation that to those who wait on Him, God will, by His Spirit, give the secret of His acceptance and presence, and then, in due time, the revelation of His saving power. The great aim would be to bring everyone in a praying and worshipping company under a deep sense of God's presence, so that when they part there will be the consciousness of having met God Himself, of having left every request with Him, and of now waiting in stillness while He works out His salvation.

It is this experience that is indicated in our text. The fulfillment of the words may, at times, be in such striking interpositions of God's power that all can join in the cry, *"Lo, this is our God...this is the LORD."* They may equally become true in spiritual experience, when God's people, in their waiting times, become so conscious of His presence that, in holy awe, souls feel, "*Lo, this is our God…this is the* LORD." It is this, alas, that is too much missed in our meetings for worship. The godly minister has no more difficult, no more solemn, no more blessed task, than to lead his people out to meet God. And, before he preaches, he must bring each one into contact with Him. "We are now here in the presence of God"—these words of Cornelius show the way in which Peter's audience was prepared for the coming of the Holy Spirit. Waiting before God, waiting for God, and waiting on God are the conditions of God showing His presence.

A company of believers gathered with the one purpose, helping each other by little intervals of silence, to wait on God alone, opening the heart for whatever God may have of new discoveries of evil, of His will, of new openings in work or methods of work, would soon have reason to say, "*Lo, this is our God; we have waited for him, and he will save us: this is the* LORD; *we have waited for him, we will be glad and rejoice in his salvation.*"

My soul, wait thou only upon God!

19

AS A GOD
OF JUDGMENT

Yea, in the way of thy judgments, O LORD, *have we waited for thee....*
For when thy judgments are in the earth,
the inhabitants of the world will learn righteousness.
—Isaiah 26:8–9

The LORD *is a God of judgment: blessed are all they that wait for him.*
—Isaiah 30:18

God is a God of mercy and a God of judgment. Mercy and judgment are forever together in His dealings. In the Flood, in the deliverance of Israel out of Egypt, in the overthrow of the Canaanites, we ever see mercy in the midst of judgment. In these, the inner circle of His own people, we see it, too. The judgment punishes the sin, while mercy saves the sinner. Or, rather, mercy saves the sinner, not in spite of, but by means of, the very judgment that came upon his sin. In waiting on God, we must beware of forgetting this—as we wait we must expect Him as a God of judgment.

"In the way of thy judgments, O Lord, have we waited for thee." That will prove true in our inner experience. If we are honest in our longing for holiness—in our prayers to be wholly the Lord's—His holy presence will stir up and discover hidden sin. It will bring us very low in the bitter conviction of the evil of our nature, its opposition to God's law, and its inability to fulfill that law. The words will come true: *"Who may abide the day of his coming?...For he is like a refiner's fire"* (Mal. 3:2). *"Oh that thou wouldest... come down....As when the melting fire burneth"* (Isa. 64:1). In great mercy, God executes, within the soul, His judgments upon sin, as He makes it feel its wickedness and guilt. Many try to flee from these judgments. The soul that longs for God, and for deliverance from sin, bows under them in humility and in hope. In silence of soul, it says, *"Rise up, Lord, and let thine enemies be scattered"* (Num. 10:35). *"In the way of thy judgments...have we waited for thee."*

Let no one who seeks to learn the blessed art of waiting on God, wonder if at first the attempt to wait on Him only reveals more of sin and darkness. Let no one despair because unconquered sins, evil thoughts, or great darkness appear to hide God's face. Was not, in His own beloved Son, the gift and bearer of His mercy on Calvary, the mercy as hidden and lost in the judgment? Oh, submit and sink down deep under the judgment of your every sin. Judgment prepares the way and breaks out in wonderful mercy. It is written, *"Zion shall be redeemed with judgment"* (Isa. 1:27). Wait on God, in the faith that His tender mercy is working out His redemption in the midst of judgment. Wait for Him; He will be gracious to you.

There is another application still, one of unspeakable solemnity. We are expecting God, in the way of His judgments, to visit this earth; we are waiting for Him. What a thought! We know of these coming judgments. We know that there are tens of thousands of professing Christians who live on in carelessness, and who, if no change comes, must perish under God's hand. Oh, will we not do our utmost to warn them, to plead with and for them, if God may have mercy on them! If we feel our lack of boldness, zeal, and power, will we not begin to wait on God more definitely and persistently as a God of judgment? Will we not ask Him to so reveal Himself in the judgments that are coming on our very friends, that we may be inspired with a new fear of Him and them, and constrained to speak and pray as never yet before? Verily, waiting on God is not meant to be a spiritual self-indulgence. Its object is to let God and His holiness, Christ and the love that died on Calvary, the Spirit and fire that burns in heaven and came to earth, get possession of us, to warn and arouse men with the message that we are waiting for God in the way of His judgments. Oh, Christian, prove that you really believe in the God of judgment!

My soul, wait thou only upon God!

20

WHO WAITS ON US

And therefore will the LORD *wait, that he may be gracious unto you, and*
therefore will he be exalted, that he may have mercy upon you:
for the LORD *is a God of judgment: blessed are all they that wait for him.*
—Isaiah 30:18

We must not only think of our waiting upon God, but also of what is more wonderful still, of God's waiting upon us. The vision of Him waiting on us will give new impulse and inspiration to our waiting upon Him. It will give us an unspeakable confidence that our waiting cannot be in vain. If He waits for us, then we may be sure that we are more than welcome—that He rejoices to find those He has been seeking for. Let us seek even now, at this moment, in the spirit of lowly waiting on

God, to find out something of what it means. *"Therefore will the* LORD *wait, that he may be gracious unto you."* We will accept and echo back the message, *"Blessed are all they that wait for him."*

Look up and see the great God upon His throne. He is love—an unceasing and inexpressible desire to communicate His own goodness and blessedness to all His creatures. He longs and delights to bless. He has inconceivably glorious purposes concerning every one of His children, by the power of His Holy Spirit, to reveal in them His love and power. He waits with all the longings of a father's heart. He waits that He may be gracious unto you. And, each time you come to wait upon Him, or seek to maintain in daily life the holy habit of waiting, you may look up and see Him ready to meet you. He will be waiting so that He may be gracious unto you. Yes, connect every exercise, every breath of the life of waiting, with faith's vision of your God waiting for you.

And if you ask: How is it, if He waits to be gracious, that even after I come and wait upon Him, He does not give the help I seek, but waits on longer and longer? There is a double answer. The one is this. God is a wise husbandman, who *"waiteth for the precious fruit of the earth, and hath long patience for it"* (James 5:7). He cannot gather the fruit until it is ripe. He knows when we are spiritually ready to receive the blessing to our profit and His glory. Waiting in the sunshine of His love is what will ripen the soul for His blessing. Waiting under the cloud of trial, that breaks in showers of blessing, is as necessary. Be assured that if God waits longer than you could wish, it is only to make the blessing doubly precious. God waited four thousand years, until the fullness of time, before He sent His Son. Our times are in His hands. He will avenge His elect speedily. He will make haste for our help and not delay one hour too long.

The other answer points to what has been said before. The giver is more than the gift; God is more than the blessing. And our being kept waiting on Him is the only way for our learning to find our life and joy in Himself. Oh, if God's children only knew what a glorious God they have, and what a privilege it is to be linked in fellowship with Him, then they would rejoice in Him! Even when He keeps them waiting, they will learn to understand better than ever. *"Therefore will the* LORD *wait, that he may be gracious unto you."* His waiting will be the highest proof of His graciousness.

"Blessed are all they that wait for him." A queen has her ladies-in-waiting. The position is one of subordination and service, and yet it is considered one of the highest dignity and privilege, because a wise and gracious sovereign makes them companions and friends. What a dignity and blessedness to be attendants-in-waiting on the everlasting God, ever on the watch for every indication of His will or favor, ever conscious of His nearness, His goodness, and His grace! *"The* LORD *is good unto them that wait for him"* (Lam. 3:25). *"Blessed are all they that wait for him."* Yes, it is blessed when a waiting soul and a waiting God meet each other. God cannot do His work without His and our waiting His time. Let waiting be our work, as it is His. And, if His waiting is nothing but goodness and graciousness, let ours be nothing but a rejoicing in that goodness, and a confident expectancy of that grace. And, let every thought of waiting become to us the simple expression of unmingled and unutterable blessedness, because it brings us to a God who waits that He may make Himself known to us perfectly as the gracious One.

My soul, wait thou only upon God!

21

THE ALMIGHTY ONE

They that wait upon the LORD *shall renew their strength;*
they shall mount up with wings as eagles; they shall run, and not be
weary; and they shall walk, and not faint.
—Isaiah 40:31

Our waiting on God will depend greatly on our faith of what He is. In our text, we have the close of a passage in which God reveals Himself as the everlasting and almighty One. It is as that revelation enters into our soul that the waiting will become the spontaneous expression of what we know Him to be—a God altogether most worthy to be waited upon.

Listen to the words, "*Why sayest thou, O Jacob…My way is hid from the* Lord…*? Hast thou not known? hast thou not heard, that the everlasting God, the* Lord, *the Creator of the ends of the earth, fainteth not, neither is weary?*" (Isa. 40:27–28). So far from it: "*He giveth power to the faint; and to them that have no might he increaseth strength. Even the youths shall faint…and the young men shall utterly fall*" (vv. 29–30). And consider that "*the glory of young men is their strength*" (Prov. 20:29). All that is deemed strong with man shall come to nothing. "*But they that wait upon the* Lord," on the Everlasting One, who does not faint, and is not weary, they "*shall renew their strength; they shall mount up with wings as eagles; they shall run, and*"—listen now, they will be strong with the strength of God, and, even as He, they will "*not be weary; and they shall walk, and*" even as He, they will "*not faint.*"

Yes, "*they shall mount up with wings as eagles.*" You know what eagles' wings mean. The eagle is the king of birds; it soars the highest into the heavens. Believers are to live a heavenly life, in the very presence and love and joy of God. They are to live where God lives; they need God's strength to rise there. It will be given to them that wait on Him.

You know how the eagles' wings are obtained. Only in one way—by the eagle birth. You are born of God. You have the eagles' wings. You may not have known it; you may not have used them; but God can and will teach you how to use them.

You know how the eagles are taught the use of their wings. See yonder cliff rising a thousand feet out of the sea. See high up a ledge on the rock, where there is an eagle's nest with its treasure of two young eaglets. See the mother bird come and stir up her nest, and with her beak push the timid birds over the precipice. See how they flutter and fall and sink toward the depth. See now how she "*fluttereth over her young, spreadeth abroad her wings, taketh them, beareth them on her wings*" (Deut. 32:11), and so, as they ride upon her wings, brings them to a place of safety. And so, she does this once and again, each time casting them out over the precipice, and then again taking and carrying them. "*So the* Lord *alone did lead him*" (v. 12). Yes, the instinct of that eagle mother was God's gift, a single ray of that love in which the Almighty trains His people to mount as on eagles' wings.

He stirs up your nest. He disappoints your hopes. He brings down your confidence. He makes you fear and tremble, as all your strength fails, and you feel utterly weary and helpless. And all the while He is spreading His strong wings for you to rest your weakness on and offering His everlasting Creator strength to work in you. And all He asks is that you sink down in your weariness and wait on Him. Allow Him in His Jehovah strength to carry you as you ride upon the wings of His omnipotence.

Dear child of God, I pray you, lift up your eyes, and behold your God! Listen to Him who says that He "*fainteth not, neither is weary*" (Isa. 40:28), who promises that you too will not faint or be weary, who asks nothing but this one thing, that you should wait on Him. And, let your answer be, With such a God, so mighty, so faithful, so tender,

My soul, wait thou only upon God!

22

ITS CERTAINTY
OF BLESSING

Thou shalt know that I am the LORD:
for they shall not be ashamed that wait for me.
—Isaiah 49:23

Blessed are all they that wait for him.
—Isaiah 30:18

What promises! How God seeks to draw us to waiting on Him by the most positive assurance that it never can be in vain; *"they shall not be ashamed that wait for me."* How strange that, though we should so often have experienced it, we are yet so slow to learn that this blessed waiting must and can be the very breath of our life—a continuous resting in God's presence and His love, an unceasing yielding of ourselves for Him to perfect His work in us. Let us once again listen and meditate, until our heart says with new conviction, *"Blessed are all they that wait for him."*

We found in the prayer of Psalm 25: *"Let none that wait on thee be ashamed"* (v. 3). The very prayer shows how we fear that it might be true. Let us listen to God's answer, until every fear is banished, and we send back to heaven the words God speaks, Yes, Lord, we believe what You say: "All they who wait for Me will *not* be ashamed." *"Blessed are all they that wait for him."*

The context of each of these two passages points us to times when God's church was in great straits, and to human eyes there were no possibilities of deliverance. But, God interposes with His word of promise, and pledges His almighty power for the deliverance of His people. And it is as the God who has Himself undertaken the work of their redemption that He invites them to wait on Him, and assures them that disappointment is impossible.

We, too, are living in days in which there is much in the state of the church, with its profession and its formalism, that is indescribably sad. Amid all we praise God for, there is, alas, much to mourn over! Were it not for God's promises, we might well despair. But, in His promises the living God has given and bound Himself to us. He calls us to wait on Him. He assures us we will not be put to shame. Oh, that our hearts might learn to wait before Him, until He Himself reveals to us what His promises mean. In the promises, He reveals Himself in His hidden glory! We will be irresistibly drawn to wait on Him alone. May God increase the company of those who say: *"Our soul waiteth for the LORD: he is our help and our shield"* (Ps. 33:20).

This waiting upon God on behalf of His church and people will depend greatly upon the place that waiting on Him has taken in our personal life. The mind may often have beautiful visions of what God has promised to do, and the lips may speak of them in stirring words, but these are not really the measure of our faith or power. No, it is what we really know of God in our personal experience, conquering the enemies within, reigning and ruling, revealing Himself in His holiness and power in our innermost being. It is this that will be the real measure of the spiritual blessing we expect from Him, and bring to our fellowmen.

It is as we know how blessed the waiting on God has become to our own souls, that we will confidently hope in the blessing to come on the church around us. The keyword of all our expectations will be, He has said: "All they who wait on Me will not be ashamed." From what He has done in us, we will trust Him to do mighty things around us. *Blessed are all they that wait for him.* Yes, blessed even now in the waiting. The promised blessings for ourselves, or for others, may tarry. The unutterable blessedness of knowing and having Him who has promised—the divine Blesser, the living Fountain of the coming blessings—is even now ours. Do let this truth acquire full possession of your souls, that waiting on God is itself the highest privilege of man, the highest blessedness of His redeemed child.

Even as the sunshine enters with its light and warmth, with its beauty and blessing, into every little blade of grass that rises upward out of the cold earth, so the everlasting God meets, in the greatness and the tenderness of His love, each waiting child, to shine in his heart *the light of the knowledge of the glory of God in the face of Jesus Christ* (2 Cor. 4:6). Read these words again, until your heart learns to know what God waits to do to you. Who can measure the difference between the great sun and that little blade of grass? And yet, the grass has all of the sun it can need or hold.

Do believe that in waiting on God, His greatness and your littleness suit and meet each other most wonderfully. Just bow in emptiness and poverty and utter weakness, in humility and meekness, and surrender to His will before His great glory, and be still. As you wait on Him, God draws near. He will reveal Himself as the God who will mightily fulfill His every promise. And, let your heart continually take up the song: *Blessed are all they that wait for him.*

My soul, wait thou only upon God!

23

FOR UNLOOKED-FOR THINGS

For since the beginning of the world men have not heard,
nor perceived by the ear, neither hath the eye seen, O God, beside thee,
what he hath prepared for him that waiteth for him.
—Isaiah 64:4

The American Standard Version has the thought: "*Neither hath the eye seen a God besides thee, who worketh for him that waiteth for him.*" In the King James Version, the thought is that no eye has seen the thing that God has prepared. In the American Standard Version, no eye has seen a God, besides our God, who works for him who waits for Him. To both, the two thoughts are common: that our place is to wait upon God, and that what the human heart cannot conceive will be revealed to us. The difference is the following: in the American Standard Version, it is *the* God who works; in the King James Version, *the thing* He is to work. In 1 Corinthians 2:9, *"But as it is written, Eye hath not seen, nor ear heard, neither have entered into the heart of man, the things which God hath prepared for them that love him,"* the reference is in regard to the things that the Holy Spirit is to reveal, as in the King James Version, and in this chapter we will keep to that.

The previous verses in Isaiah, especially Isaiah 63:15, refer to the low state of God's people. The prayer has been poured out, *"Look down from heaven"* (v. 15). *"Why hast thou…hardened our heart from thy fear? Return for thy servants' sake"* (v. 17). And 64:1–2, still more urgent, *"Oh that thou wouldest rend the heavens, that thou wouldest come down…as when the melting fire burneth…to make thy name known to thine adversaries!"* Then follows the plea from the past, *"When thou didst terrible things which we looked not for, thou camest down, the mountains flowed down at thy presence"* (v. 3). *"For"*— this is now the faith that has been awakened by the thought of things we looked not for, He is still the same God—*"neither hath the eye seen, O God, beside thee, what he hath prepared for him that waiteth for him."*

God alone knows what He can do for His waiting people. As Paul expounds and applies it: *"The things of God knoweth no man, but the Spirit of God"* (1 Cor. 2:11). *"But God hath revealed them unto us by his Spirit"* (v. 10).

The need of God's people, and the call for God's intervention, is as urgent in our days as it was in the time of Isaiah. There is now, as there was then, as there has been at all times, a few who seek after God with their whole hearts. But, if we look at Christendom as a whole, at the state of the church of Christ, there is infinite cause for beseeching God to rend the heavens and come down. Nothing but a special interposition of almighty power will avail. I fear we do not have a proper conception of what the so-called Christian world is in the sight of God. Unless God comes down *"as when the melting fire burneth…to make [His] name known to [His] adversaries"* (Isa. 64:2), our labors are comparatively fruitless.

Look at the ministry: how much it is in the wisdom of man and of literary culture; how little in demonstration of the Spirit and of power. Think of the unity of the body: how little there is of the manifestation of the power of a heavenly love binding God's children into one. Think of holiness—the holiness of Christlike humility and crucifixion to the world. How little the world sees that they have men among them who live in Christ in heaven, in whom Christ and heaven live!

What is to be done? There is only one thing. We must wait upon God. And what for? We must cry, with a cry that never rests, *"Oh that thou wouldest rend the heavens...[and] come down, that the mountains might flow down at thy presence"* (Isa. 64:1). We must desire and believe, we must ask and expect, that God will do unlooked-for things. We must set our faith on a God of whom men do not know what He has prepared for them who wait for Him. The wonder-doing God, who can surpass all our expectations, must be the God of our confidence.

Yes, let God's people enlarge their hearts to wait on a God able to do exceeding abundantly above what we can ask or think. (See Eph. 3:20.) Let us band ourselves together as His elect who cry day and night to Him for things men have not seen. He is able to arise and to make His people a name and a praise in the earth. *"The LORD will wait, that he may be gracious unto you...blessed are all they that wait for him"* (Isa. 30:18).

My soul, wait thou only upon God!

24

TO KNOW HIS GOODNESS

The LORD is good unto them that wait for him.
—Lamentations 3:25

There is none good but God. (See Matt. 19:17.) His goodness is in the heavens. *"Oh how great is thy goodness, which thou hast laid up for them that fear thee"* (Ps. 31:19). *"O taste and see that the LORD is good"* (Ps. 34:8). And here is now the true way of entering into and rejoicing in this goodness of God—waiting upon Him. The Lord is good—even His children often do not know it, for they do not wait in quietness for Him to reveal it. But, to those who persevere in waiting, whose souls do wait, it will come true. One might think that it is just those who have to wait who might doubt it. But, this is only when they do not wait, but grow impatient.

The truly waiting ones will all say, *"The* LORD *is good unto them that wait for him."* If you want to fully know the goodness of God, give yourself more than ever to a life of waiting on Him.

At our first entrance into the school of waiting upon God, the heart is mainly set on the blessings which we wait for. God graciously uses our needs and desires for help to educate us for something higher than we were thinking of. We were seeking gifts; He, the Giver, longs to give Himself and to satisfy the soul with His goodness. It is just for this reason that He often withholds the gifts, and that the time of waiting is made so long. He is constantly seeking to win the heart of His child for Himself. He wishes that we would not only say, when He bestows the gift, "How good is God!" but that long before it comes, and even if it never comes, we should all the time be experiencing: it is good that a man should quietly wait. *"The* LORD *is good unto them that wait for him."*

What a blessed life the life of waiting then becomes, the continual worship of faith, adoring, and trusting His goodness. As the soul learns its secret, every act or exercise of waiting becomes just a quiet entering into the goodness of God, to let it do its blessed work and satisfy our every need. And, every experience of God's goodness gives new attractiveness to the work of waiting. Instead of only taking refuge in time of need, there comes a great longing to wait continually and all day. And, however duties and engagements occupy the time and the mind, the soul gets more familiar with the secret art of always waiting. Waiting becomes the habit and disposition, the very second nature and breath of the soul.

Dear Christian, begin to see that waiting is not one among a number of Christian virtues, to be thought of from time to time. But, it expresses that disposition that lies at the very root of the Christian life. It gives a higher value and a new power to our prayers and worship, to our faith and surrender, because it links us, in unalterable dependence, to God Himself. And, it gives us the unbroken enjoyment of the goodness of God: *"The* LORD *is good unto them that wait for him."*

Let me stress once again that you must take time and trouble to cultivate this much needed element of the Christian life. We get too much secondhand religion from the teaching of men. That teaching has great value, even as the preaching of John the Baptist sent his disciples away from himself to the living Christ, if it leads us to God Himself. What our faith needs is—more of God.

Many of us are too occupied with our work. As with Martha, the very service we want to render the Master separates us from Him. It is neither pleasing to Him nor profitable to ourselves. The more work, the more need of waiting upon God. The doing of God's will would then be, instead of exhausting, our meat and drink, our nourishment and refreshment and strength. "*The* LORD *is good unto them that wait for him.*" How good is known only by those who prove it in waiting on Him. How good none can fully tell but those who have proved Him to the utmost.

My soul, wait thou only upon God!

25

QUIETLY

It is good that a man should both hope
and quietly wait for the salvation of the LORD.
—Lamentations 3:26

"Take heed, and be quiet; fear not, neither be fainthearted" (Isa. 7:4). "In quietness and in confidence shall be your strength" (Isa. 30:15). Such words reveal to us the close connection between quietness and faith. They show us what a deep need there is of quietness, as an element of true waiting upon God. If we are to have our whole heart turned toward God, we must have it turned away from man, from all that occupies and interests, whether of joy or sorrow.

God is a being of such infinite greatness and glory, and our nature has become so estranged from Him, that it requires our whole heart and desires set upon Him, even in some little measure, to know and receive Him. Everything that is not God, that excites our fears or stirs our efforts or awakens our hopes or makes us glad, hinders us in our perfect waiting on Him. The message is one of deep meaning: *"Take heed, and be quiet"*; *"In quietness…shall be your strength"*; *"It is good that a man should…quietly wait."*

Scripture abundantly testifies how the very thought of God in His majesty and holiness should silence us: *"The Lord is in his holy temple: let all the earth keep silence before him"* (Hab. 2:20); *"Hold thy peace at the presence of the Lord God"* (Zeph. 1:7); *"Be silent, O all flesh, before the Lord: for he is raised up out of his holy habitation"* (Zech. 2:13).

As long as the waiting on God is chiefly regarded as an end toward more effectual prayer, and the obtaining of our petitions, this spirit of perfect quietness will not be obtained. But, when it is seen that waiting on God is itself an unspeakable blessedness—one of the highest forms of fellowship with the Holy One—the adoration of Him in His glory will of necessity humble the soul into a holy stillness, making way for God to speak and reveal Himself. Then, it comes to the fulfillment of the precious promise, that all of self and self-effort will be humbled: *"The haughtiness of men shall be bowed down, and the Lord alone shall be exalted in that day"* (Isa. 2:11).

Let everyone who wants to learn the art of waiting on God remember the lesson, *"Take heed, and be quiet"* (Isa. 7:4). *"It is good that a man… quietly wait."* Take time to be separate from all friends and all duties, all cares and all joys; time to be still and quiet before God. Take time not only to secure stillness from man and the world, but from self and its energy. Let the Word and prayer be very precious. But remember, even these may hinder the quiet waiting. The activity of the mind in studying the Word or giving expression to its thoughts in prayer, the activities of the heart, with its desires and hopes and fears, may so engage us that we do not come to the still waiting on the All-glorious One; our whole being is prostrate in silence before Him.

Though at first it may appear difficult to know how thus quietly to wait, with the activities of mind and heart for a time subdued, every effort after it will be rewarded. We will discover that it grows upon us, and the little season of silent worship will bring a peace and a rest that give a blessing not only in prayer, but all day.

"It is good that a man should…quietly wait for the salvation of the LORD." Yes, it is good. The quietness is the confession of our meekness. It will not be done with all our willing and running (see Rom. 9:16), with all our thinking and praying. We must receive it from God. It is the confession of our trust that our God will, in His time, come to our help—the quiet resting in Him alone. It is the confession of our desire to sink into our nothingness and to let Him work and reveal Himself. Do let us wait quietly. In daily life, let there be, in the soul that is waiting for the great God to do His wondrous work, a quiet reverence, an abiding watching against too deep engrossment with the world. Then, the whole character will come to bear the beautiful stamp—quietly waiting for the salvation of God.

My soul, wait thou only upon God!

26

IN HOLY EXPECTANCY

Therefore I will look unto the LORD;
I will wait for the God of my salvation: my God will hear me.
—Micah 7:7

Have you ever heard of a little book, *Expectation Corners?* It tells of a king who prepared a city for some of his poor subjects. Not far from them were large storehouses, where everything they could need was supplied if they sent in their requests. But, on one condition—that they should be on the lookout for the answer, so that when the king's messengers came with the answer to their petitions, they should always be found waiting and ready to receive them. The sad story is told of one desponding person who never expected to get what he asked, because he was too unworthy. One day, he was taken to the king's storehouses, and there, to his amazement, he saw, with his address on them, all the packages that had been made up for him and sent. There was the garment of praise and the oil of joy and the eye salve and so much more. They had been to his door but found it closed; he was not on the lookout. From that time on, he learned the lesson Micah would teach us today. *"I will look unto the* LORD*; I will wait for the God of my salvation: my God will hear me."*

I have said more than once: waiting for the answer to prayer is not the whole of waiting, but only a part. Today, I want to take in the blessed truth that it is a part, and a very important one. When we have special petitions, in connection with which we are waiting on God, our waiting must be very definitely in the confident assurance, *"My God will hear me."*

A holy, joyful expectancy is of the very essence of true waiting. And, this is not only true in reference to the many varied requests every believer has to make, but most especially to the one great petition which ought to be the chief thing every heart seeks for itself—that the life of God in the soul may have full sway, that Christ may be fully formed within, and that we may be filled to all the fullness of God. This is what God has promised. This is what God's people too little seek, very often because they do not believe it possible. This is what we ought to seek and dare to expect, because God is able and waiting to work it in us.

But, God Himself must work it. And for this end our working must cease. We must see how entirely it is to be the faith of the operation of God, who raised Jesus from the dead. Just as much as the resurrection, the perfecting of God's life in our souls is to be directly His work. And, waiting has to become, more than ever, a tarrying before God in stillness of soul, counting upon Him who raises the dead and calls the things that are not as though they were. (See Rom. 4:17.)

Just notice how the threefold use of the name of God in our text points us to Himself as the one from whom alone is our expectation. *"I will look unto the* LORD*; I will wait for the God of my salvation: my God will hear me."* Everything that is salvation, everything that is good and holy, must be the direct, mighty work of God Himself within us. In every moment of a life in the will of God, there must be the immediate operation of God. And, the one thing I have to do is this: to look to the Lord, to wait for the God of my salvation, to hold fast the confident assurance, *"my God will hear me."*

God says, *"Be still, and know that I am God"* (Ps. 46:10).

There is no stillness like that of the grave. In the grave of Jesus, in the fellowship of His death, in death to self with its own will and wisdom, its own strength and energy—there is rest. As we cease from self and our soul becomes still to God, God will arise and show Himself. *"Be still, and know"*; then you will know *"that I am God."* There is no stillness like the stillness Jesus gives when He speaks. *"Peace, be still"* (Mark 4:39). In Christ, in His death, in His life, in His perfected redemption, the soul may be still, and God will come in, take possession, and do His perfect work.

My soul, be thou still only unto God!

27

FOR REDEMPTION

Simeon...was just and devout, waiting for the consolation of Israel:
and the Holy Ghost was upon him....Anna, a prophetess...spake of
him to all them that looked for redemption in Jerusalem.
—Luke 2:25, 36, 38

ere we have the mark of a waiting believer. *"Just,"* righteous in all his conduct; *"devout,"* devoted to God, ever walking as in His presence; *"waiting for the consolation of Israel,"* looking for the fulfillment of God's promises: *"and the Holy Ghost was upon him."* In the devout waiting, he had been prepared for the blessing. And Simeon was not the only one. Anna spoke to all who looked for redemption in Jerusalem. This was the one mark, amid surrounding formalism and worldliness, of a godly band of men and women in Jerusalem. They were waiting on God, looking for His promised redemption. And now that the consolation of Israel has come, and the redemption has been accomplished, do we still need to wait? We do indeed. But, will not our waiting, who look back to it as come, differ greatly from those who looked forward to it as coming? It will, especially in two aspects. We now wait on God in the full power of the redemption, and we wait for its full revelation.

Our waiting is now in the full power of the redemption. Christ said, "In that day you will know that you are in Me. Abide in Me." The Epistles teach us to present ourselves to God as *"dead indeed unto sin, but alive unto God through Jesus Christ"* (Rom. 6:11), *"blessed…with all spiritual blessings in heavenly places in Christ"* (Eph. 1:3). Our waiting on God may now be in the wonderful consciousness maintained by the Holy Spirit within us, that we are accepted in the Beloved, that the love that rests on Him rests on us, that we are living in that love, in the very nearness and presence and sight of God.

The old saints took their stand on the Word of God, and waiting, hoping on that Word, we rest on the Word, too—but, oh, under what exceedingly greater privileges, as one with Christ Jesus! In our waiting on God, let this be our confidence: in Christ we have access to the Father. How sure, therefore, we may be that our waiting cannot be in vain.

Our waiting differs, too, in this, that while they waited for a redemption to come, we see it accomplished and now wait for its revelation in us. Christ not only said, *"Abide in me"* (John 15:4), but also *"I in you"* (v. 4). The Epistles not only speak of us in Christ, but of Christ in us, as the highest mystery of redeeming love. As we maintain our place in Christ day by day, God waits to reveal Christ in us in such a way that He is formed in us, that His mind and disposition and likeness acquire form and substance in us, so that by each it can in truth be said, *"Christ liveth in me"* (Gal. 2:20).

My life in Christ up there in heaven and Christ's life in me down here on earth—these two are the complement of each other. And, the more my waiting on God is marked by the living faith, *I in Christ*, the more the heart thirsts for and claims the Christ in me. The waiting on God, which began with special needs and prayer, will increasingly be concentrated, as far as our personal life is concerned, on this one thing: Lord, reveal Your redemption fully in me; let Christ live in me. Our waiting differs from that of the old saints in the place we take, and the expectations we entertain. But, at root it is the same: waiting on God, from whom alone is our expectation.

Learn one lesson from Simeon and Anna. How utterly impossible it was for them to do anything toward the great redemption—toward the birth of Christ or His death. It was God's work. They could do nothing but wait. Are we as absolutely helpless in regard to the revelation of Christ in us? We are indeed. God did not work out the great redemption in Christ as a whole and leave its application in detail to us.

The secret thought that it is so is the root of all our feebleness. The revelation of Christ in every individual believer, and in each one the daily revelation, step by step and moment by moment, is as much the work of God's omnipotence as the birth or resurrection of Christ. Until this truth enters and fills us, and we feel that we are just as dependent upon God for each moment of our life in the enjoyment of redemption as they were in their waiting for it, our waiting upon God will not bring its full blessing. The sense of utter and absolute helplessness, the confidence that God can and will do all, are the marks of our waiting as of theirs. As gloriously as God proved Himself to them the faithful and wonder-working God, He will to us, too.

My soul, wait thou only upon God!

28

FOR THE COMING OF HIS SON

[Be] ye yourselves like unto men that wait for their lord.
—Luke 12:36

Until the appearing of our Lord Jesus Christ:
which in its own times he shall show, who is the blessed and only
Potentate, the King of kings, and Lord of lords.
—1 Timothy 6:14–15 asv

Turned to God from idols to serve the living and true God; and to
wait for his Son from heaven.
—1 Thessalonians 1:9–10

W aiting on God in heaven, and waiting for His Son from heaven—these two God has joined together, and no man may put them asunder. The waiting on God for His presence and power in daily life will be the only true preparation for waiting for Christ in humility and true holiness. The waiting for Christ coming from heaven to take us to heaven will give the waiting on God its true tone of hopefulness and joy. The Father, who, in His own time, will reveal His Son from heaven, is the God who, as we wait on Him, prepares us for the revelation of His Son. The present life and the coming glory are inseparably connected in God and in us.

There is sometimes a danger of separating them. It is always easier to be engaged with the Christianity of the past or the future than to be faithful in the Christianity of today. As we look to what God has done in the past, or will do in time to come, the personal claim of present duty and present submission to His working may be avoided. Waiting on God must always lead to waiting for Christ as the glorious consummation of His work. And, waiting for Christ must always remind us of the duty of waiting upon God as our only proof that the waiting for Christ is in spirit and in truth.

There is such a danger of our being more occupied with the things that are coming than with Him who is to come. There is such scope in the study of coming events for imagination and reason and human ingenuity, that nothing but deeply humble waiting on God can save us from mistaking the interest and pleasure of intellectual study for the true love of Him and His appearing. All you who say you wait for Christ's coming, be sure that you wait on God now. All you who seek to wait on God now to reveal His Son in you, see to it that you do so as men waiting for the revelation of His Son from heaven. The hope of that glorious appearing will strengthen you in waiting upon God for what He is to do in you now. The same omnipotent love that is to reveal that glory is working in you even now to prepare you for it.

"*The blessed hope and appearing of the glory of the great God and our Saviour Jesus Christ*" (Titus 2:13 ASV), is one of the great bonds of union given to God's church throughout the ages. "*He shall come to be glorified in his saints, and to be marvelled at in all them that believed*" (2 Thess. 1:10 ASV). Then, we will all meet, and the unity of the body of Christ will be seen in its divine glory. It will be the meeting place and the triumph of divine love. Jesus receiving His own and presenting them to the Father. His own meeting Him and worshipping, in speechless love, that blessed face. His own meeting each other in the ecstasy of God's own love. Let us wait, long for, and love the appearing of our Lord and heavenly Bridegroom. Tender love to Him and tender love to each other is the true and only bridal spirit.

I am very afraid that this is sometimes forgotten. A beloved brother in Holland was speaking about the expectancy of faith being the true sign of the bride. I ventured to express a doubt. An unworthy bride, about to be married to a prince, might only be thinking of the position and the riches that she was to receive. The expectancy of faith might be strong and true love utterly lacking. It is not when we are most occupied with prophetic subjects, but when in humility and love we are clinging close to our Lord and His followers, that we are in the bride's place. Jesus refuses to accept our love except as it is love to His disciples. Waiting for His coming means waiting for the glorious coming manifestation of the unity of the body, while we seek here to maintain that unity in humility and love. Those who love most are the most ready for His coming. Love to each other is the life and beauty of His bride, the church.

And how is this to be brought about? Beloved child of God, if you want to learn how to properly wait for His Son from heaven, live even now waiting on God in heaven. Remember how Jesus lived ever waiting on God. He could do nothing of Himself. It was God who perfected His Son through suffering and then exalted Him. It is God alone who can give you the deep spiritual life of one who is really waiting for His Son: wait on God for it. Waiting for Christ Himself is so different from waiting for things that may come to pass! The latter any Christian can do; the former, God must work in you every day by His Holy Spirit. Therefore, all you who wait on God, look to Him for grace to wait for His Son from heaven in the Spirit which is from heaven. And, you who want to wait for His Son, wait on God continually to reveal Christ in you.

The revelation of Christ in us, as it is given to them who wait upon God, is the true preparation for the full revelation of Christ in glory.

My soul, wait thou only upon God!

29

FOR THE PROMISE
OF THE FATHER

He charged them not to depart from Jerusalem,
but to wait for the promise of the Father.
—Acts 1:4 ASV

In speaking of the saints in Jerusalem at Christ's birth—with Simeon and Anna—we saw how the call to waiting is no less urgent now, though the redemption they waited for has come, than it was then. We wait for the full revelation in us of what came to them, but what they could scarcely comprehend. In the same way, it is with waiting for the promise of the Father. In one sense, the fulfillment can never come again as it came at Pentecost. In another sense, and that in as deep a reality as with the first disciples, we need to wait daily for the Father to fulfill His promise in us.

The Holy Spirit is not a person distinct from the Father in the way two persons on earth are distinct. The Father and the Spirit are never without or separate from each other. The Father is always in the Spirit; the Spirit works nothing but as the Father works in Him. Each moment, the same Spirit that is in us is in God, too. And, he who is most full of the Spirit will be the first to wait on God most earnestly to further fulfill His promise and to still strengthen him mightily by His Spirit in the inner man. The Spirit in us is not a power at our disposal. Nor is the Spirit an independent power, acting apart from the Father and the Son. The Spirit is the real, living presence and the power of the Father working in us. Therefore, it is he who knows that the Spirit is in him who waits on the Father for the full revelation and experience of the Spirit's indwelling. It is he who waits for His increase and abounding more and more.

See this in the apostles. They were filled with the Spirit at Pentecost. When they, not long after, on returning from the council where they had been forbidden to preach, prayed afresh for boldness to speak in His name, a fresh coming down of the Holy Spirit was the Father's fresh fulfillment of His promise.

At Samaria, by the Word and the Spirit, many had been converted, and the whole city was filled with joy. At the apostles' prayer, the Father once again fulfilled the promise. (See Acts 8:14–17.) Even so to the waiting company—"We are all here before God" (see Acts 10:33)—in Cornelius' house. And so, too, in Acts 13. It was when men, filled with the Spirit, prayed and fasted, that the promise of the Father was afresh fulfilled, and the leading of the Spirit was given from heaven: *"Separate me Barnabas and Saul"* (Acts 13:2).

So also we find Paul, in Ephesians, praying for those who have been sealed with the Spirit, that God would grant them the spirit of illumination. And later on, that He would grant them, according to the riches of His glory, to be strengthened with might by the Spirit in the inner man.

The Spirit given at Pentecost was not something that God failed with in heaven, and sent out of heaven to earth. God does not, cannot, give away anything in that manner. When He gives grace or strength or life, He gives it by giving Himself to work it—it is all inseparable from Himself. Much more so is the Holy Spirit. He is God, present and working in us. The true position in which we can count upon that working with an unceasing power is as we, praising for what we have, still unceasingly wait for the Father's promise to be still more mightily fulfilled.

What new meaning and promise does this give to our lives of waiting! It teaches us to continually keep the place where the disciples tarried at the footstool of the throne. It reminds us that, as helpless as they were to meet their enemies, or to preach to Christ's enemies until they were endued with power, we, too, can only be strong in the life of faith, or the work of love, as we are in direct communication with God and Christ. They must maintain the life of the Spirit in us. This assures us that the omnipotent God will, through the glorified Christ, work in us a power that can bring unexpected things to pass, impossible things. Oh, what the church will be able to do when her individual members learn to live their lives waiting on God— when together, with all of self and the world sacrificed in the fire of love, they unite in waiting with one accord for the promise of the Father, once so gloriously fulfilled, but still unexhausted!

Come and let each of us be still in the presence of the inconceivable grandeur of this prospect: the Father waiting to fill the church with the Holy Spirit. And willing to fill me, let each one say.

With this faith, let a hush and a holy fear come over the soul, as it waits in stillness to take it all in. And, let life increasingly become a deep joy in the hope of the ever-fuller fulfillment of the Father's promise.

My soul, wait thou only upon God!

30

CONTINUALLY

Therefore turn thou to thy God: keep mercy and judgment,
and wait on thy God continually.
—Hosea 12:6

Continuity is one of the essential elements of life. Interrupt it for a single hour in a man, and it is lost; he is dead. Continuity, unbroken and ceaseless, is essential to a healthy Christian life. God wants me to be, and God waits to make me; I want to be, and I wait on Him to make me, every moment, what He expects of me—what is well pleasing in His sight. If waiting on God is the essence of true faith, the maintenance of the spirit of entire dependence must be continuous. The call of God, *"wait on thy God continually,"* must be accepted and obeyed. Although there may be times of special waiting, the disposition and habit of soul must be there unchangeably and uninterrupted.

This continual waiting is indeed a necessity. To those who are content with a feeble Christian life, it appears to be a luxury beyond what is essential to be a good Christian. But, all who are praying the prayer, "Lord, make me as holy as a pardoned sinner can be made! Keep me as near to You as it is possible for me to be! Fill me as full of Your love as You are willing to do!" feel at once that it is something that must be had. They feel that there can be no unbroken fellowship with God, no full abiding in Christ, no maintaining of victory over sin and readiness for service, without waiting continually on the Lord.

The continual waiting is a possibility. Many think that with the duties of life it is out of the question. They cannot always be thinking of it. Even when they wish to, they forget.

They do not understand that it is a matter of the heart and that what the heart is full of, occupies it, even when the thoughts are otherwise engaged. A father's heart may be continuously filled with intense love and longing for a sick wife or child at a distance, even though pressing business requires all his thoughts. When the heart has learned how entirely powerless it is for one moment to keep itself or bring forth any good, when it has learned how surely and truly God will keep it, when it has, in despair of itself, accepted God's promise to do for it the impossible, it learns to rest in God. In the midst of occupations and temptations, it can wait continually.

This waiting is a promise. God's commands are enablings. Gospel precepts are all promises, a revelation of what our God will do for us. When you first begin waiting on God, it is with frequent intermission and failure. But, do believe God is watching over you in love and secretly strengthening you in it. There are times when waiting appears like just losing time, but it is not so. Waiting, even in darkness, is unconscious advance, because it is God you have to do with, and He is working in you. God, who calls you to wait on Him, sees your feeble efforts and works it in you. Your spiritual life is in no respect your own work; as little as you begin it, can you continue it.

It is God's Spirit who has begun the work in you of waiting upon God. He will enable you to wait continually.

Waiting continually will be met and rewarded by God Himself working continually. We are coming to the end of our lessons. I hope that you and I might learn one thing: God must, God will work continually. He ever does work continually, but the experience of it is hindered by unbelief. But, He, who by His Spirit teaches you to wait continually, will bring you also to experience how, as the Everlasting One, His work is never ceasing. In the love and the life and the work of God, there can be no break, no interruption.

Do not limit God in this by your thoughts of what may be expected. Do fix your eyes upon this one truth: in His very nature, God, as the only Giver of life, cannot do anything other than work in His child every moment. Do not look only at the one side: "If I wait continually, God will work continually." No, look at the other side. Place God first and say, "God works continually; every moment I may wait on Him continually." Take time until the vision of your God working continually, without one moment's intermission, fills your being. Your waiting continually will then come of itself. Full of trust and joy, the holy habit of the soul will be, *"on thee do I wait all the day"* (Ps. 25:5). The Holy Spirit will keep you ever waiting.

My soul, wait thou only upon God!

31

ONLY

My soul, wait thou only upon God; for my expectation is from him.
He only is my rock and my salvation.
—Psalm 62:5–6

I t is possible to be waiting continually on God, but not only upon Him. There may be other secret confidences intervening and preventing the blessing that was expected. And so the word *only* must come to throw its light on the path to the fullness and certainty of blessing. *"My soul, wait thou only upon God....He only is my rock."*

Yes, *"my soul, wait thou only upon God."* There is but one God, but one source of life and happiness for the heart; *"He only is my rock"*; *"My* soul, *wait thou only upon God.*" You desire to be good; "*There is none good but...God*" (Matt. 19:17), and there is no possible goodness but what is received directly from Him. You have sought to be holy; "*There is none holy as the* LORD" (1 Sam. 2:2), and there is no holiness but what He by His Spirit of holiness every moment breathes in you. You would gladly live and work for God and His kingdom, for men and their salvation. Hear how He said,

> The everlasting God, the LORD, the Creator of the ends of the earth, fainteth not, neither is weary....He giveth power to the faint; and to them that have no might he increaseth strength....They that wait upon the LORD shall renew their strength. (Isa. 40:28–39, 31)

He only is God; He only is your Rock: "*my soul, wait thou only upon God.*"

"*My soul, wait thou only upon God.*" You will not find many who can help you in this. There will be enough of your brothers to draw you to put trust in churches and doctrines, in schemes and plans and human appliances, in means of grace and divine appointments. But, "*my soul, wait thou only upon God*" Himself. His most sacred appointments become a snare when trusted in. The brazen serpent becomes Nehushtan (see 2 Kings 18:4); the ark and the temple a vain confidence. Let the living God alone, none and nothing but He, be your hope.

"*My soul, wait thou only upon God.*" Eyes and hands and feet, mind and thought, may have to be intently engaged in the duties of this life. "*My soul, wait thou only upon God.*" You are an immortal spirit, created not for this world but for eternity and for God. Oh, my soul, realize your destiny. Know your privilege, and "*wait thou only upon God.*" Let not the interest of spiritual thoughts and exercises deceive you; they very often take the place of waiting upon God. "*My soul, wait thou,*" your very self, your innermost being, with all its power, "*wait thou only upon God.*" God is for you; you are for God. Wait only upon Him.

Yes, "*my soul, wait thou only upon God.*" Beware of two great enemies: the world and self. Beware of allowing any earthly satisfaction or enjoyment, however innocent it appears, keep you back from saying, "*I* [will] *go...unto God my exceeding joy*" (Ps. 43:4). Remember and study what Jesus said about denying self: "*Let* [a man] *deny himself*" (Matt. 16:24). Tersteegen, a German Protestant devotional writer, said, "The saints deny themselves in everything." Pleasing self in little things may be strengthening it to assert itself in greater things.

"*My soul, wait thou only upon God.*" Let Him be all your salvation and all your desire. Say continually and with an undivided heart, "*From him cometh my* [expectation]. *He only is my rock...I shall not be greatly moved*" (Ps. 62:1–2). Whatever your spiritual or temporal needs are, whatever the desire or prayer of your heart, whatever your interest in connection with God's work in the church or the world—in solitude or in the rush of the world, in public worship or other gatherings of the saints, "*my soul, wait thou only upon God.*" Let your expectations be from Him alone. "*He only is my rock.*"

"*My soul, wait thou only upon God.*" Never forget the two foundation truths on which this blessed waiting rests. If you are ever inclined to think this waiting only is too hard or too high, they will recall you at once. They are your absolute helplessness and the absolute sufficiency of your God. Oh, enter deeply into the entire sinfulness of all that is of self, and do not think of letting self have anything to say one single moment. Enter deeply into your utter and unceasing inability to ever change what is evil in you, or to bring forth anything that is spiritually good. Enter deeply into your relationship of dependence on God, to receive from Him every moment what He gives. Enter deeper still into His covenant of redemption, with His promise to restore more gloriously than ever what you have lost. And, by His Son and Spirit, He will unceasingly give you His actual divine presence and power. And thus, wait upon your God continually and only.

"*My soul, wait thou only upon God.*" No words can tell, no heart can conceive, the riches of the glory of this mystery of the Father and of Christ. Our God, in the infinite tenderness and omnipotence of His love, waits to be our life and joy. Oh, my soul, let it no longer be necessary that I repeat the words, "Wait upon God." But, let all that is in me rise and sing, *"Truly my soul waiteth upon God"* (Ps. 62:1). *"On thee do I wait all the day"* (Ps. 25:5).

My soul, wait thou only upon God!

MOMENT BY MOMENT

I the LORD *do keep it; I will water it every moment.*
—Isaiah 27:3

Dying with Jesus, by death reckoning mine;
Living with Jesus, a new life divine;
Looking to Jesus till glory doth shine,
Moment by moment, O Lord, I am Thine.

Chorus:

Moment by moment I'm kept in His love;
Moment by moment I've life from above;

Looking to Jesus till glory doth shine;
Moment by moment, O Lord, I am Thine.

Never a battle with wrong for the right,
Never a contest that He doth not fight;
Lifting above us His banner so white,
Moment by moment, I'm kept in His sight.

Never a trial that He is not there,
Never a burden that He doth not bear,
Never a sorrow that He doth not share,
Moment by moment, I'm under His care.

Never a heartache, and never a groan,
Never a teardrop, and never a moan;
Never a danger but there on the throne,
Moment by moment, He thinks of His own.

Never a weakness that He doth not feel,
Never a sickness that He cannot heal;
Moment by moment, in woe or in weal,
Jesus, my Saviour, abides with me still.

WITH CHRIST IN THE
SCHOOL OF PRAYER

CONTENTS

PREFACE

Of all the traits of a life like Christ, there is none higher and more glorious than conformity to Him in the work that now engages Him without ceasing in the Father's presence: His all-powerful intercession. The more we abide in Him and grow to be like Him, the more His priestly life will work in us. Our lives will become what His is—a life that continuously prays for men.

The place and power of prayer in the Christian life is too little understood. As long as we view prayer simply as the means of maintaining our own Christian lives, we will not fully understand what it is really supposed to be. But when we learn to regard it as the highest part of the work entrusted to us—the root and strength of all other work—we will see that there is nothing we need to study and practice more than the art of praying

It is my prayer that God may use this book to make clearer to some of His children the wonderful place of power and influence that He is saving for them. The Father waits to hear every prayer of faith. He wants to give us whatever we ask for in Jesus' name. God intends prayer to have an answer, and no one has yet fully conceived what God will do for the child who believes that his prayer will be heard. God hears prayer.

Many complain that they don't have the power to pray in faith an effective prayer that accomplishes much. The message I want to give them is that the blessed Jesus is waiting and longing to teach them this.

May God open our eyes to understand the holy ministry of intercession to which, as His royal priesthood, we have been set apart. May He give us a large and strong heart to believe what mighty influence our prayers can exert. And may all fear of our being able to fulfill our vocation vanish as we see Jesus, living eternally to pray, living in us to pray, and guaranteeing the results of our prayer lives.

—*Andrew Murray*

1

THE ONLY TEACHER

And it came to pass, that, as he was praying in a certain place,
when he ceased, one of his disciples said unto him, Lord, teach us to pray.
—Luke 11:1

The disciples had learned to understand something of the connection between Christ's wondrous life in public and His secret life of prayer. They had been with Him and had seen Him pray. They had learned to believe in Him as a Master in the art of prayer. None could pray like Him. And so they went to Him with the request, *"Lord, teach us to pray."* In later years they would tell us that there were few things more wonderful or blessed that He taught them than His lessons on prayer.

It is still true today that disciples who see Him feel the need of repeating the same request, "*Lord, teach us to pray.*" As we grow in the Christian life, the thought and the faith of the Beloved Master in His never failing intercession become more precious, and the hope of being like Christ in His intercession gains an attractiveness never before known. As we see Him pray and remember that there is none who can pray or teach like Him, we feel the petition of the disciples, "*Lord, teach us to pray,*" is just what we need. Everything He is and has is our very own. Because He Himself is our life, we should feel assured that if we ask, He will be delighted to take us into closer fellowship with Himself and teach us to pray as He prays.

Go, my brothers! Go to the Blessed Master and ask Him to enroll your names in that school that He always keeps open for those who long to study the divine art of prayer and intercession! Yes, let us say to the Master as they did of old, "*Lord, teach us to pray.*" As we meditate, we will find each word of our petition full of meaning.

"*Lord, teach us to pray.*" Yes, to pray. This is what we need to be taught. Though in its beginnings prayer is so simple that the feeblest child can pray, it is at the same time the highest and holiest work to which man can rise. Prayer is fellowship with the Unseen and Most Holy One. The powers of the eternal world have been placed at prayer's disposal. It is the very essence of true religion and the channel of all blessings. It is the secret of power and life not only for ourselves, but for others, for the church, and for the world. It is to prayer that God has given the right to take hold of Him and His strength. It is on prayer that the promises wait for their fulfillment, the kingdom waits for its coming, and the glory of God waits for its full revelation. How slothful and unfit we are for this blessed work.

Only the Spirit of God can enable us to do it right. How speedily we are deceived into resting in a form of prayer, while the power is still missing! Our early training, the teaching of the church, the influence of habit, the stirring of the emotions—how easily these lead to prayer that has no spiritual power and achieves little. Who wouldn't cry out for someone to teach him true prayer that takes hold of God's strength and achieves much, to which the gates of heaven are really opened wide?

Jesus has opened a school in which He trains those of His redeemed ones who especially desire to have power in prayer. Enter it with the petition, "Lord, this is just what we need to be taught! Oh, teach us to pray!"

"Lord, teach us to pray." Yes, us, Lord. We have read in Your Word about the power Your believing people of long ago had when they prayed and what mighty wonders were done in answer to their prayers. This took place under the old covenant, in the time of preparation. Now, in these days of fulfillment, how much more will You give Your people a sure sign of Your presence? We have heard the promises given to Your apostles of the power of prayer in Your Name and have seen how gloriously they experienced their truth. We know for certain they can become true to us, too. We hear continually, even in these days, what glorious tokens of Your power You still give to those who trust You completely. Lord, teach us to pray with power, too! The promises are for us; the powers and gifts of the heavenly world are for us. Oh, teach us to pray so that we may receive abundantly! To us, too, You have entrusted Your work. On our prayers, too, the coming of Your kingdom depends. In our prayers, too, You can glorify Your Name. *"Lord, teach us to pray."* We offer ourselves as learners. We want only You to teach us.

"Lord, teach us to pray." Yes, we feel the need now of being taught to pray. At first there is no work that appears so simple; later on, none that is more difficult. And the confession is forced from us: we do not know how to pray as we should (Rom. 8:26). It is true we have God's Word with its clear and sure promises, but sin has so darkened our minds that we don't always know how to apply the Word. In spiritual matters we do not always seek the most important things. In temporal matters we are still less able to use the wonderful liberty our Father has given us to ask for what we need.

Even when we know what to ask for, so much is still needed to make prayer acceptable. It must be to the glory of God, in full surrender to His will, in full assurance of faith, in the name of Jesus, and with a perseverance that, if need be, refuses to be denied. All this must be learned. It can only be learned in the school of much prayer, for practice makes perfect.

Amid the painful consciousness of ignorance and unworthiness, in the struggle between believing and doubting, the heavenly art of effective prayer is learned. There is One—the Beginner and Finisher of faith and prayer—who watches over our praying and sees to it that in all who trust Him for it, education in the school of prayer is carried on to perfection. Let the deep undertone of all our prayers be the teachableness that comes from faith in Him as a perfect Teacher, and we can be sure that we will be taught. We will learn to pray in power. Yes, we can depend on His teaching us to pray.

"Lord, teach us to pray." No one can teach like Jesus. A pupil needs a teacher who knows his work, who has the gift of teaching, who in patience and love will descend to the pupil's needs. Blessed be God! Jesus is all this and much more. It is Jesus, praying Himself, who teaches us to pray. He knows what prayer is. He learned it amid the trials and tears of His earthly life. In heaven it is still His beloved work. His life there is prayer. Nothing delights Him more than to find those whom He can take with Him into the Father's presence, clothing them with power to pray down God's blessing to those around them, training them to be His fellow workers in the intercession by which the kingdom is to be revealed on earth.

He knows how to teach, whether it is by the urgency of felt need, by the confidence that joy inspires, by the studying of the Word, or by the testimony of another believer who knows what it is to have prayer heard. By His Holy Spirit, He has access to our hearts and teaches us to pray by showing us the sin that hinders the prayer or by giving us the assurance that we please God. He teaches by giving not only thoughts of what to ask or how to ask, but by breathing into us the very spirit of prayer and living within us as the Great Intercessor. We can most joyfully say, "Who teaches like Him?" Jesus never taught His disciples how to preach, only how to pray. To know how to speak to God is more than knowing how to speak to man. Power with God is the first thing, not power with men. Jesus loves to teach us how to pray.

What do you think, my beloved fellow disciples? Wouldn't it be just what we need, to ask the Master for a month to give us a course of special lessons on the art of prayer? As we meditate on the words He spoke on earth, let us yield ourselves to His teaching in the fullest confidence that with such a Teacher we will make progress. Let us take time not only to meditate, but to pray, to sit at the foot of the throne and be trained for the work of intercession. Let us do so in the assurance that despite our stammerings and fears, He is carrying on His work most beautifully. He will breathe His own life, which is all prayer, into us. As He makes us partakers of His righteousness and His life, He will make us partakers of His intercession, too. As the members of His body—as a holy priesthood (1 Pet. 2:5)—we will take part in His priestly work of praying to and getting results from God for men. Yes, even though we are unknowing and weak, let us most joyfully say, *"Lord, teach us to pray!"*

Lord, teach us to pray.

Blessed Lord, You live eternally to pray and can teach me, too, to live eternally to pray! You want me to share Your glory in heaven by sharing this unceasing prayer with You, standing as a priest in the presence of my God.

Lord Jesus, enroll my name among those who confess that they don't know how to pray as they should, and who especially ask You for a course of teaching in prayer. Lord, teach me to be patient in Your school, so that You will have time to train me. I am ignorant of the wonderful privilege and power of prayer, of the need for the Holy Spirit to be the spirit of prayer. Lead me to forget my thoughts of what I think I know, and make me kneel before You in true teachableness and poverty of spirit.

Fill me, Lord, with the confidence that with You for my Teacher, I will learn to pray. Then I will not be afraid, because my Teacher prays continuously to the Father and by His prayer rules the destinies of His church and the world. Unfold for me everything I need to know about the mysteries of the prayer world. When there is something I may not know, teach me to be strong in faith, giving glory to God.

Blessed Lord, I know that You won't put that student to shame who trusts You. And with Your grace, that student won't shame you, either. Amen.

2

THE TRUE WORSHIPPERS

*The hour cometh, and now is, when the true worshippers shall
worship the Father in spirit and in truth:
for the Father seeketh such to worship him. God is a Spirit:
and they that worship him must worship him in spirit and in truth.*
—John 4:23–24

hese words of Jesus to the woman of Samaria are His first
recorded teaching on the subject of prayer. They give us some
wonderful first glimpses into the world of prayer. The Father seeks worshippers. Our worship satisfies His loving heart and is a joy to Him. He
seeks true worshippers but finds many who are not the way He would like
them. True worship is that which is in spirit and truth. The Son has come

to open the way for this worship in spirit and in truth and to teach it to us. One of our first lessons in the school of prayer must be to understand what it is to pray in spirit and in truth and to know how we can attain it.

To the woman of Samaria our Lord spoke of a threefold worship. First there is the ignorant worship of the Samaritans: *"ye worship ye know not what"* (John 4:22). Second is the intelligent worship of the Jew, having the true knowledge of God: *"we know what we worship: for salvation is of the Jews"* (v. 22). The new, spiritual worship that He Himself has come to introduce is third: *"the hour cometh, and now is, when the true worshippers shall worship the Father in spirit and in truth."*

The words *"in spirit and in truth"* do not mean earnestly, from the heart, or in sincerity. The Samaritans had the five books of Moses and some knowledge of God. There was doubtless more than one among them who honestly and earnestly sought God in prayer. The Jews had the true, full revelation of God in that portion of His Word that had been given. There were godly men among them who called on God with their whole hearts, but not *"in spirit and truth"* in the full meaning of the words. Jesus said, *"The hour is coming, and now is"* (John 5:25). Only in and through Him will the worship of God be in spirit and truth.

Among Christians, one still finds the three classes of worshippers. Some in their ignorance hardly know what they're asking for. They pray earnestly, but receive little. There are others having more correct knowledge who try to pray with all their minds and hearts. They often pray most earnestly and yet do not attain the full blessedness of worship in spirit and truth. It is into the third class we must ask our Lord Jesus to take us. He must teach us how to worship in spirit and truth. This alone is spiritual worship; this makes us the kind of worshippers the Father seeks. In prayer, everything will depend on our understanding and practicing worship in spirit and truth.

"God is a Spirit: and they that worship him must worship him in spirit and in truth." The first thought suggested here by the Master is that there must be harmony between God and His worshippers. This is according to a principle that prevails throughout the universe: correspondence between

an object and the organ to which it reveals or yields itself. The eye is receptive to light, the ear to sound. The man who truly wants to worship God—to find, know, possess, and enjoy God—must be in harmony with Him and have the capacity for receiving Him. Because God is Spirit, we must worship in spirit.

What does this mean? The woman had asked our Lord whether Samaria or Jerusalem was the true place of worship. He answers that henceforth worship is no longer to be limited to a certain place: "*Woman, believe me, the hour cometh, when ye shall neither in this mountain, nor yet at Jerusalem, worship the Father*" (John 4:21). God is Spirit, not bound by space or time. In His infinite perfection, He is the same always and everywhere. His worship must not be confined by place or form, but be spiritual as God Himself is spiritual.

This is a lesson of deep importance. How much our Christianity suffers from being confined to certain times and places! A man who seeks to pray earnestly only in the church or in the prayer closet spends the greater part of his time in a spirit entirely at variance with that in which he prayed. His worship was the work of a fixed place or hour, not of his whole being. God is a Spirit. What He is, He is always and in truth. Our worship must be the same: It must be the spirit of our lives.

"*God is a Spirit: and they that worship him must worship him in spirit and truth*." The second thought that comes to us is that this worship in the spirit must come from God Himself. Because God is Spirit, He alone has Spirit to give. He sent His Son to fit us for such spiritual worship by giving us the Holy Spirit. It is of His own work that Jesus speaks when He said twice, "*The hour cometh*" (vv. 21, 23), and then adds, "*and now is*" (v. 23).

Jesus came to baptize with the Holy Spirit, which could not stream forth until He was glorified (John 1:33; 7:37–38; 16:7). When Jesus had made an end of sin, He entered into the Holiest of all with His blood. There on our behalf He received the Holy Spirit (Acts 2:33) and sent Him down to us as the Spirit of the Father. It was when Christ had redeemed us and we had received the position of children that the Father sent the Spirit of His Son into our hearts to cry, "*Abba, Father*" (Gal. 4:6). The worship in spirit is the worship of the Father in the Spirit of Christ, the Spirit of Sonship.

This is the reason why Jesus uses the name of Father here. We never find one of the Old Testament saints personally appropriating the name of child or calling God his Father. The worship of the Father is only possible for those to whom the spirit of the Son has been given. The worship in spirit is only possible for those to whom the Son has revealed the Father and who have received the spirit of Sonship. It is only Christ who opens the way and teaches the worship in spirit.

Worship in spirit and in truth. In truth does not only mean in sincerity. Nor does it only signify accordance with the truth of God's Word. The expression is one of deep and divine meaning. Jesus is *"the only begotten of the Father, full of grace and truth"* (John 1:14). *"The law was given by Moses, but grace and truth came by Jesus Christ"* (v. 17). Jesus said, *"I am the…truth, and the life"* (John 14:6). The Old Testament was all shadow and promise. Jesus brought and gives the reality, the substance of things hoped for. In Him the blessings and powers of the eternal life are our actual possession and experience.

Jesus is full of grace and truth. The Holy Spirit is the Spirit of truth, through whom the grace that is in Jesus is ours, a positive communication out of the divine life. And so worship in spirit is worship in truth. This actual living fellowship with God is a real correspondence and harmony between the Father who is a spirit and the child praying in the spirit.

The woman of Samaria could not immediately understand what Jesus said to her. Pentecost was needed to reveal its full meaning. We are inadequately prepared to grasp such teaching at our first entrance into the school of prayer. We will understand it better later on. Let us begin by taking the lesson as He gives it. We are carnal and cannot bring God the worship He seeks.

But Jesus has given us the Spirit. Let our attitudes in prayer be what Christ's words have taught us. Let there be the deep confession of our inability to bring God the worship that is pleasing to Him, the childlike teachableness that waits for Him to instruct us, and the simple faith that yields itself to the breathing of the Spirit. Above all, let us hold on tightly to this blessed reality: the secret of prayer in spirit and truth is in the knowledge of the Fatherhood of God, the revelation of His infinite Fatherliness in our hearts, and the faith in His infinite love for us as His children. This is the new and living way Christ opened up for us. To have Christ the Son, and the Spirit of the Son, dwelling within us and revealing the Father makes us true, spiritual worshippers.

Lord, teach us to pray.

Blessed Lord, I adore the love with which You taught the woman who had refused You a cup of water what the worship of God must be. I rejoice in the assurance that You will instruct any disciple, who comes to You with a heart that longs to pray in spirit and truth, with the same love. O my Holy Master, teach me this blessed secret!

Teach me that worship in spirit and truth is not anything from man, but comes only from You. It is not only a thing of times and seasons, but the outflowing of a life in You. Teach me to get near to God in prayer with the attitude that I am ignorant and have nothing in myself to offer Him. But, at the same time, remind me of the provision that You, my Savior, make for the Spirit's breathing in my childlike stammerings.

I bless You because in You I am a child, and I have a child's liberty of access to the Father. In You I have the spirit of Sonship and of worship in truth.

Teach me above all, blessed Son of the Father, the revelation of the Father that gives confidence in prayer. Let the infinite Fatherliness of God's heart be my joy and strength for a life of prayer and of worship. Amen.

3

ALONE WITH GOD

*But thou, when thou prayest, enter into thy closet, and when thou hast
shut thy door, pray to thy Father which is in secret; and thy Father
which seeth in secret shall reward thee openly.*
—Matthew 6:6

After Jesus had called his first disciples, He gave them their
first public teaching in the Sermon on the Mount. There He
explained the kingdom of God—its laws and its life—to them. In that
kingdom, God is not only King, but Father. He not only gives all, but is
Himself all. The knowledge and fellowship of Him alone is its blessedness. Hence it came as a matter of course that the revelation of prayer and
the prayer life was a part of His teaching concerning the new kingdom

He came to establish. Moses gave neither command nor regulation with regard to prayer. Even the prophets said little about prayer. It is Christ who teaches us to pray.

The first thing the Lord teaches His disciples is that they must have a secret place for prayer. Everyone must have some solitary spot where he can be alone with his God. Every teacher must have a schoolroom. We have learned to know and accept Jesus as our only Teacher in the school of prayer. He has already taught us at Samaria that worship is no longer confined to specific times and places. Worship—true, spiritual worship—is a thing of the spirit and the life. A man's whole life must be worship in spirit and truth. But Jesus wants each one to choose for himself a fixed spot where he can meet Him daily. That inner chamber, that solitary place, is Jesus' schoolroom. That spot can be anywhere. It can even change from day to day if we're traveling. But that secret place must be somewhere with quiet time for the pupil to place himself in the Master's presence. Jesus comes there to prepare us to worship the Father.

A teacher always wants his schoolroom to be bright, attractive, and filled with the light and air of heaven. He wants it to be a place where his pupils long to come and love to stay. In His first words on prayer in the Sermon on the Mount, Jesus seeks to set the inner chamber before us in its most attractive light. If we listen carefully, our main purpose in being there becomes obvious. Jesus uses the name of Father three times: *"pray to thy Father"; "thy Father...shall reward thee"; "Your Father knoweth what things ye have need of"* (Matt. 6:8).

The first thing in closet prayer is to meet the Father. The light that shines in the closet must be the light of the Father's countenance. The atmosphere in which we breathe and pray is God's Father love, God's infinite Fatherliness. Thus, each thought or petition we breathe out will be in simple, hearty, and childlike trust in the Father. The Master teaches us to pray by bringing us into the Father's living presence. What we pray there must be of value. We should listen carefully to hear what the Lord has to say to us.

First, *"pray to thy Father which is in secret."* God is a God who hides Himself to the carnal eye. As long as in our worship of God we are chiefly occupied with our own thoughts and exercises, we will not meet Him who is a Spirit, the Unseen One. But to the man who withdraws himself from all that is of the world and man and waits for God alone, the Father will reveal Himself. As he shuts out the world and its life, surrendering himself to be led by Christ into God's presence, the light of the Father's love will fall on him.

The secrecy of the inner chamber and the closed door, the entire separation from everything around us, is an image of the inner spiritual sanctuary, the secret of God's tabernacle. It is there within the veil that our spirit truly comes into contact with the Invisible One. Thus we are taught at the very beginning of our search for the secret of effective prayer to remember that it is in the inner chamber, where we are alone with the Father, that we learn to pray properly. The Father is in secret. In these words, Jesus teaches us where He is waiting for us and where He is always to be found.

Christians often complain that their private prayer is not what it should be. They feel weak and sinful, and their hearts are cold and dark. It is as if they have no faith or joy in what little they have to pray about. They are discouraged and kept from prayer by the thought that they cannot come to the Father as they ought to or as they wish. Child of God, listen to your Teacher! He tells you that when you go to private prayer your first thought must be that the Father is waiting for you there in secret. Don't let a cold and prayerless heart keep you from the presence of the loving Father. The Lord is concerned about you the way a father is concerned about his children. Do not think about how little you have to give to God, but about how much He wants to give to you. Just place yourself before His face and look up into it. Think of His wonderful, tender, concerned love. Tell Him how sinful, cold, and dark everything is. The Father's loving heart will give light and warmth to yours. Do what Jesus said. Just shut the door and pray to the Father in secret. Isn't it wonderful to be able to go alone to the infinite God? Just look up and say, "My Father!"

"And thy Father which seeth in secret shall reward thee." Here Jesus assures us that secret prayer cannot be fruitless. Its blessing will be evident in our lives. All we have to do is entrust our lives on earth to God when we are in secret and alone with Him. He will reward us openly and see that the answers to our prayers are made manifest in His blessing upon us. Our Lord teaches us that because God meets us in secret with infinite Fatherliness and faithfulness, we should meet Him with childlike simplicity of faith and be confident that our prayers will receive a blessing. "He that cometh to God must believe...that he is a rewarder of them that diligently seek him" (Heb. 11:6). The blessing of the closet does not depend on the strong or fervent feeling with which I pray, but on the love and power of the Father to whom I there entrust my needs. Remember your Father sees and hears in secret. Go there and stay there; then leave in confidence. God will answer. Trust Him and depend on Him for it. Prayer to the Father cannot be in vain. He will reward you openly.

Further confirming this faith in the Father love of God, Christ speaks a third word: "Your Father knoweth what things ye have need of, before ye ask him" (Matt. 6:8). At first sight it might appear as if this thought made prayer less necessary: God knows what we need far better than we do. But as we get a deeper insight into what prayer really is, this truth will help to strengthen our faith. It will teach us that we do not need to compel an unwilling God to listen to us with the multitude and urgency of our words. It will lead to a holy thoughtfulness and silence in prayer as it suggests the question: Does my Father really know that I need this? Once we have been led by the Spirit to the certainty that our request is indeed something that, according to the Word, we need for God's glory, we will have the wonderful confidence to say, "My Father knows I need it and must have it." If there is any delay in the answer, we will learn to hold on in quiet perseverance.

Father, You know I need it! Christ our Teacher would like to cultivate the blessed liberty and simplicity of a child in us as we draw near to God. Look up to the Father until His Spirit works it in us. Sometimes in our prayers we are so occupied with our fervent, urgent petitions that we forget that the Father knows and hears. At those times just hold still and quietly say, "My Father sees, my Father hears, my Father knows." It will help our faith to take the answer and say, *"We know that we have the petitions that we desired of him"* (1 John 5:15).

Now that you have entered the school of Christ to be taught to pray, take these lessons, practice them, and trust Him to perfect you in them. Go to the inner chamber often. Close the door, so that you are shut off from men and shut up with God. There the Father waits for you, and there Jesus will teach you to pray. To be alone in secret with the Father should be your highest joy. To be assured that the Father will openly reward your secret prayer so that it cannot remain unblessed should be your strength day by day. And to know that the Father knows that you need what you ask should be your liberty to bring every need to Him in the assurance that He will supply it according to His riches in glory in Christ Jesus.

Lord, teach us to pray.

Blessed Savior, with my whole heart I bless You for designating the inner chamber as the school where You meet each of Your pupils alone to reveal the Father to them. Oh, my Lord, strengthen my faith in the Father's tender love and kindness, so that when I feel sinful or troubled, my first instinctive thought will be to go where the Father waits for me and where prayer can never go unblessed. Let me know that He knows my need before I ask. This will allow me, in great faith, to trust that He will give what His child requires. May the place of secret prayer become the most beloved spot on earth to me!

Lord, hear me as I pray that You would bless the prayer closets of Your believing people everywhere. Let Your wonderful revelation of the Father's tenderness free all Christians from the thought that prayer is a burden, and lead them to regard it as the highest privilege of their lives—a joy and a blessing. Bring back everyone who is discouraged because they cannot find You in prayer. Make them understand that all they have to do is to go to You with their emptiness, because You have everything to give, and You delight in doing it. Let their one thought be not what they have to take to the Father, but what the Father waits to give them.

Especially bless the inner chamber of all Your servants who are working for You as the place where God's truth and God's grace is revealed to them. Let them be anointed there with fresh oil daily. Let it be there that their strength is renewed and they receive in faith the blessings with which they are to bless their fellowmen. Lord, draw us all closer to You and the Father in prayer. Amen.

4

THE MODEL PRAYER

After this manner therefore pray ye: Our Father which art in heaven.
—Matthew 6:9

Every teacher knows the power of example. He not only tells the child what to do and how to do it, but shows him how it really can be done. Realizing our weakness, our heavenly Teacher has given us the very words we are to take with us as we draw near to our Father. We have in them a form of prayer that contains the freshness and fullness of the eternal life. It is so simple that a child can say it and so divinely rich that it encompasses all that God can give. A model and inspiration for all other prayer, it draws us at the same time back to itself as the deepest utterance of our souls before our God.

"Our Father which art in heaven." To appreciate this word of adoration correctly, remember that none of the saints in Scripture ever ventured to address God as his Father. This invocation places us at once in the center of the wonderful revelation that Jesus came to make: His Father is our Father, too. It is the essence of redemption: Christ delivers us from the curse so that we can become the children of God. It explains the miracle of regeneration: the Spirit in the new birth gives us new life. And it reveals the mystery of faith: before the redemption is accomplished or understood, the disciples speak the word that prepares them for the blessed experience yet to come. The words are the key to the whole prayer and to all prayer. It takes time and life to study them; it will take eternity to understand them fully.

The knowledge of God's Father love is the first and simplest, but also the last and highest lesson in the school of prayer. Prayer begins in a personal relationship with the living God as well as a personal, conscious fellowship of love with Him. In the knowledge of God's Fatherliness revealed by the Holy Spirit, the power of prayer will root and grow. The life of prayer has its joy in the infinite tenderness, care, and patience of an infinite Father who is ready to hear and to help. *"Our Father which art in heaven."* Wait until the Spirit has made these words spirit and truth to us, filling our hearts and lives. Then we will indeed be within the veil, in the secret place of power where prayer always prevails.

"Hallowed be thy name" (Matt. 6:9). There is something here that strikes us at once. While we ordinarily bring our own needs to God in prayer before thinking of what belongs to God and His interests, the Master reverses the order. First *"Thy name"* (v. 9), *"Thy kingdom"* (v. 10), *"Thy will"* (v. 10); then *"give us"* (v. 11), *"forgive us"* (v. 12), *"lead us...deliver us"* (v. 13). The lesson is of more importance than we think. In true worship the Father must be first, and He must be everything. The sooner we learn to forget ourselves so that He may be glorified, the richer our own blessing in prayer will be. No one ever loses anything by sacrificing for the Father. This must influence all our prayers.

There are two sorts of prayer: personal and intercessory. The latter ordinarily occupies the lesser part of our time and energy. This should not be. Christ has opened the school of prayer especially to train intercessors for the great work of bringing down, by their faith and prayer, the blessings of His work and love to the world. There can be no deep growth in prayer unless this is our aim.

A child may ask his father to provide only what he needs for himself. But this child soon learns to say, "Give some for my sister, too." The grown-up son who lives only for the father's interests and takes charge of the father's business asks more largely and gets everything he asks. Jesus wants to train us for the blessed life of consecration and service in which all our interests are subordinate to the name, the kingdom, and the will of the Father. Live for this! Let each "Our Father" be followed in the same breath by "*Thy name*," "*Thy kingdom*," "*Thy will*"!

"*Hallowed be thy name*" (Matt. 6:9). What name? This new name of *Father*. The word *Holy* is the central word of the Old Testament. *Father* is the central word of the New Testament. In this name of love, all the holiness and glory of God are revealed. And how is the name to be hallowed? By God Himself. "*I will* [hallow] *my great name, which was profaned*" (Ezek. 36:23). Our prayers must be for God to reveal the holiness, the divine power, and the hidden glory of His name in ourselves, in all His children, and in the world. The Spirit of the Father is the Holy Spirit. It is only when we yield ourselves to be led of Him that the Father's name will be hallowed in our prayers and our lives. Let us learn this prayer: "*Our Father… Hallowed be thy name*" (Matt. 6:9).

"*Thy kingdom come*" (v. 10). The Father is a King who has a kingdom. The son and heir of a king has no higher ambition than the glory of his father's kingdom. In time of war or danger, this becomes his passion; he can think of nothing else. The children of the Father are here in the Enemy's territory, where the kingdom that is in heaven has not yet been fully manifested. What is more natural than that, when they learn to hallow the Father-name, they cry with deep enthusiasm, "*Thy kingdom come.*" The coming of the kingdom is the one great event on which the revelation of the Father's glory, the blessedness of His children, and the salvation of the world depend. The coming of the kingdom also depends on our prayers.

Let us join in the deep, longing cry of the redeemed, "*Thy kingdom come,*" which we have learned in the school of Jesus.

"*Thy will be done in earth, as it is in heaven*" (Matt. 6:10). This petition is too frequently applied alone to the suffering of the will of God. In heaven God's will is done, and the Master teaches the child to ask that God's will may be done on earth just at it is in heaven, in the spirit of adoring submission and ready obedience. Because the will of God is the glory of heaven, doing His will brings the blessedness of heaven. As the will is done, the kingdom of heaven comes into the heart. And wherever faith has accepted the Father's love, obedience accepts the Father's will. The surrender to, and the prayer for, a life of heaven-like obedience is the spirit of childlike prayer.

"*Give us this day our daily bread*" (v. 11). When the child has yielded himself to the Father in the care for His name, His kingdom, and His will, he has full liberty to ask for his daily bread. A master cares for the food of his servant, as does a general for his soldiers, or a father for his child. The Father in heaven will care for the child who has given himself up in prayer to His interests. We may in full confidence say, "Father, I live for Your honor and Your work. I know You care for me." Consecration to God and His will gives wonderful liberty in prayer for temporal things. The whole earthly life is given over to the Father's loving care.

"*And forgive us our debts, as we forgive our debtors*" (v. 12). As bread is the first need of the body, so forgiveness is for the soul. God's provision for the one is as sure as for the other. We are children, but we are sinners, too. We owe our right of access to the Father's presence to the precious blood and the forgiveness it has won for us. Beware of the prayer for forgiveness becoming a formality. Only that which is sincerely confessed is really forgiven. Let us in faith accept the forgiveness as promised. It is a spiritual reality, an actual transaction between God and us, giving us entrance into all the Father's love with all the privileges of His children. Such forgiveness is impossible without a forgiving spirit toward others. In each prayer to the Father, we must be able to say that we know of no one whom we do not heartily love.

"And lead us not into temptation, but deliver us from evil" (Matt. 6:13). All our personal needs are supplied through the provision of our daily bread, the pardon of our sins, and the protection from all sin and the power of the Evil One. The prayer for bread and pardon must be accompanied by the surrender to live in holy obedience to the Father's will in all things. A prayer of belief that everything will be kept by the power of the indwelling Spirit from the power of the Evil One should also be offered.

Children of God, Jesus wants us to pray like this to the Father in heaven. Oh, let His name, kingdom, and will have the first place in our love. In response, God will provide for us, pardon us, and love us. So the prayer will lead us to the true child life: the Father giving everything to the child and being everything for the child. We will understand how Father and child—the *Thine* and the *Our*—are one. The heart that begins its prayer with the God-devoted *Thine* will have the power in faith to speak out the *Our*, too. Such prayer will indeed be the fellowship and interchange of love, always bringing us back in trust and worship to Him who is not only the Beginning, but the End. *"For thine is the kingdom, and the power, and the glory, for ever. Amen"* (v. 13). Son of the Father, teach us to pray, *"Our Father."*

Lord, teach us to pray.

Oh, Jesus. the only begotten Son. teach us to pray, *"Our Father."* We thank You for these living, blessed words that You have given us. We thank You for everyone who through these words has learned to know and worship the Father and for what these people have meant to us. Lord, we feel as if we need years in Your school to learn each separate lesson, because Your lessons are so profound. But, instead, we look to You to lead us more deeply into their meaning. Please do this, Lord. We ask it for Your name's sake; Your name is Son of the Father.

Lord, once You said, *"No man knoweth…the Father, save the Son, and he to whomsoever the Son will reveal him"* (Matt. 11:27). You also said, *"I have declared unto them thy name, and will declare it: that the love wherewith thou hast loved me may be in them*" (John 17:26). Lord Jesus, reveal the Father to us! Let His name and His infinite Father love—the love with which He loved You—be in us. Then we will be able to rightly say, "*Our Father.*" Then we will understand Your teaching, and the first spontaneous breathing of our hearts will be: "Our Father, Your name, Your kingdom, and Your will." And we will bring our needs, our sins, and our temptations to Him in the confidence that the love of such a Father cares for all.

Blessed Lord, we are Your students, and we trust You. Please teach us to pray, "*Our Father.*" Amen.

5

THE CERTAIN ANSWER
TO PRAYER

Ask, and it shall be given you; seek,
and ye shall find; knock, and it shall be opened unto you:
for every one that asketh receiveth; and he that seeketh findeth;
and to him that knocketh it shall be opened.
—Matthew 7:7–8

Ye ask, and receive not, because ye ask amiss.
—James 4:3

Our Lord returns here in the Sermon on the Mount to speak of prayer a second time. The first time He spoke of the Father who is found in secret and who rewards openly (Matt. 6:4). Jesus also gave us the pattern prayer (vv. 5–15). Here He wants to teach us what in all Scripture is considered the chief thing in prayer: the assurance that prayer will be heard and answered. Observe how He uses words that mean almost the same thing and repeats the promise each time so distinctly: *"ye shall receive"* (Matt. 21:22), *"ye shall find,"* *"it shall be opened unto you."* He then gives the law of the kingdom as grounds for such assurance: *"every one that asketh receiveth; and he that seeketh findeth; and to him that knocketh it shall be opened."* We cannot help but feel that in this sixfold repetition He wants to impress this one truth deeply on our minds: we may and must most confidently expect an answer to our prayers. Everyone who asks, receives. Next to the revelation of the Father's love, there is not a more important lesson than this in the whole course of the school of prayer.

A difference in meaning has been sought in the three words the Lord uses: *"ask," "seek," "knock."* If it was indeed His purpose for these three words to have three distinct meanings, then the first, *"ask,"* refers to the gifts we pray for. But we may ask and receive the gift without the Giver. *"Seek"* is the word Scripture uses of God Himself. Christ assures us that we can find Him. But it is not enough to find God in time of need without coming into abiding fellowship with Him. *"Knock"* refers to admission to dwell with Him and in Him. Asking and receiving the gift would thus lead to seeking and finding the Giver, and from there to the knocking on and opening of the door to the Father's home and love. One thing is sure: the Lord wants us to believe most certainly that asking, seeking, and knocking cannot be in vain. Receiving an answer, finding God, and the opening of His heart and home are the certain fruits of prayer.

That the Lord should have thought it necessary to repeat the truth in so many forms is a lesson of deep importance. It proves that He knows our hearts. He knows that doubt and distrust toward Him are natural to us and that we view prayer as religious work without expecting an answer. He also knows that we believe prayer is something spiritually too difficult for the half-hearted disciple, even though he believes that God hears prayer and answers it. At the very beginning of His instruction, He therefore endeavors to lodge this truth deeply into the hearts of those who want to learn to pray: prayer accomplishes a great deal. Ask and you will receive; everyone who asks, receives. This is the eternal law of the kingdom. If you ask and do not receive, it must be because there is something wrong or missing in the prayer. Let the Word and Spirit teach you to pray properly. But do not lose the confidence He wants to give you that everyone who asks receives.

"Ask, and it shall be given you." In Christ's school, there is no mightier encouragement of persevering in prayer than this. As a child has to prove a sum to be correct, so the proof that we have prayed correctly is our answer. If we ask and get no answer, it is because we have not learned to pray properly. Let every learner in the school of Christ therefore take the Master's Word in all simplicity: everyone who asks, receives. Christ had good reasons for speaking so unconditionally. Be careful not to weaken the Word with human wisdom. When He tells us heavenly things, believe Him. His Word will explain itself to him who believes it fully. If questions and difficulties arise, don't try to settle them before accepting the Word. Let us entrust them all to Him; He will solve them. Our work is to accept and believe His promise completely. Let our inner chamber be inscribed with that promise in letters of light.

According to the teaching of the Master, prayer consists of two parts: a human side and a divine side. The human side is the asking; the divine is the giving. Or to look at both from the human side, there is the asking and the receiving—the two halves that make up a whole. It is as if He wants to tell us that we are not to rest without an answer because it is the will of God and the rule in the Father's family that every childlike, believing petition is granted. If no answer comes, we are not to sit down in resignation and suppose that it is not God's will to give us an answer. There must be something in the prayer that is not as God would have it. We must seek for guidance to pray so that the answer will come. It is far easier for the flesh to submit without the answer than to yield itself to being searched and purified by the Spirit, until it has learned to pray the prayer of faith.

One of the terrible marks of the diseased state of Christian life these days is that there are so many who are content without the distinct experience of answer to prayer. They pray daily, they ask many things, and they trust that some of them will be heard. But they know little of direct, definite answer to prayer as the rule of daily life. The Father seeks daily communion with His children so that He can listen to and grant their petitions. He wills that we come to Him day by day with distinct requests. He wills day by day to do what I ask. It was in His answer to prayer that the saints learned to know God as the Living One and were stirred to praise and love Him. (See Psalms 34; 66:19; 116:1.) Our Teacher waits to imprint this on our minds: prayer and its answer—the child asking and the Father giving—belong to each other.

There may be cases in which the answer is a refusal because the request is not according to God's Word, such as when Moses asked to enter Canaan. But there was still an answer. God did not leave His servant in uncertainty as to His will. The gods of the heathen are dumb and cannot speak. Our Father lets His child know when He cannot give him what he asks. The child withdraws his petition as the Son did in Gethsemane. Both Moses, the servant, and Christ, the Son, knew that what they asked was not according to what the Lord had spoken. Their prayers were the humble requests that the decision be changed. By His Word and Spirit, God will teach those who are teachable and who give Him time whether their requests be according to His will or not. Withdraw the request if it is not according to God's will, or persevere until the answer comes. Prayer is supposed to have an answer. It is in prayer and its answer that the interchange of love between the Father and His child takes place.

How deeply our hearts must be estranged from God that we should find it so difficult to grasp such promises! Even though we accept the words and believe their truth, the faith of the heart that fully possesses them and rejoices in them comes so slowly. It is because our spiritual life is still so weak and our capacity for accepting God's thoughts is so feeble. Let us look to Jesus to teach us as none but He can teach. Simply take His words and trust Him by His Spirit to make them life and power within us. They will enter our inner being and allow the spiritual, divine reality of the truth they contain to take possession of us. We should not be content until every petition we offer is carried to heaven on Jesus' own words: *"Ask, and it shall be given you."*

Beloved fellow disciples in the school of Jesus, learn this lesson well! Let us take these words just as they were spoken. Do not let human reason weaken their force. Let us take them and believe them just as Jesus gives them. In due time, He will teach us how to understand them fully. Now we should begin by implicitly believing them. Take time in prayer to listen to His voice. Don't let the feeble experiences of unbelief limit what faith can expect. Let us seek not only in prayer, but at all times, to joyfully accept the assurance that man's prayer on earth and God's answer in heaven are meant for each other. Trust Jesus to teach us to pray so that the answer can come. He will do it if we hold fast to the word He gives us: *"ask, and ye shall receive"* (John 16:24).

Lord, teach us to pray.

O Lord Jesus, teach me to understand and believe what You have promised me. You know the reasons that churn in my heart when I don't receive an answer to my prayer. Then, I believe that my prayer is not in harmony with the Father's will, that perhaps You want to give me something better, or that prayer as fellowship with God should be enough blessing to me without an answer. And yet, my blessed Lord, I find in Your teaching that You said plainly that prayer may and must expect an answer. You assure us that this is the fellowship of a child with the Father: the child asks, and the Father gives.

Blessed Lord, your words are faithful and true. It must be because I am not praying correctly that my experience of answered prayer is small. It must be because I live too little in the Spirit that my prayer is too little in the Spirit, and my power for the prayer of faith is lacking.

Lord, teach me to pray! Lord Jesus, I trust You to teach me to pray in faith. Lord, teach me this lesson: everyone who asks, receives. Amen.

6

THE INFINITE
FATHERLINESS OF GOD

Or what man is there of you, whom if his son ask bread,
will he give him a stone? Or if he ask a fish, will he give him a serpent?
If ye then, being evil, know how to give good gifts unto your children,
how much more shall your Father which is in heaven give
good things to them that ask him?
—Matthew 7:9–11

In these words our Lord proceeds further to confirm what He had said about the certainty of an answer to prayer. To remove all doubt and to show us on what sure ground His promise rests, He appeals to what everyone has seen and experienced here on earth. Because we are all children, we

493

know what we expected of our fathers. Because we are fathers or continually see them in action, we consider it the most natural thing in the world for a father to listen to his child. The Lord asks us to look up from earthly parents, of whom even the best are sinners, and calculate how much more the heavenly Father will give good gifts to those who ask Him. Jesus wants us to see that because God is greater than sinful man, our assurance that He will more surely than any earthly father grant our childlike petitions ought to be greater. As much greater as God is than man, so much surer is it that prayer will be heard with the Father in heaven than with a father on earth.

Although this parable is simple and intelligible, it contains a deep and spiritual teaching. The prayer of a child owes its influence entirely to the relation in which he stands to the parent. The prayer can exert that influence only when the child is really living in that relationship and in the home, in the love, and in the service of the Father. The power of the promise, "*ask, and it shall be given you*" (Matt. 7:7), lies in the loving relationship between us as children and the Father in heaven. When we live and walk in that relationship, the prayer of faith and its answer will be the natural result. And so the lesson we have today in the school of prayer is this: live as a child of God, and you will be able to pray and most assuredly be heard as a child.

What is the true child life? The answer can be found in any home. The child who forsakes his father's house, finding no pleasure in the presence, love, and obedience of his father, and who still expects to get whatever he asks for, will surely be disappointed. Conversely, the child who finds the joy of his life in the conversation, will, honor, and love of the father will find that it is the father's joy to grant his requests. Scripture says, "*As many as are led by the Spirit of God, they are the sons of God*" (Rom. 8:14). The childlike privilege of asking for everything is inseparable from the childlike life under the leading of the Spirit. He who gives himself to be led by the Spirit in his life will be led by Him in his prayers, too. And he will find that Fatherlike giving is the divine response to childlike living.

To see what this childlike living is, in which childlike asking and believing have their grounds, we should listen to what our Lord teaches in the

Sermon on the Mount about the Father and His children. In it, the prayer promises are imbedded in the life precepts. The two are inseparable; they form one whole. The only person who can count on the fulfillment of the promise is the person who accepts all that the Lord has connected with it. It is as if in speaking the word, *"ask, and ye shall receive"* (John 16:24), He said, "I give these promises to those whom I have pictured in their childlike poverty and purity, and of whom I have said, *'They shall be called the children of God'"* (Matt. 5:9).

Will such teaching discourage the weak? If it is necessary to conform oneself to this portrait of a child, won't many give up all hope of answers to prayer? The difficulty is removed if we think again of the blessed relationship of Father and child. A child is weak; there is a great difference among children in age and talent. The Lord does not demand that we fulfill the law perfectly. All He requires is our childlike and wholehearted surrender to live as children with Him in obedience and truth. He asks nothing more, but will accept nothing less. The Father must have our whole hearts. When this is given and He sees us with honest purpose and steady will seeking to be and live as a child in everything, then our prayers will count with Him as the prayer of a child. Anyone who simply and honestly begins to study the Sermon on the Mount and takes it as his guide in life will find, notwithstanding weakness and failure, an ever growing liberty to claim the fulfillment of its promises in regard to prayer. In the names of Father and child, he has the pledge that his petitions will be granted.

This is the one chief thought on which Jesus dwells here, and which He would like all of His students to consider. He wants us to see that the secret of effective prayer is to have the heart filled with the Father love of God. It is not enough for us to know that God is a Father. It is necessary for us to take time to meditate on what that name implies. We must take the best earthly father we know, contemplating carefully the tenderness and love with which he regards the request of his child and the love and joy with which he grants every reasonable desire. Then, as we think in adoring worship of the infinite love and Fatherliness of God, we must consider with how much more tenderness and joy He regards our requests and gives us what we ask for.

The Lord wants us to see how much this divine attitude is beyond our comprehension and to feel how impossible it is for us to understand God's readiness to hear us. Then He wants us to come and open our hearts for the Holy Spirit to fill them with God's Father love. Let us do this not only when we want to pray, but let us yield heart and life to dwell in that love. The child who only wants to know the love of the father when he has something to ask will be disappointed. But whoever lets God always be the Father in everything, living his whole life in the Father's presence and love, will discover that such a life in God's infinite Fatherliness and continual answers to prayer are inseparable.

Beloved fellow disciple, we are beginning to see why we know so little about daily answers to prayer. The chief lesson the Lord has for us in His school centers on the name of the Father. We must learn to say, *"Abba, Father"* (Gal. 4:6), and *"Our Father which art in heaven"* (Matt. 6:9). Whoever can say this has the key to all prayer. The Father listens in all the compassion with which a father responds to a weak or sickly child, in all the joy with which he hears a stammering child, in all the gentle patience with which he tolerates a thoughtless child. We must meditate upon the heart of our Father until our every prayer goes upward on the faith of this divine word: *"how much more shall your Father which is in heaven give good things to them that ask him."*

Lord, teach us to pray.

Blessed Lord, though this is one of the first and simplest lessons in Your school, it is one of the hardest for our hearts to learn. We know so little of the love of the Father. Lord, teach us to live in such a way that the Father and His love may be nearer, clearer, and dearer to us than the love of any earthly father. Let Your assurance of His hearing our prayers give us much more confidence in Him than in any earthly parent, because He is infinitely greater than man.

Lord, show us that it is only our unchildlike distance from the Father that hinders the answer to prayer, and lead us on to the true life of God's children. Lord Jesus, it is fatherlike love that awakens childlike trust. Reveal the Father and His tender love to us, so that we may become childlike and experience how in the child's life lies the power of prayer.

Blessed Son of God, the Father loves You and has given You all things. And You love the Father and have done all the things He commanded You to do. You therefore have the power to ask for anything. Lord, give us Your Spirit, the Spirit of the Son. Make us childlike, as You were on earth. Let our prayers be breathed in the faith that, just as heaven is higher than earth, God's Father love and His readiness to give us what we ask for surpass anything we can imagine. Amen.

Author's Note

"Our Father which art in heaven" (Matt. 6:9). Alas! We speak it only as a reverential homage. We think of it as a figure borrowed from an earthly life, and only in some faint and shallow meaning to be used of God. We are afraid to take God as our tender Father. We think of Him as a schoolmaster or an inspector who knows nothing about us except through our lessons.

Now open the ears of your heart, timid child of God! We aren't supposed to learn to be holy as a hard lesson at school so we can make God think well of us. We are to learn it at home with the Father to help us. God loves you not because you are clever or good, but because He is your Father. The Cross of Christ does not make God love us. It is the outcome of His love for us. He loves all His children: the clumsiest, the dullest, and the worst. His love lies underneath everything. We must grasp it as the solid foundation of our religious life, not growing up into that love, but growing up out of it. We must begin there or our beginning will come to nothing. Grasp this mightily! We must go beyond ourselves for any hope, strength, or confidence. And what hope, what strength, what confidence may be ours when we begin with *"Our Father which art in heaven"*!

We need to feel the tenderness and helpfulness that lie in these words. Meditate on the words *our Father*. Say them over to yourself until you feel something of their wonderful truth. They mean that I am bound to God by the closest and tenderest relationship, and that I have a right to His love, His power, and His blessing in a way no one else could give me. Imagine the boldness with which we can approach Him! Imagine the great things we have a right to ask for! *Our Father.* It means that all His infinite love, patience, and wisdom reach down to help me. There is infinitely more implied by this relationship than the possibility of holiness.

We are to begin in the patient love of our Father. Think about how He knows us personally, as individuals with all our peculiarities, our weaknesses, and our difficulties. The master judges by the result, but our Father judges by the effort. Failure does not always mean fault. He knows how much things cost and weighs them carefully where others wouldn't. *Our Father.* Think about how His great love understands the poor beginnings of His little ones, clumsy and simple as they may seem to others. All this and infinitely more lies in this blessed relationship! Don't be afraid to claim it all as your own!

7

THE
ALL-COMPREHENSIVE GIFT

If ye then, being evil, know how to give good gifts unto your children:
how much more shall your heavenly Father give the
Holy Spirit to them that ask him?
—Luke 11:13

n the Sermon on the Mount, the Lord had already said His wonderful *"How much more?"* (Matt. 7:11). Here in Luke, where He repeats the question, there is a difference. Instead of speaking as He did then of giving *"good gifts,"* He said, *"How much more shall your heavenly Father give the Holy Spirit?"* He thus teaches us that the foremost and the best of these gifts is the Holy Spirit, or rather, that in this gift all others are comprised.

The Holy Spirit is the first of the Father's gifts and the one He delights most in bestowing. The Holy Spirit is therefore the gift we ought to seek first.

We can easily understand the unspeakable worth of this gift. Jesus spoke of the Spirit as *"the promise of the Father"* (Acts 1:4), the one promise in which God's Fatherhood revealed itself. The best gift a good and wise earthly father can bestow on a child is his own spirit. This is the great object of a father in education: to reproduce in his child his own disposition and character. If the child is to know and understand his father, if he is to enter into all his will and plans, if he is to have his highest joy in the father and the father in him, he must be of one mind and spirit with him. It is impossible to conceive of God bestowing any higher gift on His child than His own Spirit. God is what He is through His Spirit; the Spirit is the very life of God. Just think what it means for God to give His own Spirit to His child on earth.

The glory of Jesus as a Son on earth was that the Spirit of the Father was in Him. At His baptism in the Jordan, the Voice proclaiming Him the Beloved Son and the Spirit descending upon Him were united. And so the apostle said of us, *"Because ye are sons, God hath sent forth the Spirit of his Son into your hearts, crying, Abba, Father"* (Gal. 4:6). A king seeks in the whole education of his son to call forth a kingly spirit in him. Our Father in heaven desires to educate us as His children for the holy, heavenly life in which He dwells. For this purpose He gives us His own Spirit from the depths of His heart.

Jesus' whole purpose after He made atonement with His own blood was to enter into God's presence and obtain the Holy Spirit for us, sending Him down to dwell in us. Because He is the Spirit of the Father and the Son, the whole life and love of the Father and the Son are in Him. Coming down among us, He lifts us up into the fellowship of the Father and the Son. As the Spirit of the Father, He fills our hearts with the love with which the Father loved the Son and teaches us to live in it. As the Spirit of the Son, He breathes into us the childlike liberty, devotion, and obedience in which the Son lived on earth. The Father can bestow no higher or more wonderful gift that this: His own Holy Spirit, the Spirit of Sonship.

This truth naturally suggests that this first and chief gift of God must be the first and chief object of all prayer. The one necessary element in the spiritual life is the Holy Spirit. All the fullness is in Jesus. His is the fullness of grace and truth from which we receive grace for grace. The Holy Spirit is the appointed intermediary whose special work is to convey Jesus and everything there is in Him to us. He is the Spirit of life in Christ Jesus.

If we yield ourselves entirely to the will of the Spirit and let Him have His way with us, He will manifest the life of Christ within us. He will do this with a divine power, maintaining the life of Christ in us in uninterrupted continuity. If there is one thing we should pray for to draw us to the Father's throne and keep us there, it is the Holy Spirit.

The Spirit meets the believer's every need in the variety of gifts that He has to dispense. Just think of the names He bears. He is the Spirit of:

+ **Grace:** who reveals and imparts all of the grace there is in Jesus;

+ **Faith:** who teaches us to begin, go on, and increase in believing;

+ **Adoption and assurance:** who witnesses that we are God's children and inspires our confiding in Him and our confident "Abba, Father";

+ **Truth:** who leads us to accept each word of God in truth;

+ **Prayer:** through whom we speak with the Father so that we may be heard;

+ **Judgment:** who searches our hearts and convicts us of sin;

+ **Holiness:** who manifests and communicates the Father's holy presence within us;

+ **Power:** who makes us testify boldly and work effectively in the Father's service;

+ **Glory:** who is the pledge of our inheritance and prepares us for the glory to come.

Surely the child of God needs only one thing to be able to really live as a child of God: to be filled with this Spirit.

The lesson Jesus teaches in His school is this: the Father is longing to give the Holy Spirit to us if we will simply ask in childlike dependence on what He said, *"If ye…know how to give good gifts unto your children: how much more shall your heavenly Father give the Holy Spirit to them that ask him?"* In the words of God's promise, *"I will pour out my spirit* [abundantly]" (Joel 2:28), and in His command, *"Be filled with the Spirit"* (Eph. 5:18), we know what God is ready to give us. As God's children, we have already received the Spirit. But we still need to pray for His special gifts as we require them. We need to pray also for His complete possession and unceasing guidance. We are like a branch that is already filled with the sap of the vine and is crying for the continued and increasing flow of that sap. Just as the branch needs more sap to bring its fruit to perfection, the believer, rejoicing in the possession of the Spirit, still thirsts and cries for more. What the great Teacher would like us to learn in this situation is that we should expect nothing less than God's promise and God's command in answer to our prayers. We must be filled abundantly. Christ wants us to ask this in the assurance that the wonderful how much more of God's Father love is a pledge that when we ask, we will most certainly receive.

As we pray to be filled with the Spirit, we shouldn't look for the answer in our feelings. All spiritual blessings must be received, that is, accepted or taken, in faith.[1] Believe that the Father gives the Holy Spirit to His praying child. Even while I pray, I must say in faith, "I have what I ask, and the fullness of the Spirit is mine." Let us continue unshakably in this faith. On the strength of God's Word, we know that we should have what we ask.

We should be thankful that we have been heard and thankful for what we have received and now possess. Continue praying in belief that the blessing that has already been given to us will break through and fill our entire being. It is in such believing thanksgiving and prayer that our souls

---

1. The Greek word for receiving and taking is the same. When Jesus said, *"Every one that asketh receiveth"* (Matt. 7:8), He used the same verb as at the Supper, *"Take, eat"* (Matt. 26:26), or on the resurrection morning, *"Receive ye* [accept, take] *the Holy Ghost"* (John 20:22). Receiving not only implies God's bestowment, but our acceptance.

open up and the Spirit takes entire and undisturbed possession of them. Such prayer not only asks and hopes for, but also takes, holds, and inherits the full blessing. In all our prayers let us remember the lesson the Savior teaches us: one thing we can be sure of is that the Father desires to have us filled with His Spirit, and He delights in giving Him to us.

Once we have learned to believe this for ourselves, we can take the liberty and power from the treasure held for us in heaven to pray for the outpouring of the Spirit on the church, on all flesh, on individuals, or on special efforts. Once we have learned to know the Father in prayer for ourselves, we learn to pray most confidently for others, too. The Father gives the Holy Spirit most to those who ask that He be given to others.

Lord, teach us to pray.

Father in heaven, you sent Your Son to reveal Yourself to us: Your Father love and everything that love has for us. Christ has taught us that the gift above all gifts that You want to give us in answer to prayer is the Holy Spirit. O my Father, there is nothing I desire so much as to be filled with the Holy Spirit. The blessings He brings are so unspeakable. They are just what I need. He fills the heart with Your love and with Yourself. I long for this! He breathes the mind and life of Christ into me, so that I can live as He did, in and for the Father's love. I long for this! He supplies power from heaven for all my walk and work. I long for this! O Father, please give me the fullness of Your Spirit today.

Father, I base this request on the words of my Lord, "*how much more shall* [He] *give the Holy Spirit.*" I believe that You hear my prayer, and that I receive now just what I am asking for. Father, I claim and I take it! The fullness of Your Spirit is mine. I receive this gift today as a faith gift. In faith, I believe the Father works everything He has promised through the Spirit. The Father delights in breathing His Spirit into His waiting child as he fellowships with Him. Amen.

8

THE BOLDNESS
OF GOD'S FRIENDS

*And he said unto them, Which of you shall have a friend, and shall go
unto him at midnight, and say unto him, Friend, lend me three loaves;
for a friend of mine in his journey is come to me, and I have nothing
to set before him? And he from within shall answer and say, Trouble
me not: the door is now shut, and my children are with me in bed; I
cannot rise and give thee. I say unto you, Though he will not rise and
give him, because he is his friend, yet because of his importunity he will
rise and give him as many as he needeth.*
—Luke 11:5–8

The first teaching our Lord gave to His disciples was in the Sermon
on the Mount. It was nearly a year later that the disciples asked

Jesus to teach them to pray. In answer, He gave them the Lord's Prayer a second time to show them what to pray. He then spoke of how they ought to pray and repeated what He formerly said of God's Fatherliness and the certainty of an answer. But in between He added the beautiful parable of the friend at midnight to teach them the twofold lesson that God does not only want us to pray for ourselves, but for those who are perishing around us. In such intercession great boldness of entreaty is often necessary and always lawful and pleasing to God.

The parable is a perfect storehouse of instruction regarding true intercession. It contains the following:

* the love that seeks to help the needy around us, *"a friend...is come to me"*;

* the need that gives rise to the cry, *"I have nothing to set before him"*;

* the confidence that help is available, *"which of you shall have a friend... and say...Friend, lend me three loaves"*;

* the unexpected refusal, *"I cannot rise and give thee"*;

* the perseverance that takes no refusal, *"because of his importunity"*;

* the reward of such prayer, *"he will...give him as many as he needeth."*

In this we can find a perfect example of the prayer and faith in which God's blessing has so often been sought and found.

Let us confine ourselves to this chief thought: prayer is an appeal to the friendship of God. If we are God's friends and go as friends to Him, we must prove that we are friends of the needy. God's friendship to us and ours to others go hand in hand. When we go to God as this kind of friend, we may use the utmost liberty in claiming an answer.

There is a twofold use of prayer: one is to obtain strength and blessing for our own lives; the other is the higher and true glory of prayer for which Christ has taken us into His fellowship and teaching—intercession, the royal power a child of God exercises in heaven on behalf of others and even of the kingdom. We see in Scripture how it was in intercession for others that Abraham and Moses, Samuel and Elijah, and all the holy men of long ago proved that they had power with God and prevailed. It is when we give ourselves to be a blessing to others that we can count on the blessing of God for ourselves. When we go to God as a friend of the poor and the perishing, we can count on His friendliness. The righteous man who is a friend of the poor is a very special friend of God. This gives wonderful liberty in prayer.

"Lord! I have a needy friend whom I must help. As a friend I have undertaken to help him. In You I have a Friend whose kindness and riches I know to be infinite. I am sure You will give me what I ask. If I am ready to do for my friend whatever I can, even though I am a sinner, I know that You, my heavenly Friend, are ready to do so much more to give me what I ask for."

Pondering the friendship of God may not seem to reveal anything new about confident prayer after having studied the fatherhood of God. After all, a father is more than a friend. But if we consider it, pleading the friendship of God can open new wonders to us. It is so perfectly natural for a child to obtain what he asks for from his father that we almost call it the father's duty to grant him the request. But with a friend, it is as if the kindness were freer, dependent on sympathy and character rather than on nature. In addition, the relationship of a child to his father is one of perfect dependence. Two friends are more nearly on the same level. In teaching us the spiritual mystery of prayer, our Lord would rather have us approach God as those whom He has acknowledged as His friends and whose minds and lives are in sympathy with His.

But we must be living as His friends. We are still children even when we stray, but friendship depends on our conduct. *"Ye are my friends, if ye do whatsoever I command you"* (John 15:14). *"Seest thou how faith wrought with his works, and by works was faith made perfect? And the scripture was fulfilled which saith, Abraham believed God…and he was called the Friend of God"* (James 2:22–23). The Spirit, the same Spirit, that leads us also bears witness to our acceptance with God (Rom. 8:16).

In the same way, the same Spirit helps us in prayer. Life as a friend of God gives us the wonderful liberty to say, "I have a friend to whom I can go even at midnight." And how much better it is when I go in the very spirit of friendliness and kindness I look for in God, seeking to help my friend as I want God to help me. When I go to God in prayer, He always looks at the aim of my petition. If it is merely for my own comfort or joy that I seek His grace, I do not receive it. But if I want Him to be glorified in my dispensing His blessings to others, I will not ask in vain. If I ask for others, but want to wait until God has made me so rich that it is no sacrifice or act of faith to aid them, I will not receive an answer. My prayer will be heard if I can say that I have already asked for help for a needy friend. Even though I don't have what I need, I have already begun the work of love, because I know I have a Friend who will help me. We do not know how effective this plea is. When the friendship of earth looks in its need to the friendship of heaven, *"He will…give him as many as he needeth."*

But we do not always get what we ask for all at once. The one way in which man can honor and enjoy his God is through faith. Intercession is part of faith's training school. There our friendship with men and with God is tested. It is seen whether our friendship with the needy is so real that we would sacrifice our rest and go even at midnight to obtain what they needed. Our friendship with God should be so clear that we can depend on Him not to turn us away, therefore continuing to pray until He answers.

What a deep heavenly mystery persevering prayer is! The God who has promised and who longs to give the blessing holds it back. It is a matter of such deep importance to Him that His friends on earth should know and fully trust their rich Friend in heaven! Because of this, He trains them in the school of delayed answer to find out how their perseverance really does prevail. They can wield mighty power in heaven if they simply set themselves to it!

There is a faith that sees the promise and embraces it, but does not receive it (Heb. 11:13, 39). When the answer to prayer does not come and the promise we most firmly trust appears to be fruitless, the trial of faith, more precious than gold, takes place. It is in this trial that the faith that has embraced the promise is purified, strengthened, and prepared in personal, holy fellowship with the living God to see His glory. It takes and holds the promise until it has received the fulfillment in living truth of what it had requested from the unseen but living God.

Each child of God who is seeking to perform the work of love in his Father's service should take courage. The parent with his child, the teacher with his class, the Bible reader with his circle, and the preacher with his congregation all bear the burden of hungry, perishing souls. Let them all take courage. That God should really require persevering prayer is at first very strange to us. But there is a real, spiritual necessity for importunity. To teach it to us, the Master uses this almost strange parable. If the unfriendliness of a selfish earthly friend can be conquered by importunity, imagine how much more it will accomplish with our heavenly Friend! He loves to give us what we ask for, but is held back by our spiritual unfitness, our incapacity to possess what He has to give. Let us thank Him that in delaying His answer He is preparing us to assume our true position with Him and to exercise all our power. He is training us to live with Him in the fellowship of undoubting faith and trust, to be indeed the friends of God. Let us securely hold the threefold cord that cannot be broken: the hungry friend needing the help, the praying friend seeking the help, and the Mighty Friend loving to give us as much help as we need.

Lord, teach us to pray.

O my Blessed Lord and Teacher, I must come to You in prayer; Your teaching is so glorious. But it is still too high for me to grasp. I must confess that my heart is too little to take in these thoughts of the wonderful boldness I may use with Your Father as my Friend. Lord Jesus, I trust You to give me Your Spirit with Your Word, and to make the Word quick and powerful in my heart. I desire to claim this promise from Your Word: *"because of his importunity he will...give him as many as he needeth."*

Lord, teach me to know the power of persevering prayer more. I know that in it, the Father allows for the time we need for the inner life to grow and ripen, so that His grace may be made our very own. Through our persevering prayer, He trains us to exercise strong faith that does not let Him go even in the face of seeming disappointment. He wants to give us the wonderful liberty of knowing how truly He has made the dispensing of His gifts dependent on our prayers. Lord, teach me to see all this in spirit and truth!

Let it be the joy of my life to become the caretaker of my rich Friend in heaven! Let me take care of all the hungry and perishing, even at midnight, because I know my Friend always gives as much as is needed to him who perseveres. Amen.

9

PRAYER
PROVIDES LABORERS

Then saith he unto his disciples, The harvest truly is plenteous, but the
labourers are few; pray ye therefore the Lord of the harvest, that he will
send forth labourers into his harvest.
—Matthew 9:37–38

T he Lord frequently taught His disciples that they must pray and
how they should pray. But He seldom told them what to pray.
This He left to their sense of need and the leading of the Spirit. But in
the above Scripture, He expressly directs them to remember one thing. In
view of the abundant harvest and the need for reapers, they must cry to the
Lord of the harvest to send laborers. Just as in the parable of the friend at

midnight, He wants them to understand that prayer is not to be selfish; it is the power through which blessing can come to others. The Father is Lord of the harvest. When we pray for the Holy Spirit, we must pray for Him to prepare and send laborers for the work.

Why does He ask His disciples to pray for this? Could He not pray Himself? Would not one prayer of His achieve more than a thousand of theirs? Is God, the Lord of the harvest, not aware of the need? And would He not, in His own good time, send laborers without the disciples' prayers? Such questions lead us into the deepest mysteries of prayer and its power in the kingdom of God. The answer to such questions will convince us that prayer is indeed a power on which the gathering of the harvest and the coming of the kingdom do in very truth depend.

Prayer is no form or show. The Lord Jesus was Himself the truth; everything He spoke was the truth. It was when He saw the multitude and was moved with compassion on them, because they *"were scattered abroad, as sheep having no shepherd"* (Matt. 9:36), that He called on the disciples to pray for laborers to be sent to them. He did so because He really believed that their prayers were needed and would help.

The veil that hides the invisible world from us was wonderfully transparent to the holy human soul of Jesus. He had looked long and deep and far into the hidden connection of cause and effect in the spiritual world. He had marked in God's Word how God called men like Abraham, Moses, Joshua, Samuel, and Daniel, giving them authority over men in His Name. God also gave these men the authority to call the powers of heaven to their aid as they needed them. Jesus knew that the work of God had been entrusted to these men of old and to Himself for a time here upon earth. Now it was about to pass over into the hands of His disciples. He knew that when they were given responsibility for this work, it would not be a mere matter of form or show. The success of the work would actually depend on them and their faithfulness.

As a single individual, within the limitations of a human body and a human life, Jesus feels how little a short visit can accomplish among these wandering sheep He sees around Him. He longs for help to have them properly cared for. He therefore tells His disciples to begin to pray. When they have taken over the work from Him on earth, they are to make this one of their chief petitions in prayer: that the Lord of the harvest Himself would send laborers into His harvest. But since He entrusted them with the work and made it to a large extent dependent on them, He gives them authority to apply to Him for laborers and makes the supply dependent on their prayers.

How little Christians really feel and mourn the need of laborers in the fields of the world, so ripe for the harvest. How little they believe that our labor supply depends on prayer and that prayer will really provide *as many as he needeth*" (Luke 11:8). The dearth of labor is known and discussed. Efforts are sometimes made to supply the need. But how little the burden of the sheep wandering without a Shepherd is really assumed in the faith that the Lord of the harvest will send forth the laborers in answer to prayer. Without this prayer, fields ready for reaping will be left to perish. And yet it is so. The Lord has surrendered His work to His church. He has made Himself dependent on them as His body, through whom His work must be done. The power that the Lord gives His people to exercise in heaven and earth is real; the number of laborers and the measure of the harvest does actually depend on their prayer.

Why don't we obey the Master's instruction more heartily and cry more earnestly for laborers? There are two reasons. The one is that we miss the compassion of Jesus that gave rise to this request for prayer. Believers must learn to love their neighbors as themselves and to live entirely for God's glory in their relationships with fellowmen. The Father's first commandment to His redeemed ones is that they accept those who are perishing as the charge entrusted to them by their Lord. Accept them not only as a field of labor, but as the objects of loving care and interest. Soon, compassion toward the hopelessly perishing will touch your heart, and the cry will ascend with a new sincerity.

The other reason for the neglect of the command is that we believe too little in the power of prayer to bring about definite results. We do not live close enough to God to be capable of the confidence that He will answer.

We have not surrendered entirely to His service and kingdom. But our lack of faith will be overcome as we plead for help. Let us pray for a life in union with Christ, so that His compassion streams into us and His Spirit assures us that our prayers are heard.

Such prayer will obtain a twofold blessing. There will first be a desire for an increase in the number of men entirely given up to the service of God. That there are times when men actually cannot be found for the service of the Master as ministers, missionaries, or teachers of God's Word is a terrible blot upon the church of Christ. As God's children make this a matter of supplication in their own circles or churches, it will be given. The Lord Jesus is now Lord of the harvest. He has been exalted to bestow the gifts of the Spirit. He wants to make gifts of men filled with the Spirit. But His supply and distribution of these gifts depend on the cooperation of the members with Him. Prayer will lead to such cooperation and will stir those praying to believe that they will find the men and the means for the work.

The other blessing will be equally great. Every believer is a laborer. As God's children, we have been redeemed for service and have our work waiting. It must be our prayers that the Lord would fill all His people with the spirit of devotion, so that no one may be found standing idle in the vineyard. Wherever there is a complaint about the lack of fit helpers for God's work, prayer has the promise of a supply. God is always ready and able to provide. It may take time and importunity, but Christ's command to ask the Lord of the harvest is the pledge that the prayer will be heard. *"I say unto you...he will rise and give him as many as he needeth"* (Luke 11:8).

This power to provide for the needs of the world and secure the servants for God's work has been given to us in prayer. The Lord of the harvest will hear. Christ who taught us to pray this way will support the prayers offered in His name and interest. Let us set apart time and give all of ourselves to this part of our intercessory work. It will lead us into the fellowship of that compassionate heart of His that led Him to call for our prayers. It will give us the insight of our royal position as children of the King whose will counts for something with the great God in the advancement of His kingdom. We will feel that we really are God's fellow workers on earth, that we have earnestly been entrusted with a share in His work. We will become partakers in the work of the soul. But we will also share in the satisfaction of the soul as we learn how, in answer to prayer, blessing has been given that otherwise would not have come.

Lord, teach us to pray.

Blessed Lord, once again You have given us another wondrous lesson to learn. We humbly ask that you let us see these spiritual realities. There is a large harvest that is perishing as it waits for sleepy disciples to give the signal for laborers to come. Lord, teach us to view it with a heart full of compassion and pity. There are so few laborers, Lord. Show us what terrible sin the lack of prayer and faith is, considering there is a Lord of the harvest so able and ready to send them forth. Show us how He does indeed wait for the prayer to which He has promised an answer. We are the disciples to whom the commission to pray has been given. Lord, show us how You can breathe Your Spirit into us, so that Your compassion and the faith in Your promise will rouse us to unceasing, prevailing prayer.

O Lord, we cannot understand how You can entrust such work and give such power to men so slothful and unfaithful. We thank You for all those whom You are teaching day and night to cry for laborers to be sent. Lord, breathe Your Spirit into all Your children. Let them learn to live only for the kingdom and glory of their Lord and become fully awake to the faith in what their prayer can accomplish. And let our hearts be filled with the assurance that prayer offered in living faith in the living God will bring certain and abundant answer. Amen.

10

PRAYER MUST BE DEFINITE

And Jesus answered and said unto him,
What wilt thou that I should do unto thee?
—Mark 10:51

T he blind man had been crying out loud repeatedly, *"Thou son of David, have mercy on me"* (Mark 10:47, 48). The cry had reached the ear of the Lord. He knew what the man wanted and was ready to grant it to him. But before He did it, He asked him, *"What wilt thou that I should do unto thee?"* He wanted to hear not only the general petition for mercy, but the distinct expression of what the man's desire was that day. Until he verbalized it, he was not healed.

There are still petitioners to whom the Lord puts the same question who cannot get the aid they need until they answer that question. Our prayers must be a distinct expression of definite need, not a vague appeal to His mercy or an indefinite cry for blessing. It isn't that His loving heart does not understand or is not ready to hear our cry. Rather, Jesus desires such definite prayer for our own sakes because it teaches us to know our own needs better. Time, thought, and self-scrutiny are required to find out what our greatest need really is. Our desires are put to the test to see whether they are honest and real and are according to God's Word. We also consider whether we really believe we will receive the things we ask. Such reflective prayer helps us to wait for the special answer and to mark it when it comes.

So much of our prayers are vague and pointless. Some cry for mercy, but do not take the trouble to know exactly why they want it. Others ask to be delivered from sin, but do not name any sin from which a deliverance can be claimed. Still others pray for God's blessing on those around them—for the outpouring of God's Spirit on their land or on the world—and yet have no special field where they can wait and expect to see the answer. To everyone the Lord says, "What do you really want, and what do you expect Me to do?"

Every Christian has only limited power. Just as he must have his own specific field of labor in which to serve God, he must also make his prayers specific. Each believer has his own circle, family, friends, and neighbors. If he were to take one or more of these by name, he would find himself entering the training school of faith that leads to personal dealing with his God. When we have faithfully claimed and received answers in such distinct matters, our more general prayers will be believing and effectual. Not many prayers will reach the mark if we just pour out our hearts in a multitude of petitions, without taking time to see whether every petition is sent with the purpose and expectation of getting an answer.

Bow before the Lord with silence in your soul and ask such questions as these:

+ What is really my desire?

‣ Do I desire it in faith, expecting to receive an answer?

‣ Am I ready to present it to the Father and leave it there in His bosom?

‣ Is there agreement between God and me that I will get an answer?

We should learn to pray in such a way that God will see and we will know what we really expect.

The Lord warns us against the vain repetitions of the Gentiles, who expect to be heard because they pray so much. We often hear prayers of great earnestness and fervor, in which a multitude of petitions are poured forth. The Savior would undoubtedly have to respond to some of them by asking, "What do you want?"

If I am in a foreign country on business for my father, I would certainly write two different sorts of letters home. There will be family letters with typical affectionate expressions in them, and there will be business letters containing orders for what I need. There may also be letters in which both are found. The answers will correspond to the letters. To each sentence of the letters containing the family news I do not expect a special answer. But for each order I send, I am confident of an answer regarding the forwarding of the desired article. In our dealings with God, the business element must be present. Our expressions of need, sin, love, faith, and consecration must be accompanied by an explicit statement of what we are asking for and what we expect to receive. In response, the Father loves to give us a token of His approval and acceptance.

But the word of the Master teaches us more. He does not say, "What do you wish?" but "What do you will?" One often wishes for a thing without willing it. I wish to have a certain article, but the price is too high, so I decide not take it. I wish, but do not will to have it. The lazy man wishes to be rich, but does not will it. Many people wish to be saved, but perish because they do not will it.

The will rules the whole heart and life. If I really will to have something that is within my reach, I do not rest until I have it. When Jesus asks us, "What wilt thou?" He asks whether it is our intention to get what we ask for at any price, however great the sacrifice. Do you really will to have it enough to pray continuously until He hears you, no matter how long it takes? How many prayers are wishes sent up for a short time and then forgotten! And how many are sent up year after year as a matter of duty, while we complacently wait without the answer.

One may ask if it wouldn't be better to make our wishes known to God, leaving it to Him to decide what is best, without our seeking to assert our wills. The answer is, by no means. The prayer of faith that Jesus sought to teach His disciples does not simply proclaim its desire and then leave the decision to God. That would be the prayer of submission for cases in which we cannot know God's will. But the prayer of faith, finding God's will in some promise of the Word, pleads for that promise until it comes.

In Matthew 9:28, Jesus said to the blind man, *"Believe ye that I am able to do this?"* In Mark, He said, *"What wilt thou that I should do?"* In both cases He said that faith had saved them. And He said to the Syrophenician woman, too, *"Great is thy faith: be it unto thee even as thou wilt"* (Matt. 15:28). Faith is nothing but the purpose of the will resting on God's Word and saying, "I must have it." To believe truly is to will firmly.

Such a will is not at variance with our dependence on God and our submission to Him. Rather, it is the true submission that honors God. It is only when the child has yielded his own will in entire surrender to the Father that he receives from the Father the liberty and power to will what he desires. Once the believer has accepted the will of God, as revealed through the Word and the Spirit, as his will, too, then it is the desire of God that His child use this renewed will in His service. The will is the highest power of the soul. Grace desires above everything to sanctify and restore this will to full and free exercise because it is one of the chief traits of God's image. God's child is like a son who lives only for his father's interests, seeks his father's will rather than his own, and is trusted by the father with his business. God speaks to that child in all truth, *"What wilt thou?"*

It is often spiritual sloth that, under the appearance of humility, professes to have no will. It fears the trouble of searching for the will of God or, when found, the struggle of claiming it in faith. True humility is always accompanied by strong faith. Seeking to know only the will of God, that faith then boldly claims the fulfillment of the promise, *"Ye shall ask what ye will, and it shall be done unto you"* (John 15:7).

Lord, teach us to pray.

Lord Jesus, teach me to pray with all my heart and strength that there may be no doubt with You or with me about what I have asked. I want to know what I desire so well that as my petitions are being recorded in heaven, I can also record them here on earth and note each answer as it comes. Make my faith in what Your Word has promised so clear that the Spirit may work within me the liberty to will that it will come. Lord, renew, strengthen, and sanctify my entire will for the work of effectual prayer.

Blessed Savior, I pray that You reveal to me the wonderful grace You show us, the grace that asks us to say what we desire and then promises to do it. Son of God, I cannot fully understand it. I can only believe that You have indeed redeemed us wholly for Yourself, and that You want to mold our wills, making them Your most efficient servant. Lord, I unreservedly yield my will to You as the channel through which Your Spirit is to rule my whole being. Let Him take possession of it, lead it into the truth of Your promises, and make it so strong in prayer that I may always hear Your voice saying, *"Great is thy faith: be it unto thee even as thou wilt"* (Matt. 15:28). Amen.

11

THE FAITH THAT TAKES

Therefore I say unto to you, All things whatsoever ye pray and ask for,
believe that ye receive them, and ye shall have them.
—Mark 11:24 ASV

W hat a promise! It is so large, so divine, that our little hearts cannot comprehend it. In every possible way we seek to limit it to what we think is safe or probable. We don't allow it to come in just as He gave it to us with its quickening power and energy. If we would allow it, that promise would enlarge our hearts to receive all of what His love and power are really ready to do for us.

Faith is very far from being a mere conviction of the truth of God's Word or a conclusion drawn from certain premises. It is the ear that has heard God say what He will do and the eye that has seen Him doing it. Therefore, where there is true faith, it is impossible for the answer not to come. We must do this one thing that He asks of us as we pray, "*Believe that ye receive them.*" He will see to it that He does the thing He has promised: "*Ye shall have them.*"

The essence of Solomon's prayer is, "*Blessed be the LORD God of Israel, who hath with his hands fulfilled that which he spake with his mouth to my father David*" (2 Chron. 6:4). This should be the essence of all true prayer. It is the joyful adoration of a God whose hand always secures the fulfillment of what His mouth has spoken. Let us in this spirit listen to the promise Jesus gives because each part of it has a divine message.

"*All things whatsoever.*" From the first word, our human wisdom begins to doubt and say, "This can't possibly be literally true." But if it isn't, why did the Master say it? He used the very strongest expression He could find, "*All things whatsoever.*" And He said it more than once, "*If thou canst believe, all things are possible to him that believeth*" (Mark 9:23); "*if ye have faith as a grain of mustard seed…nothing shall be impossible unto you*" (Matt. 17:20). Faith is completely the work of God's Spirit through His Word in the prepared heart of the believing disciple. It is impossible for the fulfillment not to come, because faith is the pledge and forerunner of the coming answer.

"*All things whatsoever ye pray and ask for, believe that ye receive.*" The tendency of human reason is to intervene here with certain qualifiers, such as "if expedient," "if according to God's will," to break the force of a statement that appears dangerous. Beware of dealing this way with the Master's words. His promise is most literally true. He wants His frequently repeated "*all things*" to enter our hearts and reveal how mighty the power of faith is. The Head truly calls the members of His Body to share His power with Him. Our Father places His power at the disposal of the child who completely trusts Him. Faith gets its food and strength from the "*all things*" of Christ's promise. As we weaken it, we weaken faith.

The "*whatsoever*" is unconditional except for what is implied in the believing. Before we can believe, we must find out and know what God's will is. Believing is the exercise of a soul surrendered to the influence of the Word and the Spirit. Once we do believe, nothing is impossible. Let us pray that we do not limit Christ's *"all things"* with what we think is possible. Rather, His *"whatsoever"* should determine the boundaries of our hope and faith. It is seed word that we should take just as He gives it and keep it in our hearts. It will germinate and take root, filling our lives with its fullness and bearing abundant fruit.

"All things whatsoever ye pray and ask for." It is in prayer that these *"all things"* are to be brought to God. The faith that receives them is the fruit of the prayer. There must be a certain amount of faith before there can be prayer, but greater faith is the result of prayer. In the personal presence of the Savior and in conversation with Him, faith rises to grasp what at first appeared too high. Through prayer we hold up our desires to the light of God's holy will, our motives are tested, and proof is given whether we are indeed asking in the name of Jesus and only for the glory of God. The leading of the Spirit shows us whether we are asking for the right thing and in the right spirit. The weakness of our faith becomes obvious as we pray. But we are encouraged to say to the Father that we do believe and that we prove the reality of our faith by the confidence with which we persevere. It is in prayer that Jesus teaches and inspires faith. Whoever waits to pray, or loses heart in prayer because he doesn't feel the faith needed to get an answer, will never learn that faith. Whoever begins to pray and ask will find the Spirit of faith is given nowhere so surely as at the foot of the throne.

"Believe that ye receive them." Clearly we are to believe that we receive the very things we ask. The Savior does not say that the Father may give us something else because He knows what is best. The very mountain that faith wants to remove is cast into the sea.

There is one kind of prayer in which we make known our request in everything, and the reward is the sweet peace of God in our hearts and minds. This is the prayer of trust. It makes reference to the countless desires of daily life that we cannot find out if God will give. We leave it to Him to decide whether or not to give, as He knows best.

But the prayer of faith of which Jesus speaks is something higher and different. Nothing honors the Father like the faith that is assured that He will do what He has said in giving us whatever we ask. Such faith takes its stand on the promise delivered by the Spirit. It knows most certainly that it receives exactly what it asks, whether in the greater interest of the Master's work or in the lesser concerns of daily life. Notice how clearly the Lord states this in Mark 11:23, "*Whosoever...shall not doubt in his heart, but shall believe that those things which he saith shall come to pass; he shall have whatsoever he saith.*" This is the blessing of the prayer of faith of which Jesus speaks.

"*Believe that ye receive them.*" This word of central importance is too often misunderstood. Believe that you have received what you're asking for now, while praying! You may not actually see it manifested until later. But now, without seeing it, you are to believe that it has already been given to you by the Father in heaven. Receiving or accepting an answer to prayer is just like receiving or accepting Jesus. It is a spiritual thing, an act of faith separate from all feeling. When I go to Jesus, asking Him for forgiveness for a sin, I believe He is in heaven for just that purpose, and I accept His forgiveness. In the same way, when I go to God asking for any special gift which is according to His Word, I must believe that what I desire is mine. I believe that I have it; I hold it in faith; and I thank God that it's mine. "*If we know that he hear us, whatsoever we ask, we know that we have the petitions that we desired of him*" (1 John 5:15).

"*And ye shall have them.*" The gift that we first hold in faith as ours from heaven will become ours in personal experience. But will it be necessary to pray longer once we know we have been heard and have received what we asked? Additional prayer will not be necessary when the blessing is on its way. In these cases we should maintain our confidence, proving our faith by praising God for what we have received, even though we haven't experienced it yet.

There are other cases in which faith needs to be further tried and strengthened in persevering prayer. Only God knows when everything is fully ripe for the manifestation of the blessing that has been given to faith. Elijah knew for certain that rain would come. God had promised it. And yet he had to pray the seven times. That prayer was not just for show. It was an intense spiritual reality both in the heart of Elijah as he lay there pleading and in heaven where it has its effectual work to do. It is through faith and patience we inherit the promises (Heb. 6:12). Faith says most confidently, "I have received it." Patience perseveres in prayer until the gift bestowed in heaven is seen on earth.

"*Believe that ye receive them, and ye shall have.*" Between the "*ye receive them*" in heaven and the "*shall have*" on earth, the key word is "*believe.*" Believing praise and prayer are the link. Remember that it is Jesus who said this. As we see heaven opened to us and the Father on the throne offering to give us whatever we ask for in faith, we are ashamed that we have so little availed ourselves of the privilege. We feel afraid that our feeble faith will still not be able to grasp what is so clearly placed within our reach. One thing must make us strong and full of hope: it is Jesus who brought us this message from the Father. He Himself lived the life of faith and prayer when He was on earth. When the disciples expressed their surprise at what He had done to the fig tree, He told them that the very same life He led could be theirs. They could command not only the fig tree, but the very mountain, and it would obey.

Jesus is our life. In us He is everything now that He was on earth. He really gives everything He teaches. He is the Author and the Perfecter of our faith (Heb. 12:2). He gives the spirit of faith. Don't be afraid that such faith isn't meant for us. Meant for every child of the Father, it is within the reach of anyone who will be childlike, yielding himself to the Father's will and love and trusting the Father's Word and power. Dear fellow Christian, have courage! This word comes through Jesus, who is God's Son and our Brother. Let our answer be, "Yes, blessed Lord, we do believe Your Word that we receive whatever we ask."

Lord, teach us to pray.

Blessed Lord, the Father sent You to show us all His Love and all the treasures of blessing that love is waiting to bestow. Lord, You've given us such abundant promises concerning our liberty in prayer. We are ashamed that our poor hearts have accepted so little of it. It has simply seemed too much for us to believe.

Lord, teach us to take and keep and use Your precious Word: *All things whatsoever ye pray and ask for, believe that ye receive them"* Blessed Jesus, it is in You that our faith must be rooted if it is to grow strong. Your work has completely freed us from the power of sin and has opened the way to the Father. Your love is longing to bring us into the full fellowship of Your glory and power. Your Spirit is constantly drawing us into a life of perfect faith and confidence. We are sure that through Your teaching we will learn to pray the prayer of faith. You will train us to pray so that we will believe that we really have what we ask for. Lord, teach me to know and trust and love You in such a way that I live and dwell in You. Through You, may all my prayers rise up and go before God, and may my soul have the assurance that I am heard. Amen.

12

THE SECRET OF
BELIEVING PRAYER

Jesus answering saith unto them, Have faith in God.
For verily I say unto you...whosoever...shall not doubt in his heart,
but shall believe that those things which he saith shall come to pass;
he shall have whatsoever he saith.
—Mark 11:22–23

Answer to prayer is one of the most wonderful lessons in all Scripture. In many hearts it must raise the question, "How can I ever attain the faith that knows it receives everything it asks for?" It is this question our Lord will answer today.

Before He gave that wonderful promise to His disciples, Christ shows where faith in the answer to prayer originates and finds its strength. *"Have faith in God."* This faith precedes the faith in the promise of an answer to prayer. The power to believe a promise depends entirely on faith in the promiser. Trust in the person engenders trust in what he says. We must live and associate with God in personal, loving communication. God Himself should be everything to us. His Holy Presence is revealed where our whole being is opened and exposed to His mighty influence. There the capacity for believing His promises will be developed.

The connection between faith in God and faith in His promise will become clear to us if we consider what faith really is. It is often compared to the hand or the mouth, by which we take and use what is given to us. But it is important that we understand that faith is also the ear by which we hear what is promised and the eye by which we see what is offered. The power to take depends on this. I must hear the person who gives me the promise because the very tone of his voice gives me courage to believe. I must see him because the light of his face melts all my qualms about my right to take. The value of the promise depends on the promiser. It is on my knowledge of what the promiser is that faith in the promise depends.

For this reason Jesus said, *"Have faith in God,"* before He gives the wonderful prayer promise. Let your eye be open to the living God. Through this eye we yield ourselves to God's influence. Just allow it to enter and leave its impression on our minds. Believing God is simply looking at God and what He is, allowing Him to reveal His presence to us. Give Him time and completely yield to Him, receiving and rejoicing in His love. Faith is the eye through which the light of God's presence and the vigor of His power stream into the soul. As what I see lives in me, so by faith God lives in me, too.

Faith is also the ear through which the voice of God is always heard. The Father speaks to us through the Holy Spirit. The Son is the Word—the substance of what God says—and the Spirit is the living voice. The child of God needs this secret voice from heaven to guide him and teach him, as it taught Jesus, what to say and what to do. An ear opened toward God is a believing heart that waits to hear what He says.

The words of God will be not only the words of a book, they will be spirit, truth, life, and power. They will make mere thoughts come to life. Through this opened ear, the soul abides under the influence of the life and power of God Himself. As His words enter the mind, dwelling and working there, through faith God enters the heart, dwelling and working there.

When faith is in full use as eye and ear—the faculties of the soul by which we see and hear God—then it will be able to exercise its full power as hand and mouth—the faculties by which we take God and His blessings. The power of reception will depend entirely on the power of spiritual perception. For this reason, before Jesus gave the promise that God would answer believing prayer, He said, *"Have faith in God."* Faith is simply surrender. I yield myself to the suggestions I hear. By faith I yield myself to the living God. His glory and love fill my heart and have mastery over my life.

Faith is fellowship. I give myself up to the influence of the friend who makes me a promise and become linked to him by it. When we enter into living fellowship with God Himself, in a faith that always sees and hears Him, it becomes easy and natural to believe His promise regarding prayer. Faith in the promise is the fruit of faith in the promiser. The prayer of faith is rooted in the life of faith. And in this way the faith that prays effectively is indeed a gift of God. It is not something He bestows or infuses all at once, but is far deeper and truer. It is the blessed disposition or habit of soul that grows up in us through a life of communion with Him. Surely for one who knows his Father well and lives in constant close communion with Him, it is a simple thing to believe the promise that He will do what His child wishes.

Because very many of God's children do not understand this connection between the life of faith and the prayer of faith, their experience of the power of prayer is limited. Sincerely desiring to obtain an answer from God, they concentrate wholeheartedly on the promise and try their utmost to grasp that promise in faith. When they do not succeed, they are ready to give up hope. The promise is true, but it is beyond their power to accept it in faith.

Listen to the lesson Jesus teaches us: have faith in God, the Living God. Let faith focus on God more than on the thing promised, because it is His love, His power, His living presence that will awaken and work the faith. To someone asking to develop more strength in his hands and arms, a physician would say that his whole constitution must be built up. So the cure of feeble faith can be found only in the invigoration of our whole spiritual lives through communication with God. Learn to believe in God, to hold on to God, and to let God take possession of your life. It will become easy to grasp the promise. Whoever knows and trusts God finds it easy to also trust the promise.

Note how distinctly this comes out in former saint. Every exhibition of the power of faith was the fruit of a special revelation from God. We see it in Abraham: "*The word of the* LORD *came unto Abram in a vision, saying, Fear not, Abram; I am thy shield….And he brought him forth abroad, and said….And he believed in the* LORD" (Genesis 15:1, 5–6). And later again, "*The* LORD *appeared to Abram, and said unto him, I am the Almighty God….And Abram fell on his face: and God talked with him, saying, as for me, behold, my covenant is with thee*" (Genesis 17:1, 3–4). It was the revelation of God Himself that gave the promise its living power to enter the heart and cultivate the faith. Because they knew God, these men of faith could not do anything but trust His promise. God's promise will be to us what God Himself is. The man who walks before the Lord and falls on his face to listen while the living God speaks to him will receive the promise. We have God's promises in the Bible with full liberty to claim them. Our spiritual power depends on God Himself speaking those promises to us. He speaks to those who walk and live with Him.

Therefore, have faith in God. Let faith be all eyes and ears. Surrender to God, and let Him make His full impression on you, revealing Himself fully in your soul. Consider it a blessing of prayer that you can exercise faith in God as the living, mighty God who is waiting to give us the good pleasure of His will and faith with power (2 Thess. 1:11). Regard Him as the God of love, whose delight it is to bless and impart His love. In such faithful worship of God, the power will speedily come to believe the promise, too. *"What things soever ye desire, when ye pray, believe that ye receive"* (Mark 11:24). Make God your own through faith; the promise will become yours, also.

Jesus is teaching us a precious lesson today. We seek God's gifts, but God wants to give us Himself first. We think of prayer as the means of extracting good gifts from heaven, and we think of Jesus as the means to draw ourselves up to God. We want to stand at the door and cry. Jesus wants us to enter in and realize that we are friends and children. Accept His teaching. Let every experience of the weakness of our faith in prayer incite us to have and exercise more faith in the living God, and in such faith to yield ourselves to Him. A heart full of God has power for the prayer of faith. Faith in God fosters faith in the promise, including the promise of an answer to prayer.

Therefore, child of God, take time to bow before Him, and wait for Him to reveal Himself. Take time to let your soul exercise and express its faith in the Infinite One in holy worship. As He shares Himself with and takes possession of you, the prayer of faith will crown your faith in God.

Lord, teach us to pray.

O my God, I do believe in You. I believe You are the Father, infinite in Your love and power. As the Son, You are my redeemer and my life. And as the Holy Spirit, You are my comforter, my guide, and my strength. I have faith that You will share everything You are with me and that You will do everything You promise.

Lord Jesus, increase my faith! Teach me to take time to wait and worship in God's holy presence until my faith absorbs everything there is in Him for me. Let my faith see Him as the Fountain of all life, working with almighty strength to accomplish His will in the world and in me. Let me see Him in His love, longing to meet and fulfill my desires. Let faith take possession of my heart and life to the extent that through it God may dwell there. Lord Jesus, help me! I want with my whole heart to believe in God. Fill me every moment with faith in God.

O my Blessed Savior, how can Your church glorify You and fulfill the work of intercession through which Your kingdom will come unless our whole lives consist of faith in God? Blessed Lord, speak Your Word, *"have faith in God,"* into the depths of our souls. Amen.

THE CURE OF UNBELIEF

Then came the disciples to Jesus apart, and said,
Why could not we cast him out? And Jesus said unto them, Because
of your unbelief: for verily I say unto you, If ye have faith as a grain
of mustard seed, ye shall say unto this mountain, Remove hence to
yonder place; and it shall remove; and nothing shall be impossible unto
you. Howbeit this kind goeth not out but by prayer and fasting.
—Matthew 17:19–21

W hen the disciples saw Jesus cast the evil spirit out of the epileptic whom *"they could not cure"* (Matt. 17:16), they asked the Master why they had failed. He had given them *"power and authority over all devils, and to cure diseases"* (Luke 9:1). They had often exercised that power and joyfully told how the devils were subject to them. And yet now, while He was on the Mount, they had utterly failed. Christ's casting the evil spirit out proved that there had been nothing in the will of God or in the nature of the case to make the miracle impossible. From their expression, *"Why could not we?"* it is evident that the disciples had wanted and tried to cast the spirit out. They had probably called upon it, using the Master's name. But their efforts had been in vain. They had been put to shame in front of the crowd.

Christ's answer was direct and plain, *"Because of your unbelief."* Christ's success was not a result of His having a special power to which the disciples had no access. He had so often taught them that here is one power—the power of faith—to which, in the kingdom of darkness as in the kingdom of God, everything must bow. In the spiritual world, failure has only one cause: lack of faith. Faith is the one condition on which all divine power can enter man and work through him. It is the sensitivity of man's will yielded to and molded by the will of God.

The power the disciples had received to cast out devils did not belong to them as a permanent gift or possession. The power was in Christ, to be received, held, and used by faith alone, living faith in Himself. Had they been full of faith in Him as Lord and Conqueror in the spirit world, had they been full of faith in Him as having given them authority to cast out devils in His name, their faith would have given them the victory. *"Because of your unbelief"* was, for all time, the Master's explanation and reproof of impotence and failure in His church.

Such a deficiency of faith must have a cause. The disciples may have asked, "Why couldn't we believe? Our faith has cast out devils before this. Why did we fail in believing this time?" Before they can ask, the Master answers them, *"This kind goeth not out but by prayer and fasting."*

Though faith is the simplest exercise of the spiritual life, it is also the highest. The spirit must yield itself in perfect receptivity to God's Spirit and become strengthened for this activity. Such faith depends entirely on the state of the spiritual life. Only when this is strong and in good health— when the Spirit of God has total influence in our lives—does faith have the power to do its mighty deeds.

Therefore Jesus adds, *"Howbeit this kind goeth not out but by prayer and fasting."* The faith that can overcome stubborn resistance such as you have just seen in this evil spirit, Jesus tells them, is not possible except for men living in very close fellowship with God and in very special separation from the world—in prayer and fasting. And so He teaches us two lessons of deep importance in regard to prayer. The one is that faith needs a life of prayer in which to grow and keep strong. The other is that prayer needs fasting for its full and perfect development.

Faith needs a life of prayer for its full growth. In all the different parts of the spiritual life, there is a close union between unceasing action and reaction, so that each may be both cause and effect. Thus it is with faith. There can be no true prayer without faith; some measure of faith must precede prayer. And yet prayer is also the way to more faith; there can be no higher degrees of faith except through much prayer. This is the lesson Jesus teaches here.

Nothing needs to grow as much as our faith. *"Your faith groweth exceedingly"* (2 Thess. 1:3) is said of one church. When Jesus spoke the words, *"According to your faith be it unto you"* (Matt. 9:29), He announced the law of the kingdom, which tells us that different people have different degrees of faith, that one person may have varying degrees, and that the amount of faith will always determine the amount of one's power and blessing. If we want to know where and how our faith is to grow, the Master points us to the throne of God. It is in prayer, exercising one's faith in fellowship with the living God, that faith can increase. Faith can only live by feeding on what is divine, on God Himself.

It is in the adoring worship of God—the waiting on Him and for Him in the deep silence of soul that yields itself for God to reveal Himself—that the capacity for knowing and trusting God will be developed. As we take His Word from the blessed Book and ask Him to speak it to us with His living, loving voice, the power to believe and receive the Word as God's own word to us will emerge in us. It is in prayer, in living contact with God in living faith, that faith will become strong in us. Many Christians cannot understand, nor do they feel the need, of spending hours with God. But the

Master says, and the experience of His people has confirmed, that men of strong faith are men of much prayer.

This brings us back again to the lesson we learned when Jesus, before telling us to believe that we receive what we ask for, first said, *"Have faith in God"* (Mark 11:22). It is God—the living God—into whom our faith must strike its roots deeply and broadly. Then it will be strong enough to remove mountains and cast out devils. *"If ye have faith...nothing shall be impossible unto you"* (Matt. 17:20). If we could only give ourselves up to the work God has for us in the world! As we came into contact with the mountains and the devils that are to be cast away and cast out, we would soon comprehend how much we need great faith and prayer. They alone are the soil in which faith can be cultivated. Christ Jesus is our life and the life of our faith. It is His life in us that makes us strong and ready to believe. The dying to self that much prayer implies allows a closer union to Jesus in which the spirit of faith will come in power. Faith needs prayer for its full growth.

The second lesson is that prayer needs fasting for its full growth. Prayer is the one hand with which we grasp the invisible. Fasting is the other hand, the one with which we let go of the visible. In nothing is man more closely connected with the world of sense than in his need for, and enjoyment of, food. It was the fruit with which man was tempted and fell in Paradise. It was with bread that Jesus was tempted in the wilderness. But He triumphed in fasting.

The body has been redeemed to be a temple of the Holy Spirit. In body as well as spirit, Scripture says, we are to glorify God in eating and drinking. There are many Christians to whom this eating for the glory of God has not yet become a spiritual reality. The first thought suggested by Jesus' words in regard to fasting and prayer is that only in a life of moderation and self-denial will there be sufficient heart and strength to pray much.

There is also a more literal meaning to His words. Sorrow and anxiety cannot eat, but joy celebrates its feasts with eating and drinking. There may come times of intense desire, when it is strongly felt how the body and its appetites still hinder the spirit in its battle with the powers of darkness. The need is felt of keeping it subdued. We are creatures of the senses. Our minds are helped by what comes to us in concrete form. Fasting helps to express, to deepen, and to confirm the resolution that we are ready to sacrifice anything, even ourselves, to attain the kingdom of God. And Jesus, who Himself fasted and sacrificed, knows to value, accept, and reward with spiritual power the soul that is thus ready to give up everything for Him and His kingdom.

There is still a wider application of Christ's words. Prayer is reaching out for God and the unseen. Fasting is letting go of everything that can be seen and touched. Some Christians imagine that everything that isn't positively forbidden and sinful is permissible to them. So they try to retain as much as possible of this world with its property, its literature, and its enjoyments. The truly consecrated soul, however, is like a soldier who carries only what he needs for battle. Because he frees himself of all unnecessary weight, he is easily capable of combating sin. Afraid of entangling himself with the affairs of a worldly life, he tries to lead a Nazarite life as one specially set apart for the Lord and His service. (See Numbers 6:2–6.) Without such voluntary separation, even from what is lawful, no one will attain power in prayer. Such power comes only through fasting and prayer.

Disciples of Jesus, you have asked the Master to teach you to pray, so come now and accept His lessons! He tells you that prayer is the path to faith—strong faith that can cast out devils. He tells you, *"If ye have faith… nothing shall be impossible unto you."* Let this glorious promise encourage you to pray much. Isn't the prize worth the price? Give up everything to follow Jesus in the path He opens to us! Fast if you need to! Do anything you must so that neither the body nor the world can hinder us in our great life work—talking to God in prayer, so that we may become men of faith whom He can use in His work of saving the world.

Lord, teach us to pray.

O Lord Jesus, how continually You must reprimand us for our unbelief. Our terrible inability to trust our Father and His promises must appear quite strange to You. Lord, let Your words, *"because of your unbelief,"* sink into the very depths of our hearts and reveal how much of the sin and suffering around us is our fault. Then teach us, Blessed Lord, that faith can be gained and learned in the prayer and fasting that bring us into living fellowship with Yourself and the Father.

O Savior, you are the Author and the Perfecter of our faith (Heb. 12:2). Teach us what it means to let You live in us by Your Holy Spirit. Lord, our efforts and prayers for grace to believe have been so ineffective. We know it is because we want You to give us strength in ourselves. Holy Jesus, teach us the mystery of Your life in us—how You, by Your Spirit, live the life of faith in us, insuring that our faith will not fail. Make our faith a part of that wonderful prayer life that You give to those who expect their training for the ministry of intercession to come from not only words and thoughts, but from the Spirit of Your own life. And teach us how, in fasting and prayer, we can mature in the faith for which nothing will be impossible. Amen.

14

PRAYER AND LOVE

And when ye stand praying, forgive, if ye have ought against any: that your Father also which is in heaven may forgive you your trespasses.
—Mark 11:25

These words immediately follow the great prayer promise, *"what things soever ye desire, when ye pray, believe that ye receive them, and ye shall have them"* (Mark 11:24). We have already seen how the words that preceded that promise, *"have faith in God"* (v. 22), taught us that, in prayer, everything depends on the clarity of our relationship with God. These words that follow it remind us that our relationships with our fellowmen must be clear, too. Love of God and love of our neighbor are inseparable.

The prayer from a heart that is not right with God or with men will not succeed.

Faith and love are essential to each other. This is a thought to which our Lord frequently gave expression. In the Sermon on the Mount, when speaking of the sixth commandment, He taught His disciples that acceptable worship of the Father was impossible if everything were not right with one's brother:

> *If thou bring thy gift to the altar, and there rememberest that thy brother hath aught against thee; leave there thy gift before the altar, and go thy way; first be reconciled to thy brother, and then come and offer thy gift.*
> (Matt. 5:23–24)

After having taught us to pray, "*Forgive us our debts, as we forgive our debtors*" (Matt. 6:12), Christ added, "*If ye forgive not men their trespasses, neither will your Father forgive your trespasses*" (v. 15). At the close of the parable of the unmerciful servant, He applies His teaching in the words, "*So likewise shall my heavenly Father do also unto you, if ye from your hearts forgive not every one his brother their trespasses*" (Matt. 18:35).

Here, in Mark 11, beside the dried-up fig tree, as Jesus speaks of the power and the prayer of faith, He abruptly introduces the thought, "*When ye stand praying, forgive, if ye have ought against any: that your Father also which is in heaven may forgive you your trespasses.*" Perhaps the Lord had learned during His life that disobedience to the law of brotherly love was the great sin of even praying people, and the great cause of the ineffectiveness of their prayer. It is as if He wanted to lead us into His own blessed experience that nothing strengthens faith as much as the consciousness that we have given ourselves in love and compassion for those whom God loves.

The first lesson we are taught here is to have a forgiving disposition. We should pray, "Forgive us just as we have forgiven others." Scripture says, "*Forgiving one another...even as Christ forgave you*" (Col. 3:13). God's full and free forgiveness should be the model of our forgiveness of men; otherwise, our reluctant, half-hearted forgiveness, which is not forgiveness at all, will be God's rule with us. All of our prayers depend on our faith in God's pardoning grace. If God dealt with us while keeping our sins in mind, not one prayer would be heard. Pardon opens the door to all God's love and blessing. Because God has pardoned all our sins, our prayers can go through to obtain all we need.

The deep, sure ground of answer to prayer is God's forgiving love. When it has taken possession of our hearts, we pray in faith. But also, when it has taken possession of our hearts, we live in love. God's forgiving nature, revealed to us in His love, becomes our nature. With the power of His forgiving love dwelling in us, we forgive just as He forgives.

If great injury or injustice occurs, try first of all to assume a godlike disposition. Avoid the sense of wounded honor, the desire to maintain your rights, and the need to punish the offender. In the little annoyances of daily life, never excuse a hasty temper, a sharp word, or a quick judgment with the thought that we mean no harm, or that it is too much to expect feeble human nature to really forgive the way God and Christ do. Take the command literally: *"Even as Christ forgave you, so also do ye"* (Col. 3:13). The blood cleanses selfishness from the conscience. The love it reveals is a pardoning love that takes possession of us and flows through us to others. Our forgiving love toward men is the evidence of God's forgiving love in us. It is a necessary condition of the prayer of faith.

There is a second, more general lesson: our daily life in the world is the test of our communication with God in prayer. How often the Christian, when he comes to pray, does his utmost to cultivate certain frames of mind that he thinks will be pleasing. He doesn't understand, or he forgets, that life does not consist of a lot of loose pieces that can be picked up at random and then be discarded. Life is a whole. The hour of prayer is only a small part of daily life. God's opinion of what I really am and desire is not based on the feeling I conjure up, but on the tone of my life during the day.

My relationship with God is part of my relationships with men. Failure in one will cause failure in the other. It isn't necessary that it be a distinct consciousness of something wrong between my neighbor and myself. An ordinary current of thinking and judging—the unloving thoughts and words I allow to pass unnoticed—can hinder my prayer. The effective prayer of faith comes from a life given up to the will and the love of God. My prayer is answered by God, not as a result of what I try to be when praying, but because of what I am when I'm not praying.

All these thoughts can be gathered into a third lesson: in life among human beings, the one thing on which everything depends is love. The spirit of forgiveness is the spirit of love. Because God is love, He forgives. It is only when we are dwelling in love that we can forgive as God forgives. In love for our brothers we have the evidence of love for the Father (1 John 4:20), the basis for our confidence before God, and the assurance that our prayers will be heard. *"Let us...love...in deed and in truth....hereby we...shall assure our hearts before him....If our heart condemn us not, then have we confidence toward God. And whatsoever we ask, we receive of him"* (1 John 3:18–19, 21–22). Neither faith nor work will profit if we don't have love. Love unites us with God; it proves the reality of faith. *"Have faith in God"* (Mark 11:22) and *"have love one to another"* (John 13:35) are both essential commandments. The right relationships with the living God above me and the living men around me are the conditions for effective prayer.

This love is of special consequence when we are praying for our fellowmen. We sometimes commit ourselves to work for Christ out of zeal for His cause or for our own spiritual health, without giving ourselves in personal self-sacrificing love for those whose souls we seek. No wonder our faith is powerless and without victory! View each wretched one, however unlovable he is, in the light of the tender love of Jesus the Shepherd searching for the lost. Look for Jesus Christ in him and take him into a heart that really loves for Jesus' sake. This is the secret of believing prayer and successful effort. Jesus speaks of love as the root of forgiveness. It is also the root of believing prayer.

There is nothing as heart-searching as believing prayer, or even the honest effort to pray in faith. Don't deflect that self-examination by the thought that God does not hear your prayers. *"Ye ask, and receive not, because ye ask amiss"* (James 4:3). Let that Word of God search us. Ask whether our prayers are indeed the expression of lives completely given over to the will of God and the love of man. Love is the only soil in which faith can take root and thrive. Only in the love of fixed purpose and sincere obedience can faith obtain the blessing. Whoever gives himself to let the love of God dwell in him, whoever in daily life loves as God loves, will have the power to believe in the love that hears his every prayer. That almighty love is the Lamb who is in the midst of the throne. It is suffering and enduring love that exists with God in prayer. The merciful shall obtain mercy; the meek shall inherit the earth.

Lord, teach us to pray.

Blessed Father, you are love, and only he who dwells in love can come into fellowship with You. Your blessed Son has taught me again how deeply true this is. O my God, let the Holy Spirit flood my heart with Your love. Be a fountain of love inside me that flows out to everyone around me. Let the power of believing prayer spring out of this life of love. O my Father, grant by the Holy Spirit that this love may be the gate through which I find life in Your love. Let the joy with which I daily forgive whoever might offend me be the proof that Your forgiveness is my power and life.

Lord Jesus, Blessed Teacher, teach me how to forgive and to love. Let the power of Your blood make the pardon of my sins a reality, so that Your forgiveness of me and my forgiveness of others may be the very joy of heaven. Point out the weaknesses in my relationships with others that might hinder my fellowship with God. May my daily life at home and in society be the school in which strength and confidence are gathered for the prayer of faith. Amen.

15

THE POWER
OF UNITED PRAYER

*Again I say unto you, That if two of you shall agree on earth as
touching any thing that they shall ask, it shall be done for them of
my Father which is in heaven. For where two or three are gathered
together in my name, there am I in the midst of them.*
—Matthew 18:19–20

One of the first lessons of our Lord in His school of prayer was not to pray visibly. Go into your closet and be alone with the Father. When He has taught us that the meaning of prayer is personal, individual contact with God, He gives us a second lesson: you also need public, united prayer. He gives us a very special promise for the united prayer of two or three who agree in what they ask. As a tree has its roots hidden in the ground and its stem growing up into the sunlight, so prayer needs secrecy in which the soul meets God alone and public fellowship with those who find their common meeting place in the name of Jesus.

The reason why this must be so is plain. The bond that unites a man with his fellowmen is no less real and close than that which unites him to God: one with them. Grace renews not only our relationship with God, but our relationships with our fellow human beings, too. We not only learn to say "my Father," but also "our Father." It would be unnatural for the children of a family to always meet their father separately, never expressing their desires or their love jointly. Believers are not only members of one family, but of one body. Just as each member of the body depends on the other, the extent to which the Spirit can dwell in the body depends on the union and cooperation of everyone. Christians cannot reach the full blessing God is ready to bestow through His Spirit until they seek and receive it in fellowship with each other. It was to the hundred and twenty praying together in total agreement under the same roof that the Spirit came from the throne of the glorified Lord. In the same way, it is in the union and fellowship of believers that the Spirit can manifest His full power.

The elements of true, united prayer are given to us in these words of our Lord. The first is agreement as to the thing asked. It isn't enough to generally consent to agree with anything another may ask. The object prayed for must be some special thing, a matter of distinct, united desire. The agreement must be, as in all prayer, in spirit and in truth. In such agreement exactly what we are asking for becomes very clear. We find out whether we can confidently ask for it according to God's will and whether we are ready to believe that we have received it.

The second element is the gathering in the name of Jesus. Later, we will learn much more about the necessity and the power of the name of Jesus in prayer. Here our Lord teaches us that His name must be the center and the bond of the union that makes them one, just as a home contains and unites all who are in it. *"The name of the* LORD *is a strong tower: the righteous runneth into it, and is safe"* (Prov. 18:10). That name is such a reality to those who understand and believe in it, that to meet within it is to have Him present. Jesus is powerfully attracted by the love and unity of His disciples: *"Where two or three are gathered in my name, there am I in the midst of them."* The presence of Jesus, alive in the fellowship of His loving, praying disciples, gives united prayer its power.

The third element is the sure answer: *"It shall be done for them of my Father."* Although a prayer meeting for maintaining religious fellowship, or for our own edification, may have its use, this was not the Savior's reason for recommending it. He meant it as a means of securing special answer to prayer. A prayer meeting without recognized answer to prayer ought to be the exception to the rule. When we feel too weak to exercise the faith necessary to attain a distinct desire, we ought to seek strength in the help of others. In the unity of faith, love, and the Spirit, the power of the name and of the presence of Jesus acts more freely, and the answer comes more surely. The evidence that there has been true, united prayer is the fruit— the answer, the receiving of the thing for which we have asked. *"I say unto you…it shall be done for them of my Father which is in heaven."* What an extraordinary privilege united prayer is! What a potential power it has! Who can say what blessing might be gained by the following:

+ if the believing husband and wife knew they were joined together in the name of Jesus to experience His presence and power in united prayer (1 Pet. 3);

+ if friends were aware of the mighty help two or three praying in concert could give each other;

+ if in every prayer meeting the coming together in the name, the faith in His presence, and the expectation of the answer stood in the foreground;

+ if in every church, united, effective prayer were regarded as one of the chief purposes for which they were banded together;

+ if in the universal church the coming of the kingdom and of the King Himself were really a matter of unceasing, united crying to God!

The apostle Paul had great faith in the power of united prayer. To the Romans he wrote, "*I beseech you, brethren...for the love of the Spirit, that ye strive together with me in your prayers to God for me*" (Rom. 15:30). He expected, in answer to their combined prayers, to be delivered from his enemies and to prosper in his work. To the Corinthians he declared, "*[God] will also deliver us; ye also helping together on our behalf by your supplication*" (2 Cor. 1:10–11 ASV). He expects their prayers to have a real share in his deliverance. To the Ephesians he wrote, "*With all prayer and supplication praying at all seasons in the Spirit...for all the saints, and on my behalf, that utterance may be given unto me*" (Eph. 6:18–19 ASV). He makes the power and success in his ministry dependent on their prayers. With the Philippians he expects that his trials will become his salvation and increase the progress of the Gospel, "*through your supplication and the supply of the Spirit of Jesus Christ*" (Phil. 1:19 ASV). When telling the Colossians to continue praying constantly, he adds, "*Withal praying for us also, that God may open unto us a door for the word*" (Col. 4:3 ASV). And to the Thessalonians he wrote, "*Finally, brethren, pray for us, that the word of the Lord may run and be glorified...and that we may be delivered from unreasonable...men*" (2 Thess. 3:1–2 ASV).

It is quite evident that Paul perceived himself as the member of a body whose sympathy and cooperation he depended on. He counted on the prayers of these churches to gain for him what otherwise might not be given. To him the prayers of the church were as real a factor in the work of the kingdom as the power of God.

Who can say what power a church could develop and exercise if it would assume the work of praying day and night for the coming of the kingdom, for God's power, or for the salvation of souls? Most churches think their members gather simply to take care of and edify each other. They don't know that God rules the world by the prayers of His saints, that prayer is the power by which Satan is conquered, and that through prayer the church on earth has access to the powers of the heavenly world. They do not remember that Jesus has, by His promise, made every assembly in His name a gate to heaven, where His presence is to be felt, and His power experienced by the Father fulfilling their desires.

We cannot sufficiently thank God for the blessed week of united prayer with which Christendom, in our days, opens every year. It is of unspeakable value as proof of our unity and our faith in the power of united prayer, as a training school for the enlargement of our hearts to take in all the needs of the church, and as a help to united persevering prayer. But it has been a special blessing as a stimulus to continued union in prayer in the smaller circles. When God's people realize what it means to meet as one in the name of Jesus, with His presence in the midst of a body united in the Holy Spirit, they will boldly claim the promise that the Father will do what they agree to request.

Lord, teach us to pray.

Blessed Lord, you ask so earnestly for the unity of Your people. Teach us how to encourage our unity with Your precious promise regarding united prayer. Show us how to join together in love and desire, so that Your presence is in our faith in the Father's answer.

Oh, Father, we pray for those smaller circles of people who meet together so that they may become one. Remove all selfishness and self-interest, all narrowness of heart and estrangement that hinders their unity. Cast out the spirit of the world and the flesh through which Your promise loses all its power. Let the thought of Your presence and the Father's favor draw us all nearer to each other.

Grant especially, blessed Lord, that Your church may believe that it is by the power of united prayer that she can bind and loose in heaven, cast out Satan, save souls, remove mountains, and hasten the coming of the kingdom. And grant, good Lord, that my prayer circle may indeed pray with the power through which Your name and Word are glorified. Amen.

16

THE POWER OF
PERSEVERING PRAYER

And he spake a parable unto them to this end, that men ought always to pray, and not to faint; saying, There was in a city a judge, which feared not God, neither regarded man: and there was a widow in that city; and she came unto him, saying, Avenge me of mine adversary. And he would not for a while: but afterward he said within himself, Though I fear not God, nor regard man; yet because this widow troubleth me, I will avenge her, lest by her continual coming she weary me. And the Lord said, Hear what the unjust judge saith. And shall not God avenge his own elect, which cry day and night unto him, though he bear long with them? I tell you that he will avenge them speedily. Nevertheless when the Son of man cometh, shall he find faith on the earth?
—Luke 18:1–8

O f all the mysteries of the prayer world, the need for persevering prayer is one of the greatest. We cannot easily understand why the Lord, who is so loving and longing to bless us, should have to be petitioned time after time, sometimes year after year, before the answer comes. It is also one of the greatest practical difficulties in the exercise of believing prayer. When our repeated prayers remain unanswered, it is easy for our lazy flesh—maintaining the appearance of pious submission—to think that we must stop praying because God may have a secret reason for withholding His answer to our request. Faith alone can overcome difficulty. Once faith has taken its stand on God's Word and the name of Jesus and has yielded itself to the leading of the Spirit to seek only God's will and honor in its prayer, it need not be discouraged by delay. It knows from Scripture that the power of believing prayer is considerable; real faith can never be disappointed. It knows that to exercise its power, it must be gathered up, just like water, until the stream can come down in full force.

Prayer must often be heaped up until God sees that its measure is full. Then the answer comes. Just as each of ten thousand seeds is a part of the final harvest, frequently repeated, persevering prayer is necessary to acquire a desired blessing. Every single believing prayer has its influence. It is stored up toward an answer that comes in due time to whoever perseveres to the end. Human thoughts and possibilities have nothing to do with it; only the Word of the living God matters. Abraham for so long *"in hope believed against hope"* (Rom. 4:18 ASV) and then *"through faith and patience inherit[ed] the promises"* (Heb. 6:12). Wait and pray often for the coming of the Lord to fulfill His promise.

When the answers to our prayers do not come at once, we should combine quiet patience and joyful confidence in our persevering prayer. To enable us to do this, we must try to understand two words in which our Lord describes the character and conduct of our God and Father toward those who cry day and night to Him: *"He bear long with them....He will avenge them speedily."*

The Master uses the word *speedily*. The blessing is all prepared. The Father is not only willing, but is most anxious to give them what they ask. His everlasting love burns with His longing desire to reveal itself fully to His beloved and to satisfy their needs. God will not delay one moment longer than is absolutely necessary. He will do everything in His power to hasten the answer.

But why—if this is true and God's power is infinite—does it often take so long to get an answer to prayer? And why must God's own elect so often, in the midst of suffering and conflict, cry day and night? *"He bear long with them."* Of course the husbandman longs for his harvest. But he knows it must have its full term of sunshine and rain, so he has plenty of patience (James 5:7). A child so often wants to pick the half-ripe fruit, while the farmer knows to wait until the proper time.

In his spiritual nature, man, too, is under the law of gradual growth that reigns in all created life. Only on the path of development can he reach his divine destiny. And only the Father, who determines the times and seasons, knows the moment when the soul or the church is ripened to that fullness of faith in which it can really take and keep a blessing. As a father who longs to have his only child home from school and yet waits patiently until the time of training is completed, so it is with God and His children.

Insight into this truth should lead the believer to cultivate the corresponding attitudes of patience, faith, waiting, and praise, which are the secrets of his perseverance. By faith in the promise of God, we know that we have the petitions we have asked of Him. Faith holds the answer in the promise as an unseen spiritual possession. It rejoices in it and praises God for it. But there is a difference between this kind of faith and the clearer, fuller, riper faith that obtains the promise as a present experience. It is in persevering, confident, and praising prayer that the soul grows up into full union with its Lord in which it can possess the blessing in Him.

There may be things around us that have to be corrected through prayer before the answer can fully happen. The faith that has, according to the command, believed that it has received, can allow God to take His time. It knows it has and must succeed. In quiet, persistent, and determined perseverance, it continues in prayer and thanksgiving until the blessing comes. And so we see a combination of what at first sight appears to be so contradictory: the faith that rejoices in God's answer as a present possession combined with the patience that cries day and night until that answer comes. The waiting child meets God triumphantly with his patient faith.

The great danger in this school is the temptation to think that it may not be God's will to give us what we desire. If our prayers agree with God's Word and are led by the Spirit, don't give way to these fears.

Learn to give God time. He needs time with us. In daily fellowship with Him, we must give Him time to exercise the full influence of His presence in us. Day by day, as we are kept waiting, it is necessary that faith be given time to prove its reality and fill our beings entirely. God will lead us from faith to vision; we will see His glory.

Don't let delay shake your faith, for it is faith that will provide the answer in time. Each believing prayer is a step nearer to the final victory! It ripens the fruit, conquers hindrances in the unseen world, and hastens the end. Child of God, give the Father time! He is longsuffering over you. He wants your blessing to be rich, full, and sure. Give Him time, but continue praying day and night. And above all, remember the promise, *"I tell you that he will avenge them speedily."*

The blessing of such persevering prayer is indescribable. There is nothing that examines the heart more closely than the prayer of faith. It teaches you to discover, confess, and give up everything that hinders the coming of the blessing—everything that is not in accordance with the Father's will. It leads to closer fellowship with Him who alone can teach you to pray. Complete surrender becomes possible under the covering of the blood and the Spirit. Christian, give God time! He will perfect whatever concerns you (Ps. 138:8)!

Let your attitude be the same whether you are praying for yourself or for others. All labor, physical or mental, needs time and effort. We must give ourselves up to it. Nature reveals her secrets and yields her treasures only to diligent and thoughtful labor. However little we can understand it, spiritual husbandry is always the same: the seed we sow in the soil of heaven, the efforts we put forth, and the influence we seek to exert in the world above all require our complete surrender in prayer. Maintain great confidence that when the time is right, we will reap abundantly if we don't give up (Gal. 6:9).

Let us especially learn this lesson as we pray for the church of Christ. She is indeed like a poor widow in the absence of her Lord, apparently at the mercy of her adversary and helpless to correct the situation. When we pray for His church or any portion of it that is under the power of the world, let us ask Him to visit her with mighty workings of His Spirit to prepare her for His coming. Pray in the assured faith that prayer does help. Unceasing prayer will bring the answer. Just give God time. And remember this day and night: *"Hear what the unjust judge saith. And shall not God avenge His own elect, which cry day and night unto him, though he bear long with them? I tell you that he will avenge them speedily."*

Lord, teach us to pray.

O Lord my God, teach me how to know Your way and in faith to learn what Your beloved Son has taught: *"He will avenge them speedily."* Let Your tender love and the delight You have in hearing and blessing Your children lead me implicitly to accept the promise that we may have whatever we ask for, and that the answer will be seen in due time. Lord, we understand nature's seasons; we know how to wait for the fruit we long for. Fill us with the assurance that You won't delay one moment longer than is necessary, and that our faith will hasten the answer.

Blessed Master, you have said that God's elect appeal to Him day and night. Please teach us to understand this. You know how quickly we become tired. Perhaps we feel that the divine majesty of the Father is so far beyond the reach of our continued prayer that is isn't becoming for us to plead with Him too much. O Lord, teach me how real the labor of prayer is! I know that here on earth, when I fail at something, I can often succeed by renewed and more continuous effort and by taking more time and thought. Show me how, by giving myself more entirely to prayer—by actually living in prayer—I can obtain what I have asked for.

Above all, O blessed Teacher, Author and Perfecter of my faith (Heb. 12:2), let my whole life be one of faith in the Son of God who loved me and gave Himself for me (Gal. 2:20)!

In You my prayer gains acceptance, and I have the assurance of the answer. Lord Jesus, in such faith I will pray always, ceasing never. Amen.

Author's Note

The need of persevering prayer appears to be at variance with the faith that knows that it has received what it asks. (See Mark 11:24.) One of the mysteries of the divine life is the harmony between sudden, complete possession and slow, imperfect appropriation. Here persevering prayer appears to be the school in which the soul is strengthened for the boldness of faith. Considering the diversity of operations of the Spirit, there may be some in whom faith takes the form of persistent waiting. For others, triumphant thanksgiving appears the only proper expression of the assurance of having been heard.

17

PRAYER IN HARMONY WITH GOD

Father, I thank thee that thou hast heard me.
And I knew that thou hearest me always.
—John 11:41–42

Thou art my Son; this day have I begotten thee.
Ask of me, and I shall give thee.
—Psalm 2:7–8

In the New Testament we find a distinction made between faith and knowledge. *"To one is given by the Spirit the word of wisdom; to another the word of knowledge by the same Spirit; to another faith by the same Spirit"* (1 Cor. 12:8–9). In a child or an uninformed Christian, there may be much faith with little knowledge. Childlike simplicity accepts the truth without difficulty and often cares little to give any reason for its faith but this: God said it. But it is the will of God that we should love and serve Him, not only with all the heart but also with all the mind (Matt. 22:37). He wants us to develop an insight into the divine wisdom and beauty of all His ways, words, and works. Only in this way will the believer be able to fully approach and rightly adore the glory of God's grace. And only thus can our hearts intelligently understand the treasures of wisdom and knowledge that exist in redemption, preparing us to join in the highest note of the song that rises before the throne: *"O the depth of the riches both of the wisdom and knowledge of God!"* (Rom. 11:33).

This truth has its full application in our prayer lives. While prayer and faith are so simple that the newborn convert can pray with power, more mature Christians may find in the doctrine of prayer some of their deepest questions. How extensive is the power of prayer? How can God grant such mighty power to prayer? How can prayer be harmonized with the will of God? How can God's sovereignty and our will—God's liberty and ours—be reconciled? These and similar questions are appropriate subjects for Christian meditation and inquiry. The more earnestly and reverently we approach such mysteries, the more we will fall down in adoring wonder to praise Him who has in prayer given such power to man.

One of the difficulties with regard to prayer is the result of the perfection of God. He is absolutely independent of everything outside of Himself. He is an infinite being who owes what He is to Himself, alone. With His wise and holy will, He has determined Himself and everything that is to be. How can our prayers influence Him? How can He be moved by prayer to do what He otherwise would not do? Isn't the promise of an answer to prayer simply a condescension to our weakness? Is the power of prayer anything more than an accommodation of our mode of thought, because the accomplishments of deity are never dependent of any outside action? And isn't the real blessing of prayer simply the influence it exerts on us?

Seeking answers to such questions provides the key to the very being of God in the mystery of the Holy Trinity. If God were only one Person, shut up within Himself, there could be no thought of nearness to Him or influence on Him. But in God there are three Persons: Father and Son, who have in the Holy Spirit their living bond of unity and fellowship. When the Father gave the Son a place next to Himself as His equal and His counselor, He opened a way for prayer and its influence into the very inmost life of Deity itself.

On earth, just as in heaven, the whole relationship between Father and Son is that of giving and taking. If the taking is to be as voluntary and self-determined as the giving, the Son must ask and receive. *"Thou art my Son; this day have I begotten thee. Ask of me, and I shall give thee."* The Father gave the Son the place and the power to influence Him. The Son's asking wasn't just for show. It was one of those life movements in which the love of the Father and the Son met and completed each other. The Father had determined that He would not be alone in His counsels: their fulfillment would depend on the Son's asking and receiving. Thus asking was in the very Being and Life of God. Prayer on earth was to be the reflection and the outflow of this.

Jesus said, *"I knew that thou hearest me always"* (John 11:42). Just as the Sonship of Jesus on earth cannot be separated from His Sonship in heaven, His prayer on earth is the continuation and the counterpart of His asking in heaven. His prayer is the link between the eternal asking of the only begotten Son in the bosom of the Father and the prayer of men on earth. Prayer has its rise and its deepest source in the very being of God. In the bosom of the Deity, nothing is ever done without prayer—the asking of the Son and the giving of the Father.

This may help us to understand how the prayer of man, coming through the Son, can have an effect on God. God's decrees are not made without reference to the Son, His petition, or a petition sent up through Him. The Lord Jesus is the First Begotten, the Head and Heir of all things. As the Representative of all creation, He always has a voice in the Father's decisions. In the decrees of the eternal purpose, room was always left for the liberty of the Son as Mediator and Intercessor. The same holds true for the petitions of all who draw near to the Father through the Son.

If Christ's liberty and power to influence the Father seem to be at variance with the immutability of the divine decrees, remember that God doesn't have a past, as man does, to which He is irrevocably bound. The distinctions of time have no meaning to Him who inhabits eternity. Eternity is an ever present now, in which the past never passes and the future is always present. To meet our human comprehension of time, Scripture must speak of past decrees and a coming future.

In reality, the unchanging nature of God's plan is still in perfect harmony with His liberty to do whatever He wills. The prayers of the Son and His people weren't included in the eternal decrees simply for show. Rather, the Father listens with His heart to every prayer that rises through the Son. God really does allow Himself to be moved by prayer to do what He otherwise would not have done.

This perfect, harmonious union of divine sovereignty and human liberty is an unfathomable mystery because God as the Eternal One transcends all our thoughts. But let it be our comfort and strength to know that in the eternal fellowship of the Father and the Son, the power of prayer has its origin and certainty. Through our union with the Son, our prayers are taken up and can have their influence in the inner life of the Blessed Trinity. God's decrees are no iron framework against which man's liberty struggles vainly. God Himself is living love, who in His Son who became flesh has entered into the tenderest relationship with all that is human. Through the Holy Spirit, He takes up everything human into the divine life of love, leaving Himself free to give every human prayer its place in His government of the world.

In the light of such thoughts, the doctrine of the Blessed Trinity is no longer an abstract speculation, but the living manifestation of how man is taken up into the fellowship of God, his prayer becoming a real factor in God's rule of this earth. We can catch a glimpse of the light shining out from the eternal world in words such as these: *"Through him we…have access by one Spirit unto the Father"* (Eph. 2:18).

Lord, teach us to pray.

Everlasting God, in deep reverence I worship before the holy mystery of Your divine being. If it pleases You, most glorious God, to reveal some of that mystery to me, I would bow with fear and trembling rather than sin against You as I meditate on Your glory.

Father, I thank You for being not only the Father of Your children here on earth, but the Father of Jesus Christ through eternity. Thank You for hearing our prayers and for having given Christ's asking a place in Your eternal plan. Thank You also for sending Christ to earth and for His blessed communication with You in heaven. There has always been room in Your counsel for His prayers and the answers to those prayers. And I thank You above all that through Christ's true human nature on Your throne above, and through Your Holy Spirit in our human nature here below, a way has been opened by which every human cry of need can be received into the life and love of God, always obtaining an answer.

Blessed Jesus, as the Son, You have opened this path of prayer and assured us of an answer. We beseech You to teach us how to pray. Let our prayers be the sign of our sonship, so that we, like You, know that the Father always hears us. Amen.

18

PRAYER IN HARMONY WITH THE DESTINY OF MAN

And he saith unto them, Whose is this image and superscription?
—Matthew 22:20

And God said, Let us make man in our image, after our likeness.
—Genesis 1:26

W hose is this image?" It was with this question that Jesus foiled His enemies when they tried to trick Him, settling the matter of responsibility in regard to paying taxes. The question and the principle it involves are universally applicable, particularly to man himself. Bearing God's image decides man's destiny. He belongs to God, and prayer to God is what he was created for. Prayer is part of the wondrous likeness he bears to His divine original. It is the earthly likeness of the deep mystery of the fellowship of love in which the Trinity has its blessedness.

The more we meditate on what prayer is and on the wonderful power it has with God, the more we have to ask how man is so special, that such a place in God's plan has been allotted to him. Sin has so degraded him that we can't conceive of what he was meant to be based on what he is now. We must turn back to God's own record of man's creation to find what God's purpose was and what capacities man was given to fulfill that purpose.

Man's destiny appears clearly in God's language at creation. It was to fill, to subdue, and to have dominion over the earth and everything in it. These three expressions show us that man was intended, as God's representative, to rule here on earth. As God's deputy, he was to fill God's place, keeping everything in subjection to Him. It was the will of God that everything done on earth should be done through man, i.e., the history of the earth was to be entirely in his hands.

In accordance with such a destiny was the position he was to occupy and the power at his disposal. When an earthly sovereign sends a representative to a distant province, that representative advises the sovereign as to the policy to be adopted there. The sovereign follows that advice, doing whatever is necessary to enact the policy and maintain the dignity of his empire. If the sovereign, however, doesn't approve of the policy, he replaces the representative with someone who better understands his desires for the empire. But as long as the representative is trusted, his advice is carried out.

As God's representative, man was to have ruled. Everything was to have been done according to his will. On his advice and at his request, heaven was to have bestowed its blessing on earth. His prayer was to have been the natural channel through which the Lord in heaven and man, as lord of this world, communicated. The destinies of the world were given into the power of the wishes, the will, and the prayers of man.

With the advent of sin, all this underwent a terrible change: Man's fall brought all creation under the curse. Redemption brought the beginning of a glorious restoration. In Abraham, God began to make Himself a people from whom kings—not to mention the Great King—would emerge. We see how Abraham's prayer power affected the destinies of those who came into contact with him. In Abraham we see how prayer is not only the means of obtaining blessing for ourselves, but it is the exercise of a royal prerogative to influence the destinies of men and the will of God that rules them. We do not once find Abraham praying for himself. His prayers for Sodom and Lot, for Abimelech, and for Ishmael prove that a man who is God's friend has the power to control the history of those around him.

This had been man's destiny from the first. But Scripture tells us more: God could entrust man with such a high calling because He had created him in His own image and likeness. The external responsibility was not committed to him without the inner fitness. The root of man's inner resemblance to God was in his nature to have dominion, to be lord of all. There was an inner agreement and harmony between God and man, an embryonic godlikeness, which gave man a real fitness for being the mediator between God and His world.

Man was to be prophet, priest, and king, to interpret God's will, to represent nature's needs, to receive and dispense God's bounty. It was in bearing God's image that he could bear God's rule. He was indeed so much like God—so capable of entering into God's purposes and carrying out His plans—that God could trust him with the wonderful privilege of asking for and obtaining what the world might need.

Although sin has for a time frustrated God's plans, prayer still remains what it would have been if man had never fallen: the proof of man's godlikeness, the vehicle of his communication with the Father, and the power that is allowed to hold the Hand that holds the destinies of the universe. Man is of divine origin, created for and capable of possessing kinglike liberty. His prayer is not merely a cry for mercy. It is the greatest execution of his will.

What sin destroyed, grace has restored. What the first Adam lost, the second has won back. In Christ, man regains his original position, and the church, abiding in Christ, inherits the promise: *"Ask what ye will, and it shall be done unto you"* (John 15:7). To begin with, such a promise does by no means refer to the grace or blessing we need for ourselves. It has reference to our position as the fruit-bearing branches of the Heavenly Vine, who, like Him, only live for the work and glory of the Father. It is for those who abide in Him, who have forsaken themselves for a life of obedience and self-sacrifice in Him, and who have completely surrendered to the interests of the Father and His kingdom. They understand how their redemption through Christ has brought them back to their original destiny, restoring God's image and the power to have dominion.

Such men indeed have the power—each in his own area—to obtain and dispense the powers of heaven here on earth. With holy boldness they may make known what they will. They live as priests in God's presence. They are kings possessing the powers of the world to come.[2] They enter upon the fulfillment of the promise: *"Ask what ye will, and it shall be done unto you."*

Church of the living God! Your calling is higher and holier than you know! God wants to rule the world through your members. He wants you to be His kings and priests. Your prayers can bestow and withhold the blessings of heaven. In His elect who are not content just to be saved, but who surrender themselves completely, the Father will fulfill all His glorious counsel through them just as He does through the Son. In His elect, who cry day and night to Him, God wants to prove how wonderful original destiny was. Man was the image bearer of God on earth, which was indeed given to him to rule. When he fell, everything fell with him. Now the whole creation groans and travails in pain together (Rom. 8:22).

---

2. "God is seeking priests among the sons of men. A human priesthood is one of the essential parts of His eternal plan. To rule creation by man is His design. Priesthood is the appointed link between heaven and earth, the channel of communication between the sinner and God. Such a priesthood, insofar as expiation is concerned, is in the hands of the Son of God alone; insofar as it is to be the medium of communication between Creator and creature, is also in the hands of redeemed men—of the church of God. God is seeking kings. Not out of the ranks of angels. Fallen man must furnish Him with the rulers of His universe. Human hands must wield the scepter, human heads must wear the crown."—*The Rent Veil*, by Dr. H. Bonar

But now man is redeemed. The restoration of the original dignity has begun. It is God's purpose that the fulfillment of His eternal purpose and the coming of His kingdom should depend on His people. They abide in Christ and are ready to accept Him as their Head, their great Priest-King. In their prayers they boldly say what they desire God to do for them. As God's image bearer and representative on earth, redeemed man has the power to determine the history of this earth through his prayers. Man was created and then redeemed to pray, and by his prayer to have dominion.

Lord, teach us to pray.

[Lord,] *what is man, that thou art mindful of him? and the son of man, that thou visitest him? For thou hast made him a little lower than the angels, and hast crowned him with glory and honour. Thou madest him to have dominion over the works of thy hands; thou hast put all things under his feet.…O* LORD *our Lord, how excellent is thy name in all the earth!*   (Ps. 8:4–6, 9)

Lord God, man has sunk so low because of sin. And how terribly it has darkened his mind. He doesn't even know his divine destiny: to be Your servant and representative. How sad it is that, even when their eyes are opened, men are so unready to accept their calling! They could have such power with God and with men, too!

Lord Jesus, through You, the Father has again crowned man with glory and honor, opening the way for us to be what He wants us to be. O Lord, have mercy on Your people—Your heritage! Work mightily with us in Your church! Teach Your believing disciples to accept and to go forth in their royal priesthood. Teach us to use the power of prayer, to which You have given such wonderful promises, to serve Your kingdom, to have rule over the nations, and to make the name of God glorious on the earth. Amen.

19

POWER FOR PRAYING AND WORKING

Verily, verily, I say unto you, He that believeth on me,
the works that I do shall he do also; and greater works than these shall
he do; because I go unto my Father. And whatsoever ye shall ask in my
name, that will I do, that the Father may be glorified in the Son.
If ye shall ask any thing in my name, I will do it.
—John 14:12–14

The Savior opened His public ministry in the Sermon on the Mount with the same subject He uses here in His parting address from the Gospel of John: prayer. But there is a difference. The Sermon on the Mount is directed to disciples who have just entered His school, scarcely knowing that God is their Father, whose prayers have reference chiefly to their personal needs. In His closing address, He speaks to disciples whose training time is coming to an end, who are ready as His messengers to take over His place and His work.

Christ's first lesson had been: be childlike, pray believingly, and trust the Father to give you everything good. Here He points to something higher. The disciples are now His friends. He has told them everything He knows about the Father. They are His messengers into whose hands the care of His work and kingdom on earth is to be entrusted. Now they must assume that role, performing even greater works than Christ in the power of His approaching exaltation. Prayer is to be the channel through which that power is received. With Christ's ascension to the Father, a new epoch for both their working and their praying commences.

This connection comes out clearly in our text from John, chapter fourteen. As His body here on earth, as those who are one with Him in heaven, the disciples are now to do greater works than He had done. Their successes and their victories are to be greater than His. Christ mentions two reasons for this. One is that He was going to the Father to receive all power; the other is that they could now ask for and expect that power in His Name. *"Because I go unto my Father. And"*—notice this *and*—*"And whatsoever ye shall ask …that will I do."* His going to the Father brings a double blessing: the disciples could ask for and receive everything in His name, and as a consequence, would do the greater works. This first mention of prayer in our Savior's parting words teaches us two most important lessons: Whoever wants to do the works of Jesus must pray in His name. Whoever prays in His name must work in His name.

In prayer the power for work is obtained. When Jesus was here on earth, He did the greatest works Himself. Devils that the disciples could not cast out fled at His word. When He went to be with the Father, He was no longer here in body to work directly. The disciples were now His body. All His work from the throne in heaven must and could be done here on earth through them.

573 With Christ in the School of Prayer

Now that Christ was leaving the scene and could only work through commissioners, it might have been expected that the works would be fewer and weaker. He assures us of the contrary: *"Verily, verily, I say unto you, He that believeth on me, the works that I do shall he do also; and greater works than these shall he do; because I go unto my Father."* His approaching death was to be a breaking down of the power of sin. With the resurrection, the powers of the eternal life were to take possession of the human body and obtain supremacy over human life. With His ascension, Christ was to receive the power to communicate the Holy Spirit completely to His Body. The union—the oneness between Himself on the throne and those on earth—was to be so intensely and divinely perfect that He meant it as the literal truth: *"greater works than these shall he do, because I go unto my Father."*

And how true it was! Jesus, during three years of personal labor on earth, gathered little more than five hundred disciples, most of whom were so powerless that they weren't much help to His cause. Men like Peter and Paul did much greater things than He had done. From the throne He could do through them what He Himself in His humiliation could not yet do. He could ask the Father, receiving and bestowing new power for the greater works. And what was true for the disciples is true for us: as we believe and ask in His name, the power comes and takes possession of us also to do the greater works.

Alas! There is little or nothing to be seen of the power to do anything like Christ's works, not to mention anything greater. There can only be one reason: the belief in Him and the believing prayer in His name are absent. Every child of God must learn this lesson: prayer in the name of Jesus is the only way to share in the mighty power that Jesus has received from the Father for His people. It is in this power alone that the believer can do greater works. To every complaint about difficulties or lack of success, Jesus gives this one answer: *"He that believeth on me...greater works than these shall he do; because I go unto my Father. And whatsoever ye shall ask in my name, that will I do."* If you want to do the work of Jesus, believe and become linked to Him, the Almighty One. Then pray the prayer of faith in His name. Without this our work is just human and carnal. It may have some use in restraining sin or in preparing the way for a blessing, but the real power is missing. Effective working first needs effective praying.

The second lesson is this: whoever prays must work. It is for power to work that prayer has such great promises. Power for the effective prayer of faith is gained through working. Our blessed Lord repeats no less than six times those unlimited prayer promises that evoke anxious questions as to their real meaning: *"whatsoever," "any thing," "what ye will," "ask and ye shall receive"* (John 14:13–14; 15:7, 16; 16:23–24). Many a believer has read these with joy and hope, and in deep earnestness of soul has attempted to plead them for his own need, and has come out disappointed. The simple reason was that he separated the promise from its context.

The Lord gave the wonderful promise of the free use of His name with the Father in conjunction with doing His works. The disciple who lives only for Jesus' work and kingdom, for His will and honor, will be given the power to appropriate the promise. Anyone grasping the promise only when he wants something very special for himself will be disappointed, because he is making Jesus the servant of his own comfort. But whoever wants to pray the effective prayer of faith because he needs it for the work of the Master will learn it, because he has made himself the servant of his Lord's interests. Prayer not only teaches and strengthens one for work, work teaches and strengthens one for prayer.

This is true in both the natural and the spiritual worlds. *"Unto every one which hath [more] shall be given"* (Luke 19:26). Whoever is *"faithful over a few things, I will make...ruler over many things"* (Matt. 25:21). With the small amount of grace we have already received, let us give ourselves to the Master for His work! It will be to us a real school of prayer. When Moses had to take full charge of a rebellious people, he felt the need, but also the courage, to speak boldly to God and to ask great things of Him. (See Exodus 33:12, 15, 18.) As you give yourself entirely to God for His work, you will feel that these great promises are exactly what you need, and that you may most confidently expect nothing less.

Believer in Jesus! You are called—you are appointed—to do the works of Jesus, and even greater works. He has gone to the Father to get the power to do them in and through you. Remember His promise: *"Whatsoever ye shall ask in my name, that will I do."* Give yourself and live to do the works of Christ, and you will learn how to obtain wonderful answers to prayer. You will learn to do not only what He did, but much more. With disciples full of faith in Himself, boldly asking great things in prayer, Christ can conquer the world.

Lord, teach us to pray.

O my Lord, once again, I am hearing You say things that are beyond my comprehension. I can do nothing but accept them and keep them in simple, childlike faith as Your gift to me. You have said that because of Your going to be with the Father, anyone who believes in You can do not only the things You have done, but greater things as well.

Lord, I worship You as the Glorified One and eagerly await the fulfillment of Your promise. May my whole life be one of continued believing in You. Purify and sanctify my heart. Make it so tenderly susceptible to Yourself and Your love that believing in You will become its very breath.

You have said that because You went to the Father, You will do whatever we ask You to do. You want Your people to share Your power. From Your throne, You want to work through them, as members of Your body, in response to their believing prayer in Your name. You have promised us power in our prayers to You and power in our work here on earth.

Blessed Lord, forgive us for not believing You and Your promise more. Because of our lack of faith, we have failed to demonstrate how You are faithful to fulfill that promise. Please forgive us for so little honoring Your all-prevailing name in heaven or on earth.

Lord, teach me to pray so that I can prove Your game is all-powerful with God, with men, and with devils. Teach me to work and to pray in a way that glorifies You, and do Your great works through me. Amen.

20

THE MAIN PURPOSE
OF PRAYER

I go unto my Father. And whatsoever ye shall ask in my name, that
will I do, that the Father may be glorified in the Son.
—John 14:12–13

hat the Father may be glorified in the Son." It is to this end that
Jesus on His throne in glory will do everything we ask in His
name. Every answer to prayer He gives will have this as its object. When
there is no prospect of this object being obtained, He will not answer. It
follows as a matter of course that with us, as with Jesus, this must be the
essential element in our petitions. The glory of the Father must be the
aim—the very soul and life—of our prayers.

This was Jesus' goal when He was on earth: *"I seek not mine own* [honor], *but the* [honor] *of the Father which hath sent me"* (John 5:30). In such words we have the keynote of His life. The first words of His High Priestly Prayer voice it: *"Father...glorify thy Son, that thy Son also may glorify thee....I have glorified thee on the earth....Glorify thou me with thine own self"* (John 17:1, 4–5). His reason for asking to be taken up into the glory He had with the Father is a twofold one: He has glorified Him on earth; He will still glorify Him in heaven. All He asks is to be able to glorify the Father more.

As we begin to share Jesus' feeling on this point, gratifying Him by making the Father's glory our chief object in prayer, too, our prayers cannot fail to get an answer. The Beloved Son has said that nothing glorifies the Father more than His doing what we ask. Therefore, Jesus won't miss any opportunity to do what we request. Let us make His aim ours! Let the glory of the Father be the link between our asking and His doing!

Jesus' words come indeed as a sharp twoedged sword, dividing the soul and the spirit and quickly discerning the thoughts and intents of the heart (Heb. 4:12). In His prayers on earth, His intercession in heaven, and His promise of an answer to our prayers, Jesus makes His first object the glory of His Father. Is this our object, too? Or are self-interest and self-will the strongest motives urging us to pray? A distinct, conscious longing for the glory of the Father must animate our prayers.

The believer does at times desire it. But he doesn't desire it enough. The reason for this failure is that the separation between the spirit of his daily life and the spirit of his hour of prayer is too wide. Desire for the glory of the Father is not something we can arouse and present to our Lord when we prepare ourselves to pray. Only when the whole life in all its parts is given up to God's glory can we really pray to Christ's glory, too. *"Do all to the glory of God"* (1 Cor. 10:31); ask *"all to the glory of God."* These twin commands are inseparable. Obedience to the former is the secret of grace for the latter. Living for the glory of God is the condition of the prayers that Jesus can answer.

This demand that prayer be to the glory of God is quite right and natural. Only the Lord is glorious. There is no glory but His, and what He allots to His creations. Creation exists to show forth His glory. Everything that doesn't glorify Him is sinful, dark, and dead. It is only in the glorifying of God that creatures can find glory. What the Son of Man did—giving Himself wholly to glorify the Father—is nothing but the simple duty of every redeemed one. He will also receive Christ's reward.

We cannot attain a life with God's glory as our only aim by any effort of our own. It is only in the man Christ Jesus that such a life can be found. Yes, blessed be God! His life is our life. He gave Himself for us. He is now our life. It is essential to discover, confess, and deny the self because it takes God's place. Only the presence and rule of the Lord Jesus in our hearts can cast out all self-glorification, replacing it with His own God-glorifying life and Spirit. It is Jesus, who longs to glorify the Father in hearing our prayers, who will teach us to live and to pray to the glory of God.

What power is there that can urge our slothful hearts to yield themselves to our Lord to work this in us? Surely nothing more is needed than a glimpse of how worthy of glory the Father is. Our faith should learn to bow before Him in adoring worship, ascribing to Him alone the kingdom, the power, and the glory (Matt. 6:13), yielding ourselves to life in His light. Surely we will be stirred to say, "To Him alone be glory." And we will look to our Lord Jesus with new intensity of desire for a life that refuses to recognize anything but the glory of God. When there isn't enough prayer to be answered, the Father is not glorified. It is our duty to live and pray so that our prayers can be answered. For the sake of God's glory, let us learn to pray well.

What a humbling thought it is, that so often there is earnest prayer in which the desire for our own joy or pleasure is far stronger than any desire for God's glory. No wonder there are so many unanswered prayers! Here we have the secret. God cannot be glorified when that glory is not the object of our prayers. Whoever wants to pray the prayer of faith must give himself to live literally so that the Father in all things is glorified in him. This must be his aim; without it there cannot be a prayer of faith.

"How can ye believe," said Jesus, *"which receive honour one of another, and seek not the honour that cometh from God only?"* (John 5:44). When we

seek our own glory among men, we make faith impossible. Only the deep, intense self-sacrifice that gives up its own glory and seeks the glory of God wakens in the soul that spiritual susceptibility to divine faith. The surrender to God and the expectation that He will show His glory in hearing us are essential. Only he who seeks God's glory will see it in the answer to his prayer. How do we accomplish this? Let us begin with a confession. The glory of God hasn't really been an all-absorbing passion in our lives and our prayers. How little we have lived in the likeness of the Son and in sympathy with Him for God and His glory alone. Take time to allow the Holy Spirit to reveal how deficient we have been in this. True knowledge and confession of sin are the sure path to deliverance.

And then let us look to Jesus. In death He glorified God; through death He was glorified with Him. It is by dying—being dead to self and living for God—that we can glorify Him. This death to self, this life to the glory of God, is what Jesus gives and lives in each one who can trust Him for it. Let the spirit of our daily lives consist of the decision to live only for the glory of the Father as Christ did, the acceptance of Him with His life and strength working it in us, and the joyful assurance that we can live for the glory of God because Christ lives in us. Jesus helps us to live this way. The Holy Spirit is waiting to make it our experience, if we will only trust and let Him. Don't hold back through unbelief! Confidently do everything for the glory of God! Our obedience will please the Father. The Holy Spirit will seal us within with the consciousness that we are living for God and His glory.

What quiet peace and power will be in our prayers when we know that we are in perfect harmony with Christ, who promises to do what we ask, *"that the Father may be glorified in the Son."* With our whole beings consciously yielded to the inspiration of the Word and Spirit, our desires will no longer be ours. They will be His, and their main purpose will be the glory of God. With increasing liberty we will be able in prayer to say, "Father! You know we ask it only for Your glory." Answers to prayer, instead of being mountains we cannot climb, will give us greater confidence that we are heard. And the privilege of prayer will become doubly precious because it brings us into perfect unison with the Beloved Son in the wonderful partnership He proposes: "You ask, and I do, *'that the Father may be glorified in the Son.'*"

Lord, teach us to pray.

Blessed Lord Jesus, once again I am coming to You. Every lesson You give me convinces me all the more deeply that I don't know how to pray properly. But every lesson also inspires me with hope that You are going to teach me what prayer should be. O my Lord, I look to You with courage. You are the Great Intercessor. You alone pray and hear prayer for the sole purpose of glorifying the Father. Teach me to pray as You do.

Savior, I want to be nothing, yielding myself totally to You. I am giving myself to be crucified with You. Through the Spirit the works of self will be made dead. Let Your life and Your love of the Father take possession of me. A new longing is filling my soul that every day and every hour prayers to the glory of the Father will become everything to me. O my Lord, please teach me this!

My God and my Father, accept the desire of Your child who has seen that Your glory is alone worth living for. Show me Your glory. Let it overshadow me and fill my heart! May I dwell in it as Christ did. Tell me what pleases You, fulfill in me Your own good pleasure, so that I may find my glory in seeking the glory of my Father. Amen.

21

THE ALL-INCLUSIVE CONDITION

If ye abide in me, and my words abide in you,
ye shall ask what ye will, and it shall be done unto you.
—John 15:7

In all God's relations with us, the promise and its conditions are inseparable. If we fulfill the conditions, He fulfills the promise. What He is to be to us depends on what we are willing to be to Him: *"Draw nigh to God, and he will draw nigh to you"* (James 4:8). Therefore, in prayer, the unlimited promise *"ask what ye will"* has one simple and natural condition, *"if ye abide in me."* It is Christ whom the Father always hears. God is in Christ. To reach God, we must be in Christ, too. Fully abiding in Him, we

584 ⌒ Andrew Murray: Collected Works on Prayer

have the right to ask whatever we want and the promise that we will get an answer.

There is a terrible discrepancy between this promise and the experience of most believers. How many prayers bring no answer? The cause must be either that we do not fulfill the condition or that God does not fulfill the promise. Believers are not willing to admit either and therefore have devised a way of escape from the dilemma. They put a qualifying clause into the promise that our Savior did not put there—if it be God's will. This maintains both God's integrity and their own. If they could only accept it and hold fast to it as it stands, trusting Christ to make it true! And if only they would confess their failure in fulfilling the condition as the one explanation for unanswered prayer. God's Spirit would then lead them to see how appropriate such a promise is to those who really believe that Christ means it. The Holy Spirit would then make our weakness in prayer a mighty motivation for us to discover the secret and obtain the blessing of fully abiding in Christ.

"If ye abide in me." As a Christian grows in grace and knowledge of the Lord Jesus, he is often surprised to find how God's words grow, too, into new and deeper meaning. He can look back to the day when some word of God was opened up to him, and he rejoiced in the blessing he had found in it. After a time, some deeper experience gave it a new meaning, and it was as if he never had seen what it contained. And yet once again, as he advanced in the Christian life, the same word stood before him as a great mystery, until the Holy Spirit led him still more deeply into its divine fullness.

The Master's precious *"abide in me"* is one of these ever growing, never exhausted words. Step by step, it opens the fullness of the divine life to us. As the union of the branch with the vine is one of never ceasing growth, so our abiding in Christ is a life process in which the divine life takes more and more complete possession of us. The young believer may really be abiding in Christ to the limited extent that is possible for him. If he reaches onward to attain what the Master means by full abiding, he will inherit all the promises connected with it.

In the growing life of abiding in Christ, the first stage is that of faith. As the believer sees that Christ's command is really meant for him, his great aim is simply to believe that abiding in Christ is his immediate duty and a blessing within his reach. He is especially occupied with the love, power, and faithfulness of the Savior. He feels his one basic need is to believe.

It isn't long before he sees something more is needed. Obedience and faith must go together. But faith can't simply be added to obedience; it must be revealed in obedience. Faith is obedience at home, looking to the Master; obedience is faith going out to do His will.

The privilege and the blessings of this abiding are often of more interest than its duties and its fruit. Much self-will passes unnoticed. The peace that a young disciple enjoys in believing leaves him. In practical obedience the abiding must be maintained: *"If ye keep my commandments, ye shall abide in my love"* (John 15:10). Before, the truth that the mind believed was enough to let the heart rest on Christ and His promises. Now, in this stage, his chief effort is to get his will united with the will of his Lord, with his heart and life brought entirely under Christ's rule.

And yet there still seems to be something missing. The will and the heart are on Christ's side; the disciple obeys and loves his Lord. But why does the fleshly nature still have so much power? Why aren't his spontaneous actions and emotions what they should be? Where is the beauty of holiness, the zeal of love, and the conformity with Jesus and His death, in which the life of self is lost? There must surely be something which he has not yet experienced through abiding in Christ.

Faith and obedience are just the pathway to blessing. Before giving us the parable of the vine and the branches, Jesus had very distinctly told what that full blessing is. Three times over He said, *"If ye love me, keep my commandments"* (John 14:15), promising a threefold blessing with which He would crown such obedient love: the indwelling of the Holy Spirit, the manifestation of the Son, the Father and Son coming to make Their abode within us.

As our faith grows into obedience, and in obedience and love our whole being reaches out and clings to Christ, our inner lives open up. The capacity is formed within us of receiving the life and the Spirit of the glorified Jesus, through a distinct and conscious union with Christ and with the Father. The word is fulfilled in us: *"at that day ye shall know that I am in my Father, and ye in me, and I in you"* (John 14:20). God and Christ exist in each other, not only in will and in love, but in identity of nature and life. We come to understand that because of this union between the Father and the Son, so we are in Christ, and Christ is in us in exactly the same way.

After Jesus had spoken thus, He said, *"Abide in me, and I in you'* (John 15:4). Accept, consent to receive that divine life of union with Myself, in virtue of which, as you abide in Me, I also abide in you, even as I abide in the Father. So that your life is Mine and Mine is yours." True abiding consists of two parts: occupying a position into which Christ can come and abide, and abiding in Him so that the soul lets Him take the place of the self to become our life. Like little children who have no cares, we find happiness in trusting and obeying the love that has done everything for us.

To those who thus abide, the promise *"ask what ye will"* comes as their rightful heritage. It cannot be otherwise. Christ has full possession of them. He dwells in their love, their wills, and their lives. Not only have their wills been given up, Christ has entered them, dwelling and breathing there by His Spirit. These people pray in Him. He prays in them, and the Father always hears Him. What they ask will be done for them.

Beloved fellow believer, let us confess that because we do not abide in Christ as He would like us to, the church is impotent in the face of infidelity, worldliness, and heathendom. In the midst of such enemies, the Lord could make her more than a conqueror. (See Rom. 8:37.) We must believe that He means what He promises and accept the conviction the confession implies.

But don't be discouraged. The abiding of the branch in the Vine is a life of never ceasing growth. The abiding—as the Master meant it—is within our reach, for He lives to give it to us. Let us but be ready to count all things as loss (see Phil. 3:8) and to say, "What I have attained so far is hardly anything. I want to learn to perceive Christ the same way He perceives me." Let us not be occupied so much with the abiding as with Him to whom the abiding links us and His fullness. Let it be Christ—the whole Christ, in His obedience and humiliation, in His exaltation and power—in whom our soul moves and acts. He Himself will fulfill His promise in us.

As we abide and grow into fuller and fuller abiding, let us exercise our right—the will to enter into God's will. Obeying what that will commands, let us claim what it promises. Let us yield to the teaching of the Holy Spirit. He will show each of us what the will of God is so that we may claim it in prayer. And let us be content with nothing less than the personal experience of what Jesus gave when He said, *"If ye abide in me...ye shall ask what ye will, and it shall be done unto you."*

Lord, teach us to pray.

Beloved Lord, make Your promise in all its simplicity new to men. Teach me to accept it, letting the only limitation on Your holy giving be my own willingness. Lord, let each word of Your promise be, in a new way, made quick and powerful in my soul.

You say, *"Abide in me."* O my Master, my Life, my All—I do abide in You. Allow me to grow up in all Your fullness. It is not the effort of faith, trying to cling to You and trusting You to protect me; nor my will, obeying You and keeping Your commandments, that alone can satisfy me. Only You Yourself, living in me as You do in the Father, can satisfy me. It is You, my Lord, no longer before me and above me, but united with me, that I need. I trust You for this.

You say, *"Ask what ye will."* Lord, I know that a life of complete, deep abiding will renew, sanctify, and strengthen my will in such a way that I will have the desire and the liberty to ask for great things. Lord, let my will—dead in Your death, living in Your life—be bold and large in its petitions.

You say, *"It shall be done."* O Jesus, You are *"the Amen, the faithful and true witness"* (Rev. 3:14). Give me in Yourself the joyous confidence that You will make this promise even more wonderfully true to me than ever before, because it has not entered into the heart of man to conceive what God has prepared for those who love Him. (See 1 Cor. 2:9.) Amen.

Author's Note

Many books and sermons on prayer emphasize the blessing of prayer as a spiritual exercise, even if there is no answer. God's fellowship ought to be more important to us than the gift we ask for. But a careful examination of what Christ said about prayer reveals that He wanted us to think of prayer more as the means to an end. The answer was to be the proof that we and our prayers are acceptable to the Father in heaven. It is not that Christ would have us consider the gifts of higher value than the fellowship and favor of the Father. By no means. But the Father intends the answer to be a token of His favor and of the reality of our fellowship with Him.

Daily answer to prayer is the proof of our spiritual maturity. It shows that we have attained the true abiding in Christ, that our will is truly one with God's will. It also reveals that our faith is strong enough to see and take what God has prepared for us, that the name of Christ and His nature have taken full possession of us, and that we have been found fit to take a place among those whom God admits to His counsels, according to whose prayer He rules the world. Prayer is very blessed; the answer is more blessed still. It is the response from the Father that our prayers, our faith, and our wills are indeed as He would wish them to be.

I make these remarks with the one desire of leading my readers to put together for themselves everything that Christ has said about prayer. Accept the truth that when prayer is what it should be, or rather when we are what we should be, the answer must be expected. It will bring us out from those refuges where we have comforted ourselves with unanswered prayer. It will show us the place of power to which Christ has appointed

His church, that place that it occupies so little. It will reveal the terrible weakness of our spiritual lives as the cause of our not praying boldly in Christ's name. It will urge us mightily to rise to a life in full union with Christ and in the fullness of the Spirit as the secret of effective prayer. And it will so lead us to realize our destiny: *"In that day....Verily, verily, I say unto you, Whatsoever ye shall ask the Father in my name, he will give it you....Ask, and ye shall receive, that your joy may be full"* (John 16:23–24). Prayer that is really in union spiritually with Jesus is always answered.

22

THE WORD AND PRAYER

If ye abide in me, and my words abide in you, ye shall ask what ye will, and it shall be done unto you.
—John 15:7

The vital connection between the Word and prayer is one of the simplest and earliest lessons of the Christian life. As that newly converted heathen put it: "I pray—I speak to my Father; I read—my Father speaks to me." Before prayer, God's Word strengthens me by giving my faith its justification and its petition. And after prayer, God's Word prepares me by revealing what the Father wants me to ask. In prayer, God's Word brings me the answer, for in it the Spirit allows me to hear the Father's voice.

Prayer is not monologue, but dialogue. Its most essential part is God's voice in response to mine. Listening to God's voice is the secret of the assurance that He will listen to mine. *"Incline thine ear, and hear"* (Dan. 9:18). *"Give ear unto me"* (Isa. 51:4) and *"hearken unto me"* (v. 4) are words that God speaks to man as well as man to God. His hearkening will depend on ours.

My willingness to accept His words will determine the power my words have with Him. What God's words are to me is the test of what He Himself is to me. It shows the uprightness of my desire to meet Him in prayer.

It is this connection between His Word and our prayers that Jesus points to when He said, *"If ye abide in me, and my words abide in you, ye shall ask what ye will, and it shall be done unto you."* The deep importance of this truth becomes clear if we notice the expression that this one replaces. More than once Jesus had said, *"Abide in me, and I in you"* (John 15:4). His abiding in us was the complement and the crown of our abiding in Him. But here, instead of *"ye in me, and I in you"* (John 14:20), He said, *"Ye...in me, and my words...in you."* The abiding of His words is the equivalent of Himself abiding.

What a view this opens up to us of the place the words of God in Christ are to have in our spiritual lives, especially in our prayers. A man's words reveal himself. In his promises, he gives himself away, binding himself to the one who receives his promises. In his commands, he proclaims his will, seeking to make himself master of those whose obedience he claims, to guide and use them as if they were part of himself. Through our words, spirit holds fellowship with spirit. If a man's words are heard, accepted, held fast, and obeyed, he can impart himself to someone else through them. But with human beings, this can happen only in a limited sense.

God, however, is the infinite Being in whom everything is life, power, spirit, and truth, in the very deepest meaning of the words. When God reveals Himself in His words, He does indeed give Himself—His love and His life, His will and His power—to those who receive these words, in a reality passing comprehension. In every promise, He gives us the power to grasp and possess Himself. In every command, He allows us to share His will, His holiness, and His perfection. God's Word gives us God Himself. That Word is nothing less than the Eternal Son, Christ Jesus. Therefore, all of Christ's words are God's words, full of a divine, quickening life and power. "*The words that I speak unto you, they are spirit, and they are life*" (John 6:63).

Those who study the deaf and mute tell us how much the power of speaking depends on that of hearing, and how the loss of hearing in children is followed by a loss of speaking, too. This is also true in a broader sense: our speech is based on what we hear. In the highest sense, this is true of our conversation with God. To offer a prayer—to utter certain wishes and appeal to certain promises—is an easy thing that man can learn with human intelligence. But to pray in the Spirit—to speak words that reach and touch God, affecting and influencing the powers of the unseen world—depends entirely on our hearing God's voice. We must listen to the voice and language that God uses and, through the words of God, receive His thoughts, His mind, and His life into our hearts. The extent to which we listen will determine the extent to which we learn to speak in the voice and the language that God hears. The ear of the learner, wakened morning by morning, prepares him to speak to God. (See Isa. 50:4.)

This hearing the voice of God is something more than the thoughtful study of the Word. One can study and gain knowledge of the Word having little real fellowship with the living God. But there is also a reading of the Word, in the very presence of the Father and under the leading of the Spirit, in which the Word comes to us in living power from God Himself. It is to us the very voice of the Father, a real, personal fellowship with Himself The living voice of God enters the heart, bringing blessing and strength, and awakening the response of a living faith that reaches back to the heart of God.

The power both to obey and believe depends on hearing God's voice this way. The chief thing isn't knowing what God has said we must do, but that God Himself says it to us. Neither the law nor the book nor the knowledge of what is right works obedience. This can be accomplished only by the personal influence of God through His living fellowship. The presence of God Himself as the Promiser, not the knowledge of what He has promised, awakens faith and trust in prayer. It is only in the full presence of God that disobedience and unbelief become impossible.

"If ye abide in me, and my words abide in you, ye shall ask what ye will, and it shall be done unto you." In these words, the Savior gives Himself. We must have the words in us—taken up into our wills and lives, reproduced in our inner natures and conduct. They must abide in us. Our lives must be one continuous display of the words that fill us. The words reveal Christ inside and our lives reveal Him outside. As the words of Christ enter our very hearts, becoming and influencing our lives, our words will enter His heart and influence Him. My prayer will depend on my life: whatever God's words are to me and in me will determine what my words will be to God and in God. If I do what God says, God will do what I say.

The Old Testament saints understood this connection between God's words and ours quite well. Their prayer really was a loving response to what they had heard God speak. If the word were a promise, they counted on God to do as He had spoken. *"Do as Thou hast said"* (2 Sam. 7:25; 1 Chron. 17:23); *"For thou, O Lord God, hast spoken it"* (2 Sam. 7:29); according to Thy promise; according to Thy word. In such expressions they showed that what God spoke in promise was the root and the life of what they spoke in prayer. If the word was a command, they simply did as the Lord had spoken: *"So Abram departed, as the Lord had spoken"* (Gen. 12:4). Their lives were fellowship with God, the exchange of word and thought. What God spoke they heard and did; what they spoke God heard and did. In each word, He speaks to us, and the whole Christ gives Himself to fulfill it. For each word, He asks no less than that we give the whole man to keep that word and to receive its fulfillment.

"If…my words abide in you." The condition is simple and clear. In His words His will is revealed. As the words abide in me, His will rules me. My will becomes the empty vessel that His will fills and the willing instrument that His will rules. He fills my inner being. In the exercise of obedience and faith, my will becomes stronger and is brought into deeper inner harmony

with Him. Because He can fully trust it to will nothing but what He wills, He is not afraid to give the promise, *"If…my words abide in you, ye shall ask what ye will, and it shall be done unto you."* To all who believe it and act upon it, He will make it literally true.

Disciples of Christ, while we have been excusing our unanswered prayers with a fancied submission to God's wisdom and will, the real reason has been that our own feeble lives have been the cause of our feeble prayers! Nothing can make men strong but the word coming from God's mouth. By that we must live. The word of Christ makes us one with Him and fits us spiritually for touching and taking hold of God. We must love and live in that Word, letting it abide in and become part of us.

All that is of the world passes away. Whoever does God's will lives forever. Let us yield heart and life to the words of Christ, the words in which He gives Himself, the personal living Savior. His promise will become our rich experience: *"If ye abide in me, and my words abide in you, ye shall ask what ye will, and it shall be done unto you."*

Lord, teach us to pray.

Blessed Lord, I see why my prayer has not been more believing and effective. I was more occupied with my speaking to You than with Your speaking to me. I did not understand that the secret of faith is this: there can be only as much faith as there is of the living Word dwelling in the soul.

Your Word taught me so clearly to be *"swift to hear"* and *"slow to speak"* (James 1:19), and not to be hasty to say just anything to God. Lord, teach me that it is only when I take Your Word into my life that my words can be taken into Your heart. Teach me that if Your Word is a living power within me, it will be a living power with You, also. Show me that what Your mouth has spoken Your hand will perform.

Lord Jesus, deliver me from the uncircumcised ear! Give me the opened ear of the learner, wakened morning by morning to hear the Father's voice.

Just as You speak only what You hear from the Father, may my speaking be the echo of Your speaking to me. *"When Moses was gone into the tabernacle...to speak with him, then he heard the voice of one speaking unto him from off the mercy seat"* (Num. 7:89). Lord, may it be so with me, too. Let my life and character reveal that Your words abide and are seen in me. May this be my preparation for the complete blessing: *"Ye shall ask what ye will, and it shall be done unto you."* Amen.

23

OBEDIENCE: THE PATH TO POWER IN PRAYER

Ye have not chosen me, but I have chosen you, and ordained you,
that ye should go and bring forth fruit,
and that your fruit should remain: that whatsoever ye shall ask of the
Father in my name, he may give it you.
—John 15:16

The effectual fervent prayer of a righteous man availeth much.
—James 5:16

The promise of the Father's giving whatever we ask is here once again renewed, showing us to whom such wonderful influence in the council chamber of the Most High is to be granted. *"I have chosen you,"* the Master said, *"and ordained you, that ye should go and bring forth fruit, and that your fruit should remain."* He then adds, to the end *"that whatsoever ye* [the fruit-bearing ones] *shall ask of the Father in my name, he may give it you."* This is nothing but a fuller expression of what He meant by the words, *"If ye abide in me"* (John 15:7). He had spoken of the object of this abiding as the bearing of *"fruit"* (v. 2), *"more fruit"* (v. 2), and *"much fruit"* (vv. 5, 8). In this, God would be glorified and the mark of discipleship would be seen. He now adds that the reality of the abiding, as seen in fruit abounding and abiding, is the qualification for praying so as to obtain what we ask. Entire dedication to the fulfillment of our calling is the key to effective prayer and the unlimited blessings of Christ's wonderful prayer promises.

There are Christians who fear that such a statement is at variance with the doctrine of free grace. But surely it doesn't disagree with free grace rightly understood or the many express statements of God's blessed Word. Take the words of John:

> Let us...love...in deed and in truth. And hereby we...shall assure our hearts before him....And whatsoever we ask, we receive of him, because we keep his commandments, and do those things that are pleasing in his sight. (1 John 3:18–19, 22)

Or take the often quoted words of James, *"The effectual fervent prayer of a righteous man availeth much."* This describes a man of whom, according to the definition of the Holy Spirit, it can be said, *"He that doeth righteousness is righteous, even as he is righteous"* (1 John 3:7). Mark the spirit of so many of the Psalms, with their confident appeal to the integrity and righteousness of the supplicant. In Psalm 18 David said,

> The LORD rewarded me according to my righteousness; according to the cleanness of my hands hath he recompensed me....I was also upright before him, and I kept myself from mine iniquity. Therefore hath the LORD recompensed me according to my righteousness. (Ps. 18:20, 23–24. See also Psalms 7:3–5; 15:1–2; 17:3, 6; 26:1–6; 119:121, 153.)

If we carefully consider these scriptures in the light of the New Testament, we find them in perfect harmony with the explicit teaching of the Savior's parting words: *"If ye keep my commandments, ye shall abide in my love"* (John 15:10); *"Ye are my friends, if ye do whatsoever I command you"* (v. 14). The words are indeed meant literally: *"I…ordained you, that ye should go and bring forth fruit, and that"* then, *"whatsoever ye shall ask of the Father in my name, he may give it you."*

Let us seek to enter into the spirit of what the Savior teaches us here. There is a danger in our evangelical religion of looking too much at what it offers from one side, as a certain experience obtained in prayer and faith. There is another side that God's Word puts very strongly, that of obedience as the only path to blessing. What we need to realize is that in our relationship to God He is the Infinite Being who created and redeemed us. The first sentiment that ought to motivate us is that of subjection: surrender to His supremacy, His glory, His will, and His pleasure ought to be the first and uppermost thought of our lives.

The question is not, however, how we are to obtain and enjoy His favor, for in this the main thing may still be self. What this Being in the very nature of things rightfully claims, and is infinitely and unspeakably worthy of, is that His glory and pleasure should be my only object. Surrender to His perfect and blessed will—a life of service and obedience—is the beauty and the charm of heaven. Service and obedience were the thoughts that were uppermost in the mind of the Son when He was on earth. Service and obedience must become the chief objects of our desires and aims, even more so than rest, light, joy, or strength. In them we will find the path to all the higher blessedness that awaits us.

Note what a prominent place the Master gives it, not only in this fifteenth chapter, in connection with the abiding, but in the fourteenth, where He speaks of the indwelling of the Trinity. John 14:15 says, *"If ye love me, keep my commandments,"* and the Spirit will be given to you by the Father. Then verse 21, *"He that hath my commandments, and keepeth them, he it is that loveth me."* He will have the special love of the Father and the special manifestation of Christ. Verse 23 is one of the highest of all the great and precious promises: *"If a man love me, he will keep my words: and my Father [and I]…will come…and make up our abode with him."* Could words put it more clearly that obedience is the way to the indwelling of the Spirit, to His revealing the Son within us, and to His preparing us to be the abode, the home of the Father? The indwelling of the Trinity is the heritage of those who obey.

Obedience and faith are simply two parts of one act—surrender to God and His will. As faith strengthens itself in order to be obedient, it is in turn strengthened by obedience. Faith is made perfect by works. Often our efforts to believe are unsuccessful because we don't assume the only position in which a large faith is legitimate or possible—that of entire surrender to the honor and the will of God. The man who is entirely consecrated to God and His will finds the power to claim everything that His God has promised to be for him.

The application of this in the school of prayer is very simple but very solemn. *"I have chosen you,"* the Master said, *"and ordained you, that ye should go and bring forth fruit,"* *"much fruit"* (John 15:5, 8), *"and that your fruit should remain,"* that your life might be one of abiding fruit and abiding fruitfulness, *"that"* as fruitful branches abiding in me, *"whatsoever ye shall ask of the Father in my name, he may give it you."*

How often we've tried to pray an effective prayer for grace to bear fruit and have wondered why the answer didn't come. It was because we were reversing the Master's order. We wanted to have the comfort, the joy, and the strength first, so we could do the work easily and without any feeling of difficulty or self-sacrifice. But He wanted us to do what He said in the obedience of faith, without worrying about whether we felt weak or strong, or whether the work was hard or easy. The path of fruit bearing leads us to the place and the power of successful prayer.

Obedience is the only path that leads to the glory of God. Obedience doesn't replace faith or supply its shortcomings. But faith's obedience gives access to all the blessings our God has for us. In the Gospel of John, the baptism of the Spirit (John 14:16), the manifestation of the Son (see verse 21), the indwelling of the Father (see verse 23), the abiding in Christ's love (see John 15:10), the privilege of His holy friendship (see verse 14), and the power of effective prayer (see verse 16), all wait for the obedient.

Now we know the great reason why we have not had power in faith to pray successfully. Our lives weren't as they should have been. Simple obedience—abiding fruitfulness—was not its chief mark. We wholeheartedly approve of the divine appointment of men to whom God gives the power to rule the world. At their request, He does what otherwise would not have taken place. Their will guides the path in which God's will is to work. These men must have learned obedience themselves. Their loyalty and submission to authority must be above all suspicion. If we approve the law, that obedience and fruit bearing are the path to prevailing prayer, we must with shame acknowledge how little our lives have exemplified this.

Let us yield ourselves to take up the appointment the Savior gives us. If we concentrate on our relationship to Him as our Master, we should no longer begin each new day with thoughts of comfort, joy, or blessing. Our first thought should be: "I belong to the Master." Every moment I must act as His property, as a part of Himself, as one who only seeks to know and do His will. I am a servant, a slave of Jesus Christ. Let this be the spirit that animates me. If He says, "No longer do I call you servants, *'but I have called you friends'* (John 15:15)," let us accept the place of friends, because, *"Ye are my friends, if ye do whatsoever I command you"* (v. 14).

The one thing He commands us as His branches is to bear fruit. Live to bless others, to testify of the life and the love there is in Jesus. In faith and obedience give your whole life to that which Jesus chose us for and appointed us to—fruit bearing. Think of His electing us to this, accepting your appointment as coming from Him who always gives us everything He demands of us. We will grow strong in the confidence that a life of fruit bearing and abiding is within our reach. And we will understand why this fruit bearing alone can be the path to the place of all-effective prayer. The man who, in obedience to Christ, proves that he is doing what his Lord wills, will receive whatever he desires from the Father. *"Whatsoever we ask, we receive of him, because we keep His commandments, and do those things that are pleasing in his sight"* (1 John 3:22).

Lord, teach us to pray.

Blessed Master, teach me to understand fully what I only partly realize, that only by obeying the will of God can we obtain His promises and use them effectively in our prayers. Show me how bearing fruit perfects the deeper growth of the branch into the Vine, allowing us to experience that perfect union with God in which we can ask for whatever we want.

O Lord, reveal to us how with all the hosts of heaven, with all the saints here on earth, and even with Yourself on earth, that obedience to God is the highest privilege. It gives access to oneness with the Father Himself in that which is His highest glory—His all-perfect will. And show us how, if we keep Your commandments and bear fruit according to Your will, our spiritual natures will grow to the full stature of a perfect man, having power to ask and receive anything.

O Lord Jesus, reveal Yourself to us! Through Your purpose and power, make Your wonderful promises the daily experience of everyone who completely yields himself to You and Your words. Amen.

24

THE ALL-POWERFUL PLEA

And whatsoever ye shall ask in my name, that will I do....
If ye shall ask any thing in my name, I will do it....That whatsoever ye
shall ask of the Father in my name, he may give it you....Verily, verily,
I say unto you, Whatsoever ye shall ask the Father in my name, he
will give it you. Hitherto have ye asked nothing in my name: ask, and
ye shall receive....At that day ye shall ask in my name.
—John 14:13–14; 15:16; 16:23–24, 26

U ntil now the disciples had not asked in the name of Christ, nor had He Himself ever used the expression. Here in His parting words, He repeats the word unceasingly in connection with those promises of unlimited meaning: *"whatsoever," "any thing."* He wanted to teach them

603

and us that His name is our only, but also our completely sufficient, plea. The power of prayer and its answer depend on the right use of the name.

What is a person's name? It is a word or expression in which a person is represented to us. When I mention or hear a name, it brings to mind the whole man, what I know of him, and also the impression he has made on me. The name of a king includes his honor, his power, and his kingdom. His name is the symbol of his power. And so each name of God embodies and represents some part of the glory of the Unseen One. The name of Christ is the expression of everything He has done and everything He is and lives to do as our Mediator.

What does it mean to do a thing in the name of another? It is to come with his power and authority, as his representative and substitute. Using another's name always presupposes a common interest. No one would give another the free use of his name without first being assured that his honor and interests were as safe with that other person as with himself. What does it mean when Jesus gives us power over His name—the free use of it—with the assurance that whatever we ask in it will be given to us? The ordinary comparison of one person giving another, on some special occasion, the liberty to ask something in his name, comes altogether short here. Jesus solemnly gives to all His disciples a general and unlimited power to use His name at all times for everything they desire. He could not do this if He did not know that He could trust us with His interests and that His honor would be safe in our hands.

The free use of someone else's name is always a token of great confidence and close union. Someone who gives his name to another stands aside to let that person act for him. Someone who takes the name of another gives up his own as of no value. When I go in the name of another, I deny myself. I take not only his name, but himself and what he is, instead of myself and what I am.

Such use of a person's name may be the result of a legal union. A merchant leaving his home and business gives his chief clerk a general power by which he can withdraw thousands of dollars in the merchant's name. The clerk does this, not for himself, but only in the interests of the business. Because the merchant knows and trusts him as wholly devoted to his interests and business, he dares put his name and property at his clerk's command.

When the Lord Jesus went to heaven, He left His work—the management of His kingdom on earth—in the hands of His servants. He also gave them His name to draw all the supplies they needed for the due conduct of His business. Christ's servants have the spiritual power to use the name of Jesus only insofar as they yield themselves to live only for the interests and the work of the Master. The use of the name always supposes the surrender of our interests to Him whom we represent.

Another use of a name may be because of a life union—in the case of the merchant and his clerk, the union is temporary. Oneness of life on earth gives oneness of name: a child has the father's name because he has his life. Often the child of a good father is honored or helped by others for the sake of the name he bears. But this would not last long if it were found that it was only a name and that the father's character was not present in it. The name and the character or spirit must be in harmony. When such is the case, the child will have a double claim on the father's friends. The character secures and increases the love and esteem extended at first for the name's sake.

It is the same with Jesus and the believer: we are one; we have one life and one Spirit with Him. For this reason we may proceed in His name. Our power in using that name, whether with God, men, or devils, depends on the measure of our spiritual life union with Christ. Our use of His name rests on the unity of our lives with Him.

The name and the Spirit of Jesus are one. "*Whatsoever ye shall ask in my name*" means "in My nature." With God, things are requested according to their nature. Asking in Christ's name doesn't mean that at the end of some request we say, "This I ask in the name of Jesus Christ." It means we are praying according to His nature, which is love that doesn't seek its own will, but only the will of God and the good of all creatures. Such asking is the cry of Christ's own Spirit in our hearts.

The union that gives power to the use of the name may be the union of love. When a bride whose life has been one of poverty becomes united to the bridegroom, she gives up her own name to be called by his, and has the full right to use it. She purchases in his name, and that name is not refused. This is done because the bridegroom has chosen her for himself, counting on her to care for his interests because they are now one.

The heavenly Bridegroom does nothing less. Having loved us and made us one with Himself, what can He do but give those who bear His name the right to present it before the Father or to come with it to Himself for all they need? No one really gives himself up to live in the name of Jesus without receiving in ever increasing measure the spiritual capacity to ask for and receive in that name whatever he desires. My bearing of the name of another shows that I have given up my own name and, with it, my own independent life. But just as surely, it shows I have possession of everything belonging to the name I have taken instead of my own.

The common comparison to a messenger sent to ask in the name of another, or a guilty person using the name of a guardian in his appeal, is defective. We are not praying in the name of someone who is absent. Jesus Himself is with the Father. When we pray to the Father, it must be in Jesus' name. The name represents the person. To ask in His name is to ask in full union of interest, life, and love with Himself, as one who lives in and for Him.

Let the name of Jesus have undivided supremacy in my heart and life! My faith will grow to the assurance that what I ask for in that name cannot be refused. The name and the power of asking go together. When the name of Jesus has become the power that rules my life, its power in prayer with God will be seen, too.

Everything depends on my own relationship to the name. The power it has on my life is the power it will have in my prayers. There is more than one expression in Scripture that can make this clear. *"Do all in the name of the Lord Jesus"* (Col. 3:17) is the counterpart of "ask all." To do all and ask all in His name go together. *"We will walk in the name of the Lord our God"* (Mic. 4:5) means the power of the name must rule in the whole life. Only then will it have power in prayer. God looks not to our lips, but to our lives to see what the name is to us. When Scripture speaks of *"men that have* [given] *their lives for the name of our Lord Jesus"* (Acts 15:26) or of one *"ready...to die...for the name of the Lord Jesus"* (Acts 21:13), we see what our relationship to the name must be. When it is everything to me, it will obtain everything for me. If I let it have all I have, it will let me have all it has.

"Whatsoever ye shall ask in my name, that will I do." Jesus means that promise literally. Christians have sought to limit it because it looked too free. It was hardly safe to trust man so unconditionally. They did not understand that the phrase *"in my name"* is its own safeguard. It is a spiritual power that no one can use further than his living and acting in that name allows.

As we bear the name before men, we have the power to use it before God. Let us plead for God's Holy Spirit to show us what the name means, and what the right use of it is. It is through the Spirit that the name, which is above every name in heaven (see Phil. 2:9), will take the place of supremacy in our hearts and lives, too. Disciples of Jesus, let the lessons of this day go deeply into your hearts. The Master said, "Only pray in my name; whatsoever you ask will be given." Heaven is opened to you! The treasures and powers of the spiritual world are placed at your disposal to help those around you.

Learn to pray in the name of Jesus. He says to us, as He said to the disciples, *"Hitherto have ye asked nothing in my name: ask, and ye shall receive"* (John 16:24). Let each disciple of Jesus seek to avail himself of the rights of his royal priesthood to use the power placed at his disposal for his work. Let Christians awake and hear this message: your prayers can obtain what would otherwise be withheld! They can accomplish what would otherwise remain undone! Oh, awake, and use the name of Jesus to open the treasures of heaven for this perishing world!

Lord, teach us to pray.

Blessed Lord, it seems as if each lesson You give me has such depth of meaning that if I could just learn that one, I would be able to pray properly.

Right now I feel as if I only need to pray for one thing: Lord, please teach me what it is to pray in Your name. Teach me to live and act, to walk and speak, to do everything in the name of Jesus, so that my prayer cannot be anything else but in that blessed name, too.

Lord, teach me to fully grasp the precious promise that whatever I ask in Your name You will do, and the Father will give. I realize that I haven't fully attained, and that I don't completely understand, the wondrous union You mean when You say, *"In my name."* Let me hold on to the promise until it fills my heart with the undoubting assurance that I can ask for anything in the name of Jesus.

O my Lord, let the Holy Spirit teach me this! You did describe Him as *"the Comforter…whom the Father will send in my name"* (John 14:26). He knows what it is to be sent from heaven in Your name, to reveal and to honor the power of that name in Your servants, and to use that name alone to glorify You. Lord Jesus, let Your Spirit dwell in me and fill me! I yield my whole being to His rule and leading. Your name and Your Spirit are one. Through Him, Your name will be the strength of my life and my prayer. Then I will be able to forsake everything for Your name's sake, speaking to men and to God in Your name, and proving that this, indeed, is the name above every name.

Lord Jesus, please teach me by Your Holy Spirit to pray in Your name. Amen.

25

THE HOLY SPIRIT
AND PRAYER

*And in that day ye shall ask me nothing. Verily, verily,
I say unto you, Whatsoever ye shall ask the Father in my name, he
will give it you. Hitherto have ye asked nothing in my name: ask, and
ye shall receive, that your joy may be full.*
—John 16:23–24

*At that day ye shall ask in my name: and I say not unto you, that I
will pray the Father for you: for the Father himself loveth you.*
—John 16:26–27

Praying in the Holy Ghost, keep yourselves in the love of God.
—Jude 20–21

The words of John to little children, young men, and fathers suggest the thought that often in the Christian life there are three great stages of experience. (See 1 John 2:12–14.) The first, that of the newborn child, is filled with the assurance and the joy of forgiveness. The second, the transition stage of struggle and growth in knowledge and strength, is comparable to young men growing strong. God's Word is doing its work in them and giving them victory over the Evil One. The final stage of maturity and ripeness is that of the fathers, who have entered deeply into the knowledge and fellowship of the Eternal One.

In Christ's teaching on prayer, three similar stages in prayer life are apparent. The Sermon on the Mount describes the initial stage. All of His teaching is comprised in one word: *Father.* Pray to your Father; your Father sees, hears, knows, and will reward. How much more than any earthly father He is! Simply be childlike and trustful.

Then comes something like a transition stage of conflict and conquest. Words like these refer to it: *"This kind goeth not out but by prayer and fasting"* (Matt. 17:21); *"Shall not God avenge his own elect, which cry day and night unto him?"* (Luke 18:7).

Finally, we have in the parting words a higher stage: the children have become men. They are now the Master's friends, from whom He has no secrets, and to whom He said, *"All things that I have heard of my Father I have made known unto you"* (John 15:15). In the frequently repeated *"whatsoever ye shall ask,"* He hands them the keys of the kingdom. Now the time has come for the power of prayer in His name to be proved.

The contrast between this final stage and the previous preparatory ones is marked most distinctly in the words: *"Hitherto have ye asked nothing in my name"*; *"At that day ye shall ask in my name."* *"At that day"* means the day of the outpouring of the Holy Spirit. The great work Christ was to do on the cross—the mighty power and the complete victory to be manifested in His resurrection and ascension—would allow the glory of God to come down from heaven as never before, to dwell in men. The Spirit of the glorified Jesus was to come and be the life of His disciples. And one of the signs of that wonderful, new flow of the Spirit was to be a power in prayer that was up to that time unknown. Prayer in the name of Jesus—asking for and obtaining everything—is to be the evidence of the reality of the Spirit's indwelling.

The coming of the Holy Spirit indeed began a new epoch in the prayer world. To understand this, we must remember who He is, what His work is, and why His not being given until Jesus was glorified is significant. It is in the Spirit that God exists, for He is Spirit. It is in the Spirit that the Son was begotten of the Father, because in the fellowship of the Spirit, the Father and the Son are one. The Father's prerogative is eternal, continuous giving to the Son. The Son's right and blessedness is to ask and receive eternally. Through the Spirit, this communion of life and love is maintained. This has been true from all eternity.

It is especially true now, when the Son as Mediator lives to pray. The great work that Jesus began on earth of reconciling God and man in His own body, He carries on in heaven. To accomplish this, He took the conflict between God's righteousness and our sin into His own person. On the cross, He ended the struggle once and for all in His own body. Then He ascended to heaven, where He carries out the deliverance He obtained and manifests His victory in each member of His body. This is why He lives to pray. In His unceasing intercession, He places Himself in living fellowship with the unceasing prayer of His redeemed ones. Or rather, it is His unceasing intercession that shows itself in their prayers, giving them a power they never had before.

He does this through the Holy Spirit. This Spirit of the glorified Jesus was not manifested and could not be until Jesus had been glorified (John 7:39). This gift of the Father was something distinctively new, entirely different from what the Old Testament saints had known. The work that the blood effected in heaven when Christ entered within the veil was totally true and new. The redemption of human nature into fellowship with His resurrection power and His glory was intensely real. The taking up of our humanity through Christ into the life of the triune God was an event of such inconceivable significance that the

Holy Spirit was indeed no longer only what He had been in the Old Testament.

That *"the Holy Ghost was not yet...because that Jesus was not yet glorified"* (John 7:39) was literally true. The Holy Spirit had come from Christ's exalted humanity to testify in our hearts of what Christ had accomplished. Just as Jesus, after having come to earth as a man, returned to heaven with power He didn't have before, so the Holy Spirit came to us with a new life that He hadn't had before. He came to us with that new life—as the Spirit of the glorified Jesus. Under the Old Testament He was invoked as the Spirit of God. At Pentecost He descended as the Spirit of the glorified Jesus, bringing down and communicating to us the full fruit and power of the accomplished redemption.

Christ's continuing intercession maintains the effectiveness and application of His redemption. The Holy Spirit descending from Christ to us draws us up into the great stream of His ascending prayers. The Spirit prays for us without words in the depths of a heart where even thoughts are at times formless. He takes us up into the wonderful flow of the life of the triune God. Through the Spirit, Christ's prayers become ours, and ours are made His. We ask for what we desire, and it is given to us. We then understand from experience, *"Hitherto have ye asked nothing in my name....At that day ye shall ask in my name."*

What we need in order to pray in the name of Christ—to ask that we may receive that our joy may be full—is the baptism of this Holy Spirit. This is more than the Spirit of God under the Old Testament. This is more than the Spirit of conversion and regeneration the disciples had before Pentecost. This is more than the Spirit with a portion of Christ's influence and power. This is the Holy Spirit, the Spirit of the glorified Jesus in His exaltation and power, coming to us as the Spirit of the indwelling Jesus, revealing the Son and the Father within us (John 14:16–23). This Spirit cannot simply be the Spirit of our hours of prayer. It must be the Spirit of our whole lives and walks, glorifying Jesus in us by revealing the completeness of His work and making us wholly one with Him and like Him. Then we can pray in His name, because we are truly one with Him. Then we have that immediate access to the Father of which Jesus said, *"I say not unto you, that I will pray the Father for you"* (John 16:26).

Oh, we need to understand and believe that to be filled with the Spirit of the Glorified One is the one need of God's believing people. Then we will be able, *"with all prayer and supplication* [to be] *praying at all seasons in the Spirit"* (Eph. 6:18 ASV) and *"praying in the Holy Ghost,* [to] *keep* [ourselves] *in the love of God." "At that day ye shall ask in my name."*

Once again, we learn this lesson: what our prayers achieve depends on what we are and what our lives are. Living in the name of Christ is the secret of praying in the name of Christ; living in the Spirit is necessary for praying in the Spirit. Abiding in Christ gives the right and power to ask for what we desire. The extent of our abiding is equivalent to our power in prayer. The Spirit dwelling within us prays, not always in words and thoughts, but in a breathing and a being that is deeper than utterance. (See Rom. 8:26.) There is as much real prayer in us as there is of Christ's Spirit. Let our lives be full of Christ and full of His Spirit, so that the wonderfully unlimited promises to our prayers will no longer appear strange.

> *Hitherto have ye asked nothing in my name: ask, and ye shall receive, that your joy may be full....At that day ye shall ask in my name.... Verily, verily, I say unto you, Whatsoever ye shall ask the Father in my name, he will give it you.*

Lord, teach us to pray.

O my God, in holy awe I bow before You, the Three in One. Again I see how the mystery of prayer is the mystery of the Holy Trinity. I adore the Father who always hears. I adore the Son who lives eternally to pray. And I love the Holy Spirit who comes from the Father and the Son, lifting us up into the fellowship of that blessed, never ceasing asking and receiving. I bow, my God, in adoring worship before the infinite power that, through the Holy Spirit, takes us and our prayers into Your divine life and its fellowship of love.

O my blessed Lord Jesus, teach me to understand this lesson: the indwelling Spirit streaming from You and uniting us to You is the Spirit of prayer. Teach me how, as an empty, wholly consecrated vessel, to yield myself to His being my life. Teach me to honor Him and to trust Him, as a living Person, to lead my life and my prayer. Teach me especially in prayer to wait in holy silence, giving Him time to breathe His unutterable intercession within me. And teach me that through Him it is possible to *"pray without ceasing"* (1 Thess. 5:17) and to pray without failing, because He makes me a partaker of the never ceasing and never failing intercession in which You appear before the Father.

O Lord, fulfill in me Your promise, *"At that day ye shall ask in my name....Verily, verily, I say unto you, Whatsoever ye shall ask the Father in my name, he will give it."* Amen.

Author's Note

Prayer has often been compared to breathing. We have to carry out the comparison fully to see how wonderful the place is which the Holy Spirit occupies. With every breath, we expel impure air that would soon cause our death and inhale fresh air to which we owe our life. In confession we release our sins, and in prayer we release the needs and desires of our hearts. And we inhale the fresh air of the promises, the love, and the life of God in Christ. We do this through the Holy Spirit, who is the breath of our life.

He is also the breath of God. The Father breathes Him into us to unite Himself with our lives. Just as every expiration is followed by the inhaling of the next breath, so God inhales His breath, and the Spirit returns to Him laden with the desires and needs of our hearts.

Thus the Holy Spirit is the breath of the life of God and the breath of the new life in us. As God breathes Him out, we receive Him in answer to prayer; as we breathe Him back again, He rises to God carrying our petitions. It is though the Holy Spirit that the Father and the Son are one, and that the intercession of the Son reaches the Father. He is our Spirit of prayer. True prayer is the living experience of the truth of the Holy Trinity. The Spirit's breathing, the Son's intercession, and the Father's will become one in us.

26

CHRIST, THE INTERCESSOR

But I have prayed for thee, that thy faith fail not.
—Luke 22:32

I say not unto you, that I will pray the Father for you.
—John 16:26

He ever liveth to make intercession for them.
—Hebrews 7:25

All growth in the spiritual life is connected with clearer insight into what Jesus is to us. The more I realize that Christ must be everything to me and in me, that everything in Christ is indeed for me, the more I learn to live the real life of faith. This life dies to self and lives wholly in Christ. The Christian life is no longer a vain struggle to live right, but a resting in Christ to find strength in Him as life. He helps us fight and gain the victory of faith!

This is especially true of the life of prayer. It, too, comes under the law of faith alone and is seen in the light of the fullness and completeness there is in Jesus. The believer understands that prayer is no longer a matter of strain or anxious care, but an experience of what Christ will do for him and in him. It is a participation in the life of Christ, which is the same on earth as in heaven, always ascending to the Father as prayer. So he begins to pray. Such a believer not only trusts the merits of Jesus, or His intercession, by which our unworthy prayers are made acceptable, but also trusts in that near and close union through which He prays in us and we in Him. Having Him within us, we abide in Him and He in us through the Holy Spirit perfecting our union with Him, so that we ourselves can come directly to the Father in His name.

The whole of salvation is Christ Himself. He has given Himself to us. He Himself lives in us. Because He prays, we pray, too. Just like the disciples, when they saw Jesus praying and asked Him to make them partakers of what He knew of prayer, we know that He makes us participate with Himself in the life of prayer. He is now our Intercessor on the throne.

This comes out quite clearly in the last night of His life. In His High Priestly Prayer (see John 17), He shows us how and what He has to pray to the Father and what He will pray when He ascends to heaven. In His parting address he had repeatedly connected His going to the Father with their new life of prayer. The two would be ultimately connected. His entrance on the work of His eternal intercession would be the commencement and the power of their new prayer life in His name. It is the sight of Jesus in His intercession that gives us power to pray in His name. All right and power of prayer is Christ's; He makes us share in His intercession.

To understand this, think first of His intercession. He lives to intercede. The work of Christ on earth as Priest was just a beginning. As Aaron, who offered the blood sacrifice, Jesus shed His blood. As Melchizedek, He now lives within the veil to continue His work for the power of the eternal life.

"It is Christ that died, yea rather...who is even at the right hand of God, who also maketh intercession for us" (Rom. 8:34). That intercession is an intense reality—a work that is absolutely necessary—and without which the continued application of redemption cannot take place. Through the incarnation and resurrection of Jesus, the wondrous reconciliation took place, and man became partaker of the divine life and blessedness.

But the real, personal use of this reconciliation cannot take place without the unceasing exercise of His divine power by the Head in heaven. In all conversion and sanctification, in every victory over sin and the world, there is a real exercise of Christ's power. This exercise takes place only through His prayer: He asks of the Father and receives from the Father. *"He is able also to save them to the uttermost...[because] he ever liveth to make intercession"* (Heb. 7:25). He receives every need of His people in intercession, extending to them what the Godhead has to give. His mediation on the throne is as real and indispensable as it was on the cross. Nothing takes place without Christ's intercession. It engages all His time and all His power. It is His unceasing occupation at the right hand of the Father.

We participate, not only in the benefits of His work, but in the work itself. This is because we are His body. The Head and the members are one: *"The head [cannot say] to the feet, I have no need of you"* (1 Cor. 12:21). We share with Jesus everything He is and has. *"The glory which thou gavest me I have given them"* (John 17:22). We are partakers of His life, His righteousness, and His work. We share His intercession, too. He cannot do it without us.

"Christ...is our life" (Col. 3:4); *"Yet not I, but Christ liveth in me"* (Gal. 2:20). The life in Him and in us is identical; it is one and the same. His life in heaven is a life of continuous prayer. When it descends and takes possession of us, it does not lose its character. It becomes a life of continuous prayer in us, too. It is a life that without ceasing asks and receives from God.

This is not as if there were two separate currents of prayer rising upward—one from Him and one from His people. A substantial life union is also a prayer union. What He prays passes though us, and what we pray passes through Him. He is the angel with the golden censer. *"There was given unto him much incense"*—the secret of acceptable prayer—*"that he should offer it with the prayers of all saints upon the golden altar"* (Rev. 8:3). We live and abide in Him, the Interceding One.

The Only Begotten is the only One who has the right to pray. To Him alone it was said, *"Ask, and it shall be given you"* (Matt. 7:7). Just as the fullness for all things dwells in Him, a true fullness in prayer dwells in Him, too. He alone has the power of prayer. Growth of the spiritual life consists of a deeper belief that all treasures are in Him, and that we, too, are in Him. We receive each moment what we possess in Him. Prayer life is the same. Our faith in the intercession of Jesus must not only be in His praying for us when we do not or cannot pray. As the Author of our lives and our faith, He draws us to pray in unison with Him. Our prayers must be a work of faith in the sense that as we know that Jesus communicates His whole life in us, He also breathes our praying into us.

To many a believer, it was a new epoch in his spiritual life when it was revealed to him how truly and entirely Christ was his life, standing responsible for his remaining faithful and obedient. It was then that he really began to live a life of faith. No less blessed will be the discovery that Christ is responsible for our prayer lives, too. As the center and embodiment of all prayer, it is communicated by Him through the Holy Spirit to His people.

"He ever liveth to make intercession" as the Head of the Body. He is the Leader in that new and living way that He has opened up as the Author and the Perfecter of our faith (Heb. 12:2). He provides everything for the life of His redeemed ones by giving His own life in them. He cares for their lives of prayer by taking them up into His heavenly prayer life, giving and maintaining His prayer life within them. *"I have prayed for thee,"* not to render thy faith needless, but *"that thy faith fail not."* Our faith and prayer of faith is rooted in His. If we pray with and in the eternal Intercessor,

abiding in Him, then we can *"ask what* [we] *will, and it shall be done unto* [us]" (John 15:7).

The thought of our fellowship in the intercession of Jesus reminds us of what He has taught us more than once before. All these wonderful prayer promises have the glory of God, in the manifestation of His kingdom and the salvation of sinners, as their aim. As long as we pray chiefly for ourselves, the promises of the last night must remain a sealed book to us. The promises are given to the fruit-bearing branches of the Vine, to disciples sent into the world to live for perishing men as the Father sent Him, to His faithful servants and intimate friends who take up the work He leaves behind. Like their Lord, they have become seed corn, losing their lives to multiply them. (See John 12:24.)

Let us each find out what our work is and which souls are entrusted to our special prayers. Let us make our intercession for them our lives of fellowship with God. We will not only discover the truth to the promises of power in prayer. We will begin to realize how our abiding in Christ and His abiding in us makes us share in His own joy of blessing and saving men.

Oh, most wonderful intercession of our Blessed Lord Jesus! We not only owe everything to that intercession, but in it we are taken up as active partners and fellow workers! Now we understand what it is to pray in the name of Jesus, and why it has such power. To pray in His name, in His Spirit, in Himself, and in perfect union with Him is the active and effective intercession of Christ Jesus. When will we ever be wholly taken up into it?

Lord, teach us to pray!

Blessed Lord, in lowly adoration I again bow before You. All of Your work of redemption has now passed into prayer. You are completely occupied with praying, to maintain and dispense what You purchased with Your blood. You live to pray. And because we abide in You, we have direct access to the Father. Our lives can be lives of unceasing prayer, and the answers to our prayers are certain.

Blessed Lord, You have invited Your people to be Your fellow workers in a life of prayer. You have united Yourself with Your people. As Your Body, they share the ministry of intercession with You. Only through this ministry can the world be filled with the fruit of Your redemption and the glory of the Father. With more liberty than ever I come to You, my Lord, and plead with You to teach me to pray. Your life is prayer; Your life is mine. Lord, teach me to pray in You and like You.

And, O my Lord, let me know, just as You promised Your disciples, that You are in the Father, I am in You, and You are in me. Let the uniting power of the Holy Spirit make my whole life an abiding in You and in Your intercession. May my prayer be its echo, so that the Father hears me in You and You in me. Lord Jesus, in everything, let Your mind be in me! In everything, let my life be in You! In this way, I will be prepared to be the channel through which Your intercession pours its blessing on the world. Amen.

27

CHRIST,
THE HIGH PRIEST

*Father, I will that they also, whom thou hast given me,
be with me where I am.*
—John 17:24

In His parting address, Jesus gives His disciples the full revelation of what the new life was to be when the kingdom of God had come in power. They were to find their calling and their blessedness in the indwelling of the Holy Spirit, in union with Jesus, the Heavenly Vine, and in their witnessing and suffering for Him. As He described their future life, the Lord had repeatedly given the most unlimited promises as to the power their prayers might have.

Now in closing, He Himself proceeds to pray. To let His disciples have the joy of knowing what His intercession for them in heaven as their High Priest will be, He gives them this precious legacy of His prayer to the Father. He does this because, as priests, they are to share in His work of intercession, and they must know how to perform this holy work.

In the teaching of our Lord on this last night, found in John 17, we recognize that these astonishing prayer promises have not been given for our benefit, but in the interest of the Lord and His kingdom. Only from the Lord Himself can we learn what prayer in His name is to be and what it can obtain. To pray in His name is to pray in perfect unity with Himself. The High Priestly Prayer will teach everyone that prayer in the name of Jesus may ask for and expect everything. This prayer is ordinarily divided into three parts. Our Lord first prayed for Himself (see verses 1–5), then for His disciples (see verses 6–19), and last for all the believing people of all ages (see verses 20–26). The follower of Jesus who gives himself to the work of intercession, and who would like to know how much of a blessing he can pray down upon his circle in the name of Jesus, should in all humility let himself be led of the Spirit to study this wonderful prayer as one of the most important lessons of the school of prayer.

First of all, Jesus prayed for Himself, for His being glorified, so that He may glorify the Father. "Father! Glorify Your Son. And now, Father, glorify Me." (See verse 1.) He presented reasons for His praying this way. A holy covenant was concluded between the Father and the Son in heaven. The Father promised Him power over all flesh as the reward for His work. Now Jesus had done the work, He had glorified the Father, and His one purpose was to further glorify Him. With the utmost boldness He asked the Father to glorify Him, so that He would now be and do for His people everything He has undertaken.

Disciple of Jesus, here you have the first lesson in your work of priestly intercession, to be learned from the example of your Great High Priest. To pray in the name of Jesus is to pray in unity and in sympathy with Him. The Son began His prayer by clarifying His relationship to the Father, speaking of His work and obedience and His desire to see the Father glorified.

You should pray like this. Draw near to the Father in Christ. Plead His finished work. Say that you are one with it, that you trust it, and live in it. Say that you, too, have given yourself to finish the work the Father has given you to do and to live alone for His glory. Then ask confidently that the Son may be glorified in you.

This is praying in the name, in the very words, and in the Spirit of Jesus, in union with Jesus Himself. Such prayer has power. If with Jesus you glorify the Father, the Father will glorify Jesus by doing what you ask in His name. It is only when your own personal relationship, like Christ's, is clear with God—when you are glorifying Him and seeking everything for His glory—that, like Christ, you will have power to intercede for those around you.

Our Lord next prayed for the circle of His disciples. He spoke of them as those whom the Father has given Him. Their distinguishing characteristic was that they have received Christ's Word. He said He was now sending them into the world in His place, just as the Father had sent Him. He asked two things for them: that the Father would keep them from the Evil One and that He would sanctify them through His Word.

Just like the Lord, each believing intercessor has his own immediate circle for whom he prays first.

Parents have their children, teachers their pupils, pastors their flocks, and all believers have those whose care lies on their hearts. It is of great consequence that intercession should be personal, pointed, and definite. Our first prayer must always be that they receive the Word.

But this prayer will not work unless we say to the Lord, "I have given them Your Word." This gives us liberty and power in intercession for souls. Don't just pray for them, but speak to them. When they have received the Word, pray for their being kept from the Evil One and for their being sanctified through that Word. Instead of being hopeless or judging, or giving up on those who fall, let us pray, "Father, keep them in Your name! Sanctify them through Your truth!" Prayer in the name of Jesus accomplishes much: *"What ye will…shall be done unto you"* (John 15:7).

Next our Lord prayed for a still wider circle. *"Neither pray I for these alone, but for them also which shall believe on me through their word"* (John 17:20). His priestly heart enlarged itself to embrace all places and all time. He prayed that everyone who belongs to Him may everywhere be one, as God's proof to the world of the divinity of His mission. He then prayed that they may always be with Him in His glory. Until then, He asked, *"That the love wherewith thou last loved me may be in them, and I in them"* (v. 26).

The disciple of Jesus who has first proved the power of prayer in his own circle cannot confine himself within its limits. He then prayed for the universal church and its different branches. He prayed especially for the unity of the Spirit and of love. He prayed for its being one in Christ, as a witness to the world that Christ, who has made love triumph over selfishness and separation, is indeed the Son of God sent from heaven. Every believer ought to pray that the unity of the Church, not in external organizations, but in spirit and in truth, is manifested.

Jesus said, *"Father, I will"* or "I desire." Based on His right as Son, the Father's promise to Him, and His finished work, He could do so. The Father had said to Him, *"Ask of me, and I shall give thee"* (Ps. 2:8). He simply availed Himself of the Father's promise. Jesus has given us a similar promise: *"what ye will…shall be done unto you"* (John 15:7). He asks me in His name to say what I will, what I desire. Abiding in Him, in a living union with Him in which man is nothing and Christ is everything, the believer has the liberty to take up that word of his High Priest. In answer to the question, *"What wilt thou?"* (Matt. 20:21; Mark 10:51; Luke 18:41) to say, *"'Father, I will'* all that You have promised."

This is nothing but true faith. It honors God that I have such confidence in saying that what I desire is indeed acceptable to Him. At first sight, our hearts shrink from the expression. We feel neither the liberty nor the power to speak in such a manner. But grace will most assuredly be given to each one who loses his will in his Lord's. Whoever gives up his will entirely will find it again renewed and strengthened with a divine strength.

"Father, I will." This is the keynote of the everlasting, ever active, all-powerful intercession of our Lord in heaven. It is only in union with Him that our prayers are effective and accomplish much. If we abide in Him, living, walking, and doing all things in His name; if we take each separate petition, tested and touched by His Word and Spirit, and cast it into the mighty stream of intercession that goes up from Him to be presented before the Father; then we will have the full confidence that we receive what we ask for. The cry *"Father, I will"* will be breathed into us by the Spirit Himself. We will lose ourselves in Him and become nothing, finding that in our impotence we have power to succeed.

Disciples of Jesus, you are called to be like your Lord in His priestly intercession! When will we awaken to the glory of our destiny to pray to God for perishing men and be answered? When will we shake off the sloth that clothes itself in the pretense of humility and yield ourselves wholly to God's Spirit that He might fill our wills with light and power to know, to take, and to possess everything that our God is waiting to give?

Lord, teach us to pray.

O my Blessed High Priest, who am I that You should invite me to share Your power of intercession? And why, O my Lord, am I so slow of heart to understand, believe, and exercise this wonderful privilege to which You have redeemed Your people? O Lord, give me Your grace that my life's work may become praying without ceasing, to draw down the blessing of heaven on all my surrroundings on earth.

Blessed Lord, I come now to accept my calling, for which I will give up everything and follow You. Into Your hands I will believingly yield my whole being. Form, train, and inspire me to be one of Your prayer force, those who watch and strive in prayer, who have power and victory. Take possession of my heart, and fill it with the desire to glorify God in the gathering, sanctification, and union of those whom the Father has given You. Take my mind, and give me wisdom to know when prayer can bring a blessing. Take me wholly and prepare me as You would a priest to stand always before God and to bless His name.

Blessed Lord, now and through all my spiritual life, let me want everything for You and nothing for myself. Let it be my experience that the person who has and asks for nothing for himself receives everything, including the wonderful grace of sharing Your everlasting ministry of intercession. Amen.

28

CHRIST, THE SACRIFICE

And he said, Abba, Father, all things are possible unto thee; take away this cup from me: nevertheless not what I will, but what thou wilt.
—Mark 14:36

W hat a contrast within the space of a few hours! What a transition from the quiet elevation of "[lifting] *up his eyes to heaven, and* [saying]...*Father, I will*" (John 17:1, 24) to falling on the ground and crying in agony, "My Father! *'not what I will.'*" In the one we see the High Priest within the veil in His all-powerful intercession; in the other, the sacrifice on the altar opening the way through the rent veil. The High Priestly *"Father, I will"* (v. 24) precedes the sacrificial *"Father...not what I will,"* but this was only to show what the intercession would be once the sacrifice was brought. The prayer before the throne, *"Father, I will,"* had its origin and its power in the prayer at the altar, *"Father...not what I will."* From the entire surrender of His will in Gethsemane, the High Priest on the throne has the power to ask what He will and the right to make His people share that power, asking what they will.

For everyone who wants to learn to pray in the school of Jesus, this Gethsemane lesson is one of the most sacred and precious. To a superficial scholar, it may appear to take away the courage to pray in faith. If even the earnest supplication of the Son was not heard, if even He had to say *"Not what I will,"* how much more we must need to say it! Thus it appears impossible that the promises that the Lord had given only a few hours previously, *"Whatsoever ye shall ask"* (John 14:13) and *"What ye will"* (John 15:7), could have been meant literally.

A deeper insight into the meaning of Gethsemane would teach us the sure way to the assurance of an answer to our prayers. Gaze in reverent and adoring wonder on this great sight: God's Son praying through His tears and not obtaining what He asks. He Himself is our Teacher and will open up to us the mystery of His holy sacrifice, as revealed in this wondrous prayer.

To understand the prayer, let us note the infinite difference between what our Lord prayed earlier as royal High Priest and what He here prayed in His weakness. There He prayed to glorify the Father and to glorify Himself and His people as the fulfillment of distinct promises that had been given to Him. He asked what He knew would be according to the Word and the will of the Father. He could boldly say, *"Father, I will"* (John 17:24).

Here, He prayed for something in regard to which the Father's will is not yet clear to Him. As far as He knew, it was the Father's will that He should drink the cup. He had told His disciples of the cup He must drink. A little later He would again say, *"The cup which my Father hath given me, shall I not drink it?"* (John 18:11). It was for this He had come to this earth. But in the unutterable agony of soul that gripped Him as the power of darkness overcame Him, He began to taste the first drops of death—the wrath of God against sin. His human nature, as it shuddered in the presence of the awful reality of being made a curse, gave utterance in this cry of anguish. Its desire was that, if God's purpose could be accomplished without it, He might be spared the awful cup: *"Let this cup pass from me"* (Matt. 26:39). That desire was the evidence of the intense reality of His humanity.

The *"not as I will"* (v. 39) kept that desire from being sinful. He pleadingly cries, *"All things are possible unto thee,"* and returns again to still more earnest prayer that the cup may be removed. *"Not what I will,"* repeated three times, constitutes the very essence and worth of His sacrifice. He had asked for something of which He could not say, "I know it is Your will." He had pleaded God's power and love and had then withdrawn his plea in His final, *"Thy will be done"* (v. 42). The prayer that the cup should pass away could not be answered. The prayer of submission that God's will be done was heard and gloriously answered in His victory first over the fear, and then over the power of death.

In this denial of His will, this complete surrender of His will to the will of the Father, Christ's obedience reached its highest perfection. From the sacrifice of the will in Gethsemane, the sacrifice of the life on Calvary derives its value. It is here, as Scripture says, that He learned obedience and became the Author of everlasting salvation to everyone who obeys Him. Because in that prayer He *"became obedient unto death, even the death of the cross"* (Phil. 2:8), God exalted Him highly and gave Him the power to ask what He will (Phil. 2:8–9). It was in that *"Father...not what I will,"* that He obtained the power for the *"Father, I will"* (John 17:24). By Christ's submittal in Gethsemane, He secured for His people the right to say to them, *"Ask what ye will"* (John 15:7).

Let us look at the deep mysteries that Gethsemane offers. First, the Father offers His Well-Beloved the cup of wrath. Second, the Son, who is always so obedient, shrinks back and implores that He may not have to drink it. Third, the Father does not grant the Son His request, but still gives the cup. And last, the Son yields His will, is content that His will is not done, and goes out to Calvary to drink the cup. O Gethsemane! In you I see how my Lord could give me such unlimited assurance of an answer to my prayers. He won it for me by His consent to have His petition unanswered.

This is in harmony with the whole scheme of redemption. Our Lord always wins for us the opposite of what He suffered. He was bound so that we could go free. He was made sin so that we could become the righteousness of God. (See 2 Cor. 5:21.) He died so that we could live. He bore God's curse so that God's blessing would be ours. He endured God's not answering His prayer, so that our prayers could find an answer. He said, *"Not what I will,"* so that He could say to us, *"If ye abide in me…ask what ye will, and it shall be done unto you"* (John 15:7).

"If ye abide in me": here in Gethsemane the word acquired new force and depth. Christ is our Head, who stands in our place and bears what we would otherwise have had to bear forever. We deserved that God should turn a deaf ear to us and never listen to our cries. Christ came and suffered for us. He suffered what we had merited. For our sins, He suffered beneath the burden of that unanswered prayer. But now His suffering succeeds for me. What He has borne is taken away from me. His merit has won for me the answer to every prayer, if I abide in Him.

Yes, in Him, as He bows there in Gethsemane, I must abide. As my Head, He not only once suffered for me, but He always lives in me, breathing and working His own nature in me. The Spirit through which He offered Himself to God is the Spirit that dwells in me, too. He makes me a partaker of the very same obedience and the sacrifice of the will to God. That Spirit teaches me to yield my will entirely to the will of the Father, to give it up even unto death. He teaches me to distrust whatever is of my own mind, thought, and will, even though it may not be directly sinful. He opens my ear to wait in great gentleness and teachableness of soul for what the Father day by day has to speak and to teach. He shows me how union with God's will—and the love of it—is union with God Himself. Entire surrender to God's will is the Father's claim, the Son's example, and the true blessedness of the soul.

The Spirit leads my will into the fellowship of Christ's death and resurrection. My will dies in Him and in Him is made alive again. He breathes into it a holy insight into God's perfect will, a holy joy in yielding itself to be an instrument of that will, and a holy liberty and power to lay hold of God's will to answer prayer. With my whole will, I learn to live for the interests of God and His kingdom and to exercise the power of that will—crucified but risen again—in nature and in prayer, on earth and in heaven, with men and with God.

The more deeply I enter into the *"Father...not what I will"* of Gethsemane, and into Him who said it, the fuller is my spiritual access to the power of His *"Father, I will"* (John 17:24). The soul experiences that the will has become nothing in order that God's will may be everything. It is now inspired with a divine strength to really will what God wills and to claim what has been promised to it in the name of Christ.

Listen to Christ in Gethsemane as He calls, *"If ye abide in me...ye shall ask what ye will, and it shall be done unto you"* (John 15:7). Be of one mind and spirit with Him in His giving up everything to God's will; live like Him in obedience and surrender to the Father. This is abiding in Him— the secret of power in prayer.

Lord, teach us to pray

Blessed Lord Jesus, Gethsemane was the school where You learned to pray and to obey. It is still Your school, where You lead all Your disciples who wish to learn to obey and to pray just like You. Lord, teach me there to pray in the faith that You have atoned for and conquered our self-will and can indeed give us grace to pray like you.

O Lamb of God, I want to follow You to Gethsemane! There I want to become one with You and abide in You, as You to the very death yield Your will to the Father. With You, through You, and in You, I yield my will in absolute and entire surrender to the will of the Father. Conscious of my own weakness and the secret power with which self-will would assert itself and again take its place on the throne, I claim in faith the power of Your victory. You have triumphed over it and delivered me from it. In Your death, I will daily live. In Your life, I will daily die. Abiding in You, may my will, through the power of Your eternal Spirit, become a finely tuned instrument that yields to every touch of the will of my God. With my whole soul, I say with You and in You. *"Father…not as I will, but as thou wilt"* (Matt. 26:39).

Blessed Lord, open my heart, and the hearts of all Your people, to fully take in the glory of the truth: that a will given up to God is a will God accepts for use in His service, to desire, determine, and will what is according to God's will. Let mine be a will that, by the power of the Holy Spirit, exercises its royal prerogative in prayer. Let it loose and bind in heaven and on earth, asking whatever it chooses, and saying it will be done. Amen. O Lord Jesus, teach me to pray.

29

OUR BOLDNESS
IN PRAYER

And this is the confidence that we have in him, that,
if we ask any thing according to his will, he heareth us:
and if we know that he hear us, whatsoever we ask,
we know that we have the petitions that we desired of him.
—1 John 5:14–15

One of the greatest hindrances to believing prayer is undoubtedly this: many don't know if what they ask is according to the will of God. As long as they are in doubt on this point, they cannot have the boldness to ask in the assurance that they will certainly receive. They soon begin to think that once they have made known their requests and receive no answer, it is best to leave it to God to do "*according to his good pleasure*" (Eph. 1:9). The words of John, "*If we ask anything according to his will, he heareth us,*" as they understand them, make certainty as to an answer to prayer impossible, because they cannot be sure of what the will of God really may be. They think of God's will as His hidden counsel: how can man fathom the purpose of a God who is wise in all things?

This is the very opposite of John's purpose in writing this. He wanted to stir boldness and confidence in us, until we had the full assurance of faith in prayer. He said that we should have the boldness to say to the Father that we know we are asking according to His will, and we know that He hears us. With such boldness, He will hear us no matter what we ask for, as long as it is according to His will. In faith, we should know that we have the answer. And even as we are praying, we should be able to receive what we have asked.

John supposed that when we pray, we first find out if our prayers are according to the will of God. They may be according to God's will, and yet not be answered at once, or without the persevering prayer of faith. It is to give us courage to persevere and to be strong in faith that He tells us we can have boldness or confidence in prayer, because if we ask anything according to His will, He hears us. It is evident that if we are uncertain whether our petitions are according to His will, we cannot have the comfort of His promise, "*We know that we have the petitions that we desired of him.*"

But this is just the difficulty. More than one believer says, "I do not know if what I desire is according to the will of God. God's will is the purpose of His infinite wisdom. It is impossible for me to know whether He considers something else better for me than what I desire. He may have reasons for withholding what I asked." Everyone should understand that with such thoughts the prayer of faith becomes an impossibility. There may still be a prayer of submission or of trust in God's wisdom. But there cannot be a prayer of faith.

The great mistake here is that God's children do not really believe that it is possible to know God's will. Or if they believe this, they do not take the time and trouble to find it out. What we need is to see clearly how the Father leads His waiting, teachable child to know that his petition is according to His will. Through God's holy Word—taken up and kept in the heart, the life, and the will—and through God's Holy Spirit—accepted in His dwelling and leading—we will learn to know that our petitions are according to His will.

First, let us consider the Word. There is a secret will of God, with which we often fear that our prayers may be at variance. But this is not the will of God that we should be concerned with in our prayers. His will as revealed in His Word should be our concern. Our notions of a secret will that makes decrees, rendering the answers to our prayers impossible, are erroneous. Childlike faith in what He is willing to do for His children simply accepts the Father's assurance that it is His will to hear prayer and to do what faith in His Word desires and accepts. In the Word, the Father has revealed in general promises the great principles of His will with His people. The child has to take the promise and apply it to the special circumstances in His life to which it has reference. Whatever he asks within the limits of that revealed will, he may confidently expect, knowing it to be according to the will of God.

In His Word, God has given us the revelation of His will. He shows us His plans for us, His people, and for the world. With the most precious promises of grace and power, He carries out these plans through His people. As faith becomes strong and bold enough to claim the fulfillment of the general promise in the special case, we may have the assurance that our prayers are heard, because they are according to God's will. Take the words of John in the verse following our text as an illustration: "If any man see his brother sin a sin which is not unto death, he shall ask, and [God] shall give him life" (1 John 5:16). This is the general promise. The believer who pleads on the grounds of this promise, prays according to the will of God, and John wants him to feel the boldness to know that he has the petition for which he asks.

God's will is something spiritual and must be spiritually discerned. It is not a matter of logic that we can argue about. Not every Christian has the same gift or calling. While the general will revealed in the promises is the same for everyone, each person has a specific, individual role to fulfill in God's purpose. The wisdom of the saints is in knowing this specific will of God according to the measure of grace given us, and to ask in prayer just what God has prepared and made possible for each. The Holy Spirit dwells in us to communicate this wisdom. The personal application of the general promises of the Word to our specific personal needs is given to us by the leading of the Holy Spirit.

It is this union of the teaching of the Word and the Spirit that many do not understand. This causes a twofold difficulty in knowing what God's will may be. Some seek the will of God in an inner feeling or conviction and expect the Spirit to lead them without the Word. Others seek it in the Word, without the living leading of the Holy Spirit. The two must be united. Only in the Word and in the Spirit can we know the will of God and learn to pray according to it. In the heart, the Word and Spirit must meet. Only by indwelling can we experience their teaching. The Word must abide in us; our heart and life must be under its influence daily.

The quickening of the Word by the Spirit comes from within, not from without. Only he who yields himself entirely, in his whole life, to the supremacy of the Word and the will of God can expect to discern what that Word and will permit him to ask boldly in specific cases. The same is true of the Spirit. If I desire His leading in prayer to assure me what God's will is, my whole life must be yielded to that leading. Only in this way can mind and heart become spiritual and capable of knowing God's holy will. He who through Word and Spirit lives in the will of God by doing it will know to pray according to that will in the confidence that He hears.

If Christians could only see what incalculable harm they do themselves by thinking that because their prayers are possibly not according to God's will, they must be content without answers. God's Word tells us that the great reason for unanswered prayers is that we do not pray right: "*Ye ask and receive not, because ye ask amiss*" (James 4:3). In not granting an answer, the Father tells us that there is something wrong in our praying. He wants us to discover it and confess it, and so to teach us true believing and effective prayer. He can only attain this object when He brings us to the place where we see that we are to blame for the withholding of the answer. Our aims, our faith, or our lives are not what they should be. God is frustrated as long as we are content to say: "Perhaps it is because my prayer is not according to His will that He does not hear me."

Oh, let us no longer throw the blame for our unanswered prayers on the secret will of God, but on our own faulty praying! Let that word, "*Ye... receive not, because ye ask amiss,*" be a lantern of the Lord, searching heart and life to prove that we are indeed those to whom Christ gave His promises of certain answers! Let us believe that we can know if our prayers are according to God's will! Let us yield our hearts to the indwelling of the Word of the Father, to have Christ's Word abiding in us. We should live day by day with the anointing that teaches all things. If we yield ourselves unreservedly to the Holy Spirit as He teaches us to abide in Christ and to dwell in the Father's presence, we will soon understand how the Father's love longs for the child to know His will. In the confidence that His will includes everything His power and love have promised to do, we should know, too, that He hears all of our prayers. "*This is the confidence that we have...that, if we ask any thing according to his will, he heareth us.*"

Lord, teach us to pray.

Blessed Master, with my whole heart I thank You for the blessed lesson that the path to a life full of answers to prayer is through the will of God. Lord, teach me to know this blessed will by living it, loving it, and always doing it. In this way, I will learn to offer prayers according to that will. In their harmony with God's blessed will, I will find boldness in prayer and confidence in accepting the answer.

Father, it is Your will that Your child should enjoy Your presence and blessing. It is Your will that everything in Your child's life should be in accordance with Your will and that the Holy Spirit should work this in him. It is Your will that Your child should live in the daily experience of distinct answers to prayer, in order to enjoy living and direct fellowship with You. It is Your will that Your name should be glorified in and through

Your children, and that it will be in those who trust You. O my Father, let this will of Yours be my confidence in everything I ask.

Blessed Savior, teach me to believe in the glory of this will. That will is the eternal love that, with divine power, works out its purpose in each human will that yields itself to it. Lord, teach me this! You can make me see how every promise and every command of the Word is indeed the will of God, and that its fulfillment is given to me by God Himself. Let His will become the sure rock on which my prayer and my assurance of an answer always rest. Amen.

Author's Note

There is often great confusion as to the will of God. People think that what God wills must inevitably take place. This is by no means the case. God wills a great deal of blessings to His people that never come to them. He wills it most earnestly, but they do not will it. Hence, it cannot come to them. This is the great mystery of man's creation with a free will and the renewal of his will in redemption. God has made the execution of His will dependent on the will of man. God's will as revealed in His promises will be fulfilled as much as our faith allows. Prayer is the power by which something comes to pass that otherwise would not have taken place. And faith is the power that determines how much of God's will is done in us. Once God reveals to a soul what He is willing to do for it, the responsibility for the execution of that will rests with us.

Some are afraid that this is putting too much power into the hands of man. But all power is put into the hands of man through Christ Jesus. (See Luke 10:19.) The key to all prayer and all power is His. When we learn to understand that He is just as much one with us as with the Father, we see how natural, right, and safe it is that such power is given. Christ the Son has the right to ask whatever He chooses. Through our abiding in Him and His abiding in us, His Spirit breathes in us what He wants to ask and obtain through us. We pray in His name. The prayers are as much ours as they are His.

Others fear that to believe that prayer has such power limits the liberty and the love of God. Oh, if we only knew how we are limiting His liberty and His love by not allowing Him to act in the only way in which He chooses to act, now that He has taken us up into fellowship with Himself! Our prayers are like pipes, through which water is carried from a large mountain stream to a town some distance away. Such water pipes don't make the water willing to flow down from the hills, nor do they give it its power of blessing and refreshment. This is its very nature. All they do is to determine its direction.

In the same way, the very nature of God is to love and to bless. His love longs to come down to us with its quickening and refreshing streams. But He has left it to prayer to say where the blessing is channeled. He has committed it to His believing people to bring the living water to the desert places. The will of God to bless is dependent on the will of man to say where the blessing goes.

30

THE MINISTRY
OF INTERCESSION

An holy priesthood, to offer up spiritual sacrifices,
acceptable to God by Jesus Christ.
—1 Peter 2:5

Ye shall be named the Priests of the LORD.
—Isaiah 61:6

T he spirit of the Lord GOD is upon me; because the LORD hath *anointed me"* (Isa. 61:1); these are the words of Jesus. As the fruit of His work, all redeemed ones are priests—fellow partakers with Him of His anointing with the Spirit as High Priest. This anointing is *"like the precious ointment...upon the beard, even Aaron's beard: that went down to the skirts of his garments"* (Ps. 133:2). Like every son of Aaron, every member of Jesus' body has a right to the priesthood. But not everyone exercises it. Many are still entirely ignorant of it. And yet it is the highest privilege of a child of God, the mark of greatest nearness and likeness to Him who *"ever liveth to [pray]"* (Heb. 7:25). Do you doubt this? Think of what constitutes priesthood.

There is, first, the work of the priesthood. This has two sides: one Godward, the other manward. *"Every high priest...is ordained for men in things pertaining to God"* (Heb. 5:1), or as it is said by Moses, *"The LORD separated the tribe of Levi...to stand before the LORD to minister unto him, and to bless in his name"* (Deut. 10:8). (See also Deuteronomy 21:5 and 33:10; Malachi 2:6.) On the one hand, the priest had the power to draw nigh to God, to dwell with Him in His house, and to present Him with the blood of the sacrifice or the burning incense. This work he did not do, however, on his own behalf, but for the sake of the people whose representative he was. This is the other side of his work. He received people's sacrifices, presented them to God, and then came out to bless in His name, giving the assurance of His favor and teaching them His law.

A priest is thus a man who does not live for himself. He lives with God and for God. His work as God's servant is to care for His house, His honor, and His worship, making known to men His love and His will. He lives with men and for men. (See Heb. 5:2.) His work is to find out their sins and needs, bring these before God, offer sacrifice and incense in their names, obtain forgiveness and blessing for them, and then to come out and bless them in His name.

This is the high calling of every believer. They have been redeemed with the one purpose of being God's priests in the midst of the perishing millions around them. In conformity to Jesus, the Great High Priest, they are to be the ministers and stewards of the grace of God.

Secondly, there is the walk of the priesthood, in harmony with its work. As God is holy, so the priest was to be especially holy. This means not only separated from everything unclean, but holy unto God—being set apart and given up to God for His use. Separation from the world and being given up to God were indicated in many ways.

It was seen in the clothing. The holy garments, made according to God's own orders, marked the priests as His. (See Exodus 28.) It was seen in the command as to their special purity and freedom from all contact with death and defilement. Much that was allowed to an ordinary Israelite was forbidden to them. Priests could have no bodily defects or blemishes. Bodily perfection was to be the model of wholeness and holiness in God's service. The priestly tribes were to have no inheritance with the other tribes. God was to be their inheritance. Their lives were to be ones of faith—set apart unto God—they were to live on Him as well as for Him. All this is symbolic of what the character of the New Testament priest is to be. Our priestly power with God depends on our personal life and walk. Jesus must be able to say of our walk on earth, "[They] *have not defiled their garments*" (Rev. 3:4).

In our separation from the world, we must prove that our desire to be holy to the Lord is wholehearted and entire. The bodily perfection of the priest must have its counterpart in our also being without spot or blemish (Eph. 5:27; 1 Pet. 1:19). We must be *"the man of God…perfect, thoroughly furnished unto all good works"* (2 Tim. 3:17). *"Perfect and entire, wanting nothing"* (James 1:4). (See also Leviticus 21:17-21 and Ephesians 5:27.) Above all, we must consent to give up all inheritance on earth. We must forsake everything and—like Christ—have need only of God and keep everything for Him alone. This marks the true priest, the man who only lives for God and his fellowmen.

Thirdly, there is the way to the priesthood. God had chosen all of Aaron's sons to be priests. Each of them was a priest by birth. Yet he could not begin his work without a special act of ordinance—his consecration. Every child of God is a priest by right of his birth—his blood relationship to the Great High Priest. But he can exercise his power only as he accepts and realizes his consecration.

With Aaron and his sons it took place in the following way, according to Exodus 29: after being washed and clothed, they were anointed with the holy oil. Sacrifices were then offered, and the right ear, the right hand, and the right foot were touched with the blood. They and their garments were then sprinkled with the blood and the oil together. In the same way, as the blood and the Spirit work more fully in the child of God, the power of the holy priesthood will also work in him. The blood will take away all sense of unworthiness; the Spirit will take away all sense of unfitness.

Notice what was new in the application of the blood to the priest. If he had ever as a penitent sought forgiveness by bringing a sacrifice for his sin, the blood was sprinkled on the altar, but not on his person. But now, for priestly consecration, there was to be closer contact with the blood. The ear, hand, and foot were by a special act brought under its power, and the whole being sanctified for God. When the believer is led to seek full priestly access to God, he feels the need of a fuller and more enduring experience of the power of the blood. Where he had previously been content to have the blood sprinkled only on the mercy seat as what he needed for pardon, he now needs a more personal sprinkling and cleansing of his heart from an evil conscience. Through this, he has *"no more conscience of sins"* (Heb. 10:2); he is cleansed from all sin. As he gets to enjoy this, his consciousness is awakened to his wonderful right of intimate access to God and of the full assurance that his intercessions are acceptable.

As the blood gives the right, the Spirit gives the power for believing intercession. He breathes into us the priestly spirit and a burning love for God's honor and the saving of souls. He makes us one with Jesus to the extent that prayer in His name is a reality. The more the Christian is truly filled with the Spirit of Christ, the more spontaneous will be his giving himself up to the life of priestly intercession.

Beloved fellow Christians, God needs priests who can draw close to Him, live in His presence, and by their intercession draw down the blessings of His grace on others. And the world needs priests who will bear the burden of the perishing ones and intercede on their behalf.

Are you willing to offer yourself for this holy work? You know the surrender it demands—nothing less than the Christlike giving up of everything, so that the salvation of God's love may be accomplished among men. Don't be one of those who are content with being saved, just doing enough work to keep themselves warm and lively! Let nothing keep you back from giving yourselves to be wholly and only priests of the Most High God!

The thought of unworthiness or of unfitness need not keep you back. In the blood, the objective power of the perfect redemption works in you. In the Spirit, the full, subjective, personal experience of a divine life is secured. The blood provides an infinite worthiness to make your prayers acceptable. The Spirit provides a divine fitness, teaching you to pray exactly according to the will of God.

Every priest knew that when he presented a sacrifice according to the law of the sanctuary, it was accepted. Under the covering of the blood and the Spirit, you have the assurance that all the wonderful promises of prayer in the name of Jesus will be fulfilled in you. Abiding in union with the Great High Priest, *"ye shall ask what ye will, and it shall be done unto you"* (John 15:7). You will have power to pray the effective prayer of the righteous man that accomplishes a great deal (James 5:16). You will not only join in the general prayer of the church for the world, but be able in your own sphere to take up your own special work in prayer. As priests, you will work on a personal basis with God to receive and know the answer, and so to bless in His name.

Come, brother, come! Be a priest, only a priest, and all priest! Walk before the Lord in the full consciousness that you have been set apart for the holy ministry of intercession. This is the true blessedness of conformity to the image of God's Son.

Lord, teach us to pray.

O my blessed High Priest, accept the consecration in which my soul responds to Your message! I believe in the holy priesthood of Your saints. I believe that I am a priest, having the power to appear before the Father in prayer that will bring down many blessings on the perishing souls around me. I believe in the power of Your precious blood to cleanse me from all sin. It gives me perfect confidence in God and brings me near to Him in the full assurance of faith that my intercession will be heard.

I believe in the anointing of the Spirit. It comes down to me daily from You, my Great High Priest, to sanctify me. It fills me with the consciousness of my priestly calling and with the love of souls. It also teaches me what is according to God's will and how to pray the prayer of faith.

I believe that just as You are in all things in my life, You are in my prayer life, drawing me up into the fellowship of Your wondrous work of intercession.

In this faith, I yield myself today to my God as one of His anointed priests. I stand before Him to intercede on behalf of sinners, and then return to bless them in His name.

Holy Lord Jesus, accept and seal my consecration! Lay Your hands on me and consecrate me Yourself to this holy work. Let me walk among men with the consciousness and the character of a priest of the Most High God.

And to Him who loved us—who washed us from our sins in His own blood, and who made us kings and priests before God, His Father—to Him be glory and power forever! Amen.

31

A LIFE OF PRAYER

Rejoice evermore. Pray without ceasing. In every thing give thanks.
—1 Thessalonians 5:16–18

Our Lord told the parable of the widow and the unjust judge to teach us that men ought to pray without ceasing. The widow persevered in seeking one definite thing. The parable appears to refer to persevering in prayer for some special blessing, when God delays or appears to refuse. The Epistles, which speak of continuing in prayer, watching for the answer, and praying always in the Spirit, appear to refer to something different—the whole life being one of prayer. As the soul longs for the manifestation of God's glory to us, in us, through us, and around us, the inmost life of the soul is continually rising upward in dependence, faith, longing desire, and trustful expectation.

What is needed to live such a life of prayer? The first thing is undoubtedly an entire sacrifice of one's life to God's kingdom and glory. If you try to pray without ceasing because you want to be very pious and good, you will never succeed. Yielding ourselves to live for God and His honor enlarges the heart and teaches us to regard everything in the light of God and His will. We instinctively recognize in everything around us the need for God's help and blessing, and an opportunity for His being glorified.

Everything is weighed and tested by the one thing that fills the heart: the glory of God. The soul has learned that only what is of God can really glorify Him. Through the heart and soul, the whole life becomes a looking up, a crying from the inmost heart, for God to prove His power and love and reveal His glory. The believer awakes to the consciousness that he is one of the watchmen on Zion's walls, whose call really does touch and move the King in heaven to do what would otherwise not be done. He understands how real Paul's exhortations were: *"Praying always with all prayer and supplication in the Spirit...for all saints; and for me"* (Eph. 6:18–19) and *"Continue in prayer...withal praying also for us"* (Col. 4:2–3). To forget oneself—to live for God and His kingdom among men—is the way to learn to pray without ceasing.

This life devoted to God must be accompanied by the deep confidence that our prayers are effective. In His prayer lessons, our Blessed Lord insisted on faith in the Father as a God who most certainly does what we ask. *"Ask, and ye shall receive"* (John 16:24). To count confidently on an answer is the beginning and the end of His teaching. (Compare Matthew 7:8 and John 16:24.)

As we gain the assurance that our prayers are effective and that God does what we ask, we dare not neglect the use of this wonderful power. Our souls should turn wholly to God, and our lives should become prayer. The Lord needs and takes time, because we and everyone around us are creatures of time, subject to the law of growth. But know that not one single prayer of faith can possibly be lost, and that sometimes there is a necessity for accumulating prayer. Know that persevering prayer pleases God. Prayer becomes the quiet, persistent living of our lives of desire and faith in the presence of our God.

Don't limit such free and sure promises of the living God with your reasoning any longer! Don't rob them of their power, and ourselves of the wonderful confidence they are meant to inspire! The hindrance is not in God, not in His secret will, and not in the limitations of His promises. It is in us. We are not what we should be to obtain the promise. Open your whole heart to God's words of promise in all their simplicity and truth! They will search us and humble us. They will lift us up and make us glad and strong. To the faith that knows it gets what it asks for, prayer is not a work or a burden, but a joy and a triumph. It becomes a necessity and a second nature.

This union of strong desire and firm confidence is nothing but the life of the Holy Spirit within us. The Holy Spirit dwells in us, hides Himself in the depths of our being, and stirs our desires for the unseen and the divine—God Himself. It is always the Holy Spirit who draws out the heart to thirst for God and to long for His being recognized and glorified. Sometimes He speaks through us in groanings that cannot be uttered (see Rom. 8:26), sometimes in clear and conscious assurance, sometimes in distinct petitions for the deeper revelation of Christ to ourselves, and sometimes in pleas for a soul, a work, the church, or the world. Where the child of God really lives and walks in the Spirit—where he is not content to remain carnal, but tries to be a fit, spiritual organ for the Divine Spirit to reveal the life of Christ and Christ Himself—there the never ceasing life of intercession of the Blessed Son must reveal and repeat itself. Because it is the Spirit of Christ who prays in us, our prayers must be heard. Because it is we who pray in the Spirit, there is need of time, patience, and continual renewing of the prayer until every obstacle is conquered, and the harmony between God's Spirit and ours is perfect.

The chief thing we need for a life of unceasing prayer is to know that Jesus teaches us to pray. We have begun to understand a little of what His teaching is. It isn't the communication of new thoughts or views, the discovery of failure or error, or the arousal of desire and faith, however important all this may be. Jesus' teaching takes us up into the fellowship of His own prayer life before the Father. This is how Jesus really teaches. It was the sight of Jesus praying that made the disciples ask to be taught to pray. The faith of Jesus' continuous prayer truly teaches us to pray.

We know why: He who prays is our Head and our life. All He has is ours and is given to us when we give ourselves completely to Him. By His blood, He leads us into the immediate presence of God. The inner sanctuary is our home; we live there. Living so close to God and knowing we have been taken there to bless those who are far away, we cannot help but pray.

Christ makes us partakers with Himself of His prayer power and prayer life. Our true aim must not be to work a great deal and pray just enough to keep the work right. We should pray a great deal and then work enough for the power and blessing obtained in prayer to find its way through us to men. Christ lives to pray eternally; He saves and reigns. He communicates His prayer life to us and maintains it in us if we trust Him. He is responsible for our praying without ceasing. Christ teaches us to pray by showing us how He does it, by doing it in us, and by leading us to do it in Him and like Him. Christ is everything—the life and the strength—for a never ceasing prayer life. Seeing Christ's continuous praying as our example enables us to pray without ceasing. Because His priesthood is the power of an endless life—that resurrection life that never fades and never fails—and because His life is our life, praying without ceasing can become the joy of heaven here on earth. The apostle said, "*Rejoice evermore. Pray without ceasing. In every thing give thanks.*" Supported by never ceasing joy and never ceasing praise, never ceasing prayer is the manifestation of the power of the eternal life where Jesus always prays.

The union between the Vine and the branch is indeed a prayer union. The highest conformity to Christ—the most blessed participation in the glory of His heavenly life—is that we take part in His work of intercession. He and we live forever to pray. In union with Him, praying without ceasing becomes a possibility—a reality, the holiest and most blessed part of our holy and blessed fellowship with God. We abide within the veil in the presence of the Father. What the Father says, we do. What the Son asks, the Father does. Praying without ceasing is the earthly manifestation of heaven, a foretaste of the life where they rest neither day nor night in their song of worship and adoration.

Lord, teach us to pray.

O my Father, with my whole heart I praise You for this wondrous life of continuous prayer, continuous fellowship, continuous answers, and continuous oneness with Him who lives to pray forever! Oh, my God, keep me abiding and walking in the presence of Your glory, so that prayer may be the spontaneous expression of my life with You.

Blessed Savior, with my whole heart I praise You for coming from heaven to share my needs and my pleas, so that I could share Your all-powerful intercession. Thank You for taking me into Your school of prayer, teaching me the blessedness and the power of a life that is totally comprised of prayer. And most of all, thank You for taking me up into the fellowship of Your life of intercession. Now through me, too, Your blessings can be dispensed to those around me.

Holy Spirit, with deep reverence I thank You for Your work in me. Through You I am lifted up into communication with the Son and the Father, entering the fellowship of the life and love of the Holy Trinity.

Spirit of God, perfect Your work in me! Bring me into perfect union with Christ, my Intercessor! Let Your unceasing indwelling make my life one of unceasing intercession. And let my life unceasingly glorify the Father and bless those around me. Amen.

THE MINISTRY
OF INTERCESSION

CONTENTS

INTRODUCTION

A friend who heard that this book was being published asked how it differed from my previous one on the same subject, *With Christ in the School of Prayer*. An answer to that question may be the best introduction I can give to the present volume.

Any acceptance the former work has had must be attributed, as far as the contents go, to the prominence it gives to two great truths: the first is the certainty that prayer will be answered. Some believe that to ask and expect an answer is not the highest form of prayer. They maintain that fellowship with God is more than supplication, which is often selfish. To worship is more than to beg. With others, the thought that prayer is so often unanswered is so prominent that they think more of the spiritual benefit derived from the exercise of prayer than the actual gifts to be obtained by it. While admitting the measure of truth in these views, when kept in their true place, *The School of Prayer* points out how our Lord continually spoke of prayer as a means of obtaining what we desire. It illustrates how He seeks in every possible way to awaken in us the confident expectation of an answer to prayer. I was led to show how prayer—in which a man could enter into the mind of God, could assert the royal power of a renewed will and bring down to earth what, without prayer, would not have been given—is the highest proof of man's having been made in the likeness of God's Son. He is found worthy of entering into fellowship with Him, not only in adoration and worship, but in having his will actually taken up into the rule of the world and becoming the intelligent channel through which God can fulfill His eternal purpose. The book sought to reiterate and enforce the precious truths Christ preaches so continually: the blessing of prayer is that you can ask and receive what you will; the highest exercise and the glory of prayer is that persevering importunity can prevail and obtain what God at first could not and would not give.

With this truth there was a second one that came out very strongly as we studied the Master's words. In answer to the question—But why, if the answer to prayer is so positively promised, are there such numerous unanswered prayers?—we found that Christ taught us that the answer depended upon certain conditions. He spoke of faith, of perseverance, of praying in His name, of praying in the will of God. But all these conditions were summed up in the central one: *"If ye abide in me...ask what ye will, and it shall be done unto you"* (John 15:7). It became clear that the power to pray the effectual prayer of faith depended upon the life. It is only to a man given up to live as entirely in Christ and for Christ as the branch in the vine and for the vine that these promises can come true. *"In that day,"* Christ said, the Day of Pentecost, *"ye shall ask...in my name"* (John 16:23). It is only in a life full of the Holy Spirit that the true power to ask in Christ's name can be known. This led to the emphasizing of the truth that the ordinary Christian life cannot appropriate these promises. It needs a spiritual life, altogether sound and vigorous, to pray in power. The teaching naturally led to press the need of a life of entire consecration. More than one person has told me how it was in the reading of the book that he first saw what the better life was that could be lived, and must be lived, if Christ's wonderful promises are to come true to us.

In regard to these two truths, there is no change in the present volume. One only wishes that one could present them with such clearness and force as to help every beloved fellow Christian to some right impression of the reality and the glory of our privilege as God's children: *"ask what ye will, and it shall be done unto you"* (John 15:7). The present volume owes its existence to the desire to enforce two truths, of which formerly I had no such impression as now.

The one is that Christ actually meant prayer to be the great power by which His church should do its work and that the neglect of prayer is the great reason the church has not greater power over the masses in Christian and in heathen countries. In the first chapter, I have stated how my convictions in regard to this have been strengthened and what gave occasion to the writing of the book. It is meant to be, on behalf of myself and my brothers in the ministry and all God's people, a confession of shortcoming and of sin. At the same time, it is a call to believe that things can be different and that Christ waits to fit us by His Spirit to pray as He would have us. This call, of course, brings me back to what I spoke of in connection with the former volume: that there is a life in the Spirit, a life of abiding in Christ, within our reach, in which the power of prayer—both the power to pray and the power to obtain the answer—can be realized in a measure which we could not have thought possible before. Any failure in the prayer life, any desire or hope really to take the place Christ has prepared for us, brings us to the very root of the doctrine of grace as manifested in the Christian life. It is only by a full surrender to the life of abiding, by the yielding to the fullness of the Spirit's leading and quickening, that the prayer life can be restored to a truly healthy state. I feel deeply how little I have been able to put this in the volume as I could wish. I have prayed and am trusting that God, who chooses the weak things, will use it for His own glory.

The second truth that I have sought to enforce is that we have far too little conception of the place that intercession, as distinguished from prayer for ourselves, ought to have in the church and the Christian life. In intercession, our King upon the throne finds His highest glory; in it we will find our highest glory, too. Through it, He continues His saving work and can do nothing without it; through it, alone we can do our work, and nothing avails without it. In it, He ever receives from the Father the Holy Spirit and all spiritual blessings to impart; in it, we too are called to receive in ourselves the fullness of God's Spirit, with the power to impart spiritual blessing to others. The power of the church to truly bless rests on intercession: asking and receiving heavenly gifts to carry to men. Because this is so, it is no wonder that where—owing to lack of teaching or spiritual insight—we put the trust in our own diligence and effort—to the influence of the world and the flesh—and work more than we pray, the presence and power of God are not seen in our work as we would wish.

Such thoughts have led me to wonder what could be done to rouse believers to a sense of their high calling in this and to help train them to take part in it. And so this book differs from the former one in the attempt to open a practicing school and to invite all who have never taken systematic part in the great work of intercession to begin and give themselves to it. There are tens of thousands of workers who have known and are proving wonderfully what prayer can do. But there are tens of thousands who work with little prayer. Many more do not work at all because they do not know how or where they might all be added to the host of intercessors who are to bring down the blessings of heaven to earth. For their sakes, and the sake of all who feel the need of help, I have prepared helps and hints for a school of intercession for a month at the end of this book.

I have asked those who want to join to begin by giving at least ten minutes a day to this work. It is in doing that we learn to do; it is as we take hold and begin that the help of God's Spirit will come. It is as we daily hear God's call, and at once put it into practice, that the consciousness will begin to live in us: I too am an intercessor. We will feel the need of living in Christ and being full of the Spirit if we do this work correctly. Nothing will so test and stimulate the Christian life as the honest attempt to be an intercessor. It is difficult to conceive of how much we ourselves and the church will gain if, with our whole hearts, we accept the post of honor God is offering us. With regard to the school of intercession, I am confident that the result of the first month's course will be to awaken the feeling of how little we know how to intercede; a second and a third month may only deepen the sense of unfitness. This will be a great blessing. The confession, "*We know not how to pray as we ought*" (Rom. 8:26 ASV) is the introduction to the experience, "*The Spirit…maketh intercession for us*" (v. 26). Our sense of ignorance will lead us to depend on the Spirit praying in us, to feel the need of living in the Spirit.

We have heard a great deal about systematic Bible study, and we praise God for thousands and thousands of Bible classes and Bible readings. Let all the leaders of such classes try to start prayer classes—helping their students to pray in secret and training them to be, above everything, people of prayer. Let ministers ask what they can do in this. The faith in God's Word can nowhere be so exercised and perfected as in the intercession that asks, expects, and looks out for the answer. Throughout Scripture, in the life of every saint, of God's own Son, throughout the history of God's church, God is, first of all, a prayer-hearing God. Let us try to help God's children to know their God and encourage all God's servants to labor with the assurance: the chief and most blessed part of my work is to ask and receive from my Father what I can bring to others.

It will now easily be understood that what this book contains will be nothing but the confirmation and the call to put into practice the two great lessons of the former one. "*Ask what ye will, and it shall be done unto you*" (John 15:7). "*What things soever ye desire…believe that ye receive them*" (Mark 11:24). These great prayer promises, as part of the church's enduement of power for her work, are to be taken as literally and actually true: "*If ye abide in me, and my words abide in you*" (John 15:7), "*In that day ye shall ask…in my name.*" (John 16:23). These great prayer conditions are universal and unchangeable. A life abiding in Christ and filled with the Spirit, a life entirely given up as a branch for the work of the vine, has the power to claim these promises and to pray the effectual prayer that avails much (James 5:16). Lord, teach us to pray.

—*Andrew Murray*

1

THE LACK OF PRAYER

Ye have not, because ye ask not.
—James 4:2

And he saw that there was no man,
and wondered that there was no intercessor.
—Isaiah 59:16

There is none that calleth upon thy name,
that stirreth up himself to take hold of thee.
—Isaiah 64:7

The entire morning session of a convention I recently attended was devoted to prayer and intercession. Great blessing was found, both in listening to what the Word teaches of their need and power and in joining in continued, united supplication. Many felt that we knew too little of persevering, importunate prayer, and that it is, indeed, one of the greatest needs of the church.

We pray too little! There is even a lack of hope for any great change, due to force of habit and the pressured feeling that prayer is a duty.

What I have heard lately regarding prayer has made a deep impression on me. What affected me the most was that God's servants should feel hopeless about the prospect of an entire change being made. I prayed God would give me words that might help to direct attention to the problem and to stir up faith, awakening the assurance that God, by His Spirit, will enable us to pray as we should. Real deliverance can be found from a failure that hinders our own joy in God and our power in His service.

Let me begin, for the sake of those who have never had their attention directed to the matter, by giving some examples that prove how universal the sense of shortcoming in prayer is.

Dr. Whyte, of Free St. George's, Edinburgh, made an address to ministers. In it, he said that as a young minister, he had thought that he should spend as much of his free time as possible with his books in his study. This was because he wanted to feed his people with the very best he could prepare for them. But he had now learned that prayer was of more importance than study. He remembered that deacons were elected to take charge of the collections, so that the apostles could *"give* [themselves] *continually to prayer, and to the ministry of the word"* (Acts 6:4). At times, when the deacons of his congregation brought him his salary, he had to ask himself whether he had been as faithful in his responsibilities as they had been in theirs. He felt as if it were almost too late to regain what he had lost and urged his brothers to pray more. What a solemn confession and warning from one of the high places: we pray too little!

During a convention several years ago, I was discussing the subject of prayer in conversation with a well-known London minister. He maintained that if so much time must be given to prayer, it would involve the neglect of the responsibilities of his position. "There is the morning mail, before breakfast, with ten or twelve letters that must be answered. Then there are committee meetings waiting, with countless other engagements, more than enough to fill up the day. It is difficult to see how it can all be done."

My answer was, in substance, that it was simply a question of whether the call of God for our time and attention was of more importance than that of man. If God was waiting to meet us and to give us blessing and power from heaven for His work, it was a shortsighted policy to put other work in the place that God and waiting on Him should have.

At one of our ministerial meetings, the superintendent of a large district put the case this way: "I rise in the morning and, before breakfast, have half an hour with God in the Word and in prayer. I go out and am occupied all day with a multiplicity of engagements. I do not think many minutes elapse without my breathing a prayer for guidance or help. After my day's work, I return in my evening devotions and speak to God about the day's work. But of the intense, definite, importunate prayer of which Scripture speaks, I know little." What, he asked, must I think of such a life?

Imagine the difference between a man whose profits are just enough to maintain his family and keep up his business, and another whose income enables him to extend the business and to help others. There can be an earnest Christian life in which there is prayer enough to keep us from backsliding, just maintaining the position we have, without much growth in spirituality or Christ-likeness. This prayer attitude is more defensive—seeking to ward off temptation—than aggressive—reaching out after higher attainment. If we are to grow in strength, with some large experience of God's power to sanctify ourselves and to bring down real blessing on others, there must be more definite and persevering prayer. The Scriptures, teaching about "cry[ing] *day and night*" (Luke 18:7), "*continuing stedfastly in prayer*" (Rom. 12:12 ASV), watching thereunto prayer (Eph. 6:18), and being heard for his importunity (see Luke 11:8), must, in some degree, become our experience if we are really to be intercessors.

Another example: a pastor of quite a large church who had many responsibilities once said to me, "I see the importance of much prayer, and yet my life hardly leaves room for it. Are we to submit? Or tell us how we can attain what we desire?" I admitted that the difficulty was universal. A most honored South African missionary, now gone to his rest, had the same complaint. I recalled his words: "In the morning at five, the sick people are at the door waiting for medicine. At six, the printers come, and I have to set them to work and teach them. At nine, the school calls me, and till late at night, I am kept busy with a large correspondence."

In my answer, I quoted a Dutch proverb: "'What *is* heaviest must *weigh* heaviest'—must have the first place." The law of God is unchangeable; as on earth, so in our traffic with heaven, we only get as we give. Unless we are willing to pay the price and sacrifice time, attention, and what appear to be legitimate or necessary duties for the sake of the heavenly gifts, we need not look for a large experience of the power of the heavenly world in our work. The whole company present joined in the sad confession; it had been thought over, and mourned over, times without number. Yet somehow, there they were, all these pressing claims and all the ineffectual resolves to pray more barring the way. I do not need to say to what further thoughts our conversation led; the substance of them will be found in some of the later chapters in this volume.

Let me call just one more witness. In the course of my journey, I met with one of the Cowley Fathers who had just been holding retreats for clergy of the English Church. I was interested to hear from him the line of teaching he follows. In the course of conversation, he used the expression: "the distraction of business," and it came out that he found it one of the great difficulties he had to deal with in himself and others. Of himself, he said that by the vows of his order he was bound to give himself specially to prayer. But he found it exceedingly difficult. Every day he had to be at four different points of the town he lived in; his predecessor had left him the charge of a number of committees where he was expected to do all the work. It was as if everything conspired to keep him from prayer.

All this testimony clarifies the fact that prayer does not have the place it should have in our ministerial and Christian life. The shortcoming is one of which all are willing to confess, and the difficulties in the way of deliverance are such as to make a return to a true and full prayer life almost impossible. Blessed be God: *"The things which are impossible with men are possible with God"* (Luke 18:27). *"God is able to make all grace abound toward you; that ye, always having all sufficiency in all things, may abound to every good work"* (2 Cor. 9:8). Do let us believe that God's call to much prayer need not be a burden and cause of continual self-condemnation. He means it to be a joy. He can make it an inspiration, giving us strength for all our work and bringing down His power to work through us in our fellowmen. Do not be afraid to fully admit to the sin that shames us, and then to face it in the name of our Mighty Redeemer. The light that shows us our sin and condemns us for it will show us the way out of it into the life of liberty that is well pleasing to God. If we allow this one matter, unfaithfulness in prayer, to convict us of the lack in our Christian lives, God will use the discovery to bring us not only the power to pray that we long for, but the joy of a new and healthy life, of which prayer is the spontaneous expression.

And what is the way by which our sense of the lack of prayer can be made the means of blessing, the entrance on a path in which the evil may be conquered? How can our fellowship with the Father, in continual prayer and intercession, become what it ought to be, if we and the world around us are to be blessed? As it appears to me, we must begin by going back to God's Word, to study what place God means prayer to have in the life of His child and His church. A fresh sight of what prayer is according to the will of God, of what our prayers can be, through the grace of God, will free us from those feeble, defective views in regard to the absolute necessity of continual prayer, which lie at the root of our failure. As we get an insight into the reasonableness and rightness of this divine appointment and come under the full conviction of how wonderfully it fits in with God's love and our own happiness, we will be freed from the false impression of its being an arbitrary demand. With our whole heart and soul, we will consent to it and rejoice in it, as the only possible way for the blessing of heaven to come to earth. All thought of task and burden, of self-effort and strain, will pass away in the blessed faith—that as simple as breathing is in the healthy, natural life, praying will be in the Christian life that is led and filled by the Spirit of God.

As we occupy ourselves with and accept this teaching of God's Word on prayer, we will be led to see how our failures in the prayer life were owing to failure in the Spirit life. Prayer is one of the most heavenly and spiritual of the functions of the Spirit life. How could we try or expect to fulfill it so as to please God, except as our souls are in perfect health, and our lives are truly possessed and moved by God's Spirit? The insight into the place God means prayer to have, and that it only can have in a full Christian life, will show us that we have not been living the true, the abundant life. It will show us that any thought of praying more and effectually will be vain, except as we are brought into a closer relationship with our Blessed Lord Jesus.

Christ is our life. Christ lives in us in such reality that His life of prayer on earth, and of intercession in heaven, is breathed into us in just such measure as our surrender and our faith allow and accept it. Jesus Christ is the Healer of all diseases, the Conqueror of all enemies, the Deliverer from all sin. If our failures teach us to turn afresh to Him, and to find in Him the grace He gives to pray as we should, this humiliation may become our greatest blessing. Let us all unite in praying to God that He would visit our souls and fit us for that work of intercession, which is at this moment the greatest need of the church and the world. It is only by intercession that that power can be brought down from heaven, which will enable the church to conquer the world. Let us stir up the slumbering gift that is lying unused and seek to gather, train, and band together as many as we can to be God's remembrancers and to give Him no rest until He makes His church a joy in the earth. Nothing but intense, believing prayer can meet the intense spirit of worldliness, which is complained of everywhere.

2

THE WORKING OF
THE SPIRIT AND PRAYER

*If ye then, being evil, know how to give good gifts
unto your children: how much more shall your heavenly
Father give the Holy Spirit to them that ask him?*
—Luke 11:13

Christ had just said in Luke 11:9, "*Ask, and it shall be given.*" God's giving is inseparably connected with our asking. He applies this especially to the Holy Spirit. As surely as a father on earth gives bread to his child, so God gives the Holy Spirit to those who ask Him. The whole working of the Spirit is ruled by one great law: God must give it, and we must ask for it. When the Holy Spirit was poured out at Pentecost with a flow that never ceases, it was in answer to prayer. The inflow into the believer's heart and His outflow in the rivers of living water still depend on the law, *"Ask, and it shall be given."*

In connection with our confession of the lack of prayer, what we need is some understanding of the place prayer occupies in God's plan of redemption. Nowhere is this seen more clearly than in the first half of the Acts of the Apostles. The story of the birth of the church in the outpouring of the Holy Spirit, and of the first freshness of its heavenly life in the power of that Spirit, will teach us how prayer on earth, whether as cause or effect, is the true measure of the presence of the Spirit of heaven.

We begin with the well-known words, *"These all continued with one accord in prayer and supplication"* (Acts 1:14). And further, from chapter 2: *"And when the day of Pentecost was fully come, they were all with one accord in one place....And they were all filled with the Holy Ghost....And the same day there were added unto them about three thousand souls"* (vv. 1, 4, 41). The great work of redemption had been accomplished. The Holy Spirit had been promised by Christ *"not many days hence"* (Acts 1:5). He had sat down on His throne and received the Spirit from the Father. But all this was not enough. One thing more was needed: the disciples' ten days of united, continued supplication. It was intense, continued prayer that prepared the disciples' hearts, opened the windows of heaven, and brought down the promised gift. The power of the Spirit could no more be given without Christ sitting on the throne than it could descend without the disciples on the footstool of the throne.

For all ages, the law is laid down here, at the birth of the church, that the power of the Spirit must be prayed down from heaven. The amount of believing, continued prayer will determine the amount of the Spirit's working in the church. Direct, definite, determined prayer is what we need. See how this is confirmed in Acts, chapter 4. Peter and John had been brought before the council and threatened with punishment. When they returned to their Christian brothers and reported what had been said to them, *"they lifted up their voice to God with one accord"* (Acts 4:24) and prayed for boldness to speak the Word.

And when they had prayed, the place was shaken…and they were all filled with the Holy Ghost, and they spake the word of God with boldness. And the multitude of them that believed were of one heart and of one soul.…And with great power gave the apostles witness of the resurrection of the Lord Jesus: and great grace was upon them all.

(Acts 4:31–33)

It is as if the story of Pentecost is repeated a second time over—with the prayer, the shaking of the house, the filling with the Spirit, the speaking God's Word with boldness and power, the great grace upon all, and the manifestation of unity and love—to imprint indelibly on the heart of the church that it is prayer that lies at the root of her spiritual life and power. The measure of God's giving the Spirit is our asking. He gives as a father to him who asks as a child.

Go on to Acts, the sixth chapter. There we find that, when murmuring arose as to the neglect of the Grecian Jews in the distribution of alms, the apostles proposed the appointment of deacons to serve the tables. "We," they said, "*will give ourselves continually to prayer, and to the ministry of the word*" (Acts 6:4). It is often said that there is nothing in honest business, when it is kept in its place as entirely subordinate to the kingdom, which must ever be first, preventing fellowship with God. Work like ministering to the poor should certainly not hinder the spiritual life. And yet the apostles felt it would hinder them in their giving themselves to the ministry of prayer and the Word. What does this teach? That the maintenance of the spirit of prayer is not enough for those who are the leaders of the church. To keep the communication between the King and His servants clear and fresh, to draw down power and blessing—not only for the maintenance of our own spiritual life, but for those around us—and to continually receive instruction and empowerment for the great work to be done, the apostles, as the ministers of the Word, felt the need to be free from other duties in order to give themselves to much prayer.

James wrote, "*Pure religion and undefiled before God and the Father is this, To visit the fatherless and widows in their affliction*" (James 1:27). If ever any work were a sacred one, it was that of caring for these Grecian widows.

And yet, even these duties might interfere with the apostles' special calling to give themselves to prayer and the ministry of the Word. In the kingdom of heaven, as on earth, there is power in the division of labor. While some, like the deacons, had to care especially for serving the tables and ministering the alms of the church here on earth, others had to be set free for that steadfast continuance in prayer that would uninterruptedly secure the downflow of the powers of the heavenly world. The minister of Christ is set apart to give himself as much to prayer as to the ministry of the Word. Faithful obedience to this law is the secret of the church's power and success. As before, so after Pentecost, the apostles were men given up to prayer.

Acts, chapter 8, shows the intimate connection between the Pentecostal gift and prayer, from another point of view. In Samaria, Philip had preached with great blessing, and many had believed. But the Holy Spirit had, as yet, fallen on none of them. The apostles sent down Peter and John to pray for them that they might receive the Holy Spirit. The power for such prayer was a higher gift than preaching. It was the work of the men who had been in closest contact with the Lord in glory, the work that was essential to the perfection of the life that preaching and baptism, faith and conversion had only begun. Surely of all the gifts of the early church for which we should long, there is none more needed than the gift of prayer—prayer that brings down the Holy Spirit on believers. This power is given to the men who say, *"We will give ourselves…to prayer"* (Acts 6:4).

The outpouring of the Holy Spirit in the house of Cornelius at Caesarea (Acts 10) provides another testimony to the wondrous interdependence of the action of prayer and the Spirit, and another proof of what will come to a man who has given himself to prayer. Peter went up at midday to pray on the housetop. And what happened? He saw heaven opened, and there came the vision that revealed to him the cleansing of the Gentiles. Then came the message of the three men from Cornelius, a man who *"prayed to God alway"* (v. 2) and had heard from an angel, *"Thy prayers…are come up…before God"* (v. 4). The Spirit said to Peter, *"Go with them"* (v. 20). It is Peter, praying, to whom the will of God is revealed, to whom guidance is given as to going to Caesarea, and who is brought into contact with a praying and prepared company of hearers. No wonder that in answer to all this prayer a blessing comes beyond all expectation, and the Holy Spirit is poured out upon the Gentiles. A much-praying minister will receive an entrance into God's will he would otherwise know nothing of. He will be brought to praying people where he does not expect them and will receive blessing above all he asks or thinks. The teaching and the power of the Holy Spirit are both unalterably linked to prayer.

Our next reference will show us faith in the power that the church's prayer has with its glorified King, as it is found not only in the apostles, but in the Christian community. In Acts 12, we have the story of Peter in prison on the eve of execution. The death of James had aroused the church to a sense of real danger, and the thought of losing Peter, too, had awakened all her energies. She took herself to prayer: *"Prayer was made without ceasing of the church unto God for him"* (v. 5). That prayer achieved much; Peter was delivered. When he came to the house of Mary, he found *"many were gathered together praying"* (v. 12). Stone walls and double chains, soldiers and keepers, and the iron gate all gave way before the power from heaven brought down to his rescue through prayer. The whole power of the Roman Empire, as represented by Herod, was impotent in the presence of the power the church of the Holy Spirit wielded in prayer. They stood in close and living communication with their Lord in heaven; they knew that the words, *"All power is given unto me,"* and *"Lo, I am with you alway"* (Matt. 28:18, 20), were absolutely true. They had faith in His promise to hear them no matter what they asked. Because of this, they prayed in the assurance that the powers of heaven could work on earth, and would work at their request and on their behalf. The early church believed in prayer and practiced it.

Just one more illustration of the place and the blessing of prayer among men filled with the Holy Spirit. In Acts, chapter 13, we have the names of five men at Antioch who had given themselves specially to ministering to the Lord with prayer and fasting. Their giving themselves to prayer was not in vain. As they ministered to the Lord, the Holy Spirit met them and gave them new insight into God's plans. He called them to be fellow workers with Himself in an undertaking for which He had called Barnabas and Saul.

Their part and privilege would be to support these men with renewed fasting and prayer and to let them go, *"sent forth by the Holy Ghost"* (Acts 13:4).

God in heaven would not send forth His chosen servants without the cooperation of His church; men on earth were to have a real partnership in the work of God. It was prayer that fitted and prepared them for this. It was to praying men that the Holy Spirit gave authority to do His work and use His name. It was to prayer that the Holy Spirit was given. It is still prayer that is the only secret of true church expansion, being guided from heaven to find and send forth God-called and God-empowered men. Through prayer, the Holy Spirit will reveal the men He has selected; through prayer, He will give these men the honor of knowing that they are men, *"sent forth by the Holy Ghost."* It is prayer that is the link between the King on the throne and the church at His footstool—the human link that has its divine strength in the power of the Holy Spirit, who comes in answer to it.

As one looks back on these chapters in the history of the early church, how clear these two great truths stand out: where there is much prayer, there will be much of the Spirit; and where there is much of the Spirit, there will be ever increasing prayer. So clear is the living connection between the two that when the Spirit is given in answer to prayer, it awakens more prayer to prepare for the fuller revelation and communication of His divine power and grace. If prayer was, thus, the power by which the early church flourished and triumphed, is there any reason why it should not be the one great need of the church today?

Let these be considered facts in our church work:

+ Heaven is still as full of stores of spiritual blessing as it was in the apostles' time.

+ God still delights to give the Holy Spirit to *"them that ask him."*

+ Our lives and work are still as dependent on the direct impartation of divine power as they were in those early times.

+ Prayer is still the appointed means for drawing down these heavenly blessings in power on ourselves and those around us.

✦ God is still seeking men and women who will, in addition to all their other work of ministering, specially give themselves to persevering prayer.

And we—you, my reader, and I—may have the privilege of offering ourselves to God to labor in prayer, bringing down these blessings to this earth. Let us beseech God to make all this truth so living in us that we will not be able to rest until it has mastered us, and our whole hearts become so filled with it that we will regard the practice of intercession as our highest privilege. Let us find in it the only sure measurement for blessing on ourselves, on the church, and on the world.

3

A MODEL
OF INTERCESSION

*And he said unto them, Which of you shall have a friend,
and shall go unto him at midnight, and say unto him, Friend,
lend me three loaves; for a friend of mine in his journey is come to me, and
I have nothing to set before him? And he from within shall answer and
say, Trouble me not...I cannot rise and give thee. I say unto you, Though
he will not rise and give him, because he is his friend, yet because of his
importunity he will rise and give him as many as he needeth.*
—Luke 11:5–8

*I have set watchmen upon thy walls, O Jerusalem, which shall never
hold their peace day nor night: ye that make mention of the* Lord,
keep not silence. And give him no rest.
—Isaiah 62:6–7

We have seen what power prayer has in the previous chapter. It is the one power on earth that commands the power of heaven. The story of the early days of the church is God's great object lesson—to teach His church what prayer can do, how it alone, but most surely, can draw down the treasures and powers of heaven into the life on earth.

Let us briefly recall the lessons we learned. Did we not see the following:

+ That prayer is both indispensable and irresistible?
+ That untold power and blessing are stored for us in heaven?
+ That this power will make us a blessing to men and fit us to do any work or face any danger?
+ That this power is to be sought in prayer continually and persistently?
+ That those who have the heavenly power can pray it down upon others?
+ That in all the ministries of Christ's church, prayer is the one secret of success?
+ That it can defy all the power of the world and fit men to conquer that world for Christ?

Yes, it is the power of the heavenly life—the power of God's own Spirit, the power of Omnipotence—that waits for prayer to bring it down.

In all the prayer of the apostles, there was little thought of personal needs or happiness. It was their desire to witness for Christ and bring Him and His salvation to others; it was the thought of God's kingdom and glory that possessed these disciples. If we desire to be delivered from the sin of neglecting prayer, we must enlarge our hearts for the work of intercession. Praying constantly for ourselves will come to failure. Only in intercession for others will our faith, love, and perseverance be aroused, and the power of the Spirit, which can fit us for saving men, be found.

We are asking how we may become more faithful and successful in prayer; let us see how the Master teaches us in the parable of the friend at midnight. His lesson is that intercession for the needy requires the highest exercise of our power of believing and prevailing prayer. Intercession is the most perfect form of prayer, in that it is the prayer Christ prays on His throne. Let us learn what the elements of true intercession are.

1. An urgent need. Here intercession has its origin. The friend came at midnight—an untimely hour. He was hungry and could not buy bread. If we are to learn to pray properly, we must open our eyes and hearts to the needs around us.

We often hear of the millions of unsaved souls living in midnight darkness, perishing for lack of the Bread of life. We also hear of the many nominal Christians who are almost as unenlightened and indifferent as those who are unsaved. We see millions in the Christian church who know little of a walk in the light of God or in the power of a life fed by bread from heaven. We all have our own circles—congregations, schools, friends, missions—in which the great complaint is that the light and life of God are too little known. Surely, if we believe what we profess—that God alone is able to help, that God certainly will help in answer to prayer—all these needs ought to make us intercessors, people who give their lives to prayer for those around them.

Let us take time to seriously consider these needs. Each Christless soul will go down into utter darkness, perishing from hunger, even though there is bread to spare. Unknown millions of souls are dying without the knowledge of Christ. Our own neighbors and friends—souls entrusted to us—are dying without hope. Christians all around us are living a sickly, feeble, and fruitless spiritual life. Surely there is a need for prayer. Nothing but prayer to God for help will avail.

2. The willing love. The friend took his weary, hungry friend into his house and into his heart, too. He did not excuse himself by saying he had no bread; even though it was midnight, he sent to find some for him. He sacrificed his night's rest and his comfort to find the needed bread. "*Love...
seeketh not its own*" (1 Cor. 13:4–5 ASV). It is the very nature of love to give up and forget self for the sake of others. It takes their needs and makes them its own, finding its real joy in living and dying for others, as Christ did.

It is the love of a mother for her prodigal son that makes her pray for him. The true love in us will become the spirit of intercession. It is possible to do a great deal of faithful, earnest work for our brothers and sisters without having true love for them. Take into consideration a physician who may be thoroughly interested in his patients, yet does not feel any special love for them. This comes from a love of his profession and a high sense of faithfulness to his duty. In the same way, servants of Christ may devote themselves to their work with self-sacrificing enthusiasm, without their Christlike love for souls being strong enough. It is this lack of love that causes so much shortcoming in prayer. Only as our focus on being diligent and thorough in our prayer lives becomes saturated with the tender compassion of Christ will true love begin compelling us to pray. We will then not be able to rest from our work if there are still souls who are not saved. True love must pray.

3. The sense of impotence. We often speak of the power of love. In one sense, love does not have power, but this truth has its limitations, which must not be forgotten. The strongest love may be utterly impotent. A mother might be willing to give her life for her dying child, and yet not be able to save it. The friend at midnight was most willing to give his friend bread, but he had none. It was this sense of impotence, of his inability to help, that sent him pleading, "*A friend of mine...is come to me, and I have nothing to set before him.*" This sense of impotence with God's servants is the very strength of the life of intercession.

As the consciousness of this thought, "*I have nothing to set before* [them]," takes possession of the minister, missionary, teacher, or worker, intercession will become their only hope and refuge. I may have knowledge and truth, a loving heart, and the readiness to give myself for those under my charge, but I cannot give them the Bread of heaven. Despite all my love and zeal, "*I have nothing to set before* [them]." Blessed is the man who has made that "*I have nothing*" the motto of his ministry. As he thinks of the Judgment Day and the danger in it for unsaved souls, as he realizes that a supernatural power and life is necessary to save men from sin, as he feels his utter inadequacy to give them life, that "*I have nothing*" urges him to pray. When the desolation of hungry souls in the midnight darkness comes upon him, intercession appears to him as his only hope, the one thing in which his love can take refuge.

Let us take this lesson to heart, as a warning to all those who are strong and wise, and for the encouragement of those who are weak: The sense of our impotence is the soul of intercession. The simplest, weakest Christian can pray down blessing from an Almighty God.

4. The faith in prayer. What he does not have himself, another can supply. He has a rich friend near, who will be both able and willing to give him bread. He is sure that if he only asks, he will receive. This faith makes him leave his home at midnight. He knows that when he does not have any to give, he can ask his friend.

We need this simple, confident faith that God will give us what we ask for. Where it really exists, there will be no mistake about whether or not we should pray. God's Word provides everything needed to stir and strengthen such faith in us. Just as the heaven our natural eyes can see is one great ocean of sunshine, with its light and heat, giving beauty and fruitfulness to earth, Scripture shows us God's true heaven, filled with spiritual blessings—divine light, love, and life; heavenly joy, peace, and power—all shining down on us. It shows us how God is waiting, delighting to bestow these blessings in answer to prayer. In a thousand promises and testimonies, it urges us to believe that prayer will be heard, and that what we cannot possibly do ourselves for those whom we want to help, can be done by prayer. Have no doubt that prayer will be heard, that through prayer, the poorest and weakest can dispense blessings to the needy, and that each of us, though poor, may yet be making many rich.

5. The importunity that prevails. The faith of the friend meets a sudden and unexpected obstacle: the rich friend refuses to hear, "*I cannot rise and give thee.*" The loving heart had not counted on this disappointment; it cannot accept it. The supplicant presses his threefold plea: here is my needy friend; you have abundance; I am your friend. He refuses to accept a denial. The love that opened his house at midnight, and then left it to seek help, must win.

This is the central lesson of the parable. In our intercession, we may find that there is difficulty and delay with the answer. It may be as if God says, "*I cannot…give thee.*" It is not easy, against all appearances, to maintain our confidence that He will hear and to persevere in full assurance that we will have what we ask for. And yet, this is what God looks for from us. He so highly prizes our confidence in Him, it is so essentially the highest honor the creature can show the Creator, that He will do anything to train us in the exercise of this trust in Him. Blessed is the man who is not staggered by God's delay or silence or apparent refusal, but is strong in faith, giving glory to God. Such faith perseveres, importunately, if need be, and cannot fail to inherit the blessing.

6. The certainty of a rich reward. "*I say unto you…because of his importunity he will…give him as many as he needeth.*" If we could only learn to believe in the certainty of an abundant answer! A prophet of old said, "*Let not your hands be weak: for your work shall be rewarded*" (2 Chron. 15:7). Those who find it difficult to pray should fix their eyes on the reward and, in faith, learn to trust the divine assurance that their prayers cannot be in vain. If we can come to believe in God and His faithfulness, intercession will become the very first thing we take refuge in when we seek blessing for others, and the very last thing for which we cannot find time. And it will become a thing of joy and hope, because, all the time we pray, we know that we are sowing seed that will bring forth fruit a hundredfold. Disappointment is impossible: "*I say unto you…he will rise and give him as many as he needeth.*"

Take courage! Time spent in prayer will yield more than that given to work. Prayer alone gives work its worth and its success. Prayer opens the way for God Himself to do His work in us and through us. Let our chief work, as God's messengers, be intercession; in it, we secure the presence and power of God to go with us.

"*Which of you shall have a friend…at midnight, and say unto him, Friend, lend me three loaves?*" This Friend is none other but our God. Do let us learn that in the darkness of midnight—at the most unlikely time and in our greatest need—when we have "*nothing to set before*" those we love, we

have a rich Friend in heaven, the Everlasting God and Father, who is waiting to be asked for help. Let us confess our lack of prayer before Him,
admitting that it proves our weak faith and is the symptom of a life that is
still too much under the power of self, the flesh, and the world. The Lord
Jesus, who related this parable of the Friend at midnight, waits to make us
all importunate friends.

Therefore, let us give ourselves to be intercessors. Let us cry with
importunity to God when we see people who need help, when the spirit
of compassion stirs within us, when we feel our own powerlessness to
help, or when we see obstacles in the way of our getting an answer. God
alone can help. And in answer to our prayers, He will help. In addition, we
should do our utmost to train the next generation of Christians in what we
have learned. Let us teach those who come after us how to enter the good
land—the blessed life of unceasing prayer. Moses could not enter the land
of Canaan, but there was one thing he could do—he could, at God's bidding, *"charge Joshua, and encourage him, and strengthen him"* (Deut. 3:28).

The model intercessor is the model Christian worker. The secret of
successful work is to give away daily what we ourselves are receiving from
God. Intercession is the blessed link between our impotence and God's
omnipotence.

4

BECAUSE OF HIS IMPORTUNITY

I say unto you, Though he will not rise and give him,
because he is his friend, yet because of his importunity he will rise and
give him as many as he needeth.
—Luke 11:8

And he spake a parable unto them to this end,
that men ought always to pray, and not to faint....Hear what the
unjust judge saith. And shall not God avenge his own elect,
which cry day and night unto him, though he bear long with them?
I tell you that he will avenge them speedily.
—Luke 18:1, 6–8.

Our Lord Jesus thought it was so important for us to realize the need for perseverance and importunity in prayer that He gave us two parables to teach us this. That should prove that in such persevering and importuning we have, at once, prayer's greatest difficulty and its highest power. Christ wants us to know that prayer will not always be easy and smooth. We must expect difficulties, which can only be conquered by determined persistence.

In the parables, our Lord presents the difficulty as belonging to the persons to whom the petition was addressed, and the importunity as needed to overcome their reluctance to hear. In our communion with God, the difficulty is not on His side, but on ours. In connection with the first parable, He tells us that our Father is more willing to give good things to those who ask Him than any earthly father would be to give his child bread. In the second, He assures us that God longs to avenge His elect speedily. The need of urgent prayer cannot be because God must be made willing or disposed to bless; the need lies altogether in ourselves. But because it was not possible to find any earthly illustration of a loving father or a willing friend from whom the needed lesson of importunity could be taught, He takes the unwilling friend and the unjust judge to instill in us the faith that perseverance in prayer can overcome every obstacle.

The difficulty is not in God's love or power, but in ourselves and our own incapacity to receive the blessing. And yet, because of this difficulty—our lack of spiritual preparedness—God has difficulty, too. His wisdom and His righteousness—indeed His love—dare not give us what would do us harm if we received it too soon or too easily. The sin, or the consequences of sin, that makes it impossible for God to answer immediately is a barrier on God's side as well as on ours. To break through this power of sin in ourselves, or in those for whom we pray, is what makes the striving and the conflict of prayer such a reality. Men of all ages have prayed, quite correctly, with the sense that there were difficulties in the heavenly world to overcome. As they pleaded with God for the removal of the unknown obstacles, and in that persevering supplication were brought into a state of utter brokenness and helplessness, they became entirely resigned to Him, in union with His will, with the faith that could take hold of Him. Then, the hindrance in themselves and in heaven were together overcome. As God conquered them, they conquered God. As God prevails over us, we prevail with God.

God has created us in such a way that the clearer our insight into the reasonableness of a demand, the heartier our surrender to it. One great cause of our negligence in prayer is that there appears to be something arbitrary, or at least something incomprehensible, in the call to such continued prayer. If we could be brought to see that this apparent difficulty is a divine necessity, and the source of unspeakable blessing, we would be ready to give ourselves with gladness of heart to persevering prayer. Let us attempt to understand how the difficulty that the call to importunity presents is one of our greatest privileges.

I do not know whether you have ever noticed what part difficulties play in our natural life. They call out man's powers as nothing else can. They strengthen and ennoble character. What is education, for example, but a daily developing and disciplining of the mind as increasingly difficult problems are presented to the pupil to be overcome? The moment a lesson has become easy, the pupil is moved on to one that is more advanced. In the meeting and the mastering of difficulties, our highest attainments are to be found.

It is the same in our relationship with God. Just imagine what the result would be if the child of God had only to ask and receive and go away. What unspeakable loss to the spiritual life would result! Difficulty and delay require persevering prayer to obtain the true blessing and blessedness of the heavenly life. As we persevere, we learn how little we delight in fellowshipping with God, and how little living faith we have in Him. We discover how earthly and unspiritual our heart still is, how little we have of God's Holy Spirit. We come to know our own weakness and unworthiness. We yield to God's Spirit to pray in us and to take our place in Christ Jesus, and we abide in Him as our only plea with the Father. There, our own will, strength, and goodness are crucified. There, we rise in Christ to newness of life, with our whole wills dependent on God and His glory.

Let us begin to praise God for the need and the difficulty of importunate prayer. They are one of His choicest means of grace.

Consider what our Lord Jesus owed to the difficulties in His path. In Gethsemane, it was as if the Father chose not to hear. Jesus prayed even more earnestly, until "He was heard." In the way He opened up for us, He learned obedience by the things He suffered and so was made perfect. His will was given up to God; His faith in God was tried and strengthened; the Prince of this world, with all his temptations, was overcome. This is the new and living way He consecrated for us. It is in persevering prayer that we walk with and are made partakers of His very Spirit. Prayer is a form of crucifixion, of our fellowship with Christ's cross, of our giving up our flesh to the death. O Christians! Shouldn't we be ashamed of our reluctance to sacrifice the flesh, our own will, and the world, as evidenced in our reluctance to pray much? Can we learn the lesson that both nature and Christ teach? The difficulty of importunate prayer is our highest privilege; to overcome it will bring us our richest blessings.

There are various elements of importunity. The most important are perseverance, determination, and intensity. Beginning with the refusal to at once accept a denial, importunity grows to the determination to persevere, to spare no time or trouble, until an answer comes. It then rises to the intensity in which the whole being is given to God in supplication, and the boldness comes to grasp God's strength. It can be quiet and restful at one time, and passionate and bold at another. It can take time and be patient, and then claim at once what it desires. No matter what its form, it always means and knows that God hears prayer, and it will be heard. .

Remember its wonderful appearances in the Old Testament. Think of Abraham, as he pleads for Sodom. Time after time, he renews his prayer, until the sixth time, he has to say, *"Let not the Lord be angry"* (Gen. 18:32). He does not cease until he has heard God's answer for each of his requests, until he has learned how far he can go, has entered into God's mind, and rests in God's will. For his sake, Lot was saved. *"God remembered Abraham, and sent Lot out of the midst of the overthrow"* (Gen. 19:29). Shouldn't we, who have redemption and promises for the unsaved that Abraham never knew, begin to plead more with God on their behalf?

Think of Jacob, when he feared meeting Esau. The angel of the Lord met him in the dark and wrestled with him. (See Gen. 32:24–32.) When the angel saw that he could not win, he said, *"Let me go"* (v. 26). And Jacob answered, *"I will not let thee go, except thou bless me"* (v. 26). The angel blessed him then and there. The boldness that said, *"I will not let thee go,"* forcing the blessing from the reluctant angel, was so pleasing in God's sight that Jacob was given a new name: *"Israel* [he who strives with God]: *for as a prince hast thou power with God and with men, and hast prevailed"* (v. 28).

Through all the ages, God's children have understood what Christ's two parables teach: God holds Himself back and tries to get away from us, until what is of flesh, self, and sloth in us is overcome, and we so prevail with Him that He can and must bless us. Why do so few of God's children desire this honor: being princes of God, strivers with God, who prevail? What our Lord taught us, *"What things soever ye desire…believe that ye receive them"* (Mark 11:24), is nothing but His restatement of Jacob's words, *"I will not let thee go, except thou bless me"* (Gen. 32:26). This is the opportunity He teaches, and we must learn to claim and take the blessing.

Think of Moses when Israel had made the golden calf. Moses returned to the Lord and said, *"Oh, this people have sinned a great sin….Yet now, if thou wilt forgive their sin—; and if not, blot me, I pray thee, out of thy book which thou hast written"* (Exod. 32:31-32). That was importunity—Moses would rather have died than not have his people given to him. When God heard him, He promised Moses that He would send His angel to go with the people. But Moses went to Him again and would not be content until, in answer to his prayer, God promised He Himself would go with them. (See Exod. 33:2–3, 12–15, 17–18.) He said, *"I will do this thing also that thou hast spoken"* (Exodus 33:17). After that, when in answer to Moses' prayer, *"show me thy glory"* (v. 18), God made His goodness pass before him, Moses once again began pleading, *"Let my Lord, I pray thee, go among us"* (Exod. 34:9). And he was there with the Lord forty days and forty nights (v. 28). Of these days he said, *"I fell down before the LORD, as at the first, forty days and forty nights: I did neither eat bread, nor drink water, because of all your sins which ye sinned"* (Deut. 9:18).

As an intercessor, Moses used importunity with God and prevailed. He proves that the man who truly lives near to God, and with whom God speaks face to face, becomes partaker of that same power of intercession that there is in Him who is at God's right hand and ever lives to pray.

Think of Elijah in his prayer, first for fire and then for rain. In the former, you have the importunity that claims and receives an immediate answer. In the latter, bowing himself down to the earth, his face between his knees, his answer to the servant who had gone to look toward the sea and come with the message, *"There is nothing,"* was *"Go again seven times"* (1 Kings 18:43). Here was the importunity of perseverance. He had told Ahab there would be rain. He knew it was coming, and yet he prayed until the seven times were fulfilled. Of Elijah and his prayers, we are taught, *"Pray one for another....[Elijah] was a man subject to like passions as we are.... The effectual fervent prayer of a righteous man availeth much"* (James 5:16-17). Where is the Lord God of Elijah, this God who draws out such effectual prayer and hears it so wonderfully? His name be praised—He is still the same! Let His people simply believe that He still waits to be inquired of! Faith in a prayer-hearing God will make a prayer-loving Christian.

Remember the marks of the true intercessor, as the parable taught us: a sense of human need, a Christlike love in the heart, a consciousness of personal impotence, faith in the power of prayer, courage to persevere in spite of refusal, and the assurance of an abundant reward. These characteristics constitute a Christian intercessor and release the power of prevailing prayer. They constitute the beauty and the health of Christian life, fitting a man for being a blessing in the world and making him a true Christian worker, who does, indeed, get from God the bread of heaven to dispense to the hungry. These dispositions elicit the highest—the heroic—virtues of the life of faith.

There is nothing to which the nobility of natural character owes so much as it does to the spirit of enterprise and daring, which in travel, war, politics, or science, battles with difficulties and conquers. No labor or expense is too great for the sake of victory. Shouldn't we Christians be able to face difficulties through prayer? As we labor and strive in prayer, our renewed will asserts its royal right to claim, in the name of Christ, what it will, wielding its God-given power to influence the destinies of men. Shouldn't men of the world sacrifice ease and pleasure in their pursuits to fight their way through to the place where they find liberty for the captive and salvation for the perishing?

Let each servant of Christ learn to know his calling. His King ever lives to pray. The Spirit of the King ever lives in us to pray. The blessings that the world needs must be called down from heaven in persevering, importunate, believing prayer. It is from heaven, in answer to such prayer, that the Holy Spirit will take complete possession of us to do His work through us. Let us acknowledge how vain all of our own work has been, due to our meager prayer. Let us change our method, so that more prayer, much prayer, unceasing prayer, is the proof that we look to God for everything and that we believe that He hears us.

5

THE LIFE THAT CAN PRAY

If ye abide in me, and my words abide in you,
ye shall ask what ye will, and it shall be done unto you.
—John 15:7

The effectual fervent prayer of a righteous man availeth much.
—James 5:16

Beloved, if our heart condemn us not, then have we confidence toward
God. And whatsoever we ask, we receive of him, because we keep his
commandments, and do those things that are pleasing in his sight.
—1 John 3:21–22

Here on earth, the success of someone asking a favor for others depends entirely on his character and the relationship he bears to the person for whom he is interceding. What he is gives weight to what he asks. It is no different with God. Our power in prayer depends on our lives. Where our lives are right we will know to pray so as to please God, and prayers will secure the answer. The scriptures quoted above all point in this direction. *"If ye abide in me,"* our Lord said, *"ye shall ask…and it shall be done unto you."* It is the prayer of a righteous man, according to James, that avails much. We receive *"whatsoever we ask,"* John said, because we obey and please God. All lack of power to pray correctly and perseveringly, all lack of power in prayer with God, indicates some lack in the Christian life. As we learn to live the life that pleases God, God will give us what we ask for. Let us learn from our Lord Jesus, in the parable of the vine, what the healthy, vigorous Christian life is, and how it may ask and receive whatever it desires. Hear His voice: *"If ye abide in me, and my words abide in you, ye shall ask what ye will, and it shall be done unto you."* And again at the close of the parable: *"Ye have not chosen me, but I have chosen you, and ordained you, that ye should go and bring forth fruit, and that your fruit should remain: that whatsoever ye shall ask of the Father in my name, he may give it you"* (John 15:16).

What sort of life is it, according to the parable, that we must lead to bear fruit, and then to ask and receive whatever we desire? What must we be or do, that will enable us to pray as we should, and to receive what we ask for? The answer is in these words: the branch life gives power for prayer. We are branches of Christ, the Living Vine. We must simply live like branches—abide in Christ—then we will ask what we will, and it will be done unto us.

We all know what a branch is. Its essential characteristic is that it is simply a growth of the vine, produced by it and appointed to bear its fruit. It has only one reason for existence: it is there at the bidding of the vine, that through it the vine may bear and ripen its precious fruit. Just as the vine lives solely and wholly to produce the sap that makes the grape, so the branch has the singular object of receiving that sap and bearing the grape.

Its only work is to serve the vine, in order that through it the vine may do its work.

Is the believer—the branch of Christ, the Heavenly Vine—as literally, as exclusively, to live only that Christ may bear fruit through him? Is a true Christian, as a branch, to be just as absorbed in and devoted to the work of bearing fruit to the glory of God as Christ the Vine was on earth and is now in heaven? This, and nothing less, is indeed what is meant. It is to this branch life that the unlimited prayer promises of the parable are given. It is this branch life—existing solely for the Vine—that will have the power to pray properly. When we abide in Him and His words abide—kept and obeyed—in our hearts and lives and are absorbed into our very beings, then we will have the grace to pray correctly and the faith to receive the answer.

Let us take Christ's words, *"any thing"* (John 14:14), *"whatsover"* (v. 13), and *"what ye will"* and accept them in their simple, literal truth and their infinite, divine grandeur. They are wonderfully repeated six times in the promises of our Lord's farewell discourse. (See John 14:13–14; 15:7, 16; 16:23–24.) Because they appear altogether too large for us to take them literally, we qualify them to meet our human ideas of what appears right. This is because we separate them from that life of absolute and unlimited devotion to Christ's service to which they were given.

God's covenant is always: give all and take all. Whoever is willing to be wholly branch, and nothing but branch, must be ready to place himself absolutely at the disposal of Jesus, the Vine of God, to bear His fruit, and to live every moment only for Him. This person will receive a divine liberty to claim Christ's *"whatsoever"* in all its fullness, and a divine wisdom and humility to use it right. He will live and pray, claiming the Father's promises as Christ did, only for God's glory in the salvation of men. He will use his boldness in prayer only for power in intercession and getting men blessed. The unlimited devotion of the branch life to fruitbearing and the unlimited access to the treasures of the Vine life are inseparable. It is only the life abiding wholly in Christ that can pray the effective prayer in the name of Christ.

Think, for a moment, of the men of prayer in Scripture, and see in them the life that could pray in such power. We spoke of Abraham as an intercessor. What gave him such boldness? He knew that God had chosen and called him away from his home and people to walk before Him, that all nations might be blessed in him. He knew that he had obeyed and forsaken everything for God. Implicit obedience, to the very sacrifice of his son, was the law of his life. He did what God asked of him: he dared to trust God to do whatever he asked. We spoke of Moses as an intercessor. He, too, had forsaken everything for God, *"esteeming the reproach of Christ greater riches than the treasures in Egypt"* (Heb. 11:26). He lived at God's disposal; he *"was faithful in all his house, as a servant"* (Heb. 3:5). How often it is written of him, *"according to all that the LORD commanded [Moses], so did he"* (Exod. 40:16). No wonder he was so very bold. His heart was right with God, and he knew God would hear him. This is no less true of Elijah, the man who took his stand for the Lord God of Israel. The man who is ready to risk everything for God can count on God to do everything for him.

Men pray as they live, because it is the life that prays. The life that, with wholehearted devotion, gives up everything for God and to God can claim everything from God. Our God longs exceedingly to prove Himself the Faithful God and Mighty Helper of His people. He only waits for hearts that are completely turned from the world to Himself and are open to receive His gifts. The man who loses all will find all; he will dare to ask and, then, take it. The branch that only and truly lives abiding in Christ, the Heavenly Vine, the branch that is entirely given up, like Christ, to bear fruit in the salvation of men, the branch that has Christ's words taken into and abiding in its life, may and dares ask what it will; it will be done. We may not yet have attained that full devotion to which our Lord had trained His disciples, neither may we equal them in their power of prayer. We may, nevertheless, take courage in remembering that every new step we take in our Christian life toward the perfect branch life, and every surrender to live for others in intercession, will be met from above by a corresponding liberty to pray with greater boldness and expect larger answers. The more we pray, and the more conscious we become of our unfitness to pray in power, the more we will be urged and helped to press on toward the key to power in prayer—a life abiding in Christ, entirely at His disposal.

Is there anyone concerned about why they have failed to attain this blessed branch life, so simple and yet so mighty? Do they wonder how to reach it? Let me point them to one of the most precious lessons of the parable of the Vine, one that is all too little noticed. Jesus said, *"I am the true vine, and my Father is the husbandman"* (John 15:1). It is, indeed, something very wonderful that we have Christ, the glorified Son of God, whose divine fullness of life and grace we can share. But there is something more wonderful still. We have the Father, as the Husbandman, watching over our abiding in the Vine, over our growth and fruitbearing. It is not left to our faith or our faithfulness to maintain our union with Christ. God—the Father of Christ, who united us with Him—will see to it that the branch is what it should be. He will enable us to bring forth just the fruit we were appointed to bear. Hear what Christ said of this, *"Every branch that beareth fruit, he purgeth it, that it may bring forth more fruit"* (v. 2). More fruit is what the Father seeks; more fruit is what the Father Himself will provide. It is for this that He, as the Vinedresser, cleanses the branches.

Think for a moment what this means. It is said that of all fruit-bearing plants on earth, there is none that produces fruit so full of spirit—from which spirit can be so abundantly distilled—as the vine. And of all fruit-bearing plants, there is none that is so prone to overgrowth, and for which pruning and cleansing are so indispensable. The one great work that a vinedresser must do for the branch every year is to prune it. Other plants can, for a time, bear fruit without pruning. But the vine must have it. Therefore, the branch that desires to abide in Christ and bring forth much fruit—that desires to be able to ask whatsoever it will—must trust in and yield to the divine cleansing.

What exactly does the vinedresser cut away with his pruning knife? Nothing but the wood that the branch has produced: true, honest wood, with the vine's true nature in it. This must be cut away. And why? Because it draws away the strength and life of the vine and hinders the flow of the juice to the grape. The more it is cut down, the less wood there is in the branch, and the more sap that goes to the grape. The wood of the branch must decrease, that the fruit for the vine may increase. In obedience to the law of all nature, death is the way to life, and gain comes through sacrifice. The rich and luxuriant growth of wood must be cut off and discarded in order that more abundant life may be seen in the cluster.

Child of God, branch of the Heavenly Vine, there is a part of you that may appear perfectly innocent and legitimate, but it depletes your interest and your strength to such an extent that it must be pruned and cleansed away. We know what power in prayer men like Abraham, Moses, and Elijah had, and we know what fruit they bore. But how often do we remember what it cost them? How God had to separate them from their surroundings and repeatedly draw them from trusting in themselves, so they would seek their lives in Him alone. We will bear much fruit only when our own will, strength, effort, and pleasure—even where these appear perfectly natural and sinless—are cut down, leaving our entire being free and open to receive the sap of the Heavenly Vine, the Holy Spirit. It is in the surrender of what human nature holds fast in the full and willing submission to God's holy pruning knife—that we will become what Christ chose and appointed us for: fruit bearers, to whom whatever is requested from the Father in Christ's name will be given.

Christ tells us in the next verse what the pruning knife is: *"Ye are clean through the word which I have spoken unto you"* (John 15:3). As He said later, *"Sanctify them through thy truth: thy word is truth"* (John 17:17). *"The word of God is…sharper than any twoedged sword, piercing even to the dividing asunder of soul and spirit"* (Heb. 4:12). Christ had spoken such heart-searching words to His disciples on love and humility, being the least and—like Himself— the servant of all, denying self, taking the cross, and losing the life. Through His Word, the Father had cleansed them, cutting away all confidence in themselves or the world, preparing them for the inflowing and filling of the Spirit of the Heavenly Vine. We cannot cleanse ourselves; God is the Vinedresser. We may confidently entrust ourselves to His care.

Beloved Christians—ministers, missionaries, teachers, workers, believers old and young—are you mourning your lack of prayer and, as a consequence, your lack of power in prayer? O come and listen to your beloved Lord as He tells you to be a branch, united to and identified with the Heavenly Vine; your prayers will then be effective and powerful. Are you despairing because you do not, you cannot, live this branch life, abiding in Him? Come and listen again. For you to bear *"more fruit"* (John 15:2) is not only your desire, but the Father's, too. He is the Husbandman who cleanses the fruitful branch, so it can bear more fruit. Cast yourself upon God to do in you what is impossible for man. Count upon a divine cleansing to cut down and take away all that self-confidence and self-effort that has been the cause of your failure. The God who gave you His beloved Son to be your Vine, who made you His branch, will do His work of cleansing to make you fruitful in every good work, including the work of prayer and intercession.

The life that can pray is a branch entirely given up to the Vine and the Vine life. All responsibility for its cleansing is cast on the Vinedresser. A branch abiding in Christ, trusting and yielding to God for His cleansing, can bear much fruit. In the power of such a life we will love prayer; we will know how to pray; we will pray and receive whatever we ask.

6

IS RESTRAINING PRAYER A SIN?

Thou…restrainest prayer before God.
—Job 15:4

What profit should we have, if we pray unto him?
—Job 21:15

*God forbid that I should sin against the
LORD in ceasing to pray for you.*
—1 Samuel 12:23

> *Neither will I be with you any more,*
> *except ye destroy the accursed from among you.*
> —Joshua 7:12

Any deep quickening of the spiritual life of the church will always be accompanied by a deeper sense of sin. This will not be caused by theology, which can only give expression to what God has already worked in the life of His people. Nor will this deeper sense of sin only be seen in stronger expressions of self-reproach, which often consists of the harboring of sin and unbelief. But the true sense of the hatefulness of sin and the hatred of it will be proved by the intensity of desire for deliverance and the struggle to know to the very utmost what God's power to save is. It is no less than a holy jealousy, to sin against God in nothing.

If we are to deal effectively with the lack of prayer, we must look at it from this point of view and ask, "Is restraining prayer a sin?" And if it is, how should it be discovered, confessed, cast out by man, and cleansed away by God? Jesus is a Savior from sin. Only when we truly know sin can we truly know the power that saves from sin. The life that can pray effectively is the life of the cleansed branch—the life that knows deliverance from the power of self. To see that our prayer-sins are indeed sins is the first step to a true and divine deliverance from them.

In the story of Achan (see Joshua 7), we have one of the strongest proofs in Scripture that it is sin that robs God's people of His blessing, and that God will not tolerate it. It is, at the same time, the clearest indication of the principles under which God deals with sin and removes it. Let us see, in the light of the story, if we can learn how to look at the sin of prayerlessness, and at the sinfulness that lies at the root of it. The words I have quoted above, "*Neither will I be with you any more, except ye destroy the accursed thing from among you,*" take us into the very heart of the story. They suggest a series of precious lessons around the truth they express: the presence of sin makes the presence of God impossible.

1. The presence of God is the great privilege of God's people and their only power against the Enemy. God had promised to bring Moses into the promised land. Moses proved that he understood this when, after the sin of the golden calf, God spoke of withdrawing His presence and sending an angel. Moses refused to accept anything less than God's presence. *"For wherein shall it be known here that I and thy people have found grace in thy sight? is it not in that thou goest with us?"* (Exodus 33:16). This gave Caleb and Joshua their confidence: the Lord is with us. This gave Israel their victory over Jericho: the presence of God. Throughout Scripture, this is the great, central promise: "I am with thee." The wholehearted believer is separated from the worldling and worldly Christians around him by living consciously hidden in the secret of God's presence.

2. Defeat and failure always result from the loss of God's presence. It was thus at Ai. God had brought His people into Canaan with the promise to give them the land. When the defeat at Ai took place, Joshua felt at once that the cause must be in the withdrawal of God's power. He had not fought for them. His presence had been withheld.

In the Christian life and the work of the church, defeat is always a sign of the loss of God's presence. If we apply this truth to our failures in the prayer life, considering our failure in work for God, we are led to see that it all simply goes back to our not standing in clear and full fellowship with God. His nearness, His immediate presence, has not been the chief thing sought after and trusted in. He could not work in us as He desired. Loss of blessing and power is always caused by the loss of God's presence.

3. The loss of God's presence always results from some hidden sin. Just as, in nature, pain is a warning sign of some hidden evil in the system, defeat is God's voice telling us there is something wrong. He has given Himself so wholly to His people, He delights so in being with them, and would so gladly reveal His love and power in them, that He never withdraws unless He is compelled to do so by their sin.

The church is complaining about many defeats today; she has so little power in the civilized world; the preaching of the gospel everywhere is paralyzed by the scarcity of money and men; powerful conversions are rare;

and the number of holy, consecrated, spiritual Christians, devoted to the service of God and their fellowmen is small. This all stems from a lack of the effective prayer that brings the Holy Spirit in power to ministers, believers, missionaries, and unsaved souls. Can we deny that our lack of prayer is the sin causing God's presence and power to be so far from us?

4. God Himself will discover the hidden sin. We may think we know what the sin is, but only God can discover its real and deep meaning. When He spoke to Joshua before naming the sin of Achan, God first said, *"They have also transgressed my covenant which I commanded them"* (Josh. 7:11). God had commanded that all the booty of Jericho—gold, silver, and everything else—was to be consecrated unto the Lord, be placed in His treasury (Josh. 6:19). Israel had broken this consecration vow; it had not given God what was due Him; it had robbed God.

We need God to show us how our lack of prayer indicates an unfaithfulness to our consecration vow: to give God all of our hearts and lives. Our limited prayers, with the excuses we make for them, are a greater sin than we know. It shows that we have little taste or relish for fellowship with God; that our faith rests more on our own work and efforts than on the power of God. It demonstrates that we have little sense of the heavenly blessings God waits to shower down on us, that we are not ready to sacrifice the ease and confidence of the flesh for perseveringly waiting on God. And finally, it proves that the spirituality of our life—our abiding in Christ—is altogether too weak to make us prevail in prayer. When the pressure of work for Christ is allowed to be the excuse for our not finding time to seek and secure His own presence and power in it as our chief need, our sense of absolute dependence on God is not right. It shows we have no deep understanding of the divine and supernatural work of God in which we are only His instruments, no true entrance into the heavenly, altogether otherworldly, character of our mission, and no full surrender to and delight in Christ Jesus Himself.

If we would allow God's Spirit to show us that all this comes from negligence in prayer, and of misplaced priorities, all our excuses would fall away. We would fall down and cry, "We have sinned! We have sinned!"

Samuel once said, *"As for me, God forbid that I should sin against the* LORD *in ceasing to pray for you"* (1 Sam. 12:23). Ceasing from prayer is sin against God. May God reveal this to us.

5. When God reveals sin, it must be confessed and cast out. When the defeat at Ai came, Joshua and Israel were ignorant of the cause. Because God dealt with Israel as a nation—as one body—they were all held accountable for the sin of one member. Israel as a whole was unaware of the sin, and yet suffered for it. The church may be unaware of the greatness of the sin of limited prayer, individual ministers or believers may never have considered it an actual transgression, but it nevertheless brings punishment. When the Holy Spirit begins to convict us of it, and the sin is hidden no more, then the time of heart searching begins. In our story, the combination of individual and united responsibility is very solemn. As for the individual, God took each one, *"man by man"* (Josh. 7:14). Every man felt himself under the eye of God, to be dealt with, and when Achan had been taken, he had to make confession. As for the united body, all Israel suffered as God dealt with them. Then, together, *"all Israel"* stoned and burned Achan, his family (v. 24), and *"the accursed"* (v. 15) out of their midst.

If we have reason to think that our lack of prayer is the sin in our camp, let us first confess it, both personally and unitedly. Then, let us come before God to destroy and put away the sin. The heap of stones in the valley of Achor stands at the very threshold of Israel's history in Canaan to remind us that God cannot bear sin, that God will not dwell with sin, and that, if we really want God's presence in power, sin must be put away. The solemn fact is this: although there may be many other sins, to not pray as Christ and Scripture teach us is definitely one that causes the loss of God's presence. We must bring this sin out before God and give it up to the death. Then we must yield ourselves to God and obey His voice. No fear of past failure, no threatening array of temptations, duties, or excuses must keep us back. It is a simple question of obedience.

Are we going to give ourselves up to God and His Spirit to live a life in prayer that is pleasing to Him? Surely—if God truly has been withholding His presence from us, if He really has been revealing our sin, if He really is calling for its destruction and our return to obedience—surely we can depend on His grace to accept and strengthen us for the life He desires of us. It is not a question of what you can do. It is a question of whether, with your whole heart, you give God what is due Him, surrendering yourself to let His will and grace have their way with you.

6. With sin cast out, God's presence is restored. From this day onward, there is not a word in the book of Joshua of defeat in battle. The story shows them going on from victory to victory. The securing of God's presence gives power to overcome every enemy.

This truth is so simple that the very ease with which we acquiesce to it robs it of its power. Let us pause and think about what it implies. If when God is with us, we are victorious, then the responsibility for defeat must lie in our hands. This means that some sin must be causing it. Therefore, we should immediately search out and put away that sin. We may confidently expect God's presence the moment this is done. But each of us has a solemn obligation to examine his life to find what part he may have in this evil.

God never speaks to His people about sin except with the purpose of saving them from it. The same light that shows the sin will show the way out of it. The same power that breaks down and condemns, if humbly yielded to and waited on in confession and faith, will make it possible to rise up and conquer. It is God who is speaking to His church and to us about this sin: "He...*wondered that there was no intercessor*" (Isa. 59:16); "*I wondered that there was none to uphold*" (Isa. 63:5); "*I sought for a man... that should...stand in the gap before me...but I found none*" (Ezek. 22:30). The God who speaks thus will work this change for His children who seek His face: He will make the valley of Achor—of trouble and shame, of sin confessed and cast out—a door of hope. Let us not fear or cling to the excuses and explanations that circumstances suggest. All we must do is to simply confess, "We have sinned; we are sinning; we dare not sin any longer." God does not demand impossibilities of us in prayer. He does not weary us with an impractical ideal. He asks us to pray no more than what He gives us grace to do. We may, therefore, rest assured that He will give us the grace to pray so that our intercessions will be a pleasure to Him and to us, a source of strength to our conscience and our work, and a channel of blessing to those for whom we labor.

God dealt personally with Joshua, with Israel, and with Achan. Let each of us allow Him to deal personally with us concerning this sin of too little prayer, the consequences of too little prayer in our lives and work, the deliverance from sin, and prayer's certainty and blessedness. Just bow in stillness and wait before God until He overshadows you with His presence. Let Him lead you out of the region of human reasoning, where conviction of sin can never be deep, and full deliverance can never come. Take quiet time and be still before God, so that He may take this matter in hand. *"Sit still…for [He] will not be in rest, until he [has] finished the thing this day"* (Ruth 3:18). Leave yourself in God's hands.

7

WHO SHALL DELIVER?

*Is there no balm in Gilead; is there no physician there? why then is not
the health of the daughter of my people recovered?*
—Jeremiah 8:22

*Return, ye backsliding children, and I will heal your backslidings.
Behold, we come unto thee; for thou art the LORD our God.*
—Jeremiah 3:22

Heal me, O LORD, and I shall be healed.
—Jeremiah 17:14

*Wretched man that I am! who shall deliver me from
the body of this death? I thank God through Jesus Christ our Lord....*

The law of the Spirit of life in Christ Jesus hath made me
free from the law of sin and death.
—Romans 7:24–25; 8:2

A gentlemen once came to me for advice and help. He was evidently an earnest and well-instructed Christian man. For several years, he had been in quite difficult surroundings, trying to witness for Christ. The result was a sense of failure and unhappiness. His complaint was that he had no relish for the Word, and that, though he prayed, it was as if his heart was not in it. If he spoke to others or gave a tract, it was under a sense of duty; the love and the joy were not present. He longed to be filled with God's Spirit, but the more he sought it, the farther off it appeared to be. What was he to think of his state, and was there any way out of it?

My answer was that the whole matter appeared to be very simple: he was living under the law and not under grace. As long as he did so, there could be no change. He listened attentively, but could not see exactly what I meant.

I reminded him of the difference, the absolute contrast between law and grace. Law demands; grace bestows. Law commands, but gives no strength to obey. Grace promises and performs, doing everything for us. Law burdens, casts down, and condemns. Grace comforts, makes strong and glad. Law appeals to self to do its utmost; grace points to Christ to do all. Law requires effort and strain, urging us toward a goal we can never reach. Grace works all of God's blessed will in us. I pointed out to him how his first step should be to completely accept his failure and his inability, as God had been trying to show him, instead of striving against it. With this acceptance and confession, he could sink down before God in utter helplessness. There he would learn that, unless grace gave him deliverance and strength, he could never do better than he had done, and that grace would, indeed, work all for him. He must come out from under law, self, and effort, taking his place under grace and allowing God to do all.

In later conversations he told me the diagnosis of the disease had been correct. He admitted grace must do everything. And yet, he had such a deep belief that he must do something, at least to be faithful, to secure the work of grace, that he feared his life would not change very much. He thought he would not be strong enough to handle the strain of new difficulties into which he was now going. There was, amid all his intense earnestness, an undertone of despair. He could not live as he knew he ought to.

I have already mentioned that I had noticed this tone of hopelessness. Every minister who has come into close contact with souls seeking to live wholly for God—to *"walk worthy of the Lord unto all pleasing"* (Col. 1:10)—knows that this renders true progress impossible. There are many difficulties to be met, especially if one desires a fuller prayer life. We so often resolve to pray more and better, and then fail. We do not all have the strength of will required to change our habits. The pressure of duty is great. It is so difficult to find time for more prayer. We do not always feel real enjoyment in prayer, which would enable us to persevere. We do not have the necessary power for supplication and pleading, as we should. Instead of being a joy and a strength, our prayers are a source of continual self-condemnation and doubt. We have, at times, mourned and confessed and resolved. But to tell the honest truth, we do not expect—for we do not see the way to—any great change.

It is evident that as long as this spirit prevails, there can be very little prospect of improvement. Discouragement must bring defeat. One of the first objects of a physician is to awaken and maintain hope. Without this, he knows his medicines will often accomplish little. No teaching from God's Word as to the duty, the urgent need, or the blessed privilege of more prayer will avail, as long as something lingers inside us whispering, "There is no hope." First, we must find the hidden cause of our failure and despair, and then, realize how divinely sure deliverance is. We must, unless we are to rest content with our state, listen to and join in the question, *"Is there no balm in Gilead; is there no physician there? why then is not the health of the daughter of my people recovered?"* We must listen to, and receive into our heart, the divine promise, *"Return, ye backsliding children, and I will heal your backslidings,"* and Israel's response, *"Behold, we come unto thee: for thou art the LORD our God."* We must come with the personal prayer and have faith that there will be a personal answer. Let us begin now to claim it in regard to the lack of prayer, believing that God will help us: *"Heal me, O LORD, and I shall be healed."*

It is always important to distinguish between the symptoms of a disease and the disease itself. Weakness and failure in prayer is a sign of weakness in the spiritual life. If a patient were to ask a physician to give him something to stimulate his weak pulse, he would be told that this would do him little good. The pulse is the index of the state of the heart and the whole system. The physician is striving to have health restored. Everyone who would like to pray more faithfully and effectively must learn that his whole spiritual life is in a sickly state and needs restoration. His shortcoming in prayer is merely the symptom of his weak life of faith. Only when he realizes this will he become fully alive to the serious nature of the disease. He will then see the need for a radical change in his whole life and walk, if his prayer life—the pulse of his spiritual system—is to indicate health and vigor. God has created us in such a way that the exercise of every healthy function causes joy. Prayer is meant to be as simple and natural as breathing or working are to a healthy man. The reluctance we feel, and the failure we confess, are God's own voice calling us to acknowledge our disease, and to come to Him for the healing He has promised.

And what is the disease of which the lack of prayer is the symptom? We cannot find a better answer than is pointed out in the words, *"Ye are not under the law, but under grace"* (Rom. 6:14).

This suggests the possibility of two types of Christian life: a life partly under the law and partly under grace, and a life entirely under grace, in the full liberty from self-effort and the full experience of the divine strength that it can give. A true believer may still be living partly under the law, in the power of self-effort, striving to do what he cannot possibly accomplish. The continued failure in his Christian life results from his trusting in himself and trying to do his best. He does, indeed, pray and look to God for help, but it is still in his own strength, helped by God, that he does the work. In the Epistles to the Romans and the Galatians, Paul tells them that they *"have not received the spirit of bondage again"* (Rom. 8:15); that they are *"free from the law"* (v. 2); that they are no more servants, but sons (see Gal. 4:7); that they must beware of nothing so much as becoming *"entangled again with the yoke of bondage"* (Gal. 5:1).

Everywhere in the New Testament we see this contrast between the law and grace, between the flesh, which is under the law, and the Spirit, who is the gift of grace, through whom grace does all its work. For us, just as for the early church, the great danger is living under the law, serving God in the strength of our flesh. The great majority of Christians appear to remain in this state all their lives. This explains, to a large extent, their lack of true, holy living and power in prayer. They do not know that all failure can have but one cause: men seek to do themselves what grace alone can do in them, what grace most certainly will do.

Many will not be prepared to admit that this is their disease, that they are not living *"under grace"* (Rom. 6:14). Impossible, they say. "From the depth of my heart," a Christian cries, "I believe and know that there is no good in me, and that I owe everything to grace alone." "I have spent my life," a minister said, "and found my glory in preaching and exalting the doctrine of free grace." "And I," a missionary answers, "how could I ever have thought of seeing the heathen saved, if my only confidence had not been in the message I brought, and the power I trusted, of God's abounding grace." Surely you cannot say that our failures in prayer—and we sadly confess them—are caused by our not living under grace? This cannot be our disease.

We know it is possible for a man to be suffering from a disease without knowing it. What he believes to be a slight ailment turns out to be quite dangerous. Do not let us be too sure that we are not, to a large extent, still living *"under the law"* (v. 14) while considering ourselves to be living wholly *"under grace."* Very frequently, the reason for this mistake is the limited meaning attached to the word *grace*. Just as we limit God Himself by our little or unbelieving thoughts of Him, so we limit His grace at the very moment we are delighting in terms like the *"riches of...grace"* (Eph. 1:7) and *"grace... exceeding abundant"* (1 Tim. 1:14). The very term, "grace abounding," has been confined to the one great, blessed truth of free justification with the ever renewed pardon and eternal glory for the vilest of sinners. Yet the equally blessed truth of "grace abounding" in sanctification is not fully known.

Paul wrote, "*Much more they which receive abundance of grace...shall reign in life by one, Jesus Christ*" (Rom. 5:17). That reigning in life, as conquerors over sin, exists even here on earth. "*Where sin abounded*"—in the heart and life—"*grace did much more abound: that...grace reign through righteousness*" (vv. 5:20–21) in the whole life and being of the believer. It is of this reign of grace in the soul that Paul asks, "*Shall we sin, because we are...under grace?*" and answers, "*God forbid*" (Romans 6:15). Grace is not only pardon of, but power over, sin. Grace takes the place sin had in the life, and undertakes, as sin had reigned within the power of death, to reign in the power of Christ's life. It is of this grace that Christ spoke, "*My grace is sufficient for thee,*" and Paul answered, "*Will I rather glory in my infirmities....for when I am weak, then am I strong*" (2 Cor. 12:9–10). It is this grace that, when we are willing to confess ourselves utterly impotent and helpless, comes in to work all in us. It is of this grace that Paul taught, "*God is able to make all grace abound toward you; that ye, always having all sufficiency in all things, may abound to every good work*" (2 Cor. 9:8).

It often happens that a seeker of God and salvation will read his Bible much, and yet never see the truth of a free and full and immediate justification by faith. Once his eyes are opened and he accepts it, he is amazed to find it everywhere. In just the same way, many believers who believe in the doctrine of free grace as applied to pardon have never seen its wondrous meaning to work a whole new life in us. It can actually give us strength every moment for whatever the Father wills us to be and do. When God's light shines into our heart with this blessed truth, we know what Paul meant, "*Not I, but the grace of God*" (1 Cor. 15:10). There again you have the twofold Christian life. One part is that in which the "*not I*"—I am nothing, I can do nothing—has not yet become a reality. The other is when the wondrous exchange has been made, and grace has taken the place of our effort. Then we say and know, "*I live; yet not I, but Christ liveth in me*" (Gal. 2:20). This may then become a lifelong experience: "*The grace of our Lord was exceeding abundant with faith and love which is in Christ Jesus*" (1 Tim. 1:14).

Beloved child of God, do you believe it possible that this has been the problem in your life, the cause of your failure in prayer? You did not know how grace would enable you to pray, if you placed your whole life under its power. You sought by earnest effort to conquer your reluctance or deadness in prayer, but failed. You strove by every motive of shame or love you could think of to stir yourself to it, but it would not help. Wouldn't it be worthwhile to ask the Lord whether the message I bring you as His servant may not be more true for you than you think? Your lack of prayer is the result of a diseased state of life, and the disease is this: you have not accepted, in your daily life and in your Christian duty, the full salvation that the Word brings. *"Ye are not under the law, but under grace"* (Rom. 6:14). The provision of grace and the power by which it makes us reign in life is not only as universal and deep reaching as the demand of the law and the reign of sin, it is more *"exceeding abundant"* (1 Tim. 1:14).

In Romans 7, Paul gives us a picture of a believer's life under the law, with the bitter experience in which it ends: *"Wretched man that I am! who shall deliver me from the body of this death?"* His answer to the question, *"I thank God through Jesus Christ our Lord,"* shows that there is deliverance from a life held captive by evil habits against which he struggled in vain. That deliverance is by the Holy Spirit giving us the full experience of what the life of Christ can work in us: *"The law of the Spirit of life in Christ Jesus hath made me free from the law of sin and death."* The law of God could only deliver us into the bondage of the law of sin and death. The grace of God can bring us into, and keep us in, the liberty of the Spirit. We can be made free from the sad life under the power that held us captive and kept us from doing the righteous things we wanted to do. The Spirit of life in Christ can free us from our continual failure in prayer and enable us to *"walk worthy of the Lord unto all pleasing"* (Col. 1:10).

Oh, do not be hopeless; do not be despondent! There is a balm in Gilead; there is a Physician there; there is healing for our sickness. What is impossible with man is possible with God. (See Luke 18:27.) What you see no possibility of doing, grace will do. Confess the disease; trust the Physician; claim the healing; pray the prayer of faith: *"Heal me...and I shall be healed."* You, too, can become a person of prayer and pray the effectual prayer that avails much.

8

WILT THOU
BE MADE WHOLE?

Jesus...saith unto him, Wilt thou be made whole?
The impotent man answered him, Sir, I have no man...to put me into
the pool....Jesus saith unto him, Rise...and walk. And immediately
the man was made whole...and walked.
—John 5:6–9

Peter said...In the name of Jesus Christ of Nazareth rise up and
walk....The faith which is by him hath given him this perfect
soundness in the presence of you all.
—Acts 3:6, 16

Peter said…Aeneas, Jesus Christ maketh thee whole:
arise….And he arose immediately.
—Acts 9:34

Weakness in prayer is the mark of disease. The inability to walk is, in the Christian, as in the natural life, a terrible proof of some evil in the system that needs a physician. The lack of power to walk joyfully in the new and living way that leads to the Father and the throne of grace is especially grievous. Christ is the great Physician, who comes to every Bethesda, where those who need healing are gathered, and asks His loving, searching question, *"Wilt thou be made whole?"* For anyone still clinging to hope in the pool, or looking for some man to put him in, for anyone hoping somehow to be helped, in time, by just continuing in the use of the ordinary means of grace, His question points to a better way. He offers them healing in a way of power they have never understood. And to anyone willing to confess, not only his own powerlessness, but his failure to find any man to help him, His question brings the sure and certain hope of a near deliverance. We have seen that our weakness in prayer is part of a life afflicted with spiritual weakness. Let us listen to our Lord as He offers to restore our spiritual strength and to fit us for walking like healthy, strong men in all the ways of the Lord. Then we will be properly fit to take our place in the great work of intercession. As we see the wholeness He offers, how He gives it, and what He asks of us, we will be prepared for giving a willing answer to His question.

The Health That Jesus Offers

What are some of the marks of spiritual health? Our text leads us to one: walking. To the sick man Jesus said, *"Rise…and walk,"* and with that, restored him to his place among men in full health and vigor, able to do his share of all the work of life. It is a wonderfully suggestive picture of the restoration of spiritual health. To the healthy, walking is a pleasure; to the sick, a burden, if not an impossibility. To many Christians, movement and progress in God's way is as wearying an effort as walking is to the lame. Christ comes to say, *"Rise...and walk,"* and with His word He gives the power to do so.

Think about this walk to which He restores and empowers us. It is a life like that of Enoch and Noah, who *"walked with God"* (Gen. 6:9); a life like that of Abraham, to whom God said, *"Walk before me"* (Gen. 17:1) and who himself said, *"The* LORD, *before whom I walk"* (Gen. 24:40); a life of which David sang, *"They shall walk...in the light of thy countenance"* (Psalm 89:15), and Isaiah prophesied, *"They that wait upon the* LORD *shall renew their strength...they shall run, and not be weary; and they shall walk, and not faint"* (Isaiah 40:31). Just as God the Creator does not faint nor become weary, they who walk with Him, waiting on Him, will never be exhausted or weak. Zacharias and Elisabeth, the last of the Old Testament saints, lived this life, and of them it was said *"They were both righteous before God, walking in all the commandments and ordinances of the Lord blameless"* (Luke 1:6). This is the walk Jesus came to make possible and true for His people in greater power than ever before.

Hear what the New Testament says of it: *"That like as Christ was raised up from the dead by the glory of the Father, even so we also should walk in newness of life"* (Rom. 6:4). It is the Risen One who said to us, *"Rise...and walk."* He gives us the power of the resurrection life, which is a walk in Christ. *"As ye have therefore received Christ Jesus the Lord, so walk ye in him"* (Col. 2:6). It is a walk like Christ. *"He that saith he abideth in him ought himself also so to walk, even as he walked"* (1 John 2:6). It is a walk by the Spirit and after the Spirit. *"Walk in the Spirit, and ye shall not fulfill the lust of the flesh"* (Gal. 5:16). *"Who walk not after the flesh, but after the Spirit"* (Rom. 8:1). It is a walk worthy of God and pleasing to Him. *"That ye might walk worthy of the Lord unto all pleasing, being fruitful in every good work"* (Col. 1:10). "[I] beseech you...that as ye have received of us how ye ought to walk and to please God, so ye would abound more and more" (1 Thess. 4:1). It is a walk in heavenly love. *"Walk in love, as Christ also hath loved us"* (Eph. 5:2). It is a *"walk in the light, as he is in the light"* (1 John 1:7). It is a walk of faith, whose power comes simply from God and Christ and the Holy Spirit to the soul turned away from the world. *"We walk by faith, not by sight"* (2 Cor. 5:7).

So many believers regard such a walk as impossible, so impossible that they do not feel it a sin that they walk otherwise. Therefore, they do not long for this walk in newness of life. They have become so accustomed to the life of powerlessness that the life and walk in God's strength has little attraction. But there are some who are not like this. They wonder if these words really mean what they say, and if the wonderful life each one of them speaks of is simply an unattainable ideal, or meant to be realized in flesh and blood. The more they study them, the more they feel that they are spoken for daily life. And yet they appear too high. If only they would believe that God sent His Almighty Son and His Holy Spirit to indeed bring us and fit us for a life and walk from heaven beyond anything that man could dare to think or hope for.

How Jesus Makes Us Whole

When a physician heals a patient, he treats him externally and does something which, if possible, leaves his patient independent of his aid in the future. He restores him to perfect health and leaves him. The work of our Lord Jesus is in both respects the very opposite. Jesus works not from without, but from within, by entering into our very life by the power of His Spirit. And instead of rendering the patient independent of His future assistance, Christ's one purpose in healing—His one condition of success—is to bring us into such dependence on Him that we are not able to do without Him for one single moment. Christ Jesus Himself is our life, in a sense that many Christians have no conception of.

Our prevailing weak and sickly life is entirely due to our lack of understanding of the divine truth. As long as we expect Christ to perform single, occasional acts of grace for us from heaven, trusting Him each time to give us something that will last a little while, we cannot be restored to perfect health. But when we see how nothing is to be our own for a single moment, everything is supposed to be Christ, when we learn to accept this from Him and trust Him for it, the life of Christ becomes the health of our soul. Health is nothing but life in its normal, undisturbed action. Christ gives us health by giving us Himself as our lives. In this way, He becomes our strength for our walk. Isaiah's words find their New Testament fulfillment therein: *"They that wait upon the* LORD*...shall walk, and not faint"* (Isa. 40:31), because Christ is now the strength of their lives.

It is strange how believers sometimes think this life of dependence is too great a strain, and a loss of personal liberty. They admit a need of dependence, of much dependence, but with room left for their own wills and energy. They do not see that even a partial dependence makes us debtors and leaves us nothing to boast of. They forget that our relationship to God, and cooperation with Him, is not that He does the larger part and we the lesser, but that God does all and we do all—God all in us, we all through God. This dependence on God secures our true independence. When our will seeks nothing but the divine will, we reach a divine nobility, the true independence of all that is created. He who has not seen this must remain a sickly Christian, letting self do part and Christ part. He who accepts the life of unceasing dependence on Christ, as life and health and strength, is made whole. As God, Christ can enter into and become the life of His creature. As the Glorified One who received the Holy Spirit from the Father to bestow, He can renew the heart of the sinful creature and make it His home. By His presence, He can maintain it in full health and strength.

All of you who would rather walk and please God, so that in your prayer life, your heart does not condemn you, listen to Christ's words: *"Wilt thou be made whole?"* He can give you soul health. He can give you a life that can pray and know that it is pleasing the Father. If you desire this, come and hear how you can receive it.

What Christ Asks of Us

The story of the man at Bethesda invites us to notice three things very specially. Christ's question first appeals to the will, asking for the expression of its consent. He then listens to the man's confession of his utter helplessness. Then, comes the ready obedience to Christ's command that rises up and walks.

The first step is, *"Wilt thou be made whole?"* There could be no doubt about the answer of the lame man. Who would not be willing to have his sickness removed? But in the spiritual life, there is a greater need to press the question. Some will not admit that they are so sick. Some will not believe that Christ can make a man whole. Some will believe it for others, but they are sure it is not for them. At the root of all this lies the fear of the self-denial and the sacrifice that will be needed. They are not willing to entirely forsake their walks in the world, to give up all self-will, self-confidence, and self-pleasing. The walk in Christ and like Christ is too straight and hard; they do not will it; they do not will to be made whole. My brother and sister, if you are willing, speak it out: "Lord, at any price, I will!" It is Christ's will to make you clean and whole. But you must will it also. If you desire to be delivered from your sickness, say to Him without fear, "I will, I will!"

Then comes the second step. Christ wants us to look up to Him as our only Helper. *"I have no man…to put me into"* must be our cry. Here on earth there is no help for me. Weakness may grow into strength in the ordinary way, if the body is in a sound state. But sickness requires special measures. Your soul is sick; your inability to walk the Christian walk joyfully is a sign of disease. Don't be afraid to confess it. Admit that there is no hope for restoration unless Christ's mercy heals you. Give up the idea of growing out of your sickly condition into a healthy one, of growing out from under the law into a life under grace. A few days ago, I heard a student say, "Do not think of growing into a missionary. Unless God forbids you, take the step. The decision will bring joy and strength, will set you free to mature in everything needed to be a missionary, and will be a help to others." It is just the same in the Christian life. Delay and struggle will hinder you. Simply confess that you cannot bring yourself to pray as you should, because you cannot give yourself the healthy, heavenly life that loves to pray, that knows to count on God's Spirit to pray in us. Come to Christ to heal you. In one moment, He can make you whole. There may not be a sudden change in your feelings or in what you are in yourself. But in heavenly reality, Christ will come in, in response to your surrender and faith, to take charge of your inner life and fill it with Himself and His Spirit.

The third thing Christ asks is the surrender of faith. When He spoke to the lame man, His command had to be obeyed. The man believed that there was truth and power in Christ's word; in that faith, he rose and walked. By faith he obeyed. And what Christ said to others was for him, too: *"Go thy way; thy faith hath made thee whole"* (Mark 10:52). Christ asks this faith of us, too, in order for His word to change our sickness into strength, fitting us for that walk in newness of life for which we have been quickened in Him. If we do not believe this, if we will not take courage and say with Paul, *"I can do all things through Christ which strengtheneth me"* (Phil. 4:13), we cannot obey. But if we will listen to the word that describes the walk that is not only possible, but livable, as proved by God's time-honored saints, if we fix our eye on the mighty, living, loving Christ, who speaks in power, *"Rise...and walk,"* we will take courage and obey. We will rise and begin to walk in Him and His strength. In faith, apart from and above all feeling, we will accept and trust an unseen Christ as our strength, and go on in the strength of the Lord God. We will know Christ as the strength of our lives. We will know and tell and prove that Jesus Christ has made us whole.

Can it really happen? Yes, it can. He has done it for many; He will do it for you. Beware of forming wrong conceptions of what must take place. When the lame man was made whole, he still had to learn how to use his newfound strength. If he wanted to dig, build, or learn a trade, he had to begin at the beginning. Do not expect to be immediately proficient in prayer or any other part of the Christian life. But do expect and be confident of this one thing: because you have trusted yourself to Christ to be your health and strength, He will lead and teach you. Begin to pray in a quiet sense for your ignorance and weakness but with a joyful assurance that He will work in you what you need. Rise and walk each day in a holy confidence that He is with you and in you. Just accept Jesus Christ the Living One, and trust Him to do His work.

Will you do it? Have you done it? Even now Jesus speaks, *"Rise...and walk."* Answer Him: "Amen, Lord! At Your word I come. I rise to walk with You, in You, and like You."

9

THE SECRET OF
EFFECTUAL PRAYER

What things soever ye desire, when ye pray,
believe that ye receive them, and ye shall have them.
—Mark 11:24

Here we have a summary of the teaching of our Lord Jesus on prayer. Nothing will convince us more of the sin of our negligence in prayer, revealing its causes and giving us courage to expect entire deliverance, than the careful study and believing acceptance of that teaching. The more heartily we enter into the mind of our blessed Lord, simply thinking about prayer as He thought, the more surely His words will become living seeds. They will grow and produce their fruit in us—a life corresponding exactly to the divine truth they contain. Do let us believe this: Christ, the living Word of God, gives, in His words, a divine quickening power that brings what they say, which works in us what He asks, and which actually enables us to do everything He demands. Learn to regard His teaching on prayer as a definite promise of what He, by His Holy Spirit dwelling in you, is going to work into your very being and character.

Our Lord gives us the five components, or essential elements, of true prayer. There must be, first, the heart's desire; then, the expression of that desire in prayer; with that, the faith that carries the prayer to God; in that faith, the acceptance of God's answer; then comes the experience of the desired blessing. It might help us to learn to pray believingly if we would each take a definite request to the Lord. Or perhaps better still, we might all unite and take the one thing to Him that has been occupying our attention: our failure in prayer. We could take, as the object of our desire and supplication, the grace of supplication. Together, we could ask and receive in faith the power to pray just as, and as much as, God expects of us. Let us meditate on our Lord's words in the confidence that He will teach us how to pray for this blessing.

1. "What things soever ye desire." Desire is the secret power that moves the whole world of living men and directs the course of each. It is, therefore, the soul of prayer. The cause of insufficient or unsuccessful prayer is very often found in the lack or weakness of desire. Some may doubt this; they are sure that they have very earnestly desired what they ask. But their desire may not be as wholehearted as God would have it, as the heavenly worth of these blessings demands. It may, indeed, be the lack of desire that is the cause of failure. What is true of God is true of each of His blessings. And the more spiritual the blessing, the truer it is. *"Ye shall seek me, and find me, when ye shall search for me with all your heart"* (Jer. 29:13).

Of Judah in the days of Asa it is written, *"They...sought him with their whole desire"* (2 Chron. 15:15). A Christian may often have very earnest desires for spiritual blessings. But besides these, there may be other desires in his daily life occupying a large place in his interests and affections. The spiritual desires are not all-absorbing. He wonders if his prayer is being heard. It is simply that God wants the whole heart. *"The Lord our God is one Lord: and thou shalt love the Lord thy God with all thy heart"* (Mark 12:29–30). The law is unchangeable: God offers Himself, gives Himself away, to the wholehearted who give themselves wholly away to Him. He always gives us according to our hearts' desires, not as we think it, but as He sees it. If there are other desires that occupy our heart more than Himself and His presence, He allows these to be fulfilled, and the desires that engage us at the hour of prayer cannot be granted.

We desire the gift of intercession, grace, and power to pray correctly. Our hearts must be drawn away from other desires; we must give ourselves wholly to this one. We must be willing to live completely in intercession for the kingdom. By fixing our eyes on the blessedness and the need of this grace, by believing with certainty that God will give it to us, by giving ourselves up to it for the sake of the perishing world, desire may be strengthened, and the first step taken toward the possession of the coveted blessing. Let us seek the grace of prayer, as we seek the God with whom it will link us, *"with [our] whole desire"* (2 Chron. 15:15). We can depend on the promise, *"He will fulfill the desire of them that fear him"* (Psalm 145:19). Let us not be afraid to say to Him, "I desire it with my whole heart."

2. *"What things soever ye desire, when ye pray."* The desire of the heart must become the expression of the lips. Our Lord Jesus more than once asked those who cried to Him for mercy, *"What wilt thou?"* (Mark 10:51). He wanted them to say what they desired. To speak it out loud aroused their whole being into action. It brought them into contact with Him and awakened their expectation. To pray is to enter into God's presence, to claim and secure His attention, to have distinct dealing with Him in regard to some request. Prayer is to commit our needs to His faithfulness and to leave them there. It is in so doing that we become fully conscious of what we are seeking.

There are some who often carry strong desires in their hearts, without bringing them to God in the clear expression of definite and repeated prayer. Others go to the Word and its promises to strengthen their faith, but do not give sufficient attention to that pointed asking of God that helps to assure the soul that the matter has been put into God's hands. Still others come in prayer with so many requests and desires that it is difficult for them to say what they really expect God to do. If you desire from God this great gift of faithfulness in prayer and the power to pray properly, begin by exercising yourself in prayer about just that. Say to yourself and to God, "I would like to ask You for the grace of intercession. I am asking You for it now and will continue to ask for it until I receive it. As plain and pointed as words can make it, I am saying, 'My Father! I do desire, I do ask of You, and I expect You to grant me this request.'"

3. "What things soever ye desire, when ye pray, believe." Because it is only by faith that we can know God, receive Jesus Christ, or live the Christian life, faith is the life and power of prayer. If we are to enter a life of intercession in which there is joy and power and blessing, if we are to have our prayers for this grace of prayer answered, we must relearn what faith is. We must begin to live and pray in faith as never before.

Faith is the opposite of sight, and the two are contrary to each other. "*We walk by faith, not by sight*" (2 Cor. 5:7). If the unseen is to get full possession of us, and our heart, life, and prayer are to be full of faith, there must be a withdrawal from, a denial of, the visible. The spirit that seeks to enjoy as much as possible that which is superficially innocent or legitimate, that gives the first place to the calls and duties of worldly life, is inconsistent with strong faith and close contact with the spiritual world. "*We look not at the things which are seen*"—the negative side needs to be emphasized if the positive, "*but at the things which are not seen*" (2 Cor. 4:18), is to become natural to us. In praying, faith depends on our living in the invisible world.

This faith is especially important to knowing God. The great reason for our lack of faith is our lack of knowledge of God and our weak communication with Him. "*Have faith in God*" (Mark 11:22), Jesus said when He spoke of removing mountains. Only as a soul comes to know God, becoming occupied with His power, love, and faithfulness, denying self and the world, and allowing the light of God to shine on it, will unbelief become impossible. All the mysteries and difficulties connected with answers to prayer will, however little we may be able to solve them intellectually, be swallowed up in the adoring assurance: "This God is our God. He will bless us. He does indeed answer prayer. And the grace to pray that I am asking for, He will delight to give."

4. "*What things soever ye desire, when ye pray, believe that ye receive,*" now as you pray. Faith has to accept the answer, as given by God in heaven, before it is found or felt on earth. This point causes difficulty, and yet it is the very essence, the real secret, of believing prayer. Try to take it in. Spiritual things can only be spiritually understood or appropriated. The spiritual, heavenly blessing of God's answer to your prayers must be spiritually recognized and accepted before you feel anything of it. It is faith that accomplishes this. A soul that not only seeks an answer, but seeks first the God who gives the answer, receives the power to know that it has what it has asked of Him. If the soul knows that it has asked according to His will and promises, that it has come to and found Himself to give it, then it does believe that it has received. "*We know that he* [hears] *us*" (1 John 5:15).

There is nothing as heart searching as the faith, "*Believe that ye receive.*" As we strive to believe and find we cannot, it leads us to discover what is hindering us. Blessed is the man who holds nothing back and lets nothing hold him back. With his eyes and heart on God alone, he refuses to rest until he has believed what our Lord bids him, that he has received. Here is the place where Jacob becomes Israel and the power of prevailing prayer is born out of human weakness and despair. Here is where the real need for persevering and importunate prayer comes in. It will not rest, go away, or give up, until it knows it is heard and believes that it has received.

Are you praying for "*the spirit of grace and of supplications*" (Zech 12:10)? Ask for it with a strong desire and believe in God who hears prayer. Do not be afraid to press on and believe that your life can indeed be changed, that the world with its pressures and responsibilities that hinder prayer, can be overcome. Believe that God gives you your heart's desire and the grace to pray both in measure and in spirit, just as the Father would have His child do. "*Believe that ye receive.*"

5. "*What things soever ye desire, when ye pray, believe that ye receive them, and ye shall have them.*" The receiving from God in faith—the believing acceptance of the answer with the perfect, praising assurance that it has been given—is not necessarily the experience or subjective possession of the gift we have asked for. At times, there may be a long interval of time between our asking and our actually receiving. In other cases, the believing supplicant may immediately experience the actual enjoyment of what he has received. It is especially in the former case that we need to have faith and patience: faith to rejoice in the assurance of the answer bestowed and received, and to begin acting on that answer even though nothing is felt; patience to wait if, for the present, there is no sensible proof of its reality. We can count on it: *"Ye shall have,"* in tangible reality.

If we apply this to the prayer for the power of faithful intercession—the grace to pray earnestly and perseveringly for souls around us—let us learn to grasp the divine assurance that as surely as we believe, we receive. Faith may, therefore, rejoice in the certainty of an answered prayer. The more we praise God for it, the sooner the experience will come. We may begin at once to pray for others in the confidence that grace will be given to us to pray more perseveringly and more believingly than we have ever done before. If we do not find any immediate growth or power in prayer, we must not be hindered or discouraged. We have accepted, apart from feeling, a spiritual, divine gift by faith; in that faith we are to pray, doubting nothing. The Holy Spirit may, for a little time, be hiding Himself within us. But we can count on Him to pray in us, even though it is with groanings that cannot find expression. In due time, we will become conscious of His presence and power. As sure as there is desire, prayer, faith, and faith's acceptance of the gift, there will also be the manifestation and experience of the blessing we sought.

Beloved Christians, do you truly desire that God would enable you to pray in such a way that your life would be free from continual self-condemnation, and that the power of His Spirit would come down in answer to your petition? Come and ask it of God. Kneel down and pray for it in a single, definite sentence. When you have done so, remain kneeling in faith, believing in God who answers. Believe that you do now receive what you have prayed; believe that you have received. If you find it difficult to do this, remain kneeling and say that you are doing it on the strength of His own word. If it costs time, struggle, and doubt, fear not. While you are there at His feet, looking up into His face, faith will come. *"Believe that ye receive."* At His bidding you dare to claim the answer. Begin a new prayer life in that faith, even though it may be weak. Let this one thought be its strength: you have asked and received grace in Christ to prepare you, step by step, to be faithful in prayer and intercession. The more simply you hold on to this and expect the Holy Spirit to work it in you, the more surely and fully this word will be made true to you: you will have it. God Himself who gave the answer will work it in you.

10

THE SPIRIT
OF SUPPLICATION

I will pour upon the house of David...
the spirit of grace and of supplications.
—Zechariah 12:10

The Spirit also helpeth our infirmities: for we know not
what we should pray for as we ought: but the Spirit itself maketh
intercession for us with groanings which cannot be uttered.
And he that searcheth the hearts knoweth what is the mind
of the Spirit, because he maketh intercession for the saints
according to the will of God.
—Romans 8:26–27

With all prayer and supplication in the Spirit, and watching thereunto
with all perseverance and supplication for all saints.
—Ephesians 6:18

Praying in the Holy Ghost.
—Jude 20

The Holy Spirit has been given to every child of God to be his life. He dwells in him, not as a separate Being in one part of his nature, but as his very life. He is the divine power or energy by which his life is maintained and strengthened. All that a believer is called to be or to do, the Holy Spirit can and will work in him. If he does not know or yield to the Holy Guest, the Blessed Spirit cannot work. His life will be a sickly one, full of failure and sin. As he yields, waits, and obeys the leading of the Spirit, God works in him everything that is pleasing in His sight.

The Holy Spirit is, in the first place, a Spirit of prayer. He was promised as a *"Spirit of grace and of supplications,"* the grace for supplication. He was sent forth into our hearts as *"The Spirit of adoption, whereby we cry, Abba, Father"* (Rom. 8:15). He enables us to say, in true faith and growing understanding of its meaning, *"Our Father which art in heaven"* (Matt. 6:9). *"He maketh intercession for the saints according to...God."* As we pray in the Spirit, our worship is as God desires it to be, *"In spirit and in truth"* (John 4:23). Prayer is the breathing of the Spirit in us. Power in prayer comes from the power of the Spirit in us, waited on and trusted in. Failure in prayer comes from the weakness of the Spirit's work in us. Our prayers are the index of the measure of the Spirit's work in us. For us to pray right, the life of the Spirit must be right in us. For praying the effective, prevailing prayer of the righteous man, everything depends on the indwelling of the Spirit.

There are three very simple lessons that we must know if we want to enjoy the blessing of being taught to pray by the Spirit of prayer.

The first is to believe that the Spirit dwells in us. (See Eph. 1:13.) Deep in the inmost recesses of his being, hidden and unfelt, every child of God has the holy, mighty Spirit of God dwelling in him. He knows it by the faith that accepts God's promise and believes that of which he sees, as yet, no sign. "We...receive the promise of the Spirit through faith" (Gal. 3:14). As long as we measure our prayer power by what we feel or think we can accomplish, we will be discouraged when we hear how much we ought to pray. But when we quietly believe that, in the midst of all our weakness, the Holy Spirit as a Spirit of supplication is dwelling within us, for the very purpose of enabling us to pray in the manner and measure that God desires, our hearts will be filled with hope. We will be strengthened in the assurance that lies at the very root of a happy and fruitful Christian life— God has made an abundant provision for our being what He wants us to be. We will begin to lose our sense of burden, fear, and discouragement about our ever praying sufficiently, because we see that the Holy Spirit Himself will pray, is praying, in us.

The second lesson is to beware, above everything, of grieving the Holy Spirit. (See Eph. 4:30.) If you grieve Him, how can He work in you the quiet, trustful, and blessed sense of that union with Christ that makes your prayer pleasing to the Father? Beware of grieving Him by sin, by unbelief, by selfishness, and by unfaithfulness to His voice in conscience. Do not think that grieving Him is a necessity. That assumption cuts away the very sinews of your strength. Do not consider it impossible to obey the command, "Grieve not the Holy Spirit" (v. 30). He Himself is the very power of God that makes it possible for you to be obedient. Your will can, in the power of the Spirit, at once reject any sin that rises up against your will, such as sloth, pride, self-will, or the passions of the flesh. Cast these on Christ and His blood, and your communion with God will be immediately restored. Each day, accept the Holy Spirit as your Leader and Life and Strength. You can depend on Him to make your heart everything it should be. There, in your heart, this Unseen and Unfelt One, who is known only by faith, provides the love, faith, and power of obedience you need. This is because He is revealing Christ, who is actually your Life and Strength, unseen within you. Do not grieve the

Holy Spirit by distrusting Him just because you do not feel His presence in you.

Especially in the matter of prayer, do not grieve Him. When you trust Christ to bring you into a new, healthy prayer life, do not expect to be able, all at once, to pray as easily, powerfully, and joyfully as you would like to. No, it may not come all at once. But just bow quietly before God in your ignorance and weakness. The best and most sincere prayer comes when you put yourself before God just as you are and count on the hidden Spirit praying in you. *"We know not what we should pray for as we ought"*; ignorance, difficulty, and struggle characterize our prayers all along. But *"the Spirit...helpeth our infirmities."* How? *"The Spirit itself,"* deeper down than our thoughts or feelings, *"maketh intercession for us with groanings which cannot be uttered."* When you cannot find words, when your words appear cold and powerless, just believe the Holy Spirit is praying in you. Be quiet before God; give Him time. In due season you will learn to pray. Beware of grieving the Spirit of prayer by not honoring Him in patient, trustful surrender to His intercession in you.

The third lesson is to *"be filled with the Spirit"* (Eph. 5:18). We have seen the meaning of this great truth: it is only the healthy spiritual life that can pray right. The command comes to each of us: *"Be filled with the Spirit."* While some are content with a small measure of the Spirit's indwelling, it is God's will that we should be filled with the Spirit. That means that our whole beings ought to be entirely yielded to the Holy Spirit, to be possessed and controlled by Him alone. We can count on and expect the Holy Spirit to take possession of and fill us. Our failure in prayer has been caused by our not having accepted the Spirit of prayer to be our lives. We have not yielded wholly to Him, whom the Father gave as the Spirit of His Son, to work the life of the Son in us. Let us, to say the very least, be willing to receive Him, to yield ourselves to God, and to trust Him for it. Let us not again willfully grieve the Holy Spirit by declining, by neglecting, by hesitating to seek to have Him as fully as He is willing to give Himself to us. If we believe that prayer is the great need of our work and of the church, if we truly desire to pray more, let us turn to the very source of all power and blessing. Let us believe that the Spirit of prayer, in His fullness, is for us.

We all know the place the Father and the Son have in our prayers. It is to the Father we pray and from whom we expect the answer. It is in the merit, name, and life of the Son, it is abiding in Him and He in us, that we trust we will be heard. But have we understood that in the Holy Trinity all three Persons have an equal place in prayer and that faith in the Holy Spirit of intercession is as indispensable as faith in the Father and the Son? How clearly this is stated in the words, *"Through him we...have access by one Spirit unto the Father"* (Eph. 2:18). As much as prayer must be to the Father, and through the Son, it must be by the Spirit. And the Spirit can pray in us only when He lives in us. It is only as we give ourselves to the Spirit living and praying in us that the glory of the prayer-hearing God and the blessed mediation of the Son can be known by us in their power.

Our last lesson is to pray in the Spirit for all saints. (See Eph. 6:18.) The Spirit, who is called *"the spirit...of supplications"* is also the Spirit of intercession. It is said of Him: *"The Spirit itself maketh intercession for us with groanings which cannot be uttered."* *"He maketh intercession for the saints."* Christ *"also maketh intercession for us"* (Rom. 8:34). The thought is essentially that of mediation—one pleading for another. When the Spirit of intercession takes full possession of us, all selfishness vanishes, and we no longer want to have Him for ourselves alone, apart from His intercession for others. We can begin to avail ourselves of our wonderful privilege to pray for others. We long to live the Christ life of unselfishly yielding our heart unceasingly to God to obtain His blessing for those around us. Intercession then becomes not an incidental or occasional part of our prayers, but their one great object. Our prayers for ourselves takes their true place as the means for preparing us to exercise our ministry of intercession more effectively.

I have humbly asked God to give me what I may give each of my readers—divine light and help to forsake the life of failure in prayer and to enter into the life of intercession that the Holy Spirit can enable them to lead. It can be done by a simple act of faith, claiming the fullness of the Spirit, that is, the full measure of the Spirit that you are capable in God's sight of receiving and He is willing to bestow. Will you not, right now, accept this by faith?

Let me remind you of what takes place when you accept Christ. Most of us sought peace, for a time, in our efforts and struggles to give up sin and please God. But peace was not to be found thus. The peace of God's pardon came by faith, trusting God's promise concerning Christ and His salvation. You had heard of Christ as the gift of God's love; you knew that He was for you, too; you had experienced His grace. But it wasn't until, in faith in God's Word, you accepted Him as God's gift to you, that you found the peace and joy that He can give. Believing in Him and His saving love made all the difference and changed you from someone who had always grieved Him into someone who loved and served Him. But you still experience times when you feel that you love and serve Him so poorly.

At the time you accepted Christ, you knew little about the Holy Spirit. Later you heard of His dwelling in you, and of His being the power of God in you, making it possible for you to be everything the Father intends you to be. His indwelling and inworking were still vague and indefinite and hardly a source of joy or strength. You did not yet know how much you might need Him, and, still less, what you might expect of Him. But you have learned from your failures. Now you begin to see how you have been grieving Him by not trusting and not following Him, by not allowing Him to work all God's pleasure in you.

All this can be changed. Just as after seeking Christ—praying to Him, and trying without success to serve Him—you found rest in accepting Him by faith, you can yield yourself to the full guidance of the Holy Spirit in just the same way. Claim and accept Him to work in you whatever God desires. Will you do it? Just accept Him in faith as Christ's gift. Let Him be the Spirit of your whole life—including your prayer life—and you can count on Him to take charge. You can then begin, even though you feel weak and unable to pray properly, to bow before God in silent assurance that He will teach you to pray.

My dear fellow Christians, just as you consciously accepted Christ by faith to pardon your sins, you can now, in the same faith, consciously accept Christ who gives the Holy Spirit to do His work in you. *"Christ hath redeemed us...that we might receive the promise of the Spirit through faith"* (Gal. 3:13–14). Kneel down, and simply believe that the Lord Jesus Christ, who baptizes with the Holy Spirit, is now, in response to your faith, beginning to bless you with a full experience of the power of the indwelling Spirit. Depend most confidently on Him, regardless of your feelings or your experience, to do His work as the Spirit of supplication and intercession. Renew that act of faith each morning and each time you pray. Trust Him, despite all appearances, to work in you—be sure He is working— and He will show you how the joy of the Holy Spirit can be the power of your life.

"I will pour [out]...the spirit of...supplications." Are you beginning to see that the mystery of prayer is the mystery of the divine indwelling? God in heaven gives His Spirit to be the divine power praying in our hearts, drawing us upward to our God. God is a Spirit, and nothing but a similar life and Spirit within us can have communion with Him. Man was created for this communion with God, so that God could dwell and work in him and be the life of his life. It was this divine indwelling that sin lost. Christ came to exhibit it in His life, to win it back for us in His death, and then to impart it to us by coming again from heaven in the Spirit to live in His disciples. Only this indwelling of God through the Spirit can explain and enable us to appropriate the wonderful promises given to prayer. God gives the Spirit as a Spirit of supplication, too, to maintain His divine life within us as a life in which prayer continually rises to heaven.

Without the Holy Spirit, no man can call Jesus, Lord; cry, *"Abba, Father"* (Gal. 4:6); worship in spirit and truth; or pray without ceasing. The Holy Spirit is given to the believer to be and do everything in him that God wants him to be and do. He is given to him especially as the Spirit of prayer and supplication. Is it clear that everything in prayer depends on our trusting the Holy Spirit to do His work in us? We must yield ourselves to His leading and depend only and entirely on Him.

We read, *"Stephen [was] a man full of faith and of the Holy Ghost"* (Acts 6:5). The two always go together in exact proportion to each other.

As our faith sees and trusts the Spirit in us to pray, and waits on Him, He will do His work. And our faith—the longing desire and the earnest supplication—our definite faith is all the Father seeks. Let us know the Holy Spirit, and in the faith of Christ who unceasingly gives Him, cultivate the assured confidence that we can learn to pray as the Father desires us to pray.

11

IN THE NAME OF CHRIST

Whatsoever ye shall ask in my name, that will I do.
—John 14:13

If ye shall ask any thing in my name, I will do it.
—John 14:14

I have chosen you...that whatsoever ye shall ask of the
Father in my name, he may give it you.
—John 15:16

Verily, verily, I say unto you, Whatsoever ye shall ask the Father in
my name, he will give it you. Hitherto have ye asked nothing in my

name: ask, and ye shall receive, that your joy may be full.
—John 16:23–24

At that day ye shall ask in my name.
—John 16:26

I n my name" is repeated six times. Our Lord knew how slowly our hearts would take this in. He longed so much for us to really believe that His name is the power in which every knee should bow, and in which every prayer could be heard, that he did not weary of saying it over and over, *"In my name."* Between the wonderful *"whatsoever ye shall ask,"* and the divine *"I will do it," "the Father…will give it,"* the simple link is, *"In my name."* Our asking and the Father's giving are equal in the name of Christ. Everything in prayer depends upon our comprehending this: *"In my name."*

A name is a word by which we call to mind the whole being and nature of an object. When I speak of a lamb or a lion, the name at once suggests the different nature peculiar to each. The name of God is meant to express His whole divine nature and glory. Therefore, the name of Christ means His whole nature, His person and work, His disposition and Spirit. To ask in the name of Christ is to pray in union with Him. When a sinner first believes in Christ, he knows and thinks only of His merit and inter-cession. To the very end, that is the one foundation of our confidence. And yet, as the believer grows in grace and enters more deeply and truly into union with Christ—that is, as he abides in Him—he learns that to pray in the name of Christ also means to pray in His Spirit. It means to pray in the possession of His nature, as the Holy Spirit imparts it to us. As we grasp the meaning of the words, *"At that day ye shall ask in my name"*—the day when, in the Holy Spirit, Christ came to live in His disciples—we will no longer be staggered at the greatness of the promise, *"Whatsoever ye shall ask in my name, that will I do."* We will get some insight into the unchangeable necessity and certainty of the law that whatever is asked in the name of Christ, in union with Him and out of His nature and Spirit, must be given.

As Christ's prayer nature lives in us, His prayer power becomes ours, too. Our attainment and experience are certainly not the ground of our confidence. Rather, the honesty and wholeheartedness of our surrender to everything that Christ seeks to be in us will determine our spiritual fitness and power to pray in His name. *"If ye abide in me,"* He said, *"...ye shall ask what ye will"* (John 15:7). As we live in Him, we get the spiritual power to avail ourselves of His name. The branch wholly given up to the life and service of the Vine can count on His sap and strength for its fruit. In the same way, the believer, who, in faith, allows the Spirit to possess his whole life, can avail himself of all the power of Christ's name.

Here on earth, Christ as man came to reveal what prayer is. To pray in the name of Christ, we must pray as He prayed on earth, as He taught us to pray, in union with Him, as He now prays in heaven. We must study Him in love and accept Him in faith as our Example, our Teacher, and our Intercessor.

Christ, Our Example

Prayer in Christ and prayer in us cannot be two different things. Just as there is but one God who is a Spirit and who hears prayer, there is but one spirit of acceptable prayer. We must realize that Christ spent a great deal of time in prayer. The great events of His life were all connected with special prayer. It is important for us to learn of His absolute dependence on, and unceasing direct communication with, the heavenly world if we are able to live a heavenly life or to exercise heavenly power around us. It is foolish and fruitless to attempt to work for God and heaven without first, in prayer, getting the life and the power of heaven to possess us. Unless this truth lives in us, we cannot avail ourselves of the mighty power of the name of Christ. His example must teach us the meaning of His name.

Of His baptism we read, *"Jesus also being baptized, and praying, the heaven was opened"* (Luke 3:21). In prayer, heaven was opened to Him; it came down to Him with the Spirit and the voice of the Father. In power, He was led into the wilderness; in fasting and prayer, this spirit was tested and fully appropriated. Early in His ministry, Mark recorded, *"And in the morning…a great while before day, he went out, and departed into a solitary place, and there prayed"* (Mark 1:35). Somewhat later, Luke said, *"Multitudes came together to hear, and to be healed….And he withdrew himself into the wilderness, and prayed"* (Luke 5:15–16). He knew how the holy service of preaching and healing could exhaust the spirit. He knew that too much contact with men could cloud the fellowship with God. He knew that time was needed for the Spirit to rest and root in Him and that no pressure of duty among men could free Him from the absolute need of much prayer. If anyone could have been satisfied with always living and working in the spirit of prayer, it would have been our Master. But He could not. He needed to have His supplies replenished by continual, prolonged seasons of prayer. To use Christ's name in prayer surely includes following His example and praying as He did.

Of the night before choosing His apostles we read: *"He went out into a mountain to pray, and continued all night in prayer to God"* (Luke 6:12). The first step toward creating the church and choosing men to be His witnesses and successors called Him to a special prayer of long duration. Everything had to be done according to the pattern established on the mount. *"The Son can do nothing of himself….The Father…showeth him all things that himself doeth"* (John 5:19–20). In the night of prayer, it was shown to Him.

In the night between the feeding of the five thousand—when Jesus knew that they wanted to take Him by force and make Him King—and the walking on the sea, He withdrew again into the mountain, Himself alone, to pray. (See Matt. 14:23; Mark 6:46; John 6:15.) It was God's will He had come to do and God's power He was to reveal. This power was not a possession of His own; it had to be prayed for and received from above. His first announcement of His approaching death, after He had elicited from Peter the confession that He was the Christ, is introduced by the words, *"And it came to pass, as he was alone praying"* (Luke 9:18). The introduction to the story of the Transfiguration is, He *"went up into a mountain to pray"* (v. 28). The request of the disciples, *"Lord, teach us to pray*" (Luke 11:1), follows from, "*It came to pass, that, as he was praying in a certain place*" (v. 1). In His own personal life, in His communion with the Father, in everything He is and does for men, the Christ whose name we are to use is a Man of prayer. Prayer gives Him His power of blessing and transfigures His very body with the glory of heaven. His own prayer life enables Him to teach others how to pray. How much more must it be prayer—prayer alone, much prayer—that can fit us to share His glory of a transfigured life, or make us the channel of heavenly blessing and teaching to others? To pray in the name of Christ is to pray as He prays.

As the end of His life approached, Christ prayed even more. When the Greeks asked to see Him, and He spoke of His approaching death, He prayed. At Lazarus's grave, He prayed. In the last night, He prayed His prayer as our High Priest, so that we might know what His sacrifice would win and what His everlasting intercession on the throne would be. In Gethsemane, He prayed His prayer as the Lamb giving itself to the slaughter. Even on the cross, He prayed—a prayer of compassion for His murderers, a prayer of atoning suffering in the thick darkness, a prayer in death of confident resignation of His spirit to the Father.

Christ's life and work, His suffering and death were all prayer. They were all dependence on God, trust in God, receiving from God, surrender to God. Your redemption, believer, is a redemption brought about by prayer and intercession, because your Christ is a praying Christ. The life He lives for you, the life He lives in you, is a praying life that delights to wait on God and receive everything from Him. To pray in His name is to pray as He prayed. Christ is our example because He is our Head, our Savior, and our Life. By virtue of His Deity and His Spirit, He can live in us. We can pray in His name, because we abide in Him and He in us.

Christ, Our Teacher

Christ was what He taught. His teaching was the revelation of how He lived, and—praise God—of the life He was to live in us. His teaching of the disciples was to awaken their desires, preparing them for what He would, by the Holy Spirit, be and work in them. Let us believe very confidently that everything He was in prayer, and everything He taught, He himself will give. He came to fulfill the law. But much more than that, He will fulfill the Gospel in everything taught to us about what to pray and how.

What to pray. It has sometimes been said that direct petitions, as compared with the exercise of fellowship with God, are but a subordinate part of prayer, that in the prayer of those who pray best and most, they occupy an insignificant place. If we carefully study everything that our Lord said about prayer, we see that this is not His teaching. In the Lord's Prayer, in the parables on prayer, in the illustration of a child asking for bread, of our seeking and knocking, in the central thought of the prayer of faith, *"What things soever ye…pray, believe that ye receive them"* (Mark 11:24), in the often repeated *"whatsoever"* of the last evening—everywhere our Lord urges and encourages us to offer definite petitions, and to expect definite answers. It is only because we confine prayer too much to our own needs that it is necessary to free it from the appearance of selfishness by giving the petitions a subordinate place. If believers could awaken to the glory of the work of intercession, they would see that in the definite pleading for definite gifts for definite spheres and persons, lies our highest fellowship with our glorified Lord and our only real power to bless men. It would be clear that there can be no truer fellowship with God than these definite petitions and their answers, by which we become the channels of His grace and life to men. It is then that our fellowship with the Father is the same as the Son has in His intercession.

How to pray. Our Lord taught us to pray in secret, in simplicity, with our eyes on God alone, in humility, and in the spirit of forgiving love. But the chief truth He reiterated was this: to pray in faith. And He defined that faith, not only as a trust in God's goodness or power, but as the definite assurance that we have received the very things we ask for. In the case of a delayed answer, He insisted on perseverance and urgency. We must be followers of those *"who through faith and patience inherit the promises"* (Heb. 6:12). This faith accepts the promise and knows it has what it has requested; this patience obtains the promise and inherits the blessing. We then learn to understand why God, who promises to avenge His elect speedily, bears with them in seeming delay. It is so that their faith may be purified from everything that is of the flesh and tested and strengthened to become that spiritual power that can do all things, even casting mountains into the heart of the sea.

Christ, Our Intercessor

We have gazed on Christ in His prayers; we have listened to His teaching as to how we must pray. To know fully what it is to pray in His name, we must know Him, too, in His heavenly intercession.

Just think what this means: all His saving work is still carried on in heaven, just as on earth, in unceasing communication with, and direct intercession to, the Father, who is All in All. Every act of grace in Christ has been preceded by, and owes its power to, intercession. God has been honored and acknowledged as its Author. On the throne of God, Christ's highest fellowship with the Father, and His partnership in the Father's rule of the world, is in intercession. Every blessing that comes down to us from above bears this stamp of God: through Christ's intercession. His intercession is nothing but the fruit and the glory of His atonement. When He gave Himself as a sacrifice to God for men, He proved that His whole heart had the one object of glorifying God in the salvation of men. In His intercession, this great purpose is realized: He glorifies the Father by asking and receiving everything from Him. He saves men by bestowing on them what He has obtained from the Father. Christ's intercession is the Father's glory, His own glory, and our glory.

And now this Christ, the Intercessor, is our life. He is our Head and we are His body. His Spirit and life breathe in us. On earth, as in heaven, intercession is God's chosen, God's only, channel of blessing. Let us learn from Christ what glory there is in it, what the way to exercise this wondrous power is, and what part it is to take in our work for God.

The glory of it. By it, beyond anything, we glorify God. By it we glorify Christ. By it we bring blessing to the church and the world. By it we obtain our highest nobility—the godlike power of saving men.

The way to it. Paul wrote, "*Walk in love, as Christ also hath loved us, and hath given himself…a sacrifice to God* [for us]" (Eph. 5:2). If we live as Christ lives, we will give ourselves—our whole lives—to God, to be used by Him for men. When we have done this, we will no longer seek anything for ourselves, but for men. And when we ask God to use us, and to impart to us what we can bestow on others, intercession will become to us, as it is in Christ in heaven, the great work of our lives. And if we ever think that the call is too high, or the work too great, faith in the interceding Christ, who lives in us, will give us the victory. We will listen to Him who said, "*The works that I do shall he do also; and greater works than these shall he do*" (John 14:12). We will remember that we are not under the law, with its impotence, but under grace with its omnipotence, working all in us. We will believe again in Him who said to us, "*Rise…and walk*" (John 5:8) and gave us His life as our strength. We will claim afresh the fullness of God's Spirit as His sufficient provision for our needs and rely on Him to be in us the Spirit of Intercession, who makes us one with Christ. Oh, let us only keep our place—giving up ourselves, like Him, in Him, to God for men.

Then, we will understand the role intercession is to have in God's work through us. We will no longer try to work for God and ask Him to follow it with His blessing. We will do what the friend at midnight did, what Christ did on earth, and forever does in heaven—we will first get from God and then turn to men to give what He gave us. As with Christ, we will make our chief work to receive from the Father. Giving to men will then be in power.

Servants of Christ, children of God, be of good courage. Let no fear of weakness or poverty make you afraid—ask in the name of Christ. His name is Himself, in all His perfection and power. He is the living Christ and will Himself make His name a power in you. Do not fear to plead the name. His promise is a threefold cord that cannot be broken. "*Whatsoever ye shall ask in my name*"—"*it shall be done unto you*" (John 15:7).

12

MY GOD WILL HEAR ME

Therefore will the L<small>ORD</small> *wait, that he may be gracious unto you…
blessed are all they that wait for him.…He will be very gracious unto
thee at the voice of thy cry; when he shall hear it, he will answer thee.*
—Isaiah 30:18–19

The L<small>ORD</small> *will hear when I call unto him.*
—Psalm 4:3

I have called upon thee, for thou wilt hear me, O God.
—Psalm 17:6

I will look unto the LORD;
I will wait for the God of my salvation: my God will hear me.
—Micah 7:7

The power of prayer rests in the faith that God hears it. In more than one sense, this is true. It is this faith that gives a man courage to pray. It is this faith that gives him power to prevail with God. The moment I am assured that God hears me, I feel drawn to pray and to persevere in prayer. I feel the strength to claim and take in faith the answer God gives. The main reason for the lack of prayer is the lack of the living, joyous assurance: *"My God will hear me."* If only God's servants had a vision of the living God waiting to grant their requests—to bestow all the heavenly gifts of the Spirit they are in need of—how everything would be set aside to make room for this one power that can ensure heavenly blessing—the prayer of faith!

When a man can and does say, in living faith, *"My God will hear me,"* nothing can keep him from prayer. He knows that what he cannot do or get done on earth, can and will be done for him from heaven. Let each one of us bow in stillness before God and wait on Him to reveal Himself to us as the prayer-hearing God. In His presence, the wondrous thoughts gathering round the central truth will be revealed to us.

1. *"My God will hear me."* What a blessed certainty! We have God's word for it in numberless promises. We have thousands of witnesses who will attest to the fact that they have found it to be true. We have had the experience of it in our lives. We have known it to be true. We have had the Son of God come from heaven with the message that if we ask, the Father will give. We have had Christ Himself praying on earth and being heard. And we have Him in heaven now, sitting at the right hand of God and making intercession for us. God hears prayer—God delights to hear prayer. He has allowed His people to be tried a thousand times over that they might be compelled to cry to Him and learn to know Him as the Hearer of prayer.

Let us confess with shame how little we have believed this wondrous truth. How seldom we have received it into our hearts and allowed it to possess and control our whole beings. That we accept a truth is not enough. The living God, of whom the truth speaks, must, in its light, be so revealed that our whole life is spent in His presence. Our consciousness must be as clear as a little child's toward its earthly parent—I know for certain my father hears me.

Beloved child of God! You know by experience how little an intellectual understanding of truth has profited you. Beseech God to reveal Himself to you. If you want to live a different prayer life, bow each time before you pray in silence to worship God. Wait there until some right sense of His nearness and readiness to answer comes to you. You will begin to pray with the words, *"My God will hear me."*

2. *"My God will hear me."* What a wondrous grace! Think of God in His infinite majesty, His altogether incomprehensible glory, His unapproachable holiness, sitting on a throne of grace, waiting to be gracious, inviting, and encouraging you to pray with His promise: *"Call upon me, and I will answer [you]"* (Psalm 91:15). Think of yourself—your nothingness and helplessness as a person, your wretchedness and transgressions as a sinner, your feebleness and unworthiness as a saint—and praise the glory of that grace that allows you to say boldly of your prayers for yourself and others, *"My God will hear me."* Think of how you are not left to yourself and of what you can accomplish in this wonderful fellowship with God. God has united you with Christ; in Him and His name, you have your confidence. On the throne, He prays with you and for you; on the footstool of the throne, you pray with Him and in Him. His worth, and the Father's delight in hearing Him, are the measure of your confidence—your assurance of being heard.

There is more. Think of the Holy Spirit, the Spirit of God's own Son, sent into your heart to cry, *"Abba, Father"* (Gal. 4:6). The Holy Spirit is to be in you a Spirit of supplication when you do not know how to pray as you ought. (See Rom. 8:26.) Think, in all your insignificance and unworthiness, of your being as acceptable as Christ Himself. Think, in all your ignorance and feebleness, of the Spirit making intercession according to God within you. Then, cry out, "What wondrous grace! Through Christ I have access to the Father, by the Spirit. I can, I do believe it: '*My God will hear me*.'"

3. "*My God will hear me*." What a deep mystery! Sometimes, difficulties arise that cannot help but perplex even the honest heart. There is the question as to God's sovereign, all-wise, all-disposing will. How can our wishes, often so foolish, and our will, often so selfish, overrule or change that perfect will? Is it not better to leave all to His disposal, who knows what is best and loves to give us the very best? Or how can our prayers change what He has ordained before? Then, there is the question as to the need of persevering prayer and waiting long for the answer. If God is infinite love and delights more to give than we to receive, what is the need for the pleading, wrestling, urgency, and long delay of which Scripture and experience speak? Arising out of this, there is still another question—that of the multitude of apparently vain and unanswered prayers. How many have pleaded for loved ones, and they appeared to die unsaved. How many cry for years for spiritual blessing, and no answer comes. To think of all this tries our faith and makes us hesitate as we say, "*My God will hear me*."

Beloved, prayer, in its power with God, and His faithfulness to His promise to hear it, is a deep, spiritual mystery. To the above questions, answers can be given that remove some of the difficulty. But after all, the first and the last that must be said is this: as little as we can comprehend God can we comprehend this, one of the most blessed of His attributes, that He hears prayer. It is a spiritual mystery—nothing less than the mystery of the Holy Trinity. God hears because we pray in His Son, because the Holy Spirit prays in us.

If we have believed and claimed the life of Christ as our health, and the fullness of the Spirit as our strength, let us not hesitate to believe in the power of our prayers, too. The Holy Spirit can enable us to believe and rejoice in it, even where every question is not yet answered. He will do this as we lay our questionings in God's bosom, trust His faithfulness, and give ourselves humbly to obey His command to pray without ceasing. Every art unfolds its secrets and its beauty only to the man who practices it. To the humble soul who prays in the obedience of faith, who practices prayer and intercession diligently because God asks it, the secret of the Lord will be revealed. To this soul, the thought of the deep mystery of prayer, instead of being a weary problem, will be a source of rejoicing, adoration, and faith, in which the unceasing refrain is ever heard: *"My God will hear me."*

4. *"My God will hear me."* What a solemn responsibility! How often we complain about darkness, feebleness, and failure, as if there were no help for them. God has promised, in answer to our prayers, to supply our every need (see Phil. 4:19) and give us His light and strength and peace. If we only realized the responsibility of having such a God, and such promises, with the sin and shame of not fully availing ourselves of them. How confident we should feel that the grace, which we have accepted and trusted to enable us to pray as we should, will be given.

There is more. This access to a prayer-hearing God is especially meant to make us intercessors for our fellowmen. Even as Christ obtained His right of prevailing intercession by giving Himself as a sacrifice to God for men and through it receives the blessings He dispenses, so, if we have truly given ourselves to God, we share His right of intercession and are able to obtain the powers of the heavenly world, too. The power of life and death is in our hands. (See 1 John 5:16.) In answer to prayer, the Spirit can be poured out; souls can be converted; believers can be established. In prayer, the kingdom of darkness can be conquered, souls are brought out of prison into the liberty of Christ, and the glory of God is revealed. Through prayer, the sword of the Spirit—the Word of God—can be wielded in power, and in public preaching as in private speaking, the most rebellious are made to bow at Jesus' feet.

What a responsibility the church has in giving herself to the work of intercession! What a responsibility every minister, missionary, and worker, set apart for the saving of souls, has in yielding himself wholly to act out and prove his faith: *"My God will hear me."* And what a call on every believer, instead of burying and losing this talent, to seek to use it to the very utmost in prayer and supplication for all saints and for all men. My God will hear me. The deeper our entrance into the truth of this wondrous power God has given to us, the more wholehearted our surrender to the work of intercession will be.

5. *"My God will hear me."* What a blessed prospect! I see that all the failures of my past life have been due to the lack of this faith. My failure, especially in the work of intercession, has had its deepest root in this—I did not live in the full faith of the blessed assurance, *"My God will hear me."* Praise God! I begin to see it; I believe it. All can be different. Or, rather, I see Him; I believe Him. *"My God will hear me."* Yes, me, even me! Commonplace and insignificant though I be, filling but a very little place, so that I will hardly be missed when I go—even I have access to this Infinite God, with the confidence that He hears me. One with Christ, led by the Holy Spirit, I dare to say, "I will pray for others, for I am sure my God will listen to me: *'My God will hear me.'*" What a blessed prospect before me—every earthly and spiritual anxiety is exchanged for the peace of God, who cares for all and hears prayer. What a blessed prospect in my work—to know that even when the answer is long in coming, and there is a call for much patient, persevering prayer, the truth remains infallibly sure: *"My God will hear me."*

And what a blessed prospect for Christ's church if we could all give prayer its place, give faith in God its place or, rather, give the prayer-hearing God His place! This is the one great thing that those who, in some measure, begin to see the urgent need of prayer should pray for in the first place. When God, at first, and then time after time, poured forth the Spirit on His praying people, He laid down the law for all time: as much of prayer, so much of the Spirit. Let each one who can say, *"My God will hear me,"* join in the fervent supplication that throughout the church, truth may be restored to its true place, and the blessed prospect will be realized: a praying church overflowing with the power of the Holy Spirit.

6. *"My God will hear me."* What a need of divine teaching! We need this, both to enable us to hold this word in living faith, and to make full use of it in intercession. It has been said, and it cannot be said too often or too earnestly, that the one necessary thing for the church of our day is the power of the Holy Spirit. It is just because this is so, from the divine side, that we may also say that from the human side, the one necessary thing is more prayer—more believing, persevering prayer. There is much to be confessed and taken away in us if the Spirit is to work freely. But the upward look, the deep dependence, the strong crying to God, and the effectual prayer of faith that avails—all these are sadly lacking. And all these are essential.

Shouldn't we all try to learn the lesson that will make prevailing prayer possible—the lesson of a faith that always sings, *"My God will hear me"*? Simple and elementary as it is, it requires practice, patience, time, and heavenly teaching to learn it correctly. Under the impression of a bright thought or a blessed experience, it may look as if we knew the lesson perfectly. But the need of making this our first prayer—that God who hears prayer would teach us to believe it, and so to pray correctly—will continually recur. If we desire it, we can count on Him. He delights in hearing prayer and answering it. He gave His Son that He might always pray for us and with us, and His Holy Spirit to pray in us. We can be sure there is not a prayer that He will hear more certainly than this: that He so reveal Himself as the prayer-hearing God, that our whole being may respond, *"My God will hear me."*

13

PAUL: A PATTERN OF PRAYER

Go…and inquire…for one called Saul, of Tarsus: for, behold, he prayeth.
—Acts 9:11

*For this cause I obtained mercy, that in me first Jesus Christ
might show forth all longsuffering, for a pattern to them which should
hereafter believe on him to life everlasting.*
—1 Timothy 1:16

God took His own Son and made Him our example and our
pattern. It sometimes is as if the power of Christ's example is

lost in the thought that He, in whom is no sin, is not man as we are. Our Lord took Paul, a man of like passions with ourselves, and made him a pattern of what He could do for one who was the chief of sinners (1 Tim. 1:15). And Paul, the man who, more than any other, has set his mark on the church, has always been thought of as an exemplary man. In his mastery of divine truth and his teaching of it; in his devotion to his Lord and his self-consuming zeal in His service; in his deep experience of the power of the indwelling Christ and the fellowship of His cross; in the sincerity of his humility and the simplicity and boldness of his faith; in his missionary enthusiasm and endurance—in all this, and so much more, *"the grace of our Lord was exceeding abundant"* (1 Tim. 1:14). Christ gave him, and the church has accepted him, as a pattern of what Christ would have, of what Christ would work. Seven times Paul speaks of believers following him: *"Wherefore I beseech you, be ye followers of me"* (1 Cor. 4:16); *"Be ye followers of me, even as I also am of Christ"* (1 Cor. 11:1). (See also in Philippians 3:17; 4:9; 1 Thessalonians 1:6; 2 Thessalonians 3:7–9.)

If Paul, as a pattern of prayer, is not studied or appealed to as much as he is in other respects, it is not because he is not a remarkable proof of what grace can do, or because we do not, in this respect, stand in as much need of the help of his example. A study of Paul as a pattern of prayer will bring a rich reward of instruction and encouragement. The words our Lord used of Paul at his conversion, *"Behold, he prayeth,"* may be taken as the keynote of his life from then on. Christ at the right hand of God, in whom we are blessed with all spiritual blessings (Eph. 1:3), was everything to him. To pray and expect the heavenly power in his work and on his work, coming directly from heaven by prayer, was the simple outcome of his faith in the Glorified One. In this, too, Christ meant him to be a pattern, so that we might learn that just as Christ and His gifts and the unworldliness of the powers that work for salvation are known and believed, prayer will become the spontaneous rising of the heart to the only source of its life. Let us see what we know of Paul.

Paul's Habits of Prayer

These habits are revealed almost unconsciously. He wrote in Romans 1, "*God is my witness...that without ceasing I make mention of you always in my prayers....For I long to see you, that I may impart unto you some spiritual gift, to the end ye may be established*" (vv. 9, 11). In Romans 10: "*My heart's desire and prayer to God for Israel is, that they might be saved*" (v. 1); in Romans 9: "*I have great heaviness and continual sorrow of heart. For I could wish that myself were accursed from Christ for my brethren.*" (vv. 2–3).

In 1 Corinthians 1:4, he wrote, "*I thank my God always on your behalf, for the grace of God which is given you by Jesus Christ.*" In 2 Corinthians 6:4–5: "*Approving ourselves as the ministers of God...in watchings, in fastings.*"

In Galatians 4:19 he wrote, "*My little children, of whom I travail in birth again until Christ be formed in you.*" In Ephesians 1:16: "*[I] cease not to give thanks for you, making mention of you in my prayers.*" In Ephesians 3:14, 16: "*I bow my knees unto the Father...that he would grant you...to be strengthened with might by his Spirit in the inner man.*" In Philippians 1: "*I thank my God upon every remembrance of you, always in every prayer of mine for you all making request with joy....For God is my record, how greatly I long after you all in the bowels of Jesus Christ. And this I pray*" (vv. 3–4, 8–9). In Colossians 1: "*We give thanks to God...praying always for you....For this cause we also, since the day we heard it, do not cease to pray for you, and to desire*" (vv. 3, 9). In Colossians 2:1: "*I would that ye knew what great conflict I have for you...and for as many as have not seen my face in the flesh.*"

In 1 Thessalonians 1:2, Paul again wrote, "*We give thanks to God always for you all, making mention of you in our prayers.*" In 1 Thessalonians 3:9–10: "*We joy for your sakes before our God; night and day praying exceedingly that we...might perfect that which is lacking in your faith.*" In 2 Thessalonians 1:3, 11: "*We are bound to thank God always for you....Wherefore also we pray always for you.*" In 2 Timothy 1:3: "*I thank God...that without ceasing I have remembrance of thee...night and day.*" In Philemon 4: "*I thank my God, making mention of thee always in my prayers.*"

These passages taken together give us the picture of a man whose words, *"pray without ceasing"* (1 Thess. 5:17), were simply the expression of his daily life. He had such a sense of the insufficiency of simple conversion; of the need of the grace and the power of heaven being brought down for the young converts in prayer; of the need of much and unceasing prayer, day and night, to bring it down; of the certainty that prayer would bring it down, that his life was continual and most definite prayer. He had such a sense that everything must come from above, and such a faith that it would come in answer to prayer, that prayer was neither a duty nor a burden but the natural turning of the heart to the only place from which it could possibly obtain what it sought for others.

The Contents of Paul's Prayers

It is of as much importance to know what Paul prayed, as how frequently and earnestly he did so. Intercession is a spiritual work. Our confidence in it will greatly depend on our knowing that we ask according to the will of God. The more distinctly we ask heavenly things—which we feel God alone can bestow, which we are sure He will bestow—the more direct and urgent our appeal to God alone will be. The more impossible the things are that we seek, the more we will turn from all human work to prayer and to God alone.

In the Epistles, in addition to where he speaks of his praying, we have a number of distinct prayers in which Paul uttered his heart's desire for those to whom he wrote. In these we see that his first desire was always that they might be *"established"* in the Christian life (Rom. 1:11). As much as he praised God when he heard of conversion, he knew how feeble the young converts were, how their establishing would avail nothing without the grace of the Spirit prayed down. If we look at some of his major prayers, we will see what he asked and obtained.

Take the two prayers in Ephesians: the one for light, the other for strength. In the former (see Ephesians 1:16), he prays for the Spirit of wisdom to enlighten them to know what their calling and inheritance was. (See Eph. 1:17–18.) It was also so they would know about the mighty power of God working in them. (See v. 19.) Spiritual enlightenment and knowledge was their great need, to be obtained for them by prayer. In the latter (see Ephesians 3:14), he asks that the power they had been led to see in Christ might work in them. He asks that they be strengthened with divine might, so as to have the indwelling Christ (see vv. 16–17), the love that passes knowledge, and the fullness of God actually come on them. (See v. 19.) These were things that could only come directly from heaven. These were things he asked and expected. If we want to learn Paul's art of intercession, we must ask nothing less for believers in our day.

Look at the prayer in Philippians 1:9–11. There, too, it is first for spiritual knowledge; then comes a blameless life, and then a fruitful life to the glory of God. It is also so in the beautiful prayer in Colossians 1:9–11: first, spiritual knowledge and understanding of God's will, then the strengthening with all might to all patience and joy.

Or take the two prayers in 1 Thessalonians. The one: *"The Lord make you to increase and abound in love one toward another...to the end he may stablish your hearts unblameable in holiness"* (1 Thessalonians 3:12–13). The other: *"The very God of peace sanctify you wholly; and I pray God your whole spirit and soul and body be preserved blameless"* (1 Thessalonians 5:23). The very words are so high that we hardly understand, still less believe, still less experience what they mean. Paul so lived in the heavenly world—he was so at home in the holiness and omnipotence of God and His love—that such prayers were the natural expression of what he knew God could and would do. *"Lord...stablish your hearts unblameable in holiness"; "God... sanctify you wholly"*—the man who believes in these things and desires them will pray for them for others. The prayers are all a proof that Paul seeks for them the very life of heaven on earth. No wonder that he is not tempted to trust in any human means but looks for it from heaven alone. Again, I say, the more we take Paul's prayers as our pattern and make his desires our own for believers for whom we pray, the more prayer to the God of heaven will become as our daily breath.

Paul's Requests for Prayer

These are no less instructive than his own prayers for the saints. They prove that he does not consider prayer any special prerogative of an apostle. He calls the humblest and simplest believer to claim his right. They prove that he does not think that only the new converts or feeble Christians need prayer. He himself is, as a member of the body, dependent on his fellow Christians and their prayers. After he had preached the Gospel for twenty years, he still asked for prayer that he might speak as he ought to. Not once and for all, not for a time, but day by day, without ceasing, must grace be sought and brought down from heaven for his work. United, continued waiting on God is to Paul the only hope of the church. With the Holy Spirit, a heavenly life—the life of the Lord in heaven—entered the world. Nothing but unbroken communication with heaven can keep it up.

Listen to how he asks for prayer, and with what earnestness:

I beseech you, brethren, for the Lord Jesus Christ's sake, and for the love of the Spirit, that ye strive together with me in your prayers to God for me; that I may be delivered from them that do not believe in Judaea; and…may come unto you with joy by the will of God.

(Rom. 15:30–32)

How remarkably the prayers of Romans 15:5–6; 13 were answered. The remarkable fact that the Roman world power had proved its antagonism to God's kingdom, then all at once became Paul's protector, and secured him a safe convoy to Rome, can only be accounted for by these prayers.

In 2 Corinthians 1:10–11 he wrote, *"In whom we trust that he will yet deliver us; ye also helping together by prayer for us."* In Ephesians 6:18–20: *"Praying always with all prayer and supplication in the Spirit…for all saints; and for me…that I may open my mouth boldly…that therein I may speak boldly, as I ought to speak."* In Philippians 1:19: *"I know that this [trouble] shall turn to my salvation through your prayer, and the supply of the Spirit of Jesus Christ."* In Colossians 4:2–4: *"Continue in prayer…withal praying also for us, that God would open unto us a door of utterance, to speak the mystery of Christ…*

that I may make it manifest, as I ought to speak." In 1 Thessalonians 5:25: *"Brethren, pray for us."* In Philemon 22: *"I trust that through your prayers I shall be given unto you."*

We saw how Christ prayed and taught His disciples to pray. We see how Paul prayed and taught the churches to pray. As the Master, so the servant calls us to believe and to prove that prayer is the power both of the ministry and the church. We have a summary of his faith in these remarkable words concerning something that caused him grief: *"This shall turn to my salvation through your prayer, and the supply of the Spirit of Jesus Christ"* (Phil. 1:19). As much as he looked to his Lord in heaven, he looked to his fellow believers on earth to secure the supply of that Spirit for him. The Spirit from heaven and prayer on earth were to him, as to the twelve after Pentecost, inseparably linked. We often speak of apostolic zeal and devotion and power—may God give us a revival of apostolic prayer.

Let me ask once again, does the work of intercession take the place in the church it ought to have? Is it commonly understood that everything depends on getting from God that *"supply of the Spirit of Jesus Christ"* for and in ourselves that can give our work its real power to bless? This is Christ's divine order for all work—His own and that of His servants. This is the order Paul followed: first come every day, as having nothing, and receive from God *"the supply of the Spirit"* in intercession; then go and impart what has come to you from heaven.

In all His instructions, our Lord Jesus spoke more often to His disciples about their praying than their preaching. In the farewell discourse, He said little about preaching but much about the Holy Spirit and their asking whatsoever they would in His name. (See John 14:13.) If we are to return to this life of the first apostles and of Paul, and really accept the truth that our only strength is intercession, we must have the courage to confess past sins and to believe that there is deliverance. To break through old habits, to resist the clamor of pressing duties that have always had their way, to make every other call subordinate to this one, whether others approve or not, will not be easy at first. But the men or women who are faithful will not only be rewarded themselves, but they will become benefactors to their fellow

Christians: "*Thou shalt be called, The repairer of the breach, The restorer of paths to dwell in*" (Isa. 58:12).

But is it really possible? Can it indeed be that those who have never been able to face, much less overcome, the difficulty can become mighty in prayer? Tell me, was it really possible for Jacob to become Israel—a prince who prevailed with God? It was. The things that are impossible with men are possible with God. (See Luke 18:27.) Have you not received from the Father, as the great fruit of Christ's redemption, the Spirit of supplication, the Spirit of intercession? Just pause and think what that means. And will you still doubt whether God is able to make you strivers with God (see Rom. 15:30), princes who prevail with Him? Oh, let us abandon all fear, and in faith claim the grace for which we have the Holy Spirit dwelling in us—the grace of supplication, the grace of intercession. Let us quietly, perseveringly believe that He lives in us and will enable us to do our work. Let us in faith not fear to accept and yield to the great truth that intercession, as it is the great work of the King on the throne, is the great work of His servants on earth. We have the Holy Spirit, who brings the Christ life into our hearts, to fit us for this work. Let us at once realize and arouse the gift within us. As we daily set aside our time for intercession and count on the Spirit's enabling power, the confidence that we can, in our measure, follow even as he followed Christ will grow.

14

GOD SEEKS INTERCESSORS

I have set watchmen upon thy walls, O Jerusalem,
which shall never hold their peace day nor night:
ye that make mention of the LORD, keep not silence.
And give him no rest...till he make Jerusalem a praise in the earth.
—Isaiah 62:6–7

And he saw that there was no man,
and wondered that there was no intercessor.
—Isaiah 59:16

And I looked, and there was none to help;
and I wondered that there was none to uphold.
—Isaiah 63:5

There is none that calleth upon thy name,
that stirreth up himself to take hold of thee.
—Isaiah 64:7

And I sought for a man…that should…stand in the gap before me for
the land, that I should not destroy it: but I found none.
—Ezekiel 22:30

I have chosen you, and ordained you,
that ye should go and bring forth fruit…that whatsoever ye shall ask of
the Father in my name, he may give it you.
—John 15:16

In the study of the starry heavens, much depends on proper understanding of magnitudes. Without some sense of the size of the heavenly bodies, which appear so small to the eye, and of the almost unlimited extent of the regions in which they move, though they appear so near, there can be no true knowledge of the heavenly world or its relation to this earth. It is even so with the spiritual heavens and the heavenly life in which we are called to live. It is especially so in the life of intercession, that most wondrous fellowship between heaven and earth. Everything depends on the proper understanding of magnitudes.

Just think of the three that come first. There is a world, with its needs entirely dependent on and waiting to be helped by intercession. There is a God in heaven, with His all-sufficient supply for all those needs, waiting to be asked. There is a church, with its wondrous calling and its sure promises, waiting to be roused to a sense of its wondrous responsibility and power.

God seeks intercessors. There is a world with its perishing millions, with intercession as its only hope. So much love and work are comparatively vain, because there is so little intercession. There are millions living as if there had never been a Son of God to die for them. Every year, millions pass into the outer darkness without hope. Millions bear the Christian name, but the great majority of them live in utter ignorance or indifference. Millions of feeble, sickly Christians, thousands of wearied workers, could be blessed by intercession, could help themselves to become mighty in intercession. Churches and missions sacrificing life and labor with little result often lack the power of intercession. Souls, each one worth more than worlds—worth nothing less than the price paid for them in Christ's blood—are within reach of the power that can be won by intercession. We surely have no conception of the magnitude of the work to be done by God's intercessors, or we would cry to God above everything to give us the spirit of intercession.

God seeks intercessors. There is a God of glory able to meet all these needs. We are told that He delights in mercy, that He waits to be gracious, that He longs to pour out His blessing. We are told that the love that gave the Son up to death is the same love that each moment hovers over every human being. And yet He does not help. And there they perish. It is as if God does not move. If He does so love and long to bless, there must be some inscrutable reason for His holding back. What can it be? Scripture says it is because of our unbelief. (See Matthew 13:58, 17:20). It is the faithlessness and consequent unfaithfulness of God's people. He has taken them into partnership with Himself. He has honored them, and bound Himself, by making their prayers one of the standard measures of the working of His power. Lack of intercession is one of the chief reasons for the lack of blessing. Oh, that we would turn our eyes and heart from everything else and fix them on God who hears prayer. Let the magnificence of His promises, His power, and His purpose of love overwhelm us! How our whole lives and hearts would become intercession.

God seeks intercessors. There is a third magnitude to which our eyes must be opened: the wondrous privilege and power of the intercessors. There is a false humility which makes a great virtue of self-depreciation, because it has never seen its utter nothingness. If it knew that, it would never apologize for its feebleness, but glory in its utter weakness as the one condition of Christ's power resting on it. It would judge itself, its power, and influence before God in prayer as little by what it sees or feels as we judge the size of the sun or stars by what the eye can see. Faith sees man created in God's image and likeness to be God's representative in this world and have dominion over it. Faith sees man redeemed and lifted into union with Christ: abiding in Him, identified with Him, and clothed with His power in intercession. Faith sees the Holy Spirit dwelling and praying in the heart, making, in our sighings, intercession to God. Faith sees the intercession of the saints as part of the life of the Holy Trinity: the believer as God's child asking of the Father, in the Son, through the Spirit. Faith sees something of the divine fitness and beauty of this scheme of salvation through intercession. Faith wakens the soul to a consciousness of its wondrous destiny, and arms it with strength for the blessed self-sacrifice it calls to.

God seeks intercessors. When He called His people out of Egypt, He separated the priestly tribe to draw near to Him, stand before Him, and bless the people in His name. From time to time, He sought and found and honored intercessors, for whose sake He spared or blessed His people. When our Lord left the earth, He said to the inner circle He had gathered around Him, an inner circle of special devotion to His service, to which access is still free to every disciple: "*I have chosen you, and ordained you… that whatsoever ye shall ask of the Father in my name, he may give it you.*" We have already noticed the three wonderful words repeated six times: "*whatsoever,*" "*in my name,*" "*it shall be done*" (John 15:7). In them, Christ placed the power of the heavenly world at their disposal, not for their own selfish use, but in the interest of His kingdom. We know how wondrously they used it. And since that time, down through the ages, these men have had their successors, men who have proved how surely God works in answer to prayer. And we may praise God that in our day, too, there is an ever increasing number who begin to see and prove that in church and mission, in all societies, large and small, intercession is the chief thing. They see that it is the power that moves God and opens heaven. They are learning, and long to learn better so that all may learn, that in our work for souls, intercession must take the first place. Those who have received from heaven, in the power of the Holy Spirit, what they are to communicate to others will be best able to do the Lord's work.

God seeks intercessors. Though God had His appointed servants in Israel—watchmen set by Himself to cry to Him day and night and give Him no rest—He often had to wonder and complain that there was no intercessor. He wondered why there was no one who stirred himself up to take hold of His strength. And He still waits and wonders in our day that there are not more intercessors. He still wonders why all of His children do not give themselves to this highest and holiest work, and why many of them who do so, do not engage in it more intensely and perseveringly. He wonders why ministers of His Gospel complain that their duties do not allow them to find time for this, which He considers their first, highest, most delightful, and alone effective work. He wonders why His sons and daughters, who have forsaken home and friends for His sake, come so short in what He meant to be their abiding strength: receiving day by day all they need to impart to the non-believers. He wonders why multitudes of His children have little conception of what intercession is. He wonders why even more have learned that it is their duty, seek to obey it, but confess that they know little about taking hold of God or prevailing with Him.

God seeks intercessors. He longs to dispense larger blessings. He longs to reveal His power and glory as God, His saving love, more abundantly. He seeks intercessors in larger number, in greater power, to prepare the way of the Lord. He seeks them. Where could He seek them but in His church? And how does He expect to find them? He entrusted to His church the task of telling about their Lord's need, of encouraging, training, and preparing them for His holy service. And He always comes again, seeking fruit, seeking intercessors. In His Word, He has spoken of the *"widow indeed...[who] trusteth in God, and continueth in supplications and prayers night and day"* (1 Tim. 5:5).

God seeks intercessors. He looks to see if the church is training the great army of aged men and women, whose time of outward work is past, but who can strengthen the army of the *"elect, which cry day and night unto him"* (Luke 18:7). He looks to the great host of the Christian endeavor—the three or four million young lives given in the solemn pledge: "I promise the Lord Jesus Christ that I will strive to do whatever He would like to have me do"—and wonders how many are being trained to pass from the

772 ⌒ *Andrew Murray: Collected Works on Prayer*

brightness of the weekly prayer meeting and its confession of loyalty, on to the secret intercession that is to save souls. He looks to the thousands of young men and women in training for the work of ministry and mission. He gazes longingly to see if the church is teaching them that intercession—power with God—must be their first care. The church should seek to train and help them to do it. He looks to see whether ministers and missionaries are understanding their opportunity and laboring to turn the believers of their congregation into those who can help together by their prayers (see 2 Chron. 20:4), and can strive with them in their prayers. (See Rom. 15:30.) As Christ seeks the lost sheep until He finds it, God seeks intercessors.

God seeks intercessors. He will not, He cannot, take the work out of the hands of His church. And so He comes, calling and pleading in many ways. Now, He does so by a man whom He raises up to live a life of faith in His service and to prove how actually and abundantly He answers prayer. Then, He does so by the story of a church that makes prayer for souls its starting point and bears testimony to God's faithfulness. Sometimes, He does so in a mission that proves how special prayer can meet special need and bring down the power of the Spirit. Or other times, He does so by a season of revival coming in answer to united, urgent supplication. In these and many other ways, God is showing us what intercession can do. He is beseeching us to awaken and train His great host to be, every one, a people of intercession.

God seeks intercessors. He sends His servants out to call them. Let ministers make this a part of their duties. Let them make their church a training school of intercession. Give the people definite objects for prayer. Encourage them to make a definite time for it, even if it is only ten minutes every day. Help them to understand the boldness they may use with God. Teach them to expect and look for answers. Show them what it is first to pray and get an answer in secret, and then carry the answer and impart the blessing. Tell everyone who is master of his own time that he is as the angels: free to tarry before the throne and then go out and minister to the heirs of salvation. Sound out the blessed tidings that this honor is for all God's people. There is no difference. That servant girl, this day laborer, that bedridden invalid, this daughter in her mother's home, these men in business—all are called; all, all, are needed. God seeks intercessors.

God seeks intercessors. As ministers begin the work of finding and training intercessors, it will urge them to pray more themselves. Christ made Paul a pattern of His grace before He made him a preacher of it. It has been well said, "The first duty of a clergyman is humbly to beg of God that all he would have done in his people may be first truly and fully done in himself." The effort to bring this message of God may cause much heart searching and humiliation. All the better. The best practice in doing a thing is helping others to do it. Oh, servants of Christ, be as watchmen who cry to God day and night. Let us awake to our holy calling. Let us believe in the power of intercession. Let us practice it. Let us seek on behalf of our people to get from God Himself the Spirit and the life we preach. With our spirits and lives given up to God in intercession, the Spirit and life that God gives them through us cannot fail to be the life of intercession, too.

15

THE COMING REVIVAL

Wilt thou not revive us again: that thy people may rejoice in thee?
—Psalm 85:6

O LORD, revive thy work in the midst of the years.
—Habakkuk 3:2

Though I walk in the midst of trouble, thou wilt revive me...
thy right hand shall save me.
—Psalm 138:7

I dwell...with him also that is of a contrite and humble spirit...
to revive the heart of the contrite ones.
—Isaiah 57:15

Come, and let us return unto the LORD: *for he hath torn,*
and he will heal us.....He [will] *revive us.*
—Hosea 6:1–2

The coming revival—one frequently hears these words. There are many teachers who see signs of its approach and confidently herald its speedy appearance. In the increase of mission interest, in the tidings of revivals in heathen places where Christian doors are opening, in the hosts of our young, in victories already secured—wherever believing hopeful workers enter—they are given the assurance of a time of power and blessing such as we have never known. They are told that the church is about to enter into a new era of increasing spirituality and larger extension.

There are others who, while admitting the truth of some of these facts, fear that the conclusion drawn from them are one-sided and premature. They see the interest in missions increased but point out to how small a circle it is confined. They also note how utterly out of proportion it is to what it ought to be. To the great majority of church members, to the greater part of the church, it is as yet anything but a life question. They remind us of the power of worldliness and formality. They contrast the increase of the money-making and pleasure-loving spirit among professing Christians, to the lack of spirituality in so many, many of our churches. They declare that the continuing and apparently increasing estrangement of many from God's day and Word is proof that the great revival has certainly not begun and is hardly thought of by most. They say that they do not see the deep humiliation, the intense desire, and the fervent prayer that appear as forerunners of every true revival.

These are two opposing views that are equally dangerous. We must guard against both superficial optimism, which is never able to gauge the extent of the evil, and hopeless pessimism, which neither praises God for what He has done nor trusts Him for what He is ready to do.

Optimism will lose itself in happy self-congratulation, as it rejoices in its zeal and diligence and apparent success. It will never see the need of confession and great striving in prayer so we can be prepared to meet and conquer the hosts of darkness. Pessimism virtually gives over the world to Satan and almost prays and rejoices to see things get worse. It will hasten the coming of Him who is to make all right. May God keep us from either error and fulfill the promise, *"Thine ears shall hear a word behind thee, saying, This is the way, walk ye in it, when ye turn to the right hand, and when ye turn to the left"* (Isa. 30:21).

Let us listen to the lessons suggested by the passages we have quoted. They may help us to pray the prayer correctly *"O Lord, revive thy work."*

1. *"O Lord, revive thy work."* Read again the passages of Scripture at the beginning of the chapter, and see how they all contain the one thought: revival is God's work. He alone can give it; it must come from above. We are frequently in danger of looking at what God has done and is doing and to count on that as the pledge that He will at once do more. And all the time He may be blessing us by the measure of our faith or self-sacrifice and cannot give more until we discover and confess what is hindering Him. Or we may be looking at all the signs of life and good around us. We may be congratulating ourselves on all the organizations and agencies that are being created. All the while, the need of God's mighty and direct intervention is not properly felt, and entire dependence on Him is not cultivated.

Regeneration—the giving of divine life—we all acknowledge to be God's act, a miracle of His power. The restoring or reviving of the divine life, in a soul or a church, is as much a supernatural work. To have the spiritual discernment that can understand the signs of the heavens, and predict the coming revival, we need to enter deep into God's mind and will. We need God to reveal its conditions and to prepare those who are to pray for it or are to be used to bring it out. *"Surely the Lord God will do nothing, but he revealeth his secret unto his servants the prophets"* (Amos 3:7). It is God who is to give the revival. It is God who reveals His secret. It is the spirit of absolute dependence on God, giving Him the honor and the glory, that will prepare for it.

2. *"O Lord, revive thy work."* A second lesson suggested is that the revival God is to give will be given in answer to prayer. It must be asked and received directly from God Himself. Those who know anything about the history of revivals will remember how often this has been proved. Both international and local revivals have been distinctly linked to special prayer. In our own day, there are numerous congregations and missions where special or permanent revivals are—all glory be to God—connected with systematic, believing prayer. The coming revival will be no exception. An extraordinary spirit of prayer, urging believers to much secret and united prayer, pressing them to labor fervently (see Col. 4:12) in their supplications, will be one of the surest signs of approaching showers and floods of blessing.

Let all who are burdened by the lack of spirituality, the low state of the life of God in believers, listen to the call that comes to us. If there is to be revival—a mighty, divine revival—it will need wholeheartedness in prayer and faith. Let not one believer think himself too weak to help or imagine that he will not be missed. The gift that is in him may be so inspiring that, for his friends or neighborhood, he will be God's chosen intercessor.

Let us think of the need of souls, of all the sins among God's people, of the lack of power in so much of the preaching, and begin to cry, "*Wilt thou not revive us again: that thy people may rejoice in thee?*" And let us have this truth lodged deep in our hearts: every revival comes, as Pentecost came, as the fruit of united, continued prayer. The coming revival must begin with a great prayer revival. It is in the closet, with the door shut, that the sound of abundant revival will be first heard. An increase in the secret prayer of ministers and members will be the sure herald of blessing.

3. "O LORD, revive thy work." A third lesson our texts teach is that the revival is promised to the humble and contrite. We want the revival to break down and save the proud and the self-satisfied. God will give this but only on the condition that those who see and feel the sin of others take their burden of confession and bear it. All who pray for and claim in faith God's reviving power for His church should humble themselves with the confession of its sins. The need of revival always points to previous decline. And the decline was always caused by sin. Humiliation and contrition have always been the conditions for revival. In all intercession, confession of man's sin and God's righteous judgment is always an essential element.

We continually see this throughout the history of Israel. It comes out in the reformations under the pious kings of Judah. We hear it in the prayer of men like Ezra, Nehemiah, and Daniel. In Isaiah, Jeremiah, and Ezekiel, as well as in the minor prophets, it is the keynote of all the warnings and promises. If there is no humiliation and forsaking of sin, there can be no revival or deliverance. *"These men have set up their idols in their heart…should I be inquired of at all by them?"* (Ezek. 14:3). *"To this man will I look, even to him that is poor and of a contrite spirit, and trembleth at my word"* (Isa. 66:2). Amid the most gracious promises of divine visitation, there is this note: *"Be ashamed and confounded for your own ways, O house of Israel"* (Ezek. 36:32).

We find the same in the New Testament. The Sermon on the Mount promises the kingdom to the poor and those who mourn. In the epistles to the Corinthians and Galatians, the religion of man—of worldly wisdom and confidence in the flesh—is exposed and denounced. Without this worldliness being confessed and forsaken, all the promises of grace and the Spirit will be vain. In the epistles to the seven churches, we find five of which He has something against. In each of these, the keyword of His message is—not to the unconverted, but to the church—repent! All the glorious promises that each of these epistles contain, down to the last one, with its *"open the door, I will come in"*; *"to him that overcometh will I grant to sit with me in my throne"* (Rev. 3:20–21), are dependent on that one word: repent!

And if there is to be a revival in our churches, to yield a holy, spiritual membership, won't that trumpet sound need to be heard—repent? Was it only in Israel, in the ministry of kings and prophets, that there was so much evil in God's people to be cleansed away? Was it only in the church of the first century that Paul and James and our Lord Himself had to speak such sharp words? Or is there not in the church of our days an idolatry of money, talent, and culture? Is there not a worldly spirit, making it unfaithful to its one and only Husband and Lord, a confidence in the flesh that grieves and resists God's Holy Spirit? Is there not a confession of the lack of spirituality and spiritual power?

Let all who long for the coming revival, who seek to hasten it by their prayers, pray this above everything—that the Lord may prepare His prophets to go before Him at His bidding. *"Cry aloud, spare not, lift up thy voice like a trumpet, and show my people their transgression"* (Isa. 58:1). Every deep revival among God's people must have its roots in a deep sense and confession of sin. Until those who would lead the church in the path of revival bear faithful testimony against the sins of the church, people will be found unprepared.

Men would gladly have a revival as the outgrowth of their agencies and progress. God's way is the opposite. It is out of death, acknowledged as the desert of sin, confessed as utter helplessness, that He revives. He revives the heart of the contrite one.

4. "O LORD, revive thy work." There is a final thought suggested by the text from Hosea. It is as we return to the Lord that revival will come. For if we had not wandered from Him, His life would be among us in power. *"Come, and let us return unto the LORD: for he hath torn, and he will heal us; he hath smitten, and he will bind us up....He [will] revive us...and we shall live in his sight"* (Hosea 6:1–2). As we have said, there can be no return to the Lord where there is no sense or confession of wandering. *"Let us return unto the LORD"* must be the keynote of the revival. Let us return, acknowledging and forsaking whatever there has been in the church that is not entirely according to His mind and spirit. Let us return, yielding up and casting out whatever power of God's two great enemies—confidence in the flesh or the spirit of the world—has been in our faith.

Let us return and acknowledge how undividedly God must have us to fill us with His Spirit and use us for the kingdom of His Son. Oh, let us return in the surrender of a dependence and a devotion that has no measure but the absolute claim of Him who is the Lord. Let us return to the Lord with our whole heart, that He may make and keep us wholly His. He will revive us, and we will live in His sight. Let us turn to the God of Pentecost, as Christ led His disciples to turn to Him, and the God of Pentecost will turn to us.

The great work of intercession is needed for this returning to the Lord. It is here that the coming revival must find its strength. Let us begin as individuals to plead with God, confessing whatever we see of sin or hindrance in ourselves or others. If there were no other sin, surely the lack of prayer is matter enough for repentance, confession, and returning to the Lord. Let us seek to foster the spirit of confession, supplication, and intercession in those around us. Let us help to encourage and train those who think themselves too weak. Let us lift up our voices to proclaim the great truths.

The revival must come from above. It must be received in faith from above and brought down by prayer. The revival comes to the humble and contrite, and it is up to them to bring it to others. If we return to the Lord with our whole hearts, He will revive us. On those who see these truths rest the solemn responsibility of giving themselves up to witness for them and to act them out.

And as each of us pleads for the revival throughout the church, let us especially cry to God for our own neighborhood or sphere of work. Let there be, with every minister and worker, *"great searchings of heart"* (Judg. 5:16), as to whether they are ready to give as much time and strength to prayer as God desires. Let them, even as they are, in public, leaders of their larger or smaller circles, give themselves, in secret, to take their places in the front rank of the great intercession host. They must prevail with God before the great revival, the floods of blessing, can come. Of all who speak or think or long for revival, let none hold back in this great work of honest, earnest, definite pleading: *"O LORD, revive thy work."* *"Wilt thou not revive us again?"*

Come, and let us return to the Lord. He will revive us! And let us know, let us follow on to know the Lord. *"His going forth is prepared as the morning; and he shall come unto us as the rain, as the latter…rain unto the earth"* (Hos. 6:3). Amen. So be it.

THE SECRET
OF INTERCESSION

CONTENTS

INTRODUCTION

This little book has been prepared with the view of rousing Christians to some right sense of the solemn duty, the high privilege, and the wonderful power of intercession. It seeks to point out what a place intercession has in God's plan for the extension of His kingdom and for the strengthening of the life of His children so that they may receive from Him the heavenly blessings He has to bestow and then go forth to impart them to the world around.

The Dutch original has been found helpful in encouraging Christians to realize their high calling and in helping them to take their place among the Lord's remembrancers who call upon Him day and night. This translation is issued with the hope and prayer that it may be used in Bible classes and prayer meetings to foster that spirit of devotion and prayer that is so essential to the Christian life.

—Andrew Murray

1

INTERCESSION

Pray one for another.
—James 5:16

What a mystery of glory there is in prayer! On the one hand we see God in His holiness, love, and power waiting and longing to bless man. On the other hand there is sinful man, a worm of the dust, bringing down from God by prayer the very life and love of heaven to dwell in his heart.

But the glory of intercession is so much greater: when a man is bold and asks from God what he desires for others. He seeks to bring down on one soul, or it may be on hundreds and thousands, the power of the eternal life with all its blessings.

Intercession! Would one not say that this is the very holiest exercise of our boldness as God's children? It is the highest privilege and enjoyment connected to our communion with God. It is the power of being used by God as instruments for His great work of making men His habitation and showing forth His glory.

Would one not think that the church would count intercession as one of the chief means of grace? The church should seek above everything to cultivate in God's children the power of an unceasing prayerfulness on behalf of the perishing world.

One would expect believers, who have to some extent been brought into the secret, to feel what strength there is in unity and what assurance there is that God will certainly avenge His own elect who cry day and night to Him. It is when Christians cease from looking for help in external union and aim at all being bound together to the throne of God by an unceasing devotion to Jesus Christ, and an unceasing continuance in supplication for the power of God's Spirit, that the church will put on her beautiful garments and put on her strength, too, and overcome the world.

Our gracious Father, hear our prayers and teach Your church, and teach each of us, what is the glory, what is the blessing, what is the all-prevailing power of intercession. Give us, we pray You, the vision of what intercession means to You, as essential for carrying out Your blessed purpose, what it means to ourselves as the exercise of our royal priesthood, and what it will mean to Your church, and to perishing men, in the bringing down of the Spirit in power. For Jesus' sake. Amen.

2

THE OPENING OF THE EYES

*And Elisha prayed, and said, L*ORD*...open his eyes, that he may
see....Elisha said, L*ORD*, open the eyes of these men, that they may see.*
—2 Kings 6:17, 20

How wonderfully the prayer of Elisha for his servant was
answered! The young man saw the mountain full of chariots
of fire and horsemen about Elisha. The heavenly host had been sent by God
to protect His servant.

A second time Elisha prayed. The Syrian army had been smitten with
blindness and so led into Samaria. There Elisha prayed for the opening of
their eyes, and lo, they found themselves hopeless prisoners in the hand of
the enemy.

We wish to use these prayers in the spiritual sphere. First of all, to ask that our eyes may see the wonderful provisions that God has made for His church in the baptism with the Holy Spirit. All the powers of the heavenly world are at our disposal in the service of the heavenly kingdom. How little the children of God live in the faith of that heavenly vision—the power of the Holy Spirit on them, with them, and in them—for their own spiritual lives and as their strength joyfully to witness for their Lord and His work!

But we will find that we need that second prayer too, that God may open the eyes of those of His children who do not as yet see the power that the world and sin have upon His people. They are as of yet unconscious of the feebleness that marks the church, making it impotent to do the work of winning souls for Christ and building up believers for a life of holiness and fruitfulness. Let us pray especially that God may open all eyes to see what the great and fundamental need of the church is, in intercession that brings down His blessing, that the power of the Spirit may be known unceasingly in its divine efficacy and blessing.

Our Father, who is in heaven, You who are so unspeakably willing to give us the Holy Spirit in power, hear our humble prayer.
Open our eyes, we pray You, that we may realize fully the low estate of Your church and people, and as fully what treasures of grace and power You are willing to bestow in answer to the fervent prayer of a united church. Amen.

3

MAN'S PLACE IN GOD'S PLAN

The heaven, even the heavens, are the LORD's: but the earth hath he given to the children of men.
—Psalm 115:16

God created heaven as a dwelling for Himself: perfect, glorious, and most holy. The earth He gave to man as his dwelling: everything very good but only as a beginning with the need of being kept and cultivated. The work God had done, man was to continue and perfect.

Think of the iron and the coal hidden away in the earth, of the steam hidden away in the water. It was left to man to discover and to use all of this, as we see in the network of railways that span the world and the steamers that cover the ocean. God had created all to be used. He made the discovery and the use dependent on the wisdom and diligence of man. What the earth is today, with its cities and habitations, with its cornfields and orchards, it owes to man. The work God had begun and prepared was by man to be carried out in fulfillment of God's purpose. And so nature teaches us the wonderful partnership to which God calls man for the carrying out of the work of creation to its destined end.

This law holds equally good in the kingdom of grace. In this great redemption God has revealed the power of the heavenly life and the spiritual blessings of which heaven is full. But He has entrusted to His people the work of making these blessings known and making men partakers of them.

What diligence the children of this world show in seeking for the treasures that God has hidden in the earth for their use! Will not the children of God be equally faithful in seeking for the treasures hidden in heaven, to bring them down in blessing on the world? It is by the unceasing intercession of God's people that His kingdom will come and His will will be done on earth as it is in heaven. (See Matt. 6:10.)

Ever blessed Lord, how wonderful is the place You have given man, in trusting him to continue the work You have begun. We pray that You will open our hearts for the great thought that, through the preaching of the Gospel and the work of intercession, Your people are to work out Your purpose. Lord, open our eyes. For Jesus' sake. Amen.

4

INTERCESSION IN
THE PLAN OF REDEMPTION

Thou that hearest prayer, unto thee shall all flesh come.
—Psalm 65:2

When God gave the world into the power of man, made in His own image, who should rule over it as a viceroy under Him, it was His plan that Adam should do nothing except that which was with God and through God. God Himself would do all His work in the world through Adam. Adam was to be the owner, master, and ruler of the earth. When sin entered the world, Adam's power was proven to be a terrible reality. It was through him that the earth, with the whole race of man, was brought under the curse of sin.

When God made the plan of redemption, His object was to restore man to the place from which he had fallen. God chose His servants of old who, through the power of intercession, could ask what they would and it should be given to them. When Christ became man, it was so that, as man, both on earth and in heaven, He might intercede for man. Before He left the world, He imparted this right of intercession to His disciples in the sevenfold promise of the Farewell Discourse (see John 15–17), that whatever they would ask He would do for them.

God's intense longing to bless seems in some sense to be graciously limited by His dependence on the intercession that rises from the earth. He seeks to rouse the spirit of intercession that He may be able to bestow His blessing on mankind. God regards intercession as the highest expression of His people's readiness to receive and to yield themselves wholly to the working of His almighty power.

Christians need to recognize intercession as their true nobility and their only power with God—the right to claim and expect that God will hear prayer. It is only as God's children begin to see what intercession means in regard to God's kingdom that they will realize how solemn their responsibility is.

Each individual believer will be led to see that God waits for him to take his part. He will feel in very truth that the highest, the most blessed, the mightiest of all human instrumentalities for the fulfillment of the petition, *"As in heaven, so in earth"* (Luke 11:2), is the intercession that rises day and night. Christian warriors are pleading with God for the power of heaven to be sent down into the hearts of men. Oh, that God might burn into our hearts this one thought: intercession in its omnipotent power is according to His will and is most certainly effectual!

5

GOD SEEKS INTERCESSORS

And he saw that there was no man,
and wondered that there was no intercessor.
—Isaiah 59:16

From the start God had among His people intercessors to whose voice He had listened and given deliverance. Here we read of a time of trouble when He sought for an intercessor but in vain. And He wondered! Think of what that means: the amazement of God that there should be none who loved the people enough or who had sufficient faith in His power to deliver, to intercede on their behalf. If there had been an intercessor, He would have given deliverance; without an intercessor, His judgments came down. (See Isaiah 64:7; Ezekiel 22:30–31.)

Of what infinite importance is the place the intercessor holds in the kingdom of God! Is it not indeed a matter of wonder that God should give men such power? Yet there are so few who know what it is to take hold of His strength and pray down His blessing on the world.

Let us try to realize the position. When God had in His Son completed the new creation and Christ had taken His place on the throne, the work of the extension of His kingdom was given into the hands of men. He ever lives to pray. Prayer is the highest exercise of His royal prerogative as Priest-King upon the throne. All that Christ was to do in heaven was to be in fellowship with His people on earth. In His divine condescension God has willed that the working of His Spirit shall follow the prayer of His people. He waits for their intercession, showing the preparation of heart, to what extent they are ready to yield to His Spirit's control.

God rules the world and His church through the prayers of His people. That God should have made the expansion of His kingdom to such a large extent dependent on the faithfulness of His people in prayer is a stupendous mystery and yet an absolute certainty. God calls for intercessors; in His grace He has made His work dependent on them. He waits for them.

Our Father, open our eyes to see that You do invite
Your children to have a part in the extension of Your kingdom by their
faithfulness in prayer and intercession. Give us such an insight into
the glory of this holy calling that with our whole hearts we may yield
ourselves to its blessed service. Amen.

6

CHRIST AS INTERCESSOR

Wherefore he is able also to save them to the uttermost that come unto God by him, seeing he ever liveth to make intercession for them.
—Hebrews 7:25

When God had said in Isaiah that He wondered that there was no intercessor, there followed the words: *"Therefore his arm brought salvation unto him"* (Isa. 59:16). *"The Redeemer shall come to Zion"* (v. 20). God Himself would provide the true intercessor, in Christ His Son, of whom it had already been said, *"He bare the sin of many, and made intercession for the transgressors"* (Isa. 53:12).

In His life on earth Christ began His work as intercessor. Think of the high-priestly prayer on behalf of His disciples and of all who should through them believe in His name. Think of His words to Peter, *"I have prayed for thee, that thy faith fail not"* (Luke 22:32): a proof of how intensely personal His intercession is. And on the cross He spoke as intercessor: *"Father, forgive them"* (Luke 23:34).

Now that He is seated at God's right hand, He continues, as our Great High Priest, the work of intercession without ceasing. But with this difference: He gives His people power to take part in it. Seven times in His farewell discourse He repeated the assurance that what they asked He would do.

The power of heaven was to be at their disposal. The grace and power of God waited for man's bidding. Through the leading of the Holy Spirit they would know what the will of God was. They would learn in faith to pray in His name. He would present their petition to the Father, and through His and their united intercession, the church would be clothed with the power of the Spirit.

Blessed Redeemer, what wonderful grace that You call us to share in Your intercession! We pray that You will arouse in Your redeemed people a consciousness of the glory of this their calling, and of all the rich blessing that Your church in its impotence can, through its intercession in Your name, bring down upon this earth. May Your Holy Spirit work in Your people a deep conviction of the sin of restraining prayer, of the sloth and unbelief and selfishness that is the cause of it, and of Your loving desire to pour out the Spirit of prayer in answer to their petitions. For Your name's sake. Amen.

7

THE INTERCESSORS
GOD SEEKS

I have set watchmen upon thy walls,
O Jerusalem, which shall never hold their peace day nor night:
ye that make mention of the LORD, keep not silence.
—Isaiah 62:6

W atchmen are ordinarily placed on the walls of a city to give notice to the rulers of coming danger. God appoints watchmen not only to warn men—often they will not hear—but also to summon Him to come to their aid whenever need or enemy may be threatening. The great mark of the intercessors are that they are not to hold their peace day or night, to take no rest, and to give God no rest, until the deliverance comes. In faith they may count upon the assurance that God will answer their prayers.

It is of this that our Lord Jesus said, *"Shall not God avenge his own elect, which cry day and night unto him?"* (Luke 18:7). From every land the voice is heard that the church of Christ, under the influence of the power of the world and the earthly mindedness it brings, is losing its influence over its members. There is but little proof of God's presence in the conversion of sinners or the holiness of His people. With the great majority of Christians there is an utter neglect of Christ's call to take a part in the extension of His kingdom. The power of the Holy Spirit is but little experienced.

Amid all the discussions as to what can be done to interest young and old in the study of God's Word or to awaken love for the services of His house, one hears but little of the indispensable necessity of the power of the Holy Spirit in the ministry and the membership of the church. One sees but little sign of the conviction and confession that it is owing to the lack of prayer that the workings of the Spirit are so feeble and that only by united, fervent prayer a change can be brought about. If ever there was a time when God's elect should cry day and night to Him, it is now. Will you not, dear reader, offer yourself to God for this blessed work of intercession and learn to count it as the highest privilege of your life to be a channel through whose prayers God's blessing can be brought down to earth?

> *Ever blessed Father, hear us, we pray You, and raise up intercessors, such as You would have. Give us, we ask You, men and women to act as Your remembrancers, taking no rest and giving You no rest, until Your church again becomes a praise in the earth. Blessed Father, let Your Spirit teach us how to pray. Amen.*

8

THE SCHOOL
OF INTERCESSION

Who in the days of his flesh,
when he had offered up prayers and supplications with strong crying
and tears…and was heard in that he feared.
—Hebrews 5:7

C hrist, as Head, is Intercessor in heaven; we, as the members of His body, are partners with Him on earth. Let no one imagine that it cost Christ nothing to become an intercessor. He could not be our example without this. What do we read of Him?

When thou shalt make his soul an offering for sin, he shall see his seed….He shall see of the travail of his soul….Therefore will I divide

him a portion with the great...because he hath poured out his soul unto
death.   (Isa. 53:10–12)

Notice the thrice-repeated expression in regard to the pouring out of
His soul.

The pouring out of the soul—that is the divine meaning of intercession. Nothing less than this was needed if His sacrifice and prayers were to
have power with God. This giving of Himself to live and die that He might
save the perishing was a revelation of the spirit that has power to prevail
with God.

If we, as helpers and fellow laborers with the Lord Jesus, are to share
His power of intercession, there will need to be with us as well the travail of
soul that there was with Him, the giving up of our lives and their pleasures
for the one supreme work of interceding for our fellowmen. Intercession
must not be a passing interest. It must become an ever growing object of
intense desire for which, above everything, we long and live. It is the life of
consecration and self-sacrifice that will indeed give power for intercession.
(See Acts 15:26; 20:24; Philippians 2:17; Revelation 12:11.)

The longer we study this blessed truth and think of what it means
to exercise this power for the glory of God and the salvation of men, the
deeper our convictions will become that it is worth giving up everything to
take part with Christ in His work of intercession.

Blessed Lord Jesus, be pleased to teach us how to unite with You in
calling upon God for the souls You have bought. Let Your love fill us
and all Your saints, that we may learn to plead for the power of Your
Holy Spirit to be made known. Amen.

9

THE POWER IN
THE NAME OF JESUS

Hitherto have ye asked nothing in my name: ask, and ye shall receive,
that your joy may be full....At that day ye shall ask in my name.
—John 16:24, 26

During Christ's life upon earth the disciples had known but little of the power of prayer. In Gethsemane, Peter and the others had utterly failed. They had no conception of what it was to ask in the name of Jesus and to receive. The Lord promises them that in that day that was coming they would be able to pray with such a power in His name that they might ask what they would and it should be given to them.

"*Hitherto have ye asked nothing in my name: ask, and ye shall receive, that your joy may be full....At that day ye shall ask in my name.*" Therefore you will receive. These two conditions are still found in the church. With the great majority of Christians there is such a lack of knowledge of their oneness with Christ Jesus, and of the Holy Spirit as the Spirit of prayer, that they do not even attempt to claim the wonderful promises Christ here gives. But where God's children know what it is to abide in Christ and in vital union with Him and to yield to the Holy Spirit's teaching, they begin to learn that their intercession avails much. God will give the power of His Spirit in answer to their prayers.

It is faith in the power of Jesus' name, and in our right to use it, that will give us the courage to follow on when God invites us to the holy office of intercessor. When our Lord Jesus, in His Farewell Discourse, gave His unlimited prayer promise, He sent the disciples out into the world with this consciousness: "He who sits upon the throne, and who lives in my heart, has promised that what I ask in His name I will receive. He will do it."

Oh, if Christians but knew what it is to yield themselves wholly and absolutely to Jesus Christ and His service, how their eyes would be opened to see that intense and unceasing prayerfulness is the essential mark of the healthy spiritual life. The power of all-prevailing intercession will indeed be the portion of those who live only in and for their Lord!

Blessed Savior, give us the grace of the Holy Spirit so that we might live in You and with You and for You; allow us to boldly look to You for the assurance that our prayers are heard. Amen.

10

PRAYER, THE WORK
OF THE SPIRIT

God hath sent forth the Spirit of his Son into your hearts,
crying, Abba, Father.
—Galatians 4:6

We know what *"Abba, Father"* meant in the mouth of Christ in Gethsemane. It was the entire surrender of Himself to the very death that the holy will of God's love in redemption of sinners might be accomplished. In His prayer He was ready for any sacrifice, even to the yielding of His life. In that prayer we have revealed to us the heart of Him whose place is at the right hand of God, with the wonderful power of intercession that He exercises there and the power to pour down the Holy Spirit.

The Holy Spirit has been bestowed by the Father to breathe the very spirit of His son into our hearts. Our Lord would have us yield ourselves as wholly to God as He did, to pray like Him, that God's will of love should be done on earth at any cost. As God's love is revealed in His desire for the salvation of souls, so also the desire of Jesus was made plain when He gave Himself for them. And He now asks of His people that that same love should fill them too so that they give themselves wholly to the work of intercession and, at any cost, pray down God's love upon the perishing.

And if anyone should think that this is too high and beyond our reach, the Holy Spirit is actually given into our hearts so that we may pray as Jesus did in His power and in His name. It is the man who yields himself wholly to the leading of the Holy Spirit who will feel urged, by the compulsion of a divine love, to the undivided surrender to a life of continual intercession because he knows that it is God who is working in him.

Now we can understand how Christ could give such unlimited promises of answer to prayer to His disciples; they were first going to be filled with the Holy Spirit. Now we understand how God can give such a high place to intercession in the fulfillment of His purpose of redemption. It is the Holy Spirit who breathes God's own desire into us and enables us to intercede for souls.

Abba Father! Oh, grant that by Your Holy Spirit there may be maintained in us the unceasing intercession for love for the souls for whom Christ died. Give, oh, give to Your children the vision of the blessedness and the power that come to those who yield themselves to this high calling. Amen.

11

CHRIST, OUR EXAMPLE
IN INTERCESSION

*He shall divide the spoil with the strong; because...he bare the sin of
many, and made intercession for the transgressors.*
—Isaiah 53:12

"H e...*made intercession for the transgressors.*" What did that mean
to Him? Think of what it cost Him to pray that prayer effectually. He had to pour out His soul as an offering for sin and to cry in
Gethsemane, "*Father...thy will be done*" (Matt. 26:42).

Think what moved Him so to sacrifice Himself to the very uttermost!
It was His love for the Father—that His holiness might be manifest. It was
also His love for souls—that they might be partakers of His holiness.

Think of the reward He won! As Conqueror of every enemy, He is seated at the right hand of God with the power of unlimited and assured intercession. And He would see His seed, a generation of those of the same mind as Himself, whom He could train to share in His great work of intercession.

And what does this mean for us, when we indeed seek to pray for the transgressors? That we, too, will yield ourselves wholly to the glory of the holiness and the love of the Father. Therefore we can also say, "Your will be done; cost what it may, we, too, will sacrifice ourselves, even to pouring out our souls unto death."

The Lord Jesus has united us in partnership with Himself in carrying out the great work of intercession. He in heaven and we on earth must be of one mind. We must have only one aim in life. That aim is that we should love the Father and the lost by consecrating our lives to intercession for God's blessing. The burning desire of Father and Son for the salvation of souls must be the burning desire of our hearts, too.

What an honor! What a blessedness! What a power for us to do the work because He lives, and by His Spirit He pours forth His love into our hearts!

> *Everlasting God of love, open our eyes to the vision of the glory of Your Son, as He ever lives to pray. And open our eyes to the glory of that grace which enables us in His likeness also to live, that we may pray for the transgressors. Father, for Jesus' sake. Amen.*

12

GOD'S WILL AND OURS

Thy will be done.
—Matthew 26:42

It is the high prerogative of God that everything in heaven and earth is to be done according to His will and as the fulfillment of His desires. When He made man in His image, it was, above all, that his desires were to be in perfect accord with the desires of God. This is the high honor of being in the likeness of God. We are to feel and wish just as God. In human flesh man was to be the embodiment and fulfillment of God's desires.

When God created man with the power of willing and choosing what he should be, He limited Himself in the exercise of His will. And when man had fallen and yielded himself to the will of God's enemy, God in His infinite love set about the great work of winning man back to make the desires of God his own. As in God, so in man, desire is the great moving power. And just as man had yielded himself to a life of desire after the things of the earth and the flesh, God had to redeem him and to educate him into a life of harmony with Himself. His one aim was that man's desire should be in perfect accord with His own.

The great step in this direction was when the Son of the Father came into this world to reproduce the divine desires in His human nature and in His prayer to yield Himself up to the perfect fulfillment of all that God wished and willed. The Son, as man, said in agony and blood, "*Thy will be done,*" and made the surrender even to being forsaken by God. He did this so that the power that had deceived man might be conquered and deliverance procured. It was in the wonderful and complete harmony between the Father and the Son when the Son said, "*Thy will be done,*" that the great redemption was accomplished.

And now the great work of appropriating that redemption is that believers have to say, first of all for themselves and then in lives devoted to intercession for others: "*Thy will be done in earth, as it is in heaven*" (Matt. 6:10). As we plead for the church—its ministers and its missionaries, its strong Christians or its young converts—for the unsaved, whether nominally Christian or heathen, we have the privilege of knowing that we are pleading for what God wills and that through our prayers His will is to be done on earth as in heaven.

13

THE BLESSEDNESS OF
A LIFE OF INTERCESSION

Then hear thou from the heavens their prayer and their
supplication, and maintain their cause.
—2 Chronicles 6:35

What an unspeakable grace to be allowed to deal with God in intercession for the supply of other's needs! To be able to take part in Christ's great work as Intercessor is such a blessing. It is wonderful to be in close union with Him and to mingle my prayers with His! What an honor to have power with God in heaven over souls and to obtain for them what they do not even know or think!

What a privilege, as a steward of the grace of God, to bring to Him the state of the church or of individual souls, of the ministers of the Word, or of His messengers away in heathendom, and plead on their behalf until He entrusts me with the answer!

What blessedness, in union with other children of God, to strive together in prayer until the victory is gained over difficulties here on earth or over the powers of darkness in high places!

It is indeed worth living for to know that God will use me as an intercessor to receive and dispense here on earth His heavenly blessing and, above all, the power of His Holy Spirit.

This is truly the life of heaven, the life of the Lord Jesus Himself in His self-denying love, taking possession of me and urging me to yield myself wholly to bear the burden of souls before Him and to plead that they may live.

Too long have we thought of prayer simply as a means for the supplying of our need in life and service. May God help us to see what a place intercession takes in His divine counsel and in His work for the kingdom. May our hearts indeed feel that there is no honor or blessedness on earth at all equal to the unspeakable privilege of waiting upon God, bringing down from heaven, and opening the way on earth for the blessings He delights to give!

Oh, my Father, let Your life indeed flow down to this earth, and fill the hearts of Your children! As the Lord Jesus pours out His love in His unceasing intercession in heaven, let it even be so with us also upon earth, a life of overflowing love and never ending intercession. Amen.

14

THE PLACE OF PRAYER

These all continued with one accord in prayer and supplication.
—Acts 1:14

The last words that Christ spoke before He left the world give us the four great notes of His church: *"Wait for the promise of the Father"* (Acts 1:4). *"But ye shall receive power, after that the Holy Ghost is come upon you: and ye shall be witnesses unto me both in Jerusalem…and unto the uttermost part of the earth"* (Acts 1:8).

United and unceasing prayer, the power of the Holy Spirit, living witnesses to the living Christ from Jerusalem to the uttermost part of the earth—such are the marks of the true Gospel, of the true ministry, of the true church of the New Testament.

A church of united and unceasing prayerfulness, a ministry filled with the Holy Spirit, the members living witnesses to a living Christ with a message to every creature on earth—such was the church that Christ founded and such was the church that went out to conquer the world.

When Christ had ascended to heaven, the disciples knew at once what their work was to be: continuing with one accord in prayer and supplication. They were to be bound together by the love and Spirit of Christ into one body. It was this that gave them their wonderful power in heaven with God and upon earth with men.

Their one duty was to wait in united and unceasing prayer for the power of the Holy Spirit as the enduement from on high for their witness to Christ to the ends of the earth. A praying church, a Spirit-filled church, a witnessing church with all the world as its sphere and aim—such is the church of Jesus Christ.

As long as it maintained this character, it had power to conquer. But alas, as it came under the influence of the world, how much it lost of its heavenly, supernatural beauty and strength! How unfaithful in prayer, how feeble the workings of the Spirit, how formal its witness to Christ, and how unfaithful to its worldwide mission!

Blessed Lord Jesus, have mercy upon Your church and give, we pray You, the Spirit of prayer and supplication as of old, that Your church may prove what power from You rests upon her and her testimony for You to win the world to Your feet. Amen.

15

PAUL AS AN INTERCESSOR

I bow my knees unto the Father…that he would grant you…
to be strengthened with might by his Spirit.
—Ephesians 3:14, 16

W̲e think of Paul as the great missionary, the great preacher, the great writer, the great Apostle *"in labours more abun-dant"* (2 Cor. 11:23). We do not sufficiently think of him as the intercessor who sought and obtained, by his supplication, the power that rested upon all his other activities and brought down the blessing that rested on the churches that he served.

We see above what he wrote to the Ephesians. Think of what he said to the Thessalonians: *"Night and day praying exceedingly that we…might perfect that which is lacking in your faith....To the end he may stablish your hearts unblameable in holiness"* (1 Thess. 3:10, 13). To the Romans: *"Without ceasing I make mention of you always in my prayers"* (Rom. 1:9). To the Philippians: *"Always in every prayer of mine for you all making request with joy"* (Phil. 1:4). And to the Colossians: *"We...do not cease to pray for you"* (Col. 1:9); *"I would that ye knew what great conflict I have for you"* (Col. 2:1).

Day and night he cried to God in his intercession for them that the light and the power of the Holy Spirit might be in them. As earnestly as he believed in the power of his intercession for them so also did he believe in the blessing that theirs would bring upon him. *"Now I beseech you...that ye strive together with me in your prayers to God for me"* (Rom. 15:30). *"[God] will yet deliver us; ye also helping together by prayer for us"* (2 Cor. 1:10–11). *"Praying...for me...that I may open my mouth boldly"* (Eph. 6:18–19). *"This shall turn to my salvation through your prayer"* (Phil. 1:19).

The whole relationship between pastor and people depends on the united, continual prayerfulness. Their whole relationship to each other is a heavenly one, spiritual and divine, and can only be maintained by unceasing prayer. When ministers and people waken up to the consciousness that the power and blessing of the Holy Spirit is waiting for their united and unceasing prayers, the church will begin to know something of what apostolic Christianity is.

Ever blessed Father, we do most humbly ask You, restore again graciously to Your church the spirit of supplication and intercession. For Jesus' sake. Amen.

16

INTERCESSION FOR LABORERS

The harvest truly is plenteous, but the labourers are few;
pray ye therefore the Lord of the harvest, that he will send forth
labourers into his harvest.
—Matthew 9:37–38

The disciples understood very little of what these words meant. Christ gave them as a seed to be lodged in their hearts for later use. At Pentecost, as they saw how many of the new converts were ready in the power of the Spirit to testify about Christ, they must have felt how the ten days of continuous, united prayer had brought this blessing. This was an example of the fruit of the Spirit's power: laborers in the harvest.

Christ meant to teach us that however large the field may be and however few the laborers, prayer is the best, the sure, the only means for supplying the need.

What we have to understand is that it is not only in time of need that the prayer must be sent up but that the whole work is to be carried on in the spirit of prayer. This way the prayer for laborers will be in perfect harmony with the whole of our lives and efforts.

In the China Inland Mission, the number of missionaries had gone up to two hundred. At a conference held in China, these missionaries felt so deeply the need for more laborers for the districts that were unprovided for that after much prayer, they felt at liberty to ask God to give them within a year one hundred additional laborers and ten thousand pounds to meet the expenses. They agreed to continue in prayer day by day throughout the year. At the end of the time, the one hundred suitable men and women had been found along with eleven thousand pounds.

The churches all complain about the lack of laborers and funds to meet the needs of the world, its open fields, and its waiting souls. Does not Christ's voice call us to the united and unceasing prayer of the first disciples? God is faithful, by the power of His Spirit, to supply every need. Let the church take the posture of united prayer and supplication. God hears prayer.

Blessed Lord Jesus, teach Your church what it means to live and labor for You in the Spirit of unceasing prayerfulness, that our faith may rise to the assurance that You will indeed, in a way surpassing all expectation, meet the crying needs of a dying world. Amen.

17

INTERCESSION
FOR INDIVIDUAL SOULS

Ye shall be gathered one by one, O ye children of Israel.
—Isaiah 27:12

In our bodies every member has its appointed place. This is also true in society and in the church. The work must always aim at the welfare and the highest perfection of the whole through the cooperation of every individual member.

In the church the thought is too often found that the salvation of men is the work of the minister, whereas he generally only deals with the crowd and will seldom reach the individual. This is the cause of a twofold evil. The individual believer does not understand that it is necessary for him to testify to those around him for the nourishment and the strengthening of his own spiritual life and for the ingathering of souls. Unconverted souls suffer unspeakable loss because Christ is not personally brought to them by each believer they meet. The thought of intercession for those around us is all too seldom found. Its restoration to its right place in the Christian life—how much that would mean to the church and its missions!

Oh, when will Christians learn the great truth that what God in heaven desires to do needs prayer on earth as its indispensable condition. It is as we realize this that we will see that intercession is the chief element in the conversion of souls. All of our efforts are in vain without the power of the Holy Spirit given in answer to prayer. It is when ministers and people unite in a covenant of prayer and testimony that the church will flourish and that every believer will understand the part he has to take.

What can we do to stir up the spirit of intercession? There is a twofold answer. Let every Christian, as he begins to get an insight into the need and the power of intercession, begin by exercising it on behalf of single individuals. Pray for your children, for your relatives and friends, for all with whom God brings you into contact. If you feel that you do not have the power to intercede, let the discovery humble you and drive you to the mercy seat. God wants every redeemed child of His to intercede for the perishing. It is the vital breath of the normal Christian life—the proof that it is born from above.

Then pray intensely and persistently that God may give the power of His Holy Spirit to you and His children around you, that the power of intercession may have the place that God will honor.

18

INTERCESSION FOR MINISTERS

And for me.
—Ephesians 6:19

Praying also for us.
—Colossians 4:3

Finally, brethren, pray for us.
—2 Thessalonians 3:1

These expressions of Paul suggest how strong his conviction must
have been that the Christians had power with God and that their

prayers would indeed bring new strength to him in his work. He had such a sense of the actual unity of the body of Christ. He saw unity in the interdependence of each member, even the most honorable, and in the life that flowed through the whole body. This encouraged him to rouse Christians for their own sakes, for his sake, and for the sake of the kingdom of God, with his call: "*Continue in prayer, and watch in the same with thanksgiving; withal praying also for us*" (Col. 4:2–3).

The church depends upon the ministry to an extent that we very little realize. The place of the minister is so high, as the steward of the mysteries of God and as the ambassador for God to beseech men in Christ's name to be reconciled to Him, that unfaithfulness or inefficiency must bring a terrible blight on the church that he serves. If Paul, after having preached for twenty years in the power of God, still needed the prayers of the church, how much more does the ministry in our day need it?

The minister needs the prayers of his people. He has a right to them. He is in very truth dependent on them. It is his task to train Christians for their work of intercession on behalf of the church and the world. He must begin with training them to pray for himself. He may have to begin still farther back and learn to pray more for himself and for them. Let all intercessors who are seeking to enter more deeply into their blessed work give a larger place to the ministry, whether of their own church or of other churches.

Let them plead with God for individual ministers and for special circles. Let them continue in prayer and watch therein, that ministers may be people of power, of prayer, and full of the Holy Spirit. Oh friends, pray for the ministry!

Our Father who is in heaven, we humbly pray that You would arouse believers to a sense of their calling to pray in the spirit of faith for the ministers of the Gospel. Amen.

19

PRAYER FOR ALL SAINTS

*With all prayer and supplication in the Spirit, and watching thereunto
with all perseverance and supplication for all saints.*
—Ephesians 6:18

Notice how Paul repeats the words in the intensity of his desire
to reach the hearts of his readers. *"With all prayer and supplication...watching thereunto with all perseverance and supplication."* It is *"all
prayer...all perseverance and [all] supplication."* The words take thought, if
they are to meet with the needed response. Paul felt so deeply the unity of
the body of Christ, and he was so sure that the unity could only be realized
in the exercise of love and prayer. Therefore, he pleaded with the believers
at Ephesus unceasingly and fervently to pray for all saints, not only in their

immediate circle, but in all the church of Christ of whom they might hear. Unity is strength. As we exercise this power of intercession with all perseverance, we will be delivered from self with all its feeble prayers and lifted up to that enlargement of heart in which the love of Christ can flow freely and fully through us.

The great lack in true believers is often that in prayer they are occupied with themselves and with what God must do for them. Let us realize that we have here a call to every believer to give himself without ceasing to the exercise of love and prayer. It is as we forget ourselves, in the faith that God will take charge of us, and yield ourselves to the great and blessed word of calling down the blessing of God upon our fellow believers that the whole church will be fitted to do its work in making Christ known to every creature. This alone is the healthy and the blessed life of a child of God who has yielded himself wholly to Christ Jesus.

Pray for God's children and the church around you. Pray for all the work in which they are engaged or ought to be. Pray at all seasons in the Spirit for all of God's saints. There is no blessedness greater than that of abiding communion with God. There is no way that leads to the enjoyment of this more surely than the life of intercession for which these words of Paul appeal so pleadingly.

20

MISSIONARY INTERCESSION

And when they had fasted and prayed,
and laid their hands on them, they sent them away.
—Acts 13:3

The supreme question of foreign missions is how to multiply the number of Christians who will individually and collectively exert this force of intercession for the conversion and transformation of men. Every other consideration and plan is secondary to that of wielding the forces of prayer.

We take for granted that those who love this work and bear it upon their hearts will follow the scriptural injunction to pray unceasingly for its triumph. To such, not only the morning watch and the hours of stated devotion, but all times and seasons, will witness an attitude of intercession that refuses to let God go until He crowns His workers with victory.

Missions have their roots in the love of Christ, which was proven on the cross and now lives in our hearts. As men are so earnest in seeking to carry out God's plans for the natural world, so God's children should be at least as wholehearted in seeking to bring Christ's love to all mankind. Intercession is the chief means appointed by God to bring the great redemption within the reach of all.

Pray for the missionaries that the Christ life may be clear and strong. Pray also that they may be people of prayer and filled with love, in whom the power of the spiritual life is made manifest.

Pray for the native Christians that they may know the glory of the mystery among the heathen so that with Christ in them, they will know the hope of glory.

Pray for the baptism classes and all the pupils in schools that the teaching of God's Word may be in power. Pray especially for the native pastors and evangelists that the Holy Spirit may fill them to be witnesses for Christ among their fellow countrymen.

Pray, above all, for the church of Christ that it may be lifted out of its indifference and that every believer may be brought to understand that the one object of his life is to help to make Christ King on the earth.

Our gracious God, our eyes are on You. Will You not in mercy hear our prayers and by the Holy Spirit reveal the presence and the power of Christ in the work of Your servants? Amen.

21

THE GRACE OF INTERCESSION

Continue in prayer, and watch in the same with thanksgiving...
praying also for us.
—Colossians 4:2–3

Nothing can bring us nearer to God and lead us deeper into
His love than the work of intercession. Nothing can give us
a higher experience of the likeness of God than the power of pouring out
our hearts into the bosom of God in prayer for men around us. Nothing
can so closely link us to Jesus Christ, the great Intercessor, and give us the
experience of His power and Spirit resting on us as the yielding of our
lives to the work of bringing the great redemption into the hearts and lives
of our fellowmen. There is nothing in which we will know more of the

powerful working of the Holy Spirit than the prayer breathed by Him into our hearts, *"Abba, Father"* (Gal. 4:6), in all the fullness of meaning that it had for Christ in Gethsemane. Nothing can so help us to prove the power and the faithfulness of God to His Word as when we reach out in intercession to the multitudes either in the church of Christ or in the darkness of heathenism. We pour out our souls as living sacrifices before God. Our one persistent plea is that He will, in answer to our prayers, open the windows of heaven and send down His abundant blessing. God will be glorified, our souls will reach their highest destiny, and God's kingdom will come.

There is nothing that will so help us to understand and to experience the living unity of the body of Christ and the irresistible power that it can exert as the daily and continued fellowship with God's children. His children stand together in the persistent plea that God will arise and have mercy upon Zion and make her a light and a life to those who are sitting in darkness. Oh, my friends, how little we realize what we are losing in not living in fervent intercession! What could we possibly lose for ourselves and for the world if we allow God's Spirit, as a Spirit of grace and of supplication, to master our whole being?

In heaven Christ lives to pray. His whole communion with His Father is prayer: an asking and receiving of the fullness of the Spirit for His people. God delights in nothing so much as in prayer. Will we not learn to believe that the highest blessings of heaven will be unfolded to us as we pray more?

Blessed Father, pour down the Spirit of supplication and intercession on Your people. For Jesus Christ's sake. Amen.

22

UNITED INTERCESSION

There is one body, and one Spirit.
—Ephesians 4:4

Our own bodies teach us how essential for their health and
strength it is that every member should take its full share in
seeking the welfare of the whole. It is even so in the body of Christ. There
are, alas, too many who look upon salvation only in connection with their
own happiness. There are those, again, who know that they live not unto
themselves. They truly seek in prayer and work to bring others to share in
their happiness; however, they do not yet understand that in addition to
their personal circle or church, they have a calling to enlarge their hearts to
take the whole body of Christ Jesus into their love and their intercessions.

Yet this is what the Spirit and the love of Christ will enable them to do. It is only when intercession for the whole church, by the whole church, ascends to God's throne that the Spirit of unity and power can have its full sway. The desire that has been awakened for closer union between the different branches of the church of Christ is cause for thanksgiving. And yet the difficulties are so great and, in the case of different nationalities of the world, so apparently inseparable that the thought of a united church on earth appears beyond reach.

Let us bless God that there is a unity in Christ Jesus that is deeper and stronger than any visible manifestation could make it. There is a way in which even now, amidst all diversity of administrations, the unity can be practically exemplified and utilized as the means of an unthought-of accession of divine strength and blessing in the work of the kingdom. It is in the cultivation and increase of the Spirit and in the exercise of intercession that the true unity can be realized. As believers are taught what is the meaning of their calling as a royal priesthood, they are led to see that God is not confined in His love or promises to their limited spheres of labor. God invites them to enlarge their hearts and like Christ—we may say like Paul too—to pray for all who believe, or can yet be brought to believe, that this earth and the church of Christ in it will, by intercession, be bound to the throne of heaven as it has never yet been.

Let Christians and ministers agree and bind themselves together for this worldwide intercession. It will strengthen the confidence that prayer will be heard and that their prayers too will become indispensable for the coming of the kingdom.

23

UNCEASING INTERCESSION

Pray without ceasing.
—1 Thessalonians 5:17

How different the standard of the average Christian is, with regard to a life in the service of God, from that which Scripture gives us. The average Christian's chief thought is personal safety: grace to pardon our sins and to live such a life as may secure our entrances into heaven. How high above this is the Bible standard: a Christian surrendering himself with all his powers, with his time and thought and love wholly yielded to the glorious God who has redeemed him, whom he now delights in serving, in whose fellowship is heaven begun.

To the average Christian the command *"Pray without ceasing"* is simply a needless and impossible life of perfection. Who can do it? We can get to heaven without it. To the true believer, on the contrary, it holds out the promise of the highest happiness, of a life crowned by all the blessings that can be brought down on souls through his intercession. And as he perseveres, it becomes increasingly his highest aim upon earth, his highest joy, his highest experience of the wonderful fellowship with the holy God.

"Pray without ceasing!" Let us take that word in full faith as a promise of what God's Spirit will work in us, of how close and intimate our union to the Lord Jesus can be, and of our likeness to Him in His ever blessed intercession at the right hand of God. Let it become to us one of the chief elements of our heavenly calling to be consciously the stewards and administrators of God's grace to the world around us. As we think of how Christ said, *"I in them, and thou in me"* (John 17:23), let us believe that just as the Father worked in Him, so Christ, the interceding High Priest, will work and pray in us. As the faith of our high calling fills our hearts, we will begin literally to feel that there is nothing on earth for one moment to be compared with the privilege of being God's priests. This privilege includes walking without intermission in His holy presence, bringing the burden of the souls around us to the footstool of His throne, and receiving at His hands the power and blessing to dispense to our fellowmen.

This is indeed the fulfillment of the Word of old, which said that man was created in the likeness and the image of God. (See Gen. 1:27.)

24

INTERCESSION, THE LINK BETWEEN HEAVEN AND EARTH

Thy will be done, as in heaven, so in earth.
—Luke 11:2

When God created heaven and earth, He meant heaven to be the divine pattern to which earth was to be conformed. *"As in heaven, so in earth"* was to be the law of its existence. This truth calls us to think of what constitutes the glory of heaven. God is all in all there. Everything lives in Him and to His glory. We then think of what this earth has now become with all its sin and misery. Here on earth the great majority of the race is without any knowledge of the true God, and the remainder are nominal Christians who are for the greater part utterly indifferent to His claims and estranged from His holiness and love. What a revolution, what a miracle is needed if the Word is to be fulfilled: *"As in heaven, so in earth."*

How is this word ever to come true? Through the prayers of God's children. Our Lord teaches us to pray for it. Intercession is to be the great link between heaven and earth. The intercession of the Son, begun upon earth, continued in heaven, and carried on by His redeemed people upon earth, will bring about the mighty change: *"As in heaven, so in earth."* As Christ said, *"I come to do thy will, O God"* (Heb. 10:9). He prayed the great prayer in Gethsemane, *"Thy will be done"* (Matt. 26:42). So His redeemed ones, who yield themselves fully to His mind and Spirit, make His prayer their own and unceasingly send up the cry, *"Thy will be done, as in heaven, so in earth."*

Every prayer of a parent for a child, of a believer for the saving of the lost, or for more grace to those who have been saved is part of the great unceasing cry going up day and night from this earth, *"as in heaven, so in earth."*

But it is when God's children not only learn to pray for their immediate circles and interests, but enlarge their hearts to take in the whole church and the whole world, that their united supplication will have power with God. Then the day will be hastened when it will indeed be *"as in heaven, so in earth"*—the whole earth filled with the glory of God. Child of God, will you not yield yourself, like Christ, to live with this one prayer: *"Father...Thy will be done, as in heaven, so in earth"* (Luke 11:2)?

> *"Our Father, which art in heaven, Hallowed be Thy name. Thy kingdom come, Thy will be done, as in heaven, so in earth"* (Luke 11:2). *Amen.*

25

THE FULFILLMENT OF
GOD'S DESIRES

For the LORD hath chosen Zion...for his habitation....
Here will I dwell; for I have desired it.
—Psalm 132:13–14

Here you have the one great desire of God that moved Him in the work of redemption. His heart longed for man to dwell with Him and in Him. To Moses He said: *"And let them make me a sanctuary; that I may dwell among them"* (Exod. 25:8). And just as Israel had to prepare the dwelling for God, even so His children are now called to yield themselves for God to dwell in them and to win others to become His habitation. As the desire of God toward us fills the heart, it will waken within us the desire to gather others around us to become His dwelling too.

What an honor! What a high calling to count my worldly business as entirely secondary and to find my life and my delight in winning souls in whom God may find His heart's delight! *"Here will I dwell; for I have desired it."*

Above all, this is what I can do through intercession. I can pray for God to give His Holy Spirit to those around me. It is God's great plan that man himself will build Him a habitation. It is in answer to the unceasing intercession of His children that God will give His power and blessing. As this great desire of God fills us, we will give ourselves wholly to labor for its fulfillment.

Think of David when he thought of God's desire to dwell in Israel, how he said, *"I will not give sleep to mine eyes, or slumber to mine eyelids, until I find out a place for the* LORD, *an habitation for the mighty God of Jacob"* (Ps. 132:4-5). And will we not, to whom it has been revealed what that indwelling of God may be, give our lives for the fulfillment of His heart's desire?

Oh, let us begin, as never before, to pray for our children, for the souls around us, and for all the world. Not only because we love them, but also because God longs for them and gives us the honor of being the channels through whom His blessing is brought down. Children of God, awake to the realization of what it means that God is seeking to train you as intercessors through whom the great desire of His loving heart can be satisfied!

Oh, God, who has said of human hearts, "Here will I dwell; for I have desired it," teach us, we pray You, to pray, day and night, that the desire of Your heart may be fulfilled. Amen.

26

THE FULFILLMENT OF MAN'S DESIRES

Delight thyself also in the LORD; and he shall give thee
the desires of thine heart.
—Psalm 37:4

God is love, an ever flowing fountain out of which streams the unceasing desire to make His creatures the partakers of all the holiness and the blessedness there is in Himself. This desire for the salvation of souls is indeed God's perfect will, His highest glory.

God imparts to all His children, who are willing to yield themselves wholly to Him, this loving desire to have His place in their hearts. In this, the likeness and image of God consist: to have a heart in which His love takes complete possession and leads us to find spontaneously our highest joy in loving as He does.

Thus our text finds its fulfillment: *"Delight thyself also in the* Lord*,"* and in His life of love, *"and he shall give thee the desires of thine heart."* Count upon it that the intercession of love, rising up to heaven, will be met with the fulfillment of the desire of our hearts. We may be sure that as we delight in what God delights in, such prayer is inspired by God and will have its answer. And our prayers become unceasingly, "Your desires, oh, my Father, are mine. Your holy will of love is my will, too."

In fellowship with Him we get the courage, with all our wills and strength, to bring before His throne the persons or the circles in which we are interested with an ever growing confidence that our prayers will be heard. As we reach out in yearning love, we will receive the power to take hold of the will of God to bless and to believe that God will work out His own blessed will in giving us the desire of our hearts. He will do this because the fulfillment of His desire has been the delight of our souls.

We then become, in the highest sense of the word, God's fellow laborers. Our prayers becomes part of God's divine work of reaching and saving the lost. And we learn to find our happiness in losing ourselves in the salvation of those around us.

Our Father, teach us that nothing less than delighting ourselves in You and in Your desires toward men can inspire us to pray right and give us the assurance of an answer. Amen.

27

MY GREAT DESIRE

One thing have I desired of the Lord, that will I seek after; that I may dwell in the house of the Lord all the days of my life, to behold the beauty of the Lord, and to inquire in his temple.
—Psalm 27:4

Here we have man's response to God's desire to dwell in us. When the desire of God toward us begins to rule the life and heart, our desires are fixed on one thing, and that is, to dwell in the house of the Lord all the days of our lives. Dwelling thus means to behold the beauty of the Lord, to worship Him in the beauty of holiness, and then to inquire in His temple and learn what it means that God has said, "*I the Lord have spoken it, and will do it*" (Ezek. 22:14), and *"I will yet for this be inquired of by the house of Israel, to do it for them"* (Ezek. 36:37).

The more we realize the desire of God's love to give His rest in the heart, and the more our desire is thus quickened to dwell every day in His temple and behold His beauty, the more the Spirit of intercession will grow upon us to claim all that God has promised in His new covenant. Whether we think of our churches and countries, of our homes and schools, of our nearer or wider circles; whether we think of the saved and all their needs, or the unsaved and their danger; the thought that God is indeed longing to find His home and His rest in the hearts of men, if He is only *"inquired of,"* will rouse our whole beings to strive for Zion's sake not to hold our peace. All the thoughts of our feebleness and unworthiness will be swallowed up in the wonderful assurance that He has said of human hearts: *"This is my rest for ever; here will I dwell; for I have desired it"* (Ps. 132:14).

Our faith begins to sees how high our calling is and how indispensable God has made fervent, intense, persistent prayer as the condition of His purpose being fulfilled. We are then drawn to give up our lives to a closer walk with God. We will wait unceasingly upon Him and will become a testimony to our fellow believers of what God will do in them and in us.

Is it not wonderful beyond all thought, this divine partnership in which God commits the fulfillment of His desires to our keeping? Shame on us that we have so little realized it!

> *Our Father in heaven, we ask You, give, give in power, the Spirit of grace and supplication to Your people. For Jesus' sake. Amen.*

28

INTERCESSION DAY
AND NIGHT

*And shall not God avenge his own elect, which cry day and night unto
him, though he bear long with them?*
—Luke 18:7

When Nehemiah heard of the destruction of Jerusalem, he
cried to God, "*Hear the prayer of thy servant, which I pray
before thee now, day and night*" (Neh. 1:6). God said of the watchmen set
on the walls of Jerusalem: they "*shall never hold their peace day nor night*"
(Isa. 62:6). And Paul wrote, "*Night and day praying exceedingly....To the
end he may stablish your hearts unblamable in holiness before God, even our
Father*" (1 Thess. 3:10, 13).

Is such prayer night and day really needed and really possible? Most assuredly, when the heart is first so entirely possessed by the desire that it cannot rest until this is fulfilled. The life has so come under the power of the heavenly blessing that nothing can keep it from sacrificing all to obtain it.

When a child of God begins to get a real vision into the need of the church and of the world, a vision of the divine redemption that God has promised in the outpouring of His love into our hearts, a vision of the power of true intercession to bring down the heavenly blessing, a vision of the honor of being allowed as intercessors to take part in that work, it comes as a matter of course that he regards the work as the most heavenly thing on earth—as intercessor to cry day and night to God for the revelation of His mighty power.

Let us learn from David, who said, *"For the zeal of thine house hath eaten me up"* (Ps. 69:9). Let us learn from Christ our Lord, of whom these words were so intensely true, that there is nothing so much worth living for as this one thought: how to satisfy the heart of God in His longing for human fellowship and affection and how to win hearts to be His dwelling place. And we also will not give ourselves any rest until we have found a place for the Mighty One in our hearts and yielded ourselves to the great work of intercession for so many after whom the desires of God are going out.

God grant that our hearts may be so brought under the influence of these divine truths that we may completely yield ourselves to be devoted to Christ. May our longing to satisfy the heart of God be the chief object of our lives.

Lord Jesus, the great Intercessor, who finds in it all Your glory, breathe, we pray You, from Your own Spirit into our hearts. For Your name's sake. Amen.

29

THE HIGH PRIEST AND HIS INTERCESSION

We have such an high priest.
—Hebrews 8:1

He is able also to save them to the uttermost that come unto God by him, seeing he ever liveth to make intercession for them.
—Hebrews 7:25

I n Israel, what a difference there was between the high priest and the priests and Levites. The high priest alone had access to the Holiest of

All. He bore on his forehead the golden crown engraved with "Holiness to the Lord," and by his intercession on the great Day of Atonement, he bore the sins of the people. The priests brought the daily sacrifices and stood before the Lord and came out to bless the people. The difference between high priest and priest was great. But still greater was the unity; the priests formed one body with the high priest, sharing with him the power to appear before God to receive and dispense His blessing to His people.

It is even so with our Great High Priest. He alone has power with God, in a never ceasing intercession, to obtain from the Father what His people need. And yet, infinite though the distance be between Him and the royal priesthood that surrounds Him for His service, the unity and the fellowship into which His people have been taken up with Him is no less infinite than the apparent diversity. The blessing that He obtains from His Father for us, He holds for His people to receive from Him through their fervent supplication, to be dispensed to the souls among whom He has placed them as His witnesses and representatives.

As long as Christians simply think of being saved and of a life that will make that salvation secure, they never can understand the mystery of the power of intercession to which they are called.

But once they realize that salvation means a vital life union with Jesus Christ; an actual sharing of His life dwelling and working in us; and the consecration of our whole being, to live and labor, to think and will, and find our highest joy in living as a royal priesthood; the church will put on her strength and prove, in dealings with God and man, how truly the likeness and the power of Christ dwell in her.

Oh, God, that you would open our hearts to know and prove what our royal priesthood is—what the real meaning is of our living and praying in the name of Jesus, that what we ask will indeed be given to us! Oh Lord Jesus, our Holy High Priest, breathe the Spirit of Your own holy priesthood into our hearts. Amen.

30

A ROYAL PRIESTHOOD

Call unto me, and I will answer thee, and show thee great and mighty things, which thou knowest not.
—Jeremiah 33:3

As you plead for the great mercies of the new covenant to be bestowed, take with you these thoughts.

The infinite willingness of God to bless: His very nature is a pledge of it. He delights in mercy. He waits to be gracious. His promises and the experience of His saints assure us of it.

Why then does the blessing so often tarry? In creating man with a free will and making him a partner in the rule of the earth, God limited

Himself. He made Himself dependent on what man would do. Man by his prayer would hold the measure of what God could do in blessing.

Think of how God is hindered and disappointed when His children do not pray or pray but little. The low, feeble life of the church, the lack of the power of the Holy Spirit for conversion and holiness, is all owing to the lack of prayer. How different would be the state of the church and of heathendom if God's people were to take no rest in calling upon Him!

And yet God has blessed, just up to the measure of the faith and the zeal of His people. It is not for them to be content with this as a sign of His approval, but rather to say, "If He has thus blessed our feeble efforts and prayers, what will He not do if we yield ourselves wholly to a life of intercession?"

What a call to penitence and confession that our lack of consecration has kept back God's blessing from the world! He was ready to save men, but we were not willing for the sacrifice of a wholehearted devotion to Christ and His service.

Children of God, God counts upon you to take your place before His throne as intercessors. Awake, I pray you, to the consciousness of your holy calling as a royal priesthood. Begin to live a new life in the assurance that intercession, in both the likeness to and the fellowship with the interceding Lord Jesus in heaven, is the highest privilege a man can desire. In this spirit take up the word with large expectations: *"Call unto me, and I will answer thee, and show thee great and mighty things, which thou knowest not."*

Let each one who has read thus far say whether he is not willing, whether he does not long to give himself wholly to this blessed calling and in the power of Jesus Christ to make intercession, supplication for God's church and people and for a dying world, the one chief object of his life? Is this asking too much? Is it too much to yield your life for this holy service of the royal priesthood to that blessed Lord who gave Himself for us?

31

INTERCESSION,
A DIVINE REALITY

And another angel came…and there was given unto him much incense, that he should offer it with the prayers of all saints upon the golden altar which was before the throne.
—Revelation 8:3

Are the thoughts to which this little book has given utterance not a sufficiently grave indictment of the subordinate place given to intercession in the teaching and practice of the church with its ministers and members? Is it not of such supreme importance as to make it an essential, altogether indispensable element in the true Christian life? To those who take God's Word in its full meaning, there can be no doubt about the answer. Intercession is, by amazing grace, an essential element in God's redeeming purpose, so much so that without it, the failure of its accomplishment may lie at our door.

Christ's intercession in heaven is essential to His carrying out the work He began upon earth, but He calls for the intercession of the saints in the attainment of His object. Just think of what we read: *"And all things are of God, who hath reconciled us to himself by Jesus Christ, and hath given to us the ministry of reconciliation"* (2 Cor. 5:18). As the reconciliation was dependent on Christ's doing His part, so in the accomplishment of the work He calls on the church to do her part. We see how Paul regarded intercession day and night as indispensable to the fulfillment of the work that had been entrusted to him. It is but one aspect of that mighty power of God that works in the heart of His believing people.

Intercession is indeed a divine reality. Without it the church loses one of its chief beauties and loses the joy and the power of the Spirit life for achieving great things for God. Without it, the command to preach the Gospel to every creature can never be carried out. Without it, there is no power for the church to recover from her sickly, feeble life and conquer the world. And in the life of the believer, minister, or member, there can be no entrance into the abundant life and joy of daily fellowship with God, except as he takes his place among God's elect—the watchmen and remembrancers of God, who cry to Him day and night. Church of Christ, awake, awake! Listen to the call, *"Pray without ceasing"* (1 Thess. 5:17). Take no rest, and give God no rest. Let the answer be, even though it is with a sigh from the depths of the heart, *"For Zion's sake will I not hold my peace"* (Isa. 62:1). God's Spirit will reveal to us the power of a life of intercession as a divine reality, an essential and indispensable element of the great redemption and therefore also of the true Christian life.

May God help us to know and to fulfill our calling!

PRAYER GUIDE

CONTENTS

PRAY WITHOUT CEASING

Who can do this? How can one who is surrounded by the cares of daily life do this? How can a mother love her child without ceasing? How can the eyelid without ceasing hold itself ready to protect the eye? How can I breathe and feel and hear without ceasing? Because all these are the functions of a healthy, natural life. And so, if the spiritual life be healthy, under the full power of the Holy Spirit, praying without ceasing will be natural.

Pray without Ceasing

Does it refer to continual acts of prayer, in which we are to persevere until we obtain, or to the spirit of prayerfulness that should animate us all the day? It includes both. The example of our Lord Jesus shows us this.

We have to enter our closet for special seasons of prayer; we are at times to persevere there in tenacious prayer. We are also all the day to walk in God's presence, with the whole heart set upon heavenly things. Without set times of prayer, the spirit of prayer will be dull and feeble. Without the continual prayerfulness, the set times will not avail.

Pray without Ceasing

How can I learn it? The best way of learning to do a thing—in fact the only way—is *to do it.* Begin by setting apart some time every day, say ten or fifteen minutes, in which you say to God and to yourself that you come to Him now as an intercessor for others. Let it be after your morning or evening prayer, or any other time.

If you cannot secure the same time every day, do not be troubled. Only see that you do your work. Christ chose you and appointed you to pray for others.

If at first you do not feel any special urgency or faith or power in your prayers, do not let that hinder you. Quietly tell your Lord Jesus of your feebleness; believe that the Holy Spirit is in you to teach you to pray, and be assured that if you begin, God will help you. God cannot help you unless you begin and keep on.

Pray without Ceasing

How do I know what to pray for? If once you begin and think of all the needs around you, you will soon find enough. But to help you, this book is issued with subjects and hints for prayer for a month. It is meant that we should use it month by month, until we know more fully how to follow the Spirit's leading and have learned, if need be, to make our own list of subjects. Then we can dispense with it. In regard to the use of these helps, a few words may be needed.

HOW TO USE THIS BOOK

Y ou will notice for every day two headings: the one, **What to Pray**, and the other, **How to Pray**. If the subjects only were given, one might fall into the routine of mentioning names and things before God, and the work would become a burden. The hints under the heading, **How to Pray**, are meant to remind you of the spiritual nature of the work, of the need for Divine help, and to encourage faith in the certainty that God, through the Spirit, will give us grace to pray aright and will also hear our prayer. One does not at once learn to take his place boldly and to dare to believe that he will be heard. Therefore take a few moments each day to listen to God's voice reminding you of how certainly even you will be heard; calling on you to pray in that faith in your Father, and to claim and take the blessing you plead for. And let these words about **How to Pray** enter your hearts and occupy your thoughts at other times, too. The work of intercession is Christ's great work on earth, entrusted to Him because

He gave Himself as a sacrifice to God for men. The work of intercession is the greatest work a Christian can do. Give yourself as a sacrifice to God for men, and the work will become your glory and your joy, too.

What to Pray

Scripture calls us to pray for many things: for all saints, for all men, for kings and all rulers, for all who are in adversity, for the sending forth of laborers, for those who labor in the Gospel, for all converts, for believers who have fallen into sin, for one another in our own immediate circles. The church is now so much larger than when the New Testament was written; the number of forms of work and workers is so much greater; and the needs of the church and the world are so much better known, that we need to take time and thought to see where prayer is needed and to what our hearts are most drawn. The scriptural calls to prayer demand a large heart, taking in all saints, all men, and all needs. An attempt has been made in these helps to indicate what the chief subjects are that need prayer and that ought to interest every Christian.

It will be felt difficult by many to pray for such large spheres as are sometimes mentioned. Let it be understood that in each case we may make special intercession for our own circle of interest coming under that heading. And it is hardly necessary to say further that where one subject appears of more special interest or urgency than another, we are free for a time, day after day, to take up that subject. If only time be really given to intercession, and if only the spirit of believing intercession be cultivated, the object is attained. While, on the other hand, the heart must be enlarged at times to take in all, the more pointed and definite our prayer can be, the better.

Answers to Prayer

When we pray for all saints, or for missions in general, it is difficult to know when or how our prayer is answered, or whether our prayer has had any part in bringing the answer. It is of extreme importance that we should prove that God hears us, and to this end take note of what answers to look for, and when they come. On the day of praying for all saints, take the saints of your congregation or in your prayer meeting, and ask for a revival among them. In connection with missions, take some special station or missionary you are interested in, or more than one, and plead for blessing. Expect and look for its coming, that you may praise God.

Prayer Circles

In publishing this invitation to intercession, there is no desire to add another to the many existing prayer unions or prayer bands. The first objective is to stir the many Christians who practically, through ignorance of their calling or unbelief as to their prayer availing much, take but very little part in the work of intercession; the second purpose is to help those who do pray to some fuller comprehension of the greatness of the work and the need to giving their whole strength to it. There is a circle of prayer that asks for prayer on the first day of every month for the fuller manifestation of the power of the Holy Spirit throughout the church. I have given the words of that invitation as subject for the first day and taken the same thought as keynote throughout. The more one thinks of the need and the promise, and the greatness of the obstacles to be overcome in prayer, the more one feels it must become his life's work and daily focus, that to which every other interest is subordinated.

But while not forming a large prayer union, it is suggested that it may be found helpful to have small prayer circles to unite in prayer, either for one month, with some special objective introduced daily along with the others, or through a year or longer, with the intention of strengthening each other in the grace of intercession. If a minister were to invite some of his neighboring brethren to join for some special requests along with the printed subjects for supplication, or a number of the more earnest members of his congregation to unite in prayer for revival, some might be trained to take their place in the great work of intercession who now stand idle because no man has hired them.

Who Is Sufficient for These Things?

The more we study and try to practice this grace of intercession, the more we become overwhelmed by its greatness and our feebleness. Let every such impression lead us to listen: *"My grace is sufficient for thee"* (2 Corinthians 12:9), and to answer truthfully: *"Our sufficiency is of God"* (2 Corinthians 3:5). Take courage; it is in the intercession of Christ you are called to take part. The burden and the agony, the triumph and the victory are all His. Learn from Him; yield to His Spirit in you to know how to pray. He gave Himself a sacrifice to God for men, that He might have the right and power of intercession. *"He bare the sin of many, and made intercession for the transgressors"* (Isaiah 53:12). Let your faith rest boldly on His finished work. Let your heart wholly identify itself with Him in His death and His life. Like Him, give yourself to God as a sacrifice for men; it is your highest nobility; it is your true and full union with Him; it will be to you, as to Him, your power of intercession. Beloved Christian, come and give your whole heart and life to intercession, and you will know its blessedness and its power. God asks nothing less; the world needs nothing less; Christ asks nothing less; let us offer to God nothing less.

A MONTHLY GUIDE
TO PRAYER

DAY ONE

What to Pray:
For the Power of the Holy Spirit

I bow my knees unto the Father...that he would grant you,
according to the riches of His glory, to be strengthened with might by
his Spirit in the inner man.
—Ephesians 3:14, 16

Wait for the promise of the Father.
—Acts 1:4

Pray for the fuller manifestation of the grace and energy of the blessed Spirit of God in the removal of all that is contrary to God's revealed will, so that we will not grieve the Holy Spirit, but that He may work in mightier power in the church for the exaltation of Christ and the blessing of souls.

God has one promise to and through His exalted Son, our Lord has one gift to His church, the church has one need, and all prayer unites in this one petition—the power of the Holy Spirit. Make it your prayer.

DAY ONE

How to Pray:
As a Child Asks a Father

If a son shall ask bread of any of you that is a father, will he give him
a stone?...How much more shall your heavenly Father give the Holy
Spirit to them that ask him?
—Luke 11:11, 13

Ask as simply and trustfully as a child asks for bread. You can do this, because *"God hath sent forth the Spirit of his Son into your hearts, crying, Abba, Father"* (Galatians 4:6). This Spirit is in you to give you childlike confidence. In the faith of His praying in you, ask for the power of that Holy Spirit everywhere. Mention places or groups where you specially ask it to be seen.

DAY TWO

What to Pray:
For the Spirit of Supplication

The Spirit itself maketh intercession for us.
—Romans 8:26

I will pour [out]...the spirit of...supplications.
—Zechariah 12:10

The evangelization of the world depends first upon a revival of prayer. Deeper than the need for people—deep down at the bottom of our spiritless life—is the need for the forgotten secret of prevailing, worldwide prayer.

Every child of God has the Holy Spirit within him or her to pray. God waits to give the Spirit in full measure. Ask for yourself, and all who join, for the outpouring of the Spirit of supplication. Ask it for your own prayer circle.

DAY TWO

How to Pray:
In the Spirit

Praying always with all prayer and supplication in the Spirit.
—Ephesians 6:18

Praying in the Holy Ghost.
—Jude 20

On His resurrection day, our Lord gave His disciples the Holy Spirit to enable them to wait for the full outpouring on the Day of Pentecost. It is only in the power of the Spirit already in us, acknowledged and yielded to, that we can pray for His fuller manifestation. Say to the Father, the Spirit of His Son in you is urging you to plead His promise.

DAY THREE

What to Pray:
For All Saints

With all prayer and supplication in the Spirit, and watching thereunto with all perseverance and supplication for all saints.
—Ephesians 6:18

Every member of a body is interested in the welfare of the whole and exists to help and complete the others. Believers are one body and ought to pray, not so much for the welfare of their own church or society, but first of all, for all the saints. This large, unselfish love is the proof that Christ's Spirit and love is teaching them to pray. Pray first for all and then for the believers around you.

DAY THREE

How to Pray:
In the Love of the Spirit

By this shall all men know that ye are my disciples,
if ye have love one to another.
—John 13:35

[I pray] that they all may be one...
that the world may believe that thou hast sent me.
—John 17:21

I beseech you, brethren...for the love of the Spirit,
that ye strive together with me in your prayers to God for me.
—Romans 15:30

Above all things have fervent [love] among yourselves.
—1 Peter 4:8

I f we are to pray, we must love. Let us say to God that we do love all His saints. Let us say we love especially every child of His we know. Let us pray with fervent love, in the love of the Spirit.

DAY FOUR

What to Pray:
For the Spirit of Holiness

[God] stablish your hearts unblameable in holiness.
—1 Thessalonians 3:13

God...sanctify you wholly.
—1 Thessalonians 5:23

God is the Holy One. His people are a holy people. He speaks, "I am holy; I am the Lord who makes you holy." Christ prayed, "Sanctify them; make them holy through Your truth." Paul prayed, "Establish them in Your holiness."

Pray for all saints, God's holy ones, throughout the church, that the Spirit of holiness may rule them, especially for new converts, for the saints in your own neighborhood or congregation, and for any you are especially interested in. Think of their special needs, weaknesses, or sins, and pray that God may make them holy.

DAY FOUR

How to Pray:
Trusting in God's Omnipotence

And he said, The things which are impossible
with men are possible with God.
—Luke 18:27

With men it is impossible, but not with God:
for with God all things are possible.
—Mark 10:27

The things that are impossible with people are possible with God. When we think of the great things for which we ask, how impossible they seem in light of our own insignificance. Prayer is not only wishing, or asking, but also believing and accepting. Be still before God and ask Him to help you to know Him as the Almighty One. Leave your petitions with Him who does wonders.

DAY FIVE

What to Pray:
The God's People May Be Kept from the World

Holy Father, keep through thine own name those whom thou hast given me....I pray not that thou shouldest take them out of the world, but that thou shouldest keep them from the evil. They are not of the world, even as I am not of the world.
—John 17:11, 15–16

At Gethsemane, Christ asked three things for His disciples: that they might be kept as those who are not of the world; that they might be sanctified; that they might be one in love. You cannot do better than pray as Jesus prayed. Ask for God's people that they may be kept separate from the world and its spirit; that they, by the Holy Spirit, may live as those who are not of the world.

DAY FIVE

How to Pray:
Having Confidence before God

*Beloved, if our heart condemn us not, then have we confidence toward
God. And whatsoever we ask, we receive of him, because we keep his
commandments, and do those things that are pleasing in his sight.*
—1 John 3:21–22

Learn these words by heart. Get them into your heart. Join the
ranks of those who, with John, draw near to God with an assured
heart. Their hearts do not condemn them, having confidence toward God.
In this spirit, pray for your brother who sins. (See 1 John 5:16.) In the quiet
confidence of an obedient child, plead for those of your brothers who may
be giving way to sin. Pray for all to be kept from the evil. And say often,
"What we ask, we receive, because we abide and do."

DAY SIX

What to Pray:
For the Spirit of Love in the Church

[I pray] that they all may be one; as thou, Father, art in me, and I in thee....That the world may know that thou hast sent me, and hast loved them, as thou hast loved me....That the love wherewith thou hast loved me may be in them, and I in them.
— John 17:21, 23, 26

The fruit of the Spirit is love.
—Galatians 5:22

Believers are one in Christ, as He is one with the Father. The love of God rests on them and can dwell in them. Pray that the power of the Holy Spirit may so work this love in believers that the world may see and know God's love in them. Pray much for this.

DAY SIX

How to Pray:
As One of God's "Remembrancers"

*I have set watchmen upon thy walls... which shall never hold
their peace day nor night: ye that make mention of the* Lord,
keep not silence. And give him no rest.
—Isaiah 62:6–7

Study these words until your whole soul is filled with the consciousness: *I am appointed as an intercessor.* Enter God's presence in that
faith. Study the world's need with that thought: *It is my work to intercede.*
The Holy Spirit will teach you what to pray for and how to pray. Let it be
an abiding consciousness: *My great lifework, like Christ's, is intercession: to
pray for believers and those who do not yet know God.*

DAY SEVEN

What to Pray:
For the Holy Spirit's Power on Ministers

I beseech you...that ye strive together with me
in your prayers to God for me.
—Romans 15:30

He will yet deliver us; ye also helping together by prayer for us.
—2 Corinthians 1:10–11

W hat a great host of ministers there are in Christ's church! What need they have of prayer! What an influence they might be if they were all clothed with the power of the Holy Spirit. Pray definitely for this; long for it. Think of your own minister, and ask it very especially for him. Connect every thought of the ministry, in your town or neighborhood or the world, with the prayer that all may be filled with the Spirit. Plead for them the promise, *"Tarry...until ye be endued with power from on high"* (Luke 24:49). *"Ye shall receive power, [when] the Holy Ghost is come upon you"* (Acts 1:8).

DAY SEVEN

How to Pray:
In Secret

But thou, when thou prayest, enter into thy closet, and when thou hast shut thy door, pray to thy Father which is in secret.
—Matthew 6:6

He went up into a mountain apart to pray,
and when evening was come, he was there alone.
—Matthew 14:23

Take time and realize, when you are alone with God: *Here I am now, face to face with God, to intercede for His servants.* Do not think you have no influence or that your prayers will not be missed. Your prayers and faith will make a difference. Cry in secret to God for His ministers.

DAY EIGHT

What to Pray:
For the Spirit on All Christian Workers

Ye also helping together by prayer for us,
that for the gift bestowed upon us by the means of many persons
thanks may be given by many on our behalf.
—2 Corinthians 1:11

What a multitude of workers are in our churches and missions, railways, government offices, armed forces, schools, businesses, hospitals, and community organizations! God be praised for this! How much they would accomplish if each were living in the fullness of the Holy Spirit. Pray for them; it makes you a partner in their work, and you will praise God each time you hear of blessing anywhere.

DAY EIGHT

How to Pray:
With Definite Petitions

What wilt thou that I shall do unto thee?
—Luke 18:41

The Lord knew what the man wanted, and yet He asked him. The utterances of our wishes emphasize our petitions to God and so awaken faith and expectation. Be very definite in your petitions, so as to know what answer you may look for. Just think of the great host of workers, and ask and expect God definitely to bless them in answer to the prayers of His people. Then ask still more definitely for workers around you.

Intercession is not the breathing out of pious wishes; its aim is—through believing, persevering prayer—to receive and bring about blessing.

DAY NINE

What to Pray:
For God's Spirit on Our Mission Work

As they ministered to the Lord, and fasted, the Holy Ghost said,
Separate me Barnabas and Saul....And when they had fasted and
prayed, and laid their hands on them, they sent them away. So they,
being sent forth by the Holy Ghost, departed.
—Acts 13:2–4

Pray that our mission work may all be done in this spirit: waiting on God, hearing the voice of the Spirit, sending forth men with fasting and prayer. Pray that, in our churches, our mission interest and work may be in the power of the Holy Spirit and of prayer. A Spirit-filled, praying church will send out Spirit-filled missionaries, mighty in prayer.

DAY NINE

How to Pray:
Take Time

I give myself unto prayer.
—Psalm 109:4

We will give ourselves continually to prayer.
—Acts 6:4

Be not rash with thy mouth,
and let not thine heart be hasty to utter any thing before God.
— Ecclesiastes 5:2

[He] continued all night in prayer to God.
— Luke 6:12

Time is one of the prime estimates of value. The time we give is a proof of the interest we feel.

We need time with God to realize His presence, to wait for Him to make Himself known, to consider and feel the needs we plead for, to take our place in Christ, to pray until we can believe that we have received. Take time in prayer, and pray for blessing on the mission work of the church.

DAY TEN

What to Pray:
For God's Spirit on Our Missionaries

*Ye shall receive power, after that the Holy Ghost is
come upon you: and ye shall be witnesses unto me...
unto the uttermost part of the earth.*
—Acts 1:8

What the world needs today is not only more missionaries but the outpouring of God's Spirit on everyone whom He has sent out to work for Him in the foreign field.

God always gives His servants power equal to the work He asks of them. Think of the greatness and difficulty of this work— casting Satan out of his strongholds—and pray that everyone who takes part in it may receive and do all his work in the power of the Holy Spirit. Think of the difficulties of your missionaries, and pray for them.

DAY TEN

How to Pray:
Trusting God's Faithfulness

He is faithful that promised.
—Hebrews 10:23

She judged him faithful who had promised.
—Hebrews 11:11

Just think of God's promises to His Son concerning His kingdom, to the church concerning the heathen, to His servants concerning their work, to yourself concerning your prayers; and pray in the assurance that He is faithful. He only waits for prayer and faith to fulfill them. *"Faithful is he that calleth you* [to pray] *who also will do* [what He has promised]*"* (1 Thessalonians 5:24).

Take individual missionaries, make yourself one with them, and pray until you know that you are heard. Oh, begin to live for Christ's kingdom as the one thing worth living for!

DAY ELEVEN

What to Pray:
For More Laborers

Pray ye therefore the Lord of the harvest, that he will send forth
labourers into his harvest.
—Matthew 9:38

W hat a remarkable call by the Lord Jesus for help from His disciples in getting the need supplied. What an honor put upon prayer. What a proof that God wants prayer and will hear it.

Pray for laborers, for all students in theological seminaries, training classes, Bible institutes, that they may not go unless He calls them and sends them forth. Pray that our churches may train their students to seek for the sending forth of the Holy Spirit. Pray that all believers may hold themselves ready to be sent forth or to pray for those who can go.

DAY ELEVEN

How to Pray:
In Faith, Doubting Nothing

Jesus answering saith unto them, Have faith in God....
Whosoever shall say unto this mountain, Be thou removed,
and be thou cast into the sea; and shall not doubt in his heart,
but shall believe that those things which he saith shall come to pass;
he shall have whatsoever he saith.
—Mark 11:22–23

Have faith in God! Ask Him to make Himself known to you as the faithful, mighty God who works all in all. You will be encouraged to believe that He can provide suitable and sufficient laborers, however impossible this appears. But remember, He does so in answer to prayer and faith.

Apply this to every opening where a good worker is needed. The work is God's. He can provide the right worker—but He must be asked and waited on.

DAY TWELVE

What to Pray:
For the Spirit to Convict the World of Sin

I will send [the Comforter] unto you. And when he is come,
he will reprove the world of sin.
—John 16:7–8

God's one desire—the one objective of Christ's being manifested—is to take away sin. The first work of the Spirit on the world is the conviction of sin. Without that, no deep or abiding revival, no powerful conversion can come about. Pray for it, that the gospel may be preached in such power of the Spirit, that people may see that they have rejected and crucified Christ and cry out, *"What shall we do?"* (Acts 2:37). Pray earnestly for a mighty power of conviction of sin wherever the Gospel is preached.

DAY TWELVE

How to Pray:
Stir Yourself to Take of God's Strength

Let him take hold of my strength, that he may make peace with me.
—Isaiah 27:5

There is none that calleth upon thy name, that stirreth
up himself to take hold of thee.
—Isaiah 64:7

Stir up the gift of God, which is in thee.
—2 Timothy 1:6

First, take hold of God's strength. God is a Spirit. I cannot take hold of Him and hold Him fast, except by the Spirit. Take hold of God's strength, and hold on until it has done for you what He promised. Pray for the Spirit's power to convict of sin.

Second, stir up the power that is in you by the Holy Spirit to take hold. Give your whole heart and will to it, and say, *"I will not let [You] go, except [You] bless me"* (Genesis 32:26).

DAY THIRTEEN

What to Pray:
For the Spirit of Burning

And it shall come to pass, that he that is left in Zion...shall be called
holy...when the Lord shall have washed away the filth of the daughters
of Zion...by the spirit of judgment, and by the spirit of burning.
—Isaiah 4:3–4

A washing by fire! A cleansing by judgment! Those who have passed through this will be called holy. The power of blessing for the world, the power of work and intercession that will avail, depends upon the spiritual state of the church. And that can only rise higher as sin is discovered and then put away. Judgment must begin at the house of God. There must be conviction of sin for sanctification. Beseech God to give His Spirit as a spirit of judgment and a spirit of burning to discover and burn out sin in His people.

DAY THIRTEEN

How to Pray:
In the Name of Christ

Whatsoever ye shall ask in my name, that will I do....
If ye shall ask any thing in my name, I will do it.
—John 14:13–14

A sk in the name of your Redeemer God, who sits upon the throne. Ask what He has promised, what He gave His blood for, so that sin may be put away from among His people. Ask—the prayer is after His own heart—for the spirit of deep conviction of sin to come among His people. Ask for the spirit of burning. Ask in the faith of His name—the faith of what He wills, of what He can do—and look for the answer. Pray that the church may be blessed, to be made a blessing in the world.

DAY FOURTEEN

What to Pray:
For the Church of the Future

That...the children...might not be as their fathers...a generation that set not their heart aright, and whose spirit was not stedfast with God.
—Psalm 78:6, 8

I will pour my spirit upon thy seed, and my blessing upon thine offspring.
—Isaiah 44:3

Pray for the generations who are to come after us. Think of the young men, women, and children of this age, and pray for all the agencies at work among them. Pray that in associations, societies, and unions, in homes and schools, Christ may be honored and the Holy Spirit will have control of them. Pray for the youth of your own neighborhood.

DAY FOURTEEN

How to Pray:
With the Whole Heart

[The Lord] grant thee according to thine own heart.
—Psalm 20:4

Thou hast given him his heart's desire.
—Psalm 21:2

I cried with my whole heart; hear me, O Lord.
—Psalm 119:145

God lives and listens to every petition with His whole heart. Each time we pray, the whole infinite God is there to hear. He asks that in each prayer the whole man be there, too. He asks that we cry with our whole hearts. Christ gave Himself to God for men. And so, He takes up every need into His intercession. If once we seek God with our whole hearts, the whole heart will be in every prayer with which we come to God. Pray with your whole heart for the young.

DAY FIFTEEN

What to Pray:
For Schools and Colleges

As for me, this is my covenant with them, saith the Lord;
my spirit that is upon thee, and my words which I have put in thy
mouth, shall not depart out of thy mouth, nor out of the mouth of thy
seed, nor out of the mouth of thy seed's seed, saith the Lord,
from henceforth and for ever.
—Isaiah 59:21

The future of the church and the world depends, to an extent we little conceive, on the education of the day. The church may be seeking to evangelize the heathen and be giving up her own children to secular and materialistic influences. Pray for schools and colleges, and that the church may realize and fulfill its momentous duty of caring for its children. Pray for godly teachers.

DAY FIFTEEN

How to Pray:
Not Limiting God

They...limited the Holy One of Israel.
—Psalm 78:41

He did not many mighty works there because of their unbelief.
—Matthew 13:58

Is any thing too hard for the LORD?
—Genesis 18:14

Ah, Lord GOD!...Thou hast made the heaven and the earth by thy great
power and stretched out arm, and there is nothing too hard for thee....
Behold, I am the LORD...is there any thing too hard for me?
—Jeremiah 32:17, 27

Beware, in your prayers, above everything, of limiting God, not only by unbelief, but also by fancying that you know what He can do. Expect unexpected things, above all that we ask or think. (See Ephesians 3:20.) Each time you intercede, be quiet first and worship God in His glory. Think of what He can do, of how He delights to hear Christ, of your place in Christ, and expect great things.

DAY SIXTEEN

What to Pray:
For the Power of the Holy Spirit in Our Sunday Schools

Thus saith the LORD, Even the captives of the mighty shall be taken away, and the prey of the terrible shall be delivered: for I will contend with him that contendeth with thee, and I will save thy children.
—Isaiah 49:25

Every part of the work of God's church is His work. He must do it. Prayer is the confession that He will, if we surrender ourselves into His hands, work in us and through us. Pray for the hundreds of thousands of Sunday school teachers, that those who know God may be filled with His Spirit. Pray for your own Sunday school. Pray for the salvation of the children.

DAY SIXTEEN

How to Pray:
Boldly

We have a great high priest...Jesus the Son of God....Let us therefore
come boldly unto the throne of grace.
—Hebrews 4:14, 16

W hat are these hints to help us in our work of intercession doing for us? Making us conscious of our weakness in prayer. Thank God for this. It is the very first lesson we need on the way to pray the effectual prayer that avails much. (See James 5:16.) Let us persevere, taking each subject *"boldly unto the throne of grace"* (Hebrews 4:16). As we pray, we will learn to pray, to believe, and to expect with increasing boldness. Hold fast your assurance; it is at God's command you come as an intercessor. Christ will give you grace to pray correctly.

DAY SEVENTEEN

What to Pray:
For Kings and Rulers

I exhort therefore, that, first of all, supplications, prayers, intercessions, and giving of thanks, be made for all men; for kings, and for all that are in authority; that we may lead a quiet and peaceable life in all godliness and honesty.
—1 Timothy 2:1–2

What faith in the power of prayer! A few feeble and despised Christians are to influence the mighty Roman emperors and help in securing peace and quietness. Let us believe that prayer is a power that is taken up by God in His rule of the world. Let us pray for our country and its rulers. Let us pray for all the rulers of the world, for rulers in cities or districts in which we are interested. When God's people unite in this, they may count upon their prayers having an effect in the unseen world more than they know. Let faith hold this fast.

DAY SEVENTEEN

How to Pray:
The Prayer before God as Incense

Another angel came and stood at the altar, having a golden censer;
and there was given unto him much incense, that he should offer it
with the prayers of all saints upon the golden altar which was before
the throne. And the smoke of the incense, which came with the prayers
of the saints, ascended up before God out of the angel's hand.
And the angel took the censer, and filled it with fire of the altar,
and cast it into the earth: and there were voices, and thunderings,
and lightnings, and an earthquake.
—Revelation 8:3–5

The same censer brings the prayer of the saints before God and casts fire upon the earth. The prayers that go up to heaven have their share in the history of this earth. Be sure that your prayers enter God's presence.

DAY EIGHTEEN

What to Pray:
For Peace

I exhort therefore, that, first of all, supplications...be made for all men;
for kings, and for all that are in authority; that we may lead a quiet
and peaceable life in all godliness and honesty.
For this is good and acceptable in the sight of God our Saviour.
—1 Timothy 2:1–3

He maketh wars to cease unto the end of the earth.
—Psalm 46:9

What a terrible sight: the military armaments in which the nations find their pride. What a terrible thought: the evil passions that may at any moment bring on war. And what a prospect the suffering and desolation that must come. God can, in answer to the prayers of His people, give peace. Let us pray for it and for the rule of righteousness on which alone it can be established.

DAY EIGHTEEN

How to Pray:
With Understanding

What is it then? I will pray with the spirit,
and I will pray with the understanding.
—1 Corinthians 14:15

We need to pray with the spirit, as the vehicle of the intercession of God's Spirit, if we are to take hold of God in faith and power. We need to pray with the understanding, if we are really to enter deeply into the needs we bring before Him. Take time to understand intelligently, in each subject, the nature, the extent, the urgency of the request, the ground and way and certainty of God's promise as revealed in His Word. Let the mind affect the heart. Pray with the understanding and with the spirit.

DAY NINETEEN

What to Pray:
For the Holy Spirit on Christendom

Having a form of godliness, but denying the power thereof.
—2 Timothy 3:5

Thou hast a name that thou livest, and art dead.
—Revelation 3:1

There are five hundred million nominal Christians. The state of the majority is unspeakably awful. Formality, worldliness, ungodliness, rejection of Christ's service, ignorance, and indifference—to what an extent does all this prevail! We pray for the heathen; oh, let us pray for those bearing Christ's name; many are in worse than heathen darkness.

Do you not feel as if you ought to begin to give up your life and to cry day and night to God for souls? In answer to prayer, God gives the power of the Holy Spirit.

DAY NINETEEN

How to Pray:
In Deep Stillness of Soul

My soul waiteth upon God: from him cometh my salvation.
—Psalm 62:1

Prayer has its power in God alone. The nearer a man comes to God Himself, the deeper he enters into God's will. The more he takes hold of God, the more power he has in prayer.

God must reveal Himself. If it pleases Him to make Himself known, He can make the heart conscious of His presence. Our posture must be that of holy reverence, of quiet waiting and adoration.

As your month of intercession passes on, and you feel the greatness of your work, be still before God. Thus you will get power to pray.

DAY TWENTY

What to Pray:
For God's Spirit on the Unsaved

Behold, these shall come from far...and these from the land of Sinim.
—Isaiah 49:12

Princes shall come out of Egypt;
Ethiopia shall soon stretch out her hands unto God.
—Psalm 68:31

Pray for the unsaved, who are yet without the Word. Think of China, with her billion people, many million a month dying without Christ. Think of Africa, with its two hundred million. Think of thirty million a year going down into the darkness. If Christ gave His life for them, will you not do the same? You can give yourself to intercede for them. Just begin, if you have never yet begun, with this simple monthly school of intercession. The ten minutes you give will make you feel this is not enough. God's Spirit will draw you on. Persevere, however weak you are. Ask God to give you some country or tribe to pray for. Can anything be nobler than to do as Christ did? Give your life for the unsaved.

DAY TWENTY

How to Pray:
With Confident Expectation of an Answer

Call unto me, and I will answer thee,
and show thee great and mighty things, which thou knowest not.
—Jeremiah 33:3

Thus saith the Lord God;
I will yet for this be inquired of by the house of Israel, to do it for them.
—Ezekiel 36:37

Both texts refer to promises definitely made, but their fulfillment depends on prayer; God would *"be inquired of"* to do it.

Pray for God's fulfillment of His promises to His Son and His church. Expect the answer. Plead for the unsaved. Plead God's promises.

DAY TWENTY-ONE

What to Pray:
For God's Spirit on the Jews

I will pour upon the house of David, and upon the inhabitants of Jerusalem, the spirit of grace and of supplications: and they shall look upon me whom they have pierced.
—Zechariah 12:10

Brethren, my heart's desire and prayer to God for Israel is, that they might be saved.
—Romans 10:1

Pray for the Jews. Their return to the God of their fathers stands connected, in a way we cannot tell, with wonderful blessing to the church, and with the coming of our Lord Jesus. Do not think that God has foreordained all this, and that we cannot hasten it. In a divine and mysterious way, God has connected His fulfillment of His promise with our prayers. His Spirit's intercession in us is God's forerunner of blessing. Pray for Israel and the work done among them. *"Even so, come, Lord Jesus"* (Revelation 22:20)! Amen.

DAY TWENTY-ONE

How to Pray:
With the Intercession of the Holy Spirit

We know not what we should pray for as we ought: but the Spirit itself maketh intercession for us with groanings which cannot be uttered.
—Romans 8:26

In your ignorance and weakness, believe in the secret indwelling and intercession of the Holy Spirit within you. Yield yourself to His life and leading habitually. He will help your infirmities in prayer. Plead the promises of God even where you do not see how they are to be fulfilled. God knows the mind of the Spirit, because He makes intercession for the saints according to the will of God. Pray with the simplicity of a little child. Pray with the holy awe and reverence of one in whom God's Spirit dwells and prays.

DAY TWENTY-TWO

What to Pray:
For All Who Are Suffering

Remember them that are in bonds, as bound with them; and them
which suffer adversity, as being yourselves also in the body.
—Hebrews 13:3

What a world of suffering we live in! How Jesus sacrificed all and identified Himself with it! Let us in our measure do so, too. The persecuted Russians, Poles, and Germans, the famine-stricken millions of India, the poverty and wretchedness of our great cities, and so much more—what suffering among those who know God and those who do not know Him. And then, in ten thousand homes and hearts, what sorrow. In our neighborhood, how many need help or comfort? Let us have hearts for, let us think of, the suffering. It will stir us to pray, to work, to hope, to love more. And in an unknown way and time, God will hear our prayers.

DAY TWENTY-TWO

How to Pray:
Praying Always, and Not Fainting

He spake a parable unto them to this end,
that men ought always to pray, and not to faint.
—Luke 18:1

Do you not begin to feel prayer is really the help for this sinful world? What a need there is of unceasing prayer. The very greatness of the task makes us despair! What can our ten minutes of intercession avail? It is right we feel this. This is the way in which God is calling and preparing us to give our lives to prayer. Give yourselves wholly to God for people, and amid all your work, your hearts will be drawn out to men in love, drawn up to God in dependence and expectation. To hearts thus led by the Holy Spirit, it is possible to pray always and not to faint.

DAY TWENTY-THREE

What to Pray:
For the Holy Spirit in Your Own Work

I also labour, striving according to his working,
which worketh in me mightily.
—Colossians 1:29

Y ou have your own special work; make it a work of intercession.
Paul labored, striving according to the working of God in him.
Remember, God is not only the Creator, but also the great Workman who
works all in all. You can only do your work in His strength by His working in you through the Spirit. Intercede much for those among whom you
work until God gives you life for them.

Let us all intercede, too, for each other, for every worker throughout
God's church, however solitary or unknown.

DAY TWENTY-THREE

How to Pray:
In God's Very Presence

Draw nigh to God, and he will draw nigh to you.
—James 4:8

The nearness of God gives rest and power in prayer. God's nearness is given to him who makes it his first objective. "*Draw nigh to God*"; seek the nearness to Him, and He will give it; "*he will draw nigh to you.*" Then it becomes easy to pray in faith.

Remember that when God first takes you into the school of intercession, it is almost more for your own sake than that of others. You have to be trained to love, wait, pray, and believe. Only persevere. Learn to set yourself in His presence, to wait quietly for the assurance that He draws near. Enter into His holy presence, remain there, and spread your work before Him. Intercede for the souls you are working among. Receive a blessing from God—His Spirit into your own heart—for them.

DAY TWENTY-FOUR

What to Pray:
For the Spirit on Your Own Congregation

Beginning at Jerusalem.
—Luke 24:47

Each one of us is connected with some congregation or circle of believers who are to us the part of Christ's body with which we come into most direct contact. They have a special claim on our intercession. Let it be a settled matter between God and you that you are to labor in prayer on their behalf. Pray for your ministers and all leaders or workers. Pray for the believers according to their needs. Pray for conversions. Pray for the Spirit's power to manifest itself. Band yourself with others to join in secret in specific petitions. Let intercession be a definite work, carried on as systematically as preaching or Sunday school. And pray expecting an answer.

DAY TWENTY-FOUR

How to Pray:
Continually

I have set watchmen...which shall never hold their peace day nor night.
—Isaiah 62:6

His own elect, which cry day and night unto him.
—Luke 18:7

Night and day praying exceedingly that we might…
perfect that which is lacking in your faith.
—1 Thessalonians 3:10

A widow indeed, and desolate, trusteth in God,
and continueth in supplications and prayers night and day.
—1 Timothy 5:5

When the glory of God, and the love of Christ, and the need of souls are revealed to us, the fire of this unceasing intercession will begin to burn in us for those who are near and those who are far off.

DAY TWENTY-FIVE

What to Pray:
For More Conversions

He is able also to save them to the uttermost...
seeing he ever liveth to make intercession.
—Hebrews 7:25

We will give ourselves continually to prayer,
and to the ministry of the word....And the word of God increased;
and the number of the disciples multiplied.
—Acts 6:4, 7

Christ's power to save, and save completely, depends on His unceasing intercession. The apostles' withdrawing of themselves from other work to give themselves continually to prayer was followed by the number of the disciples multiplying exceedingly. As we, in our day, give ourselves to intercession, we will have more and mightier conversions. Let us plead for this. Christ is exalted to give repentance. The church exists with the divine purpose and promise of having conversion. Let us not be ashamed to confess our sin and feebleness and cry to God for more conversions in Christian and heathen lands, of those whom you know and love. Plead for the salvation of sinners.

DAY TWENTY-FIVE

How to Pray:
In Deep Humility

Truth, Lord: yet the dogs eat of the crumbs.
Then Jesus answered and said unto her, O woman, great is thy faith:
be it unto thee even as thou wilt.
—Matthew 15:27–28

You feel unworthy and unable to pray correctly. To accept this heartily, and still to be content to come and be blessed in your unworthiness, is true humility. It proves its integrity by not seeking for anything but simply trusting His grace; thus, it is the strength of a great faith and gets a full answer. *"Yet the dogs"*; let that be your plea as you persevere for someone possibly possessed by the devil. Let not your littleness hinder you for a moment.

DAY TWENTY-SIX

What to Pray:
For the Holy Spirit on Young Converts

Peter and John...prayed for them, that they might receive the Holy Ghost: (for as yet he was fallen upon none of them: only they were baptized in the name of the Lord Jesus.)
—Acts 8:14–16

Now he which stablisheth us with you in Christ, and hath anointed us, is God; Who hath also...given the earnest of the Spirit in our hearts.
—2 Corinthians 1:21–22

How many new converts remain feeble? How many fall into sin? How many backslide entirely? If we pray for the church, its growth in holiness and devotion to God's service, pray especially for young converts. How many stand alone, surrounded by temptation. How many have no teaching on the Spirit in them and the power of God to establish them. How many are in persecuted lands, surrounded by Satan's power. If you pray for the power of the Spirit in the church, pray especially that every young convert may know that he may claim and receive the fullness of the Spirit.

DAY TWENTY-SIX

How to Pray:
Without Ceasing

*As for me, God forbid that I should sin against
the LORD in ceasing to pray for you.*
—1 Samuel 12:23

It is sin against the Lord to cease praying for others. When once we begin to see how absolutely indispensable intercession is, just as much a duty as loving God or believing in Christ, and how we are called and bound to it as believers, we will feel that to cease intercession is grievous sin. Let us ask for grace to take up our places as priests with joy and give our lives to bring down the blessings of heaven.

DAY TWENTY-SEVEN

What to Pray:
That God's People Realize Their Calling

I will bless thee...and thou shalt be a blessing...
in thee shall all families of the earth be blessed.
—Genesis 12:2–3

God be merciful unto us, and bless us; and cause his face to shine upon
us...that thy way may be known upon earth, thy saving health among
all nations.
—Psalm 67:1–2

Abraham was only blessed so that he might be a blessing to all the earth. Israel prays for blessing, so that God may be known among all nations. Every believer, just as much as Abraham, is only blessed so that he may carry God's blessing to the world.

Cry to God that His people may know this: that every believer is only to live for the interests of God and His kingdom. If this truth were preached, believed, and practiced, what a revolution it would bring in our mission work! What a host of willing intercessors we would have! Plead with God to work it by the Holy Spirit.

DAY TWENTY-SEVEN

How to Pray:
As One Who Has What He Asks for Others

Peter said...but such as I have give I thee.
—Acts 3:6

The Holy Ghost fell on them, as on us at the beginning....
God gave them the like gift as he did unto us.
—Acts 11:15, 17

As you pray for this great blessing on God's people, the Holy Spirit taking entire possession of them for God's service, yield yourself to God and claim the gift anew in faith. Let each thought of weakness or shortcoming only make you the more urgent in prayer for others. As the blessing comes to them, you, too, will be helped. With every prayer for conversions or mission work, pray that God's people may know how wholly they belong to Him.

DAY TWENTY-EIGHT

What to Pray:
That All God's People May Know the Spirit

The Spirit of truth; whom the world...knoweth [not]: but ye know him; for he dwelleth with you, and shall be in you.
—John 14:17

Know ye not that your body is the temple of the Holy Ghost?
—1 Corinthians 6:19

The Holy Spirit is the power of God for the salvation of people. He only works as He dwells in the church. He is given to enable believers to live wholly as God would have them live, in the full experience and witness of Him who saves completely. Pray God that every one of His people may know the Holy Spirit. Pray that He, in all His fullness, is given to them. Pray that they do not expect to live as their Father would have them live without having Him in His fullness, without being filled with Him. Pray that all God's people everywhere may learn to say, I believe in the Holy Spirit.

DAY TWENTY-EIGHT

How to Pray:
Laboring Fervently in Prayer

Epaphras, who is one of you, a servant of Christ, saluteth you,
always labouring fervently for you in prayers, that ye may stand perfect
and complete in all the will of God.
—Colossians 4:12

To a healthy man, labor is a delight; he labors fervently in what interests him. The believer who is in full health, whose heart is filled with God's Spirit, labors fervently in prayer. For what? That his brothers may stand perfect and complete in all the will of God. That they may know what God wills for them, how He calls them to live, and be led, and walk by the Holy Spirit. Labor fervently in prayer that all God's children may know this as possible, as divinely sure.

DAY TWENTY-NINE

What to Pray:
For the Spirit of Intercession

I have chosen you, and ordained you,
that ye should go and bring forth fruit...that whatsoever ye shall ask of
the Father in my name, he may give it you.
—John 15:16

Hitherto have ye asked nothing in my name....
At that day ye shall ask in my name.
—John 16:24, 26

Hasn't our school of intercession taught us how little we have prayed in the name of Jesus? He promised His disciples, "In that day, when the Holy Spirit comes upon you, you will ask in My name." Aren't there tens of thousands with us mourning the lack of the power of intercession? Let our intercession today be for them and all God's children, that Christ may teach us through the Holy Spirit in us what it is to live in His fullness and to yield ourselves to His Intercession work within us. The church and the world need nothing so much as a mighty Spirit of intercession to bring down the power of God on earth. Pray for the descent from heaven of the Spirit of Intercession for a great prayer revival.

DAY TWENTY-NINE

How to Pray:
Abiding in Christ

If ye abide in me, and my words abide in you, ye shall ask what ye will, and it shall be done unto you.
—John 15:7

Our acceptance with God, our access to Him, is all in Christ. As we consciously abide in Him, we have the liberty—not a liberty to our old nature or our self-will, but the divine liberty from all self-will—to ask what we will, in the power of the new nature, and it will be done. Let us keep this place, and believe even now that our intercession is heard and that the Spirit of supplication will be given all around us.

DAY THIRTY

What to Pray:
For the Holy Spirit with the Word of God

Our gospel came not unto you in word only, but also in power,
and in the Holy Ghost, and in much assurance.
—1 Thessalonians 1:5

Them that have preached the gospel unto you with
the Holy Ghost sent down from heaven.
—1 Peter 1:12

So many Bibles are being circulated. So many sermons on the Bible are being preached. So many Bibles are being read in homes and schools. How little blessing when it comes *"in word only"*; what divine blessing and power when it comes *"in the Holy Ghost,"* when it is preached *"with the Holy Ghost sent down from heaven."* Pray for Bible circulation, and preaching, teaching, and reading, that it may all be in the Holy Spirit, with much prayer. Pray for the power of the Spirit with the Word in your own neighborhood, wherever it is being read or heard. Let every mention of *"the Word of God"* waken intercession.

DAY THIRTY

How to Pray:
Watching and Praying

Continue in prayer, and watch in the same with thanksgiving; Withal
praying also for us, that God would open unto us a door of utterance.
—Colossians 4:2–3

D o you not see how all depends upon God and prayer? As long
as He lives, loves, hears, and works, as long as there are souls
with hearts closed to the Word, as long as there is work to be done in
carrying the Word, pray without ceasing. Continue steadfastly in prayer,
watching therein with thanksgiving. These words are for every Christian.

DAY THIRTY-ONE

What to Pray:
For the Spirit of Christ in His People

I am the vine, ye are the branches.
—John 15:5

For I have given you an example,
that ye should do as I have done to you.
—John 13:15

As branches we are to be so like the Vine, so entirely identified with it, that all may see that we have the same nature, life, and spirit. When we pray for the Spirit, let us not only think of a Spirit of power, but the very disposition and temper of Christ Jesus. Ask for and expect nothing less. For yourself, and all God's children, cry for it.

DAY THIRTY-ONE

How to Pray:
Striving in Prayer

Yea, [Jacob] had power over the angel, and prevailed:
he wept, and made supplication.
—Hosea 12:4

That ye strive together with me in your prayers to God for me.
—Romans 15:30

I would that ye knew what great conflict I have for you.
—Colossians 2:1

All the powers of evil seek to hinder us in prayer. Prayer is a conflict with opposing forces. It needs the whole heart and all our strength. May God give us grace to strive in prayer until we prevail.

ABOUT THE AUTHOR

Andrew Murray (1828–1917) was an amazingly prolific Christian writer. He lived and ministered as both a pastor and author from the towns and villages of South Africa. Some of Murray's earliest writings were written to provide nurture and guidance to Christians, whether young or old in the faith; they were actually an extension of his pastoral work. Once books such as *Abide in Christ, Like Christ,* and *With Christ in the School of Prayer* were written, Murray became widely known, and new books from his pen were awaited with great eagerness throughout the world.

He wrote to give daily practical help to many of the people in his congregation who lived out in the farming communities and could only come into town for church services on rare occasions. As he wrote these books of instruction, Murray adopted the practice of placing many of his more devotional books into thirty-one separate readings to correspond with the days of the month.

At the age of seventy-eight, Murray resigned from the pastorate and devoted most of his time to his manuscripts. He continued to write profusely, moving from one book to the next with an intensity of purpose and a zeal that few men of God have ever equaled. He often said of himself, rather humorously, that he was like a hen about to hatch an egg; he was restless and unhappy until he got the burden of the message off his mind.

During these later years, after hearing of pocket-sized paperbacks, Andrew Murray immediately began to write books to be published in that fashion. He thought it was a splendid way to have the teachings of the Christian life at your fingertips, where they could be carried around and read at any time of the day.

One source has said of Andrew Murray that his prolific style possesses the strength and eloquence that are born of deep earnestness and a sense of the solemnity of the issues of the Christian life. Nearly every page reveals an intensity of purpose and appeal that stirs men to the depths of their souls. Murray moves the emotions, searches the conscience, and reveals the sins and shortcomings of many of us with a love and hope born out of an intimate knowledge of the mercy and faithfulness of God.

For Andrew Murray prayer was considered our personal home base from which we live our Christian lives and extend ourselves to others. During his later years, the vital necessity of unceasing prayer in the spiritual life came to the forefront of Andrew Murray's teachings. It was then that he revealed the secret treasures of his heart concerning a life of persistent and believing prayer.

Countless persons the world over have hailed Andrew Murray as their spiritual father and given credit for much of their Christian growth to the influence of his priceless devotional books.